Lars Qvortrup (Ed)

Virtual Interaction: Interaction in Virtual Inhabited 3D Worlds

Section Editors:
Erik Granum, Berit Holmqvist, Søren Kolstrup,
Kim Halskov Madsen

Springer

Lars Qvortrup
Department of Literature, Culture and Media,
University of Southern Denmark, Campusvej 55, DK-5230 Odense M,
Denmark

ISBN 978-1-84996-863-8

British Library Cataloguing in Publication Data
Virtual interaction : interaction in virtual inhabited 3D worlds
1.Interactive multimedia 2.Virtual reality
I.Qvortrup, Lars
006.7

ISBN 978-1-84996-863-8 ISBN 978-1-4471-3698-9 (eBook)
DOI 10.1007/978-1-4471-3698-9

Library of Congress Cataloging-in-Publication Data
Virtual interaction : interaction in virtual inhabited 3D worlds / Lars Qvortrup (ed.).
p. cm.
Includes bibliographical references.
ISBN 978-1-84996-863-8
1. Interactive multimedia. 2. Virtual reality. I. Qvortrup, Lars.

QA76.76.I59 V57 2000
006.7--dc21 00-34425

Originally published by Springer-Verlag London Berlin Heidelberg in 2001
Softcover reprint of the hardcover 1st edition 2001

Typesetting: Ian Kingston Editorial Services, Nottingham, UK

34/3830-543210 Printed on acid-free paper SPIN 10769428

Virtual Interaction: Interaction in Virtual Inhabited 3D Worlds

Springer-Verlag London Ltd.

Contents

5 Methods for Designing Interactive Inhabited Virtual Worlds

List of Contributors

Peter Bøgh Andersen
Department of Computer Science
Aalborg University
Fredrik Bajers Vej 7E
DK-9200 Aalborg East
Denmark
Email:
pba@cs.auc.dk

Jørgen Callesen
Department of Information and Media Science
InterMedia-Aarhus
Aarhus University
Aabogade 34
DK-8200 Aarhus N
Denmark
Email:
callesen@imv.au.dk

Hanne Dankert
Department of Communication, Journalism and Computer Science
Roskilde University
P.O.Box 260
DK-4000 Roskilde
Denmark
Email:
hanned@ruc.dk

Erik Granum
Computer Vision and Media Technology
InterMedia-Aalborg
Aalborg University
Niels Jernes Vej 14
DK-9220 Aalborg East
Denmark
Email:
eg@vision.auc.dk

Bjarne Horn
Department of Information and Media Science
InterMedia-Aarhus
Aabogade 34
DK-8200 Aarhus N
Denmark
Email:
bjarne@dukk.dk

Jens F. Jensen
InterMedia-Aalborg
Aalborg University
Niels Jernes Vej 14
DK-9220 Aalborg East
Denmark
Email:
jensf@intermedia.auc.dk

Edvin Vestergaard Kau
Department of Information and Media Science
InterMedia-Aarhus
Aabogade 34
DK-8200 Aarhus N
Denmark
Email:
ekau@imv.aau.dk

Torunn Kjølner
Department of Dramaturgy
InterMedia-Aarhus
Aarhus University
Aabogade 34
DK-8200 Aarhus N
Denmark
Email:
dratk@hum.au.dk

Kristian Knak
AGENCY.COM Interactive TV
Andreas Bjørns Gade 8, 5. tv.
DK-1428 København K
Denmark
Email:
kknak@agency.com

Søren Kolstrup
Department of Information and Media Science
InterMedia-Aarhus
Aabogade 34
DK-8200 Aarhus N
Denmark
Email:
S_Kolstrup@imv.aau.dk

Niels Lehmann
Department of Dramaturgy
InterMedia-Aarhus
Aarhus University
Aabogade 34
DK-8200 Aarhus N
Denmark
Email:
dranl@hum.au.dk

Claus B. Madsen
Computer Vision and Media Technology
InterMedia-Aalborg
Aalborg University
Niels Jernes Vej 14
DK-9220 Aalborg East
Denmark
Email:
cbm@vision.auc.dk

Kim Halskov Madsen
Department of Information and Media Science
InterMedia-Aarhus
Aabogade 34
DK-8200 Aarhus N
Denmark
Email:
halskov@imv.au.dk

Thomas B. Moeslund
Computer Vision and Media Technology
InterMedia-Aalborg
Aalborg University
Niels Jernes Vej 14
DK-9220 Aalborg East
Denmark
Email:
tbm@vision.auc.dk

Michael Mogensen
Department of Information and Media Science
InterMedia-Aarhus
Aarhus University
Aabogade 34
DK-8200 Aarhus N
Denmark
Email:
michaelm@imv.au.dk

Bradley Music
Natural Language Group
Microsoft
1 Microsoft Way
Redmond, WA 98052
USA
Email:
bradmusic@hotmail.com

Peer Mylov
InterMedia-Aalborg
Aalborg University
Niels Jernes Vej 14
DK-9220 Aalborg East
Denmark
Email:
mylov@intermedia.auc.dk

Costanza Navarretta
CST
Njalsgade 80
DK-2300 Copenhagen C
Denmark
Email:
costanza@cst.ku.dk

Peter Øhrstrøm
Department of Communication
Aalborg University
Kroghstraede 3
DK-9220 Aalborg East
Denmark
Email:
poe@hum.auc.dk

Patrizia Paggio
CST
Njalsgade 80
DK-2300 Copenhagen C
Denmark
Email:
patrizia@cst.ku.dk

Lars Qvortrup
Department of Literature,
Culture and Media
University of Southern Denmark
Campusvej 55
DK-5230 Odense M
Denmark
Email:
larsq@litcul.sdu.dk

Claus A. Foss Rosenstand
InterMedia-Aalborg
Aalborg University
Niels Jernes Vej 14
DK-9220 Aalborg East
Denmark
Email:
clausr@intermedia.auc.dk

Mikael B. Skov
InterMedia-Aalborg
Aalborg University
Niels Jernes Vej 14
DK-9220 Aalborg East
Denmark
Email:
mskov@intermedia.auc.dk

Jan Stage
InterMedia-Aalborg
Aalborg University
Niels Jernes Vej 14
DK-9220 Aalborg East
Denmark
Email:
jans@intermedia.auc.dk

Jørgen Stigel
InterMedia-Aalborg
Aalborg University
Niels Jernes Vej 14
DK-9220 Aalborg East
Denmark
Email:
stigel@intermedia.auc.dk

Ernest Holm Svendsen
Department of Information and Media Science
InterMedia-Aarhus
Aabogade 34
DK-8200 Aarhus N
Denmark
Email:
ernest@bodhi.dk

Mads Wibroe
Ronkedor ApS
Badevej 15
DK-8240 Risskov
Denmark
Email:
wibroe@imv.au.dk

Niels Erik Wille
Department of Communication, Journalism and Computer Science
Roskilde University
P.O.Box 260
DK-4000 Roskilde
Denmark
Email:
new@ruc.dk

1 Introduction – Welcome into the Interface

Lars Qvortrup

Currently, computer interfaces are being revolutionized.

- From a text-based interface, interfaces are increasingly becoming multimedia-based.
- From a traditional "flat", two-dimensional interface, interfaces are developing into spatial three-dimensional worlds.
- From a position "in front" of the screen, users are moving "into" the interface.
- From an interactive relationship with "the interface", an agent-supported human machine interface mode is emerging. The user does not interact with the interface, but instead interacts "within" the interface world with an agent who is responsible for representing the intentions of the user, fulfilling his or her wishes, or – perhaps – playing games with the end-user.

This trend is increasingly seen in traditional office-oriented applications, but other application domains – computer games, chat rooms, virtual worlds etc. – have represented the frontier of development.

This trend constitutes the background for the national Danish research project "Staging of Virtual Inhabited 3D-Spaces". This project explores the nature and usages of the rapidly developing realm of interactive multimedia (IMM) systems and the virtual worlds which become available through such systems.

In order to do so, the project analyses the functional, cognitive and aesthetic nature of IMM systems and virtual worlds. Virtual worlds in a sense have their own ontology, as apparently anything can exist in them, and as conditions for existence in them extend beyond our immediate imagination. Presenting themselves as 3D stages with objects and agents (avatars, autonomous agents, actors etc.) it is the assumption of the project that interactive multimedia applications can be informed by theatre and film conventions. For instance, the theatrical metaphor is expected to provide a constant source of inspiration, as by its very nature it invites our imagination to play a dominant role in the explorative studies. When searching for structure in this "landscape" of opportunities, one can draw upon experiences and established structural conventions and languages developed for classical theatre, film, television and other aesthetic domains. Thus, to establish a common metaphorical framework of reference for participants coming from different academic disciplines, to limit the scope of the project, and yet cover a considerable and meaningful subset of the vast potential of this new culture and technology, the research project has adopted an approach which is inspired by the theatre as a guiding metaphor. Virtual worlds are seen as a new type of stage for the representation of objects, people and interactions, and interactive multimedia systems are perceived as the medium through which we can experiment with this stage in the roles of producer, actor or audience.

The results of the research project will be presented in three volumes, of which this is the first. The three publications are:

- *Virtual Interaction: Interaction in/with Virtual Inhabited 3D Worlds*
- *Virtual Space Construction: Construction of Virtual Inhabited 3D Worlds*
- *Virtual Staging: Staging of Virtual Inhabited 3D Worlds*

As already mentioned, currently human–machine interaction is being revolutionized. In order to understand computer-supported interaction it is becoming increasingly inappropriate to conceptualise this interaction as something happening "with" or "through" the interface. Increasingly, it is not appropriate to say that we are interacting "with" the interface, as a reader interacts with a book or – through a pencil – with a piece of paper. Similarly, it is not appropriate to say that we are interacting "through" the interface with other human beings, as we do on the Internet. Rather, we are entering the interface. The interface is becoming a world in which we act and find our way, and within which we interact with other human beings, represented by avatars, or with autonomous agents. This volume invites you into the interface in order to examine its core activity: interaction.

Section 1

In Section 1, the concepts of interaction and interactivity are analysed and mapped out, the virtual ontology of inhabited virtual worlds is explored, and the guiding metaphor of the theatre is examined. It appears that we use basic concepts concerning the interaction with and in virtual worlds in many different ways, and that our classification of virtual worlds and their inhabitants is unclear. In this introductory chapter the establishment of some basic conceptual order is aimed at.

In Chapter 2, by Jens F. Jensen, a basic division between interaction and interactivity is made. Interaction is action performed by agents, whether they are human users or virtual actors. Interactivity is a way to characterize a medium. Thus a medium may be more or less interactive, i.e. more or less suitable to support the interaction of agents. Adding to the confusion, the concepts of interaction and interactivity are rooted in different scientific traditions with different meanings. In *sociology* interaction is about the action-based relationship between human beings in social worlds. Interaction describes the relationship between individuals.

Accordingly, interactivity characterizes human beings' – or social agents' – ability to interact. A person or a social situation may be more or less "interactive". In *communication and media studies,* interaction describes the relationship between a reader and the text. Here, interactivity characterizes different text types according to the ways in which they support the reader's interaction with the text. Finally, in *informatics,* interaction is about the relationship between the user and the computer, cf. "human–machine interaction". Here, the focus is put on the computer as a medium for accessing the "text" understood in a wide sense, where "text" stands for the fictional sign worlds, which we today call "virtual worlds". Thus a specific program or interface may be characterized as more or less "interactive".

With the development of interfaces as worlds in which users, objects and agents interact, it becomes even more important to differentiate between the different roots of the interaction concept, and to understand and use interaction and interactivity in their different meanings. Entering the virtual world we interact with agents and avatars in a sense referring to the sociological concept. Still, however, we are not entering a real world, but interacting with a textual world, referring to the conceptualization of communication and media studies. Finally, we should not forget that these worlds are worlds within the computer as a medium. Even acting in virtual worlds is human–machine interaction. Thus, the understanding of interaction based on informatics is still relevant.

But Jensen also explores these virtual inhabited worlds in order to classify their inhabitants or agents. Basically, we can distinguish between human users, avatars and autonomous agents. Avatars are representations of the human user, either the designer of the virtual world or the end-users, accessing the already established world. Autonomous agents are agents that act according to their own program or – with a concept from an outdated ontology – their "free will". The point is, however, that no sharp division can be upheld. Avatars may continue to act in the virtual world after having been left by their user, thus also being programmed or being programmable by the user. Objects cannot be clearly distinguished from autonomous agents as they may also possess certain dynamic features, such as appearing when a user is at a certain distance or changing colour during the virtual day or year. The point is, of course, that the "ontology" must be reinvented for each new virtual world, and one interesting problem pointed out by Jensen is whether different virtual worlds can interact or enter each other, or whether agents in one world can visit other worlds.

In Chapter 3, by Peer Mylov, similar issues are analysed within a psychological perspective, i.e. with a focus on the end-user. Here, a classification scheme for interactive multimedia is suggested with three dimensions: according to Mylov there are four syntax forms (two spatial syntax forms, the individual and the schematic, and two time-based syntax forms, the temporal (with one object in time) and the linear (with several objects)), three representation forms (the concrete-iconic, the abstract-iconic, and the symbolic), and there are three interaction forms (the enactive, the mediated and the performative), giving 36 interactive multimedia classification cells.

However, Mylov adds that in talking about virtual worlds there is always also a difference between stage and back-stage. The user must always refer to an "I" or a "we", which are different from the "'I's", "'we's" and "'they's" at the virtual stage, and this difference is basic for our understanding of interacting with and in the virtual world. Then, of course, it may be discussed whether this distinction is an ontological or an epistemological distinction. With one possibility suggested by Mylov we are confronted with the ontological distinction between the lifeworld and the mediated world, a distinction which was suggested by Edmund Husserl at the beginning of the 20th century (Husserl, 1962) and, later, elaborated by Jürgen Habermas (Habermas, 1981). Another possibility, which is also touched upon by Mylov, is to observe the difference as yet another contingent distinction between "self" and "other", the "self" being constituted by a certain arbitrary position of observation, constituting the current blind spot of observation and action, but of course being observable by others as yet another mediated world (Luhmann, 1997, p. 538).

The important point is that the distinction between stage and back-stage, between virtuality and reality, must be made, and that it is absolutely basic for our understanding of virtual inhabited worlds that they constitute parallel worlds to reality. This implies that our virtual identity and actions in the virtual world always, implicitly or explicitly, reflect our real identity and real actions. This is exactly the reason why these worlds have their own virtual ontology. Consequently, it is an illusion to think that the final aim is to create full embeddedness in the virtual world, i.e. to make users forget about virtuality and make them believe that they are in a real world. This ideal should be avoided, not because it is too complicated and demanding to make absolutely realistic virtual worlds, but because it represents a basic epistemological error. Even the most realistic virtual world is an "as-if world". Although virtual worlds may look like real worlds, there must necessarily be a difference, cf. George Bateson's point that a map will only function as such in so far as it is different from the landscape (Bateson, 1979).

Finally, in this section, Chapter 4, by Kjølner and Lehmann, deals with the general conceptualization of virtual inhabited worlds. How should these new worlds be understood, not only – as emphasized by Mylov – as mediated or "other" worlds, but also as being of a rather specific nature? It is obvious that traditional metaphors – the virtual world as a text, as a medium etc. – do not fully meet our aims. Inspired by Brenda Laurel (Laurel, 1993), an alternative suggestion is to conceptualize the virtual inhabited interface world as "theatre": a stage with agents directed by a stage director for an audience in order to reach a certain aim, whether it is to educate, to entertain or to provide a useful tool for other purposes.

The starting point is that when we talk about interfaces we are not in the realm of brute natural science facts, but in the realm of institutional or social facts, cf. the distinction suggested by John Searle (1995). In the world of brute facts "X is Y"; for example, water is H_2O. In the world of institutional or social facts, "X is Y according to a convention", or to a (social) designer: something is a cocktail party if participants agree so or design it as such. Similarly, that something is virtual implies that it is designed by somebody, such as the basic fact about theatre is not whether it tells a story or consists of a certain number of actors, but simply that it is staged by somebody. Thus, the computer-as-theatre metaphor represents a specification of the stage/back-stage distinction.

In order to stabilize institutional facts, they are being transformed into material facts (thus sometimes looking like brute facts): market-place relations are being transformed into money, social relations into laws, and organizational cultures into offices, titles and written rules. Contingent relations, media, are being turned into conventions, forms, and these forms are stabilized by being materialized. Similarly, the *mise en scène* is a materialization of a dramaturgical idea. However, a form can function as a new open possibility, a medium, for new form constructions. To take the example of drama, Aristotle wrote his *Poetics*, which was the first form construction: actions performed by somebody for somebody else were conventionalized. However, his *Poetics* is again a medium for new form constructions, i.e. the writing of specific plays, which again function as media for form constructions by being staged by a stage director.

The same thing happens within the world of computers. As already emphasized by Alan Kay, because it can simulate any other medium the computer is a universal medium (Kay, 1984, p. 47). Thus, the computer is contingent. Consequently forms must be made, stabilized sign systems must be constructed in order to reduce the initial level of complexity, at which everything was possible. However, like in the world of theatre, the medium–form–medium process is an iterative process, and the transformation from medium to form into new medium/form can be done several times. A metaphor – the interface as a desktop – constitutes a form within which people can act and communicate. This form is being stabilized by the *de facto* standards produced by multinational software companies. However, in the next phase the desktop as form is used as a medium for new form constructions, e.g. for the construction of mail templates, which again are media for the writing of specific letters.

Similarly, in the current context, and very much inspired by Brenda Laurel, it is our assumption that the theatre functions very well as an initial and general form, i.e. as meta-form, a metaphor-based convention for the use of 3D interfaces. Partly, it signals the general distinction between real and virtual worlds, because everything on stage – and in the computer interface – is fiction, while the user belongs to the real world, i.e. the world of social conventions based on solid brute facts. However, it should not be forgotten that the real world is influenced by the virtual world, such as that people in the theatre are organized as "audience" and follow strict audience behaviour rules. Partly, it provides a good framework for the establishment of worlds with objects and agents, which again may be sub-categorized. However, the theatre metaphor will normally be too general to actually function as the final form for specific communication and action. Thus the theatre metaphor is used as medium for new form constructions, e.g. the city as a specific metaphorical realization of the theatre with its streets, buildings and cars as objects, and citizens, police officers etc. as agents.

In Chapter 4 these reflections are elaborated on. The basic virtue of the theatre metaphor is to emphasize the distinction between reality and virtuality. The aim of immersiveness can never be to eliminate this distinction, and even when totally "immersed" in the virtual world the I – the user – is always observing a world of representations. Particularly, there will always be a doubling of the I, between the user-I and the represented I, be it as an avatar or as a certain subjective virtual camera angle. Even the most identification-oriented virtual world is based on this doubling of the I and the world in real and fictional Is and worlds. Another issue dealt with by Kjølner and Lehmann is the widespread, uncritical use of the concept "metaphor". Is the "theatre" an interface metaphor in the same way as the "desktop" is? No, not quite. While the desktop seems to function as a sort of "model" according to which one can create a framework – what belongs to an office, what does not – the theatre is as much a construction tool, particularly when one turns toward different poetics. A "poetic" is not a list of items which belong or do not belong to the "theatre world". A poetic is rather a construction manual.

In addition to this, Kjølner and Lehmann add value to the important contribution by Laurel by extending the use of the theatre concept beyond Aristotelian and classical theatre. We may be informed and inspired by modern theatre as well, cf. Verfremdungs-techniques, performance theatre, improvisational theatre, mixed media theatre etc., which are all more closely related to interactive inhabited 3D worlds than is classical theatre. However, the most important and unchallenged contribution of Laurel is that we should look for believability rather than truthfulness. Instead of trying hard to create really intelligent agents, the important issue is to make them *appear* intelligent.

Section 2

In the Section 1 the basic elements of the virtual world have been identified and labelled, the epistemological nature of the virtual world has been analysed, and its general conceptualization framework – the theatre – has been presented. In Section 2 this world is entered. The world is inhabited by avatars and autonomous agents, who are supposed to provide us with interactive services. After having elaborated a typology of these virtual species, the main aim of the section is to discuss how such avatars and autonomous agents are designed and which properties they should have in order to create interesting interactive settings.

First, however, different types of approaches and basic concepts should be presented. According to Michael Mogensen in Chapter 5, three different approaches to – or perspectives on – agents can be identified. The first is the *design approach*, according to which the agent characteristics are a matter of design architecture. The second is the *classification approach*, making a taxonomy from a bird's-eye position. Finally, the third perspective is the *use approach*, which reflects the user–agent relationship. In the present context it is obvious that although design architecture must of course be considered as is a *sine qua non* for actually constructing autonomous agents, the starting point lies within the use perspective, simply because the question of whether the agent is autonomous cannot be answered by only looking at the agent's architecture. "An agent is autonomous", as Peter Bøgh Andersen and Jørgen Callesen say in Chapter 7, "if an observer interprets it as such."

Also, some terminological issues must be mentioned. Being inspired by robotics, the terms "behaviour" and "action" are used differently in autonomous agent theory than in humanistic and social sciences. An action is a concrete change of the agent's actuators, while a behaviour is something that causes one or more actions to occur.

Now, turning to the properties and design of agents, one important issue concerns the question of autonomy. What makes an agent appear not as a tool, but as a human-like character who can support the user or enter dialogues with him or her? Michael Mogensen provides an overview of autonomous agents and their qualities, partly with an implicit reference to Jensen's classification scheme, but partly also introducing "degree of autonomy" as a dimension. The main question raised is: which aspects of a virtual agent affect the user's experience of autonomy? In order to appear for a user as an autonomous agent, a number of design properties must be present. For instance, it is of course important that there is a coupling between the agent's perception and action, i.e. that the autonomous agent acts according to perception inputs. However, this is not sufficient. In addition to a simple cybernetic system's stimulus–response mechanism there should also be a reference to the agent's "self", and the construction of "self" should be affected by the references to and inputs from the environment, creating a so-called second-order cybernetic system (Ashby, 1962; Mingers, 1995). The autonomous agent should be able to choose specific actions or modes of practice based on its own accumulated experience, rather than being based on environmental knowledge built in by the designer. Thus a learning dimension is an important part of the agent's architecture.

However, the internal architecture is not the only factor to take into consideration when creating an experience of autonomy. The physical or aesthetic design is important as well. For instance, opacity is a central issue in order to create an illusion that the autonomous agent acts and reacts according to individual properties such as intention or will. Only then will the autonomous agent not just be a helpful piece of software, but a lifelike or even human-like character. Consequently, the aesthetic design of the agent is important, not necessarily in the sense that it looks like a human being, but in the way that it hides the internal mechanisms, i.e. behaves as an individual. Also, the knowledge and imagination of the user are important. Which fictional images does the user create when interacting with the agent, e.g. which virtual world context is created? It is very important for the construction of a belief in "reality" that social situations are produced in which the user feels engaged. This can be supported by the fictional staging or setting of the agent. Thus, although this is most often forgotten, the feeling of interacting with an agent which possesses autonomy is supported as much by creative staging and a good aesthetic design as by the technical agent architecture.

The contextuality issue is further explored in Chapter 6. Mikael Skov presents an overall architecture of an agent which can operate in and serve chat room users. The architecture suggested supports four functional aspects of the autonomous agent: it can communicate with the user; it can take care of operations and tasks delegated to the agent by the user; it can observe the operations of the user; and based on its observations it can recommend specific chat rooms or conversations in the chat room to the user. Here, the learning aspect emphasized by Mogensen is exemplified. Finally, the agent can communicate with other agents in order to make the most useful recommendations to its user. It can, so to speak, explore the world based on a certain representational intentionality.

In Chapter 7, Peter Bøgh Andersen and Jørgen Callesen take us one step further in the construction of autonomous agents and avatars. It is not enough to make agents that can act autonomously. We must make agents which can also create interesting actions, e.g. establish conflicts, based on which narrative structures emerge. This implies that we must go from the traditional robotics-based construction of autonomous agents, inspired by biology and ethology, into the construction of *actors*, a field which is informed by media and communication theory, literature, linguistics and dramaturgy.

Making the difference between agents and actors implies that one must differentiate between continuous flows of behaviours and discrete classifications of these behaviours based on sign systems. Behaviours only become accessible for human beings in the form of communication. When we as human beings interpret behaviours as something reflecting an intention, we observe the behaviour as communication. Here, we are back in Searle's differentiation between brute facts and social facts, or – rather – between what might be called brute behaviours and social behaviours. Brute behaviours are stimulus–response based behaviours referring only to external phenomena, while social behaviours are based both on observation of the environment and on self-observation, and exist for an observer as communication. The first type of behaviour is "caused" by something, while the latter is based on an intention. The leaves of the tree wave because of the storm, while the human being waves in order to establish a communicative contact. The waving – a continuous behaviour – is transformed into a discrete utterance, a sign. Translating the differentiation between brute behaviours and social behaviours – backstage and stage behaviours – into the sign concepts of Peirce, one might say that the former type of behaviour produces index signs, i.e. signs which function as such because they are caused by something (the direction of the smoke is caused by – i.e. is a sign of – westerly wind), while the latter produces symbols, i.e. signs which function as such because of a social convention, which is realized by the intentional behaviour of an individual.

From here, Bøgh Andersen and Jørgen Callesen suggest a number of necessary basic characteristics of virtual actors, such as the ability to inscribe worlds in worlds, i.e. to act according to intentions, to compare self-intentions with the potential intentions of others etc. However, before reaching this higher level of behaviour, some basic abilities must be established. One realm of behaviour research is discrete componential analysis. Here, components can be put together in strings in order to reach a certain goal, thus providing a simple planning mechanism. Adding to this, compulsion schema and force dynamics could make it possible to provide the agent with the ability to aim at accomplishing goals, while the addition of control behaviours could create a simple conflict situation between the agent and the user.

However, we are still far from creating interesting agents, i.e. actors. We should not only design the agent to reach goals or avoid obstacles. The agent should also know how to behave when aiming at reaching a goal or giving up its intention. Here, modality must be added to behaviour: not only is something done, but something is done with an intention, which may be fulfilled or not fulfilled by the behaviour. Also, the agent – or virtual actor – should be able to embed more than one world in its memory. There is the actual world, but also the intended potential world. And there are the opponent's actual and intended worlds, which should also be embedded in the memory. Here, concepts such as Bremond's forking paths of simple narratives and Ryan's "possible world" are introduced (Bremond, 1970; Ryan, 1991). All these materials are put together in a theoretical sketch of the components of an interesting virtual actor, which is able to create conflictual narrative situations or to put itself into the cognitive or intentional position of somebody else, i.e. is able to engage, entertain, educate or serve the end-user.

In Chapter 8, by Wibroe, Nygaard and Bøgh Andersen, the inspiration from Ryan is further pursued. It is a main point that the concept of "interactive story" implies that the "story" is not fixed from the beginning, but can be generated or at least modified during the development of the story. Consequently the story narrated must contain a conflict, i.e. the virtual world must have at least two inhabitants, a protagonist and an antagonist. However, this is not sufficient if it is demanded that the story should be able to change during its development. Thus, each virtual agent – or actor – should contain a planning mechanism, and it should be able to make guesses concerning the plans of the other agents and of course react accordingly. Here, Ryan's theory of representation of intention and of embeddedness is further developed. Also, the paper analyses a computer game, Diablo, in order to demonstrate the negative effects of having autonomous agents without these design properties.

While Peter Bøgh Andersen and Jørgen Callesen differentiate between the biological roots of traditional autonomous *agents* and the humanistic contributions to autonomous *actors*, in Chapter 9 Claus Madsen and Erik Granum make a distinction between what they call the high- and low-level layers of agents. The chapter focuses on the low-level layer, i.e. the level of the common formalism for all autonomous agents, irrespective of their individual properties.

In this chapter different potential architectures are discussed and a general architecture is presented, the idea being that this constitutes the "skeleton" on which individual scripts can be added, making the agents act as actors according to different roles. With the theatre metaphor it parallels the relationship between the actor as a human being and his or her roles and masks. The architecture suggested provides the agents with three basic properties: they are proactive (they can act according to their own intentions), they can communicate, and they have believable personalities. Particular focus is put on the agents' perceptual system: they can "see" within a certain field of view, they can "hear" within a certain distance and they can "feel" the presence of others. Of course, the agents can also remember – and, just as important – forget their perceptions, and they can act accordingly. Supporting the message emphasized by Kjølner and Lehmann that the important issue is to make agents *appear* intelligent, the main point of constructing agent architectures is that without a believable, or realistic, perceptual system, the agents cannot be expected to act in a believable and realistic manner. That is, the human observer will not believe in the agents as actors without believing and understanding the agent's perceptual system.

Finally, the different approaches represented in the section are reflected in a discussion by Bøgh Andersen, Granum and Madsen (Chapter 10). The construction of dramaturgically relevant "autonomous actors" implies a meeting of and collaboration between researchers and developers from, on the one side, engineering and computer science, and, on the other side, researchers and developers with a background in the humanities, i.e. media and communication studies, film theory etc. Here, the basic "divide" – and suggestions for bridging this gap – in the construction of inhabited 3D spaces is presented. This theme is further elaborated in the final chapter of the book, Claus Rosenstand's analysis of the narrative multimedia industry, where the same challenge has to be met from an organizational and managerial point of view.

Section 3

However, it is not enough to create a world and to inhabit it with autonomous, story-generating agents. We as users also want to interact with the virtual inhabitants. Basically, this can be done in two ways. One way is to enter a non-verbal interaction, i.e. to interact only with the virtual bodies of these virtual species. Here, motion capturing mechanisms can be applied. However, the end-user also wants to talk with the autonomous agents: to give them verbal instructions and to receive verbal responses. Thus Section 3 explores the potentials for creating both motion capturing and language-based interaction with and among humans, avatars and autonomous agents.

In Chapter 11, by Thomas Moeslund, the challenge of non-verbal interaction between the user and the autonomous agent is looked at and suggestions for the construction of body language tools, i.e. Motion Capturing or MoCap tools, are presented and overviewed.

The first issue dealt with is how to define MoCap. In principle, every non-textual interface is a MoCap interface, implying that the computer mouse and the joystick are MoCap devices. However, normally by MoCap we understand large-scale body motion (gestures, movements) captured by the computer through non-mechanical devices.

Within this definition, a number of MoCap devices are presented. Basically, one can differentiate between active and passive sensing devices. In active sensing devices motions are captured by attaching signal transmitters to the moving subject, such as body movement transmitters or data gloves. Passive sensing devices, which of course appear to be more "natural", capture movements of physical objects in the real world without attaching artificial signal transmitters to the moving objects. Here, the complexity needed to analyse the motion data is very high, and good tools have still not been developed.

Finally, however, the differentiation between continuous behaviours and their discrete representation as signs – the difference emphasized by Bøgh Andersen and Callesen – should be reflected by MoCap theory as well. Body movements have meanings (cf. the concept of "body language"), which implies that body movements should be interpreted. Sometimes a gesture has a specific meaning, i.e. can be translated into a discrete sign, and always meanings in a broad sense are attached to human movements.

In the following two chapters, language-based interaction with autonomous agents is overviewed and analysed. In Chapter 12, Patrizia Paggio and Bradley Music reflect on the fact that normally, natural language communication is multimodal since it includes verbal as well as non-verbal inputs. Therefore, to build systems supporting natural linguistic interaction it is important to understand the way in which gestures can interact with linguistic signs. Such an understanding will help create natural language interaction devices where speech recognition and production software are is not just added to MoCap devices, but where input coming from different modalities can be combined into a meaningful whole. In other words, the authors argue that to play a role in 3D virtual interfaces, automatic linguistic analysis as practised in the field of computational linguistics must be enriched to cope with gestural information.

Ideally, a multimodal system should analyse combined gesture and speech behaviours and translate them into an integrated meaning – and of course be able to respond in a similar fashion. The authors present a formalism allowing for such an integration, and discuss a number of examples to show how the formalism accommodates complementary, contradictory and ambiguous multimodal information. Finally, an architecture for multimodal analysis is sketched out where the system has the possibility of recovering from breakdowns in the communication. Just like human speakers, in fact, natural language interaction devices of the future must be able to recognize misunderstandings and to repair them accordingly.

The final aim of an autonomous agent with verbal communication abilities is to enter and to participate in natural discourses. Consequently, the nature of discourse must be understood and its basic functionalities implemented. In Costanza Navarretta's paper this aspect is considered, addressing issues such as what is the basic unit of a dialogue (the problem being that sometimes, but not always, the unit is a sentence)? How are dialogue units combined in, for example, acts of turn-taking? How is the context included in the dialogue, i.e. both the internal context (the dialogue history) and the external context (the social and physical environment of the dialogue)? All these and other elements are put together in a dialogue manager module, which is divided into a dialogue analysis component and a dialogue generation component.

Section 4

Still, however, one does not just enter the virtual world, taking up conversations with its inhabitants. One enters a fiction world, and according to Jørgen Stigel in Chapter 15, interactive 3D multimedia can be seen as the latest and highest link of a long chain of development of media within the aesthetic realm. Interactive 3D multimedia realizes the aesthetic project that was launched by the construction of central perspective in renaissance painting: that the user of the aesthetic artefact is in the centre of the fiction world. In painting this illusion is created by linear and atmospheric perspectives, by letting figures close to the viewer overlap figures at a distance etc. In film, movement and sound are added, and the feeling of space is constructed by letting front figures move faster than back-stage figures, by using stereo sound etc.

In interactive 3D multimedia important new possibilities are at hand. The first and obvious possibility is to create stereo vision by constructing two world representations, one for the right eye and one for the left eye, and to separate the two images by using polarized glasses or stereo glasses. The second possibility is to use a position-tracking system, thereby allowing the user to actually navigate in the virtual world and observe objects from all potential positions. Just as important, however, is the third possibility: interactiveness. The user interacts with the world and its objects through, for example, MoCap facilities, and he or she interacts with the agents and actors in the virtual world. Thus the user is not just a passive observer of the fiction world, but he or she is an active participant of the world.

This, however, raises an important issue, namely the issue of narration, in particular the experience of irreversibility of time: destiny in classical drama, the point of no return in film. As a matter of fact, Søren Kolstrup suggests in Chapter 14 that narrativity as a quality of a specific medium depends on the possibility of creating cliff-hangers in this particular medium. Consequently, one important question in this section is whether – or rather how – cliff-hangers can be combined with interactivity. In an interactive medium, is it possible to let somebody hang on a cliff for what by the audience or the user feels like hours? Wouldn't the user break the power of the narrator and simply help this person? Is it possible to create the feeling of destiny when the medium gives the user the possibility to make a second choice, i.e. to neutralize that decision which appeared to be fatal? Here, a media-specific conflict is constituted. On the one hand interactive 3D multimedia function like theatre, film and television, where time is irreversible; on the other hand a problem occurs because the user can influence the narrated structure. The challenge is how to construct an interactive cliff-hanger. Kolstrup suggests that the answer to this challenge is given as fights for control between the user and the author. As a user I want to open a door in order to solve a mystery, but I am only allowed to do so after having solved certain tasks. Or I want to run away from emerging dangers, but my avatar is glued to the spot in a way that is well known from nightmares. The second important issue in this section is to identify what interactive 3D multimedia can learn from earlier media, in particular from film and from television.

Jørgen Stigel points out that the problem regarding the conflict between narrativity and interactivity has two facets, because every narrative has two levels: the first level is the level of story-telling, constituting a relationship between the narrator (or the program designer) and the audience (or the user). One important secret of telling stories is to possess story-telling power: to let the hero hang on the cliff while telling a parallel story. To postpone the point of the joke. To know more – or less – than the audience. The second level is the level of the fiction: the relationship between the actors, the conflict between a dangerous world and the hero, whether the hero is identical to the user – i.e. is an avatar – or is one of the autonomous agents.

This doubling of the narrative into two sets of relationships – what might be called the external and internal relationships – also influences intentionality. The intention of the narrator may be different from the intention of the narrative or of the persons in the narrative. The fact that the principal character is a bad guy does not necessarily imply that the author is evil. Therefore, as pointed out above, it is important to construct actors – and not just agents – with intentions and with abilities to act according to plans at more than one level, thus creating interesting conflicts. However, the second facet must be included: the intentions of the actors, and the conflicts thereby constituted, must imply themes, which point towards a plot or a "deeper meaning" of the story. Similarly, the virtual inhabited 3D world must put the audience or the user in a situation where he or she is, on the one hand, absorbed by – embedded in – the story, and, on the other hand, at least unknowingly observing the constructedness of the virtual world (for instance the way in which a plot, through the intentions of the actors and the internal structures of the virtual world, points towards a moral or a deeper meaning).

This means that the organizing of the story-telling – the relationship between the author/director and the virtual inhabited 3D world – is just as important as the organizing of the story, i.e. the virtual inhabited 3D world. The relationship and the implicit contract between the narrator and the audience. In Chapter 15 this latter aspect is analysed with reference to the construction of a narrator–audience relationship in television. In television the narrator may be visible such as the newsreader in the news programmes or as the reporter in the middle of the event. Here the triangle between audience, narrator and fiction world (which may of course refer to the real world) is explicit. The narrator may, however, also be invisible but present, for instance as the speaker of a visualized story. Finally, the narrator may be absent, for instance in television films. In the latter case the viewer must reconstruct the narrator through the narration. Stigel suggests that four main types of virtual inhabited 3D world can be constructed. The first is the *forum*, which is a place with agents and avatars. Here the narrator only exists in the sense that somebody may have created interesting agents. This is similar to the cocktail party. Next is the *experimentarium*, in which the user can experiment with certain pre-organized situations such as family crises, exams and job interviews. Then comes the *exploratorium*, in which the user can explore interesting situations constituted by virtual environments with agents. The basic category is the computer game, but it is actually based on the classical novel, e.g. Cervantes' novel about Don Quixote. Worlds with a limited number of interesting characters and plots are created, and the hero – or the user, represented by a subjective camera or by an avatar – explores these plots, often implying a moral which can be extracted from the situation. Finally, we have the *consultarium*, which constitutes a locality with one or more agents providing services to the user. This may be a virtual library or information provision centre.

In Chapter 16, Jens F. Jensen analyses the ways in which film theory, e.g. film semiotics, can help us to understand the medium of virtual inhabited 3D worlds. Both media construct inhabited fiction spaces developing in time, but in virtual 3D worlds the user is represented by a point of view or by an avatar, which in both cases can be moved around in the 3D world. Referring to the categories of Stigel, in the film medium the movements of the camera are controlled by the narrator, the film director, while in the interactive 3D medium the camera may be controlled by the user. Still, many film techniques must be transformed into the interactive 3D medium. For instance, space is constructed by *mise en scène* techniques, with the building block of the shot: here the scene is set, the space is organized and the subject is staged in front of the camera. Also, the camera can be moved in different ways – tilting, making panorama shots etc. – and it can represent different points of view, such as the bird's-eye, first person or audience points of view. Similarly, time is constructed by montage techniques, i.e. through cuts relating one shot to the next in a montage, or through movements of the camera. Also, images and sounds are interrelated in different ways. One possibility is to let them represent two narrative worlds, such as is done with film music; another possibility is to let them represent the same world, such as is done with so-called diegetic sound, i.e. sound coming from a physical source in the visually represented world. It is obvious that interactive 3D multimedia must exploit and develop all these techniques in order to tell interesting stories, and Jensen suggests ways to proceed.

In Chapter 17, Edvin Kau, as a point of departure, compares a computer game, e.g. "The Residents' Freak Show", with a film scene from Kurosawa's "Rashomon". Both examples use point of view (POV) as a basic narrative tool. Kurosawa does so while telling five different characters' versions of the story. In "The Residents' Freak Show" the user is taken through different scenes, experiencing the show from his or her own POV, as is the case in many computer games. In one of the possible routes the game ends up by moving the player from looking from the outside into the fiction world of the show to looking from the inside out into the "real" world, where the player can see new users emerging. Thus the relationship between the narrator and the audience is analytically demonstrated, and the uses of film techniques in computer games are introduced and exemplified. This focuses the attention on the user and viewer activity at play in games as well as in cinema. In the user's relation to whole sets of gazes and possible positions he or she is in interaction with the narrative authority, which is built into the patterns of narration and style of the media. The interplay between the practice of style, the narrator and the user leads Kau to a discussion of the importance of both involvement and distance to the effectiveness of games and narratives. Commenting on the traditional discussion of realism, reference and perception in classical film theory and attempting to take it into new territory, where it can be brought to bear on computer generated virtual worlds as well as on film and television, Kau introduces the concepts of transmission and transformation. Transmission characterizes realistic productions depending on indexical qualities of visual media, and transformation characterizes worlds of fiction, be they cinematic or the result of digital imaging/3D animated models. To illustrate the points of discussion and to take it some steps further, elements of the game "Riven" and multimedia CD-ROM examples are analysed and compared with cinematic examples, taking up the question of openness and/or conclusiveness in worlds of multimedia games and fiction film. The chapter's analyses and discussions of style, narrative activity, and the play between user/viewer and narrator, as well as of fictitious space in film and multimedia, draw attention to the field of the media-specific aesthetic and rhetoric of audio-visual fictions in computer-generated virtual worlds.

In Chapter 18, Hanne Dankert and Niels Erik Wille take the general considerations into a specific genre, i.e. the documentary, and suggest ways in which an interactive 3D documentary can be constructed. By defining "documentary" as the objective or true representation of reality in literature, theatre, photography, radio or television, it is an obvious idea to use interactive 3D as a medium for documentaries. In interactive 3D multimedia, places or events of reality can be represented in ways, which not only give a very intense feeling of "being there", but which also give the user the opportunity to explore the place or event of the interactive 3D documentary on his or her own. Referring to Bill Nichols' (1991) distinction between the "expository", "observational", "interactive" and "reflexive" type of documentary, Dankert and Wille suggest ideas for realizing these four types in the interactive 3D medium. The *expository* type presents the subject as seen by the producer: here an interactive 3D documentary would be a guided tour with possibilities to take a closer look, ask questions etc. In the *observational* type the producer plays a more neutral role as the "fly on the wall". Here, the interactive 3D documentary gives users the opportunity to explore the documented world on their own. In the *interactive* type the fact is highlighted that the media-based observation of an event always influences the event. Here, in the 3D documentary interaction between the user and the world and its agents should be given high priority, demonstrating that social events can be influenced by an observer. Finally, the *reflexive* type represents a very conscious awareness of the documentary as genre, playing ironically or critically with the genre. Here, interactivity should not be limited to the relationship between the user and the virtual inhabited world. Also, the relationship between the user and the producer should be involved.

Finally in this section, in Chapter 19 Peter Øhrstrøm brings the considerations of narrative structures vs. interaction into the field of temporal logic representations. How can the narrative structure of an interactive multimedia system, i.e. a temporal series of events influenced by user interactions, be described by temporal logics? Øhrstrøm presents two different kinds of temporal logic, the "absolute" temporal logics of so-called A-logical notions (talking about past, present and future as distinctions in the reality) and the "relativistic" temporal logics of so-called B-logical notions (talking about earlier, later and 'simultaneous with' as distinctions according to something or somebody). Exemplifying this with a multimedia simulation of a Cardiac Care Unit, Øhrstrøm argues that interactive systems should be described within an A-logical manner.

It is obvious that links across the book can be identified. Thus it is obvious that Bill Nichols' four documentary genres in Chapter 18 are connected to Jørgen Stigel's four types of interactive 3Ds (Chapter 15). It seems that the observational 3D documentary is related to Stigel's forum: the user can observe a world which does not seem to be pre-organized by the producer. The interactive 3D documentary is related to the experimentarium, which the user experiments with and thus influences the virtual inhabited world. The expository 3D documentary is related to the exploratorium and the consultarium, where the virtual 3D worlds are rather pre-organized. Finally, the reflexive 3D documentary highlights the fact emphasized by Stigel, by Mylov, and by Kjølner and Lehmann that interactive 3D worlds have three constituents: the object, the user or interpretant, and the producer, i.e. that there are always two observers, and that meta-questions such as questions concerning genre must involve interaction between the user and the producer. Or, as stated by Jensen with reference to Peirce, the virtual inhabited world is a sign creating a relationship between three entities: the representational instance, the entity that is represented, and the instance which interprets the sign as a relationship between representational instance and entity.

Section 5

Finally, Section five looks at the methodological issues of designing virtual inhabited worlds supporting interaction with end-users. How can interactive software systems be modelled, and how are these issues taken from the academic laboratories into real multimedia production halls?

In Chapter 20, Horn, Svendsen and Halskov Madsen deal explicitly with the problem of designing interactive multimedia systems, as the chapter reflects the experiences of designing an interactive multimedia – or digital theatre – installation. Through motion capture equipment a person's movements are used to interact in real time with a virtual 3D figure, which is projected on a human-size screen. Here the design is far from a traditional system's design, as the design process concerns a multimodal, dynamic system involving computer systems, multimedia representation, human users, and constant interaction between the computer system and the users. One may say that the process – the interaction – is the aim of the system.

Based on experiences from the design process, an experimental design approach is suggested. Here, a basic design tool is to build scenarios in order to support the use of digital prototypes and the representation of user contexts. It seems that the conceptual framework founded by Donald Schön in the 1980s (Schön, 1983) and further developed in the 1990s provides an appropriate context for analysing/understanding such design processes oriented towards interactive multimodal and multimedia installations, by conceptualizing the design process as a series of experiments based on reflective "conversations" between the designer and the material. One is tempted to refer to the French sociologist Bruno Latour's concept of actor networks, according to which technological objects are not passive objects determined by human subjects, but that both parts participate in mutually stimulating creative interactions (Latour 1994, 1996).

In Chapter 21, Mikael Skov and Jan Stage also deal with the particular design challenge created by the extensive interaction between user and system in interactive multimedia systems. Based on a study of a design project in which software designers with different backgrounds worked with the same problem it is concluded that object-oriented design provides an adequate basis for design of interactive multimedia systems, but that it must be supplemented by the operating systems design and the mathematical-logical design approach, which may in particular strengthen the conceptual and methodical dimensions of the design process.

Finally, in Chapter 22 Claus Rosenstand takes us from the design laboratories into the multimedia industry. Two extreme ends of the multimedia industry are presented: on the one hand is the function-oriented industry, which is oriented towards conventional methods, structured work and reuse of code and approaches, and on the other hand is the content-oriented industry, which is oriented towards creativity, prefers new methods and avoids reuse of existing material. While the former has its background in the software industry, the latter is rooted in the film and media industries. The challenge of the multimedia industry is to combine these two traditions, and Rosenstand identifies a number of production issues and provides a good-practice list for multimedia managers, whose job is to personalize and support the merging of traditions. Finally, Rosenstand presents a matrix of narrative multimedia systems, identifying four different types, from the rather simplistic determined narrative to the open and complex creative narrative, and he demonstrates that different management approaches are needed to produce these different types of multimedia systems. In conclusion, there is no "better" multimedia industry. The important issue is to relate the right type of industry and management approach to the appropriate type of narrative multimedia system.

Summary

Thus the book takes the reader all the way from general theories and conceptualizations of interaction aspects of virtual inhabited 3D worlds, through theories of and methods for design of autonomous agents and suggestions for verbal and non-verbal interaction with agents, to the construction of narrative structures of such narrated inhabited worlds, ending in specific design methodology considerations and suggestions for management in the multimedia industry.

The book is written by a cross-faculty research group, and is targeted towards a cross-faculty audience, crossing the bridges of so-called "hard" and "soft" sciences. While meeting the expectations of an international ICT research community, the book speaks a language which can be understood by representatives from both sides of the gap – simply because in order to meet the challenge of the next generation of interfaces, cross-faculty approaches must be used.

We are therefore happy to invite you, the reader, into the fascinating world of virtual inhabited 3D interfaces in the present volume in order to explore its interactive challenges.

Acknowledgement

This book could not have been written without the support of the Danish Research Councils, which through their Centre for Multimedia Research funded major parts of the work on which it is based.

References

Ashby, W. R. (1962) Principles of the self-organizing system, in *Principles of Self-Organization* (eds. H. von Foerster and G. W. Zopf). New York: Pergamon.
Bateson, G. (1979) *Mind and Nature*. New York: Bantam Books.
Bremond, C. (1970) Morphology of the French folktale. *Semiotica* 2: 247–276.
Habermas, J. (1981) *Theorie des kommunikativen Handelns*. Frankfurt a. M.: Suhrkamp Verlag.
Husserl, E. (1962) *Die Krisis der europäischen Wissenschaften und die transzendentale Phänomenologie*. Husserliana VI, Den Haag: Martinus Nijhoff.
Kay, A. (1984) Computer software. *Scientific American* 251(3): 41–47.
Latour, B. (1994) On technological mediation. *Common Knowledge* 3: 29–64.
Latour, B. (1996) Om aktørnetværksteori. *Philosophia* 25, 3–4.

Laurel, B. (1993) *Computers as Theatre*. Reading, MA: Addison-Wesley.
Luhmann, N. (1997) *Die Gesellschaft der Gesellschaft*. Frankfurt a. M.: Suhrkamp Verlag.
Mingers, J. (1995) *Self-Producing Systems. Implications and Applications of Autopoiesis*. New York and London: Plenum Press.
Nichols, Bill (1991): *Representing Reality. Issues and Concepts in Documentary*. Bloomington and Indianapolis: Indiana University Press.
Ryan, M.-L. (1991) *Possible Worlds, Artificial Intelligence and Narrative Theory*. Bloomington and Indianapolis: Indiana University Press.
Schön, D. (1983) *The Reflective Practitioner*. New York: Basic Books.
Searle, J. (1995) *The Construction of Social Reality*. New York and London: Allen Lane, The Penguin Press.

SECTION 1

Avatars and Agents in Computerized Theatre

Introduction

Lars Qvortrup

The world of interactive 3D multimedia is a cross-institutional world. Here, researchers from media studies, linguistics, dramaturgy, media technology, 3D modelling, robotics, computer science, sociology etc. etc. meet. In order not to create a new tower of Babel, it is important to develop a set of common concepts and references. This is the aim of the first section of the book.

In Chapter 2, Jens F. Jensen identifies the roots of interaction and interactivity in media studies, literature studies and computer science, and presents definitions of interaction as something going on among agents and agents and objects, and of interactivity as a property of media supporting interaction. Similarly, he makes a classification of human users, avatars, autonomous agents and objects, demonstrating that no universal differences can be made. We are dealing with a continuum. While Jensen approaches these categories from a semiotic point of view, in Chapter 3 Peer Mylov discusses similar isues from a psychological point of view. Seen from the user's perspective, a basic difference is that between stage and back-stage (or rather: front-stage), i.e. between the real "I" and "we" and the virtual, representational "I" and "we". Focusing on the computer as a stage, in Chapter 4 Kjølner and Lehmann use the theatre metaphor to conceptualize the stage phenomena and the relationship between stage and front-stage.

However, while Mylov from his psychological perspective seems to prefer the ontological differentiation between lifeworld and mediated worlds, "reality" and "virtuality" as it were, Kjølner and Lehmann look at it from a dramaturgical position, where there is not necessarily any difference regarding level of reality. Rather, one may say that the organization of the so-called reality in front of or interfering with the virtual world is influenced by the virtual world, such as an audience is organized by the theatre's proscenium division between stage and front-stage. Comparing Jensen and Mylov, this also implies that both virtual and real interaction and interactivity should be studied. No matter what constitutes the difference between these two worlds, they are both important in the study of virtual 3D worlds.

Regarding future research it is important that common concepts are further developed and refined. Often, lack of understanding in this cross-institutional world is based on differences of concepts and metaphors rather than on differences of practical approaches and ideas. Also, as is convincingly argued by Kjølner and Lehmann, the theatre metaphor should be elaborated beyond its present Aristotelian limits. Other types of artistic form than the causal linearity of classical narrative should be included, and as a matter of fact interactive 3D worlds have more to do with improvisational theatre than with classical theatre. The present chapters only provide a starting point for further research.

2

Virtual Inhabited 3D Worlds: Interactivity and Interaction Between Avatars, Autonomous Agents and Users[1]

Jens F. Jensen

To The Inhabitants of Space in General

E. A. Abbott, Flatland, 1884

2.1 Introduction: From "Flatland" to "Spaceland"

> "I come," cried he, "to proclaim that there is a land of Three Dimensions." ... "The time is short, and much remains to be done before you are fit to proclaim the Gospel of Three Dimensions to your blind benighted countrymen in Flatland..."
>
> *E. A. Abbott, Flatland, 1884*

In E. A. Abbott's book, *Flatland. A Romance of Many Dimensions*, of 1884 he describes a fictional society that exists in only two dimensions in the form of a two-dimensional plane of length and breadth, therefore called 'Flatland'. This world is inhabited by intelligent human-like beings or agents in the form of geometrical figures (Abbott, 1884, p. 3):

> Imagine a vast sheet of paper on which straight Lines, Triangles, Squares, Pentagons, Hexagon, and other figures, instead of remaining fixed in their places, move freely about, on or in the surface, but without the power of rising above or sinking below it,

---

1 An earlier and shorter version of this chapter has been presented as an Invited Paper/ Invited Talk at *WebNet '99 - World Conference on the World Wide Web and Internet*', 24–30 October Honolulu, Hawaii (Jensen, 1999b). Related presentations can be found in (Jensen, 1998a, 1999a).

> very much like shadows – only hard and with luminous edges – and you will then have a pretty correct notion of my country and countrymen

reports the narrator, who is actually a square from "Flatland".

The inhabitants of this world are divided up into a rigid hierarchy: the women are straight lines, the soldiers and lowest classes of workmen are isosceles triangles with sharp angles, the middle class consists of equilateral or equal-sided triangles, the professional men and gentlemen are squares and pentagons, and hexagons and figures with any higher number of sides – which receive the honourable title of polygonal, or many-sided – make up increasing degrees of nobility. Finally, when the number of sides is so numerous and the sides so small that the figure cannot be distinguished from a circle, it reaches the highest degree of perfection and enters the highest class of all, the Circular or Priestly Order. Hence the more sides that form part of the figures, the higher they rank in the social hierarchy of Flatland.

The Flatlanders have no means of moving beyond the surface in which they live, let alone an awareness or consciousness of anything outside the two dimensions. Their perception and experience are limited to the two-dimensional world where all phenomena are described exclusively in terms of length and breadth.

At one point, the storyteller has a dream about a land of only one dimension, the straight line: "Lineland". Here the inhabitants are made up of points (women) and small straight lines (men) respectively, all moving to and fro in one and the same line that constitutes the whole of their world. To the Linelanders, then, the world-view is limited to a single point.

Later the narrator realizes that a third dimension, based on height, exists and consequently a world of three dimensions: "Spaceland". Among other things, he has a visit from an inhabitant of Spaceland, a three-dimensional sphere. The sphere tries to convince him of the existence of the third dimension and the possibility of a three-dimensional world. At first the narrator does not believe the stranger from Spaceland. Imagine what happens when a three-dimensional sphere visits or intersects a two-dimensional world. How will the inhabitants in Flatland necessarily sense and experience it? They will not see a sphere approaching from outside their surface or plane but will only sense the part of the sphere that intersects the two-dimensional world, i.e. they will see a circle. Seen from this 2D world, the sphere will first appear as a single point, then as a small circle, and as the sphere moves through the plane the circle will gradually increase in diameter. When half of the sphere has passed through the plane, the circle will get smaller until it appears as a single point and disappears altogether. Thus, the Flatlanders' experience of the three-dimensional sphere will necessarily be a two-dimensional circle that first grows in diameter and then shrinks. In other words, for the Flatlanders the third dimension will appear as movement in time.

Gradually, however, the narrator is convinced of the existence of a third dimension and another spatial world. He begins to tell his countrymen, the other Flatlanders, about the new Spaceland and the newly discovered third dimension, but none of the Flatlanders are able to conceive of this dimension since they have never learned to see it. At the end of the story, the narrator, the square from Flatland, is accused of spreading subversive thoughts and actually ends up in a (two-dimensional) jail (cf. Jensen, 1999a).

Naturally, the moral of the story – or at least one of the morals – is that we are only capable of sensing, perceiving and imagining the dimensions we know, i.e. the dimensions we have learned to perceive and are used to living in and experiencing, and that our perception and imagination are – more or less – blind to all beyond that.

Our situation today is in many ways similar to the Flatlanders. Users and producers of computer and multimedia systems are being trained first by one-dimensional text-based interfaces (Lineland) and later by two-dimensional graphic interfaces (Flatland). At this point there are only vague hints of what an expansion into a third dimension – Spaceland – might mean and what possibilities it will open up with regard to representation, aesthetics and interaction.

The history of "virtual communities" or "chat rooms" indicates the same development. It started with text-based virtual communities built up around simple text messaging. One of the first and most prominent examples is The Well, but other "virtual communities" also used text systems, like MUDs, IRC or chat rooms in online services. This world can be compared to Lineland. Later, two-dimensional worlds like the Palace arrived, with an interface composed of two-dimensional background pictures in which 2-dimensional, cartoon-like avatars move around – a veritable digital version of Abbott's Flatland. And finally, there are (aside from the 2.5-dimensional worlds like WorldsAway) the three-dimensional worlds – often inhabited by avatars and agents – which are used to communicate, interact, build, create etc. Here, the virtual communities are expanding into an Abbott-like Spaceland.

2.2 Virtual Inhabited 3D Worlds: Preliminary Definition

> Exactly: you see you do not even know what Space is. You think it is of Two Dimensions only: but I have come to announce to you a Third–height, breadth, and length.
>
> *E. A. Abbott, Flatland, 1884*

These virtual inhabited three-dimensional worlds (VI3DWs) are currently becoming a reality. They first appeared in computer games and standalone multimedia applications, but are increasingly appearing in networked-based systems, e.g. the Internet, intranets, the World Wide Web and interactive television. Considered as new media, they can be characterized by the following traits:

- VI3DWs are generated from software, drawn as interactive computer graphics in three space dimensions (plus a fourth dimension in time), i.e. they exist only in cyberspace: in the digital domain of the computers and the computer networks.
- VI3DWs are represented either in display systems based on stereovision (3D film, 3D CAVEs, hologram projections etc.) or on a two-dimensional screen, that is, in the last case 3D graphics are understood as a way of representing 3D data in 2D so that it can be viewed on a computer monitor or a TV screen.
- VI3DWs usually contain computer-generated representations of their users – *inter alia*, so that other users can see them – in the form of so-called "avatars". In

other words, this software is inhabited – inhabited by its users, designers and developers.

- These avatars can be moved around as movable computer graphics on the 3D scene and the movement is controlled interactively by the user.
- An avatar has a viewpoint that is fixed relative to the avatar.
- Consequently, as the user moves the avatar around, its viewpoint also moves. Because the background is animated, as well as the objects in the scene, the user can see the whole scene move relative to the figure. In short, the user can interactively control the viewpoint relative to the 3D space or scene.

One might call these environments "Virtual Inhabited 3D Worlds". However, they have other names as well, such as "3D Cyberspace", "distributed virtual reality", "Shared Spaces" (Bradley *et al.*, 1996), "3D Internet" (Wilcox, 1998), "3D Web", "3D chat", "inhabited digital spaces" (Damer *et al.*, 1995), "Avatar Cyberspace" (Damer *et al.*, 1998b) and "avatar virtual worlds" (Damer, 1998a).

These 3D worlds are currently enjoying rapid growth. Fully implemented existing virtual worlds include Active Worlds, WorldsAway, Biota's Nerve Garden, Blaxxun, Traveller, The Palace, Oz and Worlds Chat – and even more VI3DWs are under construction at the moment.

Some of these VI3DWs are (re)constructions of large three-dimensional "cities" with buildings, streets etc.; others are market-places, stages, TV programs, space stations; and still others are strange places that have no similarity whatsoever with anything in the non-virtual world (Jensen, 1998a, 1999a).

In these virtual worlds, it is possible to meet and have (mediated) social interactions and communication with other avatars, i.e. other users on the network, or with autonomous agents, in real time. Via these virtual interactions, a new type of virtual social practice and virtual social structure or culture is being created. It is these virtual inhabited 3D Worlds and their virtual interactions and communication that are the primary objects of this study.

2.3 What are Virtual Inhabited 3D Worlds, Anyway?

> Pooh! what do you know of Space? Define Space.
>
> *E. A. Abbott, Flatland, 1884*

In this context, VI3DWs will be considered as consisting of three basic elements or building blocks: virtual worlds, artificial life and virtual communities:

- The term "world" refers to the all-encompassing context for the totality of human activities and experiences and the term "virtual world" refers to "computer programs that implement digital worlds with their own 'physical' and 'biological' laws... VW is concerned with the simulation of worlds and the synthesis of digital universes" (Heudin, 1998; cf. below).
- The term "Alife" or "artificial life" refers to digital simulations of living systems which incorporate metaphors from biology, i.e. biologically inspired synthetic organisms.

- The term "virtual communities" refers to human social communities that form in and around digital virtual worlds, often in the form of a group of people communicating with each other through computer networks.

These three elements are brought together and integrated within VI3DWs, which are generally constituted around computer simulations of whole worlds or digital universes with artificial life forms and/or social communities.

One of the decisive features of VI3DWs is that they are, in a certain sense, purely symbolic worlds, exclusively constituted by representations, by symbols or by digital signs. Furthermore, these representations have no necessary, causal or motivated relationship to instances in the non-virtual world. Thus the concept of representation naturally plays a key role in the conceptualization and understanding of virtual inhabited 3D worlds.

"Representation" as a concept refers to all aspects of the appearance of virtual worlds including the appearance of avatars, bots, objects and other elements of the virtual world. Representation is related to the concept of sign.

A sign is "something which stands for something else to somebody" (Peirce, 1931-58). In other words, a sign is a manifest, perceivable entity (whether it is a thing, an element of behaviour, a form of appearance etc.) that is received by the sense organs of an interpretative, mental apparatus and is interpreted as referring to something else (an item, phenomenon, feeling, event in the real or virtual world etc.). The interpretative mental apparatus establishes a relationship or a "link" between the entity, which represents, and that which is represented.

The actual sign is then finally constituted as a relationship between these three entities: the representation, the entity that is represented, and the mental apparatus that interprets the first by linking it to the second (Jensen, 1993). In this way, signs can be seen as quite a distinctive class of phenomena, since they have meanings: they stand for or refer to other objects, events, concepts, emotions etc. These concepts – "sign" and "representation" – naturally play a key role in this context of what are entirely symbolic worlds; worlds which are exclusively constructed or built of representations – worlds which are, in a certain sense, nothing but signs.

Furthermore, the fundamental technique or system of representation is 3D graphics (and in some cases – or worlds – (3D) sound). As mentioned above, "3D graphics" refers to a way of representing three-dimensional data either via a display system based on stereovision or on a two-dimensional screen. Thus, in the last case – as also mentioned above – 3D graphics are understood as a way of representing 3D data in two dimensions so that it can be viewed on a screen or a computer monitor.

2.4 Basic Entities of Virtual Inhabited 3D Worlds

How I came to Spaceland, and what I saw there.

E. A. Abbott, Flatland, 1884

There are several types of representations or entities in VI3DWs. The following section will attempt to identify, define and discuss some of the key elements or basic entities that can be found within the horizon of virtual inhabited 3D worlds.

Virtual World The concept "Virtual World" covers the total virtual environment, i.e. the whole three-dimensional scene or 3D space with its set of various objects and with all its specific characteristics. The terms "virtual world", "scene" and "space" are here more or less synonymous. This "virtual 3D space" has a number of general properties:

- It is coordinate-based, i.e. every position in the space can be identified by a set of three coordinates (x, y, z).
- It is geometrically finite, i.e. it makes up a "bounded", "delimited" world.
- It is continuously navigable, i.e. the user can move seamlessly through the world without transition of any kind. The space itself, however, can be made up of several linked files, as long as they appear to the user to be seamless.
- It is defined by a set of "physical", "biological", "social" etc. rules. These rules have an affinity to physics-based laws like laws of nature, i.e. they define how one may move, interact, communicate etc. in the space, except that in this case it is the designer, the creator of the world, who has established the rules.
- Each world represents a specific vision of what a virtual world can be and which experiences it can offer its inhabitants and users. Virtual worlds thus have their own ontology since all conceivable forms of existence seem to be possible within them, or more precisely: the nature of being is here only limited by the current technology and imagination.

In these virtual worlds or 3D spaces there may be various types of interiors or elements which can roughly be divided into objects and agents, differentiated by whether or not their primary function is to carry out an action.

Objects An object can be defined as a limited relatively autonomous part of the world. Examples of objects are trees, billboards, windows, doors, posters etc. including props, i.e. the accessories or attributes of an avatar such as a hat, a bike or a cane. Objects typically consist of two basic components: (1) a model that determines what the object looks like, its size etc. and (2) some characteristics that determine where it is placed, which actions it can carry out etc. Objects can also be assigned actions; therefore, drawing a precise border between objects and agents, especially "bots" (cf. below) can, in some cases, be difficult.

Agents VI3DWs are not, however, solely composed of a space and objects; this space is also inhabited. Agents are entities that inhabit the virtual worlds and whose primary function is to carry out actions. They have two main forms, which will be described – for the moment – as relatively sharply differentiable polar opposites. This is done based on questions such as: who is controlling the agents? Who is doing the driving? On the one hand there are agents that react independently of the user, but which are controlled by software or AI, the so-called "autonomous agents" or "bots" (short for robots). On the other hand, there are agents, which directly represent and are controlled by users, the so-called "avatars".

Bots or autonomous agents A bot or an autonomous agent is a piece of software which is not directly or interactively controlled by a human user, but runs on its own, controlled either by a program or by some form of built-in intelligence. In real life, robots are often physically manifested as machines. On the Internet or the Web bots are often invisible or are only represented in a visible mode in the interface during input or output. The special thing about bots in VI3DWs is that they (most often) are represented as visible; that is, they have a sensory representation in the virtual world. In many cases, bots are similar to other users (i.e. avatars) and appear as a kind of automated or virtual avatar. Similarly, they may have some degree of built-in AI, independence, self-motivation, personality etc. Often bots are given specific assignments. In VI3DWs, they are usually used to inhabit sparsely populated spaces and thereby to provide the user or the avatar with company (automated conversational agents etc.), to show the way or to guide tours, to answer questions, to entertain by asking riddles or offer clues to puzzles, to provide information on present users or the present scene, etc.

Avatars At the pole directly opposite the bot or the autonomous agent is the avatar. Even though avatar technology is relatively new, the term "avatar" is paradoxically quite old. It comes from Sanskrit and means something like "the embodiment of a spirit in the flesh". In its modern digital virtual incarnation an "avatar" is defined in many different ways. Wilcox defines an avatar as "an electronic representation of a person in cyberspace", "[a] virtual expression of yourself, wearing your wardrobe of virtual clothes" or "an electronic version of the human form designed to let you enter cyberspace" (Wilcox, 1998). Damer defines it as "a digital body you can see", "a virtual personality in a three-dimensional world" (Damer, 1998a) or "animated 3D models of users" (Damer *et al.*, 1998b).

An avatar is, in other words, a representation of the human actor or user in the virtual universe which can be manipulated and controlled by the user in real time, even if the representation is, at the same time, bound by the limitation and laws of the virtual world in question. In this particular sense, avatars are – as Wilcox also formulates it – "extensions of ourselves". So if Marshall McLuhan's old catchphrase "media and technologies are extensions of ourselves" has ever been relevant it must be now, in relation to VI3DWs, where the slogan has been given a most concrete incarnation in avatar technology.

The avatar serves several functions. It is necessary in order for the user to be visible to others and thereby to have a "presence" in and interact with others in the virtual world. It is necessary for the user to have a position in the form of a set of three coordinates and thereby a viewpoint and *a sense* of "presence" in the three-dimensional world. It is generally necessary in order for the user to enter, move around in and experience the virtual space as well as to become a member of the virtual community. In VI3DWs, then, avatars are used (virtually) to meet new people, have new experiences, visit new places, learn, play etc.

An avatar has two important aspects: appearance and functionality. One important thing about an avatar is naturally its appearance – what it looks like – because it is synonymous with the way the user presents him- or herself in cyberspace. Another important thing is functionality, since an avatar can have many different functions. It can be equipped with animation and behaviour patterns (where "behaviour" here refers to a sequence of animations); it can show emotion via facial expression; it can carry objects, belongings or props; it can be able to prove its identity in connection with financial transactions; and, if desired, it can also give gifts and have pets.

As far as special behaviour patterns go, the components of animations and behaviour – like avatars themselves – are often selected from galleries and then personalized. Specific animations and behaviours can then be released or triggered by different factors, such as: user behaviour (a click of the mouse and the like), a time factor, collision detection, proximity to other objects or avatars, the appearance of an object, a touch sensor etc. Although by definition avatars are under the control of the user, the degree of control can vary in practice quite a bit. In certain cases the user can completely control all of the avatar's movements and communicative actions down to the smallest detail. In other cases, the user can only determine actions, behaviour patterns, gestures, moods, manipulation of objects etc. on a more general level. This behaviour is then carried out by a pre-programmed automatic system. In yet other cases, parts of the avatar's behaviour can be controlled by the user while other parts are controlled by a system or a more or less intelligent program.

Within the avatar category there are both the *user-in-avatar*, which is a representation of the human user in the virtual 3D world and the *designer-in-avatar*, which is a representation of the designer, developer or creator of the 3D world (sometimes called "God"). Virtual inhabited 3D worlds are then the only type of software where one can actually meet and speak with the author of the application – within the application itself.

Human Actor Finally, there is the human agent or user of the 3D system or world, who actually controls the avatar and/or the viewpoint of the world.

2.5 Cyber-Hybrids – the Strange Inhabitants of Virtual 3D Worlds

> Hey, that software is inhabited!
>
> *Bruce Damer, 1998a*

> O brave new worlds,
> That have such people in them!
>
> *E. A. Abbott, Flatland, 1884*

Although there is then, in principle, a differentiation in terms of definition between bots and avatars, both concepts cover a relatively wide spectrum of very different types of phenomena with differing degrees of control. There also seems to be a tendency toward the appearance of more and more hybrids – we could call them "cyber-hybrids" – combining avatars and bots. Furthermore, these hybrid forms are in many ways the most interesting and most promising in the virtual worlds at the moment. Rather than considering avatars and bots as polar opposites, it may therefore be more productive to consider them as the outer points along a continuum, between which can be found all sorts of combinations or hybrids (see Figure 2.1). The following will briefly outline a typology of the strange new hybrid

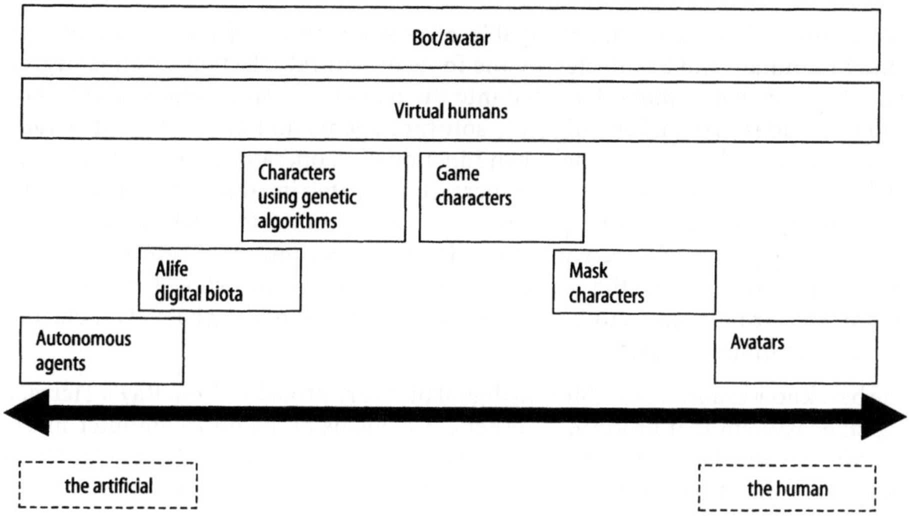

Figure 2.1 The continuum between autonomous agents and avatars.

creatures which currently populate this continuum in the virtual worlds (Wilcox, 1998).

Alife/Digital Biota Along the continuum between autonomous agents and avatars, Alife (artificial life) or digital biota is closely related to the former (see Figure 2.1). Alife and digital biota are artificial or "alien" life forms, i.e. biologically inspired, synthetic organisms in the form of quasi-autonomous software. Thus, Alife is the virtual world's counterpart to the real world's plants and primitive animal life forms. Jean-Claude Heudin (1998) describes the vision of Alife in virtual worlds in the following way: "Imagine a virtual world with digital creatures that looks like real life, sounds like real life, and even feels like real life.... This virtual world could be familiar, reproducing some parts of our reality, or unfamiliar, with strange "physical" laws and artificial life forms".

Alife as a general area of research deals with artificial living systems and the general principles of the living state. *Alife online* (1998) describes the field and its background context in the following way: "Artificial Life – literally 'life made by Man rather than by Nature'. Artificial Life ('AL' or 'Alife') is the name given to a new discipline that studies 'natural' life by attempting to recreate biological phenomena from scratch within computers and other 'artificial media'.... By extending the horizons of empirical research in biology beyond the territory currently circumscribed by life-as-we-know-it, the study of Artificial Life gives us access to the domain of life-as-it-could-be...".

With regard to the definition of "digital biota" and their boundary surfaces to creatures such as bots, agents, AI etc., Biota.org writes: "Digital Biota are a class of self-replicating autonomous software objects which includes computer viruses, artificial life programs, some cellular automata and some genetic algorithms. Once released they live or die by their own decisions as they interact with their environment. They are usually capable of reproduction – if they also have the ability to mutate and be affected by the force of natural selection to some degree then they can evolve. Biota shade out into the region of semi-autonomous objects, which includes artificial intelligence, software agents and bots. These generally have only limited control of their own functionality, operate according to outside goals, and do not reproduce.... The increase in avatar inhabited virtual environments on the Internet is one potential breeding ground for such digital biota" (Wilcox, 1999). As can be seen here, there is not only a continuum between autonomous agents and avatars; the continuum stretches across the whole field of agents and objects: from avatars, to biota and Alife, to autonomous agents, AI, bots and (semi-autonomous) objects.

The best know examples of Alife and digital biota are probably: Tom Ray's Tierra, a digital ecosystem that produces synthetic organisms based on a computer metaphor for organic life; Karl Sim's 3D virtual creatures; and Biota's Nerve Garden, a biologically-inspired multi-user collaborative 3D virtual garden hosted on the Internet – i.e. a public terrarium in cyberspace – where visitors can plant a seed and watch it grow.

Characters using genetic algorithms A bit closer to humans on the continuum between the artificial and the human are characters, which use genetic algorithms (see Figure 2.1). In other words, these characters have a built-in ability to learn from the interactions they participate in, to learn from experience and thus to continuously change their characteristics and functionality. They often have a relatively independent existence in the given virtual world where they can live out their own lives. Among the best-known examples are perhaps CyberLife's popular game "Creatures", where the user is supposed to raise the creatures from the egg stage, and the Japanese Tamagotchi.

Game Characters In the middle of the continuum, but perhaps closest to the autonomous agents, are game characters (see Figure 2.1). They are, as the name indicates, often related to games and can be regular autonomous agents with an independent existence and functionality in the universe of the game. At any given time, however, a user can take over control of a game character – for example as a tool for getting into a game, in order to learn the rules of a game or under particularly exciting and critical passages in the action – in which case the game character's status is temporarily transformed into an avatar.

Mask Characters Closer to avatars are mask characters (see Figure 2.1). Mask characters are avatars which – aside from the usual physical form and functionality of an avatar – also have a character, that can control, guide or inspire the user who is using it. For instance, the character can tell the user which high-level directions make sense in a given situation, and then, given the user's choice, improvise a course of behaviour (Hayes-Roth *et al.*, 1997). In other words, it is a "smart" avatar with an independent mental life: a consciousness or a will. As such, mask characters are used in ecommerce, learning, and entertainment as well as to teach users to play certain roles in the virtual environment. Examples are Hayes-Roth's and Extempo's "Imp Characters", which are guided by their roles, their personalities and their moods, as well as by real-time directions from the user or other software.

Virtual Humans Virtual humans are "naturalistic" copies or stand-ins for humans, where the main principle is to create the most convincing, realistic or perfect simulation of the human form and function (while normal avatars and agents may look like just about anything). Emphasis can be placed on either form (appearance) or functionality or both at once. Virtual humans are used primarily in simulations and in the testing of products and environments, but also in games and movies.

Along the continuum between autonomous agents and avatars, virtual humans cover the whole stretch (see Figure 2.1). In the bot incarnation they may appear as pure dummies which make up simple pre-programmed, animated figures in a 3D model, or they may be autonomous agents which are controlled to some degree by artificial intelligence. In the avatar incarnation they may be directly and interactively controlled by a human actor, e.g. in the form of "ergonomic avatars" in connection with virtual trials of products, processes or environments by way of simulations in cases where real life trials may be inexpedient. The same virtual human can in fact change between being a bot and an avatar. The most prominent examples in this category are perhaps the computer-generated – but very realistic – Japanese digital pop star and personality Kyoko Date, made up of 40 000 polygons (following the social logic of Abbott's *Flatland*, where the number of sides or polygons reflects the degree of perfection and supremacy, Kyoko Date must be little short of the perfect creation), and the work done on realistic avatars and virtual humans at MIRALab, Geneva.

Avatar/Bot Furthermore, there are more and more examples of agents in virtual worlds being able to switch instantly, so to speak, from the avatar mode to the bot mode (see Figure 2.1).

One example is 3D Planet's 3D-assistant, a 3D representation that can function as both an autonomous agent controlled by a program and as an avatar, depending on the situation encountered and the programs being run. The assistant functions in principle as an interface between the program that is actually running and the user, sometimes controlled by the program and sometimes controlled by the user. In this way, the 3D-assistant perhaps gives us a taste of what a so-called "assistant interface" might look like in the future.

Or one might imagine a user who participates in a communicative community represented by an avatar, but whose avatar lives on – even *after* the user has left the world and the computer – switched to some kind of "automatic pilot", continuing to interact and communicate with other agents and avatars (perhaps also running in an automatic mode). In this mode the automatic avatar might follow predetermined parameters or pre-programmed behaviours, follow some form of artificial intelligence, or even simulate or mimic what it has learned from the particular user (Wilcox, 1998).

2.6 Interactivity, Interaction and Virtual Interaction

...you must go with me – whither you know not – into the Land of Three Dimensions
E. A. Abbott, Flatland, 1884

An area of particular interest in connection with VI3DWs obviously involves the new possibilities for interaction and interactivity that arise, partly seen in relation to real life interaction, and partly in relation to interaction and interactivity (Jensen, 1997, 1998c, 1999d) in more conventional media and computer applications.

2.6.1 Interaction

The concept of "interaction" generally means "exchange", "interplay", or "mutual influence". However, if we focus on individual fields of scholarship, the concept takes on many, very different meanings. In other words, the meaning of the concept depends on the context in which it is used. Of primary importance in establishing the concept of "interaction" in the context of computers, computer media and virtual inhabited 3D worlds is how the term is understood in the academic fields of (1) sociology, (2) communication and media studies, and (3) informatics or computer science (Goertz, 1995; Jäckel, 1995; Jensen, 1999d).

(1) Concerning sociology's concept of "interaction", *Wörterbuch der Soziologie* writes: "Interaction is the most elemental unit of social events, where people adapt their behavior to each other, whether or not they follow mutual expectations or reject them. As coordinated action is not pre-programmed, a minimum of common meaning and linguistic understanding is necessary" (Krappmann, 1989, p. 310, emphasis deleted). Similarly the *International Encyclopaedia of Communications* writes: "interaction occurs as soon as the actions of two or more individuals are observed to be mutually interdependent", i.e. "interaction may be said to come into being when each of at least two participants is aware of the presence of the other, and each has reason to believe the other is similarly aware", in this way establishing a "state of reciprocal awareness" (Duncan, 1989, p. 325). Understood in this way, according to sociology, interaction makes up "a basic constituent of society" (Duncan, 1989, p. 326).

The basic model that the sociological interaction concept stems from is thus the relationship between two or more people who, in a given situation, mutually adapt their behaviour and actions to each other. The important aspects here are that limited, clear-cut social systems and specific situations are involved, where the partners in the interaction are located in the same time and space, i.e. are in close physical proximity, and "symbolic interaction" is also involved. In other words, a mutual exchange and negotiation regarding meaning takes place between partners who find themselves in the same social context. This is a phenomenon which communication and media studies would call communication, or more precisely – since the partners in the interaction are situated in the same context – face-to-face communication or interpersonal communication. Within sociology, then, it is possible to have communication without interaction (e.g. listening to the radio and/or watching TV), but not interaction without communication.

(2) As regards the concept of "interaction" in communication and media studies, there is no such clear-cut answer since there appear to be several different concepts of "interaction" involved.

If we look at the dominant trend within current communication and media studies, what might generally be called the "cultural studies" tradition, one recurring trait is that the term "interaction" is used as a broad concept that covers processes that take place between receivers on the one hand and a media message on the other. For the sake of simplicity, attention will be drawn to an example, more as a source of inspiration than as a central representative of the "cultural studies" tradition.

Wolfgang Iser wrote an essay in 1980 entitled "Interaction Between the Text and the Reader". He starts by claiming that "Central to the reading of every... work is the interaction between its structure and its recipient" (Iser, 1989, p. 160). In brief, his approach is that the work can neither be reduced to the author's text nor to the reader's subjectivity, but must be found somewhere between these two poles. And if "the virtual position of the work is between the text and the reader, its actualization is clearly the result of an interaction between the two". It seems fairly obvious that this is not "interaction" in the sociological sense. What is missing is genuine reciprocity and an exchange between the two elements involved in that the text naturally can neither adapt nor react to the reader's actions or interpretations. The concept of "interaction", as it is used here, seems to be a synonym for more noncommittal terms such as "relation", "relationship", "interpretation" or "reading".

The question immediately becomes whether it is relevant to use the concept of "interaction", with its strongly sociological connotations, in connection with these phenomena, which are actually certain types of active reception. O'Sullivan *et al.* point out a related problem in this conceptual watering down process when in *Key Concepts in Communication and Cultural Studies*, under the reference "interaction/social interaction" they warn: "The phrase "social interaction" has perhaps been used too frequently within communication studies – to the point of obscuring any one agreed interpretation. It would be inappropriate, for example, to describe an audience as 'socially interacting' when reading a book, or witnessing the death of Hamlet within a hushed and darkened theatre... because of the lack of observable reciprocation from others the social criteria are not satisfied" (O'Sullivan *et al.*, 1994, p. 155).

There are, however, also traditions within media and communication studies where the use of the concept of "interaction" comes closer to the sociological meaning, such as research in interpersonal communication, where the object of study by definition lies within a sociological framework of understanding (e.g. Corner and Hawthorn, 1989); traditional media sociology, which often takes over the sociological interaction concept and uses it in a sense that shows solidarity with the sociological meaning, primarily in relation to communication within groups of (media) audiences (e.g. McQuail, 1987, pp. 228ff); sociologically oriented media effect research and the "two-step flow"-model, which combines a mass communication model with a model for interpersonal communication within a mass media audience where the later represents "interaction" in a traditional sociological sense; "uses and gratification" studies; symbolic interactionism; and so on. In all these cases, the concept of interaction is used to designate different forms of reciprocal human actions and communication associated with the use of media.

A final example is Horton and Wohl's concept of "para-social interaction". Horton and Wohl's (1956) central insight is that the new mass media – particularly television – have an especially characteristic ability to create an illusion of apparently intimate face-to-face communication between a presenter and an individual viewer. This illusion is created by close-ups of the presenter's face and gestures, simulated direct eye contact, the use of direct address, personal small talk, a private conversational style etc. To a certain degree, the technique makes the members of the audience react – and participate – as though they were in a face-to-face interaction in a primary group. Together these conditions create what Horton and Wohl call "[the] simulacrum of conversational give and take" (Horton and Wohl, 1956, p. 215) or "intimacy at a distance". It is this relationship between the TV presenter and the viewer that they call "para-social interaction". Horton and Wohl are fully aware that this new form of (media) interaction is different from traditional social interaction and that the significant difference is precisely that media interaction is necessarily "one-sided, nondialectical, controlled by the performer, and not susceptible of mutual development" and can be characterized "by the lack of effective reciprocity" (Horton and Wohl, 1956, p. 215). Even so, their main point is that the relationship between TV performers and viewers is in principle experienced and treated in the same way as daily communication and interaction. In other words, para-social interaction "is analogous to and in many ways resembles social interaction in ordinary primary groups" (Horton and Wohl, 1956, p. 228), which is also why it can (and should) advantageously be studied as interaction in the sociological sense.

To review, then, it can be noted that the concept of interaction in media and communication studies is often used to refer to the actions of an audience or recipients in relation to media content. This may be the case *even though* no new media technology is being used which would open up the possibility for user input and two-way communication, but on the contrary, referring to traditional one-way media. These references may also occur *even though* they (often) do not refer to social situations where an interactive partner is physically present and *even though* the social situations are (often) not characterized by reciprocity and the exchange or negotiation of a common understanding. This is why we cannot speak of interaction in the strictly sociological sense.

(3) Concerning the informatic concept of "interaction", the basic model which this concept uses as its starting point is, contrary to the sociological tradition (even though the concept has been partially taken from there), the relationship between people and machines, which in this tradition is often called human–computer interaction (HCI) or man–machine interaction. Historically, this terminology originated from the transition from batch processing, where a large amount of data or programs were collected before being processed by a computer, to the so-called "dialogue mode". Using the "dialogue" function, it was possible for the user to observe partial results, menu choices and dialogue boxes and thereby continually

influence the performance of the program via new input in the form of "dialogue traffic" or – what came to be called – an "interactive mode" (Goertz, 1995). "Interaction" in the informatic sense refers, in other words, to the process that takes place when a human user operates a machine. However, it does not cover communication between two people mediated by a machine – a process often referred to as computer-mediated communication (CMC). Within informatics then (in contrast to sociology), it is possible to have (human–machine) interaction without having communication, but not (computer-mediated) communication without also having (human–computer) interaction.

A central characteristic of the informatic concept of "interaction" is that the process between the human and the machine is, to a large degree, seen as analogous with communication between people. Another important trait is the central placement of the concept of "control". For example, in 1979, when a number of the leading researchers in the field gathered for a workshop with the title "The Methodology of Interaction", it turned out that there was considerable disagreement about the definition of the "interaction" concept. After lengthy debate, they arrived at this consensus definition: "Interaction is a style of control" (Guedj, 1980, p. 69). This is another instance where the informatic concept of interaction has a complicated double relationship to that from sociology. As far as an understanding of human–machine interaction as being analogous with communication between people is concerned, it can be said to have a certain – if metaphoric – affinity with the sociological concept. On the other hand, the "control" aspect clashes with it, since control can be seen as the opposite of mutuality, reciprocity and negotiation.

The informatic concept of interaction is, as suggested, the most recent arrival of the three. Even so, as a field of research it (HCI) is perhaps the most well defined and well established, with its own conferences, journals and paradigms, and it has also had a major influence on the media concept of "interaction".

In summary, it can be said that while "interaction" in the sociological sense refers to a reciprocal relationship between two or more people, and in the informatic sense refers to the relationship between people and machines (but not communication between people mediated by machines), in communication studies it refers, among other things, to the relationship between the text and the reader, but also to reciprocal human actions and communication associated with the use of media as well as (para-social) interaction via a medium. Evidently, as far as the meaning of the concept of interaction is concerned, there is considerable disagreement and confusion.

Now, what about the concept of interactivity? While sociology does not usually use the derivative "interactivity", the concepts of "interaction" and "interactivity" in informatics appear to be synonymous – a synonymous usage that, in connection with the arrival of "new media", has also become widespread in the field of media studies. In this sense, the concept "interactivity" or the combination "interactive media" is most often used to characterize a certain trait of new media which differs from traditional media.

Without being able to go into a detailed argumentation in this context (see Jensen, 1997, 1998c, 1999d), there are good reasons to (re)establish a conceptual distinction between the concept of interaction and the concept of interactivity. It would be expedient to retain the concept of "interaction" in its original sociological sense to refer to "actions of two or more agents (or agent-like entities) observed to be mutually interdependent", and to use the concept of "interactivity" to refer to media use and mediated communication. Based on this understanding, interactivity may be defined as a measure of a medium's potential ability to let the user exert an influence on the content and/or form of the mediated communication. Thus interactivity is a way to characterize a medium, where a given medium can be more or less interactive.

2.6.2 Virtual Interaction

The concept of "virtual interaction" refers to interaction within the framework of virtual worlds. In relation to the above-mentioned general definitions, virtual interaction takes on a number of special traits. Virtual interaction as a concept has its basis in the sociological concept of interaction. Once again, interaction is connected to a specific situation and a limited and clear-cut (though here virtual) social system, and again we can speak of symbolic interaction between the participating agents. However, the special thing about interaction in virtual worlds is that the interacting partners are situated in the same time (in terms of real-time systems), but not within the same space. On the contrary, the interacting partners – understood as the human users – are physically distributed without any immediate physical proximity, i.e. the interaction itself is mediated and only the interactor's representations – e.g. the avatars – share physical proximity.

The concept of "virtual interaction" refers, in this sense, primarily to the relationship between virtual representatives of human agents situated in the same time and virtual space – i.e. in a form of "virtual proximity" – within a limited (virtual) social system: virtual representatives who mutually adapt their behaviour and actions to each other and who mutually exchange and negotiate meaning to create "symbolic interaction". Consequently, there is no face-to-face communication. On the contrary, there is a new form of face-to-interface or interface-to-interface communication. Only the avatars participate in (virtual) face-to-face communication. One of the unique traits of virtual worlds as a medium, then, is that they allow for the possibility of face-to-face communication, with all that it implies with regard to facial expression, gestures, body language etc. – in a mediated and virtual form. Thus, in virtual inhabited 3D worlds, interpersonal communication and the knowledge that this discipline represents becomes, for the first time, relevant to the computer world.

Since there is a sliding scale from representations of human users – avatars – to human-like autonomous agents, bots and animated objects, the concept of virtual interaction also covers other forms of interaction within virtual worlds. Interacting with other avatars and human-like autonomous agents naturally has a strong affinity to interaction in the sociological sense of that word. However, since a virtual world is not a real world, but, in a way, a fictional sign world or a textual world, interacting with, exploring or "reading" this world and its objects has a certain affinity to interaction as the concept is defined in communication and media studies. Finally, since virtual worlds only exist within the computer as a medium, interacting with these worlds always presupposes human–computer interaction or interactivity in the way these concepts are understood in informatics. In this way, all three concepts of interaction (and interactivity) are represented within and have relevance for VI3DWs.

2.7 Types of Virtual World Inhabitant Interaction

> Distress not yourself if you cannot at first understand the deeper mysteries of Spaceland
>
> *E. A. Abbott, Flatland, 1884*

There are several different types of virtual interactions and simulated communication which are of interest in VI3DWs. If, to begin with, for the sake of clarity, we disregard the entire population of cyber-hybrids and only examine avatars and autonomous agents as relatively pure forms, these virtual interactions can be represented by the matrix of Figure 2.2, where the redundant combinations have been eliminated.

Due to limited space, only some of the 21 different types of virtual interactions will be described and discussed below.

Human User/Avatar Interaction between a human actor and an avatar consists of the user controlling the avatar and communicating and interacting through the avatar. This depends, among other things, on how the avatar is controlled: via keyboard, mouse, joystick, some form of motion capture etc. Thus this area corresponds to a certain degree to the informatic concept of interaction, and accordingly to the traditional area of human–computer interaction, or what is called interactivity in conventional computer systems.

	Human user	Designer-in-avatar	User-in-avatar	Bot	Object	Virtual world
Human user	HU/HU					
Designer-in-avatar	D-in-A/HU	D-in-A/D-in-A				
User-in-avatar	U-in-A/HU	U-in-A/D-in-A	U-in-A/U-in-A			
Bot	Bot/HU	Bot/D-in-A	Bot/U-in-A	Bot/Bot		
Object	Ob/HU	Ob/D-in-A	Ob/U-in-A	Ob/Bot	Ob/Ob	
Virtual world	VW/HU	VW/D-in-A	VW/U-in-A	VW/Bot	VW/Ob	VW/VW

Figure 2.2 Matrix of 21 types of interaction in VI3DWs.

The interaction is, however, mutual, since the user must also adapt to the avatar's specific movements (e.g. its DOF or degrees of freedom) and abilities and its repertoire of expressions, as well as its built-in limitations. It is, for example, quite important whether the given avatar can express itself in written language, in spoken language, or through body language and facial expressions.

The relationship between human users and avatars also touches on the pivotal question of identity – a question which in virtual worlds is more than just a philosophical or existential issue. It is primarily a question of relationships between a person in real life and her or his avatar in a virtual world. The question of identity concerns, for instance, whether a person in real life can have several alternative virtual identities, techniques for validating identity, visual appearance as a key to identity etc. Identity in virtual worlds, then, concerns how it can be verified, stored, communicated, transmitted etc. (Wilcox, 1998).

Human User/Object Controlling an avatar is one thing; manipulating an object in a virtual world is quite another. How does one throw a ball or catch something? This form of interaction deals with how one interacts with a virtual object world via the computer's traditional input–output devices, but it also deals with how users implement objects in real time. This aspect also has affinity to the concept of interaction as used in informatics.

User-in-Avatar/User-in-Avatar Mutual interaction between avatars is perhaps the most interesting part of interaction forms in virtual worlds. This is the most genuine form of "virtual interaction" and as such it has affinity to the concept of interaction as used in sociology. Among other things, it deals with how avatars communicate or exchange information between each other – through written text, voice, gestures, facial expressions etc. – and how they exchange objects, including HTML documents, business cards, props or other 3D objects. However, it also deals with how changes in the position of the avatars, movements and communication are tracked and how these changes are communicated to the rest of the surrounding world. Likewise, it deals with how avatars document their identity in relation to one another, e.g. in connection with financial transactions.

User-in-Avatar/Virtual World Interaction between a user-in-avatar and a virtual world primarily concerns the physical, biological and social "rules" that are established for the world in question and the possibilities and limitations they set for the ways in which the avatar can navigate, manoeuvre through space, communicate, interact etc. within that world.

It also, however, concerns the "rights", i.e. the range of permitted actions, that the avatar has within that world: the right to chat on certain channels, the right to enter but not to change the world, the right to make changes in the world and to what extent. For example: is the avatar allowed to move objects? Leave graffiti tags on the walls? Carry out vandalism? And will these changes endure when the avatar leaves the world?

But avatar vs. virtual world interaction also concerns which types of avatar the given world permits. Is it possible, for the user to bring along his or her own tailor-made avatar designed independently and therefore new to the world? How complex is this avatar allowed to be in terms of polygons, considering the amount of calculation time that is needed for its representation? Alternatively, are only avatars designed especially for the world in question permitted or is there a specific avatar file format? It also concerns how avatars arrive in the world (is there a predetermined arrival spot?) and which objects can be brought into the world (does the world accept avatar props such as hats, bikes or dogs, or is it necessary to leave them outside the world?). This type of interaction is not just about what avatars can do in relation to the world, but also about what the surroundings can do in relation to the avatar, e.g. what does the world look like from the avatar's position? Does the world address – e.g. speak directly to – the user-in-avatar (or human actor)?

Thus this aspect carries features from the concept of interaction as used in sociology as well as media studies.

User-in-Avatar/Bot Interaction between user-in-avatar and bots concerns what bots are programmed to do and whether there are characteristics of avatar behaviour that trigger agent actions and vice versa: collision detection, proximity, visibility, touch etc. It also concerns whether agents are equipped with some form of artificial intelligence, originality or self-motivation. Bots are often used in VI3DWs to carry out standard functions such as welcoming avatars to the new world, giving guided tours or simulating interaction and communication with real avatars when no others are present. This form of virtual interaction therefore has affinity to the sociological concept of interaction, but borders on the concept of interaction as it is used in media and communication studies.

User-in-Avatar/Object Similarly, interaction between user-in-avatar and objects typically consists of avatars being affected by the object (e.g. stopped by it) or in some way being able to handle it (pick it up, carry it, move it), or conversely that an object reacts to the proximity of an avatar (becomes visible, rotates, blinks, makes a sound etc.). Also in this case various types of triggers for action, such as collision detection, closeness, visibility and touch, play an important role. Here we find ourselves in the borderland or the continuum between the concepts of interaction as they are used in sociology and media studies, respectively.

Virtual World/Bot The relationship between virtual worlds and bots concerns things such as which bots the given world allows and which rights they are given from the world creator. This type of interaction may deal with protecting the world from being changed or destroyed by invading bots. Some examples: can a virtual dog dig a hole in a lawn? Can virtual weeds in the form of biota spread throughout a garden? Can virtual termites chew holes in the woodwork?

Virtual World/Object The relationship between the virtual world and the objects deals with which types of objects the virtual world accepts and which actions can be connected to those objects. It also concerns whether or not objects endure. This last instance can allow a user to place an object in a virtual world, to give a virtual gift etc., which remains in the world even after the user/avatar has left it.

Virtual World/Virtual World Finally, interaction or relationships between Virtual Worlds concerns whether or not it is possible to jump from one virtual world to another, as well as *how* these jumps can be carried out. In other words, it concerns the technical specifications for the various network-connected worlds.

From the most general perspective it therefore also deals with whether development is moving toward universal cyberspace, where virtual worlds are compatible and interconnected, or whether there will be a multitude of incompatible, isolated islands of virtual worlds.

The world-to-world relationship can also concern more specific problems regarding worlds' relationships to each other. What happens for example if an object is thrown over the border of a world? Could it turn up in a nearby world, which might run on another server? Could it cause damage in the new world when it lands? And could it be retrieved from that world beyond (Wilcox, 1998)?

2.8 The Virtual Futures of VI3DWs

Ich bin ein Flatlander

Michael in Douglas Coupland's Microserfs, *1995*

VI3DWs are not just being met with pure positivity and great expectations. There are also researchers who criticise the whole idea of 3D interfaces. "2D is better than 3D" was, for example the headline on Jakob Nielsen's Alertbox in November 1998, "...because people are not frogs", he explained (Nielsen, 1998). And he continued: "If we *had* been frogs with eyes sitting on the sides of the head, the story might have been different, but humans have their *eyes smack in the front of their face*, looking straight out".

In arguing that 2D is more natural and intuitive than 3D, Nielsen digs up one of the world's oldest arguments – the evolutionary or perceptual aspect: "Evolution optimized *homo sapiens* for wandering the savannah – moving around a plane – and not swinging through the trees. Today this evolutionary bias shows in comparing the number of people who drive a car versus the number of helicopter pilots: 2D navigation (on the ground) vs. 3D navigation (in the air)".

This is a strange argument in itself, especially when Nielsen continues: "I do maintain that we are more capable of moving around a flat surface and that we spend most of our time doing just that". It almost sounds like a voice from Abbott's *Flatland.* It is a strange argument because moving around the surface of the Earth is not moving in 2D, since we do not find ourselves *in* the plane or surface of the Earth, but *on* it.

Contrary to Nielsen, it could be claimed that the fact that our eyes are placed in the front of our heads and that we are equipped with stereoscopic vision means that we have the ability to estimate distance and to see in depth, i.e. to see in three dimensions. Even two-dimensional realities such as paintings, photography and film have developed a whole series of techniques to construct or fake a 3D effect (Jensen,

1999c; and Chapter 16 of this volume), and correspondingly human perception has a built-in ability, as well as a tendency, to read three-dimensionality into such 2D representations. Three-dimensionality, depth and perspective are as such extremely important for everyday perception and ordinary orientation. And, at this point, there is no reason to believe that the computer as a medium will not take advantage of this perceptional bias as well.

On the other hand, there is a long *de facto* list of important critical notes about the use of 3D on computers, some of which Nielsen correctly points out – notes, which all primarily refer to today's state-of-the-art computer technology:

- Devices such as the screen and the mouse, and current interaction techniques such as scrolling, dragging and dropping, are all intended and designed for 2D interaction, not interaction in 3D.
- Navigation in a 3D space is often so confusing and difficult that users get lost.
- The 3D aspect means, among other things, that the user must also think about the "behind" factor, i.e. what is behind her? Are distant objects hidden by closer objects? Are smaller objects hidden by larger ones? and so on.
- Besides, since the user must exert extra energy and attention in order to control and navigate the 3D view there is often a tendency to produce "navigational overhead".
- Poor screen resolution makes distant objects unrecognizable and text placed in the background illegible, and so on.

Some of these problems will, in time, be solved; some of them will not. Thus many of the critical notes will still be pertinent within the foreseeable future. Consequently, there is no reason to believe, as has been prophesied, that the 3D interface built around the metaphor of a space will, during the next few years thoroughly replace the current 2D interface based on the classic windows and icons desktop metaphors. Virtual 3D worlds will most likely establish themselves as a medium or type of interface among other media and interfaces. Certain applications and domains will be suitable for 3D and implemented as 3D worlds; other applications and domains will not be suitable for 3D and will thus be implemented as some sort of 2D medium.

In many ways, virtual inhabited 3D worlds are still a medium in search of an application. However, in the foreseeable future, the most important and dominant applications of VI3DWs will probably be a new galaxy of entertainment spaces offering action (multi-player) games, adventures and exotic experiences; inhabited TV where viewers transmute into users and participants – in quiz shows, games and issue forums; virtual spaces for communication and interaction from family rooms to international political discussions; collaborative, community-building environments; collaborative workspaces (groupware); shopping and transaction spaces; virtual classrooms where students can learn together and from each other (at a distance); virtual meetings and events (virtual conferences, cyber-tradeshows, virtual exhibitions etc.); visualization spaces for physical objects that need to be understood in their solid forms (architectural sketches, design, molecular form etc.) and the like.

It is just as likely that cyber-hybrids, combining avatars and autonomous agents, will be used as advanced visible message machines always available for access in a virtual world; stand-in communicators, taking some of the information load off the user; multidimensional tools to collect data, negotiate, and act as guides in virtual environments; etc.

In the future, some of these worlds will continue to be implemented as standalone applications, while others will be implemented as distributed network-based media, and the majority of the latter group will be accessible from the Internet, World Wide Web or other forms of networked media such as interactive television or Internet-enhanced television. One likely virtual future of VI3DWs is therefore as network-based worlds.

Consequently, while the Internet and the Web have (Jensen, 1996a) until now primarily been a set of sites that could be visited, a pile of two-dimensional documents that could be surfed, it is slowly turning into a three-dimensional space with a virtual volume – for the first time giving the term "space" in "cyberspace" a literal meaning – i.e. an entirely digital environment that can be lived in and populated and in which the users can move around, communicate and interact. In other words, the Internet or the Web is likely to change from a flat, dead library into a social and communicative space: a web of human relationships – a community.

At the same time, two other aspects of the Internet or the Web are likely to change as well, the *content* and the *users*.

Most old mass media as well as most new multimedia applications are insatiable with regard to content. Given equally insatiable digital storage and broadband distribution systems, it has become difficult to produce enough content to fill media capacity. Content, like fossil fuel, is becoming a finite, even scarce, resource (cf. Jensen, 1998b).

Rather than creating a hungry "content monster", one of the basic ideas behind VI3DWs is to build a common context in which people feel comfortable expressing their own personality and appearance. One of the unique features and advantages of VI3DWs is precisely that people create their own self-authored content. As in the telephone medium, customers provide the content – in fact, *people are the content.*

Just as Andy Warhol in the heyday of the television medium proclaimed that in the future everyone would have 15 minutes of fame, the designers behind VI3DWs predict that "in the future everyone will have fifteen Megabytes of fame" (Bradley *et al.*, 1996). Users will create their own monuments of digital fame in cyberspace.

Letting users build their own spaces and make their own rules for how to govern them is seen as a way of attracting people to return to the same location again and again, in this way creating and sustaining a loyal customer base and community in 3D space. Thus it is believed that VI3DWs will "turn surfers into settlers" (Bradley *et al.*, 1996). It is the appeal of social chat, personal participation, involvement and participatory authoring which are the real attractions. It is – as Pavel Curtis once put it – *the people that are the killer app.* It is their input combined with the common, persistent context of electronic communities – in the form of VI3DWs – that will produce network settlements, i.e. one virtual future is that we are moving into an age of networked settlers. And just as VI3DWs will turn surfers into settlers, they will turn the network into a place, a place for people.

2.9 Conclusion

> So I devoted several months in privacy to the composition of a treatise on the mysteries of Three Dimensions.... Only... if possible, I spoke not of a physical Dimension, but of a Thoughtland... when I had finished my treatise (which I entitled, "Through Flatland to Thoughtland") I could not feel certain that many would understand my meaning.
>
> *E. A. Abbott, Flatland, 1884*

The most interesting aspects of any given new medium are always its unique characteristics, the characteristics that differentiate it from all the other known media. To summarize, the unique and essential qualities of VI3DWs in relation to existing media are primarily:

- that the medium makes it possible to move your personal representation and thereby to control – interactively – your represented viewpoint in the Virtual 3D World.
- that the medium makes it possible to interact and communicate with other users via representation and thereby also to interact and communicate visually and bodily with sign systems such as (virtual) body language, non-verbal signs, facial expressions etc., in this way, for the first time in the history of the computer, making the whole range of interpersonal communication, face-to-face communication, non-verbal communication etc. relevant and of interest to computer science.
- that the medium both makes it possible to communicate and interact in a – very flexible – context and to personalize communication and interaction.
- that the encounter with the computer is transformed from an experience of a two-dimensional interface, which can be clicked on, to the experience of a space in which the user feels an immersion, a presence and a community with other people.
- and, correspondingly, that the encounter with the Internet tends to change from an experience of a Web of linked 2D documents to an experience of a galaxy of interconnected virtual inhabited three-dimensional worlds; a true cyberspace where "people are the killer app".

But why not let E. A. Abbott have the last word:

> "Either this is madness or it is Hell." "It is neither," calmly replied the voice of the Sphere, "it is Knowledge; it is Three Dimensions... open your eye once again and try to look steadily." I looked, and, behold, a new world! There stood before me, visibly incorporate, all that I had before inferred, conjectured, dreamed, of perfect Circular beauty... I could see... a beautiful harmonious Something – for which I had no words; but you, my Readers in Spaceland, would call it the surface of the Sphere...
>
> *E. A. Abbott, Flatland, 1884*

References

Abbott, E. A. (1963, org. 1884) *Flatland. A Romance of Many Dimensions.* Totowa, NJ: Barnes & Noble.

Alive online (1998) *Introduction to Artificial Life.* http://alife.santafe.edu/alife/alife-def.html/.

Andersen, P. B., Holmqvist, B. and Jensen, J. F. (eds.) (1993) *The Computer as Medium.* Cambridge: Cambridge University Press.

Bradley, L., Walker, G. and McGrath, A. (1996) *Shared Spaces.* http://vb.labs.bt.com/msss/IBTE_SS/.

Corner, J. and Hawthorn, J. (eds.) (1989) *Communication Studies. An Introductory Reader.* London: Edward Arnold.

Coupland, D. (1995) *Microserfs.* New York: Regan Books.

Damer, B., Kekenes, C. and Hoffman, T. (1995) *Inhabited Digital Spaces.* http://www.ccon.org/papers/chidemcc.html.

Damer, B. (1996) Inhabited virtual worlds. *ACM Interactions.* http://www.digitalspace.com/papers/index.html.

Damer, B. (1998a) *Avatars!* Berkeley, CA: Peachpit Press.

Damer, B. (1998b) *Inhabited Virtual Worlds.* http://www.digitalspace.com/papers/index.html.

Damer, B., Gold, S., Marcelo, K. and Revi, F. (1998a) *Inhabited Virtual Worlds in Cyberspace.* http://www.digitalspace.com/papers/index.html.

Damer, B., Gold, S. and de Bruin, J. (1998b) *Steps toward Learning in Virtual World Cyberspace: TheU Virtual University and BOWorld.* http://www.ccon.org/papers/twltpaper.html.

Duncan, S. (1989) Interaction, face-to-face. In *International Encyclopedia of Communications.* New York: Oxford University Press.

Goertz, L. (1995) Wie interaktiv sind Medien? Auf dem Weg zu einer Definition von Interaktivität. In *Rundfunk und Fernsehen,* Vol. 4.

Guedj, R. A. (ed.) (1980) *Methodology of Interaction.* Amsterdam: North-Holland.

Hayes-Roth, B. *et al.* (1997) Story-making with improvisational puppets. *ACM,* 2

Heudin, J.-C. (1998) Preface. In *Virtual World* (ed. J.-C. Heudin). Harlow: Addison Wesley Longman.

Iser, W. (1989, org. 1980) Interaction between text and reader. In *Communication Studies. An Introductory Reader* (eds. J. Corner and J. Hawthorn). London: Edward Arnold.

Horton, D. and Wohl, R. (1956) Mass communication and para-social interaction. Observation on intimacy at a distance. *Psychiatry* Vol. 19.

Jäckel, M. (1995) Interaktion. Soziologische Anmerkungen zu einem Begriff. *Rundfunk und Fernsehen,* Vol. 4.

Jensen, J. F. (1993) Computer culture. The meaning of technology and the technology of meaning. In *The Computer as Medium* (eds. P. B. Andersen, B. Holmqvist and J. F. Jensen). Cambridge: Cambridge University Press.

Jensen, J. F. (1996a) Mapping the Web. In *Proceedings of WebNet 96 – World Conference of the Web Society* (ed. H. Mauer). Charlottesville, VA: AACE.

Jensen, J. F. (1996b) Mapping interactive television. A new media typology for information traffic patterns on the superhighway to the home. Invited paper to *Interactive Television 1996. The Superhighway through the Home?,* A world conference dedicated to interactive television, Sept. 1996, Edinburgh, Scotland (unpublished).

Jensen, J. F. (1997) "Interactivity" – tracking a new concept. In *Proceedings of WebNet 97 – World Conference of the WWW, Internet & Intranet* (eds. S. Lobodzinski and I. Tomek). Charlottesville, VA: ACCE.

Jensen, J. F. (1998a) Interaction and representation in 3D-virtual worlds. In *Proceedings of WebNet 98 – World Conference of the WWW, Internet & Intranet* (eds. H. Mauer and R. G. Olson). Charlottesville, VA: AACE.

Jensen, J. F. (1998b) Communication research after the mediasaurus? Digital convergence, digital divergence. In *Nordicom Review/Special Issue, The XII Nordic Conference on Mass Communication Research,* Vol. 19.

Jensen, J. F. (1998c) Interactivity. Tracking a new concept in media and communication studies. In *Nordicom Review/Special Issue, The XII Nordic Conference on Mass Communication Research,* Vol. 19.

Jensen, J. F. (1998d) Roadmap of the information highway: Internet based education systems. In *Proceedings of the IASTED International Conference* (eds. J. Gil-Mendieta and H. M. Manza), Cancùn, Mexico.

Jensen J. F. (1999a) From "Flatland" to "Spaceland". Spatial representation, enunciation and interaction in 3D-virtual worlds. *WebNet Journal. Internet Technologies, Applications & Issues*, 1(1), Jan–Mar.

Jensen, J. F. (1999b) 3D inhabited virtual worlds. Interactivity and interaction between avatars, autonomous agents, and users. In *Proceedings of WebNet 99 – World Conference on the WWW and Internet* (eds. P. de Bra and P. Leggett). Charlottesville, VA: AACE.

Jensen, J. F. (1999c) Film theory meets 3D Internet. In *Proceedings of WebNet 99 – World Conference of the WWW and Internet* (eds. P. de Bra and P. Leggett). Charlottesville, VA: AACE.

Jensen, J. F. (1999d) "Interactivity" – tracking a new concept. In *Communication, Computer Media and the Internet. A Reader* (ed. P. Mayer). Oxford: Oxford University Press.

Jensen, J. F. (1999e) Trends in interactive content and services over multimedia networks. In *Proceedings of the IASTED International Conferences, Internet, Multimedia Systems and Applications* (ed. B. Furht). Anaheim, CA: IASTED/ACTA Press.

Jensen, J. F. (1999f) Film theory meets 3D Web. A semiotic appoach to the design and analysis of Web pages and Web sites. In *Advanced Research in Computers and Communication in Education. New Human Abilities for the Networked Society, ICCE-99* (eds. G. Cumming *et al.*). Tokyo: IOS Press.

Jensen, J. F. (1999g) The concept of "interactivity". Interactivity and interactive learning environments. In *Advanced Research in Computers and Communication in Education. New Human Abilities for the Networked Society, ICCE-99* (eds. G. Cumming *et al.*). Tokyo: IOS Press.

Jensen, J. F. (1999h) Information traffic patterns in the Networked Society. Computer networks and educational applications and services on the Internet. In *Advanced Research in Computers and Communication in Education. New Human Abilities for the Networked Society, ICCE-99* (eds. G. Cumming *et al.*). Tokyo: IOS Press.

Jensen, J. F. (1999i) The concept of "interactivity" in "interactive television" and "interactive media". In *Interactive Television. TV of the Future or the Future of TV?* (eds. J. F. Jensen and C. Toscan). Aalborg: Aalborg University Press.

Jensen, J. F. and Toscan, C. (eds.) (1999) *Interactive Television. TV of the Future or the Future of TV?* Aalborg: Aalborg University Press.

Krappmann, L. (1989) Interaktion. In *Wörterbuch der Soziologie*, Vol. 2 (eds. G. Endruweit and G. Trommsdorff). Stuttgart.

McQuail, D. (1987) *Mass Communication Theory. An Introduction.* London: Sage.

Nielsen, J. (1998) 2D is better than 3D. In Jakob Nielsen's Alertbox, 15 Novovember. `http://useit.com/alertbox/981115.html`.

O'Sullivan, T. *et al.* (1994) *Key Concepts in Communication and Cultural Studies.* London: Routledge.

Peirce, C. S. (1931–58) *Collected Papers.* Cambridge, MA: Harvard University Press.

Wilcox, S. K. (1998) *Guide to 3D Avatars.* New York: Wiley Computer Publishing.

Wilcox, S. K. (1999) *Biota.org. A new expression of life.* `http://www.biota.org/org/vision.html`.

3
Three Types of Multimedia Interactions – and Beyond

Peer Mylov

> The term "interactive multimedia" (IMM) is currently enjoying enormous popularity, not only in the computing and educational communities, but also among the general public. Despite the hyperbole in the marketplace, there seems to be little doubt that IMM technology will combine with the burgeoning electronic networks (the so-called information superhighway, or Infobahn) to deeply affect the way that humans learn, work, communicate and even relax into the next century.
>
> *Rob Philips and Nick Jenkins in Philips (1997, p. 7)*

3.1 Introduction

To understand the impact of these interactive multimedia it is first necessary to get an overview of their structure and characteristics. Interactivity is an invitation to engage in interactions, but these interactions will take place in some medium. In the following we shall present three such media based on their anchoring in the psychological constitution of the individual. They mediate interactions based on bodily actions, images and symbols. As the media may contain different sorts of units and their arrangement, this will lead us to some considerations concerning syntactic properties. Four types of syntax will be sufficient to catch the significant differences in the ordering of the content of multimedia. This also leads to a division or dichotomy in the medium for images. In return we will treat the medium for actions (interactions) as a special dimension. Interactivity as a feature of our environment means a certain measure of freedom on behalf of the user, and this might create problems in relation to the intended paths through the multimedia presentation. We shall comment on the question of narrative coherence and embark upon a further analysis of the medium for images and symbols (language) respectively, showing that they really are two autonomous substrata even if the symbolic medium may dominate. In connection with the question of syntax it will be demonstrated that interactions come in two different forms. By considering modern computer-based artworks it is possible to add a third form. After this we have three media, four types of syntax and three forms of interaction. Treating each of them as a dimension in the analysis of interactive multimedia we end up with 36 cells characterizing some specific properties of such products. With this in mind we can go on and distinguish some essential features of virtual reality and the real reality. On arriving at this point two options are available. The reader can choose between endings. In the first we realize that human life is more than a meeting with interactive multimedia. We have to situate the interactions in the more encompassing life-world and its basic forms of communicative activities. By this we have established a new perspective on the interactive multimedia and their inherent properties. In the second ending we enlarge our conception of dramatic interactions and use a grammar of motives to capture interactions in the widest possible sense.

3.2 Action, Image and Symbol

Many attempts have been made to sort out and classify media presentations where different types play together or just happen to be on the same interface. One possibility for digging a little deeper and grounding an overview is to consider the psychological forms of representation in a human being. We can speak and read, we can perceive pictures or hold them in our mind, and we can act in different ways. These three capabilities will now be our starting point when it comes to a description of the representational media. But first a brief historical note.

Following in the footsteps of the cognitive epistemologist and psychologist Jean Piaget, one of his students in Geneva left and returned to Harvard in the USA to rethink and extend the research on cognitive growth in children. By doing so he and his many collaborators adapted the European way of thinking to the more pragmatic stress on the environment and the doings of the children under study. The clinical and more qualitative investigation of cognitive structures tending toward greater equilibrium was pushed in the direction of controlled experimental psychological research of achievements and representations as the children were solving problems or learning from their activities.

This student was Jerome Bruner, who is still a leading figure in what has now become known as constructivism. From the beginning, Bruner elevated language to a dominant position in line with acting and imagining[1]. Taken as three forms of representation they were presented in a more elaborated form in the seminal work, *Studies in cognitive growth* (Bruner *et al.*, 1966). Although dedicated to Piaget it was clear in the text proper that significant divergences had occurred as Bruner and colleagues was preoccupied with “the way human beings gradually learn to represent the world in which they operate – through action, image, and symbol”. (Bruner *et al.*, 1966, p. 6) Corresponding to the internal push to growth as studied by Piaget there had to be an external pull from the empowering environment. The displacement from self-generating cognitive structures to internal forms of representation

---

1 First as an adherent of Noam Chomsky, and later as explicated in *Acts of Meaning* (Bruner, 1990), Bruner is a proponent of a new paradigm centred on the study of culturally shaped narrative thinking.

enabled Bruner *et al.* to address the interaction of external factors and individual competencies.

When we talk of the ways in which somebody can know something we try to highlight the media employed. Internal representations have to be inferred from behaviour departing from their external forms. We can know something "through doing it, through a picture or image of it, and through some such symbolic means as language." (Bruner *et al.*, 1966, p. 6) We know, for example, how to tie a knot as a habitual pattern of action. Such a representation is executed in the medium of action. Now, Bruner *et al.* were aware that the concept of internal representation was stretched a little by the introduction of *enactive representations.* As Piaget has indicated, it is not obvious that an internal action scheme "stands for" anything beyond itself. This obstacle is overcome if one thinks of actions in terms of habitual patterns which are inscribed as persistent and transferable internal forms. Enactive representations are generative, as evidenced by the flexibility of tool-use. If the hammer is absent you may use a stone or another object at hand with sufficient weight, solidity and plainness of the surface. In line with the "ecological" theory of perception (Gibson, 1979), you are more or less impressed by the affordances (immediate use values, attractions) of the things in the surroundings. Even if action is serially determined as a sequence of movements, it is characteristic of the enactive medium that it transcends the temporary links from stimulus to response. If necessary, some elements can be substituted by others in order to surpass some hindrance or impediment. Enactive representations are designed to guide and support exploration by means of the senses and externalizations in the form of pictures or the spoken or written language. Taken the other way round, language interacts with the enactive representations by facilitating or controlling the execution of behaviour in relation to some goal or task.[2]

Pictures or images (internal graphics) can be used for representation of states or actions and thereby support or guide the transactions with the environment. As a medium it has its own autonomous dealings with the two other media and mediates between inner and outer pictorial configurations. There is reason to believe that imagery emerges from early enactive representations with their embedded perceptual and action-oriented components. As demonstrated by Piaget, the perceptual world becomes more stable and de-centred in parallel with the loosening of the ties to the world of action. This *iconic representation* is dominant as a medium in the time before the advent of a full-blown language. It allows a sharp separation between the person and the world around, but the internal workings of the imagery may take over and project the creations onto the outer world in a more or less veridical fashion (maybe dream-like or psychotic). And this two-way traffic is essential in our experience of the pictorial and aural content of the external media, as when we watch a movie or listen to a piece of music. As we shall touch on in the following, images are wholes ("gestalts") which are more than the sum of their parts and organized in clusters or networks such that a certain (outer) picture will be able

2 In early Soviet psychology, A.R. Luria and L.S. Vygotsky made some impressive demonstrations of the role of spoken language in gaining control over one's own actions.

to call forth or "load" an array of associated images. As a representation an object in the iconic medium has some sort of reference to objects or agglomerates of such in the outside world, and this reference may be more or less "literal" or abstract. Instead of tying a knot (an enactive enterprise) we can look at a picture and be reminded of other things (for instance intertwined snakes or branches). But even a close study of the picture reveals that iconic and enactive representations are different worlds. As a help, the art of tying a knot may be presented as a cartoon (see the classification of multimedia below) and we can feel our way toward an enactive sequence by introducing a temporal dimension, moving from left to right in the iconic medium. In conventional signs, such as a warning of a bumpy road ahead or an electronic wiring diagram, we come further toward the medium in which language operates.

If we still insist on tying the above-mentioned knot a verbal description could pave the way. "An utterance can be, in effect, a recipe or prescription or step-by-step account to guide some action. It can represent in language a sequence of acts" (Bruner *et al.*, 1966, p. 8) Departing from the picture, or rather the cartoon, we can deliver a description in which the discrete symbols according to a linguistic syntax are arranged in a sequence corresponding to the enactive representation. By doing so we demonstrate the interplay of *symbolic representations* and the two other media, although in the symbolic medium there is the further possibility of describing abstract relations that depict neither images nor actions. Sure, we can look at a photograph and maybe discover a book on a table, but in the pictorial rendering there is no element or discrete representation of this relation between two objects. We analyse and create such abstract relations and concepts in another medium via symbolic representations.

Apart from the interactions and translation between the three media it is essential to note that a representation in one medium may be assimilated in another medium. Even if a verbal description of, for instance, driving a car may be elucidating, it is not easy to jump to the enactive representations. With time and effort the coordination and refinement of sequences of actions as represented in the symbolic medium may, so to speak, sink into the enactive medium and become routines more or less triggered and supported by linguistic props (we may rehearse an instruction until the corresponding acts are connected in a behavioural program). Moving from the enactive to the iconic and further to the symbolic medium we are distancing ourselves from the bonds to a concrete reality. But even in the enactive medium it is possible to create abstract representations, as evidenced by pantomime or ballet, i.e. artistic performance. A visit to an art gallery or watching a movie may tell the same story; it is possible to "educate" the psychological base of these media, enabling them to assimilate a still wider range of culturally produced phenomena and codes.

3.3 Multimedia Defined (Syntax and Interaction)

In the enactive medium we should find the representations for interactions between a human being and its surroundings. Actually we did so by noticing that enactive programs are essential components of perceptual activity and the production of language. But in a wider sense, interaction is also the conscious control of the presentations in media which carries contents in various modalities. We shall return to the enactive medium and its representations later on.

In the symbolic medium it was obvious that the arrangement of the units was part of the representation. In the iconic medium the same may be the case. Internally the media can use different kinds of syntax, as we can see when we compare a still picture with a film or the layout of a hierarchical chart. Therefore we proceed with an analysis of some general features of the arrangement of units in the two media, i.e. the question of syntax.

With this in mind we initially have to take a closer look at the two media to see whether they are sufficiently homogenous in respect of the units they may contain. Syntactic categories at the level of the individual media only span certain kinds of members and their arrangements. This may lead to a subdivision of a medium, as defined by Bruner *et al.* (1966).

Purchase (1999) has proposed a modification regarding the iconic representations. In fact, it is a dichotomy based on the continuum from concrete to abstract pictorial renderings as described above. Rephrasing Rudolf Arnheim (1969) in his considerations on abstractness she introduces two sorts of icons, reserving the term "symbol" as Bruner *et al.* (1966) do for language. "Icons which are perceived as being identical to the concept that they represent (e.g., photographs) have a very low level of abstraction and are here termed *concrete icons*" (Purchase, 1999, p. 249). Higher up the abstraction scale we find the other category. "These *abstract icons* are not as abstract as symbols, as there is still a perceptual relationship between object and concept, but they are not perceived as *identical* to the concept" (Purchase, 1999, p. 249). In the aural modality this distinction is of less value. It might be between recordings of real sounds and sounds that have been composed by artificial means.

Out of this come two forms of representation in the iconic medium with the abstract-iconic representation standing somewhere between the concrete-iconic and the symbolic representations. In the following exposition this dichotomy in the iconic medium according to the types of units in the representations will be considered as resulting in two (sub-)media. After this we are ready to proceed with the elaboration of a scheme for syntax.

Taking into consideration the increasing use of technology for communication, four syntactic methods for arranging icons and symbols are defined (Table 3.1) – in this context as a preliminary the enactive medium is relegated to a more secondary position.

Table 3.1 Adapted from Purchase (1999, p. 248).

Syntactic categories		
Space	*Individual*	Only a **single object** at a single moment
	Schematic	Spatial indicators represent relationships in 2D- or 3D-space
Time	*Temporal*	Only a **single object** but time is essential
	Linear	Sequence of objects represents relationship in time

Two of the syntactic categories rely on space, even if the first one, individual, needs only enough space to contain one object; the rest of the surrounding space is background. In the case of a schematic syntax the iconic medium presents an arrangement in which spatial indicators show the structure of the information. The relationships may be projected into different graphic setups.

When time is constitutive for the temporal category, even if only one object is depicted, the reason is that some objects so to speak run in time. A snapshot misses the point. In the linear category we will meet with important cultural manifestations such as books or movies; the cartoon also has its place in this category for objects to be taken in one by one in a timely sequence.

Combining the three media and the four syntactic categories yields Table 3.2.

Using time and space allows a more fine-grained classification of media products. It might be argued that it is too rigid when "any movie" is an example of the crossing of the concrete-iconic medium with the linear syntax. In some cases it is just as abstract by way of cutting, lighting and zoom effects as any cartoon strip, but we typically feel some sort of pull towards or immersion into an outer iconic reality, which in the case of books relies more on (internal) imagery and symbolic associative structures and processes. From a certain perspective a word is a picture, and this internal iconicity is a necessary precondition for the fluent reading of words that do not have an irregular spelling. But the essential feature is the elicited denotations and connotations upon recognizing the word or sentence; the iconic layer becomes transparent.

Considering the aural modality it is evident that we often have to deal with composite presentations, and that these might have different syntax or abstractness. Playing a videotape with a lecture might lead to a mixture of still pictures, text, charts or cartoons. In the aural modality we may experience speech, music or different sounds at various levels of abstractness. In cases like these a further syntactic category is needed. Purchase (1999) has added "network" to account for the arrangement and composition of mini-presentations in a whole; at the same

Table 3.2 Syntactic categories crossed with forms of representation in the visual modality of the iconic medium and the symbolic medium. Compiled from descriptions in Purchase (1999).

Visual and symbolic representations according to syntax			
Syntax	Representation		
	Concrete-iconic	Abstract-iconic	Symbolic
Individual	Photograph ("Author of book")	Road sign ("Koalas in the area")	Word ("Exit")
Temporal	Continuous film ("Waterfall")	Changing backdrop (indicating distance fallen in a cartoon)	Moving symbol (rotating cursor indicating computing)
Linear	Any movie	Cartoon strip	Any book
Schematic	Taxonomic chart (diagram of staff members using photographs)	Iconic chart (bar chart illustrating population growth)	Objects and syntax bear no close relationships to the concepts (icons representing files, windows with directories)

Table 3.3			
Network	Interactive video (fiction-based story where the receiver chooses the story line)	Interactive animation (an animated version of video-based fiction story)	Hypertext (online thesaurus with links)

time she takes a further step and inserts choices or responses from the person confronted with the presentations as a constituent. Network as a syntactic category thus has built-in interactivity. Examples are given in Table 3.3.

But interactivity is not a constituent feature of multimedia proper as evidenced by this definition:

> "multimedia communication" can be defined as the production, transmission, and interpretation of a composite text, when at least two of the minitexts use different representational systems in either modality.
>
> *Purchase (1999, p. 255)*

As a semiotician she speaks of "texts" when we in this connection prefer the more general concept of (re-)presentations or products (potential or latent presentations). Following this definition a product need not enable any receiver-control at all. But in a wider sense all products may be handled at the will of the receiver, who may browse a book or start and stop the video machine. Therefore it is necessary to make a distinction between enactive and "symbolic" interactions. By this we are not getting the whole realm of enactive representations back. Enaction in this context means actions towards a "natural" and desired outcome. It can be using a dataglove to move objects back and forth on the screen or closing a book. In "symbolic" interaction, actions on the part of the receiver are arbitrary, as in using the mouse to navigate the WWW or operating a videodisc machine. But this type of interaction is more than symbolic, as evidenced by the operative effects, and we shall choose a more suitable term stressing the instrumental aspect. Enactive representations refer to the immediate senso-motoric outlet in just handling objects according to their affordances. When the action is determined by icons of different sorts or symbols we speak of mediated interactions. Finally, all this interactivity is introduced only in order to be able to classify the underlying machinery – wishing to avoid a dominance the other way round as is usual in defining multimedia.

By departing from a small concluding note in her text we can open new vistas: "...the enactive feature of interactive devices may allow virtual reality systems to be included in this semiotic framework as 'enactive interaction in a temporal concrete-iconic representational system'" (Purchase, 1999, p. 259). Note that this is also the place for "continuous film", as for instance of a waterfall. It seems to be a mistake to link interaction with a category for just one object; the continuity does not apply to the panorama and changing environment in virtual reality worlds.

Let us suggest a remedy. The table of syntax and representational media should have three dimensions. As an illustration we depict the third dimension for linear syntax by removing network from the front plane and putting it behind the front plane for linear syntax (Table 3.4). For convenience we rotate the third dimension to the front plane.

Table 3.4 Interaction as the third dimension in syntactic arrangements of multimedia.

	Linear syntax		
Enactive	Any movie	Cartoon strip	Any book
Mediated	Interactive video	Interactive animation	Hypertext

In this way we conceive of the front plane in Table 3.2 as representing the enactive interactions and the plane behind as representing mediated interactions. By so doing we reintroduce the enactive medium as a third dimension and distinguish two levels. Later we shall see whether this dichotomy is sufficient. Choosing the individual syntax in the concrete-iconic domain as an example we can just handle the photo, i.e. release enactive habit patterns, or we can cut some parts out and use them in a collage, i.e. treat the photo as material to choose from and rearrange within certain limits. In all of the syntactic-presentational domains we can mobilize programs for handling the presentations as products and in a more abstract way manipulate them to obtain a new product. Creativity has its roots here.

3.4 Navigating in Virtuality

Now it is possible to place "navigating in a virtual reality system" in its proper domain. As both enactive interactions as a background and mediated interactions are at play in a sequential order in a rather concrete medium, the choice must fall on linear syntax with mediated interactions in the concrete-iconic medium.

It should be added that the term "linear" might seem inconvenient when the navigation goes in all directions and maybe crosses its own trail. Then it should be kept in mind that the essential determinant is the sequential order of units in the presentation, and not their spatial layout.

As to the nature of a narrative, Lydia Plowman (1996, p. 92) quotes Aristotle. He stated that the various incidents of a narrative

> must be so arranged that if any one of them is differently placed or taken away the effect of wholeness will be seriously disrupted. For if the presence or absence of something makes no apparent difference, it is no real part of the whole.
>
> *Aristotle: The Poetics (Dorsch, 1965)*

Plowman recapitulates: "Narrative coherence is identified here with a lack of redundancy and a fixed sequence. In interactive multimedia (IMM) programmes challenge these traditional definitions of narrative because it can be suspended or altered at various decision points – the foci of interactivity – and a rearrangement of discrete elements gives rise to a new text and new meanings" (Plowman, 1996, p. 92).

And this is at the heart of a constructivist view of learning with interactive multimedia (cf. the earlier reference to Bruner and Piaget). On the other side, if knowledge is considered as some sort of objective content to be transmitted to more or less motivated receivers a linear and hierarchical structure gives the authoring team the sufficient control of the learning space. Such navigation schemes are implemented with menus and buttons with or without text. “Menus typically lead to a linear sequence of screens, which are commonly accessed by navigation buttons called next, previous, continue, more, back etc. The buttons may also have representative icons, typically arrows...” (Phillips, 1997, p. 72). This stereotypical way of navigating between screens has a starting point and – if the user does not get lost in cyberspace – some finalizing situation. But “it is difficult for users to put this information in context to help synthesise their own knowledge; that is, it is difficult to make a mental picture of how screens link together” (Phillips, 1997, p. 73). Clicking one’s way through the program according to an implicit structure may make series of screens practically indistinguishable and dull.

“One possibility is to use parts of the subject material itself as the mechanism for navigation” (Phillips, 1997, p. 74). This implies the use of hotwords or interactive graphics. Maybe a full-screen graphic overview with pop-up descriptions will do. In a multimedia program teaching about carbohydrates the human body is a relevant orienting space. “The graphic of the human torso is explored by moving the mouse into objects on the screen. It was thought that it is more intuitive for students to click on an image of the mouth than to click on a button labelled ‘mouth’” (Phillips, 1997, p. 74). Departing from a concrete-iconic representation the student may expose a symbolic representation or – in other contexts – an abstract-iconic representation. The means are mediated interactions (embedding enactive interactions).

When the user navigates in interactive multimedia or virtual environments there might be a lot of redundancies and there is no fixed order. But there is a sequence in virtue of the user’s choices and later on we shall consider an example where this personal exploration is just the point. In some cases we have to witness that it is the author who does the exploring:

> Brecht used some of these devices, such as the insertion of text screens, audience participation, and changing sequences of film and drama, in his lehrstück (didactic plays) as an intended departure from Aristotelian drama and its concepts of narrative.... Brecht seems to have predated interactive multimedia by rejecting the conventions of unity and linearity associated with traditional drama but he used these various means deliberately to alienate his audience, not a suitable strategy for educational media. (Phillips, 1997, p. 96)

In general this is not a suitable strategy for most presentations, whether they are labelled educational or aesthetic. As we shall see in the following, the call for participation ranging from active reception to the highest degree of involvement is a more apt characteristic of computerized art forms.

3.5 Visual or Linguistic Processing of Mass Media

Navigating might seem a hunt for the narrative – even if the participant has to construct it in the fly from various iconic and symbolic means. But the media touch on quite different layers in the receiver. Therefore we shall present an argument for the separation of the iconic and symbolic media as ontologically different types.

Watching TV or a film in the movie theatre may seem a rather passive enjoyment if you focus on the enactive medium. Only some more or less involuntary movements reveal that something is going on internally in the other media. To get hold of this processing we could try to recount the narrative and by so doing externalize the internal scene and make it public. Unfortunately, this reduction and transformation short-circuits the access to what is really lived through in the process of receiving the impressions emitted by these carriers of audiovisual content forms.

Reception on the whole is mostly studied as a possible source of the induction of inclinations or attitudes as witnessed by the recent debate over commercials in programmes for children. In particular, bad language is taken as dangerous for adults too and often masked by a disturbing noise. Politically, such reception studies are met with great interest and from time to time proposals for legislation are put forth with the intention of prohibiting certain types of mass-distributed infotainment.

For all their merits these reception studies miss the substrate making all these effects possible. Let us turn a little inward.

"The second approach to reception studies describes reception as a process in time performed by a viewer", as Grodal (1994, p. 38) maintains. Viewing and listening to an audiovisual presentation consists of a continuous interaction between viewer and viewed. Objectifying the sequence is quite another thing for other purposes. "The need for descriptions of the internal processing is especially strong if we are to describe the subjective aspects of a narrative flow, such as feelings, emotions and aesthetic effects" (Grodal, 1994, p. 39). Analysing the story of a given narrative leads to the construction of a chain of acts and consequences progressing through time and space. Of the feelings, emotions and aesthetic perceptions only those of relevance for motives for actions or permanent mental states of the protagonists become parts of the narrative proper. Maybe we should operate with a "third meaning" comprising those parts of the input that are or could not be assimilated to the cognitive constructions behind the storyline – an unnarrativized rest or excess.

In order to stimulate or spur the emotional life of the recipient it is essential that the motor outlet is restricted or cut off. According to Grodal (1994, p. 46) this makes the feeling qualities more prominent. This is achieved by enabling identification with the protagonist or, as in melodrama, by removing the possible objects for the obvious reason that they died or disappeared. Not only sensations but also memory and imagery are charged in a way baptised by Grodal saturation.

> By the reception of fiction and other media products, saturations are the result of emotionally-toned perceptions which have not been transformed into "motor" tension, and therefore sensation, input-processing and memory-functions become visible as distinct phenomena. (Grodal, 1994, p. 46)

It should be remembered that emotions are experienced in a passive mode reflected in language with words as "being touched", "become paralysed" or "being impressed", i.e. something happened to me. Some evidence for the significance of keeping direct enactment at a minimum may be found in studies of the "working memory" in which visuo-spatial and phonological processing depends on categorically different encoding of items to be processed by a central executive in the workspace. It is suggested "that visuo-spatial working memory involves a passive short-term store which has a direct link with the processes underlying visual perception, but which can be refreshed by a form of spatial rehearsal that can be blocked or suppressed by irrelevant movements" (Richardson, 1999, p. 52). An experiment demonstrated that "subjects gave lower ratings of the vividness of a visual image when they were required to carry out a concurrent visual or spatial task, ... [and] they gave lower ratings of the vividness of an auditory image when they were required to carry out a concurrent articulatory task" (Richardson, 1999, p. 54). Rotating or traversing through images held in the working memory show a structural similarity to the corresponding operations on external objects, and as such they are sensitive to competing activities. Also the emotions are closely related to memory, which provides the percepts from the remote senses with stored information about possible consequences or outcomes. Emotions function as "output delays" producing motivational states supporting cognitive elaboration. It is generally acknowledged, as Grodal (1994, p. 47) maintains, that "emotions are not irrational forces but necessary motivators for cognition and the possible resulting actions. Cognition can be seen as hypothetical mental test acts. From this point of view, media reception is mental test acts".

In passing, we have met with the two sharply separated processing systems in working memory, one for spatial–visual and one for linguistic material. There is reason to assume that this division proceeds to much deeper layers in the cognitive and emotional constitution. As Grodal states, "if the brain could only think and remember in a propositional-linguistic form, it would imply the 'non-meaning' level of film and television only existed in the very process of perception and then was either thrown away or transformed into a propositional form; during viewing the viewer would only be able to establish connections to the previous parts of the film via the propositional form." The visual level with its own type of associations would be thrown out or be a ghost in the machine.

Interestingly enough, there is an affective side to it which can be illustrated by noticing that there are two types of felt meaning. Language as an arbitrary system of signification operates with three elements. This becomes clear if we notice that there is something to link the signifier and the signified in the following expression: sa → se (Grodal, 1994, p. 69). We have a signifier followed by a pointer to the signified which in this way is activated. Naturally, it is possible that the signified is an image with all its connections to other images and concepts. "But by an analogical representation... there is no pointing function: identification of the 'signifier' will instantaneously provide the signified, although construction of images and the associations determining them is in itself a very complicated mental process" (Grodal, 1994, p. 70). Corresponding to the saturations (associations which are connected to affect-charged phenomena) we have tensities, which are the emotional system connected with the activation of enactive response. Reading a novel creates additional tensity in virtue of the pointing function in an arbitrary system, whereas visual representation creates more intensity, which is the emotional tone associated with perceptual processes. Language is modelled on another level characterized by discrete units, while the entities are fused in the iconic medium.

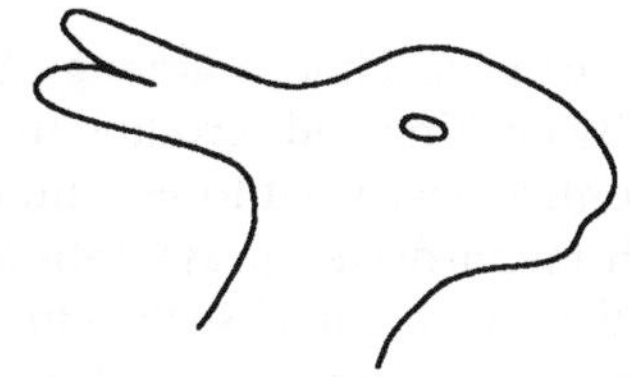

Figure 3.1 Perceptually reversible figure (duck/rabbit).

In the duck/rabbit picture (Figure 3.1) there are no elements in the same way as in language. "You could for instance take the oval area in the midst as an eye and realize that it can be eye in two contexts.... But beacon/ears are not fixed elements. They are formed from something graphical which in principle may have a vast number of uses" (Mylov, 1998, p. 283). When people were asked to make up a mental image of some such ambiguous figure they were unable to switch it from the one configuration to the other (some progress could be learned) (Richardson, 1999, p. 25). This is why there is nothing metaphoric in pictures taken by themselves. The duck does not point out of the context to the rabbit or vice versa (Mylov, 1998, p. 283).

Having concluded this argument for the separation of the iconic and symbolic media as ontologically different types, it is time to proceed with the two forms of interaction and introduce a third.

3.6 Staged or Participatory Interactions

Mediated interactions allow some user control of the presentation making predefined options available while foreclosing others. Clearly, you can intuit the influence of an author allowing you to explore the possibilities with the navigational means at your disposal. Even if at times you are totally engrossed in the hypermedia presentation, your position and perspective are those of an outsider.

To get an overview we can follow Saltz (1997) when he takes the three steps on the interactive ladder. Taking the first step we are confronted with interactive systems which "consist of simple triggers that call up images, blocks of text, extended audio or video sequences, or some combination of these" (Saltz, 1997, p. 120). As an example, you can imagine the standard WIMP interface (windows, icons, menus, pointers) which allows you to decide which part of the presentation to view when – if any. By and large the person in front of the screen is a consumer of mass-produced media to be delivered in pieces on demand.

At the next step we meet hypertext or hypermedia, which relate the user more directly to the content of the presentation. Hyperlinks in the text and sensitive pictures are the springboards to new sections judged by the authoring team to be relevant or associated with the preceding frame. In the mind of the user some coherence and meaningfulness should be maintained, even if it is possible to get lost (some products are equipped with a facility enabling the user to retrace or get an overview of the route so far). In some cases a picture invites you to a click, which elicits a new picture or an array to choose among. A mixture is the common phenomenon on "the net". By clicking and scrolling through the presentation the user has more immediate control over what to see and hear at a given moment in time than was the case with menu-driven presentations. Still, even if the user is lured by the revelations on the screen and absorbed in the content, the position is outside the work itself. There is a human–computer interface with more or less transparency, but it is only a window allowing the consumer or audience to communicate with the latent authoring.

Before taking the last step it could be useful to learn a little from the sphere of art, in which we find many sorts of interactive phenomena. To avoid a troublesome discussion we refrain from any definition or judgement of aesthetic qualities as such, even if help may be found in the literature.[3]

When, instead of fixed, immutable material objects, we focus on the performing arts, some interesting interactional features may appear. In the theatre or concert hall we may appreciate the effects of the exertions of the actors or musicians and occasionally recognize that it is fair to the work of the playwright or composer, or we may issue some other judgement of the relations between the script and its realization. The performance was an instance of an infinity of possible embodiments, and hopefully it was typical for this special type of authorial work. Writing a theatre piece or composing a score is making a (proto)type. This type has to be enacted to be sensible and experienced according to the inspired intentions of its creator. Performance is thus a delegation of responsibility to the people on the stage or in the orchestra pit. Inherently they have to deal with and decide upon the numerous ways of interpretation to be able to produce a new specimen of the type. Even if in some sense they may try to be faithful to the work itself (for instance by playing on old instruments according to the composer's original score) they may realize that performance often transpires in another medium than the symbolic. Enactive representations are the soil in which other forms of representation may grow. Later on we shall elaborate on the "life" of these media. Outside this performance we find the audience, whose encounter with the presentation is often a unique experience which is performed in their own little private theatre.

With this distinction we are in a position to separate two forms of interaction. The presence of an audience is the critical feature. "We must distinguish works of interactive computer art in which performers interact with the system while the audience looks on from those in which the audience interacts with the system directly" (Saltz, 1997, p. 119). Works in the first category are dubbed "staged interactions", while the second category is "participatory interactions". Staged interactions are performances, but participatory interactions might be. It depends on the kind of involvement and perspective. On the face of it there is no difference in the nature of

3 In Funch (1997), a thorough examination of various theories and points of view resulted in a classification of types of art appreciation. As a new type he comes up with "aesthetic experience" which transcends the ordinary stream of consciousness and as being unusual unified, luminous, and sublime visually with a permeating emotionality has far-reaching effects on the psyche and our appreciation of art in general (p. 271).

such interactions whether they are surrounded by spectators or include all available persons in the arena.

In the performing arts the aesthetic object is the live performance itself. When Saltz refers to performance as a medium we may refer back to our three media and anchor it in the enactive presentations. This is grounded by the statement that we have to do with an art form in which live human behaviour constitutes the aesthetic object. Taking interactive computer art as the latest development we can notice that the roles of the playwright, the director, the designer and the performer(s) are conflated. Computer artists "rarely delegate responsibility for the mise en scène to someone else, as a typical playwright does" (Saltz, 1997, p. 118). They maintain control by meticulously programming the computer or other devices in order to direct and frame its performance. Still, this does not put us in a position to judge whether some types of participatory interaction are performances. The critical questions will concern the perspective of the interactors on their own action as aesthetic objects and their absorption in the ongoing interactions. It is a matter of degree. Let us paraphrase an example in the spirit of Saltz (1997).

3.7 Virtual Reality and Performance

In a virtual environment you enter a three-dimensional car and explore its interior. This is incidentally one of the demos in the "cubic visualizer" (projecting pictures in stereo in a rapid rate on all of the six walls, i.e. including the floor) at the Virtual Reality Centre North (VRCN) at Aalborg University (Denmark). A tracking system tells the computers where you are and in what direction you are gazing. When you look at the dashboard all of the relevant instruments are there extended in space. You can reach out in an attempt to grab or manipulate them. Bending a little it is now possible to investigate the throttle and other things at the bottom in front of the car. As you turn around the doors will pass by and the back seats appear, covering parts of the rear window until you move further back. Sound, although lacking in this case, may easily be provided as in other industrial demos.

After this impressive experience we could ask whether it was more or less performative than inspecting a real car parked in the street. The answer is in the negative. This is not due to the virtuality of the car in the visualizing centre or depending on its degree of perfection. There may be a lack of proper shadows and no resistance when you touch an object and you may even find yourself walking through otherwise solid structures. This may detract a little from getting a total feel of the real thing. But in essence the car in both circumstances is governed by its own laws and presents itself according to your movements and perceptual focus. On the other side we have a person engaged in some project, in this case enjoying the interior of a car. These two systems interact according to the laws of nature or the programmers' skills and intentions and the capacities and wishes of a live human being. They are external to each other.

Staying in the virtual reality environment, let us now imagine that there is a person sitting on the back seat. When turning around you are amazed to discover that the person stretches out a hand and looks at you – in pain. Now you realize that there is something wrong with the hand. It is wounded and a splinter of glass points towards you. Most people would experience an urge to help this very unhappy and suffering back seat passenger. Maybe you are one of these merciful beings who immediately moves into action. If so, a significant shift occurs. Now you are a live performer in the work, and the work becomes performative, as Saltz would maintain (Saltz, 1997, p. 122). As an insider you could reflect on your performance as mandated by the performing virtual world inhabitant and evaluate it in respect of aesthetics or other qualities. By being immersed deeply in this interplay you are not merely observing or trying it out, as you need to concentrate on behaving properly at the right time at the right place. In the heat of the action you may postpone reflection or meditation to a better time.

When the passenger appealed to you and got your compassionate answer we reached the third step on the interactive ladder. Immersed in the interactive environment you performed in conjunction with another performer. In the visualizer the environment was far more interactive than hypermedia systems and it happened to launch a synchronized interaction to catch you and bring you inside the play. Now we have completed the third dimension in the analysis of interactive multimedia. Along this dimension we have enactive interactions (triggering content), mediated interactions (to choose and explore) and performative interactions (immersed in reciprocal obligation).

As the last upward step occurred in a virtual reality setup it would be tempting to suggest that only such environments possess the power to bring you wholly inside the interactions. But virtual reality is neither sufficient nor necessary. As to the first step, let us take another example (exploration of the car was the first example).

Although her work was designed for a show in the cubic visualizer Margaret Watson (1999), an American creator of interactive virtual reality art, demonstrated at VRCN one of the now popular products which implements virtual artificial surroundings with built-in interactivity. The description runs as follows:

> Liquid Meditation is a narrative virtual environment based on nature, philosophy and architecture. Constructed as a place of discovery, it was intended to offer individual investigation rather than guidance. Within the space, an immersant is given the opportunity to explore abstract water reflections. Exploration occurs within a unique architecture that structures a narrative philosophy, as well as the images of reflection. As the immersant journeys through the structure, meditative experiences within the environment foretell the upcoming revelation. Capacity to conclude the narrative is solely based on individual experience.
>
> *From a hand-out before a seminar at VRCN*

As a place for discoveries and meditations it keeps the interest and attention of the participant moving up and down staircases and through exhibition halls (`http://www.erc.msstate.edu/~watson/LIQUID/`). Many locations may reveal aesthetic objects which stand out as fascinating by virtue of their inborn ambiguity. Semir Zeki (1999), well known for his synthesis of actual knowledge on visual brain-processes, ventured into an analysis of, among other things, paintings by the classical Dutch artists. Essential to the perceptual system is the search for constancies. Colour is perceived in spite of the seemingly impossible task of correcting for changes in local lighting, shadows, texture and contrast. In spite of a fluctuating and jumpy input in two dimensions we immediately construct a stable three-dimensional visual world around us. It is veridical to a high degree and the acquisition of information in this form is essential to our survival. All of this normally goes unnoticed. What may really arouse our curiosity is the opportunity to peep through a keyhole into another world, with its possible truths. The psychological power of attraction is ambiguity. "I use the term ambiguity here to mean its ability to represent simultaneously, on the same canvas, not one but several truths, each as valid as the others" (Zeki, 1999, p. 86). Obviously, at the places to explore Watson is playing on the dissolution of the constancies, i.e. making liquid what you can expect. Even the narrative must await some possible closure originating in the explorer's private experiences.[4]

Liquid meditations is an interactive environment and as such (with a tracking system or navigating tools) sensitive to the participant's choices and wishes to explore the "unique architecture" and the images of changing reflections. It invites you to choose and explore, but it does not bring you inside as a performer internally linked with virtual agents who appeal and oblige you to (re)act properly. Its place in our classification is as linear (syntax), concrete-iconic (visual medium), and mediated interactive (enactive medium). Through this example we realize that an interactive virtual environment as such does not necessarily allow, or is not conducive to, performative interactions.

Lately it has become easy to get in touch with virtual worlds on the Net in order to explore a city or building by navigating with a pointer (e.g. mouse or joystick) and its buttons. For some it may be hard to imagine that the immersion is totally engulfing, the user being placed before a screen approximately the size of an A4 sheet of paper. Nonetheless, the latest computer games may be able to glue the user to the joystick and react with the buttons as though they were another joint on the finger.[5] In such cases we still deal with virtuality across the interface. But a work of interactive computer art does not inherently need a virtual reality interface to engage the participator in a performative work. Think of a robotic device which may be programmed to sense your movements and approach you as you face it.[6] Now you may feel tempted to play with it and thereby create a stage for a flow of interactions. As some sort of audience volunteer you are performing staged interactions. Saltz (1997, p. 122) brings us an example of a basic menu-driven interface to show that virtual reality is not necessary for performative interactions to occur.

---

4 Taking this idea of a fluent narrative seriously the Danish computer game "Englen" ("The Angel", 1999) from Deadline Multimedia, presents a town to be traversed by a patient and his paramedic. There are no obstacles to overcome, no goals to reach and no riddles to solve. You can look into the future of a person and read off his or her thoughts, which may be weird (pictured as being under the water-level). The play may leave you without any obvious sense. That is the point. When you return to some previous passage you do not have simple alternatives, as is usual, but a new story begins. By the way, as a cartoon on the screen it should be classified as abstract-iconic and mediated interactive.

5 Gregory Bateson, the biologist and one of the fathers of cybernetics, has – in *steps to an ecology of mind*" (1972) – described this "mind" by taking a blind man as an example. He or she is feeling or sensing with the end of the stick, which acts as a prolongation of the hand. As a system mind is delimited by the tools in use – not merely mediated by these artefacts.

In Luc Courchesne's "Family Portrait" from 1993 (http://www.din.umontreal.ca/courchesne/) we are faced with video projections of four people talking among themselves until a participant enters the gallery. Now one of the figures addresses the newcomer directly. It is possible to respond by selecting phrases and questions from a list on the computer monitor. When the input is inadequate the figure turns back to the ongoing conversation with the other figures. In other cases you may be engaged in an intimate exchange of personal stuff and come to know the figure. Situated inside the interactions you are performing with the figures – if they don't lose interest in you. The artist has created an interactive environment, and as an "immersant" you are not triggering or exploring when you answer or pose questions; as addressee and addresser you are engaged in performative interactions.

The next step would be to include yourself as a figure in the virtual environment. The first implementation was Myron Krueger's "Videoplace" (http://www.aec.at/prix/1990/E90gnI-videoplace.html), in which a camera directed at the participant delivered input to the computer. "Krueger's computer perceives the movements of the viewer, analyses them, and responds instantaneously with graphics, video effects, and synthesises sound" (Morgan, 1991). Projected on a screen the participant may become immersed in this "artificial reality". And it was Krueger who long ago (1973) coined this term, and his "book 'Artificial Reality', which is being published by Addison-Wesley in updated form as 'Artificial Reality II', has been instrumental in furthering his reputation as the 'Father of Artificial Reality', a major development in interactive art" (Morgan, 1991, pp. 8–9).

In "Videoplace" the participant's silhouette took its place in a 2D space inhabited by simple, flat characters. Further extensions operated with video images of the participants on the screen, but the interaction was also limited to two dimensions. Naturally, with the rapid development of computer graphics the virtual environment including the projected participant was set free to move in all three directions. As an example we shall consider "Virtual Stage", which is an extended karaoke system based on virtual reality technology. In karaoke the participant acts as the vocalist in a show with virtual characters reacting to the representation and performance delivered by the participant. "In Virtual Stage, the participant's video image – grabbed by a video camera – is composited with the rendered image of the 3D virtual environment. Participants will see the realistic video image of themselves and get a false feeling of immersion, as if existing in the VE" (Sul *et al.*, 1998, p. 42). "VE" is virtual environment, but whether the feeling of immersion is false may be an open question. Phenomenologically it is (to some extent) real, even if it is subjected to some concurrent or later instigated reflections on the status of such

---

6 Sony Corp. has created a small dog with remarkable abilities: "Communicate with AIBO; educate, love and nurture him and you will have a one of a kind artificially intelligent companion. Literally, 'cause AIBO means Artificial Intelligence roBOt, and in Japanese the word means 'companion'. And you can be sure AIBO will be a friend for life. The purpose of AIBO is to bring humans and robots closer together. AIBO's potential for learning and growth is only limited by the amount of time you spend with him. You and AIBO are bound to have many great times together". Pictures at: http://www.aibo-europe.com/.

dream-like experiences. As the participant interacts with relatively intelligent virtual characters in a reactive virtual environment and listens to a professional performance of the music, all of this aural and visual input is merged with the participant's own body-feelings. When the song is chosen from the available list the software loads a script for the music and its events, such as climax and other characteristics of the performance, and processes the other constituents of the script with the interaction data, enabling "the Virtual Stage engine" to integrate the participant's movements and vocalizing in the scenery. On screen there is help if the lyric is not known, but out there there is one's own voice to hear. This makes for a real virtual reality. But so did our virtual car in the cubic visualizer when the virtual back seat passenger appealed to you; it was interactive and sucked you into a chain of performative interactions.

3.8 Interactions, Media and Syntax

Up till now we have three types of interactions, four types of syntax and three types of media. This makes for a three-dimensional rendering with 36 cells. To avoid a crowded and barely readable figure we shall expand on the cross-section from Table 3.4. This concerns linear syntax, the three types of interaction and the three types of media (Table 3.5).

Interactive multimedia products normally resist even a three-dimensional classification as a sufficient characterization. Take as an example a movie picture of a professor lecturing to the camera for the whole time and you see that we have to involve at least two of the cells. And the types of interaction are coupled in such a way that mediated or performative interactions in most cases rest on the preceding types. At a restaurant you know how to present yourself and expect complementary performances. The roles or the scripts for visitor, waiter, doorkeeper etc. manifest themselves in close-knit patterns of behaviour. Nonetheless, you have to read about the different menus, maybe look at a series of pictures of delicious choices and after some discussion come to an agreement. But the balance goes down in the direction of performative interactions in a concrete situation in which you navigate by visual and aural means. Membership of a cell in our classification thus expresses something typical but not inclusive of the presentations.

Table 3.5 Types of interaction and types of media with linear syntax.

	Linear syntax (sequence, considered in time)		
Interactions	Media (representations)		
	Concrete-iconic	Abstract-iconic	Symbolic
Enactive	Any movie	Cartoon strip	Any book
Mediated	Interactive video	Interactive animation	Hypertext
Performative	Art: "Family Portrait" Daily life: Being at a restaurant	Computer game based on (animated) cartoon-strip	Recitation, lecture

While we judge a certain chain of interactions as a more or less successful aesthetic creation it should be kept in mind that performative interactions are also an essential part of everyday life. Or rather, daily life has a social front which becomes active when we meet with other people. Goffman (1959, p. 22) has used "the term 'performance' to refer to all the activity of an individual which occurs during a period marked by his continuous presence before a particular set of observers and which has some influence on the observers". Typically we will try to control and define the situation for those who are present. Conversely, if you happen to be a schoolteacher or an undertaker it is expected that you will only behave in accordance with the rights and obligations attached to this kind of role.

Manifesting itself in the performance is the social front, which is that part of the enactment that functions in a general and fixed fashion to define the situation for those who observe the individual. It may conveniently be divided into the setting and the personal front. Belonging to the setting we have furniture, décor, physical layout and all the stage props for the spate of human action played out before, within or upon it. Performance must normally await the arrival of the proper setting. In certain exceptional circumstances it follows with the performers, as witnessed in the funeral cortège or the royal procession to a wedding, which then takes over with its own scenery. To the personal front we may attribute "insignia of office or rank; clothing; sex, age, and racial characteristics; size and looks; posture; speech patterns; facial expressions; bodily gestures; and the like" (Goffman, 1959, p. 24). Some parts are highly temporary, such as facial expressions, which can vary during a single performance from one moment to the next, while some are relatively permanent such as gender, or in-between, such as age.

Aside from the inherently temporal aspects it may be advantageous to distinguish between the parts of the front which on the one side assure us of the performer's social status and temporary enactment, the appearance, and on the other side what may be dubbed temperament or manner. We expect that the governing Queen will be dressed and speak with an air of dignity when she presents herself to the people, even if we know that the manners may change when in company with an old schoolfriend. Normally there is consistency between setting, appearance and manner, and discrepancies will cause surprise or be considered as scandalous. We should not expect a president in the official setting to cry before the camera, or even away from the camera lens to engage in unusual erotic manoeuvres; nor might we expect, for instance, an actor with unpolished manners and plain language to appear in a highly dignified office as the head the state.

Essential to the performance is the type of region, which may be more or less concealed to an audience or public. In a theatre there is a clear division between the stage as a front region and the backstage, or in general the back region. When engaged in the front region we may be in direct contact with an audience as in a shop when serving the needs of the buyers. At other times we are busy with maintenance of the region, but still in sight of an audience. It is a matter of politeness in the direct verbal or non-verbal contact and proper behaviour (decorum) in the other parts of the region if the performance of the team is to be upheld. Backstage the teachers in their staffroom or the children in the schoolyard engage in behaviour and habits which could not be accepted in the front region.

This passage between the back and front regions and the corresponding transformation of performance has impressed many writers. To take an example we can quote George Orwell (1951, pp. 68–9) (quoted in Goffman, 1959, pp. 121–2), who watched an instance of impression management:

> It is an instructive sight to see a waiter going into a hotel dining-room. As he passes the door a sudden change comes over him. The set of his shoulders alters; all the dirt and hurry and irritation have dropped off in an instant. He glides over the carpet, with a solemn priest-like air. I remember our assistant *maître d'hôtel*, a fiery Italian, pausing at the dining-room door to address his apprentice who had broken a bottle of wine. Shaking his fist above his head he yelled (luckily the door was more or less soundproof)....
>
> Words failing him he turned to the door; and as he opened it he delivered a final insult in the same manner as Squire Western in *Tom Jones*.
>
> Then he entered the dining-room and sailed across it dish in hand, graceful as a swan. Ten seconds later he was bowing reverently to a customer. And you could not help thinking, as you saw him bow and smile, with that benign smile of the trained waiter, that the customer was put to shame by having such an aristocrat to serve him.

Earlier on, when we described the interactive computerized artwork Luc Courchesne's "Family Portrait", it was evident that the visitor transformed the backstage interactions of the projected figures to a front region performance lasting as long as the visitor behaved in a relevant and proper way. It is the same kind of metamorphosis as when a visitor knocks on the door and by entering the house changes the daily routine and perhaps not-so-peaceful atmosphere to the performance of a warm and accommodating family. Whether in direct interaction or enacting in other parts of the front region they may wish to manage the impression that everything is as it should, if not betrayed by voices or sounds from backstage or undue entrance to a region which is not controlled. Through this we learn that performative interaction is a general phenomenon as an implementation of social roles where we have to play our part. Interaction in this sense is "the reciprocal influence of individuals upon one another's actions when in one another's immediate physical presence" (Goffman, 1959, p. 15). Individuals are taken in a wider sense as including virtual operators. We have only to imbue them with sense and capability for action and we do our best to accomplish this as witnessed by the success of computerized therapeutic programs (beginning with Eliza, who would only accumulate and rephrase the input from the advice-seeker).

For an alternative ending JUMP to *Staging the Whole World.*

3.9A Back to the Life-World

What about a life behind the scenes, not only backstage but behind that and the surrounding performative interactions and media syntax? Here is what Goffman has to say:

> The claim that all the world's a stage is sufficiently commonplace for readers to be familiar with its limitations and tolerant of its presentation, knowing that at any time they will easily be able to demonstrate to themselves that it is not to be taken too

> seriously.... And so here the language and mask of the stage will be dropped. Scaffolds, after all, are to build other things with, and should be erected with an eye to taking them down. (Goffman, 1959, p. 254)

Taking down the scaffold leaves us with a building with a value in its own right. But it does not stand alone. When Jürgen Habermas (1981), in search of a suitable concept of action, browsed the social scientific literature he came up with four types of reasoned conception. Three of them serve as a doorway on the broad and elaborated concept of communicative action. Inspired by Karl R. Popper's descriptions of three separate worlds (Popper and Eccles, 1990, Ch. P2), we can see these forms of action as specific relations between agent(s) and the surroundings.

In teleological acting (*teleologischen Handelns*), which since Aristotle has been the centrepiece of theories of acting what counts is the right choice of means to achieve the desired end. When it is necessary to calculate with the presence of other people, success will depend on foreseeing their dispositions to act, and here we have to do with strategic acting (Habermas, 1981, pp. 26–7). Teleological or strategic actions happen in an objective world. It is the totality of all the facts which already exist or by goal-directed acting could be made to exist. Assertions can be true or false depending on the case and actions can be more or less successful. Other people may participate if they are of any use for the enterprise (philosophically speaking it is a brand of Utilitarianism). Only a single type of environment is relevant, i.e. the objective world.

When it comes to normative acting (*normenregulierten Handelns*) the focus is on the reciprocal expectations which members of a social group perceive as legitimate. Norms express the common understanding of what types of behaviour are right or wrong under the given circumstances. Outspoken, they concern obligations and imperatives and possible sanctions when violated. It is important to distinguish between facts in the objective world and imperatives or normative expectations in the social world. Norms and values are not facts to be evaluated according to their status as true or false. If somebody takes this attitude and situates them in the objective world it means distancing oneself from the social group – maybe for scientific reasons (as in a theory of role-behaviour in social science). Cultural values may be internalized and obtain motivational force as standards for the interpretation and formation of individual needs.

Concerning dramaturgical acting (*dramaturgischen Handelns*), we have already described some aspects of Goffman's analysis of the presentation of self in everyday life. Now we can open the third world. "From the point of view of dramaturgical action we understand social interactions as an encounter in which the participants for one another become an audience and reciprocally presents something" (Habermas, 1981, p. 136; translated). In the presentation the participant brings some parts or layers of the subjectivity out in the region in which the performance takes place. Only the performer has direct access to the subjective world, but it may be expressed in language or bodily gestures in such a way that the audience takes them as something belonging to the internal sphere. This staging of the self is superimposed on everyday activities, such as eating or working, which are done in a manner which may create a certain wanted impression and avoid unfavourable ascriptions. If we as bystanders question the validity of the expressions it becomes a matter of authenticity or sincerity. Also in this case we have to deal with two worlds.

In normative acting they were the social and objective worlds respectively. In the case of dramaturgical acting they are the social and subjective worlds, but the social world is typically regarded as something to calculate with, i.e. observed from an objective point of view.

But these three worlds, even if combined, are not an exhaustive description of human life in a society. Situated as we are in a life-world like fish in the ocean, the "worlds" are references to different types of ontology and possible interactions. Instead of water our own medium is language – remember that this was one of the three psychological-based media and inseparable from the others. Correspondingly we may assume three categorically different attitudes to what is going on around us, even if they contradict the ontology of the reference-worlds. Let us conclude with a description to put things in context.

When people in daily life act and talk to each other it is from the ideal presupposition that each one is taken as personally accountable (of sound mind) and responsible in the given social situation. In principle, a conversation rests on the assumption that every straightforward utterance is valid or that it can be supported by arguments. An utterance can refer to the social world, focusing on what is proper and right, but it can also refer to the objective world, in which matters of fact can be judged as to their truth or falsity. Besides the social world, with its norms and moral issues, and the objective world, with its facts and natural laws, there is the subjective world which should be evaluated in a different way. Every single human being "contains" (metaphorically speaking) a world which may be expressed in more or less artistic utterances or products and a wishful hope to be able to cooperate with others in binding relationships (a result of being socialized). This inner world must be judged according to the expressive efforts and the sincerity in word and deed. Thus each of the three reference-worlds has its own criteria for validity when it comes to taking a stance when other people assert something, appeal to us or reveal a little of their subjectivity. Using these reference-worlds is only possible from the perspective of the life-world, which is also the inexhaustible resource from which we get our ability to act and interact in a knowledgeable and cohesive way.

Our three types of interaction and their media, the enactive, the iconic and the symbolic, are thus situated in a wider context, the limits of which are beyond our reach. Out of this life-world emerge teleological, normative and expressive interactions with a communicative (or pseudo-communicative) intent. They are basic as mediators of our life. When it comes to multimedia presentations we may, according to their interactivity, wish to handle or control them or simply plunge into their virtual worlds. Performative, mediated and enactive interactions are degrees of personal involvement and experienced control of the presentations. Sometimes a paradox may show up. Immersed in a highly interactive virtual world we may experience ourselves as autonomous agents, when as a matter of fact the artist has foreseen and outlined the whole interaction space. But this is a species of the presentation of oneself in everyday life and as such is connected with the basic expressive interactions, albeit alloyed with a teleological component (acting toward success). In this and many other ways teleological, normative and expressive interactions as constitutive types are grounding the enactive, mediated and performative multimedia interactions. We live by interactions.

For an alternative ending JUMP to *Back to the Life-World* or JUMP to *References.*

3.9B Staging the Whole World

What about a life behind the scenes, not only backstage but behind that and the surrounding performative interactions and media syntax? Here is what Goffman has to say:

> The claim that all the world's a stage is sufficiently commonplace for readers to be familiar with its limitations and tolerant of its presentation, knowing that at any time they will easily be able to demonstrate to themselves that it is not to be taken too seriously.... And so here the language and mask of the stage will be dropped. Scaffolds, after all, are to build other things with, and should be erected with an eye to taking them down. (Goffman, 1959, p. 254)

Well, freed from the scaffolds we see the world in a new way – or a part of it. Obviously, Goffman became uneasy and headed toward the exit. But, is it really possible to get out? We only have to ask a single question in order to understand that the exit is a new entrance. Posed by Kenneth Burke (1969) it seems deceptively simple: "What is involved, when we say what people are doing and why they are doing it?" (Burke, 1969, p. xv). In other words, in our daily life with ourselves and other people we are constantly on the lookout for motives behind these doings.

In each single case the constellation or the structure of the motives is unique. To get an overview we should choose what Burke calls a representative anecdote. That is, our case must be able to unfold a terminology at a suitable level allowing us to view every concrete instance from several or maybe all possible perspectives. As our concern is with human beings acting and interacting, there are limits to the degree of reduction. To take the lowest common denominator: "the basic unit of action is the human body in purposive motion" (Burke, 1969, p. 61). A scientific reduction to sheer motion, as in behaviouristic psychology, could be informative but not generative when we consider the interplay of motives as people steer in and out of situations they try to foresee or understand. Inspired by the subject of literary criticism, Burke proposes taking the drama as the representational anecdote. Now the answer to the question may be framed in five terms as generating principles. They are:

> Act, Scene, Agent, Agency, Purpose. In a rounded statement about motives, you must have some word that names the *act* (names what took place, in thought or deed), and another that names the *scene* (the background of the act, the situation in which it occurred); also, you must indicate what person or kind of person (*agent*) performed the act, what means or instruments he used (*agency*), and the *purpose*. (Burke, 1969, p. xv)

Even if there is violent disagreement about the interpretation of a given act a complete statement about motives will offer some kind of an answer to the following:

> what was done (act), when or where it was done (scene), who did it (agent), how he did it (agency), and why (purpose) (Burke, 1969, p. xv)

It is no accident that the terms are highly ambiguous; they await deployment and articulation in the analysis of specific descriptions of actions and their circumstances, or the other way round, as the case may be. Together they form a pentad which may be treated or mistreated according to the preoccupations and traditions of the observer. Most often one of the terms is the dominant one from which some or all of the other are derived. But it is essential to note that human life is only in extreme philosophies or religious endeavours collapsed to just one term, as in radical behaviourism or total identification with a pure spirit, i.e. to scene (contingencies) or agent (a divine principle) as the distant but sole movers. It is impressive to follow how Burke places all of the major philosophical schools according to scene, agent, act or agency and purpose. To take an example, "Darwin" belongs to scene while "Marx" (maybe surprisingly) is subsumed under "agent in general"; Marxism is deemed idealistic because "there is an invitation to an idealistic philosophy whenever important economic relations have become 'idealized' or 'spiritualized'" (Burke, 1969, p. 172). As Burke elaborates: "...dialectical materialism, in its constant call upon human agents, and above all its futuristic stress upon kinds of social *unification*, is intensely idealistic. And it is our task to characterize this *from without*, in over-all terms, rather than in specifically Marxist terms, as a factual report would call for" (Burke, 1969, p. 202).

What counts is the ratio of the terms taken (preliminary) as pairs. In the scene–act ratio we follow the degree of correspondence of the setting or background and the act. To continue with the dialectic materialism we can cite Marx: "'Justice can never rise superior to the economic conditions of society and the cultural development conditioned by them'. That is, in contrast with those who would place justice as a property of personality (an attribute purely of the *agent*), the dialectical materialist would place it as a property of the *material situation* ('economic conditions'), the scene in which justice is to be enacted" (Burke, 1969, p. 13). But the strong call upon human agents displaces the ratio in the direction of agents in the scene–agent ratio. In these cases, and to a great extent in all cases, the scene is some kind of container for the other parts of the ratios. However, this does not prevent the agent from setting the scene, as evidenced by the following anecdote:

> The occasion: a committee meeting. The setting: a group of committee members bunched about a desk in an office, after hours. Not far from the desk was a railing; but despite the crowding, all the members were bunched about the chairman at the desk, inside the railing. However, they had piled their hats and coats on chairs and tables outside the pale. General engrossment in the discussion. But as the discussion continued, one member quietly arose, and opened the gate in the railing. As unnoticeably as possible, she stepped outside and closed the gate. She picked up her coat, laid it across her arm, and stood waiting. A few moments later, when there was a pause in the discussion, she asked for the floor. After being recognized by the chairman, she very haltingly, in embarrassment, announced with regret that she would have to resign from the committee.
>
> *Burke (1969, p. 11)*

She had set the scene to contain her severance as an implicit motive to be explicated in her verbal act when she announced her resignation. For the other participants the scene changed but still determined their action. Presumably they acted in accordance with the requirements of the situation. In order to set the scene according to some purpose (evidently as a first approach, the intention to quit her membership) she committed some acts by means of her body movements and verbalizations (agency). Now we see some kind of circle: scene – agent(s) – purpose – act by some agency – (new) scene. What moves us around is a dialectic emerging as the ratios change their values and merge or separate.

Taking the act–agent ratio separately we have to say that the container metaphor is not the most suitable choice. To Burke "the act–agent ratio more strongly suggests a temporal or sequential relationship than a purely positional or geometric one" (Burke, 1969, p. 16). The agent may be seen as the creator or author of his or her acts judged as being good if the agent is good or bad if issued by a bad character. Conversely, a commendable deed points to a noble character (in attitude and purpose) from whom we may expect the right choice of agency and act, i.e. means and ends according to the scene. Apart from this sequential ordering the "grammar of motives" is a question of placement in terms of the pentad and not of tracing temporal, i.e. historical or causal, relationships. The logic and dialectic embedded in a scene (a drama, a society, a philosophy) and its containments do not follow from a temporal sequence as such. Even when writing this text it readily becomes clear that the presumed logical structure, with an introduction coming first, does not correspond to the work process.

As an agency itself the pentad has a broad range of applications. To take an example, we can notice a recent development in (cultural) psychology when the "cultural-historical" school founded by the soviet psychologist L. S. Vygotsky becomes modified, and this in turn is explicated in the light of the grammar of motives. In accordance with Burke's geometry the historical dimension becomes more horizontal, and accordingly the new version is baptised "the sociocultural approach". Stating his position Wertsch (1998, pp. 23–4), one of the prominent figures, writes:

> Given that my focus has now expanded from mental functioning to a more general category of human action, I need to revisit my original formulation of sociocultural analysis.... I stated that the task of sociocultural analysis is to understand how mental functioning is related to cultural, institutional, and historical context. This formulation could now be revised to read: The task of a sociocultural approach is to explicate the relationships between human *action*, on the one hand, and the cultural, institutional, and historical contexts in which this action occurs, on the other. The specific notion of action I examine is *mediated action*. In the pentadic terms outlined by Burke, this involves focusing on agents and their cultural tools – the mediators of action.

Discussing "agency and purpose" in a separate chapter, Burke turns to pragmatism as "the philosophy of means". "In accordance with our thesis, we here seize upon the reference to *means*, since we hold that Pragmatist philosophies are generated by the featuring of the term, Agency" (Burke, 1969, p. 275). Wertsch "believe[s] that much of what we do in the human sciences is too narrowly focused on the agent in isolation and that an important way to go beyond this is to recognize the role played by "mediational means" or "cultural tools"... in human action" (Wertsch, 1998, p. 17) Departing from Vygotsky's focus on the scene–agent ratio we now have a psychological and social science of agency–act, stressing agency, i.e. a pragmatism in keeping with a dominant American tradition.

Let us now consider the pentad in some form of its possible geometrical layouts:

act

agent purpose agency

scene

As noted, the important feature is the ratios of these generating principles and their interactions. An agent may change the scene, which in its turn offers agency-enabling (affording) acts which are in correspondence with the purpose of the agent. Or as Burke (1969, p. 19) puts it:

> There is, of course, a circular possibility in the terms. If an agent acts in keeping with his nature as an agent (act–agent ratio), he may change the nature of the scene accordingly (scene–act ratio), and thereby establish a state of unity between himself and his world (scene–agent ratio). Or the scene may call for a certain kind of act, which makes for a corresponding kind of agent, thereby likening agent to scene. Or our act may change us and our scene, producing a mutual conformity. Such would be the Edenic paradigm, applicable if we were capable of total acts that produce total transformations. In reality, we are capable of but partial acts, acts that but partially represent us and that produce but partial transformations. Indeed, if all the ratios were adjusted to one another with perfect Edenic symmetry, they would be immutable in one unending "moment".

This perfect adjustment belongs to the theological notions of creation and re-creation, as when Christ's sacrifice is a conversion of God himself. "And as regards mankind, it amounts to a radical change in the very structure of the Universe, since it changed God's attitude towards men, and in God's attitude towards men resides the ultimate ground of human action" (Burke, 1969, p. 20).

Even if virtual reality is still in an early phase of development we may experience some kind of adjustment toward conformity and merging of the terms in the grammar. Larson (1996) takes the quotation (above) as evidence of the anticipatory character of Burke's work. "Enter virtual reality. It potentially alters the way we all think about, define, and apply these five key terms" (Larson, 1996, p. 98). Instead of an act with some kind of objectivity we have a virtual act which is "innately private and intrapersonal just as other nonocurring acts (e.g., dreams and fantasies) never 'really' occur and, for the most part, remain unaddressed to any audience other than the self" (Larson, 1996, p. 99) This amounts to a merging of act and agent in a way such that the act becomes "agentified". The act is realized by the agents turning their gaze or moving the glove or joystick and pressing some buttons to eliminate the enemies or whatever happens in this dreamlike world. It reminds Larson of two paradoxical meanings for the word "cleave". "In one use *to cleave* means 'to adhere closely; to stick; to cling' and in the alternate definition *to cleave* means 'to split asunder; to divide.' In virtual reality, act and agent are impossible to cleave, yet are always cloven" (Larson, 1996, p. 99). Something analogous happens to the scene. "In virtual reality, the scenes – video battles, airplane cockpits, hospital operating rooms, driving lessons, or love nests – never fully appear to VR interactants because the interactants are not on the outside looking in as in a proscenium theater – they are on the inside looking *around*" (Larson, 1996, p. 100). The scene is not a place to experience by looking in through the fourth wall. It expands and changes with the direction of the gaze or movements of the head. As far as the possibilities go, the interactant may decide to move out of the "theatre" and follow one out of an infinite number of paths. Now the scene as motivating principle is merging with the agentified act in some kind of agentified scene.

Using the agency of the VR machinery the agent is modifying the ratios in the grammar of motives. Maybe we are entitled to render the spatial layout of the pentad in this alternate form:

agent (act, scene) decisions (purpose) interactive multimedia (agency)

Remembering the internal relationship between action and agency (illustrated by Wertsch with numerous examples), we could – in spite of "the irreducible tension" – to some degree merge action and mediating means as mediated action. Now we have:

interactant ("mediated action", interactivity) (intentional) movements of body

Interactivity is a possible feature of the virtual reality world, as we saw in the example with the appeal from the back seat passenger. Following the lead of Larson (1996) we hypothesize that our performative interactions become displaced to the inner life of the interactant. Out in the open to observe are the enactive interactions which are partly the results of mediated interactions ("mediated action" could be taken as a more general term if more stress is put on the ongoing business of interaction).

Let us go to the exit with a reminder from Larson: "We need to keep in mind though that the technology to produce the primitive versions of today's virtual reality appeared on the scene only a few years ago, and new and improved versions are being developed" (Larson, 1996, p. 103). Maybe virtual communities in virtue of their social interactions would be able to exteriorize the "intrapersonal dramas" and bring us back to the (virtual) society.

References

Arnheim, R. (1969) *Visual Thinking*. Berkeley, CA: University of California Press.

Bateson, G. (1972) *Steps to an Ecology of Mind; Collected Essays in Anthropology, Psychiatry, Evolution, and Epistemology*.San Francisco, CA: Chandler.

Bruner, J. S. (1990) *Acts of Meaning*. Cambridge, MA: Harvard University Press.

Bruner, J. S., Olver, R. R. and Greenfield, P. M. (1966) *Studies in Cognitive Growth*. New York: Wiley.

Burke, K. (1969, orig. 1945) *A Grammar of Motives*. Berkeley, CA: University of California Press.

Dorsch, T. S. (transl) (1965) *Classical Literary Criticism*. Harmondsworth: Penguin.

Funch, B. S. (1997) *The Psychology of Art Appreciation*. Copenhagen: University of Copenhagen.

Gibson, J. J. (1979) *The Ecological Approach to Visual Perception*. Boston: Houghton Mifflin.

Goffman, E. (1959) *The Presentation of Self in Everyday Life*. New York: Doubleday Anchor Books.

Grodal, T. K. (1994) *Cognition, Emotion, and Visual Fiction. Theory and Typology of Affective Patterns in Film and Television*. University of Copenhagen, Department of Film and Media Studies, Copenhagen.

Habermas, J. (1981) *Theorie des kommunikativen Handelns. Band 1. Handlungsrationalität und gesellschaftliche Rationalisierung*. Frankfurt a. M.: Suhrkamp.

Larson, C. U. (1996) Dramatism and virtual reality: implications and predictions. In *Communication and Cyberspace. Social Interaction in an Electronic Environment* (eds. L. Strate, R. Jacobson and S. B. Gibson). New Jersey: Hampton Press, pp. 95–103.

Morgan, A. B. (1991) Interactivity: from sound to motion to narrative. *Art Papers* 15: 7-11.

Mylov, P. (1997) Værktøj, Design og teknologikritik (Tools, design, and critique of technology). In *Design af multimedier* (*Design of multimedia*) (ed. B. Fibiger). Aalborg: Aalborg University Press, pp. 139–176.

Mylov, P. (1998) Interaktiv grafik & lyd (Interactive graphics & sound.) In *Multimedier, Hypermedier, Interaktive medier* (*Multimedia, Hypermedia, Interactive media*) (ed. J. F. Jensen). Aalborg: Aalborg University Press, pp. 275–298.

Orwell, G. (1951) *Down and Out in Paris and London*. London: Secker and Warburg.

Phillips, R. (1997) *The Developer's Handbook to Interactive Multimedia. A Practical Guide for Educational Applications*. London: Kogan Page.

Plowman, L. (1996) Narrative, linearity and interactivity: making sense of interactive multimedia. *British Journal of Educational Technology* 27: 92–105.

Popper, K. R. and Eccles, J. C. (1990, orig. 1977) The Self and its Brain. An Argument for Interactionism. London: Routledge.

Purchase, H. C. (1999) A semiotic definition of multimedia communication. *Semiotica* 123: 247–259.

Richardson, J. T. E. (1999) *Imagery*. Hove: Psychology Press.

Saltz, D. Z. (1997) The art of interaction: interactivity, performativity, and computers. *Journal of Aesthetics and Art Criticism* 55: 117–127.

Sul, C. W., Lee, K. C. and Wohn K (1998) Virtual stage: a location-based karaoke system. *IEEE Multimedia* 42–52.

Watson, M. (1999) *Liquid Meditation*. Virtual environment product. Shown at Virtual Reality Centre North, Aalborg, Denmark.

Wertsch, J. V. (1998) *Mind as Action*. Oxford: Oxford University Press.

Zeki, S. (1999) Art and brain. *Journal of Consciousness Studies* 6: 76–96.

4

Uses of Theatre as Model: Discussing Computers as Theatre – Some Additional Perspectives

Torunn Kjølner and Niels Lehmann

For more than two thousand years, humanity has seen theatre as a powerful means of dealing with life. Not only has the staged drama been seen as a representation of human action since Aristotle defined theatre as *mimesis*, theatre has also proved an intriguing image of the world. One famous example of the use of theatre as an image of the world is, of course, Plato's idea that human beings are puppets on a stage, attached by strings to the hands of the gods. The Theatrum Mundi metaphor also drew a lot of philosophical interest throughout the Middle Ages and in the Renaissance. When William Shakespeare in 1601 wrote *As You Like It*, and let one of his characters start a monologue with "All the world's a stage, And all the men and women merely players...", he made use of a metaphor that was already a commonplace. It should perhaps be remembered that Shakespeare was well aware of this, so he gave his famous monologue to a rather displaced character in the play, Jaques, an extreme melancholic who constantly mourns about his inability to be a real fool. His desire is to be a quick-witted clown who can tell the truth through creative lies. Unfortunately, he neither sees the world from a position where this is possible nor does he have the command of language and wit to invent good puns and striking images.

A few decades into our century, sociologists, anthropologists and social psychologists started to investigate life in terms of theatre – and certainly without the melancholy and sentiment of loss typical of characters like Jaques. In this context the notion of the world as a stage was not employed to express difficulties in finding meaning and truth. On the contrary, theatrical terms were introduced as a means to produce meaning and make truth more translucent.

Early sociology, as developed by James, Mead, Durkheim and others, tried to highlight that there was more to social interaction than a meeting between individuated subjects. This type of sociology investigated how to predict social behaviour, especially if it was likely to end in a conflict. It was hardly by chance that American sociology and social psychology started to flourish in the 1930s – after the Depression. For the human sciences it seemed more important than ever to learn from the natural sciences in order to develop methods that could predict human behaviour. A burning question seemed to be: how can the human sciences contribute to avoiding another world war and another Wall Street Crash? The focus of investigation was moved from the individual character to the social context, to the actual situations where people meet. Great efforts were made to describe and understand what actually takes place when people meet. The metaphorical nature of theatre seemed to lend itself to such an undertaking. Not only could the stage represent a whole world, the meeting of individuals and their interaction seemed to constitute such a representation.

Theatre is a Greek word for a place with a view: a *theatron*, which has the same root as *theory*, was normally situated on a slanted hillside. From this "place with a view" the spectators could overlook the action, which took place on the open space in front of them. A back wall limited the viewer's gaze. On the orchestra the spectators saw a choir that danced and recited lines and actors with masks and costumes. They played different parts or roles of a drama. A "role" was a wooden stick to which a piece of papyrus was attached. On this piece of papyrus the lines and (some) actions for each character were written. Several roles connected up to form a dramatic plot. The stories told by the Greek dramatists were known. People did not come to see what happened. They knew what happened to Oedipus. They came to feel what happened, to take part in a cultural event, to be entertained – and educated. If anything, this represented "the basic theatrical situation".

Interaction is the nucleus of dramatic art. The dramatic genre differs from the epic genre in that the action takes place in the present. It differs from poetry in that it is not focused on subjective emotions and moods. The drama is told through the interaction of live performers. Aristotle noticed that in good Greek drama (or, to be precise, tragedy) the situations grew organically from each other in one line of development where we follow one main character (the protagonist) in confrontation with another character (the antagonist) through an important development of knowledge to a meaningful insight that has some important consequence for the rest of his or her life. The smallest element of dramatic action is an exchange of actions between two characters (protagonist and antagonist). A drama starts with an action that begs for an answer or some kind of reaction, which in turn can be an impulse for the protagonist to react to. Drama is a Greek word for action, but drama does not mean any kind of action. A drama is dramatic. Its actions are condensed, selected and carefully composed. According to Aristotle, the experience of drama works through composed actions and a subtle use of theatrical means. So theatre manipulates the gaze of the audience through its uses of means and through its selection of "links" between fiction and reality.

From this it can be seen that theatre could easily lend itself to the study and experience of interaction. The interaction that will take place between the dramatis personae is rehearsed and played by actors. Because it is acted out by human beings, a small amount of "additional activity" and energy become implemented in the rehearsed responses to what happens in the meeting between the actors. So there is an element of actual action and reaction in all live theatre performances, even in well-rehearsed, institutionalized, traditional theatre. There is also an element of real interaction in the meeting between the actors and the audience. These elements are, however, not predominant, and they do not have any significant impact on what happens in the play. A playwright usually has a very good idea of what kind of interaction the drama can tolerate from the audience, and in which directions the reactions may go. The degree of "real-time" interaction, or unpredicted reactions if you like, can vary, and it certainly does in different forms of theatre that we see today. Usually, though, there is a high degree of predictability in the interaction between a drama and its audience. This is due to the context and conventions of a theatre situation, and of course to how the written drama and the staged performance set up their contract of fiction with the audience.

Theatre, then, could be considered a productive model for scientific observation of the behaviour between people. The studies of mankind in social settings were in need of an understandable terminology. Ralph Linton's book *The Study of Man* (1936), a contribution to explain social behaviour as such, was a start. Inspired by the Shakespearian monologue, he introduced the term "role" and suggested that it could be considered a function of social behaviour. Sociologists and social psychologists obviously saw a paradigmatic potential in the image of the world as a stage and developed a whole range of role theories. Soon it became a part of common language to define a role as expected behaviour. Early definitions of role made clear, though, that there is a difference between role and actual behaviour. Role was rather a virtual sheet of paper on which society had written its expectations for *appropriate* behaviour in any known situation. Thus, terms lifted from dramatic theory, such as role behaviour and role conflicts, became central keys by which sociologists hoped to unlock secrets of social behaviour. This would make us capable of predicting how people would act and react in any given situation. So to understand social behaviour in terms of the theatre meant that you would be prepared for real life.

At the end of the twentieth century, and in an entirely different context, the theatre has once again drawn attention as a paradigmatic model for understanding something else. In her influential book *Computers as Theatre* (1991), Brenda Laurel urges us to think of the interaction between the computer and the human user from a histrionic point of view. Her reasons for using the theatre in this context are pretty much same as the ones sociologists had in mind when they turned their interest towards the theatre: drama is about interaction, carefully planned in terms of time and space, so it seems obvious to look for inspiration to develop virtual action in virtual spaces in the real theatre.

It seems unwise to us to overlook the advantages gained by the social sciences in terms of understanding social interaction through histrionics. Likewise, there is no doubt in our minds that Laurel's attempt to focus on interactivity in the communication between a human being and a computer in the light of theatre holds a lot of potential. Indeed, her book has proved eye-opening for many readers and designers. There is, however, always a certain danger involved in seeing something as something else: What at first seems to be a creative act of widening our outlook on something may very quickly turn into something else: a prison of a particular terminology. The use and application of metaphors and analogies can work magic as tools and images for devising new tools and ways of understanding. A metaphor quite obviously lends itself to an *experimental mode* of working. In asking what will happen *if* something is seen as this or that particular something else, one might find stunning results. One can also, of course, find satisfying answers in metaphors and analogies if one is more ontologically inclined. An *ontological mode* suggests that seeing something as *exactly* this particular something else can prove to take you a step closer to truth, even become *the* truth if you just find the right metaphor. Such an ontological mode, then, is for the metaphysically minded theoretician who hopes to find a means by which we can transgress language and by doing so get in touch with reality – unmediated.

This hope has, of course, been discussed by various theoreticians in our century. A philosopher like Jacques Derrida, for one, has shown that any attempt to create a metaphorology will necessarily make extensive use of metaphors, and for this reason he concludes that there is no escape from metaphors (Derrida, 1972).

Cognitive scientists like George Lakoff and Mark Johnson reach a similar conclusion. Our language is not only full of metaphors, they maintain, it is constituted by metaphors (Lakoff and Johnson, 1980). Only we do not see them as such because they seem to have lost their metaphorical effect. After a while a metaphor is naturalized, it loses its peculiarity and becomes a commonplace. A dead metaphor is, however, still a metaphor according to Lakoff and Johnson. That we have forgotten the metaphorical status of the words we use does not mean that the words become innocent. The world of words delimits the real world because it makes us perceive it in a certain way. Consequently we create entire perspectives on the world when we use a metaphor to understand something. One of their prime illustrations of how this happens is the way we think of illness. Here the bulk of metaphors has been imported from warfare: an illness *attacks* you, your immune *defence* starts to work, your system *fights* back. It goes without saying that there are many assumptions about the relation between the body and the world implied in this way of thinking about illness. In the light of this, and in many other examples, Lakoff and Johnson urge us to ask ourselves what it means that we choose some metaphors rather than others. Their existential and essential question then becomes: what would happen to us and the world if we chose other terms, other metaphors? In other words: words work on us and sometimes make it difficult for us to comprehend that something could have been seen in a different way.

At this point a cultural critic like Susan Sontag picks up the thread. Discussing AIDS she warns us that the image of an illness might work on you as effectively as the illness itself, and she concludes that we will also have to fight AIDS by considering our conceptualization of it critically (Sontag, 1988).

Criticizing an ontological understanding of metaphorical representation does not, however, inevitably lead to an experimental mode of using metaphors. In fact, neither Derrida, nor Lakoff and Johnson nor Sontag ask us to take this step as they all believe in the necessity of a critical investigation of the use of metaphors at work in everyday language. As Richard Rorty points out, you would more or less have to think like a poet if you want to enter an experimental mode of using metaphors (Rorty, 1989). To the artist the exploration of (or, if you will exploitation of) metaphors and powerful images is a *sine qua non* for the creation of a piece of art. The poet knows that a powerful metaphor can produce the kind of magic that allows us to see ordinary things in an entirely new perspective. Thus, he or she tries to produce an immediate effect on our way of seeing things by establishing unforeseen connections between different areas of life. The artist knows that it is productive to take an interest in metaphors "in transit", i.e. words that are losing the metaphorical value they once had in order to give them yet another twist. As Rorty believes that social change is mainly created by an attempt to redescribe ourselves in new vocabularies, he reminds us that the artistic approach could be a paradigm for intellectual work in late modernity.

It is our experience that an ontological mode of using metaphors soon leads to a prohibiting view of things which is as uncreative as it is mind-narrowing. We should, therefore, like to follow Rorty in a creative attempt to make things better. It is our guiding principle that the moment you begin to believe in your analogy you have not only reached the moment when the metaphor has lost its magic, you have also made it impossible for yourself and others to produce productive analogies.

We outline this distinction between an experimental and an ontological mode of using metaphors and analogies because it seems highly relevant for a discussion of the advantages and disadvantages of the use of theatre as a metaphor or an analogy for the interaction between computer and user. One of our points is that Brenda Laurel does not really make up her mind as to which mode she wants to employ. As far as we can see, she would prefer to be an engineer trying to come up with productive solutions to concrete problems by using her substantial knowledge of theatre. Nevertheless, she tends to become a theoretical physicist who wants to explain the nature of something when she starts to explain what theatre can do. When drawn in the direction of the ontological mode, Laurel uses theatre as a privileged way of explaining the nature of interaction. On the one hand Laurel says in the preface: "My goal in writing this book is to improve the quality of human–computer experiences through new approaches to their design" (Laurel, 1991, p. xviii). Here Laurel talks like an experimental engineer who tries to solve problems along the way and construct better relations between user and computer. She sees "theatre as an additional perspective" (Laurel, 1991, p. 10). One would think that this approach implies that she would happily see her book as part of a piecemeal science which does not rely on some grand scheme of total explanation.

On the other hand, piecemeal science is exactly what she hopes to transgress with her book: "By examining the world of human–computer activity with the same rigour and logic as Aristotle applied to the literary arts, we can arrive at a set of principles that may provide a greater acuity, robustness, and elegance than the piecemeal science that often guides the design of human–computer activity" (Laurel, 1991, p. xvii). Here Laurel seems to fathom an overall theory of interaction that can guide all our endeavours to produce good interactivity. When she adopts this mode of thinking, theatre becomes much more than just an additional model; it becomes the privileged model for understanding interactivity as such. She wants to transgress the use of theatre "as an interface metaphor" in order to use it in a much deeper way, i.e. "as a fundamental understanding of what is going on in human–computer interaction" (Laurel, 1991, p. 19) or as "a way to conceptualize human–computer interaction itself" (Laurel, 1991, p. 20). In other words she wants to take us all the way to the ontology of interaction by giving us the keys to the theatre.

The temptation to use theatre in the ontological mode can also be seen in the sociological appropriation of theatre. After the Second World War sociology took a step in a direction of a theatricalized society. In 1959, Erving Goffman published *The Presentation of Man in Everyday Life*, a book that was received with an enormous attention and gained popularity through numerous translations and reprints (Goffman, 1969). Not only theoretical social scientists and students of human behaviour, but also common people were inspired to see that we all play roles when we relate to each other and that it is in fact a difficult task to tell what is true and what is "just acting". Goffman made use of the entire theatrical vocabulary when he introduced terms like staging, roles, costumes, masks, settings and so forth. A decade or two later, most introductory books on sociology, social psychology and anthropology contained a chapter on role theory. Goffman himself had actually insisted that the terminology he borrowed from theatre had only been used as a scaffolding for a building, made to be torn down when the building was finished, but soon, as his terminology became incorporated into everyday language, the role was no longer *like* the role in the theatre; life *had become* a theatre. The world as a stage and humans as players were no longer the illusion of a mourning fictitious character. Hiding behind masks, playing contradicting roles in various situations of conflict, was what real life felt like.

Role theories after Goffman basically didn't bother about referring to the theatre. Roles gained ontological status in the study of social behaviour. This, of course, provoked critical voices to speak up. The criticism came from different directions, even from within the social sciences. The criticism did, perhaps rather expectedly, point to the fact that the role theories were not complete enough. The metaphor was not considered transparent enough for the ontological need to which it was supposed to respond. Is there not a person behind the role, the psychologist asked. If everybody just does what is expected from their roles, how does change happen?, the sociologist asked. A phenomenological approach like Bruce Wilshire (who like Derrida, Lakoff, Johnson and Sontag does not believe that metaphors can be innocent) launched a criticism of the ontologization of role theory in his 1982 book *Role Playing and Identity. The Limits of Theatre as Metaphor.* According to him "the roleplaying metaphor is exceedingly slippery and dangerous because almost inevitably when we deliberately transfer the notion of roleplaying to offstage life, we carry with us, smuggled in, the notion of fiction in the actor's portrayal. This tends to eat away from the inside our sense of reality, seriousness, and appropriateness of our "roleplaying" offstage [...] in the grip of the metaphor, we come dimly to believe that what we are doing offstage is an illicit version of what the actor is doing onstage, and so we attempt to flee our guilt and our responsibility for our unavoidable 'roleplaying'" (Wilshire, 1982, p. xvi). Consequently, Wilshire would like us to start recognizing the important differences between the fiction on stage and real-life interaction rather than seeing the one as an ontological model of the other.

Throughout Laurel's book the endeavour of the engineer trying to do things better struggles with an ontological ambition to use theatre to set interaction right. Laurel could have avoided many critical questions, we think, had she stayed with the perspective of the engineer. The belief that she presents us with an "understanding of how things work" which she finds "necessary if we are to know how to make them" (Laurel, 1991, p. 41) begs all the questions about usability. According to herself the same questions are raised by many of her critics. However, it does not seem quite fair when Donald A. Norman concludes in his foreword that "you will not find anything you can apply to your work today, or even tomorrow" (Laurel, 1991, p. xii). Even if theatre does not provide us with a privileged model of interaction, Laurel succeeds to show that there is much to be learned from theatre for people wanting to work like engineers trying to improve human–computer interaction.

Since we believe that the potential in Laurel's approach is her experimental attempt to bring the world of the theatre into dialogue with the world of computers, we would have preferred that she had not re-territorialized her thinking by ontologizing her findings – to speak with Gilles Deleuze (cf. Deleuze and Guattari, 1991). This is why, in the following section, we shall outline what in our opinion appears to be unfortunate consequences of Laurel's tendency to lose sight of her engineering ambition. What we have in mind is the fact that she becomes extremely committed to the Aristotelian poetics. This makes her overlook the potential in various theatre strategies that go beyond the rules set up by Aristotle. Finally, in Section 4.2, we shall explore an experimental mode of using theatre as a model. Had she not insisted so heavily on the Aristotelian scheme, Laurel could have found a lot of inspiration in improvisational modes of theatre productions, we believe. She does actually mention an improvisational experiment in her book. But it is remarkable, that she only employs the improvisers as "real" virtual agents in order to figure out what it takes to produce linear stories in interactive media rather than investigating what qualities the improvisation context could have led to. By taking the improvisational theatre seriously we would like to push Laurel's productive reasoning beyond its own Aristotelean limits.

4.1 Taking the Aristotelean Poetics as Paradigm

Laurel makes no secret of the fact that she takes her point of departure in the poetics formulated by Aristotle. So trying to understand what she has to offer means asking: how does she read Aristotle and what does she make of his dramaturgical suggestions? Asking these questions makes one realize, however, that the overall ambivalence of the book between a theoretical and a practical perspective on the use of dramaturgical reasoning also has a significant impact on her reading of Aristotle.

On the one hand, Laurel is very cautious. She has just chosen Aristotle's poetics because it has proved resistant against time; she tells us: "In order to build representations that have theatrical qualities in computer-based environments, a deep robust, and logically coherent notion of structural elements and dynamics is required" (Laurel, 1991, p. 36). Such a robust notion of dramatic structure is exactly what Aristotle provides, Laurel thinks. Taking a point of departure in Aristotle, therefore, "creates a disciplined way of thinking about the design of a play" (Laurel, 1991, p. 49). This is the pragmatic engineer talking. The coherency of the Aristotelean poetics appears to her to be a particularly good tool to improve human–computer activity. The Aristotelean coherence is what is needed to make improvements. So you have to eliminate "the extraneous and gratuitous" (Laurel, 1991, p. 77), or, put a little differently, you need to clarify your selections: "The important thing is to know that one is in fact exercising selectivity – to be explicit about it" (Laurel, 1991, p. 79). Opposing the commonsensical idea that creativity is only possible in absolute freedom, Laurel maintains correctly that selectivity is not opposed to creativity. On the contrary, "limitations – constraints that focus creative efforts – paradoxically increase our imaginative power by reducing the number of possibilities open to us" (Laurel, 1991, p. 101). So using the Aristotelean delimitations will only enhance our creativity, Laurel thinks.

The pragmatic conception of Aristotle as nothing but a good tool for constructing better interfaces is also at stake when Laurel attacks the normative interpretation of Aristotle known from French classicism. French classicists read Aristotle as a master who formulated all the rules needed for a perfect drama. For them, succeeding as a playwright meant accepting all these rules. They even added further restrictions. To begin with, Laurel is against this type of normativity. However, she doesn't seem to take her own criticism seriously when she also maintains that Aristotle has outlined "the nature of the drama" (Laurel, 1991, p. 38). In fact, this is exactly the argument used by the French classicists, who believed that what matters is finding the nature of a dramatic form and then fulfilling its theoretical demands. An argument for a particular form that refers to nature is at the heart of any normative poetics. Furthermore, how should the following passage be read if not as a normative prescription? "Following the causal relations through as one creates or analyses a drama automatically *reveals the ways in which things should work or exactly how they have gone awry*" (Laurel, 1991, p. 49, italics added). Here, Laurel talks like the theoretician who is so sure about her case that she acknowledges the true nature of dramatic art. Therefore she can prescribe the correct recipe. What Aristotle formulated seems to ask the status of an ontological law; an absolute norm for dramatic beauty.

This view inevitably prompts a particular question: what is the nature of the drama according to the Aristotelean paradigm? Or asked a little differently: what are the central elements in Laurel's inheritance from Aristotle?

First of all, Laurel inherits a taste for order, or organic totality. Again and again she reiterates that we need to create "organic wholeness" (Laurel, 1991, p. 90). In particular, playwrights are the ones to teach us how to create "whole actions": "In a play, the result of this successive formulation is a completed plot – a *whole action*" (Laurel, 1991, pp. 69–70). If designers could apply this particular knowledge, the interfaces they produce would become much more friendly to the users, Laurel maintains. So the central lesson to be learned from Aristotle is the following: "The *Poetics* defines form and structure in drama and narrative literature and provides an understanding of how structural elements can be combined to create organic wholes" (Laurel, 1991, p. xvii). At the top level of abstraction the organic whole means that no part of the narrative can be removed without damage to the entity.

Laurel does not, however, stay at this level of abstraction. She also inherits the Aristotelean definition of a good organic whole action, i.e. the principle of causality: "Causality is the connective tissue of plot" (Laurel, 1991, p. 73). For some reason she explains her point using *Hamlet* as her example: "An action is made up of incidents that are causally and structurally related to one another. The individual incidents that structure *Hamlet* – Hamlet fights with Laertes, for instance – are only meaningful insofar as they are woven into the action of the mimetic whole" (Laurel, 1991, p. 63). In an attempt to get a clearer image of how such a linear structure is created Laurel explains that it is a question of gradually narrowing the field of potential actions. Thus she gives us the following formula for a linear plot: "over time, dramatic potential is formulated into possibility, probability, and necessity" (Laurel, 1991, p. 69). In the phase of potential action anything can happen. As certain actions for a certain character in a certain situation are not likely to be performed, the phase of possibility will narrow the potential. When the character enters the phase of the probable, we are dealing with fewer possible actions. Finally, necessity will end all potentiality as the character is forced towards a certain inevitable concluding action.

Apart from investing in the notion of causal organicity, Laurel also inherits the notion of mimesis from Aristotle. She sees an important similarity between theatre and computers in the fact that they are both "*mimetic in nature*" (Laurel, 1991, p. 45), i.e. that producing computer programs involves finding ways of representing different things (like desktops, garbage cans and the like) which is similar to producing a performance. True as this might be, it is important to realize that this notion of representation does not necessarily lead to a demand for realism, even though it very often does in practical situations. There is no reason to believe that Aristotle had realism or naturalism in mind when he defined dramatic art as representation. But since the notion of representation even today very easily provokes an idea of art as a mirror of life, a production of iconographic images of the world seems to be highly estimated. One hundred years of theatrical realism has definitely reproduced itself in such a way. In order to match the scientific age artists looked for forms of human art that, in any detail, could be true to reality. This is also the ideal that exploits the convention of a framed stage that made it natural for the spectators to look directly into the alleged living room of the characters – and participate in their actions from a natural distance.

Laurel is surprisingly ambiguous when it comes to representative human action. Several passages seem to exclude a naturalistic interpretation of representation. Having pointed out the similarity between theatre production and computer programming, for instance, she adds that "a mimesis is a *made* thing, not an accidental or arbitrary one" (Laurel, 1991, pp. 45–46, italics added). When she discusses AI researcher Philip Agre's attempt to mimic everyday life, she concludes: "Agre wants artificial reality to be lifelike, but there are good reasons why, at least in some situations and for some purposes, artificial reality should be, well, *artificial*" (Laurel, 1991, p. 77). In another context she warns us not "to gloss over the differences between representation and reality, attempting to draw little cognitive lines from the things we see on the screen to the "real" activities [...]" (Laurel, 1991, p. 31). In other words, we should not fuse illusion and reality because representations may be without referents in the real world: "But in art as in human–computer activities, the object of a mimesis [...] may be a real thing or a virtual one; that is, a thing that exists nowhere other than in the imagination [...] *Mimetic representations do not necessarily have real-world referents*" (Laurel, 1991, p. 46). The point is, of course, that in all of these passages Laurel favours a view on representation that makes mimesis an illusionary construct that is made by someone as opposed to a direct mirroring of reality. To interpret mimesis in this way makes a lot of sense when you deal with a medium that can create virtualities for which there has never been an original in real life.

Still, when Laurel wants to be concrete, she seems to fall back on a realistic credo. She argues for instance, that "using a pebble to represent a man is not mimetic; making a doll to represent him is" (Laurel, 1991, p. 46). If a pebble cannot function as a representation of a man, it can only mean that, as a sign, it is not similar enough to its alleged referent. It is, in other words, not realistic enough. It is an ideal of similarity that makes Laurel feel uneasy with a trash can that can gobble up what has been posited within it, the visual difference between a real and a virtual desktop, and the real and the virtual folder. The latter is supposed to be magical in comparison with the real (cf. Laurel, 1991, p. 128). It is probably also her almost naturalistic interpretation of mimesis (in spite of her theoretical specifications) that lets more ideals from the conventions of realistic or naturalistic theatre survive in her thinking: the notion of absolute illusion and the framed stage. Complete illusion means that we suspend our disbelief in the illusion for the time we sit in the theatre. We accept forgetting that we watch an illusion, so to speak, and accept experiencing the action on stage *as if* it was real. To make us do so the stage machinery is usually made more or less "invisible". This is the convention that Laurel formulates when she consistently insists that "representation is all there is" and when she says that "the magic is created by both people and machines, but who, what, and where they are *do not matter* to the audience [...] when a play is "working," audience members are simply not aware of the technical aspects at all" (Laurel, 1991, p. 15). As Laurel makes her illustrations of the theatrical illusion with the stage at one end of a room and the audience at the other end, she seems very indebted to the convention of the framed stage.

In short, Laurel inherits a type of order based on causality from Aristotle and she actually combines this, by way of the Aristotelean concept of mimesis, with traditional theatre conventions. To avoid misunderstandings, however, we would like to remind our readers that we are not trying to classify Laurel as a naïve classicist whose theoretical work is of no value. We only try to point out that many of her arguments seem to lose power as examples because she is not consistent in her own references. We would simply have liked her to admit openly that the rules her arguments are built on indeed are, and must be, a set of conventions. Having made this point, we should like to add that we find the omnipresent insistence on creating order by way of selection paramount. If the ideology of George P. Landow as seen in *Hypertext 2.0. The Convergence of Contemporary Critical Theory and Technology* is in any way typical of the line of reasoning which Laurel is up against, her insistence on limitations seems more than appropriate. Landow celebrates hypertext because "digital text is always open, borderless, unfinished and displaced by the fact that it is possible for the reader to follow various links, unfinishable, capable of infinite extension" (Landow, 1997, p. 175) Valorizing this form of text, Landow urges us to "abandon conceptual systems founded upon ideas of center, margin, hierarchy, and linearity and replace them with ones of multilinearity, nodes, links, and networks" (Landow, 1997, p. 2). Faced with this celebration of a hypertextual structure, it seems more than important to remind ourselves that multimedia products rely no less on making *good* organic structures. Indeed, Laurel has a good point when she maintains that any part of an application must, like in drama, be drawn "from the circumscribed potential of the particular dramatic world. Whenever this principle is violated, the organic unity of the work is diminished, and the scheme of probability that holds the work together is disrupted" (Laurel, 1991, p. 58).

However, just as much as one wants to insist on order when reading Landow, one needs to insist that there are several forms of order, many forms of theatre that can be considered as models, when one reads Laurel. Indeed, it may be true that there are "ways in which art is 'lawful'; that is, there are formal, structural, and causal dimensions that can be identified and used both descriptively and productively" (Laurel, 1991, p. 28). But if this is so, it must also be a question of dispute on which level of abstraction one should search for, or make use of, such laws. It is understandable that Laurel infers from her belief in laws to the truthfulness of Aristotelean laws if she needs to defend her artistic approach in a non-artistic context. Needless to say, however, it seems far from necessary from our point of view.

The futility of trying to raise the laws of Aristotle to laws that hold true in any dramatic case can be seen when Laurel insists that the use of a spreadsheet can be seen as a progression along the lines of causal and linear dramaturgy (cf. Laurel, 1991, pp. 88–89) and when she tries to convince us that it would be worthwhile to use computers to turn our use of text programs into whole actions: "Computers have the potential to transform the process of writing from a series of isolated and cumbersome tasks into a whole action that retains and refreshes its connections to its inspiration, materials, and outcome" (Laurel, 1991, p. 173). To us this seems to turn the use of Aristotle into a straitjacket of particular coherence. Even if you should be in favour of a linear dramaturgy in a drama, it seems absurd to demand that the *process* of producing this kind of order should also be determined by linear development. In the process of writing you have to be able to jump from one point to another, to rewrite stuff which should have been finished in the first act according to the model, and so forth. In fact, this seems to be where a text program makes it possible to do better than other tools.

Taking other points of departure than the one suggested by Aristotle would obviously make you create other constraints and produce other forms of order. Totality doesn't necessarily include causality and directed representation. In the last part of this article we would like to discuss alternative strategies to create order and to treat other theatrical strategies as models for the creation of computer worlds. What kind of order and which rules, for instance, are explored in what seems like spontaneous interaction in improvisations? Are there tools to be considered useful for inhabited virtual 3D spaces in the creation of a drama or in devising a performance?

4.2 Additional Perspectives

As an actress Laurel knows the theatre as an art form. When she considers how theatrical strategies can be used in the production of interesting environments in the computer, she seems to reiterate the defence of art made by Aristotle in the face of his teacher Plato. The latter did not consider art in general, and theatre in particular, to be very valuable, to say the least. As he saw art as a representation of a representation of an ideal world, art was bound to be not one but two steps away from the truth. Consequently, he found art morally dangerous. It would inevitably lead people astray. So artists were bound to be *personae non gratae* in his ideal republic. Aristotle, on the other hand, argued that art in fact had a very valid social function. Theatre could, for example, cater for the purification of the emotions through a cathartic experience of watching a great tragedy. Aristotle set out to understand just *how* theatre affected people. In other words, he judged that actors could be studied as masters of rhetoric, and found that they had great help from the playwright who knew how to plot a play in order to make it work on the emotions of the spectators.

When Laurel considers how she can improve the structure of virtual environments, she thinks in terms of such a rhetoric value. She does not ask for catharsis, but she considers what is most effective in terms of user affect. This makes her insist that, like the theatre, computers should be regarded as media, not tools. It is important, however, to distinguish between the Aristotelean interest in the rhetorical aspect of theatre and the particular set of rhetorical strategies he demanded. Pioneers who were no less conscious of the rhetorical side of theatre have constantly challenged and manipulated the means of theatre in order to make new, provocative and explicit anti-Aristotelean contracts with the audience.

Of course, Laurel is aware that there have been many attacks on the Aristotelean poetics throughout the history of the theatre. The twentieth century also saw several attempts to deal with representation in non-naturalistic ways. Brecht is but one example that Laurel is aware of. His famous attempt to construct an anti-Aristotelian drama with alienation effects built into an epic structure was created to remind the audience that they were in the theatre, not in a world where things happen due to natural cause and effect. One of Brecht's main points was that the world as it is does not make sense and, as a consequence, it should not be represented as such. To him being immersed actually represents a big danger to the political and intellectual development of man. To Brecht, Aristotelian theatre, and in particular the realistic versions that were canonized around the turn of the twentieth century, naturalizes existing power structures. This made Brecht conclude that reflecting the world and being immersed mutually exclude one another.

We have seen that Laurel holds the opposite view to Brecht. To her, being involved in the action, not in technicalities, is important. So she excludes Brecht from her sources of inspiration. She does this, it seems, more from a disbelief in didactic theatre and in Brecht's political project than from a thoughtful consideration of aesthetic possibilities at hand to make represented human action work. If viewed from an aesthic angle, Brecht's epic theatre, and the multi-layered dramaturgy with which he works, may very well prove productive as an exploration of reflexive distance – both as a way of perceiving and as an effect of artistic form – which could be utilized when constructing user–computer actions. Principally such a form does not exclude getting involved in represented actions. Nor does it work against an interest in being part of an interaction with a computer. Our point is that the epic theatre of Brecht simply works according to other rules and that it has to be set up through a different fictional contract from action based on development through identification with the characters, but that these rules are no less valid. Any game, adventure story or other kind of computer program has to negotiate its formal rules with the user. So it is with aesthetics. A program can be fascinating and negotiate involvement through several means. Identification is but one. Engaging in connecting several stories and finding pleasure and insight in the linking process are the dimensions that epic theatre is made of.

Laurel's insistence on dramatic plotting for the computer rather than on epic, absurd or otherwise avant garde dramaturgical strategies, seems, in part, to stem from bad experiences with the aesthetics or effects of non-linear and participatory theatre forms. Laurel worries about what happens when people try to "eliminate linear causality from dramatic structure". She admits that it can be done for experimental reasons, and refers to what the absurdists did in the 1950s and what the participatory theatre of the 1960s did to obtain a new relationship between stage and audience. She does not, however, find any reason to bring these experiments in dialogue with "designing human–computer experience". Whether it is bad experiences that keep Laurel from investigating these alternative theatre strategies or not, this exclusion is definitely a pity. In fact, the non-linear and participatory forms of theatre hold a lot of potential for the construction of virtual worlds. They may even be better suited to the job. As a matter of fact, Laurel herself seems to point in this direction. Thus, she points out that "an apparent difference between programs and theatrical scripts is that programs are not intrinsically linear, while scripts are" (Laurel, 1991, p. 45). Apart from this insight into the non-linear nature of computer programs (which contradicts the paradigm of linear causality and seems to draw her out of the Aristotelean spell), she even notes that "whereas the action specified in a given script will not change from performance to performance, a program can lead to actions (composed of incidents) that can vary widely from session to session, depending upon the choices made and actions performed by human agents. In other words, programs generally contains more *potential* for action than plays" (Laurel, 1991, p. 68). As opposed to plays that must bring the action all the way through possibility and probability to necessity, a computer program has to stay with the potentiality. When thinking along these lines she even dreams of "worlds in which we can extend, amplify, enrich our capacities to think, feel and act" (Laurel, 1991, p. 33), a program which seems to chime more with the avant garde experiments of the 1960s than with Aristotle.

Taking theatre seriously as "an additional perspective" should lead us to an experimental mode of theatre. With her longing for an amplification of our experience Laurel starts our journey. From time to time she realizes that there is a problem with the analogy between the audience watching a theatre production and the user interacting with the computer. The interactive nature of a computer–user relationship is in fact very different from the actor–spectator relationship in the theatre. Laurel realizes this when she says that making human–computer interfaces is about "creating a jointly inhabited space" where meaning takes shape through the collaboration and successive approximations of the participants" or "a shared context for action in which both are agents" (Laurel, 1991, p. 4). If she is right in assuming that the role as an agent in a shared action is a possible position for the user, however, why then exclude an exploration of this? Indeed, theatre can provide more interesting interactive models than the actor–spectator relationship experienced in mainstream theatre. Laurel knows this, but in her book the obvious possibility, that of improvisational theatre, is only allowed a half-life as a persistent undercurrent in the argument.

When describing her work in the field of interactive fantasy, she acknowledges that the users of such a system are, in fact, like audience members who can "march up onto the stage and become various characters, altering the action by what they say and do in their roles" (Laurel, 1991, p. 16). She does not, however, further this observation or develop a possible link to improvisational or participatory theatre as a possible model for extensive experiments in this direction. In another passage Laurel admits that a program and a play cannot be homogenized completely because, to a certain extent, a program is open ended. Had she stayed with her experimental and engineering point of view, she would probably have found it worthwhile to explore the forms of theatre, which she tends to consider must fall short of what theatre really is.

In an evaluation of the experiment with interaction between a user and actors performing as virtual agents, Laurel concludes that "as theatre viewed from the outside, the entertainment value of the improvisations was largely mediocre", but that, on the other hand, "the interactor's experiences were dramatically quite powerful" (Laurel, 1991, p. 189). The second part of this commentary pinpoints, in fact, the potential in improvisational theatre. In this form of theatre you are involved not with the actions that are represented in front of you, but *in* the actions you participate in – from *within* the fiction. Educational drama has, for instance, developed many different strategies for how a participant can take part in the action and, even without being trained as an actor, become part of the narrative from within. From our experience with this kind of dramatic interaction, we have been guided to classify this theatrical form *with* an audience as an alternative to theatre *for* an audience (cf. Szatkowski *et al.*, 1999). Theatre *with* is an activity which is similar to what happens in the theatre during a rehearsal period. Staging a realistic play means to look for ultimate forms of interaction. Here, the focus is on what takes place *between* the participants – and *how* the interaction is set up so that it becomes pleasurable and interesting for the participants – and in turn for the spectators. Educational drama works on the same basic pleasure to play, to be involved in solving the dilemmas there and then to see what happens when one decides to follow certain impulses, to feel the reactions of others, to rely on the safety curtain at hand: it is – after all – just a play.

Is is far from incorrect that "putting audience on stage creates confusion" and that "the problem with the audience-as-active-participant idea is that it adds to the clutter, both psychological and physical" (Laurel, 1991, p. 17). But there is more to be said. It is only in so far that you judge improvisational theatre by the standards of the causal dramaturgy of Aristotle that you don't see that there is more to open-ended interaction than chaos. The search for essentializing the contingency of real life (for which Laurel calls) is no less at work in improvisational theatre. It is equally submitted to rules and order, though of a different kind. Unpredicted interaction only happens in our social reality, and even there one can hardly conceive of something completely unpredictable. We behave according to rules, conventions and other setups for social interaction. We can be good or bad at it, and we will hardly be able to understand why things don't always work as we thought they would, but we have no choice but to follow some rules and conventions.

Improvisational theatre takes its point of departure from such rules and should be seen as an attempt to investigate different social situations.

Good improvisation relies heavily on the ability to follow a set of rules and conventions. A lot of these rules are negotiated *before* you engage in the actual improvisation with one or several other persons, i.e. you actually learn how to improvise. Then you keep trying, just like you do when learning to play the piano. Only one thing is vitally different, of course: you need at least one more person to improvise with. If this "person" is a computer, the computer has to "know" the rules too – and be able to act and react according to certain conventions. You need to ask certain questions in order to set up theatrical fiction. Having answers to the questions *who* (are you), *where* (are you), and *what* (are you doing) is usually a good start for an improvisation. This is one of the main lessons to be learned from gurus of improvisation like Keith Johnstone and Viola Spolin (Johnstone 1981; Spolin 1983). *When* things happen is usually of minor importance and *why* things happen is a question the improviser usually has to suspend thinking about. The rule of all rules in improvisation is to avoid any anticipation of action. Every action must happen as a direct reaction to what is being said or done by the others, to the situation that is set up either before or during the play, to "facts" that have been established during the improvisation, to the space established, to sounds, light, props or whatever is either brought into the situation through active negotiation, or laid out as rules for this specific improvisation. So the ability to negotiate workable and productive rules, inside or outside the improvisation, is a prerequisite.

The rules provide the improviser with dramaturgical tools to handle a negotiation of action and plotting from within the ongoing action. Principally one can start anywhere and with very few rules. In practice, an open improvisation is almost impossible to handle for an inexperienced improviser. So rather than looking at rules as restrictions, one should consider them as possibilities to do anything at all. Just as it is easier to act more "naturally" in your own culture than in a totally unknown one, it is easier for an improviser to know "quite a lot" to be creative, present and able to listen to the given circumstances of each situation. This point cannot be overemphasized: A romantic idea of "real freedom" should be kept away from any discussion about art in general, and about theatre specifically. It easily sidetracks planning and blurs any discussion of means and objectives. As a matter of fact (or perhaps as a matter of experience) one *feels* free in an improvisation where one has a command of the matter. An inexperienced improviser *feels* much freer with a lot of rules than without them. An experienced improviser can gain the *feeling* of being a master when an improvisation with very few rules turns out successfully. Both are feelings of great satisfaction, just like winning a football match or saving the princess in a adventure game. Improvisation is based on being involved – in an activity very similar to the pleasure of playing. Improvisation does end, but it does not need to have an ending. Improvisation can be about anything, but the negotiation of rules means that it cannot be about everything.

The challenge of improvisation in terms of establishing a relation to a non-human, namely a computer, obviously lies in *how* to set up the rules, *which rules* to create, and how to "teach" the computer not to anticipate in a way that excludes the input of the user, but processes it in such a way that it looks as if the reaction was created here and now. It seems possible to work with a complex mixture of preset and randomized actions that can set up something like an improvisational situation between the computer and a user. The game of chess, which is well known to program designers, is very similar to this notion of improvisation. It is of course possible to program agents or avatars to move according to similar laws to those of a knight in chess. The problem is, on the other hand, that the *user* may want to have more material at hand than narrowly prescribed movements, as in chess.

Improvisation is used by directors as a means by which something can be learned about the characters in a play, a specific dramatic situation, the relationship between two characters, and so forth. It is, however, also an art form in its own right, and it is used extensively in drama in education. The latter field is ripe with experiences which could be utilized in the design of interactive multimedia products. In drama in education two kinds of improvisation can be seen at work at the same time. Devising a piece of educational drama means to work out plot points and turning points and anticipate ways in which these points can be reached through an active participation in the actions. The teacher can take on a role (fill a certain function) in this setup, and act so that the pupils reach an experience of suspense and relief, participate in discussions, make decisions in moral dilemmas etc. through active involvement (for examples of how this works, see for instance Bolton (1979, 1984) and O'Neill and Lambert (1982)). The fictional contract can be negotiated in as many ways as it can be in the professional theatre. Stepping in and out of the fiction is but one well-known device to make sure that there is a continued discussion and reflection of what happens and an active involvement in how things happen. So, the development of the drama is interacting with the educationally and artistically planned agenda for the setup of it.

Apart from the obvious inspirations we find in theatre *with* the participants – educational drama and improvisational theatre – we see a source of knowledge to draw from in making a performance from scratch. This is a form of "rehearsal" that is becoming known as devised theatre, or the production of post-dramatic theatre. Devised theatre has links to theatrical experiments done in laboratories and in groups, and where the main idea is to research the rules of the theatre. Questions like what happens if you do *not* tell a story, if you do *not* use actors who play roles, if you do *not* work with plotting, timing and characterization, if you indeed do not accept any Aristotelian rules at all, have been paramount, even existential, imperatives in this theatre tradition. An *experimental* mode, rather than a series of particular restrictions, has guided producers of avant garde theatre. Inspirations from other art forms – visual arts, installation, video, music videos, film and so forth – has led to many different kinds of production methods as well as types of performance, so it would make no sense to refer to this as one form of theatre from which one would be sure to find a model for human–computer design. We do want to point to some guiding principles, though, that have been become known under the concept of *devised theatre.* Some of these principles have, in our experience, indeed been useful as sources of inspiration to research possible human–computer relations.

First of all, devised theatre differs from traditional theatre in that the rehearsal period is not about staging a written play or a fully developed concept. The rehearsal period is organized as a laboratory where the main aim is to produce material. This material can be anything from a response to a theme, for instance the Tower of Babel, to investigations of technical possibilities, for instance how a performer can develop his or her movements in relation to a particular computer program. The material is judged by its degree of "artistic power" which means that one or more people from the production group always watch what happens, "judge" the results and suggest new tasks or directions for the material to be developed. After having produced a lot of material, the first steps towards a selection of what is to be left behind and what to go on with are made, and compositional questions will be discussed and investigated. Pieces of material are shifted about and new material is made to fill the gaps until there is a result to show. So, rather than having an idea or an image of a performance in mind when one starts rehearsing, devised theatre tries to take the consequence of a belief that theatre is collaborative and concrete. You have to create something concrete to see what it looks and feels like before you can decide what is interesting for this particular group to show to other people. Devised theatre certainly does not guarantee that the result *is* good, but the members have certainly researched something and reached a result that could not have been foreseen. Following this experimental attitude one of the main points is to "let the material talk by itself". One should look at the material as a "partner" in the process towards a result which is different from what you do when staging a play. It is the sharpened eye, the ability to take the right decisions, to be open to suggestions and to follow the development of the material to the end, that supplies the greatest challenges. This particular process, we suggest, could be taken as a model.

To sum up: we suggest broadening the scope to be found in Laurel's reasoning by including other forms of artistic order than the causal linearity of classical narrative. There is as much to be learned from epic, improvisational and devised theatre as we can gain from thinking along Aristotelean lines. To our minds, what seems most important to inherit from Laurel is her understanding of the need for a *rhetorical* approach to the construction of user-friendly interfaces. Laurel is at her best when she shows the importance of proper orchestration. In order to create interesting virtual environments we need to be aware of the theatrical means by which this is done. All in all it is the effect that counts. If we start thinking about agents as characters, not people, as Laurel suggests (Laurel, 1991, p. 145), we could take a lot of difficulties off the agenda, especially the questions of artificial intelligence. Instead of trying hard to create really intelligent agents, one would have to focus on making them *appear* intelligent. As Laurel puts it, thought should be inferred from the actions of the agents: "Computer-based agents, like dramatic characters, do not have to think [...]; they simply have to *provide a representation from which thought may be inferred*" (Laurel, 1991, p. 57). What we are looking for in our experiments is believability rather than truthfulness. There is nothing wrong with being tricked. In fact, we indulge in the tricks done to us when relating to fictional genres. The tricks simply have to be believable in relation to our understanding of the context that has been established. We believe (with Laurel) that it is better to renounce true to life images that will appear disappointing because they do not in fact live up to reality, and go for restrictions that will be accepted because they do not promise something that they cannot hold instead. For considerations of how to produce good human–computer interaction the particular rhetoric of improvisational theatre seems to be most promising. If we primarily think of the user as an agent partaking in an action in a virtual environment, we would probably have to conceive of the user as a visitor and the computer as a world that is populated. As we have tried to show, this is exactly how a participant would join the action in an improvisation.

References

Bolton, G. (1979) *Towards a Theory of Drama in Education.* Longman: Burnt Mill.

Bolton, G. (1984) *Drama as Education* Longman: Burnt Mill.

Deleuze, G. and Guattari, F. (1991) *Qu'est-ce que la Philosophie?* Paris: Les éditions de minuit.

Derrida, J. (1972) La mythologie blanche. In *Marges de la Philosophie*, Paris: Les éditions de minuit.

Goffman, E. (1969) *The Presentation of Self in Everyday Life.* London: Penguin.

Johnstone, K. (1981) *Impro. Improvisation and the Theatre.* London: Methuen.

Lakoff, G. and Johnson, M. (1980) *Metaphors We Live By*, London: University of Chicago Press.

Landow, G. P. (1997) *Hypertext 2.0. The Convergence of Contemporary Critical Theory and Technology*, London: Johns Hopkins University Press.

Laurel, B. (1991) *Computers as Theatre.* New York, Addison-Wesley.

Linton, R. (1936) *The Study of Man.* New York: Appleton-Century.

O'Neill, C. and Lambert, A. (1982) *Drama Structures. A Practical Handbook for Teachers.* London: Hutchinson.

Rorty, R. (1989) *Contingency, Irony, and Solidarity.* New York: Cambridge University Press.

Sontag, S. (1988) *AIDS and Its Metaphors.* New York: Farrar, Straus & Giroux.

Spolin, V. (1983) *Improvisation for the Theater.* Evanston, IL: Northwestern University Press.

Szatkowski, J. *et al.* (1999) Dramaturgy in virtual theatre. Part of *Puppet. The Educational Puppet Theatre of Virtual Worlds*, Periodic Progress Report, unpublished.

Wilshire, B. (1982) *Role Playing and Identity. The Limits of Theatre as Metaphor.* Bloomington, IL: Indiana Press.

SECTION 2

Construction of Interactive Lifelike Agents and Actors

Introduction

Erik Granum

In the context of the present book, autonomous agents are inhabitants of virtual worlds. Special versions of such agents may be called avatars, if some or all of their autonomy has been exchanged for an interface to allow a user in the real world to be in some sort of control of the agent. Then the avatar may function as the representative of the user in the virtual world.

However, the major point of this section is the agents themselves, and the following six chapters explore the agent concept from rather diverse points of view.

In Chapter 5, Mogensen structures a suggestive discussion around three basic perspectives on agents: the construction, classification and use perspectives, respectively. Mogensen derives two important projections of autonomous agents: the entity-oriented and the relation-oriented views. The analysis of Mogensen is conceptual and "top-down", and thus in contrast to Chapter 9, by Madsen and Granum, who explicitly take a "bottom-up" approach. They suggest concrete and implemented examples of interactive autonomous agents in order to learn from experience how practical issues may inform agent design and interaction. Starting with an example of a simple interactive agent, "Bouncy" the bouncing dog, alternative architectures of autonomous agents are described and discussed. The various operational elements of a practical design of a virtual environment with autonomous agents are described. In a sense this approach is in accordance with Mogensen's relation-oriented view, which claims that the competencies of agents are products of the agents' interaction with the environments. The abilities of the agents are produced through the environment.

The importance of the environment is also evident from Chapter 6. Skov provides the example of "community chat rooms" on the Internet, which use autonomous agents to facilitate communication between individual users. Agents are available for each user and an agent is servicing each chat room where users may join in to "socialize". The user agents operate on the basis of a user profile and a registration of how the user exploits the suggestions made by the agent on which information sources to pursue and which contacts to establish. Chat room agents correspondingly maintain a list of the usual communication and activity of the chat room and a list describing the current activities.

While Skov's agents are adapting to the users' wishes, in Chapter 7 Andersen and Callesen want to "feed" the user, or spectator, with stories "told" by the agents. Andersen and Callesen are concerned that agent behaviours are boring to observe unless these behaviours are based on narrative structures informed by literature, theatre and film. Approaching the problem also in a "top-down" fashion they present five different ways of analysing behaviour using linguistic evidence. This provides an interesting complement to the implementation-oriented discussion on agent architectures in Chapter 9.

Andersen and Callesen use a series of examples to demonstrate how agents may be turned into actors and how interesting behaviours are structured. One of the aspects discussed is the necessity of higher order mutual modelling of agents' "knowledge world" and "intention world". In order to create interesting plots, agent A should "figure out" what agent B "knows" about agent A's intentions etc. Eventually Andersen and Callesen "put it all together" in a structure with symbolic and non-symbolic processes at three levels ranging from "the discrete" (conceptual) to "the continuous" (operating on the physical world). Interestingly, this has clear correspondences to the bottom-up based modelling of Madsen and Granum.

In Chapter 8, Wibroe *et al.* apply the structures of "Agents and Actors" to analyse "Games and Stories", and discuss how tellable stories can be made interesting and how suspense is created. A particular computer game is described and analysed in some depth, revealing a lack of narrative structure and a tellable design, which again confirms the necessity of turning agents into actors.

This section has contributions from both media science (i.e. humanities) and computer engineering and science (natural sciences) and a contrast in approach can be noticed – in particular between Chapters 6 and 9 and the other papers.

Different cultures have been confronted in the book, and many of the current research questions are revealed through this confrontation. To illustrate this Chapter 10 presents and discusses some of the inconsistencies between the views of people from the different disciplines. For example, in the virtual worlds (or the virtual theatre):

- Who is performing (acting) and for whom?
- Is there inherently an audience?
- How can story-time and plot-time be handled in the virtual worlds?
- How can relations of dramaturgical importance of processes be added to the scale from "discrete" to "continuous", from concepts to physical properties?

Confused? Then read the "last episode" of this section.

A number of research issues have become evident from the chapters in this section.

Mogensen insists on being "in-conclusive" when summarizing his observations. The main problem that remains seems to be establishing an understanding of a structure relating the user-experienced autonomy to the designer-experienced autonomy. This connects to "externalizing the inner states of agents" as Andersen and Callesen put it. Also, it seems more important in the general case that the reasoning of autonomous agents can be inferred from observations rather than ensuring the optimality of the reasoning and decision-making processes. All in all this points to a need for new approaches to agent design.

Andersen and Callesen also address the fundamental problem of combining autonomy with the necessary control to ensure narrative behaviours and tellable stories to develop. It may well be possible to design agents that tend to show some narrative behaviour, but a number of the premises for their discussion may be disputable.

Madsen and Granum point to extending the capability (and complexity) of agents by introducing episodic memory for handling temporal information. Adding to this the "embedded possible worlds" of Ryan as described by Andersen and Callesen, we would indeed have agents with potentially very subtle behaviours. Whether this is consistent with the dramaturgical focus and simplicity required in a virtual theatre, and whether this allows "externalization of inner states" is another matter.

In any case, there are sufficient research questions and challenges to keep Mr Humanist and Mr Engineer occupied for a number of years.

5

Agents: Dependent Autonomy and Transparent Automatons?

Michael Mogensen

5.1 Introduction

In many research fields relating to computer science and engineering the usage of the term "agent" has become pervasive. The term is also used in many other fields stretching from sociology to chemistry. The most abstract meaning of the word could be defined as something that does something or causes something to happen, i.e. produces an effect or change.[1] In relation to technology this definition includes almost any artefact depending on how strictly causing and doing are understood.[2] Research fields related to artificial intelligence, robotics and software employ more narrow understandings of the term, but even within each community the conceptual meanings associated with the term "agent" are differentiated and intensively debated.

This chapter identifies three perspectives in the debate: construction, classification and use. On the basis of these three points of view different understandings of agents and their autonomy are discussed. The discussion has three foci. Firstly, differences between designers' and users' experiences of autonomy are examined, and secondly the relations between experiences of autonomy and properties of artefacts are considered. Thirdly, two general approaches to artefacts and action are outlined and juxtaposed: an entity-oriented approach and a relation-oriented approach. Finally, possible consequences of discussion for design are considered.

---

1 The *Oxford Advanced Learner's Dictionary* (Cowie, 1989) notes several meanings. Among them are "person who does something or causes something to happen" and "force or substance that produces an effect or change".

2 In the following it is just taken for granted that intentional action is routinely ascribed to artefacts. However, no analysis is made of either the differences (and parallels) between the doings of humans and of artefacts (acts, actions, behaviours, operations, performances etc.) or the central role that concepts like intention, will and consciousness play in these matters.

Two limiting features of this chapter should be noted. Firstly, my purpose is to discuss – not to report findings or establish conclusions. Secondly, the scope of this discussion is general. It is not limited to agents in 3D virtual worlds or for that matter to fictional agents in these worlds. Many of the examples and considerations are, on the contrary, drawn from domains where "the task" is not entertainment or interesting experiences, but more practical matters like information acquisition or controlling and monitoring the physical environment. Obviously domains like computer games and navigation of ships differ radically in regard to the consequences of errors and the demands on representations. I see such differences as very important in relation to both the design and experiences of agents and their autonomy, but my choice here has been to approach the question in a general, domain-independent way. While such an approach misses important aspects, my hope is that it also catches some that otherwise would have been dimmed.

5.2 Three Perspectives on Agents

Numerous proposals to pin down a specific understanding of the concept of an agent can be found in the literature concerning artificial agents. In the subsequent subsections three such understandings are outlined. This is neither meant to be an exhaustive account of the discussion nor of the three understandings outlined. The purpose is only to highlight three important perspectives on the issue. The understandings outlined serve only as typical illustrations of these three perspectives.

5.2.1 The Construction Perspective

Maes (1994a) describes agents from a design or construction perspective. From this perspective the content of the agent concept is a matter of architecture. The content can be seen as an alternative to the Deliberative Thinking paradigm in artificial intelligence research. While the latter emphasizes explicit knowledge, rational choice and problem solving, the alternative agent paradigm emphasizes "...a more direct coupling of perception to action, distributedness and decentralization, dynamic interaction with the environment and intrinsic mechanisms to cope with resource limitations and incomplete knowledge...". In this paradigm, an agent implements a new system architecture based on distributed modules (often called "behaviours") working in parallel "...on representations which are close to raw sensory data..." and without any global internal model or planning activity with one hierarchical goal structure. The functionality and behaviour of the agents are "...viewed as an emergent property of the intensive interaction of the system with its environment..." and of the interaction between behaviours generated by the individual modules. The agent paradigm is behaviour-based as opposed to knowledge-based and bottom-up not top-down (Maes, 1994b).

While this outline captures the central ideas in the agent paradigm seen as a matter of construction, the division between the paradigms is not as clear-cut as implied. In the construction of applications, ideas from both the agent and AI paradigms are very often applied in so-called hybrid architectures.

5.2.2 The Classification Perspective

A second perspective – the classification perspective – can be found in (Jennings and Wooldridge, 1995, 1998). From their taxonomic, bird's-eye perspective they propose four attributes to define, what they label as "intelligent agents".[3] An intelligent agent has to be *autonomous*, *responsive*, *proactive* and *social*. These attributes are understood in the following way:

- **Autonomy** is a property of a device with the capability to "...operate without the direct intervention of humans or others, and have some kind of control over their actions and internal state..."
- **Responsive** is the capability to "...perceive their environment....and respond in a timely fashion to changes that occur in it..."
- **Proactive** is the ability to "...exhibit opportunistic, goal-directed behavior and take the initiative where appropriate..."
- **Social** is the ability to "...interact, when they deem appropriate, with other artificial agents and humans in order to complete their own problem solving and help others with their activities."

The last three properties are seen together as a capability of flexibility. In a later paper (Jennings *et al.*, 1998) a fifth attribute – more or less implicit in the four above – is added to the definition, namely *situatedness*, meaning that "...the agent receives sensory input from its environment and that it can perform actions which change the environment in some way". Other possible properties are mentioned (adaptability, mobility, veracity, benevolence and rationality), but are not deemed necessary in a minimum definition of the agent paradigm.

5.2.3 The Use Perspective

The third perspective approaches the agent concept from a use or human–machine interaction point of view. An example of this perspective can be found in (Maes, 1994c). By replacing the metaphor of *direct manipulation*, where users initiate all tasks explicitly and monitor all events, with the metaphor of the *personal assistant*, a new style of human–computer interaction is proposed. The new style can be labelled indirect management and involves the user in collaboration with the agent, which is capable of initiating communication, monitoring events and performing tasks on behalf of the user.

Also viewing agents from a use perspective, Lieberman (1997) defines the generic term "agent" as "...any program that can be considered by the user to be acting as an

---

3 To illustrate the extent of confusion regarding the term "agent", Jennings and Wooldridge (1998) classifies software daemons as agents while Jennings *et al.* (1998) later conclude that such systems "*are certainly examples of situated, autonomous systems, (but) we would not consider them to be agents...*"! The process is the following: first the generic term "agent" is qualified with the term "intelligent", whose meaning is specified, to isolate a certain type of "agents". Later the term "agent" is reserved for these "intelligent agents" and thereby eliminating all other types of "agents" in the earlier sense.

assistant or helper, rather than as a tool...". He also proposes a narrower definition of *autonomous interface agents*, demanding that these agents have the ability both to change objects in the interface without explicit instruction from the user and to operate in parallel, i.e. concurrently, with the user.[4]

5.3 Designer and User Experiences of Autonomy

How do the three perspectives outlined in the previous section relate to the concept of autonomy? It seems to be present in all three, but in different ways and to differing degrees.

Let us take the classification perspective in Jennings and Wooldridge (1995, 1998) as a starting point, i.e. that autonomy is the capability to "...operate without the direct intervention of humans or others, and have some kind of control over their actions and internal state...". A similar understanding is widespread in research papers on autonomous agents. For example, Maes (1994b) defines an agent as autonomous "...if it decides itself how to relate its sensor data to motor commands in such a way that its goals are attended to successfully". This understanding of autonomy is in full compliance with the colloquial meaning of the word as a matter of self-governing and ability to act independently. Autonomy is seen in the light of the relation between an agent and a human (or another agent). But the agent is a distinct, independent unit with a certain degree of closure and an ability to act. The level of autonomy is understood as a function of what the artefact *can do without* human (or outside-) intervention and what the human (or other agents) *cannot do* to the artefact, namely change certain states or initiate certain actions which are under the agent's own control. Both relations can be seen as negative limitations, and link autonomy closely to action – or more specifically to the possibilities for action – and control.

However, if one compares the construction perspective with the use perspective, it becomes clear that the autonomy of agents respectively in relation to designers and to end-users in the context of a "normal" use situation can involve different kinds of autonomy. The autonomous agents exert independence from both designers and users, but not in the same way.

In the construction perspective the autonomy of an artefact is tied up with specific types of system architecture. This architecture is used both as an instrument to generate new functionality and as a special way to make the functionality work. In the construction phase, designers of autonomous agents equip agents with independent but interacting behaviour modules and situate them in an environment. These agents, their behaviours and their associated control systems are repeatedly tested, modified and reconstructed, until the resulting interactional performance of the individual agents as well as of groups of such agents is deemed satisfactory. In this process the agents can be seen as exhibiting a kind of design emergence. The designers get more

4 In Lieberman's understanding the autonomy of an agent is linked to this possibility of running concurrently with the user's activities, i.e. the ability to change objects in the interface is not a sufficient criteria for autonomy.

out than they put in, in the sense that the total performance is not specified in every detail or predicted in advance – it is experienced on the basis of experiment.

Examples of such emergent functionality are numerous. Maes (1994a) reports on a system in which individual competence modules (sand-board, pick-up-sander and put-down-sander) interact to achieve a global goal (board-sanded) without any single module to do the global planning alone and explicitly. Another example is in Pirjanian (1998), where the global goal of a robot (move as fast as possible from A to B) is achieved without an explicit model of the environment or a precompiled plan. In this robot the individual behaviours (avoid-obstacles, maintain-heading and move-fast) are continuously fused through a voting mechanism selecting between possible actions on the basis of received input from each module.[5]

This emergence can be seen as involving autonomous or independent action performed by the agent artefact. It seems however that the artefact performs two distinct types of actions. Firstly it participates in the construction of its own functionality, and secondly it decides how this functionality is performed. These two types of autonomy could be called *functional* autonomy and *executive* autonomy.

The first type is clearly described by Maes (1994a): "...one cannot simply tell these agents how to achieve a goal. Instead one has to find an interaction loop involving the system and the environment which will converge (in an environment which has the expected properties) towards the desired goal". It is to this search for a functional interaction loop that the agent embryo contributes through the feedback it provides for the designer. The agent takes part in the decisions about *what* it can and will do.

In the construction phase the agents also exert executive autonomy. It decides *how* to do what it does. This kind of autonomy is what the artefact later should exert "in production" – that is after the construction phase. But this autonomy is not only autonomy from its later users, but also from its designer. As stated clearly by Norvig and Russell (1995): "An agent is autonomous to the extent that its action choices depend on its own experience, rather than on knowledge of the environment that has been built-in by the designer".

Some agent systems are furthermore able to change their behaviour in the use context beyond the level of flexible achievement of a given goal, i.e. gradually to perform in a better way. These systems could be said also to exhibit *adaptive* autonomy.

All three kinds of autonomy – functional, executive and adaptive – can be seen as a kind of letting go of control from the designers' side. Part of the creative work is in

---

5 Note that this fusion of behaviours is not described as emergence by Pirjanian (1998). On the contrary, it is seen as "appropriate coordinated" behaviours identified through a top-down analysis of the global goal/task. Although the two examples deal with respectively choice and fusion of behaviours, I think they are similar in relation to the question of "emerging" functionality. Of course, the sense of such an alignment is dependent upon the understanding of "emergence". I use the term in a loose sense, in which it denotes that the global functionality of the system is impossible to understand if one does not take the interactions of the whole system and its environment into account. Even if the global functionality is designed and therefore anticipated, it is not a mere aggregate of individual parts of the system.

fact handed over to the artefacts, either during or after the construction phase. And for the adherents of the agent paradigm this under-specification of the agent from the designers' side is one of the design principles that make the agents robust. They are not as "brittle" as their AI ancestors, because their level of built-in knowledge is lower. Their actions will not fail as often, because they contain fewer presuppositions that can break down. On the other hand this robustness is traded for the loss of formal analysis and thereby optimal solutions.

Other aspects of autonomy are seen if we apply the use perspective. As shown by the citations from Lieberman (1997), the users' considerations can be seen as having an impact on what autonomy and action are.[6] Seen from this view, the users' experiences are necessary to understand the artefact's autonomy. The autonomy has to be experienced.

Such experiences could be differentiated in short-term experiences (immediate interpretations, impressions, feelings and perceptions) and in more permanent experiences (lasting understandings and attitudes). In the following I will focus on the former type of experience, and ask how such an immediate experience of autonomy in an artefact can be described.

In trying to answer that question one could start to ask, when an artefact is experienced or felt to do something – autonomously or not. Tentatively, I will claim that such experiences of an acting artefact must include the following two features as a minimum:

- A degree of "otherness" or differentiation must be involved in the experience, i.e. *you* have a relation to *something*. A relation that can lie anywhere in the range from a focus of perception to a conscious reflection. The crucial point is that you experience a presence of something.
- The experienced other must exert some degree of power, i.e. must be experienced as making a difference. It has consequences or effects beyond being present.

When these two features are both present, I think they equal the core of an experience of agency, i.e. the experience of an entity doing something.

Note, however, that such experiences of action do not necessarily involve an experience of a separate, autonomous centre making decisions. An artefact can be experienced as doing something (e.g. moving, calculating or playing) without an experience of decisions being made in regard to the performed actions. In other words, I think a third feature is present in the experience of autonomy:

- A distinct focus – either conscious or intuitively felt – on the reasons or causes of the consequences inherent in the experienced action. That is a presence of a "why?" or a "how?" in the experience.

Such experiences of autonomously acting entities are not only present among users but also among designers. However, if one takes a specific artefact it is easy to see that the

---

6 The perspective is ambiguous with regard to the status of these "considerations" or "ways of seeing". Are they products of the distribution of roles between human and artefact or are they subjective attitudes of the users? This question is dealt with in the next section.

autonomy experiences of designers and users can be very different, both in respect to the entities that are seen as acting and in what they are doing and to what degree the reasons for the actions matter. Both parties might agree that they experience "The robot is moving from A to B". But users will not necessarily have experiences like "The system architecture decides how to move the robot from A to B" (i.e. executive autonomy) or "The system architecture has established a capability to move the robot from A to B" (i.e. functional autonomy). The system architecture will normally not be an object or agent in the users' experiences. Neither will "making decisions" necessarily be present for the users, and if they are they most likely will be attributed to other entities than the system architecture (the robot, its brain, its design etc.).

The point here is simply that user-experienced autonomy does not necessarily coincide with designer-experienced autonomy. Experiences of functional or executive autonomy will rarely be identical or similar unless something is deliberately done to make the designers' and end-users' experiences coincide: an identity that can sometimes be desired, sometimes be irrelevant and at other times directly undesired.

5.4 System Properties and Experiences of Autonomy

While the possibility of such differences between designers and users is obvious, it could, however, be argued that the users' experiences of action and autonomy are intimately connected to the properties of a system; that is, to the artefact itself, regardless of how its designers might experience it. Such an argument could refer to specific properties of the architecture, physical interface or output of artefacts that directly produce users' experiences of autonomous action – or at least will tend to do so. Or they could refer to the role distribution between human and artefact, i.e. to what actions it is possible for the two parties to perform.

With regard to the physical interface and output of a system, the following list of artefact properties could be seen as producers of experienced agency, autonomy or even animacy:

- **Opacity**. Suchman (1987) notes that "...the description of computational artifacts as interactive is supported by their reactive, linguistic and internally opaque properties". If the artefact is opaque (i.e. not transparent) and thereby irreducible to smaller parts, it is hard to resist an ascription of action to the entire artefact, and from that follows easily ascription of intention and then personification.
- **Initiation** of changes. Movement or changes generated by an artefact can contribute to an experience of a "free will" resident in the artefact and thereby of a necessity of cooperation with an independent unit.
- **Unpredictability**. If the artefact is unpredictable this free will effect is reinforced, while it is weakened if its operations can be predicted.
- **Competence** and relevance of response/feedback. If the received responses from the artefact are meaningful, correct and useful, it facilitates the ascription of autonomy as well as general human competencies to the artefact.
- **Personification**. The use of natural language, dialogs, presentation as human (e.g. with a face or name) or other elements in the interface of the artefact which

imitates aspects of human interaction and communication, naturally contributes to expectations of human competencies in the artefact.

These properties are of course only significant in so far as they have effects on human beings. But the properties seem very hard to differentiate from the experiences they cause, i.e. from that which they are supposed to produce. All the properties have to be experienced as such to produce their effect. That is, an artefact is *seen as* opaque, unpredictable, competent or anthropomorphic. It is hard to say where the physical interface and output of the agent end and the experiences start. Although movement and changes in the interface have to be perceived too, they seem more "objective". But, firstly, they have to occur without direct (now and here) user input, to appear as initiated by the artefact. And secondly, the experience of a sequence of changes initiated by a system – whether it is deliberative or behaviour-based – can vary greatly from one user to another (or for a single user at different points in time). A computer deleting files in the trash can, making a backup file at regular intervals, or monitoring system resources can be experienced as "doing something for you". But familiarity with and/or knowledge of the functioning of these "actions" will tend to make them unnoticed. They are pushed to the background or the fringe of experience. They become operations that are not really experienced as "performed", but rather as stable, predictable or even "invisible" features of the system, i.e. they do not interfere with the "tool-ness" of the system – they do not involve conscious interpretation, fundamental change of attention or an experience of delegation or cooperation. Like incoming email, the changes are just there, because they always are – the tool is a dynamic tool, but not necessarily an agent.

On the other hand non-changes – stable or static features of the system – can appear as maintained by an agent with great effort, if you try to change them and fail. If you try to change the font in an electronic text and think that you are doing it the right way but do not succeed, then the situation can appear as though the machine actively maintains the current font. You *have* changed the font, but the machine counteracts you. You may not only consider what you could do differently, but also why the machine is not cooperating.

These considerations make it clear that several factors affect the user's experience of agency and autonomy, which are not ascribable to the artefact as material properties. They include factors in the use context, such as the users' current knowledge, goals, preferences and activities. These factors seem to be brought to the artefact by the users and their surroundings and they affect its properties. An example of such factors is lack of knowledge of the inner workings of an artefact. It will tend to reinforce the experience of opacity and vice versa.[7] The more knowledge you have of the individual active facilities in an application, the less "entity-like" the whole application will appear. Likewise, current work activities can make initiatives from the artefact invisible if they are irrelevant for the task, and changing requirements of precision due to changes of work

7 This also entails that the range of possibilities in an artefact for "opening" it or "seeing through" it, i.e. getting knowledge about it, can effect the subsequent experiences of autonomy and animacy. For example, the possibility in Microsoft Word 98 to access the rules used in AutoCorrect supports the possibility for this function to be experienced as an unperformed feature of the system, because it gives you the possibility to know why some objects in the interface are changed.

activity can affect the experience of an artefacts' "inherent" competence. A GPS system can be experienced as able to produce the exact position on the open sea, while it is experienced as having inappropriate abilities in a harbour. The GPS does the same thing, but the requirements of an exact position change.

Some of these factors present in an interaction evolve in relation to the specific artefact (e.g. familiarity), but others have their origin in situations totally disparate from the specific artefact (e.g. knowledge of similar artefacts).

Do these points made with respect to outer properties also hold for the properties of system architectures? In general I think a system or an agent can be experienced by a user as an autonomous agent or not, regardless of the architecture used for its construction. Several kinds of functionality (e.g. sorting incoming email or animating a character in a game) can be achieved through deliberate architectures as well as through architectures using behaviour-based techniques. And this can be done in a way that would make it impossible, or at least totally irrelevant, for a given user to try to distinguish the two implementations.[8] Of course a systematic comparison could reveal differences in style (e.g. one of two compared characters in a computer game could move more "confidently"), but such differences do not necessarily have any consequences on experiences of agency. In practice, experience is not a comparative exercise – it is an experience of *this* artefact.

Reactive architectures seem to demand that user interaction is targeted at *what* artefacts do and not at *how* they do it, and at what artefacts *might* do instead of at what they *have to* or *will* do – a demand that is due to the fuzzy, emergent and uncertain way that these architectures do what they do.

These architectures could be argued to involve two problems that entail experiences of agency by the users: reduced possibilities for providing feedback and control facilities. The composite and self-regulated character of automated technology can make it hard or impossible for a user to intervene in and monitor an ongoing process in relation to the actions and states of the tools as well as to the task as a whole. But agents applying reactive techniques seem to worsen these problems as well as the possibilities to deal with them.

Firstly, it is possible in an expert system to provide transparency through user feedback that displays the designer's intentions behind a given state or action, but it is not obvious how or if this can be done for reactive systems. In these systems the events evolving from the interaction between individual modules are not possible to specify in advance and are often based on continuous values, and consequently any explicit rationale behind the events they generate are equally hard to provide. This situation adds to the general uncertainty of interactions between artefact, users and environment.

Secondly, a reactive architecture in principle excludes the possibility of direct command. In relation to interface agents, Maes (1994c) suggests a partial solution to this problem (through instruction by example and adjustment of certain parameters), but basically both the user and the designer are reduced to either a trainer or

8 Which is not to say, that one implementation could not be "better" (e.g. more efficient or simpler) than another or that all kinds of functionality can be implemented in both ways.

a designer of a space of possibilities. Reactive agents can be stopped, but when they are allowed to act, they can only be guided – not commanded.[9]

But user interaction that consists in setting parameters for behaviours, instructing by example or guiding artefacts through manipulation of their environment, will not guarantee experiences of artefact agency or autonomy, and neither will the delegation of tasks to traditional, deliberate and automated artefacts. A system or an agent can be experienced as autonomous or not regardless of the architecture used for its construction. Certain input can from the system's or designer's point of view be seen as "handling a request" or "a perturbation", because the input might be treated in many ways depending on the situation. That is to say it is treated "autonomously". One user might agree in this view because she is uncertain of the agent's reaction. However, another might see it as "an invocation" because he is certain (based on explicit knowledge of the situation and the agent or just based on familiarity with them) that the agent will react in a particular way.

This finally leads to the question of the relation between experiences of autonomy and role distribution. The role of an artefact could be seen as its possibility of action in relation to a user. Formulated as different role types in regard to a given activity the following could be listed (some adapted from Endsley (1996)):

- **Object**: The artefact only does what it is explicitly told to do.
- **Informer**: The artefact describes situations and states.
- **Adviser**: The artefact pre- or proscribes actions.
- **Assistant**: The artefact acts, if the user accepts its proposals.
- **Partner**: The artefact acts independently, but the user can stop it.
- **Agent**: The artefact acts independently, but the user can affect it.
- **Autonomous agent**: The artefact acts without any interference from the user.

These roles can be seen as either:

- Embodied in the structure of the material artefact, as possibilities for artefact action and user intervention.
- The user's available and usable knowledge of the artefact's role and her possibilities of intervention.
- The user's actual experience of the artefact's role and her possibilities of intervention.

While these three levels can cohere in a unitary role relation, they certainly do not have to do so. Each level can affect the others through their own dynamics, but can imply different role relations. It can be possible to affect an agent performing an operation: the users can know that, but they do not experience it because they have no intention of interacting with it physically. Therefore it is instead experienced as an informer or even as an object.

The relation between system properties – be they outer, inner or role relations – and experiences of agency and autonomy is no trivial matter. In sum, the point in

9 Both of these problems seem to have parallels in the domain of process control.

this section is mainly negative: there are no links of necessity between system properties and experiences of action and autonomy.

Furthermore, the outer properties of an artefact seem inseparable from experience and use context. This relational interdependence is considered further in the next section.

5.5 Autonomy and Environment – Entities and Relations

If one compares the classification perspective with the construction and use perspectives, other differences appear which are interesting for the understanding of autonomy. In this section I will analyse and accentuate these differences. Moreover, I will argue that these differences imply that the actions of artefacts could be a function of interdependency between agents and their environment, and consequently that "autonomous action" is either a contradiction in terms, or at least that the seemingly contrastive relation between the concepts of autonomy and dependence must be modified.

In the classification perspective the agent is seen as an entity which possesses certain capabilities. These capabilities are seen as intrinsic qualities of the agent – it carries them, so to speak. Although the agent relates to and interacts with its environment, it is clearly separated from this environment by a border or interface, and it interacts with it on the basis of *its* competencies and *through* the border. This view of an agent as a capable entity with a degree of closure – a distinct inside and outside – is inherent in the concept of autonomy as outlined above. In this conception the border can be seen as a matter of control. This is clearly seen in Jennings *et al.* (1998), where the closure of agents is illustrated by an analogy with object-oriented programming. Agents encapsulate behaviour like objects in OOP encapsulate states, and must therefore be *requested* and not *invoked* to act. Such an approach to agents could be called entity-oriented.

Of course this entity-oriented view of agents is also present in the construction and use perspectives. But at the same time they involve elements of a radical different approach to the understanding of agents and autonomy – an approach that could be called relation-oriented. In the construction perspective this relation-oriented approach is present in the explanation of the origin of the agents' competencies. These competencies can only be said to reside in the artefact itself if a strict synchronic analysis is made. However, viewed diachronically these competencies are products of the interaction with the environment. Initially the artefact does not *have* abilities that are *used on* the environment. These abilities are *produced through* the environment.

This is clearly seen in the emphasis on embededness or situatedness among researchers in agent technology. The understanding of the situatedness varies. While Brooks (1994) stresses the physical grounding of input–output and rules out typed input–output, Maes (1994b) distinguishes only three environment types (physical, cyberspace and simulated environment) which can be combined in a given application. But the central importance of intense, direct, low-level interaction with the environment as a source of functionality is shared. Indeed, this is an important reason for not seeing traditional expert systems as agents – their connection with the environment is too indirect and controlled (Maes, 1994b) or disembodied (Jennings *et al.*, 1998). Agents exhibit more frequent interaction with the environment, and this interaction has a greater significance for the total performance of the system (in relation to the weight of the internal processes) and a broader scope of (low-level) modalities are involved. But in this way agents are also more dependent on environment than traditional AI architectures. In a way, autonomy or independence *from* the environment seems to be a consequence of a strong coupling *to* and thereby dependency of this environment.

Stronger senses of autonomy and autonomous agents, in which attributes like adaptability or ability of self-maintenance and self-repair are central, only underscore this state of affairs. In adaptive systems, input data are not only processed or contributory to the control systems responses. The history of relationships between input data and system responses also changes the way future input will be treated by the control system (i.e. it changes the qualitative performance of the system) and thereby makes these agents even more dependent on interactions with the environment.

If one is seeing this as a paradoxical and undesired state of affairs, it could be analysed as an argument based on a defective confusion of two kinds of environment: the human and the non-human. In this analysis, the agents are dependent on the non-human environment, but independent and autonomous from the human environment. The agents' binding to the non-human environment makes it possible for them to act autonomously in relation to humans. Humans that consequently also view or observe the agents as autonomous entities.

Of course this can be the situation. The argument can even be made in regard to different parts of the non-human environment; i.e. an agent can depend on some traits in its environment to generate independence from others.

However, it seems to me that some agents can be described reasonably as both dependent and independent of one kind of environmental feature. As an example, a robot can use sensor input of obstacles (dependence) and use them to avoid these same obstacles in a contingent way, i.e. independent of their specific properties. That is, a new encounter with the same obstacle could produce a new pattern of avoidance – the agent does not react to the environment in a fixed, predetermined way.[10]

Moreover, I do not see the mutual reinforcement of independence and dependence as a paradox. In biology, it is not a mystery that the longer and more intense the history of interaction is, the greater the gained independence can be. The paradox only emerges if agents and environments are viewed as distinct synchronic entities. The concept of "pure" autonomy could indeed be argued to be a product of this way of seeing.

Instead of locating autonomy in a separate human realm – a realm that in passing could be said to be still harder to distinguish from the non-human – I would rather put different environments on the same footing. That is, consider how and if recurrent processes of human-machine interaction can produce new "autonomous" capabilities.

---

10 Of course, such autonomy from the material environment at the same time can be viewed as autonomous behaviour by a human observer. But this would be another kind of autonomy, i.e. autonomy from the human.

The elements of a relation-oriented approach, which are present in the use perspective, are, however, even more important and radical. From this perspective, the attributes of an agent are not intrinsic to the agent, but are produced in the use situation. If an actual user does not consider or experience these attributes to be present, they are not present. The attributes are ascribed to the artefact – not inherent in it. This is not to say that such ascription is an act of arbitrary or voluntary choice from the user, but rather that the ascription is a necessary condition for the attributes to exist. Attributes are attributed.

This analysis seems reasonable if it is applied to the general description of agents in the use perspective. Terms like "assistant" and "helper" imply social roles, and they are hardly conceivable in isolation from a practical use situation. They presuppose that someone considers the artefact as helping or assisting, or at least that the artefact is incorporated in a social, goal-oriented project. But if the analysis is applied to the more specific attributes that agents are said to possess in the use perspective (e.g. ability to change objects in the interface) as well as in the classification perspective (i.e. being autonomous, responsive, proactive, social and situated) some doubt arises. Are such attributes not objective features of an artefact, i.e. present independently of an arbitrary user's subjective ascription?

Of course it is possible to describe artefacts in that way. But it presupposes that an observer first analyses the artefact's behaviour in a number of interactional situations, secondly that she is able to isolate "movement" as an invariant in these observations and thirdly generalizes the abstraction, i.e. "forgets" the interactional situations that actually produced the invariant behaviour, and instead ascribes the behaviour to the artefact alone. Such an observer can establish that somebody – the system or an agent – changes objects in an interface, and can subsequently ascribe this to the system or agent as a capability. But as argued in the previous section, a given user does not necessarily notice such changes in the interface, and if they are noticed they are not necessarily ascribed any meaning; and even if they are, it does not necessarily involve any sense of cooperation or agency.

The two descriptions or conceptions are different because their circumstances of production are different. The observer states that the artefact "objectively" generates movement, because it does so for all the instruments or participants in his observed interactions and maybe even because the participants or instruments do not have this experience in relation to a number of other artefacts, hypothesized not to be generating movement. However, our lonely, imagined user does not see the movement. To him, the artefact does not "objectively" generate movement. Obviously he did not participate in the observer's array of experiments. Had he been a participator, the observer would have been forced to acknowledge his experience as a variation with regard to the "moving" artefact and as an invariant in regard to all the artefacts. Hence the quality of "generating movement" would change from being an objective property of the artefact to a subjective ascription made by the majority of subjects. Of course, the observer could deny taking a single dissenter seriously, but if the numbers should continue to increase, he would be forced to give in. However, the point here is not about the numbers necessary to make the transition from objective property to subjective ascription possible. The points are, firstly, that the only difference between the two types of attribution is their prevalence,[11] and secondly that the concept of "objective properties" tends to hide this state of affairs.

The relational construction of an agent's abilities and agency is perhaps most obvious if successes are compared with breakdown situations. Despite all the emergent functionality, interactive systems employing autonomous agents often run into problems in the use context. In the domain of interactive fiction Blumberg and Galyean (1995) give examples of how an autonomous agent can ignore a user's attention or draw her attention away from environmental elements that are important for the story line. Another example is the Apple Data Detector's problems with differentiating structured information that has similar or identical syntax but different semantic content (Nardi *et al.*, 1998). Such examples not only pose the question of how to make these systems capable of doing the right things, they also question what the systems actually do. The two agents are respectively supposed to perform actions like "draw the user's attention to the magic wand" and "identify structured information in this document and propose relevant actions for using it". However, if the user focuses only on the character animated by the autonomous agent and the Data Detector proposes making a telephone call using an order number, none of the intended actions are performed. But something else *is* being performed. The Data Detector could be said to perform the intended action in a partial way, i.e. the action *is* performed but not in a successful way. In the case of the interactive fiction the change is more radical. Maybe the user gets another story than intended, or maybe she is just baffled.

In the latter case – total failure – designers can get two paradoxical experiences if they apply an entity-approach to the agent. The first is that the situations where the agent seems most autonomous are also the situations where its abilities seem most inappropriate. The agent is a juggernaut – out of control, following its own agenda and unable to perform the actions intended by the designers and probingly ascribed to it by the users. Secondly, the designers might experience that in other situations the same agents seem fully capable of directing attention and producing relevant proposals. Other users might understand the hints to the importance of the magic wand and they might not have order numbers with the syntax of telephone numbers present in their documents. What the agents are capable of doing changes without the slightest modification of their structure. However, if the relational approach is applied these paradoxes disappear. The realization of the actions intended by the designer does not depend on the abilities or attributes of the agent alone, but is a combined effect of user, use context and agent. The actions are only realized if the user actually changes her attention to the magic wand and evaluates the proposal to make a telephone call as relevant. If so, the artefact will appear both more competent and less autonomous.[12] It becomes a (more) transparent or tool-like agent. I think this is a common experience in interaction processes that involve

11 Note that these arguments do not exclude one from trying to reason about forces and conditions that could influence the prevalence of a certain ascription as well as the process of ascription itself.

12 This inverse proportional relation between experienced competence and autonomy further underlines the non-determined character of the relation between outer system properties and experiences of autonomy that was discussed earlier.

a transition from problematic uncertainty of an artefact's actions to a clarified interpretation of these actions.

These two types of explanation and understanding of agents as either entities or relations can be formulated as seemingly incompatible accounts of action. In the first explanation an agent can perform an action *because* it possesses the ability to do so. If the performance of the action is successful, it is due to the high quality of these abilities. In the other explanation the agent has the abilities *because* it performs the action. And it only performs the action *if* it is successful. If it is not successful – or only to a certain degree – the action disappears or changes, and with it the abilities of the agent. In the first account the agent is a stable entity, movable in time and space and with properties that are fixed across a wide variety of different situations. In the second the agent is a conditional product of use and use context – of a concrete situation at a specific moment in time and in a specific place.[13]

However, I think it is necessary to try to reconcile the two approaches into a "modified relational approach". As already noted, it seems inadequate either to explain a specific experience of an artefact on the basis of the use and use context only or on the basis of the in-built properties of an artefact only. Both have drawbacks. As a description of an artefact, the entity approach could be said to delete its history of construction and use, its observers and its situatedness, while the relation approach deletes the material and structural possibilities and constraints it embodies. While the contributions of both approaches seem necessary and interrelated, neither of their deletions seems reasonable.

In general and tentative terms the reconciliation of the two approaches could be formulated in the following way: a specific experience of an artefact must be seen as a conditional product of a number of processes which create the coherence that constitutes the experience. Experience is a process of stabilization – a stabilization that is permanently "threatened" by the dynamic character of the many processes it incorporates: short-term processes that include immediate material changes in artefacts and environment and changes in the activity of work, cooperation and interpretation; medium-term processes that include changes of knowledge (e.g. familiarity) and work practices; and long-term processes involving changes in language, institutions technology etc.

5.6 Design Consequences?

It could be argued that the radical relational approach implies that design is dead. This is to say that what actually goes on between humans and artefacts is determined here and now in the situated interaction. It can be analysed retrospectively, but it cannot be designed consciously in advance (i.e. from the past) or by actors outside the continuously performed practice. In this line of argument design equals evolution.

---

13 This opposition can be seen as a variation of a general conflict present in a number of theoretical discussions, for example the conflict between mentalistic and behaviouristic accounts of cognitive phenomena and between referential and operational approaches to linguistic meaning.

I think, however, that something can and unavoidably will be done to the future – deliberately or not, from a varying distance in time and space and with a varying level of integration in the actual situations.

In the entity approach, this design effort is realized by equipping artefacts with capabilities that can be used in the future by different users in different places. An alternative approach could be an attempt to make artefacts continuously changing entities, i.e. instead of trying to capture the general shape of the future from a specific point in time through a fixed design, one could aim at generality through a permanent adjustment of the artefacts to the particularity of processes going on here and now.

This is not a new idea – it can be seen as the central motivation behind the widespread efforts to make generic tools that are customizable to changing and specific personal, situational and organizational needs.

Flexibility in itself seems, however, to incorporate its own problems. Woods (1993) describes several of these. In general these problems can be seen as three sets of contradictions:

- **Possibilities** vs. **constraints**: A broad range of functions and customizing facilities enables the artefact to be used to do a lot of different things and to be useful in very different situations, while an artefact with only a few possible choices can be useless, insufficient or even hampering in certain situations. On the other hand, the broad range of possibilities can result in dangerous demands of activity directed towards instruments (e.g. the Turing tar pit) and heavy burdens on memory during high workloads (e.g. mode failures), which would make a more constrained system a better resource.
- **Transparency** vs. **opacity**: An open artefact, where vast numbers of states and information are displayed or at least are available, makes it possible to monitor and evaluate the current activities in all detail, while closed artefacts can result in confusion regarding the status of work and artefact. On the other hand this transparency can lead to the lack of a broad view of the situation and of relevant focus through information/data overload, which more closure could prevent.
- **Manual** vs. **automated**: Manually controlled artefacts make it possible to monitor and direct the processes in detail (e.g. direct manipulation) while automated processes can be impenetrable, crude and disturbing. On the other hand, manual control can be ineffective, slow and drag resources from the relevant activities, while automation can be effective, fast and helpful in preserving a broad view of the situation.

These sets are clearly interrelated. The first of them can be seen as a general formulation of a problem of flexibility, while the next two are specialization with the focus respectively on monitoring and on intervention. However, all three stress that (technical) flexibility in itself is no answer to the problem of accommodating the demands of changing situations. More flexibility is not equal to more control or coherence. Flexibility itself must be related to the current work demands and activity setting.

This demand is further emphasized and complicated if the social organization of work is also considered. Seen from this perspective other aspects of flexibility are highlighted. On the one hand, a single person often uses one artefact for many purposes simultaneously (e.g. performing a task and learning about the task). On the other hand, many persons use one instrument to perform many tasks simultaneously (e.g. using a radar screen to prevent collisions, to fix a position and as a mean to communicate) or cooperate to perform one task on the same instrument simultaneously. Or they use the same instrument differently at different points in time. Such combinations of instrument use and the shifts between them seem both to demand flexibility and to underline its potential risks and problems. Changing instruments is necessary to accommodate changes in work activity, but involves the risk of mode failures and of making cooperation and further shifts in work activity even more difficult.

Confronted with design tasks or breakdown situations, the entity approach and the (modified) relational approach each suggest two different foci of looking for solutions. The entity approach suggests equipping artefacts with properties like flexibility. The relational approach suggests strengthening the capability of human-machine systems to create coherence under dynamic conditions. This difference can be illustrated through the examples of breakdown situations used earlier. In the case of the agent in interactive fiction one could consider either how the agent should act to tell the story – or one could consider how to assess whether a story is told at all and what could be done if the answer is negative. Similarly, instead of considering how to make an algorithm capable of differentiating structured information with similar syntax but different semantics, one could consider which interactive mechanisms could be used to deal with the situation when the user identifies it.

If one accepts the dynamic and fluid character of artefacts in use, is it then possible to identify and design the properties of these situations such that they both allow for this dynamism and at the same time support the task of creating new coherent interpretations and work processes?

5.7 Conclusion

The purpose of the discussion above has not been to establish conclusions, but to outline some problems and contradictions with regard to the understanding of agents and their autonomy. The summary of this chapter is therefore similarly inconclusive. However, in an attempt to sharpen the arguments, the summary of the discussion is formulated as the following statements.

The autonomy of agents must be differentiated in regard to what it produces (functional, executive and adaptive autonomy) and in regard to whom or what it is independence from (designer, user or non-human environment).

User-experienced autonomy does not necessarily coincide with designer-experienced autonomy. Neither is there any necessary, fixed relationship between the technical architecture and properties of an artefact and the experience of it as an acting or autonomous entity. The outer properties of an artefact are intimately connected to the use context and the process of experience. Moreover, an experience of an artefact as acting does not entail that it is simultaneously experienced as autonomous.

The experience of an artefact as an agent is not necessarily accompanied by a loss of control. The experience of agency can have the form of facing uncontrollable entities as well as cooperative entities. With regard to the latter, the question of control becomes irrelevant. Cooperative entities can furthermore become "non-performing" background objects.

Autonomy can be understood as involving relations of both dependence and independence. Likewise, an understanding must be looked for that reconciles insights from both the entity and the relational approach to artefacts.

Specific experiences of an artefact must be understood as a combined effect of the history of the artefact's construction and use, including both social and material processes. Experiences of artefacts are constituted by the coherence established between these histories and processes.

For design processes this conclusion defocuses the problem of equipping artefacts with specific task-oriented capabilities or flexibility *per se*, and emphasizes the problem of which "capabilities" make the production of shifting coherent experiences of capabilities possible in the first place. Can artefacts be designed to be – in a primitive sense – reflexive? That is, can we incorporate in their structure an awareness of the fact that what they do is a matter of what they are made to do – both now and then?

References

Blumberg, B. and Galyean, T. (1995) Multi-level control for animated autonomous agents: do the right thing... oh, not that.... *Workshop Notes of the AAAI '95 symposium on Interactive Story Systems.*

Brooks, R. A. (1994) Elephants don't play chess. In *Designing Autonomous Agents: Theory and Practice from Biology to Engineering and Back* (ed. P. Maes). Cambridge, MA: MIT Press.

Cowie, A. P. (ed.) (1989) *Oxford Advanced Learner's Dictionary.* Oxford: Oxford University Press.

Endsley, M. R. (1996) Automation and situation awareness. In *Automation and Human Performance: Theory and Applications* (eds. R. Parasuraman and M. Mouloua). Mahwah, NJ: Lawrence Erlbaum Associates.

Jennings, N. R. and Wooldridge, M. (1995) Intelligent agents: theory and practice. *Knowledge Engineering Review* 10(2).

Jennings, N. R. and Wooldridge, M. (1998) Applications of intelligent agents. In *Agent Technology: Foundations, Applications and Markets* (eds. N. R. Jennings and M. Wooldridge). New York: Springer-Verlag.

Jennings, N. R., Sycara, K. and Wooldridge, M. (1998) A roadmap of agent research and development. In *Autonomous Agents and Multi-Agent Systems 1.* Boston, MA: Kluwer Academic.

Lieberman, H. (1997) Autonomous interface agents. In *Proceedings of the ACM Conference on Computers and Human Interface, CHI 97,* Atlanta, GA.

Maes, P. (1994a) Designing autonomous agents. In *Designing Autonomous Agents: Theory and Practice from Biology to Engineering and Back* (ed. P. Maes). Cambridge, MA: MIT Press.

Maes, P. (1994b) Modeling adaptive autonomous agents. In *Artificial Life Journal 1* (1 & 2) (ed. C. Langton). Cambridge, MA: MIT Press.

Maes, P. (1994c) Agents that reduce work and information overload. *Communications of the ACM* 37(7): 30–40.

Nardi, B. A., Miller, J. R. and Wright, D. J. (1998) Collaborative, programmable intelligent agents. *Communications of the ACM* 41(3): 96–104.

Norvig, P. and Russell, S. J. (1995) *Artificial Intelligence: A Modern Approach.* Englewood Cliffs, NJ:Prentice Hall.

Pirjanian, P. (1998) Multiple objective action selection & behavior fusion using voting. *PhD dissertation,* Aalborg University.

Suchman, L. A. (1987) *Plans and Situated Actions.* Cambridge: Cambridge University Press.

Woods, D. D. (1993) Price of flexibility in intelligent interfaces. *Knowledge-Based Systems* 4(6)

6

Enhancing the Usefulness of Community Chat Rooms: Application of Autonomous Agents

Mikael B. Skov

6.1 Introduction

Autonomous agents or software agents are widely recognized for their potential abilities to solve many of the problems associated with the Internet of retrieving and filtering information (Lieberman, 1997; Thomas and Fischer, 1996). Software agents have already been applied in various settings for identifying, filtering and retrieving relevant information for Internet users (Bradshaw, 1997; Lieberman, 1997; Theilmann and Rothermel, 1998; Thomas and Fischer, 1996). Some even argue that the introduction of autonomous agents may lead to a completely different kind of interaction with computers where you view the system as a personal assistant rather than a tool (Negroponte, 1997; Norman, 1997; Erickson, 1997). Application of software agents holds many promising advantages and opportunities; however, the development and application of software agents is still in its early years and is not yet an established field leaving plenty of room for further research and development.

Software agents on the Internet are primarily used for information filtering and retrieval. The Internet offers millions of users the opportunity to exchange electronic mail, photographs and sound clips; to search databases for books, CDs, cars and term papers; to participate in real-time audio- and videoconferencing; and to shop for products both virtual and physical (Stolterman *et al.*, 1997). The huge conglomerate of links, hyperlinks and virtual links is not just a technology for linking computers, it is also a medium for communication. The convergence of computer and communication technologies creates a social convergence as well. People meet in chat rooms and discussion groups to converse on everything from auto mechanics to postmodern art. In this way the Internet supports communication between people and the chat rooms and the communities serve as meeting places for all kinds of people. However, the introduction of virtual communities and chat rooms raises a number of potential problems for the Internet users. Hattori *et al.* (1999) specify these problems by stating three issues in the support of Internet communities. First, how can people be linked with other users and communities that share the same interest? Second, how can common contexts be visualized for users and how can users identify flows of conversations or discussions? Finally, how can users identify the objectives and roles of other users and communities? Addressing and solving some or all of these issues could enhance the usefulness of Internet communities.

This chapter presents a conceptual framework for a multiagent-supported community chat room. The agent framework addresses the three issues raised above by supporting users in identifying, retrieving and filtering for them relevant and interesting information by monitoring the activity of one or more chat rooms. Users are able to communicate with an agent and delegate specific operations or tasks to the agent, e.g. monitor when certain users enter a room. Also, the solution supports an agent's ability to observe the actions of the user and recommend chat rooms or specific conversations in chat rooms based on its understanding of the user. The agent operates and makes decisions on a user profile which is updated dynamically and which indicates the interests of the user. The agent is also able to communicate with other agents in order to make the most useful recommendations to its user. The framework includes an overall architecture of the involved agents and sketches for the interaction between the agents and the users.

6.2 Background

Software agents or autonomous agents are being used and applied in more and more environmental settings. Janca (1995) hailed in 1995 software agents as the next major computing paradigm and that by the year 2000 software agents would be pervasive in every market. In addition, Jennings and Wooldridge (1998) mention that autonomous agents are found in nearly every type of today's computer-based applications, including industrial applications, commercial applications, medical applications and within entertainment. At the start of the new millennium, software agents help people to find and retrieve useful information from large and anti-transparent data sources, software agents help and guide people to operate complex machines and technologies, and people interact and cooperate with autonomous agents in computer-based games, cf. Jennings and Wooldridge (1998). On the Internet software agents are also being applied mainly to support identification, retrieval and filtering of information, but are also used for entertainment and edutainment. In this section we will look at the characteristics of Internet-based virtual worlds and on the characteristics of software agents.

6.2.1 Virtual Communities and the Internet

Virtual worlds or virtual communities can be considered worlds, places, rooms or communities in which people meet and communicate with other people often sharing the same interests. Rheingold (1993) defines virtual communities as "social aggregations that emerge from the [Internet] when enough people carry on those public discussions long enough, with sufficient human feeling, to form webs of personal relationships in cyberspace". He continues to talk about virtual communities as "a group of people who may or may not meet one another face to face, and who exchange words and ideas through the mediation of computer bulletin boards and networks". Hence a virtual community is often associated with the Internet and serves to bring people together in a non-physical environment. Valtersson (1996) makes an explicit distinction between virtual communities developed in existing organizations and virtual communities formed by people sharing the same interest. The latter form of virtual community is often built upon active attitudes to the community and on voluntarily members in contrast to the community developed in organizations. In this chapter we will not use the distinction but merely focus on virtual communities as a whole.

The increasing number of virtual communities can be explained by the diffusion of the Internet. Today the Internet offers its users a variety of options, as described in Section 6.1. The Internet has become a technology which supports many of the needs and activities of people, one of them being communication. People meet through virtual communities on the Internet and discuss and communicate through chat rooms and discussion groups, for example. Stolterman *et al.* (1997) state that a virtual community or Internet community is first of all a social entity in which a number of people relate to one another through the use of a specific technology. In this case the technology is the Internet. In contrast to traditional society, in which communities are often evoked by closeness or organizational belonging, virtual or Internet communities are not a part of the physical world. The discussion of virtual communities often leads to philosophical distinctions and is difficult to define. In this chapter we will rely on a definition from Stolterman *et al.* (1997) stating that virtual communities are social communities made possible by the existence of the Internet. Chat rooms are one of the means for people to communicate and meet in Internet communities. Strout (1996) states that chat rooms are becoming more serious. Corporations have begun to provide chat rooms on their Web sites, giving the conversations a new spin and often attracting a different type of audience. Most contemporary chat rooms are simply text-based where people communicate through words and sentences. No additional features of communicating are offered, mainly due to problems with performance. However, more recent communities and chat rooms offer their users the chance to navigate and interact in small 3D-worlds with their own avatar. Also, more chat rooms incorporate semi-intelligent robots or agents, making it possible to chat not only with other human beings, e.g. visit Alice The Chat Robot (`http://www.alicebot.org/`).

6.2.2 The Internet, Virtual Communities and Software Agents

Most software agents on the Internet are built to find, filter and retrieve information for users based on user profiles. A number of different Internet agent solutions have been proposed. Thomas and Fischer (1996) introduce a framework called Basar that integrates agents into the use of the World Wide Web. Basar gives users the opportunity to create and use agents for locating, relocating and filtering information based on usage profiles. Lieberman (1997) presents an autonomous interface agent called Letizia that helps user in browsing the Internet. Letizia observes the actions of the user and makes dynamic and real-time recommendations for Web pages based on a profile of the user.

In Chapter 5 Mogensen discusses the agent definition problem. The literature on software agents has no specific and unified definition of the term, and Jennings and Wooldridge (1998) state that it is difficult to define and specify an agent, since some of the key concepts in agent-based computing lack universally accepted definitions. One of the more accepted definitions on the term was illustrated in Mogensen. Here a software agent should be autonomous, responsive, proactive and social:

- **Autonomous**: agents should be able to act without the direct intervention of humans (or other agents), and should have control over its own actions and internal states.
- **Responsive**: agents should perceive their environment and respond in a timely fashion to changes that occur in it.
- **Proactive**: agents should not simply act in response to their environment, but should be able to exhibit opportunistic goal-directed behaviour and take the initiative where appropriate.
- **Social**: agents should be able to interact, when they deem appropriate, with other artificial agents and humans in order to complete their own problem solving and to help others with their activities.

Some agents may, of course, have additional characteristics, and for certain types of application some attributes will be more important than others. Another view of the term "agent" is that an agent is a social construct of people implying that some might view a software component as an agent while others might view the same software component as a tool (Thomas and Fischer, 1996). Lieberman (1997) continues that an agent is a software program that can be considered by the user as an assistant or helper rather than a tool. In this paper we primarily hold the latter view of an agent, but the proposed agent solution of this paper will be discussed against the four characteristics. Nwana and Ndumu (1998) identify seven types of agents: collaborative agents, interface agents, mobile agents, information/Internet agents, reactive agents, hybrid agents and smart agents. In this paper we focus only on Internet agents (also called information agents). An Internet agent is a specialized agent performing the role of managing, manipulating or collecting information from many distributed. Internet agents are typically embedded within an Internet browser and use a host of Internet management tools such as spiders and search engines. In the remainder of this chapter we will use the term "agent" to describe Internet agents.

Most software agent solutions build upon the active use of profiles (Green *et al.*, 1998). A profile in an agent-based application is typically used to reflect basic interests and activities of users. The agent uses the information contained in the profile to operate in order to achieve its goals and intentions. The goals and intentions of a user agent are typically defined as identifying and retrieving interesting information for the user. Green *et al.* (1998) present an agent mediated collaborative web page filtering system. The system integrates a personal agent that updates the strength of each element with a user profile based upon feedback given on the items. Another agent system, Letizia, compiles a profile of the user's interests by recording the URLs chosen by the user and then reads the pages. A simple keyword frequency is used to analyse the pages (Lieberman, 1997). Finally, Basar integrates user profiles to model the preferences, interests, and tasks of a user. This is done both explicitly by asking the user and implicitly by observing the user (cf. Thomas and Fischer, 1996).

The literature comprises only a few articles on software agents in virtual community or in chat rooms. Hattori *et al.* (1999) outline a multi-agent system called CommunityOrganizer for supporting network communities. CommunityOrganizer is an agent solution able to visualize potential communities around the user. Further, they have identified three major issues in the support of Internet communities, namely bringing people together, supporting smooth communication, and finding relationships between people.

1. *Bringing people together.* This includes how can people be linked with others and with communities that share the same interests.
2. *Supporting smooth communication.* This includes support for visualizing and sharing common contexts, as well as identifying the flow of conversations or discussions.
3. *Finding relationships between people.* This includes how to identify the objectives and roles of communities and individuals.

6.3 Conceptual Framework for ChatAgent

The three issues of virtual community problems raised by Hattori *et al.* (1999) have been used in the design and development of the multi-agent solution ChatAgent. The overall goal of ChatAgent is to enhance the usefulness of Internet community chat rooms, and the three issues have been used as guidelines for the actual design and implementation process.

The design and development of ChatAgent has been done in close collaboration between the author of this paper and a Danish software house specializing in developing Internet applications and search engines. The design of ChatAgent is an attempt to test the applicability of autonomous agents on the Internet. ChatAgent monitors the conversations and actions of users of chat rooms and observes or communicates with users of the Web site, and based on this makes recommendations to the user. The overall purpose of ChatAgent is to support users in bringing them together and identifying flows of discussions in Internet community chat rooms.

We have chosen to illustrate ChatAgent by addressing three topics: the architecture, interaction and interface issues, and use of profiles. First, we will sketch the overall architecture of ChatAgent. Multi-agent systems are often complex by nature due to the multitude of connections between agents and the internal structure and behaviour of each agent (Jennings *et al.*, 1998). It is not a trivial task to delegate operations and behaviour between more agents in a system and even more difficult to handle at run time. Our architecture tries to illustrate connections and communication between agents and users and outlines the roles and behaviour of each agent in the community. Second, interaction and interface design issues are presented. Interaction with software agents may require new interaction patterns different from the ones known today. This is partly a result of viewing the system as a personal assistant rather than a tool (Negroponte, 1997; Norman, 1997; Erickson, 1997). Lieberman (1997) suggests that users should at any time be able to ignore any recommendation from the agent in order to avoid overloading the interaction. Finally, the application and use of user profiles will be described. As discussed in the previous section, most software agents behave and act upon active use of user profiles. This is also the case for the ChatAgent, where user profiles are used to indicate the basic subject interests of users.

6.3.1 Overall Architecture

We have proposed an overall architecture for the agent-based community chat room monitoring system ChatAgent (as illustrated in Figure 6.1). The architecture has been used during the design process to organize and design the internal and external characteristics of each agent. In addition, the architecture has been a valuable tool for visualizing the communications between user and agents at run time. In this chapter the architecture will serve as a tool for explaining the complex structure and behaviour of the entire system.

A web portal consists of one or more communities, as illustrated in Figure 6.1 by communities A and B. In each community a number of users operates and interacts using the different means made available by the portal. All users in the community have their own personal agent. A community could here be defined as a social community made possible by the existence of the Internet. Users may or may not be

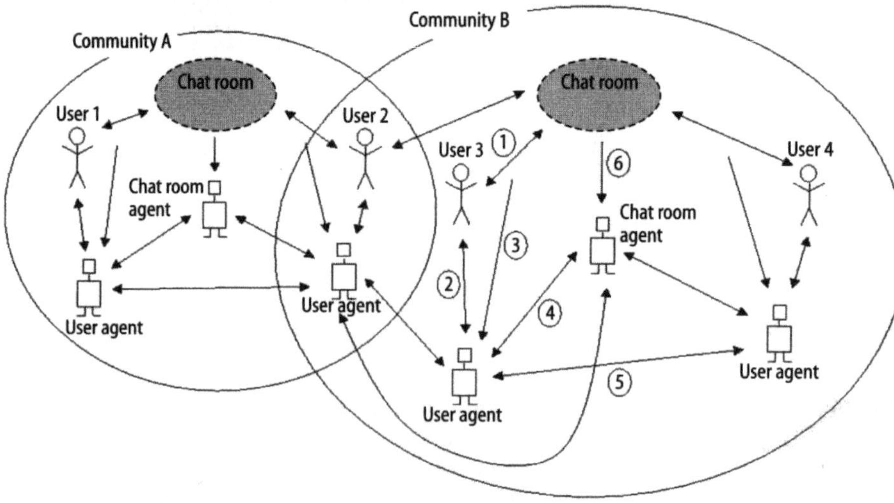

Figure 6.1 The overall architecture of ChatAgent.

aware of their "affiliation" with the community, and in this sense the community is mainly a tool for organizing the agents in the system. In addition, a chat room agent is dedicated to monitoring and controlling the activities in the chat room in each community. In the figure two communities have been illustrated. Community A consists of two users (User 1 and User 2), each associated with their own personal agent. Also, a chat room agent monitors the activities of the chat room. The user agents of the two users in the community communicate with each other and the chat room agent to retrieve information on activities in the community and the chat room. User 2 is also a part of community B. User 2's agent is able to communicate with other user agents in this community and the chat room agent. In both communities, users are able to visit the chat room for interaction with other users of the community or just for observing the conversations taking place in the chat room. As illustrated in the figure, Community B contains two other users (User 3 and User 4). Table 6.1 describes the semantics of the labelled arrows in the figure.

Table 6.1 and Figure 6.1 consist of six different kinds of arrows with different kinds of semantics. As indicated in the table, we differentiate between the kind of

Table 6.1

#	Participants	Type	Description
1	User	Observation Interaction	The user observes or communicates with other community members in the chat room. The user may only observe conversations in the chat room or observe which users enter and leave the room, or the user can communicate actively with other community members by addressing them individually or by addressing them all.
2	User, User agent	Interaction	The user can communicate with her personal agent through the user interface. The agent can continuously and dynamically present recommendations to the user and the user may inform/program the agent by evaluating recommendations.
3	User agent	Observation	The agent observes the actions of the user and thereby gains an understanding of the interests and preferences of the user. For example, the agent could observe when the user enters and leaves the chat room, which other community members the user is chatting with and categorize conversations. Also, the agent is able to observe the user's interaction with the portal as a whole.
4	User agent, Chat room agent	Communication	The user agent and the chat room agent can communicate. This communication may be initiated by either parties; e.g. the user agent asks which users are currently in the chat room.
5	User agent	Communication	The user agent may also contact other user agents to gain a richer understanding of the other user, or to initiate communication between the two users.
6	Chat room agent	Observation	The chat room agent monitors the activities in the chat room. This includes monitoring users entering and leaving the room and the discussions taking place in the chat room.

communication between agents and users and between agents and agents. The communication between users and agents is defined as interaction while communication is used for agent to agent. In addition, both users and agents observe the conversations and activities of the chat rooms.

6.3.2 Interface Design Issues and Interaction Issues

One of the first recognized requirements for the interface and the interaction of this agent solution were the necessity of using standard browser technologies. The system was meant to run for real users in real environments, so the agent solution was not designed to use advanced plug-ins or other additional software components. Problems with download time were also considered. The result is that the agent application is based upon traditional Web browser technology (Figure 6.2). The agent application runs only on the server of the community, where the community could be any kind of Web site, e.g. a corporate Web site for customers or employees.

The portal serves one or more communities by providing them with, for example, news, blackboards, chat rooms, various documents, links, email, index-based search engines or Web directories. The front page of the portal can provide the user with information on all these aspects. The overall idea is that users should be able to customize their own front page at the portal, which thus presents only the kinds of information they need, desire or want. In this way, the portal should always serve as a starting point for users when they log on to the Internet. As illustrated in the left part of Figure 6.2, the front page could include information on email, news, personal information and recommendations from the agent. Each user is defined by a set of profiles which, for example, determines the kinds of news on the front

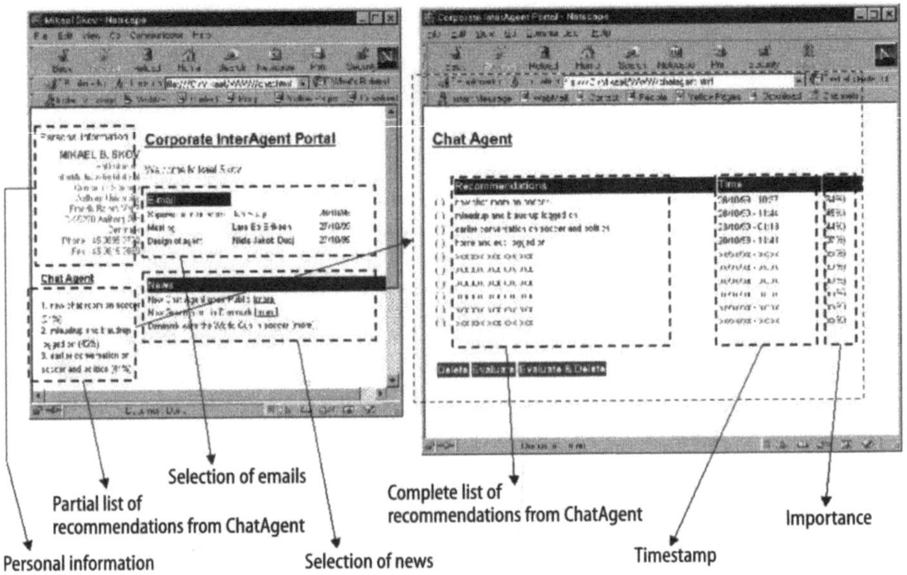

Figure 6.2 The interface of the two Web pages for the ChatAgent.

page. The user is able to see a partial selection of the recommendations from the agent. The recommendations shown are the ones the agent has assessed as having the highest importance. The interaction has been designed in such a way that users are able to ignore any recommendation made by the agent. When a user chooses to ignore a recommendation, this recommendation will eventually be removed by the agent from the list, but the ignore "action" will still be evaluated by the agent (further discussed in the subsection on user profiles). The right-hand side of the figure shows a Web page for interacting with the agent. Here the user is able to see the complete list of recommendations, their timestamps and their importance. In addition, the user is able to evaluate or delete the recommendations and thereby inform the agent about the relevance of each recommendation.

6.3.3 Usage of Profiles

As illustrated in Section 6.2, almost any agent solution is built upon extensive use of user profiles. ChatAgent is no exception. The profiles in ChatAgent are primarily used to define and describe the actions and interests of the user. A profile consists of a number of fields of any subject, e.g. football, tennis or cars. Each field in the profile is associated a value between 0 and 1, where 0 indicates no interest in the subject and 1 indicates full interest in the subject. At run time for any user, most fields would normally be zero or just above zero. The values in the profile are updated by the actions of the user on the portal. Every document linked by the portal has an additional profile that affects the user profile when the user follows a link to a document. As an example, if a user goes to a page or document that contains football news, then the user profile will be affected in the fields of football and news.

The user agent is able to observe the user by accessing the user profile at any time, thereby making the agent able to identify the basic interests of the user and making the agent able to identify significant changes in the profile. The user agent is not able to delete or update any fields in the user profile, but instead the agent holds a local mirror profile of the user in order to identify changes between the local profile and the user profile.

The chat room agent holds two profiles of the chat room. Both of these profiles have the same structure and content as the user profiles. The first profile is a long-term profile defining the basic interests of users who enter the chat room. Over a long period of time this profile will be stable and not subject to major changes. The other profile is a short-term profile defining the profiles of the users active in the chat room right now. This profile is more often changed and is not so stable, and may at certain times be very different from the long-term profile. Both profiles are updated when users enter or leave the chat room.

The user agent can at any time request a chat room agent for the short-term or long-term profiles and then perform a match between the profiles of the chat room and the profile of the user. This matchmaking is performed by an algorithm where the most significant subjects in both profiles are matched. This algorithm will not be presented further in this chapter, mainly due to its complexity.

6.4 Discussion

Having illustrated key aspects of ChatAgent we would like to discuss the solution. This discussion will involve two issues, namely can the solution be considered an agent solution and how can agent design principles be evaluated against the solution?

First, is ChatAgent really an agent system? Defining the concept of an agent has raised many discussions between researchers within the agent community. The multitude of views about agents can partly be explained by the large number of different kinds of researchers within the field (Bradshaw, 1997). Some argue for a strict definition of the term "agent" while others recommend more pragmatic definitions (Lieberman, 1997; Bradshaw, 1997). The lack of a unified definition often leads to the fact that certain software systems are referred to as agents while others totally disagree (Jennings and Wooldridge, 1998). We will try to discuss the ChatAgent against the four criteria autonomous, responsive, proactive, and social (Nwana and Ndumu, 1998). The ChatAgent is considered a multi-agent system consisting of more agents of the same type and also more than one type of agent. Both the user agent and the chat room agent can be considered autonomous. The user agent is able to act without the direct intervention of humans. The user agent makes recommendations for current or past conversations in the chat room and alerts the user when certain other users enter the chat room etc. The user has only indirect control of the user agent, the user influences the user agent by the actions in the community and the actions in the chat room and by evaluating recommendations from the agent. The user is not able to alter internal states of the agent directly. The chat room agent is also autonomous. It interacts only with other agents and has no direct interaction with humans. At all times it monitors the chat room and defines the activities and conversations of the chat room. Second, the ChatAgent can also be considered responsive. When certain activities or conversations take place in the chat room the user has to be notified within a relatively short period of time, e.g. when certain users enter the room. However, since no aspects of the system or the environment can be considered critical, the responsiveness aspect has not received the same attention as the other three aspects. Third, the ChatAgent can most definitely be considered proactive. It suggests or recommends various aspects of activities related to the chat room. These recommendation are not initiated by input from the user, but are continuously suggested by the user agent based on the agent's understanding of the user. Fourth, the last criterion is that the agent should be social. The ChatAgent interacts with both a user and other agents in order to make the best recommendations. The agent can communicate with the chat room agent to receive information about activities in the chat room, but it is also able to contact other user agents for information. Based on the four criteria for agents, we consider the ChatAgent an agent.

Second, how can ChatAgent be evaluated against other design principles? Lieberman (1997) identifies six design principles for autonomous interface agents. We will discuss two of these. First, *autonomous interface agents should suggest rather than act on behalf of the user.* Also, autonomous interface agents work best in environments where their decisions are not critical. The ChatAgent only makes suggestions to the user and the type of suggestions and the environment must be considered non-critical. The user can at any time ignore the recommendations from the agent and is still able to communicate with the chat room/other users and the rest of the Web site regardless the interaction with the agent. No interaction with the agent or negative response to the recommendations of the agent will, however, influence the behaviour and acting of the agent since its perception of the user changes on positive and negative responses and on no response. This is also supported by Ljungberg and Sørensen (1999), who have coined the term "interaction overload". We have explicitly tried to avoid this problem in the design of ChatAgent. The control of the interaction is always with the user; the agent is not allowed to take control and force the user to interact with the agent. Second, designers should *take advantage of the information the user gives the agent for free.* The actions taken by the user in the user interface constitute valuable information that the agent can use to infer the goals and interests of the user (Lieberman, 1997). The ChatAgent also monitors the actions taken by the user. First, the actions related to the use of chat rooms are monitored directly and registered for later use. Second, more profiles are generated when the user interacts with the Web site, and these profiles are actively used by the user agent to infer the basic interests of the user.

6.5 Conclusion

Software agents have proven useful and powerful in many computer-based settings. Many researchers and practitioners hold high expectations for future agent-based systems. The application of software agents seems to be very promising with respect to enhancing the usefulness of the Internet by identifying, filtering and retrieving information on behalf of users. A number of proposals for agent-based applications for the Internet have already been designed and evaluated, but the full utilization of software agents on the Internet has not been explored. We have tried to contribute to the research and development within agent-based systems on the Internet by our design of ChatAgent. This agent solution tries to enhance the usefulness of virtual communities and chat rooms by monitoring conversations in chat rooms and making recommendations to users.

Three potential problems or issues for virtual communities have been identified (as raised in the introduction). Our agent solution was partly designed and built to address and solve these problems. Table 6.2 illustrates these issues and problems, and what we tried to do in order to solve the problems.

As indicated in the table, the first issue of bringing people together is solved by having users in the same community and by recommending them to visit chat rooms where they will find other users sharing the same interests. This is done by matching the profiles of users. Second, most users are away from the Internet for shorter or longer periods, making it difficult or impossible to identify past and current conversations. ChatAgent addresses this by having your personal agent monitor the activities and conversations even when you are away. Third, agents in ChatAgent can contact other agents and communicate with them in order to find other users and communities which match the profile of the user.

Table 6.2

Issue	Problem	Solution
Bringing people together	How can people be linked with others and with communities that share the same interests?	The existence of chat rooms concerning specific topics. ChatAgent able to identify chat rooms with similar profiles to the user.
Supporting smooth communication	How to give support for visualizing and sharing common contexts, as well as identifying the flow of conversations or discussions.	The agent is able to follow and save conversations in chat rooms when the user is not logged on.
Finding relationships between people	How to identify the objectives and roles of communities and individuals.	The user agent is able to match profiles of the user with profiles of other users in the community.

There is still plenty of further research to be done in this area. One straightforward further development would to improve the abilities and skills of the user agents and chat room agents. Here you could focus on letting the agent have a more precise image of the user based not only on subject interests. An interesting and quite difficult extension to ChatAgent would be that users could borrow agents from other users, for example when entering a new community. This agent could then guide the user in this community, making it easier to orientate and navigate.

Acknowledgements

The research behind this article has been financed by the Danish Research Council's joint Multimedia Programme No. 9600869. I would like to thank the people at mindpass.com, Denmark, for a fruitful collaboration, and in particular I would like to thank Niels Jakob Buch and Michael Poulsen.

References

Bradshaw, J. M. (1997) Introduction. In *Software Agents* (ed. J. M. Bradshaw). Menlo Park, CA: AAAI Press, pp. 3–46.

Erickson, T. (1997) Designing agents as if people mattered. In *Software Agents* (ed. J. M. Bradshaw). Menlo Park, CA: AAAI Press, pp. 79–96.

Green, S., Cunningham, P. and Somers, F. (1998) Agent mediated collaborative web page filtering. In *Proceedings of Second International Workshop on Cooperative Information Agents*, Lecture Notes in Artificial Intelligence. Berlin: Springer-Verlag, pp. 195–205.

Hattori, F., Ohguro, T., Yokoo, M., Matsubara, S. and Yoshida, S. (1999) Socialware: multiagent systems for supporting network communities. *Communications of the ACM*, 42(3): 55–61.

Janca, P. C. (1995) *Pragmatic Application of Information Agents*. BIS Strategic Report.

Jennings, N. R. and Wooldridge, M. J. (1998) Applications of intelligent agents. In *Agent Technology – Foundations, Applications, and Markets* (eds. N. R. Jennings and M. J. Wooldridge). Berlin: Springer-Verlag, pp. 3–28.

Jennings, N. R., Sycara, K. and Wooldrdige, M. J. (1998) A Roadmap of agent research and development. In *Autonomous Agents and Multi-Agent Systems*. Boston, MA: Kluwer Academic Publishers, pp. 7–38.

Lieberman, H. (1997). Autonomous interface agents. In *Proceedings of the Conference on Computer-Human Interaction '97*, March, Atlanta, GA.

Ljungberg, F. and Sørensen, C. (1999) Interaction overload – managing context and modality. Submitted for publication.

Negroponte, N. (1997) Agents: from direct manipulation to delegation. In *Software Agents* (J. M. Bradshaw). Menlo Park, CA: AAAI Press, pp. 57–66.

Norman, D. A. (1997) How might people interact with agents. In In *Software Agents* (J. M. Bradshaw). Menlo Park, CA: AAAI Press, pp. 49–55.

Nwana, H. S. and Ndumu, D. T. (1998) A brief introduction to software agent technology. In *Agent Technology – Foundations, Applications, and Markets* (eds. N. R. Jennings and M. J. Wooldridge). Berlin: Springer-Verlag, pp. 29–47.

Rheingold, H. (1993) *Virtual Communities.* London: Secker & Warburg.

Stolterman, E., Ågren, A. and Croon, P. O. (1997) *Virtual Communities – Why and How Are They Studied?* Working paper.

Strout, A. (1996) Finally, cyberchat starts to get serious. In *Fortune International,* November, pp. 122–123.

Theilmann, W. and Rothermel, K. (1998) Domain Experts for Information Retrieval in the World Wide Web. *In Proceedings of 2nd International Workshop on Cooperative Information Agents,* Paris, 4–7 July, pp. 216–227.

Thomas, C. G. and Fischer, G. (1996) Using agents to improve the usability and usefulness of the World-Wide Web. In *Proceedings of the 5th International Conference on User Modeling,* Kailua-Kona, pp. 1–12.

Valtersson, M. (1996) *Virtual Communities.* Masters Thesis, Umeå University, Sweden.

7
Agents as Actors

Peter Bøgh Andersen and Jørgen Callesen

7.1 Introduction

The purpose of this chapter is to present empirically founded ideas as to the structure and design of agents that can enact interesting narratives. The chapter starts with some basic assumptions about behaviours.[1] Section 7.3 summarizes descriptions of behaviours that can count as a part of the everyday course of events. Such behaviours, however, are often boring, and they are only the raw material out of which narratives are built. Telling stories involves other techniques concerning the presentation of the behaviours to the spectator, which includes structuring the behaviours, directing how they are enacted and deciding what the agents look like. These techniques are described in Section 7.4. Finally, Section 7.5 assembles the ideas in a loose sketch for an agent design.

In contrast to most research on autonomous agents that is informed by biology and ethology, this chapter mainly draws on literature, film, animation, theatre and language theory, which is a natural choice if the agent is to perform interesting actions, i.e. not only being an agent but also an actor.

7.2 What Are Behaviours?

The main point in this section is that behaviours are social units: they are classified and segmented parts of a continuous flow of actions, and the classification is based on some sign system.

---

1 Since other chapters in this section involve robotics, we shall use the concepts from this field. In robotics, an *action* is a concrete continuous change of the robot's actuators, whereas a *behaviour* is something that causes one or more actions to occur. The reader should be aware that most of the authors quoted in this chapter would use *action* instead of *behaviour*, and vice versa. We shall sometimes say that behaviours are *enacted* via actions.

The discrete behaviours can be said to be enacted by continuous actions: they are realized as continuous trajectories. When we move, our limbs do not abruptly jump from one position to another, but must smoothly run through all intermediate positions, and when we talk, the tongue and lips must move smoothly too. However, often these trajectories neither contain objective boundaries, nor are there objective features that clearly distinguish one trajectory from another.

Consider, for example, a case where a piece of paper moves from the hand to the floor. We can say that *he lost the paper* or that *he dropped it*. We describe the same physical action but assign it to two rather different classes of behaviour. In the former case, the event was involuntarily, and he cannot be blamed. In the latter case, it was on purpose, and we can say that the loss was his fault.

Therefore, behaviours are enacted as continuous trajectories that are *articulated*[2] via some sign system, for example a natural language, and thereby made discrete. *Communicative behaviours*[3] are specialized to accomplish this process. We have to take this into account in agents if they are to tell other agents, including the audience, about their own and other agents' actions, and if they are to enact requests from other actors and promises issued by themselves. Such events are necessary in any interesting story, and the faculty to handle the continuous/discrete dichotomy must therefore be basic in agent design.

The position is thus the nominalistic one, that behaviours are different if we describe them as different, so our position lies within the *use perspective* on agents as defined in Chapter 5. An agent is autonomous if an observer interprets it as such. However, as in books and movies, the experience is produced when observers interact with the artefact, and the structure of the artefact therefore is important too. There is a difference between the experiences afforded by Donald Duck and Shakespeare, and it therefore makes sense to make qualified guesses as to which architecture can produce which experiences, which lands us in the *construction perspective* in Section 7.5.

The occurrence of communicative events simultaneously induces discrete boundaries into themselves and in the actions they communicate about.

On the one hand, the movements of tongue and lips are segmented and classified by our phonemic system so that one position of the tongue is heard as an /i/, and another one as /e/. This distinction has been known for a hundred years as the distinction between "emic" and "etic" descriptions, e.g. phonemics versus phonetics.

On the other hand, non-communicative behaviours are subject to the same dichotomy in so far as they are controlled by communicative behaviours. Although our limbs move continuously, conscious and planned movement is controlled by

2 We use the word "articulation" in the semiotic sense, where it simply means converting continuous phenomena into discrete ones. The manner in which this happens is left unspecified, and does not imply a conscious effort.

3 The term "communicative behaviour" is normally called "communicative acts" or "speech acts" in linguistics.

verbal descriptions that segment and classify our actions. For example, a part of a certain continuous movement may be classified by the sentence "He is driving towards the parking lot while avoiding the heavy traffic". This is a classification, since it rules out other descriptions, such as "He is driving home". It is also a segmentation, since the behaviour ends when the car has stopped. What happens thereafter cannot be called "He is driving towards the parking lot" but "He is heading for the supermarket".

All behaviour can to some degree be controlled or analysed by discrete representations. People can request other people to do something (including saying something), they can discuss plans and execute them afterwards, and plans can be criticized ("This is not the way to the parking lot").

However, the exact relation between discrete and continuous aspects is not clear. Early AI believed that behaviour should be fully specified by formal representations, but the idea did not have very much success and seems counter-intuitive. We do not seem to verbalize all aspects of our actions.

A more realistic idea is to view plans as constraints or resources that influence already running continuous action. There is an already ongoing bodily activity, and what plans do is to *perturb* this activity in various ways.

This approach is taken in many computer games, especially in real-time strategy games, where activity proceeds in a certain direction until the player makes a change in the world which invokes new behaviours. This can happen through direct orders to characters or by modification of the environment, e.g. by building a new house.

Apart from constraining already occurring continuous processes, discrete representations can to some degree live a life of their own, i.e. discrete representations can influence other discrete representations. This is what happens when we plan and reason logically. It may not be an innate faculty, but it can certainly be learned.

The main point, however, is that the concept of behaviours does not make sense without some sign system that can segment the continuous stream of actions. This is the guiding principle in the following sections.

7.3 How Are Behaviours Structured?

From this assumption it follows that all behaviour has discrete and continuous aspects.

The *discrete* aspect of verbal behaviour has been the main focus of linguistics in this century in two ways: one the one hand, the structure of the verbal behaviour itself (the structure of the signifier) was articulated into units such as *distinctive feature*, *phoneme*, *phrase* and *sentence*; on the other hand, the structure of the behaviour referred to was captured in terms such as *seme*, *sememe*, *semantic component* and *semantic field*. Most modern descriptive systems in grammar are of algebraic nature and focus on the discrete aspect of language (Van Valin and LaPolla, 1997).

The *continuous* aspect – how to produce coherent and relevant sequences of sounds in real time – was for a long time banned from linguistics proper, and relegated to language psychology under the headings of discourse and sentence plans, articulatory programs, etc. (Clark and Clark, 1977, pp. 223 ff.).

Now, not all behaviours are normally used to signify something, but (almost) all behaviour can be signified, i.e. we can talk about almost all behaviour (although it does not follow that we ordinarily do that or that any behaviour can be discussed with anybody. Only cyclists can discuss the art of bicycling). In its role as something we talk about, i.e. in its role as *signified*, all behaviours exhibit the discrete/continuous dichotomy.

In the following we shall give an overview of research in the structure of behaviours. Section 7.3.7 summarizes the findings. We use the Bouncy agent described in Chapter 9 of this volume to exemplify the concepts where possible.

7.3.1 Componential Analysis and AI

The discrete aspect is treated by componential semantics and lexicography (see e.g. Goddard, 1998). By analysing co-occurrence restrictions and conducting tests on native language users, it is possible to analyse the meanings of words and sentences into smaller units of meaning. Some schools assume that there is a finite collection of building blocks out of which the meanings of all languages in the world can be constructed (Goddard, 1998). For example, the meaning of *to* and *from* can be analysed as (Goddard, 1998, p. 202):

(1) X moved from A to B =
X moved for some time
Before this X was somewhere (place-A)
After this X was somewhere else (place-B).

Here *move*, *time*, *some*, *before*, *after* and *place* are assumed to be primitive. Early AI planners were built on this type of discrete componential analysis. For example, the STRIPS formalism (Fikes and Nilsson, 1971) contains three types of list: *Condition-lists*, *Add-lists* and *Delete-lists*. Given a goal, the planner selects a behaviour with the goal in its Add-list and checks whether the conditions of the behaviour are fulfilled. If they are not, the planner recursively looks for behaviours that have the unfulfilled preconditions in their add-list. The *to-from* prepositions look like this in the STRIPS formalism:

(2) Actor moves from Source to Goal =
Preconditions: Actor is at Source
Add-list: Actor is at Goal
Delete-list: Actor is at Source

Goal, Actor, and Source are variables that are instantiated when the behaviour is invoked. AI mainly consists in rearranging componential analyses so that they are useful for stringing behaviours together in a means–end hierarchy.

Bouncy does not use planning facilities, but there are a few examples of componential structure. For example, the behaviour *Go To Target* is composed of two sub-behaviours, *Avoid Obstacles* and *Approach Target*. Instead of being driven by a planning algorithm (resembling a context-free grammar), Bouncy is driven by the simpler finite state machine whose transitions are regulated by Bouncy's perceptions and moods. Some of the states are themselves finite state machines; for example, the "Interact" state is composed by three substates, "tease", "please" and "have the blues".

7.3.2 Image schemata

However, in recent years, the continuous aspects of signified behaviour has come into focus in the so-called cognitive grammar (Talmy, 1988; Johnson, 1992). The main idea is that there are dynamic phenomena that cannot be accounted for in the discrete framework, and to capture these phenomena, the notion *of image schemata* was introduced.

An image schema is (Johnson, 1992, p. 2)

> a dynamic pattern that functions somewhat like the abstract structure of an image, and thereby connects up a vast range of different experiences that manifest this same recurring structure.

An example of an image schema is the COMPULSION schema (Figure 7.1) where something applies a force to an object that sometimes cannot resist and begins to move along a trajectory, but in other cases can counteract the force so that the trajectory remains only potential.

> An actual compulsion schema exists as a *continuous, analogue* pattern of, or in, a particular experience or cognition that I have of compulsion. It is present in my perception of a jet airplane being forced down the runway, in my understanding of forces acting on continental plates, or (metaphorically) in my sense of being forced by peer pressure to join the PTA. (Johnson, 1992, p. 2)

Examples of sentences based on the compulsion schema are:

- I *pushed* the dog away (physical process)
- Her beauty made a deep *impression* on me (perception)
- His argument *forced* me to change my opinion (conversations)
- You *must* do it (social)
- It *must* be true (epistemic)

As appears, the schemata structure a vast set of different domains, and they not only control perception, but also behaviour (Johnson, 1992, p. 21).

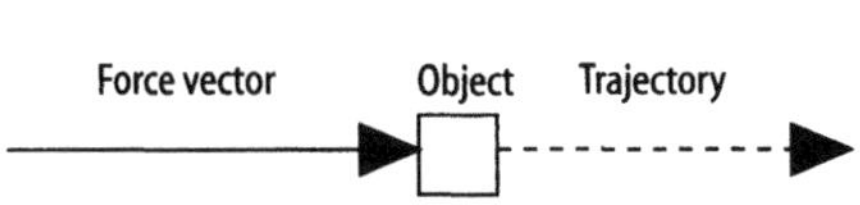

Figure 7.1 The COMPULSION schema.

In spite of the name "image schemata", they are not really rich images (Johnson, 1992, p. 24). In fact, they are a-modal, not being tied to any single perceptual modality (Johnson, 1992, p. 24). Also, they are not static objects but dynamic (Johnson, 1992, p. 29). The *from–to* meanings in (1) above correspond to the path-schema (Johnson, 1992, p. 113).

The COMPULSION schema can be formalized in various ways. A very simple one is to define a potential function with an attractor in the endpoint of the path, cf. Eqn. (7.1) and Figure 7.2.

(3) $y = \dfrac{h}{x^2 + 1}$

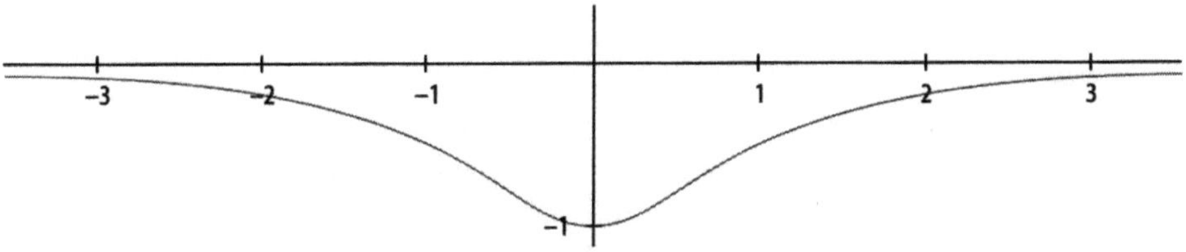

Figure 7.2 Attractor. Equation (7.1) with $h = -1$.

x measures the distance from Actor to Goal. The actor is assumed to be moved along the gradient

$$\frac{dy}{dx} = \frac{-hx}{(x^2 + 1)^2}.$$

Figure 7.3 shows three superimposed potentials that reflect the forces working on the bird.

The bird is attracted towards the mouse and repelled from the two cats. The heights of the potentials are represented by lightness: high parts (repellers) are light, low parts (attractors) are dark. Figure 7.4 shows the same situation, but now from the point of view of the male cat.

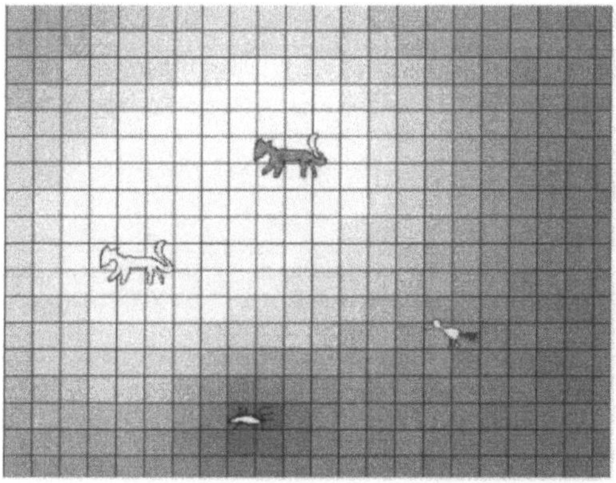

Figure 7.3 Cats and mouse seen from a bird's perspective. The cats repel, the mouse attracts.

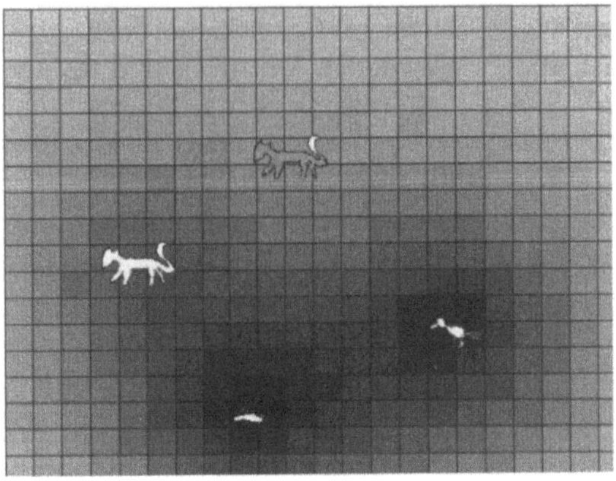

Figure 7.4 Female cat, mouse and bird from the male cat's perspective. Darker = smaller values. The cat is attracted to all three animals.

Maes (1989) describes an interesting hybrid between continuous and discrete behaviour representations, namely activation networks based on the STRIPS formalism. The network selects one behaviour among the executable behaviours that have the highest activation value. Activation values originate in the goals and in the world. For example, as shown in Figure 7.5, unsatisfied goals (A is a Y) inject activations into behaviours that contain the goal in their add-list, and true propositions (A is at X) inject activations into the behaviours of which they are preconditions. Activations can also spread inside the network. For example, unfulfilled preconditions of a behaviour (the route between X and Y is passable) spread activations to behaviours whose add-lists contain the precondition (A removes obstacle between X and Y).

Maes's activation networks are interesting because they combine the discrete with the continuous. In particular, the activation value can be used as a representation of

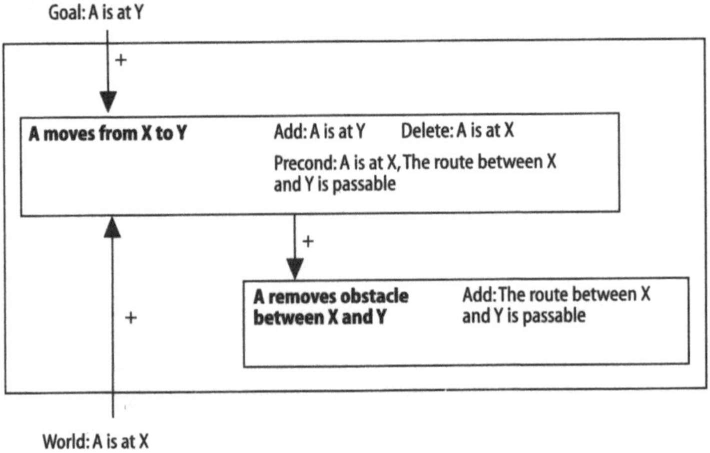

Figure 7.5 STRIPS as activation network.

Table 7.1 Four types of force dynamic patterns.

	Agonist inherently resting	Agonist inherently moving
Antagonist weaker	1. The ship kept its balance despite the waves. (ship = agonist, waves = antagonist)	2. The ship kept sailing despite the strong currents. (ship = agonist, currents = antagonist)
Antagonist stronger	3. The wind made the ship drift. (ship = agonist, wind = antagonist)	4. The storm prevented the ship from reaching harbor. (ship = agonist, storm = antagonist)

modality, low values signifying impossibility, higher ones possibility or necessity. We will elaborate on this in Sections 7.4.1 and 7.4.4.

7.3.3 Talmy's Force Dynamics.

The American linguist Leonard Talmy has elaborated a schema he calls a "force dynamic" which resemble Johnson's "compulsion schema". According to Talmy (1988), the smallest complex structure of forces seems to involve two actors and two forces. The actors are called the *agonist* and the *antagonist.* The agonist is the main character and is described as having some immanent drive towards action or rest. The antagonist tries to oppose the agonist, either by making an immobile agonist move, or by preventing a mobile agonist from moving. The force of the antagonist can be stronger or weaker than that of the agonist. This gives us the four main types in Table 7.1.

Representing meaning as gradient fields, as in Section 7.3.2, or as forces, as suggested by Talmy, has the advantage that meaning components can be fused in a straightforward way, e.g. by simple addition as in Figures 7.3 and 7.4. This is necessary, since our actual actions are more often than not the result of several concurrently working schemata. For example, in robotics, the goal-seeking behaviour and the collision avoiding behaviour must be active at the same time, and any interesting narrative must contain conflicts where the protagonist is moved by opposing forces, cf. again Figure 7.3, where the bird is simultaneously attracted by the mouse and repelled by the cat. In addition, use of potential fields of this kind is a standard method in robot motion planning (Latombe, 1991, pp. 295 ff.), so we know it can be used to control behaviour to some degree. There is also evidence that field-like forces have a neurophysiological basis (Maclennan, 1997). For concrete applications to multimedia systems, see Bøgh Andersen (1992, 1995a, 1998b).

In Section 7.3.6 we shall see that the notion of action fusion is not only relevant with physical actions, but also with symbolic ones.

7.3.4 Vendler's Verb Classes

Vendler (1957, 1967) classifies verb meanings according to their dynamic structure. According to him, there are four major types of proceses, namely *Activities* (play

Table 7.2 Vendler's four verb types.

	Static	Telic	Punctual
Activity	–	–	–
Accomplishment	–	+	–
Achievement	–	+	+
State	+	–	–

football), *Accomplishments* (drive to the parking lot), *Achievements* (win a race) and *States* (sleep, be a plumber). See also Van Valin and LaPolla (1997) for a more detailed linguistic treatment.

The processes differ in the terms of three oppositions: static/dynamic, telic/non-telic, and punctual/non-punctual, as shown in Table 7.2.

In *activities* an action is repeated an indefinite number of times. In *accomplishments* there is also action, but it stops when a certain limit has been reached (see Figure 7.6). *Achievements* denote a momentary state change, and *state* terms denote the continuation of a state of affairs. Vendler proves the existence of these types by showing that grammatical features, such as the *ing*-form, adverbials of time and duration, and, in Scandinavian languages, the auxiliary of the past participle, depend upon them. The process type is not exclusively associated with the verb, but with the sentence as a whole: *I ate apples* is an activity, whereas *I ate the apples* is an accomplishment (Figure 7.6). Like Johnson and Talmy, Vendler proves that there in fact exist definable dynamic building blocks of processes that can be assembled to control larger narratives.

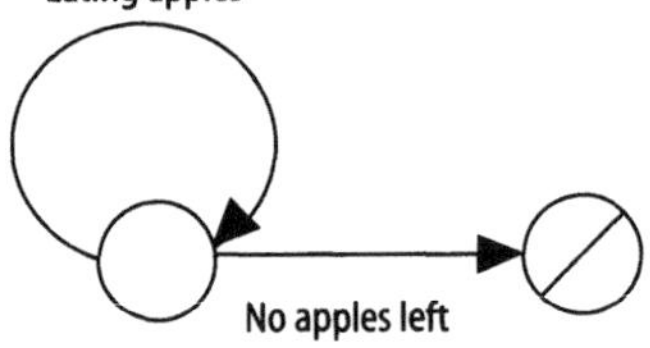

Figure 7.6 I ate the apples.

The STRIPS formalism from Section 7.3.1 only covers the two telic variants, the accomplishments and the achievements; it is hard to figure out what the delete- and add-lists for activities (play football) or states (sleep) should be. This is a problem, since activities are important in plans too: to avoid obstacles is more like an activity since it is something one always thinks about and it should be able to work together with accomplishments such as *go to goal.* The process type of *maintenance* described in the next section handles this problem.

Apart from mastering the goal-seeking behaviour, *Go To Target*, Bouncy's repertoire mostly consists of activities and states. For example, "sleep" is a state where Bouncy does not do anything, whereas "play" is more like a non-telic activity where Bouncy keeps running and jumping around.

Table 7.3 Logical analysis of four control behaviours (from Lind, 1994, p. 269).

Condition of behaviour	Explanation	Behaviour	Explanation	Result of behaviour	Explanation
pT¬p	p exists but vanishes unless maintained	d(pTp)	p is maintained	pTp	p remains
¬pT¬p	p does not exist and does not happen unless produced	d(¬pT p)	p is produced	¬pTp	p happens
pTp	p exists and remains unless destroyed	d(pT¬p)	p is destroyed	pT¬p	p vanishes
¬pTp	p does not exist but happens unless suppressed	d(¬pT¬p)	p is suppressed	¬pT¬p	p remains absent

7.3.5 Lind's Control Behaviours

Humans are not only able to classify concrete processes, but also to handle processes of processes, such as beginning, maintaining, preventing and stopping processes.

Lind (1994, draft) suggests using Von Wright's behaviour analysis for defining four basic control behaviours (T = *change*, d = *doing*, *acting*) (Table 7.3).

These types are important general control behaviours, and are also necessary in agent specification. For example, the difference between production/destruction on the one hand and maintenance/suppression on the other, can be found in Maes (1989, p. 7):

> Notice that we distinguish two types of goals: once-only goals have to be achieved only once, permanent goals have to be achieved continuously.

Compared with Vendler's classifications, Lind's *produce* and *destroy* are accomplishments, whereas his *suppress* and *maintain* are activities without any internal endpoint. Thus, avoiding obstacles while seeking a goal can be analysed as producing one state while maintaining another.

Inspired by Talmy, we can reformulate these analyses in terms of opposing forces. The advantage of entering time into the analysis is that we can bring the description closer to observation. For example, maintaining and suppressing a state p is not a one-event phenomenon as Von Wright invites us to believe. On the contrary, p and ¬p are unstable, so that in practice we will have repeated events where the controller tries to maintain p, but p keeps trying to vanish.

Table 7.4 shows the resulting nine control behaviours. A = controller, B = controlled.

Referring back to Vendler's analysis we can say that accomplishments and achievements produce a state of affairs that would otherwise not have occurred, or they destroy a state of affairs that would otherwise have persisted. Activities and states maintain, repsectively, a dynamic or static state of affairs that will cease to exist had the actor not intervened, or they prevent a state of affairs from arising.

Table 7.4 Dynamic analysis of nine control behaviours.

A	B	Resulting process	Verbs
↑	↑		1. Help (produce state)
↓	↑	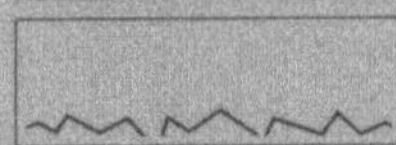	2. Suppress, prevent, forbid, avoid state
•	↑		3. Let, allow state to appear
↑	↓		4. Maintain, keep state
↓	↓		5. Help (remove state)
•	↓		6. Let, allow state to disappear
↑	•	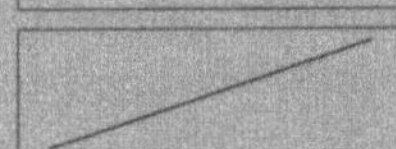	7. Produce, create state
↓	•		8. Destroy, remove state
•	•		9. Let, allow state to remain

The two new control behaviours, *help* and *let*, are indispensable in narratives. *Help* is obvious, and *let* is used in plots where the protagonist omits a behaviour and lets the situation work for him: for example, the hero may let the villain continue talking, knowing well that he is exposing himself. See Ryan (1991, p. 130) for further elaboration and examples.

Lind's control actions are useful for describing the interaction between the user and Bouncy. In some of its states, time changes the mood, but the user can influence this autonomous change. For example, when Bouncy is playing, time decreases its excitedness value, whereas the voice of the user increases it. Thus, the user can *maintain* Bouncy's level of excitation, or *let* him become bored. On the other hand, when Bouncy is sleeping, time does not make any difference, and the only way of changing Bouncy's state is for the user to *call* him. This is a case of *producing* behaviour. The Japanese *Tamagotchi* agent derives its fascination from such control actions (Figure 7.7).

7.3.6 Halliday's Process Types

Whereas the former three analyses uses the dynamic nature of the processes as their point of departure, Halliday (1994) distinguishes process types by means of

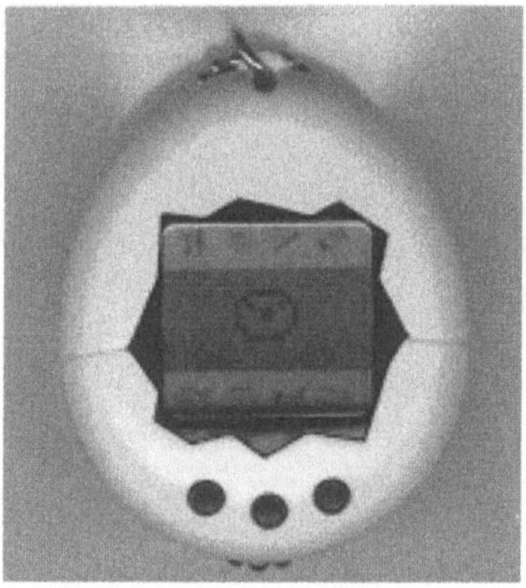

Figure 7.7 A Tamagotchi.

the semantic roles involved in the sentences describing the processes. He sets up six main types:

- *Doings*: Actor + Goal. Material processes that imply a change of state. Moving, manipulating objects etc.
- *Sensing*: Senser + Phenomenon. Mental processes like Perception (seeing or hearing something), Cognition (remember, know, believe, realize, notice, forget, or understand something), and Affection (fearing, liking or enjoying something; be puzzled or pleased by something).
- *Being*: processes of *attribution* (Carrier + Attribute: be sad, courageous, fearful) or *identification* (Identified + Identifier: be the leader of the team or the clever one).
- *Behaving*: Behaver. Psychological and physiological behaviour (watch, stare, talk, grumble, chatter, cry, laugh, frown, sigh).
- *Sayings*: Sayer + (Receiver) + (Target) + Verbiage/Quote. All symbolic exchanges of meaning (tell, ask, say, repeat, describe, praise, flatter, request, command).
- *Existing*: Existent + (Circumstance). Something that exists or happen (exist, remain, arise, occur, happen, follow, ensue, sit, stand, hang, prevail).

Halliday is the only one dealing with *sayings*. Sayings are different from other processes in two ways:

They do not rely on cause and effect, but rather on the receiver's understanding of the speaker's intention and the receiver's good-will (Posner, 1993). There is no verbal way of forcing someone to do what is requested.

Also, when verbs of communication enter into planning, it is not their own delete-list and add-list that are active, but the lists of their "Verbiage". For example, if I request somebody to give me the paper then it is the delete- and add-lists of *give* (Add(give) = I have the paper) that are effective in my plan, not those of *request*. Compare the behaviours in Table 7.5. A proper componential analysis of verbal behaviours can be found in Austin (1976) and Searle's (1994) work.

Table 7.5 Non-symbolic and symbolic behaviours.

	Preconditions	Add	Delete
Take X	I have not X I am at X	I have X	
Give X to Y	I have X I am at Y	Y has X	I have X
Ask A to B	A can hear me A can understand me	The Add-list of B	The Delete-list of B
Ask A to take X	A has not X A is at X	A has X	
Ask A to give X to Y	A has X A is at Y	Y has X	A has X

The six process types belong the to *ideational functions*, one of the three main functions postulated by Halliday. According to Halliday, an utterance is the result of three types of constraints: *textual*, *interpersonal* and *ideational* constraints. A single sentence must comply with all three of them simultaneously:

1. *Textual functions.* The utterance must cohere with the preceding utterances, and organize its contents in given and new information.
2. *Interpersonal functions.* The utterance must organize the relation between the speakers and their mutual turn-taking.
3. *Ideational functions.* The utterance must structure the situation referred to according to various principles: roles, foreground/background, superordinate/subordinate etc.

Referring back to Section 7.3.3, we can say that these three constraints must be fused into one single utterance. Some constructions can be seen as solutions of conflicts between these constraints. For example, in English there is a rule that requires heavy clauses to go behind the main sentence, and a another one saying that all sentences should have a subject. These rules can conflict, since number one removes the subject number two wants: *That she came was common knowledge* → *was common knowledge that she came.* The contradiction is solved by the pronoun *it*, which can fill the empty slot left by a sentence: *it was common knowledge that she came.* Thus behaviour fusion also occurs in verbal behaviour.

Apart from the degrees of freedom furnished by the choice of words and their order, language offers additional means for conveying connotative meanings, parallel to the denotational meanings of the utterance: pitch, stress, tone and rate. These suprasegmental properties can be manipulated in some speech synthesis systems, and are of fundamental interest especially when combined with animation engines supporting coherent facial mimics and body movements as the external traits of the agent. An example of a wave-generated skeletal animation technique for lip-syncing is shown in Figure 7.11.

Finally, one may note that Halliday offers rather detailed descriptions of how to get from his process types "down" to actual sentences. This is useful if we want the agent to verbalize its own and other's behaviours.

Bouncy is mostly in Doings, Beings and, very rudimentarily, Sensings. However, he can react to a very limited vocabulary: two states of the dataglove and two degrees of loudness from the microphone. He interprets combinations of these events in three ways: the user is calling, scolding or fondling him. Bouncy cannot use discrete symbols himself, although he can produce continuous indexes of his psychological state. For example, his excitedness controls his tail-wagging and the shape of his mouth. His psychological state can be defined as regions in a phase-space with three dimensions, <excitedness, sleepiness, mood>. If Bouncy were to describe his feelings, he would have to use critical limits in this space.

7.3.7 Summary

In the previous sections we have looked at five ways of analysing behaviour, most of which were based on linguistic evidence, and we have tried to characterize a simple autonomous agent by means of the concepts. Bouncy can be characterized as an agent whose behaviour consists primarily of *activities* and *states*, but rudimentarily employs a componential analysis. The user interaction mainly consists of *producing* and *maintaining* these behaviours, secondarily of *letting* developments run their natural course. Bouncy can *Do* physical actions, and use continuous *indexes* as symptoms of his psychological *Being*.

Since the classification schemes allow for other choices, we can also list abilities that Bouncy does not have, but possibly should have. Adding discrete representations of behaviours of type accomplishments (Section 7.3.1) would enable Bouncy to produce purposeful behaviour and describe it to the user. Adding Talmy's force dynamic could introduce an elementary plot, with Bouncy trying to accomplish some goal, being frustrated by circumstances or other dogs, but eventually succeeding. Expanding the repertoire of control actions to include suppression and destruction of a state allows the user to play the role of an adversary.

However, these enhancements are not the crucial ones for entertaining agents that can produce interesting behaviours. We discuss this question in the next section.

Figure 7.8 "The Neverhood": poses that create expectations.

7.4 How Are Interesting Behaviours Structured?

Behaviours and the characters performing them must possess special properties in order to be worthwhile looking at. Most normal behaviours are not designed to be used as signs and are therefore often boring, but theatrical and filmic behaviours have to work that way. One important feature of the characters and their behaviours is that they must keep creating expectations in the spectator.

In the game "The Neverhood" (DreamWorks Interactive, 1998, Figure 7.8) the possible behaviours are split up into a series of walks and movements, including operation of buttons and handles, which all together make up series of small gags and puzzles.

Expectations are created by the mechanics of button pushing. What will happen when the button is pushed or the handle is pulled? Expectations are also created by the poses of the character. We can't wait to see what it "looks like" when the button is pushed, because he has such a funny way of holding his hand. Furthermore, the poses are leading us to look for or think of other possible behaviours, since one hand is almost always pointing in another direction. This is a job done by a skilled animator, where each pose is "loaded" with possibilities – in fact what every theatre or film actor is trained for. Actors often show contradictory expressions which together build up a complex character – for example when the facial expression of a rich woman shows disgust for the working class hero, but her body language shows uncontrollable physical attraction. If the actor is only able to show one intended action at a time the character becomes one-dimensional.

To make the act interesting for the audience, the actor has to indicate the intended behaviour rather than show his full behaviour, as Dario Fo puts it in his famous practical book on acting techniques (Fo, 1987).

According to Bordwell (1985), the film viewer continually creates such expectations about what will happen or has happened. These expectations have the form of schemata (a murder is possible) that generates hypotheses about what one should look for next (vulnerability of the victim); the hypotheses guide the interpretation of what is actually perceived (a knife is interpreted as a weapon, not as a kitchen utensil); and cues in the material fill out slots in already existing schemata (Mr Schmidt turns out to be the murderer) or generate new ones (not a crime, after all, but a joke).

If expectations are not created, there will be no suspense or curiosity (in the broad sense) which again means that there will be no engagement. Expectations are created by a conscious use of modality: *the impossible, the possible, the actual* and *success* and *failure.* If we review the various methods for analysing behaviours above, we notice that glaring absence of any theatrical techniques. Therefore, if we use these methods in isolation we will end up with logical and causally related sequences of behaviours and outcomes that are boring because we never get the clues we need to form expectations.

This is not to say that the analyses are useless. On the contrary, if we had no possibilities of specifying behaviour sequences cohering in time and causality, we would lack the raw material out of which narrative experiences are built. If we have no way of specifying the normal, logical and expected world, we also lack the ability to create surprises, which are deviations from the normal.

In this section we shall look at semi-formalizable accounts of narrative structure and character development.

7.4.1 Bremond's Forking Paths

An early attempt to give a semi-formal account of narrative structure is found in Claude Bremond's work (Bremond, 1966, 1970).

Bremond analysed French folktales and found the basic building block shown in Figure 7.9.

The basic blocks can be assembled into larger structures, such as the *sequence*, the *enclave* and the *join.* Bremond's analysis seems limited to accomplishments and achievements. In order to use Bremond's ideas for agent design, it is necessary to specify what happens after success and failure. In the case of failure, is the behaviour tried again later (the rejected lover renews his courting), or is it given up? In the case of success, is the behaviour tried again once more (the successful gambler plays another game), or is one success sufficient? Furthermore, under which

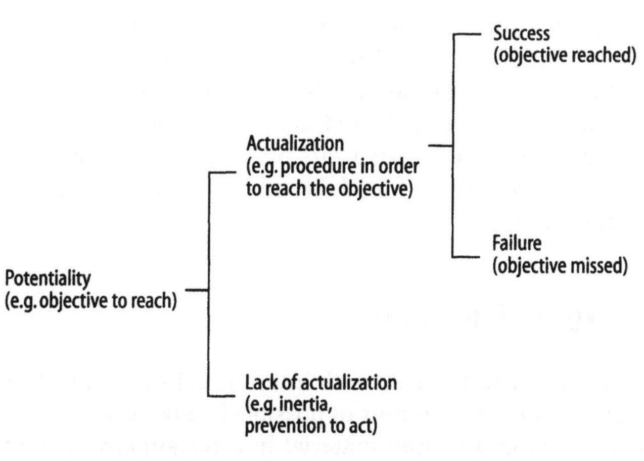

Figure 7.9 Basic narrative building block in French folktales.

Figure 7.10 "Final Fantasy VII"; Cloud Strife is raising his hand and swinging the sword after a victory over two giant dogs.

conditions are behaviours given up: after the lapse of some time-interval? After encountering a certain amount of obstacles?

Thus any behaviour should be specified with respect to its modality: is it potential? Is it actual? Does it succeed or fail? – and we need to indicate what happens in these cases. What this means is that we should not only program our autonomous agent to reach a goal and avoid obstacles; the agent should also know how to behave when it is just thinking of reaching the goal, and how to display to the audience that it has given it up again (lack of actualization). In games this is often shown as linear animated "cut-scenes" where the character makes a triumphant act, such as raising a sword after killing a monster (Figure 7.10). Another typical way of showing success or failure is by using sound effects, playing a melody, or yelling – simple ways of showing the ecstasy of victory compared with the use of body language and facial expressions in film and theatre.

To see the importance of modality, suppose the agent plays the part of a serial killer and enters the scene where the hero is placed. If the killer did not know anything about potentiality and lack of actualization, he would enter the scene, stand immobile for some time and exit. This makes poor entertainment. However, if he knew how to express his intention to add the hero to his list of victims, tension would be created, and if he knew how to signify that he gave up the intention for the time being, a relief is produced.

The remaining parts of this section elaborate on the basic problem of turning agents into actors worth looking at. However, before we continue our discussion of narrative structure, we shall discuss the basic problem of externalizing the inner states of the agent. Until recently, there has been a tendency in academia to overlook the outer expression and concentrate on designing the inner states. But the most sophisticated exploitation of modality and intention comes to nothing if the audience cannot perceive it.

7.4.2 Turning Agents into Actors

It is not enough to furnish the agent with interesting inner traits. We have to take the step from generating descriptions of possible behaviours in possible worlds to expressing behaviours in a chosen material in a certain environment. Decisions about the agent's looks, the way it moves and how it expresses its intentions will have to be made. Finally the agent has to be modelled in a style suited for live animation by a 3D engine,

This is necessarily a practical process, where the modeller will deal with aesthetic, stylistic and artistic questions as well as studies of anatomy and the physics of movement. The former approach is mainly taken by the games development industry, while the latter is taken in scientific projects, e.g. where the aim is to make precise computer-generated models of facial expressions (Parke and Waters, 1996) or body movements (Hodgins and Wooten, 1999).

The process of making systematic formal descriptions of the signifiers in animation is, although necessary, often a controversial question in both scientific and artistic communities, since it involves exact descriptions of the artist's unique and personal use of distortion and abstraction in the visualization of the character. Furthermore, 3D computer modelling is a recent art form learning from traditional animation, itself being another young tradition based on the conventions from film, TV and puppetry.

To learn more about what autonomous agents could look like as actors, it is relevant to focus on the spectrum from traditional linear animation to the colourful products from the games development industry, where any technique that seems to have some kind of potential for creating interesting, funny or entertaining characters is tried out in a pragmatic and experimental fashion.

The study of animation as an representational art form provides us with a background for understanding the various styles and possibilities in representing the characters, environments and behaviours.

In 2D animation for film, the dominant tradition is represented by Disney, where, according to Eisenstein, one important technique for giving the impression of cartoony movement, "squeeze and stretch", relies on "the metamorphosis or transition of one shape into another" (Furniss, 1998, p. 78). This is described by animation theorist O'Pray as a "protoplasmic quality", which explains our fascination of the animated figure, because it gives the spectator the awareness of the "omnipotence of plasma which contains in 'liquid form' all possibilities of future species and forms" (Wright, 1995, p. 52). Furniss describes animation as the art of creating movement in a broader sense where "an object can move fluidly and rhythmically; in short incremental bursts; slowly and hesitantly (as in working against gravity); or in a multitude of other ways that all suggest meaning to the viewer" (Furniss, 1998, p. 76), including other traditions in animation, such as puppet animation, pixellation, claymation, cut-out and collage.

In nonlinear interactive scenarios, where the spectator is represented as an animated character who can interact with characters and objects in the world, the spectator's perception of the characters at some points seems to resemble that of the puppets in the puppet theatre more than the characters in a Disney animation. The strong sense of reality in virtual 3D worlds is often created by simulating causal relations and what theatre semioticians describe as deictic relations in the diegetic universe.

> The speaking "I", for example, can address a single interlocutor, a crowd or himself, can apostrophize the gods or some absent figure (...) can turn to the audience, and so

Figure 7.11 "Half-life": the puppet-like facial expression of a guard. He is looking at you and speaks with his limited vocabulary when you push a button (Sierra On-line and Valve., 1999).

Sorry I'm on duty Mr. Freeman!
Sorry sir. I've gotta stay on my post!
Can we do this later?
Sorry sir I've gotta stay on my post!
Hey, catch me later – I'll buy you a beer!

on. He can indicate deictically his own body, the scene, the present moment, his addressee or a distant object. (Elam, 1991, p. 145)

The game "Half-life" (Sierra On-Line and Valve, 1999) uses skeletal animation combined with simple game AI techniques to increase the impression of reality created by the characters. The mouth in Figure 7.11 is animated through a bone in the jaw, programmed to follow the waveform in the sentence. The result is an effect which in glimpses is a rough version of the sophisticated techniques used in the puppet theatre. In addition, the character seems alive through continuous actions, such as breathing and random movements: a nod of the head, a movement with the arm etc. Unfortunately, the behaviours that work on the level of the story are simply randomly generated sentences chosen from a limited vocabulary, which quickly destroys the illusion that the character is real. But the guard still works as a character, a fact easily explained by film and puppet theatre theory.

The relation between the spectator and the live generated character is different from that of the film, since our ability to interact with it makes us relate more directly to its materiality. The analogy is that the spectator invades the stage in the theatre and touches the actors, sets and props.

At some point the player will observe that although the world seems "real", it is made of "dead objects". According to Metz (1974, p. 9) "it is often the criterion of touch, that of 'Materiality', confusedly present in our mind, that divides the world into object and copies", where, for example, touching the film screen or the puppet in the wax cabinet immediately destroys the illusion of reality.

This awareness of the character as an object is a phenomenon described in the theory of the puppet theatre as the invariance of the puppet (Lorenz, 1989, pp. 230–241), as "double vision" (Tillis, 1992, pp. 60–85), and as "opalization" (Jurkowski, 1988, p. 78):

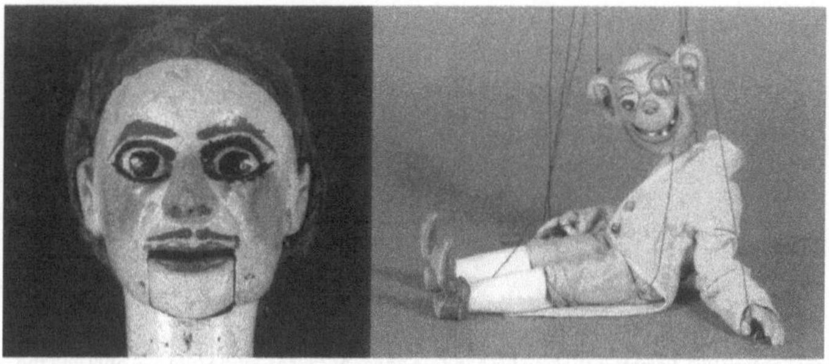

Figure 7.12 The formalization of the possible behaviours also lies in the materiality of the character. Left: Kasper, marionette (87 cm), wood/textile, Richter's Marionette Theater 1850. Right: comical character, marionette (46 cm), wood/textile, Czechoslovakia 1924/26, Spejbl und Hurvinek Theater – Joseph Skupa, puppet by Gustav Nosek (Catalog: Mobiles Puppentheater-Museum Berlin).

> There is still something more – the effect of what I choose to call "opalization", when movement fully dominates an object we feel that the character is born and present on stage. When it is the nature of the object which dominates we still see the object. The object is still the object and the character at the same time. Sometimes however this unity splits for a short while, to be regenerated after a moment. (...)

By "opalesence of the puppet" I mean the double existence of the puppet, which is perceived (and demonstrated) both as puppet and as scenic character. Clown Gustaw of Albrecht Roser is a clown character, but when his strings get entangled and he asks for help, he is a puppet; furthermore he is a puppet playing upon his awareness of being a puppet.

In the tradition of puppet theatre the object-like quality of the material, e.g. wood or clay, has been used by skilled puppeteers as an important means of expression and can serve as an inspiration for the character design and animation techniques of autonomous agents that goes beyond that of plastic Disney animation or precise naturalistic models.

The Czech artist Jiri Trnka demonstrates in his films "the ability to create expression through subtleties of movement, environment and lighting, as well as camera angle and framing, despite the inflexibility of his puppet figures", which is a way to

Figure 7.13 "Final Fantasy VII": Tifa, Barret and Cloud; Character design in 2D anime style, before the 3D modelling for the game.

Figure 7.14 "Final Fantasy VII". Barrett is shaking his hands in anger because Cloud Strife will only join the resistance movement against the powerful leaders of the city as a mercenary.

overcome the fact that "a wooden puppet generally has a rigid face, incapable of stretching to show a smile or speak" (Furniss, 1998, p. 163; cf. Figure 7.12).

In computer games development, the restriction of the material is also a major issue, especially in real-time 3D games, where the chosen 3D engine sets limits to polygon count and textures. Game designer Walter Park explains some of the advantages of the character design in the game "Final Fantasy VII" (Eidos Interactive, 1998): the use of very few polygons, large color shapes and simple surface designs in the character design gave a large freedom to use cinematographic effects (Park, 1999).

The character design in Final Fantasy VII is based on the style from Japanese anime films and the simple and naïve world of the fantasy tradition. The characters are archetypal and have few, but very distinct, features (Figure 7.13).

The main character Cloud Strife has an extreme long sword, spiky hair, elegant clothes and athletic stature like a prince. Barret Wallace has the heavily built stature of a warrior; his arm is a gun and he has extremely slender hips, like an X. Tifa Lockheart has very long legs, she has feminine and girlish features and is dressed for fighting as a teenage Amazon.

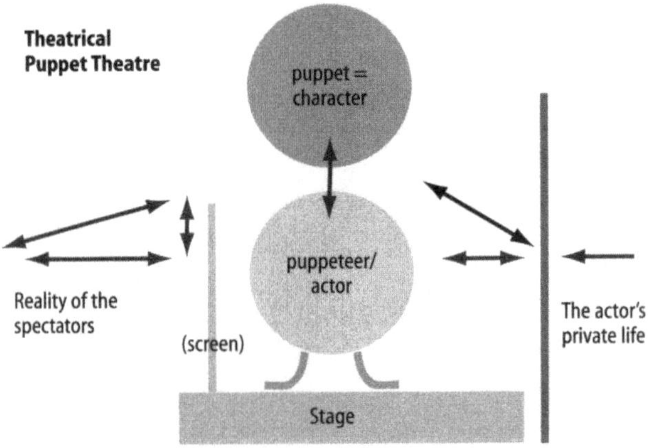

Figure 7.15 The relation between the puppet, the puppeteer and the reality of the spectator. The screen is optional.

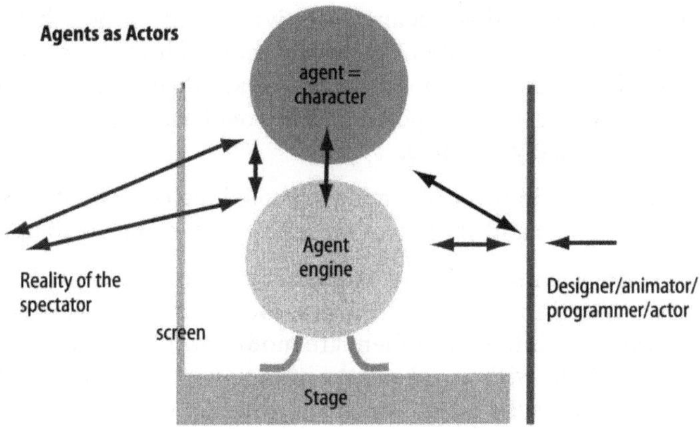

Figure 7.16 The relation between the spectator and the autonomous agent as an actor, played by an agent engine. This model is made in collaboration with dramaturgist Jette Lund.

The distinctive features of the characters make them unique and they become visually recognizable, which is important for the elaborate use of cinematic techniques, with frames ranging from close-up to panoramic throughout the game.

In the game the characters are to some extent able to express their emotions even though they are restricted by the edgy 3D design (Figure 7.14).

The theory of the puppet theatre also seems relevant to describe the special relationship between the spectator and the live animated agent, because one can draw an analogy between the puppeteer playing the puppet and the engine controlling the autonomous agent.

In the puppet theatre (Figure 7.15) the puppeteer serves (cf. Lund, 1995, p. 65) as an engine for the puppet. In some cases, he is hidden from the audience behind a screen, as in the illusionist theatre, leaving the audience speculating who is behind the screen. In modern theatre forms, the puppeteer is often visible on the stage with the puppet. The presence of the actor, hidden or visible, is the source of our fascination with the puppet and the phenomenon described as "opalization" above.

The puppet theatre is suggested as an analogy for autonomous agents in Figure 7.16. The spectator is able to go through the screen and act in the world of the agents and sometimes even to go inside them and the agent engine. In this analogy, the agent engine has to take over the function of the puppeteer to make the characters come alive, constantly revitalizing the character when the illusion of life is broken and, for a moment, it is seen as an object. In some games, where change of agent properties is a part of the gameplay and the evolving story, the spectator is also able to go inside the agent engine and thereby go inside the character. We shall return to this idea in Section 7.4.4.

7.4.3 Ryan's Possible Worlds

Bremond is not alone in emphasizing modality as a necessary ingredient of aesthetic pleasure. According to Ryan (1991), the distinction between virtual and actual worlds is a vital ingredient in any narrative, and the notion that our experience never concerns a single state of the world, but is always circumscribed by a plurality of worlds, is quite commonplace in literary theory. In fact, Ryan claims that even the simplest text presupposes that the reader is able to imagine worlds other than the one actually narrated.

In Ryan's book, a *world* in this connection is a maximal consistent set of propositions, i.e. it is a complete and consistent representation of a state of affairs.

A *System of Reality* is a set of distinct worlds. It contains a unique central world, called the *Actual World*, in which the speaker is located. Around the central world a set of satellite worlds orbit. Four of them are modal worlds: the knowledge world, the obligation world, the wish world and the intention world. These worlds contain the same propositions as the actual world, but they are tagged by different modal operators. Thus the knowledge propositions p are all prefixed by phrases such as "I firmly believe p to be true/false", "I don't know whether p", "I believe p to be probable". The obligation propositions are modified by phrases like "is allowed, obligatory, prohibited", the wish propositions by "p is good/bad", and intention-propositions by phrases like "I intend, plan to do p". All four worlds can be authentic or pretended, leaving room for authentic as well as pretended beliefs, obligations, evaluations and intentions.

In addition to the modal worlds, the Actual World is orbited by fantasy worlds: dreams and stories created by the inhabitants of the Actual World. Fantasy worlds differ from the modal worlds in that they are complete Systems of Reality that create a new actual world with modal satellites that substitute for the original System of Reality as long as the story lasts. Not only the worlds, but also the speaker and listener, are substituted and become what is known in literature theory as the *implied speaker* and *listener.*

This gives us the basic recursion that is very common in narratives: the real speaker is telling a story wherein another speaker is telling a story. In borderline cases, such as Arabian Nights, we can have up to four stories inside each other (Ryan, 1991, p. 182).

Ryan uses the following fable to illustrate her notions:

> *The Fox and the Rooster*
>
> Once a dog and a rooster went into the woods. Soon it grew dark. The rooster said, "Let us stay here all night. I will stay in this tree-top. You can sleep in the hollow trunk". "Very well", said the dog. So the dog and the rooster went to sleep. In the morning the rooster began to crow. "Cock-a-doodle-doo!". Mr Fox heard him crow. He said, "That is a rooster crowing. He must be lost in the woods. I will eat him for my breakfast." Soon Mr Fox saw the rooster in the tree-top. He said to himself: "Ha ha! Ha! ha! What a fine breakfast I shall have! I must make him come down from the tree. Ha ha! Ha! ha!" So he said to the rooster, "What a fine rooster you are! How well you sing! Will you come to my house for breakfast?" The rooster said, "Yes. thank you, I will come if my friend may come, too". "Oh yes", said Mr Fox, "I will ask your friend. Where is he?" The rooster said, "My friend is in the hollow tree. He is asleep. You must wake him". Mr Fox said to himself: "Ha ha! Ha! ha! I shall have two roosters for my breakfast!" So he puts his head into the hollow tree. Then he said, "Will you come to my house for breakfast?". Out jumped the dog, and caught Mr Fox by the nose.
>
> *Ryan (1991, p. 144, Text 6.1)*

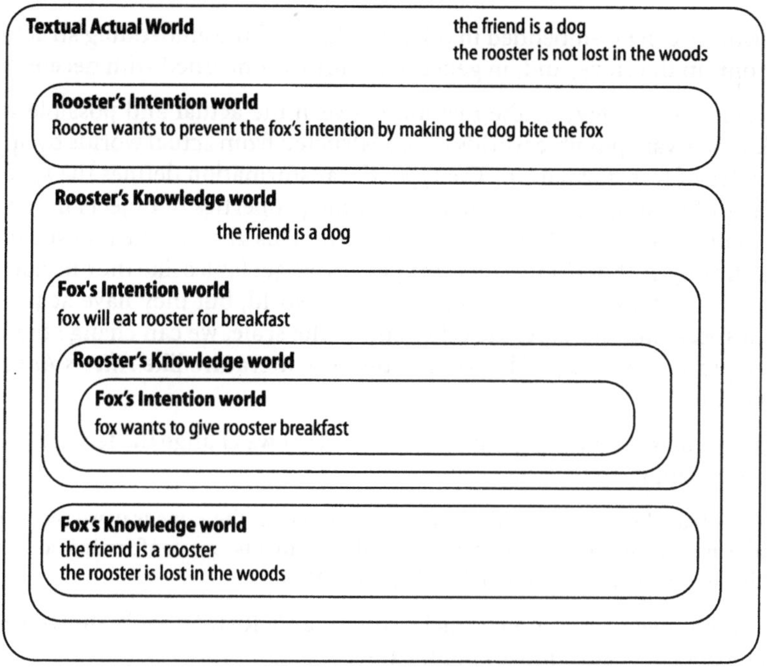

Figure 7.17 Possible worlds of "The Fox and the Rooster".

The two important modal worlds in this fable are the knowledge world and the intention world (Figure 7.17).

In the Actual World of the text, a rooster and his friend, a dog, are walking through the woods. We know that, because the author uses non-modalized sentences (*Once a dog and a rooster went into the woods*) and the author controls the actual world in text. In this world, one of its characters, the fox, believes that the rooster is lost in the woods with another rooster, which we know is not true in the textual actual world. His intention is to eat the rooster and his friend. In order to achieve this, he also intends to make the rooster follow him home by getting him to believe that the fox intends to give him breakfast. Thus, inside the intention world of the fox is embedded the knowledge world of the rooster, which again contains the intention world of the fox as conceived by the rooster: the fox intends to get the rooster to believe that the fox will offer breakfast.

Now, both the intention world and the knowledge world of the fox happen to be embedded in the knowledge world of the rooster. The rooster knows that the fox intends to eat him and seeks to accomplish this by making the rooster believe that he will get breakfast in the fox's home. The rooster controls the fox's behaviours by having the fox's modal worlds embedded in his own modal worlds.

This simple example demonstrates very clearly the importance of possible worlds in even very simple texts. If we could not reconstruct Figure 7.17 we would miss the whole point of the story. It also demonstrates the recursive structure of systems of reality: worlds can be embedded in other worlds, and the embedding structure is a major point in the story, and, in general, in stories concerned with deception.

How should we conceive of the relation between the actual and possible worlds? According to Ryan, possible worlds are constructed from actual worlds by applying simple rules of transformation. The type of transformation defines the type of the possible world. For example, we may retain the properties of objects in the actual world but enter new objects, e.g. new characters. This gives us the realistic novel. If we keep the objects but change their properties we get fables like the one above. We know roosters, dogs and foxes from the actual world, but they have acquired the ability to speak and think. At the other end of the scale, we can change the laws of nature, logic and language. This yields nonsense literature like *Alice's Adventures in Wonderland.*

The general rules for building these worlds are that we change the features dictated by the genre and keep the rest as it is:

> we reconstrue the central world of a textual universe in the same way we reconstrue the alternate possible worlds of nonfactual statements: as conforming as far as possible to our representation of AW. (Ryan, 1991, p. 51)

The example given here is extremely simple and Ryan's book shows that real fictional works are much more complicated.

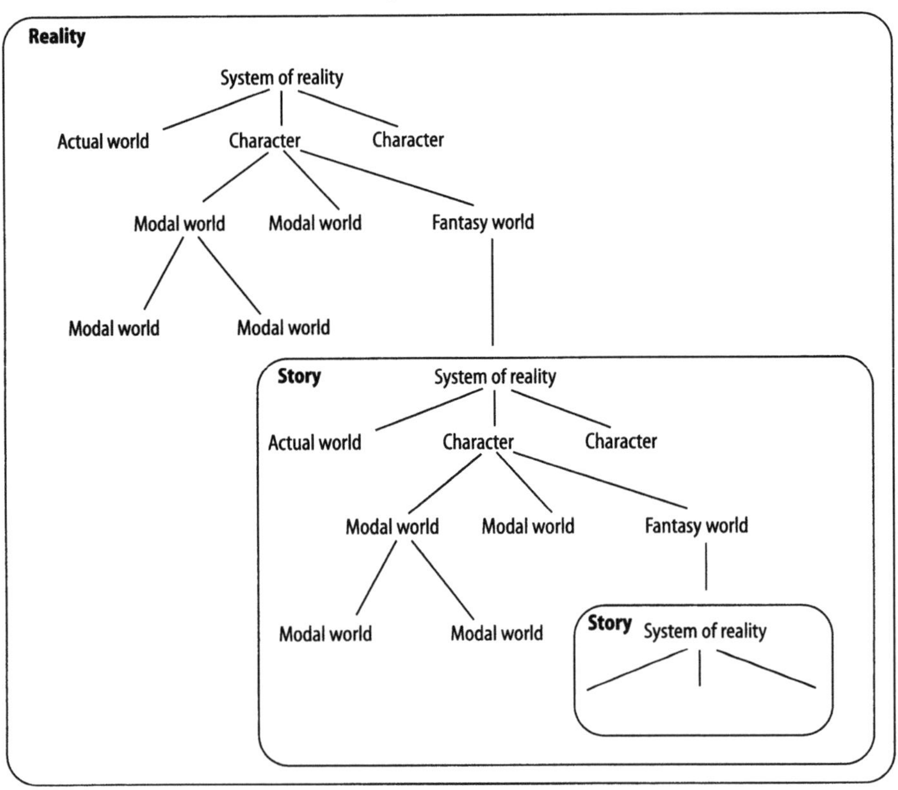

Figure 7.18 Ryan does not seem to allow nested modal worlds, but I think that her own examples indicate that this is indeed possible (adapted from Ryan (1991, p. 123).

The ability to create worlds and enter them seems to be a spontaneous faculty of humans. This ability lends credibility to Ryan's notion of worlds: when we discuss a fictive person we do not keep within the confines of the sentences of the novel. Instead, we enter a new system of reality and explore and discuss this textual world under the constraints of the transformation that created it. For example, if we have entered the world of Agatha Christie, we know that we are entitled to natural explanations of the riddles, and feel cheated if the murder turns out to have supernatural causes. On the other hand, violation of natural laws is accepted in the fantasy genre, and we accept the power of the ring in Tolkien's *The Lord of the Rings*. The reading process itself can also be characterized as "entering a world". When we become absorbed in a book or a film, we withdraw from the actual world, cease to hear and see our surroundings, forget our worries, and live for a short while in the fictive world.

This evidence from literary analysis thus shows that our interpretation of a work of art involves a basic tension between the actual world presented and a – possibly infinite – set of possible worlds that work like a huge set of projectors illuminating the present and actual by means of the dim hues and shapes of the potential. In addition, meaning seems to be recursively structured (Figure 7.18).

7.4.4 Representing and Editing the Intention World

Modal worlds are different from the textual actual world in the following important respect. In the textual actual world actions are represented as trajectories of values of object properties; for example, the movement of an agent is represented as a trajectory of its three spatial coordinates. In fact, objects can be represented as a phase space with as many dimensions as the object's degrees of freedom, and any change of the object is a trajectory in this phase space. However, in the modal worlds, it is not these physical properties of the objects that change, but rather properties of the object's actions. Thus, modal worlds can be represented by trajectories in phase spaces whose dimensions are probabilities, obligations or intentions and whose objects are actions. Actions are *reified* when they enter into the modal worlds.

> The relationship between the trajectories (episodes) of the semantic system [i.e. the actual world] and the symbols of the logic system [i.e. the modal world] seems strange: what exists as process in the semantic system, shows up as an object in the logical system. The same phenomenon lives as a process in one system, but as an entity in another. (Bøgh Andersen, 1998a, p. 177)

This sounds all very abstract, but we can in fact use Maes (1989) from Section 7.3.2 as a very concrete example. We remember that her system worked by injecting activation values into the behaviours, always choosing an executable behaviour with the highest value. The activation value is a modal value which can be interpreted as degrees of possibility – or degrees of intention if we think of the agent in anthropomorphic terms. For concrete applications of these ideas to multimedia systems, see Bøgh Andersen (1998b).

A closer reflection reveals that the idea of reification is not so counter-intuitive after all. The purpose of the modal worlds is not to execute behaviours, but to

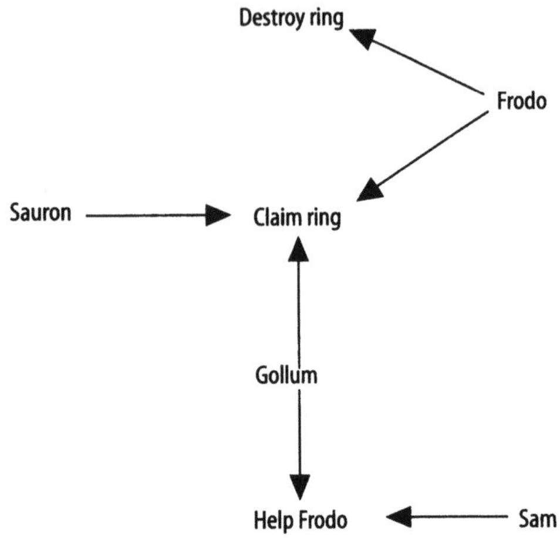

Figure 7.19 Thematic structure of *The Lord of the Rings*.

analyse possibilities and plan behaviours. Therefore, what is manipulated in these worlds are not the objects of the actual world, but rather relationships between actors and behaviours. Should I do this behaviour now? Who should do this behaviour?

In organizations, planning and execution of behaviours are often done by different departments, and it turns out that planning departments in fact do tend to reify behaviours when they describe work. In Bøgh Andersen (1997, p. 348) the manager says: "We are going to gain a step by trying to merge data input with completion". "Data input" and "completion" are names of work processes. "Completion" is a nominalization of the verb "complete", and the processes described do not involve change of work objects, but change of work processes ("merge").

In Maes's system there was only one agent, but it is natural to extend her ideas to cover assignment of a set of behaviours to a set of agents. One possibility is to reuse the dynamics from the actual world while replacing objects by actions and physical dimensions by modal dimensions. We will then obtain a representation that describes the intention worlds of the actors, and this intention world will in fact closely resemble what is known as a thematic analysis from literature theory. Consider, for example, Tolkien's *The Lord of the Rings*. There are four main characters: Sauron, Frodo, Gollum and Sam. The main theme is whether someone is to claim the right to the "ring that rules them all" or whether the ring should be destroyed. Sauron and Gollum want to claim the ring, Frodo and Sam to destroy it, although Frodo is tempted to claim it, and in fact does so in the ending. In fact, Gollum, not Frodo, becomes the agent of "destroying the ring" in the end, although not intentionally.

Figure 7.19 shows how to represent this in a dynamic modal phase space.

Figure 7.19 depicts intentions by means of forces attracting agents to behaviours. Frodo is torn between destroying and claiming the ring. In the beginning, the destroy attractor is the strongest, but in the final chapter the temptation to claim it

Figure 7.20 "half-life": the monster is attacking two enemy soldiers. One is already dead. The monster discovers you and starts hunting you instead (Sierra On-line and Valve, 1999).

grows the strongest. Gollum is divided between claiming the ring and helping Frodo to get rid of it. Only Sauron and Sam are "pure of heart": Sauron never wavers in wanting to claim the ring, Sam never in helping Frodo. Important parts of the novel can thus be described as changes of the forces attracting agents to behaviours.

Other forces must be added in order to complete the picture: for example, we need to represent "prevention" from Section 7.3.5, since Frodo and Sam want to prevent Sauron from claiming the ring, and Sauron and Gollum to prevent Frodo and Sam from destroying it.

The first person shooter game "half-life" is a good illustration of how a varied use of agent behaviour relations enhances the game. Here three groups of people with different intentions fight against each other. There are you, represented as the young scientist Mr Freeman, and your colleagues, there are the bad monsters from the underworld, and there are the soldiers conspiring against mankind, wanting to use the monsters for evil purposes.

Figure 7.21 "half-life": enemy soldiers seem intelligent by acting out collaborative skills. The pictures in the second row show close-ups of the soldiers covering the frontrunner.

In the episode of the game depicted in Figure 7.20, both you and your enemy are threatened by the same monster. The monster attacks two enemy soldiers, but when it discovers you, it starts hunting you. Thus, the <Agent – Behaviour> association <Monster – Hunting enemy soldiers> changes to <Monster – Hunting player>. However, the intentions of the characters cannot change very much, which makes the conflict between the characters very simple and the story one-dimensional. But imagine that your former enemy changes his mind and comes to help you because you were nice to him in an earlier episode of the game, i.e. the association <Monster – Hunting player > could change to <Monster – Helping player>.

Episodes like that in Figure 7.20 are an example of how the characters can change intentions in their choice of behaviour. Furthermore it shows that intention is important in the creation of conflict – a necessary ingredient in any narrative.

There are different levels of <Agent – Behaviour> associations. Consider an episode from the same game where a group of soldiers are attacking: they have the same overall intention to kill you, but carry it out in different ways. Thus, agents can be associated with the same intentional behaviour, but with different embodiments of the intention (Figure 7.21).

It is possible that representations of modality as shown in Figure 7.19 could be converted into a design tool for editing the system. The first argument is that the intention world is already a representation in which agents can analyse and plan their behaviour. The only addition needed is to allow the user/designer to do the same.

In games like "Half-life" and "Final Fantasy VII", the characters still function, although the spectator can destroy the illusion of reality for a moment by "touching" or entering the characters, as shown in Figure 7.16. In "Final Fantasy VII" the characters have different types of powers referring to their types of weapon. In one episode the main character Cloud enters a weapon shop, where the owner tells him how to use the different weapons. This is staged by a displaying a tutorial for editing the actual weapons, completely outside the world of the

Figure 7.22 "Star Craft". In real-time strategy games behaviours are often shown as icons in a menu panel. The circle with the cross means *patrol*, and the circle with the cross and the dot means *hold position*. (Blizzard Entertainment, 1998)

characters (in terms of Figure 7.16, this means contacting the agent engine), after which we enter the story world again.

The second argument is that the editing process in general seems to involve a modal process of reification where actions are turned into objects:

> The notion of instrument can be seen as a reification operation: a command such as scrolling a document is turned into an object, the scrollbar. Reification is used widely in user interfaces to turn concepts into objects that can be represented and operated upon. (Beaudouin-Lafon, unpublished, p. 5)

"Star Craft" gives a simple example of how to associate actors with behaviours: the soldiers to the left in Figure 7.22 are represented in three ways, shown in close-up on the right: as a video image that speaks simple one-liners, as dots on the map, and as little figures.

Their behaviours are presented as ongoing and continuous in real time, shown as small animated movements of the figures and dots, and as facial movements in the video image. When the soldiers are selected as individuals or as a group they can be given orders to do a behaviour by pushing the yellow buttons in the menu panel, the buttons representing reified behaviours.

7.4.5 Staging Behaviours

Another important issue is the distinction between plot and story. The *plot* denotes the sequence of events as they are presented in a novel or film, whereas the *story* denotes the sequence and the causal relationships of the events as they are assumed to have happened in the fictive Actual World. The behaviour analyses described in Section 7.3 are useful for constructing the story, but have nothing to say about how to design the plot.

Story and plot differ in time scale: the time of the story is the narrated time, whereas that of the plot is the narrating time. In a few instances the two times can coincide, but normally they are different. The narrating time is often shorter than the narrated time, and in crime stories, for example, the sequence of events are reversed: first the discovery of the crime is narrated, and as the plot unfolds we regress back in narrated time until we are confronted with the beginning: the perpetration of the crime. The interplay between plot and story is a major means for creating entertaining sequences of behaviour (Bordwell and Thompson, 1997, 1989), and this means that the agents should not only be aware of the laws of the fictive Actual World, but must also know when to present the information to the user. Creating the plot is a difficult task, since it demolishes the spectator's picture of the events as they happened in the story by hiding important events, changing the temporal order, showing ambiguous events that might lead to different conclusions etc. Spectators must work their way from the behaviours presented in the plotline to the level of the story to fully understand the overall meaning of the performed sequences of behaviours:

> It is only at the level of the *fabula* or story that the series of distinct actions and interactions of the plot are understood to form coherent *sequences* governed by the overall purposes of their agents. (Elam, 1991, p. 123)

The agent must create not only the story, but also the plot.

Besides being able to cause or prevent villainy, the agent must know the right time to disclose the act to the user. In short, agents must turn into actors, in the literal sense of the word, and always feel the gaze of the invisible audience on their backs. This statement has consequences when we turn to determining which properties should belong to the agent. In order to participate in building the story, the agent must simulate certain physical, mental and social properties, but as an actor, it should be able to control the stage too: camera angle and camera position, darkness and light, colour schemes, sound effects and music.

Consider first the requirement from Sections 7.4.1 and 7.4.2 that the agent must be able to express modality: not only that a behaviour is in progress, but also that a behaviour is impossible, possible or abandoned. This can of course be represented by dialogue, either diegetic or as asides to the audience. But more subtle means are to be preferred. Suppose our villain actor enters the stage with the goal "I want X dead". Many behaviours may have this goal on their add-lists: *drown*, *stab*, *shoot*, *push* etc. Now the villain discovers a knife on the scene and his planning mechanism determines that a precondition of "stab", namely "I have a knife", can be instantiated, i.e. the villain is building the next step of a causally connected story. The user, however, does not know this computational state of the agent.

If the agent decides on a plot that requires the user to know his state of mind, the state has to be expressed. In order to do this, the agent must not only be able to move to the knife and grasp it, but also to influence the stage so that his state is communicated. This can be done in many ways: a spotlight can hit the knife; the lighting can darken; the sound effects can cease and give way to an ominous silence; the music can change etc.

If, on the other hand, the agent decides on a plot that requires the user to be ignorant of the villain's acquisition of the knife, then the agent may cause the scene to cast a shadow on the weapon or it may move the camera to another place.

In both cases, properties of the stage must be controllable by the agent and belong to its degrees of freedom, on a par with its possibilities of locomotion and speech.

A fundamental question is thus whether we should build the whole story world first and then let the agents to act in it, or whether we should build the top of the iceberg, which is modelling the things to be shown in the plotline only.

7.5 Putting It All Together

In this section we shall put the material from the preceding sections together in a loose, but well-motivated, sketch.

The evidence presented above indicates that we need at least three layers of processes:

1. *The world of reflection, behaviour, communication and scheming.* Discrete processes are necessary for representing our ability for systematic reflection and scheming, both with respect to our behaviours (planning moves and counter-moves) and speaking (planning rhetorical structures). The act of speaking

presupposes an ability to imagine what other agents believe and intend and what they believe I believe they intend. Therefore this layer must contain recursive structures of the form shown in Figure 7.18.

2. *The world of bodies, their movements and urges.* The existence of this layer is documented by the existence of the process chunks identified by Vendler, Talmy, Johnson and others. It mediates between the layers of discrete and continuous processes, between behaviours and actions; on the one hand, it contains standardized and labelled schemata of processes that can be converted into discrete representations; on the other hand, these chunks are made of dynamic material that can be assembled into processes that can actually physically control actuators and sensors.
3. *The physical world of actions, mass, energy, velocity, etc.* This is the world in which the former two layers must ultimately be realized. Don Juan's intrigues of seduction must ultimately be realized as caressing movements of arms and hands, and ingratiating sounds produced by his silken tongue. The transition from (2) to (3) must involve some kind of arbitration mechanism which must include the possibilities of fusing several action lumps into one. Apart from the practical necessity of fusion (avoiding obstacles while striving for the door), fusion is necessary in order to generate ambiguous trajectories, be they physical or verbal actions, which again is mandatory for any plot of deception (Section 7.4.2). The deceiver always has two behaviours which must be realized simultaneously in one and the same action sequence: the real one and the faked one.

As shown in Table 7.6, there are two versions of this hierarchy, non-symbolic and symbolic processes, where the latter are a subclass of the former. Because of the symbolic processes, all processes, including the symbolic ones themselves, must live the double life of discrete and continuous phenomena, since symbolic processes cannot avoid articulating themselves and other actions into discrete elements. Without this doubling we would be able to tell stories about animals, but not fables about anthropomorphic foxes and roosters.

Table 7.6 The agent.

	Signs			
	Non-symbolic process		**Symbolic process**	
1. Discrete The world of reflection, behaviours, communication and schemes.	Planning and scheming. (Componential analysis STRIPS, Maes).		Discrete sentence representation (Syntax, Rhetorics).	
2. Discrete + continuous Fusing behaviours into actions.	Image and action schemata (Talmy, Johnson, Vendler).		Textual, interpersonal and ideational functions (Halliday)	
	Fusing	Defusing	Fusing	Defusing
3. Continuous The physical world of actions, mass, energy, velocity, inertia, collisions and gravitation.	Actuator: *Acting*	Sensor: *Seeing.*	Actuator: *Speaking and writing.*	Sensor: *Listening and reading.*

Table 7.7 The actor.

Signifier		Signified
Signified	Signifier	
Reflection	Rhetorics	Guessing the character's long-term designs
Action schemata	Communicative schemata	Enjoying suspense and surprises
Physical trajectories		Enjoying movements of bodies and rhythm of lines

The interactions between the components are unfortunately a matter of philosophical speculations, except that there is no top-down control: although I may be wrestling with a difficult chess problem, my body is still capable of executing the action schema of finding its way to the pub while avoiding bypassers, even if it receives absolutely no support from the analytical compartment – that may be completely taken by surprise by finding itself with a mug of beer in its (?) hands.

An attractive idea, consistent with the notion of agents (Maes, 1994), is that all components are themselves semi-autonomous agents that can be influenced by other components but handle the information according to their own logic. In addition, there is psychological evidence pointing in that direction (Engelkamp and Zimmer, 1994).

Although Table 7.6 may contain sufficient processes to generate normal, everyday lifelike courses of events, this is not what we are striving for. We want the agent to turn into an actor and generate interesting events, and this requires the agent to view the course of events, consisting of actions and utterances – signifieds and signifiers – as a signifier itself, produced for the benefit of an audience that are to extract pleasure from it (Table 7.7). Thus, the course of events turns into a story and must be presented as a plot to the on-looker.

Unlike everyday events, the mental reflections must become perceptible signs that enable the audience to make guesses about the character's long-term designs, emotional make-up and possible developments; the action schemata are no longer selected to merely produce the most efficient way from departure to destination, but must be contrived in such a way that the audience can enjoy suspense and surprises; and the actual physical trajectories of the actuators must replace efficient violence by sensual ballet-like brawls.

References

Austin, J. L. (1976) *How to Do Things with Words*. Oxford: Oxford University Press.

Beaudouin-Lafon, M. (unpublished) *Instrumental Interaction: a New Model for Graphical User Interfaces*. Department of Computer Science, University of Aarhus.

Blizzard Entertainment (1998) *Starcraft*. http://www.blizzard.com/starcraft/.

Bøgh Andersen, P. (1992) Vector spaces as the basic component of interactive systems. Towards a computer semiotics. *Hypermedia* 4(1): 53–76.

Bøgh Andersen, P. (1995a) The force dynamics of interactive system. Towards a computer semiotics. *Semiotica* 103(1/2): 5–45.
Bøgh Andersen, P. (1995b) Dynamic logic. In *Signs & Time* (*Zeit & Zeichen*) (eds. E. W. B. Hess-Lüttich and B. Schlieben-Lange). Tübingen: Gunter Narr Verlag, pp. 152–186.
Bøgh Andersen, P. (1997) *A Theory of Computer Semiotics. Semiotic Approaches to Construction and Assessment of Computer Systems.* Cambridge: Cambridge University Press.
Bøgh Andersen, P. (1998a) The semiotics of autopoiesis. A catastrophe-theoretic approach. *Cybernetics & Human Knowing* 2(4).
Bøgh Andersen, P. (1998b) Multimedia phase-spaces. *Multimedia Tools and Applications* 6: 207–237.
Bordwell, D. (1985) *Narration in the Fiction Film.* London: Methuen.
Bordwell, D. and Thompson, K. (1997) *Film Art. An Introduction.* New York: McGraw-Hill.
Bremond, C. (1966) La logique des possible narratifs. *Communications* 8: 60–76.
Bremond, C. (1970) Morphology of the French folktale. *Semiotica* 2: 247–276.
Clark, H. H. and Clark, E. V. (1977) *Psychology of Language.* New York: Harcourt Brace Jovanovich.
DreamWorks Interactive (1996) *The Neverhood.* `http://www.dreamworksgames.com/Games/Neverhood/`.
Eidos Interactive (1998) *Final Fantasy VII.* `http://www.eidosinteractive.com/ff7/`.
Elam, K. (1980) *The Semiotics of Theatre and Drama.* New York, London: Routledge.
Engelkamp, J. and Zimmer, H. D. (1994) *The Human Memory. A Multimodal Approach.* Seattle, Toronto, Göttingen, Bern: Hogrefe & Huber.
Fikes, R. E. and Nilsson, N. J. (1971) STRIPS: a new approach to the application of theorem proving to problem solving. In *Second International Joint Conference on Artificial Intelligence.* British Computer Society, pp. 608–619.
Fo, D. (1987) *The Tricks of the Trade* London: Routledge.
Furniss, M. (1998) *Art in Motion: Animation Aesthetics*, London: John Libbey.
Goddard, C. (1998) *Semantic Analysis.* Oxford: Oxford University Press.
Halliday, M. A. K. (1994) *An Introduction to Functional Grammar.* London: Edward Arnold.
Hodgins, J. and Wooten, W. (1999) Controlling simulated characters. In *1999 Game Developers' Conference Proceedings*, San Francisco, CA: Miller Freeman.
Johnson, M. (1992) *The Body in the Mind.* Chicago and London: University of Chicago Press.
Jurkowski, H. (1988) In *Aspects of Puppet Theatre; A Collection of Essays* (ed. P. Francis). London: Puppet Centre Trust.
Latombe, J.-C. (1991) *Robot Motion Planning.* Boston, MA: Kluwer.
Lind, M. (1990) *Representing Goals and Functions of Complex Systems.* Institute of Automatic Control Systems. DTU. 90-D-381.
Lind, M. (1994) Modeling goals and functions of complex industrial plants. *Applied Artificial Intelligence* 8: 259–283.
Lind, M. (draft). *Actions, functions and failures in dynamic environments.* Department of Automation, Technical University of Denmark.
Lorenz, K. K. (1989) Das Puppenspiel als synergetische Kunstform. In *Die Spiele der Puppe; Beiträge sur Kunst- und Socialgeschichte des Figurentheaters im 19. und 20. Jahrhundert* (Ed. M. Wegener). München: Prometh Verlag.
Lund, J. (1995) *Die Wirklichkeit – und die wirkliche Fiktion; Elemente zur Theorie des Puppentheater.* Masters thesis, University of Copenhagen, Institute of Art History and Theatre Research.
Maes, P. (1989) How to do the right thing. *Connection Science Journal* 1(3): 291–323. (Quoted from `http://pattie.www.media.mit.edu/people/pattie/cv.html#publications`).
Maes, P (1994) Modeling adaptive autonomous agents. *Artificial Life Journal* 1(1 & 2).
Maclennan, B. (1997) Field computation in motor control. In *Self-Organization, Computational Maps, and Motor Control* (eds. P. Morasso and V. Sanguinetti). Amsterdam: Elsevier, pp. 37–73.
Metz, C. (1974) *Film Language; A Semiotics of the Cinema*, New York: Oxford University Press.
Morasso, P. and Sanguinetti, V. (eds.) (1997) *Self-Organization, Computational Maps, and Motor Control.* Amsterdam: Elsevier.
Park, W. (1999) Polygon character design under technical constraints. In *1999 Game Developers Conference Proceedings*, San Francisco, CA: Miller Freeman
Parke, F. and Walters K. (1996) *Computer Facial Animation.* Massachusetts: A K Peters Wellsley.
Pirjanian, P. and Madsen, C. B. (1998) *Autonomous Agents and Agent Architectures.* Laboratory of Image Analysis, Aalborg University.

8 Games and Stories

M. Wibroe, K. K. Nygaard and P. Bøgh Andersen

8.1 Introduction

In spring 1999 one of the authors was the external examiner for a student project on interactive storytelling in a 3D environment.

The students had produced a well-structured 3D system with sound output and speech input. The graphics were very impressive, but the system was neither narrative nor interactive. The "story" ran as follows: the camera moves towards a sheep that gets scared and flees. Then the camera moves towards a signpost pointing in two directions. The user can say "castle" or "farm"; "castle" takes the user to a castle with two guards. If the user shouts, the guards face the camera, and then the "story" ends!

The students were technically very skilled and enthusiastic over the new possibilities:

> Imagine playing the role of Frodo Baggins in J. R. R. Tolkien's masterpiece, *Lord of the rings.* (Larsen and Petersen, 1999, p. 7)

But there is indeed a long way from the "Adventure of the Frightened Sheep" to Tolkien's three volumes of narrative suspense. In fact, Tolkien would have spent only a sentence or two on the sheep, whereas the students had invested their spring term in the project!

Why this gap between ambition and result?

On the one hand, the students had to design and implement the everyday and trivial aspects of a world before they could even begin to think about telling stories. Objects must be created and located (sheep, trees, birds, signposts, castle, guards), and their actions must be designed: the movement of the sheep, the flapping of the birds, and the turning of the guards. In addition, higher-level behaviours, such as moving to a goal while avoiding obstacles, must be implemented. Tolkien, on the other hand, could rely on the reader's knowledge of such everyday phenomena, and immediately begin to mould it into a fictive world designed for adventure.

Even film-makers have an easier life than the two students. Although they may have to build a castle, they can rely on the actors' ability to move, talk and smile, and trees and birds come for free.

These different working conditions are important because fictive worlds are constructed from the real world by relaxing certain constraints of the real world and leaving the rest as it is (cf. Section 7.4.3).

Thus, the real, actual, world is the raw material for building fictive worlds. The two students not only had to build the fictive world, but also to recreate the "real world" out of which the fiction is created. So in spite of the boring narrative, they got good marks for their efforts!

However, there is also another reason for the problems, namely that not all events count as narratives. In fact, it is possible to characterize rather precisely the difference between non-narrative events and narrative ones, and the "Adventure of the Frightened Sheep" definitely belongs to the former.

In this chapter, we shall discuss three issues:

- What characterizes the minimal narrative unit – which events are tellable?
- How can tellable stories be made interesting – how is suspense created?
- How can interaction be combined with narration?

It turns out that a minimal requirement for narration is a conflict of intentions, and this makes some kind of planning mechanism necessary. In addition, in order to enter scheming into the system, the agents must be able to represent the plans of the adversary to themselves. Thus we will be developing the ideas from Sections 7.3.1 and 7.4.3.

In addition, we argue that a distinction should be made between the *plot* – the sequence in which information about the story is presented – and the *story* itself – the sequence in which events happen in the fictive world.

Finally, we define two types of interaction, namely *interactive plot* and *interactive story*. In the former, which is by far the most frequent, users can only influence the sequence in which they acquire information about the story, but not the story itself. In the latter, which is the most difficult, the story can be influenced as well.

As an illustration of the concepts, we use a conventional game called Diablo that succeeds in getting most of the features wrong. Thus, the problems of Diablo count as an argument for the importance of the concepts.

8.2 The Game

Diablo represents a mixture of three game categories:

1. The *adventure genre* is the predominant element, because the game is based upon a series of quests (in this context "quest" means a mission or challenge) that the user can try to accomplish. The quests take place in a large maze, which is typical for the adventure genre.

2. The user is represented by a character that is established before the game commences. This element originates from traditional *role-playing*. Diablo enables users to establish their character within three categories, each with its own characteristics: warrior, rogue and sorcerer. The difference between them is mostly their choice of arms.
3. The game contains elements from a third genre – *real-time action*. Throughout the game users are in combat against numerous beasts, and if they fail to kill them the game cannot be completed.

The exposition of the story is enacted via numerous quests that will be analysed later. We will not deal with the variations of the different games, since the objective is to create a clear and fundamental understanding of the central aspects of the game. The following can thus be considered as a short walk-through of Diablo, from which a few less central elements have been omitted.

First the user chooses a character (warrior, rogue or sorcerer); then the game can begin. The point of departure is the town of Tristram, whose inhabitants can provide information and quests. In addition they each have different qualifications the user can make use of. For example, Griswold, the town blacksmith can repair, buy and sell different equipment.

A user who chooses to interact with the characters quickly becomes aware of the fact that something terrible has occurred in the town. "Evil" has taken possession of the maze underneath the town cathedral. From here various creatures haunt the nation and terrorize its citizens.

During the course of the game we learn that the son of King Leoric, Albrecht, has been kidnapped by evil forces. As a result of this, the king has gone insane. In the search for Albrecht, Archbishop Lazarus – the king's advisor – has led a group of the king's men into a trap in the maze, where practically everyone has been killed. From here the battle rages on through hallways and corridors. Users can kill numerous monsters, develop their character and receive various quests. At one point the user is told to rescue the king's son, who is reported to be in the custody of Lazarus. When Lazarus is finally found and killed, we learn that this was not the case after all: Albrecht has been turned over to the Prince of Darkness, Diablo, whose spirit is situated in a so-called "soulstone". His plan is his own resurrection in the flesh of the boy (who is said to be weak and compliant), and if the user does not kill Diablo, Albrecht will die. The game ends with the killing of Diablo, but by doing so the user also kills Albrecht, because the exchange of body and soul has already taken place.

From here on the game takes control, and in a filmic sequence the user's character removes the soulstone from Diablo's forehead, after which the body of Diablo is transformed into Albrecht, who then passes away. The user takes the stone (which we now presume contains Diablo's soul) and strikes it through his own forehead, presuming (at least according to our interpretation) that he can withstand the pressure of evil (any final answer to this is not provided).

A second and quite important element of the game is the development of the user's character. Users are allotted "experience points" according to their achievements, which enable them to build their character with regard to strength, speed, durability and capacity for magic. Only by killing the different monsters in the maze can the user gain sufficient strength to kill Diablo at the end of the game. To a large extent, these elements derive from computer-based role-playing games. Moreover, the development of the character depends on the user obtaining different equipment; for example, a better weapon or a new spell means an improved chance for survival.

Throughout the game users can obtain weaponry and equipment when they kill various monsters or find a locker. They can also improve equipment and magical abilities by means of Griswold and Adria – payment is in cash, naturally, for which reason the user is forced to find and collect gold throughout the game.

8.3 Theory

According to Ryan (1991), an event is *tellable* if, in a system of reality (see again Section 7.4.3), *there is a discrepancy between the actual world and a possible world or internally between possible worlds.* The former includes

> unsuccessful action, broken promises, violated interdictions, mistaken interpretation, and double, as well as single deception. (Ryan, 1991, p. 158)

The latter subsumes such widespread themes as conflicts between desire and obligation, between the intentions of the protagonist and antagonist (competition), between the desires of two agents (jealousy), or between an actor's ambitions and impotence.

A basic requirement for this to happen is that there are possible worlds at all, i.e. that an action can have more than one outcome, that acting and refraining from acting (the passive projection of the present state) result in different states, or that characters can have beliefs about the past that can differ internally or deviate from the actual past.

Thus a sequence of events without any possible worlds and with complete knowledge in all actors of the past is not tellable! We now see why the students' system was not tellable: neither sheep nor user had any intentions, therefore there could be no conflicts and no progress towards a resolution of the conflicts. On the other hand, the story of Diablo is definitely tellable: Leoric and Lazarus have conflicting intentions, and Lazarus has broken his promises to the king and deceived him.

In addition to these structural requirements, there are also substantial ones. Some themes, like religion, sex, aristocracy and mystery have en internal appeal (so that the following story ought to sell: "My god, said the Duchess, I am pregnant. Who done it?"; Ryan (1991, p. 154)). Diablo exploits all these ingredients except sex!

Events in a narrative fall into two categories, depending upon whether or not they further the resolution of the conflict. The former are called *story-functional*, the latter *descriptive*. No event is one or the other *per se*. For example, the falling of a dead leaf from a tree can be descriptive if the conflict is jealousy, but story-functional if it is about ecological issues.

Now, if we do have a tellable event, how should we tell it? According to Bordwell (1985), the plot should offer a series of time-related cues and thus be able to control the production, maintenance and destruction of the expectations of the user. This requires us to differentiate between *plot* – the sequence in which we get information about the story, and *story* – the sequence in which events take place in the fictive world.[1] In most books and movies, the two differ markedly. For example, information about the perpetrator of a murder is normally received a long time after it was committed, or, conversely, it can be hinted at before the fact in order to create suspense. Information about an event can be consciously misleading, vague or ambiguous.

The best examples of verbalizations that violate all these requirements are the stories small children tell about kindergarten or school: "And then I did this, and then he did that, and then I said something, and then the schoolmaster said something, etc.". One must really love these kids in order to avoid falling asleep.

Let us now apply these concepts to Diablo and see how it fares.

8.4 Analysis

The quests of Diablo constitute its *plot*, since they are the way in which the underlying story is revealed. The quests themselves are small narratives in their own right.

On the basis of a relatively large amount of game-plays, we have divided the various quests in Diablo into two basic categories, *Simple Exchanges* and *Breaches of Contract*, where the former is clearly dominant.

In the following we describe the characteristics of the specific quests and their importance for the narrative progression in the basic story. They are summarized in Table 8.1.

Simple exchange: These quests are about delivering something to someone and then being rewarded for your efforts by receiving an object or a piece of information. None of the agents involved in the system have any hidden motives. In some of these quests it is possible to obtain new knowledge, because the user's character – by handing over information to the town's inhabitants – gives them an opportunity to interpret/understand information they already had.

Breach of contract: In this type of quest the user is asked to do a favour in exchange for a reward. After the deed is done it turns out that one has to fight for the reward. In contrast to Simple Exchange, this type involves plotting by the other protagonists, because the involved characters to some extent have plans in conflict with those of the user.

1 The two concepts are very common in literature and film theory, but there is disagreement about the words to use. Bordwell and Thompson (1997, p. 92) use the terms *plot* and *story*, whereas the equivalents in Ryan's book are *discourse* and *plot*. Thus, Ryan's term *plot* denotes the same thing as Bordwell's *story*. We have chosen Bordwell's terms since *discourse* has strong textual connotations. Therefore, what we call *story-functional* elements are *plot-functional* in Ryan's book.

Table 8.1 The quests in a game-play categorized by type.

Type	Quest name
Simple Exchange	Chamber of Bone, Magic Rock, Halls of the Blind, Black Mushroom, Anvil of Fury, Lachdanan, Lazarus, Diablo
Breach of Contract	Snotspill, Gharbad the Weak

The different quests of the Simple Exchange type have a narrative structure that is decidedly not tellable. By this we mean that there does not exist any foundation for exciting narration in the narrative structure. The "Magic Rock" quest is an example of this. The actualized events were ("Gabriel" is the name we chose for our avatar):

1. Griswold asks Gabriel to obtain a magic rock.
2. Gabriel obtains it.
3. Gabriel hands it over to Griswold.
4. Griswold thanks Gabriel and rewards him with a ring that contains fragments of the magic stone.

The series of events can be illustrated by means of a plot diagram (Figure 8.1).

All elements in this structure have the subsequent element as a goal and the preceding element as a basis. It is difficult to tell an exciting story based on this structure because there is no clash of intentions. This is not to say that these quests cannot contribute to the overall story to a lesser extent, but in their own right they are not interesting. Thus, stories of this kind are not sufficiently complex to generate a satisfactory narration. There are no virtual events and this ultimately causes a pronounced lack of excitement.

The "Breach of Contract" type follows a narrative structure that to a greater extent generates narrative interest, because the actors plot independently and in a manner that is incompatible with the user's own plotting. "Snotspill" is an example of this type of quest. The actualized events were:

1. Gabriel meets a goblin called Snotspill.
2. Snotspill demands that Gabriel obtain a relic.
3. Gabriel meets a horde of monsters.
4. Gabriel kills the monsters.
5. Gabriel obtains the relic.
6. Gabriel gives the relic to Snotspill.

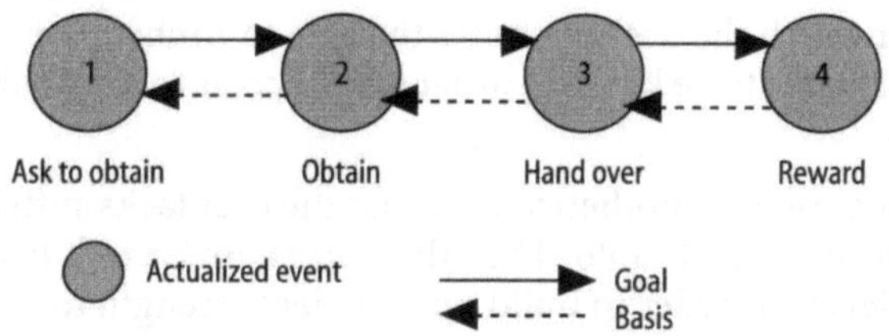

Figure 8.1 Actualized events in the "Magic Rock" quest. Compare with the "non-tellable" structure in Ryan (1991, p. 157).

7. Snotspill and his men attack Gabriel.
8. Gabriel kills Snotspill and his men.
9. Gabriel gets through to level 5.

In this quest there are a series of non-actualized events that constitute the virtual events of the story.

Virtual events:

21. Gabriel goes to level 5 without obtaining and handing over the relic.
22. Gabriel finds the relic, but is killed by the monsters.
23. Gabriel delivers the relic and continues to level 5 without any confrontations.
24. Gabriel delivers the relic and Snotspill kills him.
25. Gabriel cannot or will not hand over the relic.
26. Gabriel is caught in level 4.

The relation between the actualized and virtualized events generates a chain of sequences that are virtual stories, i.e. stories that could have unfolded had the user chosen otherwise:

Virtual embedded narratives:

A. Snotspill's passive projection: 21.
B. Snotspill's intention: 2, 3, 4, 5, 6, 7, 24.
C. Gabriel's intention: 2, 3, 4, 5, 6, 23.
D. Gabriel's passive projection: 2, 25, 26.
E. The monsters' intention: 3, 22.

The term "intention" denotes the character's own plotting, while the term "passive projection" denotes the conscious passivity of the character because it believes there to be a likely development in accordance with its self-interest. Compared with Figure 8.1, Figure 8.2 has conflicting intentions (the monsters and Snotspill, but not Gabriel, want Gabriel dead) and possible passive projections where doing nothing may be more advantageous (it may be more sound for Gabriel to decline Snotspill's request, to break his promise afterwards, or to keep the relic without delivering it to Snotspill).

The central story of Diablo is focused around two quests – "Lazarus" and "Diablo" (cf. Table 8.1). These quests are the only obligatory ones in any successful game. All other quests are chosen (more or less) arbitrarily by the system in the initial phase of the game. In principle, it is possible to move fast down through the maze to one of the final levels. Here the user has to find the "Staff of Lazarus" and deliver it to Cain in the town, after which the user can enter the gate to Archbishop Lazarus's hiding place. Here Lazarus has to be killed in order to get access to the final level, where the user kills Diablo.

However, this scenario is hypothetical, because the user lacks sufficient strength to take on either Lazarus nor Diablo. Thus the user is forced to kill a majority of the monsters on all levels in order to build up sufficient strength to deal with the final challenges.

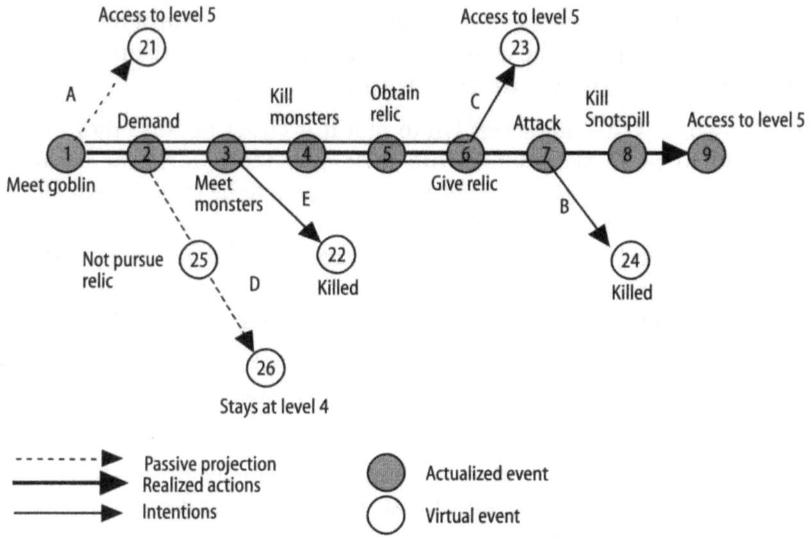

Figure 8.2 Actualized and virtual events in the "Snotspill" quest.

8.4.1 Story-Functionality

It appears from the above that only the two quests, "Lazarus" and "Diablo", are obligatory partial goals of the game. The remaining quests cannot be considered central elements of the story, because they do not directly relate to the central story and thus do not contribute actively to the narrative progression of Diablo.

In this way it makes sense to operate with a *minimal run*, where we only include the story-functional elements. The elements that together constitute the minimal run are the only ones that are essential for enactment of the story. In the minimal run, the action is limited to the fact that Archbishop Lazarus has kidnapped King Leoric's son, Albrecht, and that it is to be expected that Lazarus will sacrifice him to Diablo. When the user encounters and kills Lazarus, he will possibly see the dead body of a boy on an altar in "Lazarus's Lair". During the next visit to the town, Cain, however, tells him that the dead boy is not Prince Albrecht, who is now in the custody of Diablo who must be killed. Once Diablo is killed, the game is over.

Thus the narrative structure falls into two pieces: *the minimal run* consisting of two story-functional quests, and the *detours* consisting of quests that are not story-functional – in other aesthetic products they would be classified as loose ends!

8.4.2 Scheming

This is not the only way in which the narrative construction is insufficient. In Diablo the computer-based agents cannot be said to be actively scheming, as they should according to Ryan – at least the user does not notice it, since all agents seem to passively await the user's next move.

According to Ryan, if there is a conflict between the actual state of the universe and the subjective demands of the characters, this ought to cause them to plot against one another in order to actualize their demands.

In Ryan's theory, if the characters fail to plot it is either because they believe the actual world to be in accordance with their own ideal world, or because they passively project the course of events, believing them to be to their own advantage. If the user accepts these conventions, he or she is led to believe that the antagonists Lazarus and Diablo (whose ideal world can hardly be compatible with that of the user) fail to plot because they either see the actual world as ideal or because they assume that remaining passive will change the situation to their advantage.

But none of these assumptions is particularly probable or trustworthy when we progress to the point where the user has killed their men by the hundreds! The two villains cannot possibly see the loss of men as an advantage!

Therefore Lazarus and Diablo do not appear to be worthy adversaries of the user and the inhabitants of Tristram, and, because of these incompetent villains, a satisfactory story cannot emerge.

8.4.3 Plot and Information

One might ask whether the incompetent villains could have other causes than a faulty story; for example, the plot might be defective.

Diablo is based on a first-person perspective, as advocated by Laurel (1991), where the user gets the same information as the fictive character. But is it at all possible to picture a complex narrative when the plot is based upon a first-person perspective?

Traditionally authors make use of diverging perspectives and communicate information from different characters, which enables the reader to be differently (perhaps even better) informed than the protagonists. This is difficult to manage in a story where the user has to read the story through the protagonist's eyes.

The problem is thus which information is available for whom at a given point in the development of Diablo, i.e. it is a matter of the plot. We must expect that the evil antagonists are fully aware of what is going on in the maze – after all Diablo is supposed to be a demonic god. If this is not the case (which the passivity on their part would indicate), it is necessary, in order to maintain credibility, to account for their interpretation of the situation. Even if we stick to first-person perspective, the plot could allow for the user to overhear conversations between Lazarus and his men about the user's character and deeds.

As mentioned above, the central aspects of the plot consist of two quests – "Lazarus" and "Diablo". In this way, the plot as a whole is quite clear, and the course of action in each game is determined from the start. However, the makers of the game try (with limited success) to seduce the user to draw different conclusions from the course of action in order to create suspense about the outcome.

Basically the makers of the game have chosen not to provide the user with much information. However, the user is normally informed that the nation of Khandaras is ravaged by evil and that a number of the king's men – led by Lazarus – have taken up the fight. Lazarus has led the soldiers into a trap, and has kidnapped the king's son Albrecht. That is all one gets to know, and the gaps this creates naturally make the user wonder what else might have happened. Where is Albrecht currently, and what are Lazarus's intentions with him?

At first this may seem to be in accordance with Bordwell's plot requirements, but because only the central quests ("Lazarus" and "Diablo") are story-functional, the gaps seem to be ever present in Diablo.

With an average of less than two new pieces of information an hour, the user quickly becomes annoyed by the fact that there is so little accessible information. The user expects to be provided with more coherent information concerning specific situations within a reasonable time, and not after several hours.

The lack of control over the plot is more likely to create frustration and confusion than suspense, because the subsequent information should confirm or deny the "logical" connections and hypotheses that the user has been able to establish.

Instead, for a long period of time, the user is provided with very little information, much of which seems to have no relevance. Examples are the information that the town water supply has been contaminated, or that a caravan carrying a magic rock has passed through Tristram. These and similar incidents do not seem to relate to the central plot elements in Diablo. This, of course, could be a generally accepted effort to sidetrack the user, but in that case the makers of the game fail to guide the user back to the right track. It is not a good idea to let the user wait until the game's conclusion before learning of the more central elements of the plot!

8.4.4 Plot and Time

If we look at the temporal aspect of the plot, things are not much better. According to Bordwell, the plot should offer a series of time-related cues to control the creation of time perspective on the part of the user, but this is certainly not the case in Diablo, and that is why there is no basic sense of time in the game.

At no point do we receive any indication of a time span (for instance, it is never night in Tristram), and this prevents us from being subjected to the pressure of time.

Even when we learn that Albrecht has been handed over to Diablo, we can take our time because we have learned that time is of no consequence throughout the various quests. This is unfortunate, because the game loses a significant amount of potential for suspense. In fact, since the game does not support any sense of time at all, it is only the user's subjective understanding of various situations that determines the placement of the specific events in relation to each other.

Not only is Diablo incapable of guiding the user to essential story-functional information, but it also lacks the ability to display them in an engaging mode.

The only direct mode of displaying essential story-functional information is film sequences, but they are rare; the requisite information is usually passed on to the user by reading from a book, or through the tales of various persons. Such verbal reports can also be found in films, but here they are normally repetitions of scenes that have already displayed the highlights visually.

In Diablo, verbal information is often the only source. The problem is that verbal descriptions have relatively little dramatic effect: imagine experiencing James Bond's shown-down with Dr No only through his report to M! Such a film would not sell many tickets.

But this is what Diablo does. If only we were allowed to see to the kidnapping of Albrecht, hear him cry and Lazarus laugh his hollow laughter, our motivation for rescuing him would be immensely higher!

8.4.5 Duration of Plot and Story

Literature and film have sophisticated ways of varying the duration of plot and story. A boring period of years can be condensed into minutes, and, conversely, highly emotional scenes can be prolonged by means of slow motion and repetitions. The first-person perspective of Diablo makes such elasticity difficult. In this type of interaction, the duration of plot and story are the same, since it would spoil the illusion if the system suddenly jumped two months ahead. Many of the editing techniques of film do not apply here.

Therefore Diablo does not make much use of the reduction techniques, but when it occasionally occurs, it is not surprisingly in connection with the filmic sequences. As long as the makers of the game do not offer possibilities for interaction but control the whole sequence, it is easier for them to exploit the techniques.

Nevertheless, it would be advantageous to reduce various plot elements in Diablo. For example, moving over large distances in the game is tedious. If the user for some reason has to move from one level to another, it can easily take several minutes because the journey must be made on foot.

This problem could have been solved by offering the user magical ways of moving through levels that have already been finished. Thus, *teleportation* can be used as the *montage* of interactive games.

8.4.6 Interactivity: Plot and Story

In Diablo, as in many other games, we can distinguish between three levels of interaction: *story*, *plot*, and *kinetic*.

1. *Story interaction* denotes the user's possibilities for influencing the narrative structure of the game, i.e. the outcome of conflicts, the intentions, desires and knowledge of the actors, the plans they construct, and the strategies they employ to accomplish the plans.
2. *Plot interaction* denotes the user's possibilities to control which information is presented at what time.
3. *Kinetic interaction* encompasses the bodily movements of the actors: walking, jumping, shooting, swimming, beating, kicking etc.

The three levels of interaction roughly corresponds to the three layers defined in Section 7.5. If users can interact with the *story*, they must have access to (1) *The world of reflection, behaviour, communication and scheming.*

If users are to influence *plot*, they must have access to (2) or (3) where actions are specified and realized. If users want to learn the secrets of Diablo, they must be able to move around, avoid obstacles, flee from enemies or kill them, and they must be enabled to elicit preprogrammed verbal information from them.

Direct kinetic influence, i.e. control of the individual limb, is not usual and not very practical. Users normally have access to behaviours and not to the individual features of the actions. They do not have to specify the atomic movements of arms, hands and legs, since a simple fight would be very difficult to orchestrate. Instead, the control resides somewhere between levels (2) and (3). Sometimes users themselves have to avoid obstacles; sometimes they can just point to a place, and the avatar itself will find a path.

On the kinetic level of interaction the user's character has great freedom of movement and excellent opportunities for making use of weapons and magic. The possibilities for action on this level are very much like those known from games such as "Doom" and "Marathon".

However, as we ascend the ladder, the possibilities of interaction decrease.

For instance, the criteria for success when solving the quests (the level of the plot) are evaluated according to a set of parameters. This is not a problem in itself, but in Diablo the solutions of various quests are defined by fixed rules - and, in some instances, in a manner that seems neither logical nor obvious. Users must apply trial and error until they more or less accidentally finds the solution. Although users will eventually uncover the hidden texts, they have little more influence upon the narration than in a traditional narrative.

The interactive possibilities decrease even more when we reach the story. In fact, only one sequence of events leads to the conclusion of the story. In principle, these events can be situated far from each other in time, but they have to occur in a definite succession in order to uncover the story.

Thus, on all levels other than the kinetic one, we have a traditional linear story. We can see this if we use Laurel's (1986) classification of interaction into *frequency, range*, and *significance*. These parameters measure how *often* interaction is possible, how *many* possibilities the system sustains, and the degree to which the interactions *influence* the development of the system.

On the kinetic level, it is always possible to influence the system. A relatively large number of actions are supported and these generally have a distinct influence upon the system; for example, there is a significant difference between an untouched level in the maze, and a level where all the monsters are killed. The same is true with regard to solving the quests, but ultimately one can only uncover an already charted story, and this means that two different users of the system will probably obtain similar experiences when they play. At least the experiences will not differ more than those of two people reading the same book.

It is obvious that the influence the user is able to exert is only reflected on the kinetic level. Thus one can hardly consider the computer game Diablo an interactive story, because it only features an interactive disclosure of an already fixed story.

8.5 Remedies

Summarizing, *Diablo* contains the following 10 "faults":

Story

1. Most quests are not story-functional.
2. Some of the quests are not tellable.
3. The characters do not actively plan and scheme.

Plot

4. The central quests are sometimes presented too late in the game. The user cannot piece a coherent story together for an unacceptably long time.
5. The first-person perspective deprives the game designers of techniques for providing relevant information and for varying the relation between story and plot.
6. The system provides a thinly spread amount of partially distorted and irrelevant facts, but never exploits the noble art of conscious deceit.
7. The narration never reaches an acceptable level of suspense because it lacks time pressure.
8. Information acquisition lacks timing.
9. Emotional peaks are too often rendered by non-dramatic verbal descriptions after the fact.

Interaction

10. The system only supports kinetic interactivity. The story does not change as a result of the user's actions.

Which abilities should we add to our friends Leoric, Albrecht, Diablo, Griswold, Adria etc. (not to mention the user's character) to enable them to act a little more professionally?

Let us first reduce the ten problems to three basic deficiencies whence all evil springs.

1. The game should support *run-time construction of behaviours* and their interrelations. This will alleviate problems 1, 3, 7 and the interaction problem 10.
2. Behaviours should be specified with respect to both *story* and *plot*. This will take care of problems 4–9.
3. Characters should contain *recursive structures* that allow representation of others' plans inside one's own. Again this will alleviate problem 3.

Deficiency (3) is treated in Chapter 7, and we shall only discuss numbers (1) and (2) here. Since there are no known solutions to (1) and (2), we will only present a helpful metaphor. Thus, in opposition to the previous suggestions, what follows now is neither based on empirical evidence nor on working systems (although a simple implementation is described in Andersen (1998). A broader theoretical argument can be found in Andersen (1995)).

Run-time construction of behaviours involves two main steps, building behaviours and stringing behaviours together to make stories. If behaviours are implemented as procedures, the first step consists in assigning actual values to their formal parameters; the second step consists in constructing the hierarchical call-structure among the procedures.

However, standard programming techniques are not a good metaphor for several reasons:

1. Partially instantiated procedures must make sense which it does not do in standard programming. The reason is that a partially specified behaviour, such as "*Someone* will kill Albrecht", must be able to influence the story of Diablo. In horror movies, the suspense hinges on the even less specified "*Someone* will kill *Someone*".
2. Assignment of values to formal parameters is an important part of the story. For example, replacement of "Someone" by "Lazarus" in "*Someone* will kill Albrecht" is not a technical event "behind the scenes" but a *decision*, an important happening in the story.
3. The call structure of procedures must be variable and open to user influence.

In the following we introduce a chemical metaphor.

The atoms are the characters, the available tools and objects, and the possible behaviours. In the beginning, all atoms are scattered randomly: thus we start in a highly entropic situation.

We now define two kinds of forces working on these atoms. The first type attract characters, tools and objects to behaviours (or repel them). In this way simple narrative molecules are formed. The second type attract and repel behaviours.

The forces are assumed to work concurrently. In this way we hope to introduce order into our primordial "narrative soup".

The soup is floating in a four-dimensional container whose dimensions are: *Modality* × *Story-time* × *Plot-time* × *Urgency*. All behaviours are points in this space and can move, influenced by the forces.

Modality represents the possibility of behaviours (cf. Section 7.4.1). The highest value represents the *enactment* of the behaviour. *Story-time* represents the time of the behaviour in the fictive world, whereas *plot-time* is the time that is presented to the user. *Urgency* represents the pressure on a behaviour to be enacted. It is different from modality, since we can have behaviours that are highly desired, but nearly impossible (for example, in *The Lord of the Rings*, Frodo's destruction of the ring is highly desired but almost impossible).

Each behaviour has a "valence", i.e. it requires certain roles to be filled (Section 7.3.6). For example, "robbing" requires an agent, a victim and an object of value. Only when the behaviour has attracted items to fill these roles can it be enacted (for example, the agent = Snotspill, Victim = Gabriel, and Object = relic). The more urgent a behaviour is, the more arduously will it attract items to it.

The primary "bonding process" must have restrictions; for example, in some cases, a character can bond with only one behaviour at a time (Gabriel can only talk to one character at a time). Conversely, some behaviours can bond with only one character (only one person can carry the ring in *The Lord of the Rings*, but the role as ring-bearer oscillates between Gollum, Frodo and Sam).

In this way we can have conflicts about who is to do what. Should I fight the goblins or rescue Albrecht? Should Frodo or Sam carry the ring?

Adding material to a behaviour makes the behaviour more possible. Since the distance between a character and a behaviour makes sense (Figure 7.19), the movement of a character to and from a behaviour can be a part of the story and create suspense: that Lazarus *decides* to betray the king is an interesting event.

As indicated, these primary processes can be implemented by forces attracting and repelling story-atoms. Urgent behaviours attract characters more powerfully than less urgent ones. A character can be forced away from less urgent behaviours (which thus cannot be enacted) to more important ones (for example, Strider is removed from his patrolling duties in order to guide Frodo).

After a molecule is enacted it dissolves, and its components are free to combine with other behaviour-atoms (when Sam's obligations to Frodo are over, he can marry his Rose and have children).

Let us now turn to the formation of strands of molecules, stories. Normal means/end planning can use the techniques suggested by Maes (Section 7.3.2), where an enacted means causes its end to increase its value of possibility, i.e. enacted means attract their ends. For example, arriving at Mount Doom increases the possibility of Frodo throwing the ring into the pit. Conversely, enacted countermeasures repel the behaviours they aim at preventing.

Figure 8.3 shows the climax of *The Lord of the Rings. Being at Mount Doom* drags *Frodo throws the ring into the pit* along with it as it grows more possible. The behaviour *Gollum steals the ring* has been a constant liability all along, but is suddenly enacted to prevent Frodo from succeeding: when Gollum's behaviour approaches the "enactment" line, it repels Frodo's behaviour into the realm of impossibility.

If we want to implement normal causality, we can ensure that means precede their ends by making them repel their ends to their right. However, sequentiality need only be observed when close to enactment; as long as behaviours are virtual, the

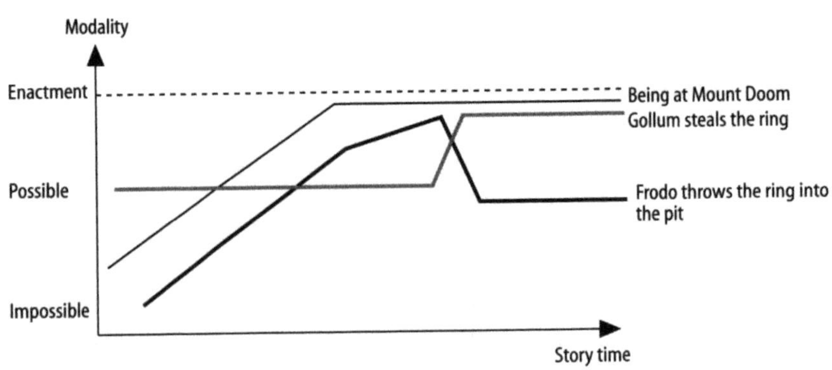

Figure 8.3 The climax of *The Lord of the Rings*.

forces regulating their chronological sequence can be very weak. Thus, sequencing slowly emerges as behaviours approach the critical limit of enactment.

Behaviours live simultaneously in two time dimensions, the story-time and the plot-time. What was said above concerns the story-time but not necessarily the plot-time. A behaviour can be enacted invisibly to the user, "backstage" in story-time, and only later be re-enacted "front-stage", e.g. as a verbal description delivered by a character.

Plot-time must be able to influence story-time. For example, if the treason of Lazarus must be enacted simultaneously in story-time and plot-time, but the user happens to be in place where he cannot see it, then plot-time can ask story-time to create a witness that observes the treason, flees to the user's location and squeals.

Designing and playing games in this architecture involves the same operation: influencing forces. Thus there is a gradual transition between design and use.

References

Aarseth, E. (1997) *Cybertext – Perspectives on Ergodic Literature.* Baltimore, MD: The Johns Hopkins University Press.

Andersen, P. Bøgh (1998) Multimedia phase-spaces. In *Multimedia Tools and Applications* 6: 207–237.

Andersen, P. Bøgh (1995) The force dynamics of interactive systems. Towards a computer semiotics. *Semiotica* 103(1/2): 5–45.

Bordwell, D. (1985) *Narration in the Fiction Film.* London: Methuen.

Bordwell, D. and Thompson, K. (1997) *Film Art. An Introduction.* New York: McGraw-Hill.

Jensen, J. F. (1997) Interaktivitet. In *Mediekultur* No. 26. SMID.

Larsen, C. B. and Petersen, B. C. (1999) *Interactive Storytelling in a Multimodal Environment.* Student Project, Intelligent Multimedia, Institute of Electronic Systems, University of Aalborg.

Laurel, B. K. (1986) Interface as mimesis. In *User Centered System Design* (eds. D. A. Norman and S. W. Draper). Hillsdale, NJ: Lawrence Erlbaum.

Laurel, B. (1991) *Computers as Theatre.* Redwood City, CA: Addison-Wesley.

Maes, P. (1989) How to do the right thing. *Connection Science Journal* 1(3), 291–323. (Quoted from `http://pattie.www.media.mit.edu/`.)

Ryan, M.-L. (1991) *Possible Worlds, Artificial Intelligence and Narrative Theory.* Bloomington & Indianapolis: Indiana University Press.

9

Aspects of Interactive Autonomy and Perception

Claus B. Madsen and Erik Granum

9.1 Introduction

The purpose of this chapter is to approach the issue of autonomous agents from a more technical, pragmatic and concrete point of view than that of the other chapters in the book. In particular, this chapter offers a contrasting perspective to Chapter 7.

Andersen and Callesen use concepts from fields such as literature, film, theatre and language theory to set some requirements for the design, or the architecture as it were, of autonomous agents. In this context it can be termed a *top-down* approach to agent design. As Andersen and Callesen point out, others have used inspiration from biology and ethology to design autonomous agents. Again a top-down approach.

The present paper takes a *bottom-up* approach. In effect, we have set out to create some concrete examples of interactive autonomous agents in order to "learn" from experience how they can be designed, and especially how practical issues inform the design of the agent architecture, the elements in it, and how they interact.

This is not to say that our work with autonomous agents is not based on any philosophy. But the philosophy is quite simple: the agents must be truly autonomous, capable of relating in a sensible manner to all aspects of a seamless, continuous, simulated virtual world. That is, the agents must relate to the spatial properties of the virtual world, the dynamics of it and the events that take place in it in a continuous and consistent manner. Here we mean as continuously as can be implemented on a computer, and consistent means not violating any expectations concerning the structure of time and space which the simulated world suggests in the observer.

What we are aiming at is a unified framework for how an agent can relate to (perceive and act on) a simulated world. That is, we are not willing to accept any kind of special cases. For example, a sheep agent and a troll agent should be based on exactly the same formalism, only "running different scripts" (playing different roles). Additionally, the mechanisms with which an agent relates to all objects in the simulated world should be the same, independently of whether the object is a house, another agent, or a real human represented by an avatar. That is, an agent should perceive and interact with an avatar exactly as it would with any other agent – no special cases.

Franklin and Graesser (1996) formulate an autonomous agent definition which is generally accepted within the community:

> An autonomous agent is a system situated within, and a part of, an environment, which senses that environment and acts on it, over time, in pursuit of its own agenda, and so as to affect what it senses in the future.

In addition to this definition, Franklin and Graesser (1996) present a set of properties which can be associated with autonomous agents according to their functionality. The agents we are interested in have three properties from this set, i.e. an agent must: (1) be proactive – the agent does not simply act in response to the environment, they should also initiate actions on their own accord, (2) be communicative – the agent communicates with other agents (possibly including people), and (3) have character – the agent has believable "personality" and emotional states.

This chapter by no means describes a completely developed agent architecture which lives up to the above goals. Rather, it can be viewed as a status report on ongoing work towards creating an architecture for a flexible autonomous agent, and a simulated virtual world in which the agent can live. We have looked in some depth at a number of issues relating to the design of autonomous agents, and this chapter attempts to present some of the experiences we have made and how these experiences have driven our efforts.

To anticipate one of the messages of the chapter, it has turned out that much of our work thus far has focused on the perceptual system of agents. In fact, we have discovered how important it is to have a thoroughly designed perceptual functionality. There may be two reasons for this:

- All the people behind the work in this chapter have some background in computer vision (computerized analysis of video images), and the application thereof for controlling robots.
- An autonomous agent will by its very nature run some kind of continuous sense–plan–act loop. Thus sensing capabilities are important, and in some manner come before much else can be investigated.

The latter issue seems to be inherent in the study of autonomous agents, whereas the former serves as information to the reader of the particular background we have for working with this problem. For years we have been studying vision-controlled robots interacting with the real world; now we have taken an interest in working with robots with personality, living in a virtual world.

The structure of the chapter is as follows. First we describe a particular autonomous agent in some detail. The agent is a character called Bouncy (Figure 9.1), and it was our first attempt at designing and implementing autonomous agents (Madsen *et al.*, 1999). In Section 9.3 we then describe some alternative formalisms, or architectures, for agents. Based on the experience gained from designing Bouncy, and the

Figure 9.1 Bouncy, an interactive dog-like bouncing ball, is a prototypical example of an interactive autonomous agent.

discussion of alternative architectures, we argue for dividing agents into two layers: a high-level and a low-level layer, or a subjective and an objective layer. This is discussed in Section 9.4. From here on the chapter focuses on the low-level, objective, layer, and presents in some depth our work with issues such as agent perception, sensory input and (spatial) memory (Section 9.5), and the use of memory for spatial reasoning (Section 9.6).

9.2 Bouncy – a Simple Interactive Agent

The main purpose of designing and implementing the Bouncy character was to gain insight into the computational models for autonomous agents, capable of partaking in believable and engaging interaction with humans (and other agents). Thus the main focus behind the design of Bouncy was *interaction*, and the entire character, or role, of Bouncy was centred on a carefully planned interaction.

Subsequently we describe the design of Bouncy focusing on the control of the agent's innate behaviours, specifically how the notions of time and perceived stimuli affect the internal state of the agent, which in turn affect agent behaviour. Bouncy is implemented as a 3D animated character. Bouncy has been demonstrated to hundreds of people, and though conceptually simple, he has been wholeheartedly accepted by people in all age groups.

9.2.1 Bouncy Scenario and Interaction

The interaction scenario comprises Bouncy in a simulated 3D virtual environment and a single human user in the real world. Bouncy moves around by bouncing up

Table 9.1 The relationship between what the user does and how Bouncy interprets the intention of what the user does.

User's behaviour		Bouncy's perception of user
Glove input	Microphone input	
None	Shouting	"Master is calling me"
Pointing	Shouting	"Master is scolding me"
Open hand	Talking	"Master is petting/comforting me"

and down (hence the name Bouncy). He is able to express various emotions (happy, sad etc.) by actuating his mouth, eyes and tail, and by the intensity with which he bounces.

Interaction with Bouncy is facilitated by several interface modalities. Bouncy is displayed to the user on a graphical display. Bouncy also produces a "bounce sound" while bouncing. Conversely, the user can communicate with Bouncy through a microphone and a dataglove, which is used to characterize the posture of the user's hand. The actions of the user are perceived by Bouncy as described in Table 9.1.

9.2.2 Bouncy Behaviour Repertoire, Control and Personality Model

Bouncy has three main behaviours, one of which is further divided into three sub-behaviours:

- **PLAY**: causes Bouncy to wander about and play
- **SLEEP**: causes Bouncy to cease any current activity, lie down and sleep
- **INTERACT**: causes Bouncy to go to and follow the user plus engage in interaction. Sub-behaviours:
  - **tease**: pay attention to user but do not approach
  - **please**: approach user, bounce, wag tail and smile
  - **have-the-blues**: stop bouncing, break eye-contact, look sad

These behaviours constitute the states in a Finite State Automaton (Figure 9.2), in which state transitions occur based on events generated in Bouncy's personality model. The above description of Bouncy's "states" clearly illustrate that the behavioural repertoire is very limited. In fact, it should be quite easy to picture the range of interactions one can have with Bouncy.

Typically, Bouncy will be bouncing around and playing, and when the user calls him, he approaches. Then if the user speaks loudly, while pointing a finger, Bouncy will gradually become sad and enter the **have-the-blues** behaviour. If the user then speaks while keeping an open hand, Bouncy will enter the **please** behaviour again. If the user does not do anything, Bouncy will get bored after a while and enter the **play** behaviour, and thus move away from the user (away from the screen) and start playing. At any point in time, Bouncy may become tired enough to go to **sleep**, a behaviour from which he wakes up after a while.

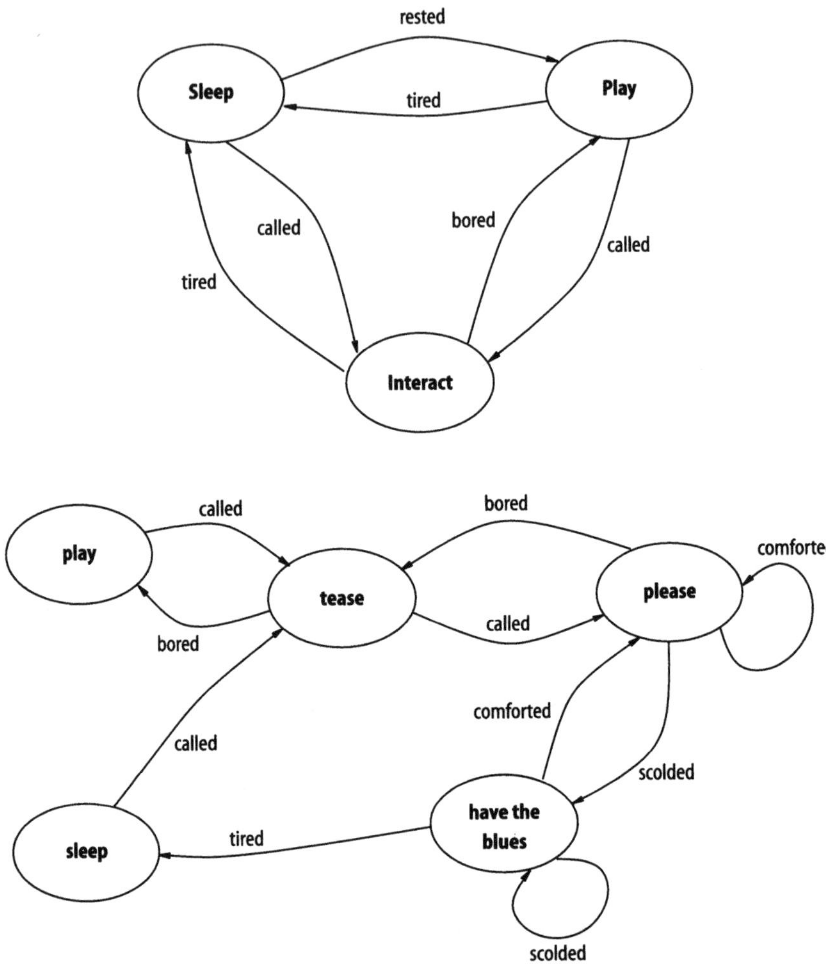

Figure 9.2 Left: the super-ordinate Finite State Automaton (FSA) of Bouncy; right: the FSA including the sub-states of the **interact** state.

The overall behaviour of Bouncy, or its dramaturgic frame, is fully described by the FSA in Figure 9.2. Yet the mechanism for determining when and why to switch from one behaviour to another is a different matter all together. In all autonomous agents this mechanism is related to the personality and the mood of the agent. These concepts are normally characterized by their static/dynamic nature:

- Personality – describes the static traits of a character, and undergoes little or no change over time
- Mood – describes the current mental state of the character at any point in time, and responds directly to changes in the character's situation

Concerning personality traits, work on autonomous agents often borrows from psychology. An often used taxonomy is the so-called five-factor model (McCrae and Costa, 1989). The model comprises extroversion, agreeableness, conscientiousness, neuroticism and openness. While it can be useful to apply these factors in

Table 9.2 Generating internal events from qualitative characterizations of the combined state of Bouncy's internal mood variables. The events drive the behaviour FSA of Bouncy (Figure 9.2). The emboldened entries indicate that the value of the corresponding variable is weighted higher than the other variables, i.e. is the determining factor.

	Excitedness	Sleepiness	Happiness
Rested		low	
Tired	low	high	low
Bored	low		
Comforted	low	not low	
Scolded		high	low

characterizing an agent, it is more doubtful whether they map well onto a computational scheme. Autonomous agents that make extensive use of this are yet to be seen, although some attempt at using personality traits explicitly in autonomous agents is demonstrated by Silva *et al.* (1999).

On the other hand an often used computational model for an agent's mood is a set of numeric variables, which change values over time. In the design of Bouncy we used three such variables: excitedness, sleepiness and happiness. All three variables range between –1 and 1. For example, a combination of excitedness being 1 and happiness being –1, would correspond to an agitated, angry Bouncy. Bouncy does not have such a state, and thus this can be characterized as a personality trait of Bouncy: it cannot be angry. Instead scolding makes it sad, i.e. it enters the **have-the-blues** state.

The FSA of Bouncy is controlled by events generated based on the values of the three described mood variables (Table 9.2). An event corresponds to "how Bouncy feels". For example, referring to the table, if excitedness is low, happiness is low, and sleepiness is high, then a **tired** event will be generated. The higher excitedness and happiness are, the higher sleepiness needs to be in order to generate the event. Depending on the current state of the FSA (Figure 9.2), the event will trigger a jump to the **sleep** state.

Naturally, the mood variables must change their values over time. Table 9.3 summarizes what happens to the mood variables as a function of time and user action, and as a function of what the current state of the FSA is. Thus, if the current state is **sleep** the excitedness variable will gradually be reset to zero, as will happiness, i.e. the **sleep** state is used to "neutralize" Bouncy's mood. And of course sleepiness is gradually reduced as a function of time. Also, if in the **sleep** state, any sound from the user will cause an increment in excitedness. This is used to make it possible for the user to "wake up" Bouncy when he is sleeping, because the **rested** event is also influenced by the value of the excitedness variable (Table 9.2). The higher the excitedness, the lower sleepiness needs to be in order to generate a **rested** event).

To summarize the behaviour control of Bouncy:

- time and user actions influence Bouncy's internal mood variables

Table 9.3 Qualitative schemes for incrementing/decrementing Bouncy's internal mood variables as a function of time, and as a function of the user's actions (sound, pet = sound plus open hand, scold = sound plus pointed finger). The **tease** state has been omitted to make the table less wide.

	Sleep		Blues			Play		Please		
	Sound	Time	Scold	Pet	Time	Sound	Time	Scold	Pet	Time
Excitedness	↑	→0	↓			↑	↓		↑	
Sleepiness		↓			↑		↑			↑
Happiness		→0	↓	↑	↓		→0	↓	↑	

Nomenclature	
Increment:	↑
Decrement:	↓
Reset:	→0

- various combinations of mood variable values generate events corresponding to "how Bouncy feels", e.g. rested, comforted.
- the events trigger state changes in the overall FSA, causing Bouncy to switch behaviour.
- the current state determines how time and user action influence the change in the mood parameters.

While the use of an FSA may seem to result in very abrupt changes in Bouncy's behaviour, the user does not really notice these changes, as Bouncy's facial expression is linked to the exact values of the happiness and excitedness (Figure 9.3).

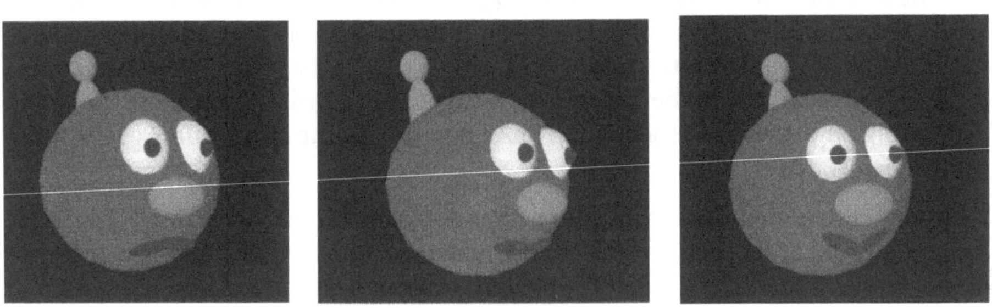

Figure 9.3 The facial expression of Bouncy is linked directly to the happiness and excitedness variables, and thus changes smoothly.

9.2.3 Extensions to the Original Bouncy Concept

In the above we have described the initial version of the Bouncy agent. Later work involved additions to the basic concepts in terms of further developing Bouncy's ability to perceive the intentions of the user. Specifically, a speech processing module was developed which enabled an analysis of the pitch and rate-of-speech of the user in order to determine whether the user utterance was intended as "approval" or "disapproval" (Brøndsted *et al.*, 1999). So far no actual speech recognition (speech to text) module has been developed for Bouncy.

Additionally, we have worked on extending Bouncy's ability to act in a virtual world with obstacles. The previously described behaviours affect the agent's "physical" degrees of freedom, in a manner where they do not interfere with each other. For example, Bouncy can smile both while bouncing and at rest. Yet there are situations where a compromise has to be made between what two or more behaviours dictate, for example when trying to approach the user (user's avatar) but the direct path is obstructed by an obstacle.

To solve this problem we have designed a formalism, Multiple Objective Action Selection (Pirjanian, 1998), for simultaneously satisfying the demands of several parallel behaviours requiring control of the agent's degrees of freedom.

Thus Bouncy can act in an environment with obstacles. Furthermore, we have experimented with flocks of Bouncys, where one Bouncy acts as leader dog and the others merely follow (Pirjanian *et al.*, 1998). Because they all are independent autonomous agents, follow-dogs may be forced to take alternative paths in order to avoid obstacles, but they will always attempt to catch up with the leader.

9.3 Alternative Autonomous Agent Architectures

In the previous section we described the architecture behind the Bouncy interactive agent. Two elements were central in this architecture: a small set of numerical mood variables and a Finite State Automaton for modelling the overall behaviour of the character. While the use of numeric mood parameters is standard in all autonomous agents (though their meaning may vary), there are alternative architectures. Two such alternatives are described in the subsequent sections.

9.3.1 The Blumberg Agent Architecture

An agent architecture has been developed by Blumberg (1997) with the explicit purpose of creating interactive characters for entertainment and educational purposes. The architecture has many similarities to the FSA approach of Bouncy, only instead of an FSA, Blumberg's agents employ a hierarchical tree structure of behaviours that the agent may engage in. It is the task of each behaviour to determine its "Level of Interest" at every point in time. An action selection mechanism then chooses which behaviour is most appropriate (Figure 9.4). Behaviours are organized in behaviour groups, and within such a group all behaviours are considered equally important. Thus all behaviours in a group compete.

The computation of the Level of Interest of a behaviour is primarily based on values produced by something called Releasing Mechanisms (RM). An RM filters the agent's sensory input so as to search for objects or events that help determine the appropriateness of a behaviour. Thus, an RM is object/event-dependent and the output is a continuous value. There are three primary phases to producing such an RM output value:

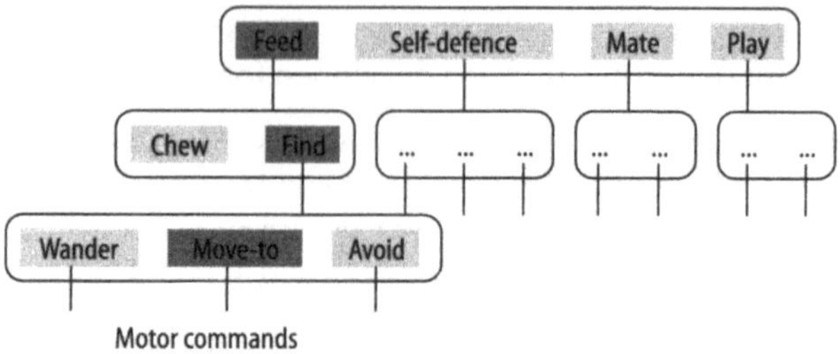

Figure 9.4 The behaviours in the top-level group compete for the control of the character at every time step. The winning behaviour may have a child group. Inside this child group all behaviours are allowed to compete. This continues all the way to the bottom of the tree. In this example the top-level behaviour Feed has won (shaded dark), allowing Chew and Find to compete, where Find has won, allowing Wander, Move-to and Avoid to compete, and among those Move-to has won.

1. Find phase: search through the sensory input for the presence of a particular object or event.
2. Filter phase: determine whether the object or event satisfies some requirements.
3. Weighting phase: determine the output value based on some criteria.

An example RM could be a "mouse detector" used for triggering the feed behaviour of a cat, which only likes white mice: (1) sift through the sensory input to see if there are any mice around, (2) if there is a mouse, determine if it is white, and (3) dependent on the distance to the white mouse compute an output value. The output value of such an RM is combined with the values of the agent's internal mood variables, for example hungriness, to produce the Level of Interest for the feed behaviour.

The description given here of the Blumberg agent architecture is quite simplified, as it contains many subtle aspects. Yet the important issues are the hierarchical organization of competing behaviours, where the competition is based on computations of behaviour Level of Interest, which in turn is based on output values from Releasing Mechanisms.

9.3.2 The JAM Agent Architecture

The Finite State Automaton approach of Bouncy and the agent architecture of Blumberg have their roots in, among others, behaviour-based systems and reactive systems thinking, which Rodney Brooks among others has advocated for many years (Brooks, 1986, 1991).

The JAM agent architecture (Huber, 1999) has its roots in more traditional AI, operating with explicit goals and plans, and reasoning about pre- and post-conditions of plans. The JAM architecture is shown schematically in Figure 9.5. The world model is a database that represents the current beliefs of the agent. The plan library is a collection of plans that the agent can use to achieve its goals. The interpreter is the agent's "brains", which reason about what the agent should do and when it should do it. The intention structure is an internal model of the goals and activities the agent currently has and keeps track of the progress that the agent has made towards accomplishing those goals. The observer is a lightweight plan that the agent executes between plan steps in order to perform functionality outside of

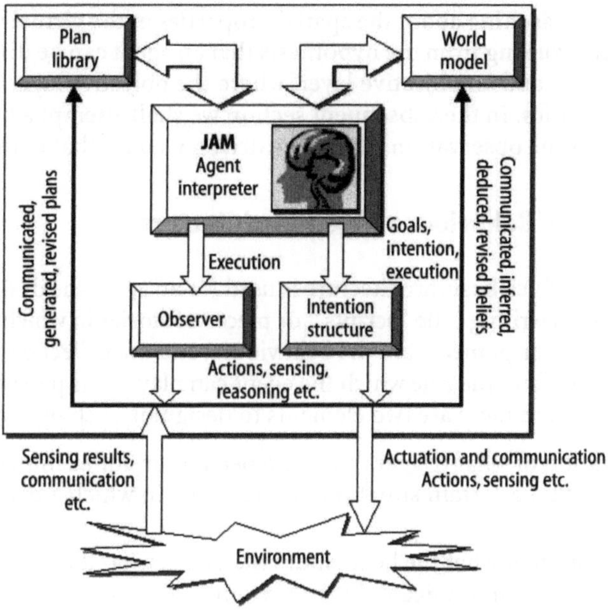

Figure 9.5 Schematic overview of the JAM agent architecture.

the scope of its normal goal/plan-based reasoning, e.g. update mood variables and process sensory input.

Changes to the world model or posting of new goals trigger reasoning to search for plans that might be applied to the situation (this list of plans is called the Applicable Plans List, or APL). The JAM interpreter selects one plan from the APL and *intends* it, i.e. commits itself to execute the plan. The act of intending the plan places the now-instantiated plan onto the agent's intention structure, where it becomes one of possibly several intentions. The newly intended plan may or may not be immediately executed, depending on the plan's utility relative to that of the intentions already on the intention structure.

9.4 Dividing Agents Into Layers

In the previous two sections we have described three different agent architectures: the Finite State Automaton (FSA) approach of Bouncy, the Blumberg agent architecture, and the JAM agent architecture. Through various projects, and over a period of approximately one year, we have accumulated experience with: (1) the FSA approach from the work with Bouncy, (2) the Blumberg architecture from implementing three specific agents using this architecture, and (3) designing and implementing a specific agent using a home-grown less formal architecture not described here.

During this work we have made some observations that have caused us to start specifically studying the interplay between an agent's perceptual system and its use of a memory for reasoning about the spatial properties of the virtual world. In fact, we are currently working from the hypothesis that an agent can be divided into two layers: a subjective and an objective layer, where the objective layer is the current focus of our activities. In the subsequent section we shall attempt a brief presentation of the gist of the observations that have driven us onto that path.

9.4.1 Scripting of Behaviour in Agent Architectures

Independently of which basic architecture is used for an agent the design of a *particular* agent involves writing little "scripts", or pieces of stories in which the agent can be involved. These script pieces are the behaviours, and the collection of behaviours in some manner defines the role which the agent can play, or its personality. In relation to this discussion there are two elements to designing such behaviours:

- a characterization of what triggers a certain behaviour, for example a way for the agent to detect that a certain situation has occurred in which a particular behaviour is relevant.
- a careful definition of what the behaviour entails, i.e. what the agent should *do* in order to exhibit or communicate this behaviour.

Using this point of view the main difference between the three described agent architectures lies in the triggering of behaviours. In the FSA approach of Bouncy, the triggering is done using characteristic sentiments defined from combinations of the mood variables. In the Blumberg architecture triggering is done via the Releasing Mechanisms and their influence on each behaviour's Level of Interest. In the JAM architecture each plan has a set of pre-conditions that must be met for the plan to be relevant.

In principle every computer program can be modelled as an FSA, and thus it cannot be argued that the JAM and Blumberg architectures can realize agents which an FSA approach cannot. Nevertheless, there are some valid arguments against using an FSA as the underlying design tool for agents that are more complex than the Bouncy example.

One way to think about this is the following. Blumberg and JAM agents can be considered as FSAs where there is a potential connection from (almost) any state to (almost) any other state. This means that the resulting agent has more freedom to switch between behaviours. This gives the Blumberg and JAM agents a higher chance of emergence, i.e. an overall behaviour of the character, which is more intriguing, unexpected and multi-faceted than with a strict FSA – something other than what the designer expected or explicitly planned, but nevertheless in accordance with the character's personality. Thus the latter two approaches are more flexible and extensible: additional behaviours can be added to the personality of an agent, without explicitly designing how the new behaviours interact with the behaviours already present.

One way to summarize the above is to say that an FSA-based design emphasizes strict scripting, by defining what the agent *should* do in a certain situation. The Blumberg and JAM agent designs emphasize emergence by focusing on what the agent *could* do.

Nevertheless, a combination of strict scripting on one hand and the chance of emergence on the other is to be preferred. Therefore scripted fixed linear sequences must be built into Blumberg or JAM agents. This is because there sometimes is a need to be able to *guarantee* a fixed sequence of events in order for a behaviour to make sense. Consider a get-acquainted-with behaviour of a dog-like creature. Such a behaviour could be triggered when an unknown object entered the dog's knowledge of the world, and a possible "script" of such a behaviour might be:

1. face the new object
2. slowly approach
3. circle the object at a safe distance
4. move close and sniff
5. engage in an appropriate interaction, for example eat, bite, lick, flee

9.4.2 Agent Perception and Memory

Another main area of observations we have made relates to the issues of agent perception: the use of memory for storing perceptual information and for reasoning about the agent's relationship to the world. In this context there are at least two relevant types of perception and thus also memory:

- spatial perception and memory – this deals primarily with the 3D structure of the virtual world and the objects in it, and is associated with the normal senses, such as vision, hearing (audio) and touching (tactile).
- episodic perception and memory – as opposed to the spatial perception the episodic perception has a much stronger relationship to a notion of time, the linear progression of events over time and their causal relationships, e.g. "one event leading to another"

While we shall not pretend to have much in-depth knowledge about the latter, there are a few comments to associate with the agent architectures presented. Each of the three architectures has the possibility of maintaining some measure of episodic memory. For example, it is easy to extend the Bouncy concept so that it will wander off and start playing if the user has made it sad and happy three times in a row. That is, each agent can keep track of its *own* decisions and what characterized the situations leading to these decisions. Similarly, all three agent architectures operate with dynamic internal mood variables, which are influenced by the passing of time (hunger increases as a function of time and activity). Thus there is some measure of explicit use of a temporal dimension. Nevertheless, to our knowledge there is still no autonomous agent research which deals with episodic perception and memory in a unified, structured manner, especially when it concerns events or episodes relating to other agents and their decisions. The main problems here are how to represent "episodes", how to identify/recognize them, and how to reason about them.

Other than what is pointed out in this section we have not yet performed thorough investigations into the area of episodic and temporal issues. This is not to say that episodic memory is not important! Even a rudimentary interplay between spatial and episodic memory is absolutely essential to create the simplest believability enhancing effects. Consider for example the get-acquainted-with behaviour described in Section 9.4.1. Imagine the following scenario:

- A dog agent sees a cat for the first time and decides to get acquainted with it.
- After having gotten to the circling stage of the behaviour the dog agent notices a human off to one side.
- The partial acquaintance with the cat and the novelty of the human might trigger the dog to start a get-acquainted-with behaviour on the human.
- The dog may be in a dilemma as to which object to further investigate first, and thus may go back and forth between the cat and the human.
- The dog may finally decide that the cat poses no threat and the human offers some promise of entertainment, if not food.

In order to enable the above simple scenario, the dog agent needs both a spatial memory and some measure of episodic memory. It needs spatial memory because it needs to remember the presence of the cat when it turns to the human and vice versa, and it needs episodic memory because it needs to remember how far into the get-acquainted-with ritual it has got with each object when switching back and forth in the dilemma situation. Having pointed this out we shall abandon the issue of episodic memory altogether, and from here on we shall deal exclusively with the spatial perception based on models of senses such as vision and audio, and the relationship of the sensory input to a spatial memory.

Concerning spatial perception, none of the agent architectures presented places any constraints on how the agent perceives the virtual world. All three architectures assume that the agent has access to whatever knowledge of the virtual world is relevant for the agent and its behaviour repertoire. Thus this is an open issue, with no constraints imposed by the architectures, and this is one reason why we have studied this area in some detail, as will be described in later sections.

Concerning spatial memory only one of the described architectures explicitly models and employs such a functionality, namely the JAM agent architecture. JAM agents have a world model which stores the beliefs of the agent. On the other hand, the two other architectures base their behaviour triggering on sensory information, and for that purpose there need not be any difference between what is actual, current sensory information, and what are memories of objects perceived in the past.

In summary, it appears that no agent architectures impose any constraints on how the perceptual system of the agent should work and how it should be backed up by a spatial memory.

9.4.3 The Objective vs. the Subjective Layer

In the previous two sections we have highlighted the areas of agent scripting and perception/memory, and pointed out our main observations regarding them. During working with developing autonomous agents we found ourselves spending a lot of time programming purpose-made sensing capabilities, the planning of agent movements etc. As a consequence, actual agent behaviour design or personality/role issues suffered. That is, every time we wanted to investigate something, too much time was wasted on reimplementing something which had already been made in another context for another agent.

This led us to adopt the working hypothesis that agents could be split into two separate layers: subjective and objective:

- subjective layer – special to a character, or an agent exhibiting a particular personality, playing a specific role
- objective layer – common to all characters, a platform providing functionalities which all agents require

Initially the purpose of designing and implementing the objective layer was to save time later when experimenting with various solutions for the subjective layer. Later the work on the objective layer took on a purpose of its own: to learn about which functionalities are the general ones, i.e. how high in the internal agent hierarchy can we go before it becomes personality or role dependent?

We have subsequently learned (see Chapter 10, which pinpoints some issues concerning engineer vs. humanist points of view), that the borderline between the objective and the subjective layer is fluent/dynamic. We have therefore decided to use the terms High Level Agent layer (HLA) and Low Level Agent (LLA). That is, the LLA is a common platform on which HLAs are built; all HLAs have an LLA beneath, but each of these LLAs is identical, the only difference being some parameters that are set concerning for example the 3D shape of the agent and how it moves.

The LLA provides the HLA with functionalities that deal with sensory input, continuous maintenance of a spatial memory, and spatial reasoning capabilities. Examples of such reasoning capabilities are path planning for moving to various places and planning of how to hide from other agents. The LLA accepts action commands from the HLA and executes them, for example "moveTo X", "follow X", "find X", "fleeFrom X" and "kill X". Essentially everything that involves physical movements in the virtual world, plus making utterances (on request from the HLA).

By nature the LLA is tightly connected to the virtual world. The actual relationship and the architecture of the LLA will be expanded upon in Section 9.5.2. First we describe three different approaches to sensory perception, where the latter is the one we are currently pursuing.

9.5 Maintaining a Spatial Memory Within the Agent

As should be evident from the discussion in the chapter thus far it is vital that agents have (access to) functionalities providing them with sensory information. They need to be able to sense the state of the virtual world in order to relate to it and act on it. In our work we have investigated three different ways of providing agents with sensory information: (1) giving the agent direct access to the geometry database of the virtual world, (2) providing agents with iconic sensory data, e.g. digital images in the case of the vision sense, and (3) higher level partly interpreted sensory information, the so-called percepts.

We applied the first approach in the case of the Bouncy agent. Bouncy had direct access to the geometry database, plus direct access to the microphone input, and the input from the dataglove. In fact the programming code for Bouncy was mixed in with the geometry handling and visualization. While this is an easy and rapid approach for implementing one particular agent, it is not a viable approach for general work on researching autonomous agents.

In the subsequent section we describe some work regarding the two other approaches to generating sensory information for agents. Regardless of the approach it has been imperative for us, that the agent's senses emulate what is intuitively expected of sensory perception; for example, the agent should have limited field-of-vision and limited range of hearing. We consider this an important element in facilitating believability and making it intuitive for the observer (and other agents) to identify with an agent's situation (what it knows and how this might influence its decisions). For this we need a sensory system based on an understandable, realistic functionality: What You Have Sensed Is What You Know – WYHSIWYK.

9.5.1 Iconic Representation of Sensory Information

A 2D digitized image (an array of pixels) is an iconic representation of visual information. Similarly audio samples are an iconic representation of sound. In the case of visual information in particular, a substantial body of research has investigated the use of iconic representations for agent sensory input (Blumberg, 1997; Monsieurs *et al.*, 1999). That is, present the agent with actual images of the virtual world, and let the agent itself recognize objects, judge distances to things etc.

To investigate this issue in the case of vision, we developed a virtual reality computer game taking place in a maze. It was a multi-player game, but the world was also populated by autonomous agents, and there was no exterior way of determining whether a character was an avatar of a human player or an agent. The objective of the game was survival in a world where there are resources (food and ammunition) and everyone can shoot at everyone.

The agents were based on a simple version of Blumberg's architecture with internal mood variables such as anger, health, and hunger. The agents had four basic behaviours: fleeFrom X, hunt X, findResource (food/ammunition), and goBeserk! The latter was a behaviour employed when the situation looked hopeless and self-preservation seemed futile.

The system could perform visual rendering of the dynamic world from the point of view of each character, agents and avatars alike. Additionally, the system could provide an overview of the entire world. Examples of such renderings are shown in Figure 9.6.

The essence here is that each agent had the 2D iconic images provided to it at a rate of approximately five images per second. From these images the agent was able to recognize objects such as doors, walls, characters and resource items, based on shape, size and colour information, i.e. typical computer vision techniques. The agent also had simulated stereo vision in order to judge distance in the virtual

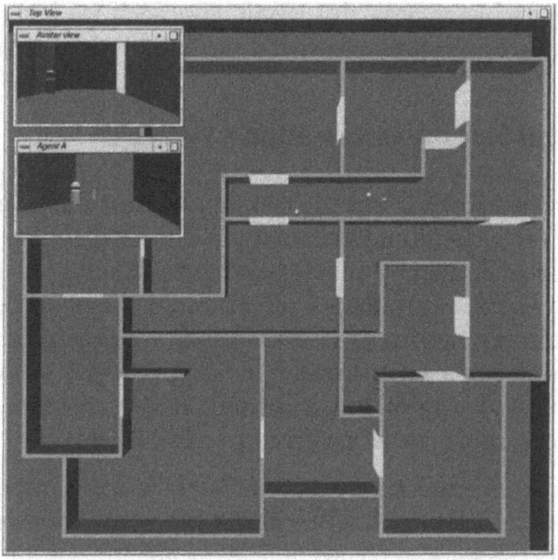

Figure 9.6 The large window shows a scenario overview, and one of the rooms contains an avatar, an agent and a resource (ammunition) item. The topmost of the smaller windows shows what the avatar sees: part of the room and a character (in this case an agent). The other small window shows what one agent sees: part of the room, a character (the avatar) and a resource item.

world. The stereo vision was emulated by utilizing the z-buffering of the graphics engine, similarly to what Monsieurs *et al.* (1999) proposed.

From the visual perception the agent maintains a spatial database at two hierarchical levels:

- inside-room level – while moving about in a room the agent builds a detailed map of the room
- room-to-room level – every room that the agent discovers and maps while roaming about gets inserted in a topological map of the world

The room-to-room level is used for planning at world level, for example going back to the place where the nearest food has been seen. The inside-room level is used for detailed interaction with other characters, for example fleeing from a character; see Section 9.6.3.

From a philosophical point of view the use of iconic representations of sensory data is highly attractive. For example, it facilitates a natural element of sensory imperfection, such as not being able to recognize an object if it is partially hidden by some other object. In fact, this approach emulates real-world sensing as closely as possible: a 3D world is projected to 2D images (e.g. on a human retina), and the 2D images are then analysed to create a *model* of the 3D world.

Nevertheless, technical problems exist. Primarily there is a substantial computational overhead associated with visual rendering of the virtual world from the point of view of all agents. Secondarily it is difficult to achieve suitable performances of the computer vision techniques for analysing the images and providing the agent with a perceived model of the environment, especially if the vision sense is to work properly in all types of environments with any kind of objects and lighting. Because of these technical problems with this iconic approach we have abandoned it in favour of using a more high-level abstract representation for sensory data.

9.5.2 Higher Level Sensory Information – Percepts

In the above described work it was the task of a Virtual Environment server (VE server) to provide each agent (and human user) with images of what they could see at any point in time. Each agent would log onto this VE server in order to subscribe to this functionality, and in turn the VE server would accept and carry out requests for movements from each agent. As such the VE server plays a very important role, in that it simulates an entire virtual world. In fact VE servers are an entire research area on their own, and cannot be completely separated from the autonomous agents since they communicate at such an extensive level.

This chapter will not address VE server issues *per se*, but it is impossible to describe agent perception and reasoning/action without giving an overview of the relationship between the VE server and the agent. Having abandoned the concept of iconic representations of sensory data, our currently ongoing work focuses on the use of so-called percepts. According to *Webster's Dictionary* a percept is "an impression of an object obtained by use of the senses". The word is related to the term "sense datum", which means "an immediate unanalysable private object of sensation". We have designed and built a VE server which Low Level Agents (LLAs) can log onto, and from which LLAs can get sensory data in the form of percepts. The VE server thus simulates, for example, the vision and the auditory senses of each agent, and gives the agent information (percepts) concerning the objects that have been sensed.

Before going into more detail with the content of percepts and the generation thereof, the relationship between the VE server, the LLA and the HLA is depicted schematically in Figure 9.7. On an overall scale the LLA is connected to the VE server, and the HLA is connected to the LLA. The LLA receives percepts from the VE server, and in turn sends movement and sound requests to the VE server. That is, if the agent wants to move, or make a sound, it must request the VE server to

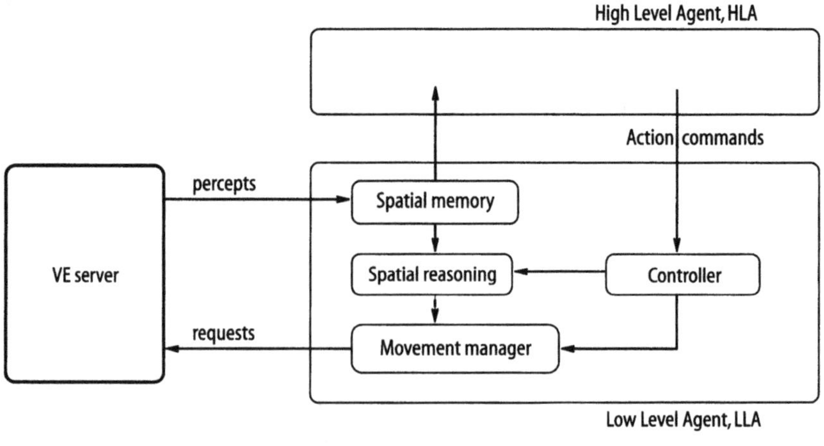

Figure 9.7 Overview of relationship between virtual world, Low Level Agent and High Level Agent.

carry out these actions. Inside the LLA percepts are used to keep the contents of a spatial memory up to date, and this spatial memory is used for planning the movements of the agent, for example planning a path from the current position to some desired position. That is, the HLA can send an action command to the LLA: "moveTo well". The LLA will then plan a path to the well, and follow the path until it arrives at the well. Section 9.6 provides more detail on the spatial reasoning.

As seen from Figure 9.7, the spatial memory of the LLA is a service provided to the HLA. The LLA uses the memory for reasoning about the geometry of the world, e.g. to avoid running into things. But the HLA uses the same memory for "affective reasoning", i.e. figuring out what a particular object in the virtual world "means" to the particular agent. Popularly speaking, a duck in the virtual world merely represents an obstacle or a special location to the LLA. But to the HLA the same duck may represent potential lunch (for a fox agent) or a playmate (for another duck agent). The LLA is the objective layer, whereas the HLA is the subjective character-dependent layer. The HLA utilizes the LLA to carry out action commands, for example "hunt duck" or "playWith duck".

Let us return to the issue of percepts. The VE server generates percepts for all agents, i.e. the front-end sensory apparatus of an agent resides in the VE server. The designed platform supports arbitrary senses, but currently four senses are implemented: (1) vision, (2) audio, (3) tactile and (4) sixth sense (Figure 9.8). The former three are emulations of the natural senses. The latter, the sixth sense, reflects a need for an agent to "feel" the presence of nearby objects, even if they are outside the agent's field of view, and even if they are not making noises. Without this sixth sense an agent would have to turn constantly to monitor the position of objects inside the agent's "personal space".

Figure 9.9 shows a screenshot from a farm scenario loaded into the VE server with a number of LLAs logged on (cows, some sheep in the background, a dog, a farmer, and a sheep in the foreground).

Having thus described the overall mechanism for generating and using percepts in our current system, we can be more specific on the contents of a percept. It is important though to stress that percept content can be anything. It is a completely flexible concept (also in our implementation), and the content listed below merely represents what we have so far identified as useful information for the agents *we* are working with.

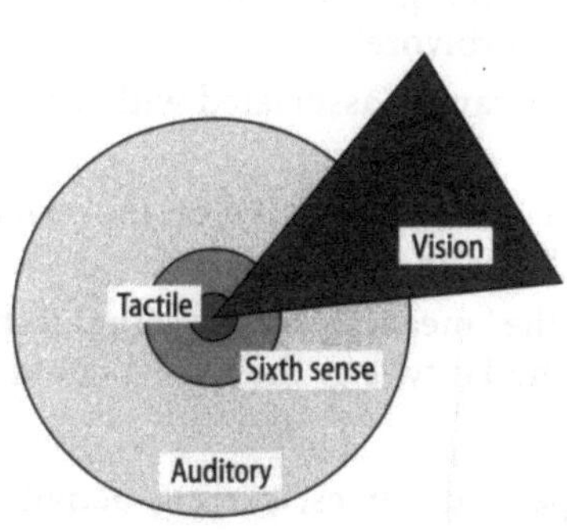

Figure 9.8 Four senses are currently implemented. The spatial properties, e.g. range and field-of-view, of each sense can be modified by the agent itself.

Figure 9.9 Visualization of the range of the agent's senses. The field of view of the vision sense is illustrated as the two lines emanating from the agent, so in the situation shown, the sheep agent is "seeing" the hay bales. Similarly, it is "aware" of the presence of the two cows, since the cows are inside the range of the sixth sense. Furthermore, the farmer and the dog in the back of the scene are within "hearing" range. The tactile sense is triggered if an object comes inside the bounding box around the agent.

Percept content:

- primarily for objective, spatial reasoning
  - ID – the name of the sensed object, e.g. "Duck01" or "Donald"
  - bounding box – the coordinates of the object's bounding box
  - position – the location of the object in the virtual world
  - orientation – how the object is oriented in the virtual world
- primarily for subjective, affective reasoning
  - sensory modality – indicates what sense caused the generation of the percept, e.g. vision
  - types – each object can belong to a number of object categories, for example "animal", "duck" and "herbivore"
  - adjectives – each object can be associated with several qualities, for example "angry" or "hungry"
  - current activity – the current activity of the sensed object, for example "waving", "eating" or "greeting"
  - speech act – indicates the "meaning" of the sound if the object was sensed with the auditory sensing modality, e.g. the sound could mean "refusal", "acceptance", "threat" etc.

The percept fields of types, adjectives, current activity and speech act can be dynamically modified by an agent. For example, a fox agent can tell the VE server that it is currently "eating". This information will then be passed via percepts to all other agents that sense (see, hear etc.) the fox. In this context it is up to the percept-receiving agent to use only as much information from the percept as is relevant given the sense modality that generated the percept. For example, an agent will be notified of the position of an object when hearing it, but it should only use the knowledge about the direction to the object that produced the sound.

In our implemented system, percepts are generated at a rate of 10 per second. This high percept rate is required for the LLA to be able to manoeuvre consistently in the virtual world. For example, to be able to follow the farmer the agent will get an update of the position of the farmer 10 times a second so that it can keep moving in the right direction in a smooth manner. This naturally presumes that the agent can "see" the farmer, i.e. that the farmer is inside the agent's field-of-view, or is close enough to be picked up by the sixth sense.

9.5.3 Spatial Memory as a Database with Entries and Queries

As seen from Figure 9.7, the Low Level Agent maintains a spatial memory, in effect by integrating all the information coming in as percepts. The very first time an object is sensed, i.e. the first time a percept is received concerning some object, the object is created as an instance in a database – the spatial memory. All the available information about the object is stored in the database.

Any subsequent percepts concerning the same object are used to update the information concerning the object in question, for example to update the knowledge of the object's position or its activities. Thus, the LLA is "born" with an empty spatial memory, which gradually gets to contain more and more entries as time passes and the agent has sensed more and more objects. There is no limit to how many objects the LLA can have in the spatial memory, and currently we have not imposed any mechanism for forgetting objects.

The spatial memory supports various queries for information. For example, the spatial memory can return the identity, and any other information, concerning an object of a certain type. This can be used by the High Level Agent to ask the spatial memory questions such as "what is the nearest object of type **hay**?".

The spatial memory also supports various events to be triggered. For example, the HLA can ask the spatial memory to generate an event, if an object of a certain identity comes within a certain range.

As explained, the contents of percepts, and thus the exact information concerning each object in the spatial memory, can be anything. It is up to the designer to decide what is useful information for various types of agent reasoning. As mentioned previously in this chapter, we are currently focusing on the Low Level Agent and its perceptual capabilities, and thus the following section describes some concrete issues relating to spatial reasoning.

9.6 Use of Spatial Memory for Spatial Reasoning

We shall discuss three issues in this context: motion/path planning, avoiding hallucinations and empathetic sensing. The path planning issue is a concrete task that an

LLA needs to be able to perform. The issue of avoiding hallucination deals with making the LLA able to notice, when the state of the virtual world does not correspond to what is recorded in the spatial memory; and empathetic sensing is a term we use to describe the fact that an agent can actually "imagine" what some other agent should be sensing, i.e. "picture the world from another character's point of view".

9.6.1 Path Planning

In order to be able to figure out how to move around in the virtual world an agent needs path planning capabilities. In our system design this functionality resides in the LLA, more specifically in the spatial reasoning module of the LLA (see Figure 9.7). In essence, path planning involves computing an obstacle free path/trajectory from the current position to some desired goal point. A goal point can be the location of some particular object, for example the stable.

Decades of path planning research in the area of mobile robotics have proven that the most flexible and efficient way to perform path planning is to use numerical potential fields composed from considering particular objects in the world to exhibit attractive or repulsive forces (Latombe, 1991).

In Chapter 7 the concept of COMPULSION schemas was described, which is exactly the concept of numerical potential fields. Once a potential field has been computed, the agent can search for a path, guided by the changing values of the potential field. In the simplest case there is only one attractive force (the goal point) and no repulsive forces. The value of the potential field at any location in the virtual world is then proportional to the distance from the location to the goal point. But note that this is not the line-of-sight distance: it is a distance that takes into account the obstacles in the world. In this case a simple gradient descent search strategy can be used to find a path to some goal point.

Figure 9.10 shows two scenarios where a pig agent has been asked to move to one of the two cows behind the fenced pen. In the first case the shortest path is left of the pen, and in the second case the shortest path is right of the pen, by passing between the farmhouse and the tree in the middle of the image. Figure 9.11 shows a longer, more complicated path generated by the pig agent. Every time a path is generated, the entire content of the agent's spatial memory is used to construct a map of the virtual world (as known to the agent at that time), and then the distance-based potential field is computed. Finally, a search algorithm is used to find the path to the desired goal, and the agent then follows the path. If the path is obstructed (e.g. because an object moved in the way), a new path is generated.

Regardless of the fact that potential fields are generally considered the most efficient tool for path planning, some researchers in the autonomous agent community employ other techniques, e.g. Monsieurs *et al.* (1999). We still claim that such techniques cannot solve path planning problems in the case where there are multiple constraints on the path, i.e. that it should not only be the shortest. This case is also discussed in Chapter 7. For example, a duck might want to go to the duck pond while simultaneously having to make sure it does not get too close to the dog. In this case the duck pond will act as an attractor and the dog as a repulsive force.

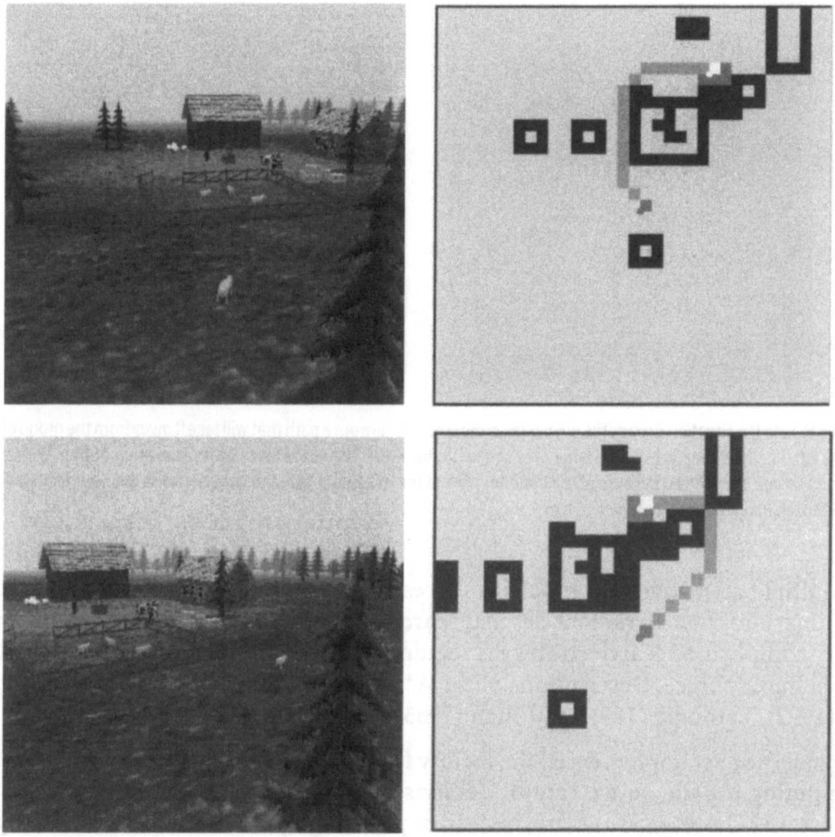

Figure 9.10 Three world snapshots and paths generated by the LLA, in this case a pig. The maps shown on the left are generated by the agent to find the path. In each map light grey represents free space, whereas black represents obstacles. The path is shown in dark grey, and the goal point is indicated by a small white square. In all paths the initial position of the agent is in the centre of the map.

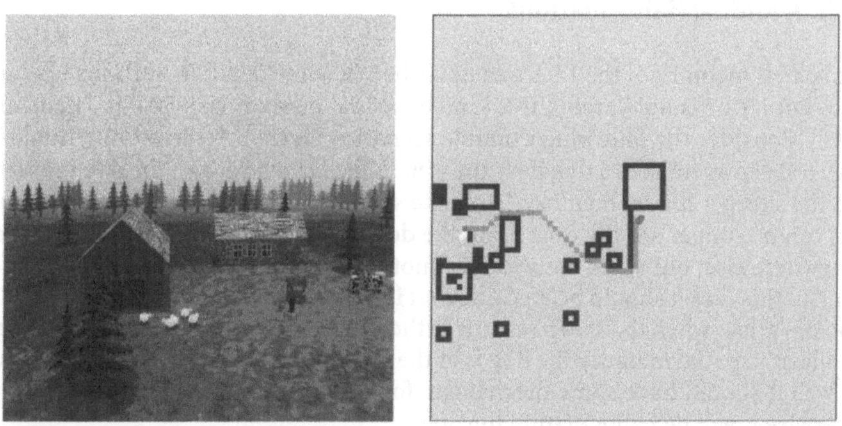

Figure 9.11 In this case the pig agent is hiding in the forest in the rear of the scene, and has planned a path to the dog near the well in the farmyard.

Figure 9.12 In the situation shown, the pig has been ordered to figure out a path that will take it *away* from the group of trees on the left, i.e. "fleeFrom forest". The large grey square in the map is the space taken up by the group of trees the agent is trying to escape from. This is because of the bounding box of the tree group being so large, which is due to a minor technical imperfection in our current VE server.

If multiple attractive and repulsive forces exist, the potential field can have local minima, and then a gradient descent search strategy is not sufficient. In this case a more complicated search strategy is required, and the classical A* search algorithm is a suitable choice. Descriptions of the A* algorithm may be found in Andersen *et al.* (1992), Latombe (1991) and Rich (1983).

We have not yet implemented the facility for combining multiple constraints when computing a path, so we cannot demonstrate this with a concrete example. But Figure 9.12 shows a case where, instead of planning a path *to* some object, the agent has been asked to plan a path *away from* some object. This path is the one which most quickly maximizes the distance to the object, and as such it can be used for planning, for example how to flee from another agent in the virtual world.

9.6.2 Avoiding Hallucinations

The spatial memory of the LLA was described in some detail in Sections 9.5.2 and 9.5.3. But if one is not careful, this kind of spatial memory can lead to "hallucinations". Consider the following example scenario (Figure 9.9 can aid in visualizing this): a sheep agent sees a dog near the well in the farmyard, and the dog is entered into the sheep's spatial memory. Then the sheep goes behind the farm house, and thus can no longer see the dog. Then the dog moves away from the well and goes somewhere else, but since the sheep cannot see the dog, the sheep does not know this. But this is as it should be, because that is the way sensing works in real life. The problem arises when the sheep returns to the well to play with the dog. According to the sheep's spatial memory the dog is at the well. So when the sheep comes back to the well it should have some mechanism for detecting that the dog has vanished. Otherwise it will be hallucinating the dog.

To solve this problem the LLA is capable of determining what it would *expect* to sense at any point in time. That is, according to the contents of the spatial memory, what would I expect to sense right now? This corresponds to people closing their eyes before entering into a room and saying: "I expect to find my computer in this room". If the computer turns out not to be there, this is noticed.

In our LLAs there is a visual imagination (an inner eye) which works on the spatial memory. This inner eye continually determines which percepts are expected right now. For example, when the sheep agent returns to the well it *expects* to see the dog. If the expected percepts concerning the dog do not arrive from the VE server, the object is marked as "vanished". It is not removed from the spatial memory, but only marked as having unknown location and other properties. If, later, a percept concerning the object is received, the "vanished" indicator is removed.

9.6.3 Empathetic Sensing

The visual imagination, the inner eye, as described in the previous section can be used for different purposes. It can be used to estimate what *other* agents can sense. Figure 9.13 shows an example where an agent is using its own spatial memory to predict which areas are invisible to another agent.

Figure 9.13 Using the internally simulated vision sense, the agent can figure out what areas of a scene are hidden from the field of view of another agent, and thus can be used for hiding. In the three examples the white area is what the other agent cannot see, and the grey area is what the other agent *can* see.

Of course, an agent cannot know exactly what another agent knows, but it is possible to make plans from the concept "according to my knowledge of the world, the other person can or cannot sense this or that". This is a fundamental prerequisite in supporting plot structures or narratives based on elements of scheming and conniving. That is, an agent can essentially reason about "I want to make sure he sees this" or "I want to make sure he does not see this". This is a concrete step towards using empathy, or putting one self in the position of others, which is critical to creating suspense and interesting plots, as pointed out in Chapter 7.

9.7 Discussion

In this chapter we have described how our desire to investigate architectures for autonomous agents in interactive virtual environments has led us to divide autonomous agents into two levels: the Low Level Agent and the High Level Agent. The paper has described some important characteristics of the LLA, i.e. its spatial memory, how it is maintained and how it is exploited for spatial reasoning. This entire development was spurred by an interest in having a platform for experimenting with the higher character level of autonomous agents – agents as actors, as it were. The purpose of the LLA is to serve as an objective layer of services, which the HLA can build upon. In the following sections we shall briefly touch upon topics concerning the use of the LLA, and finally we point out a few current activities building upon what has been described in this paper.

9.7.1 Aspects of the Interface Between High and Low Level Agent

The Low Level Agent allows the High Level Agent counterpart access to the spatial memory, and allows the HLA to query information from it. As described the spatial memory also contains information about objects, which is intended solely for affective/subjective reasoning, and as such is only relevant to the HLA. For example, the type of an object is not relevant to the LLA, but highly so to the HLA.

Conversely, the HLA may issue action commands to the LLA. These action commands are of the type "face object" (turn head in direction of object), "moveTo object", "hideFrom object", "hunt object", "playSound" etc.

Within the LLA these action commands are executed according to simple built-in scripts, which are in fact simple Finite State Automata (FSAs). These scripts form a hierarchy which can be combined in arbitrary ways. In fact, all action commands are executed using only three basic actions: moveForwards, turn and playSound. In the near future the LLA will also be able to, upon request, play various animations, i.e. make somersaults, look threatening, look sad, wave etc. The hierarchy allows the LLA to offer a specific way of carrying out an action. For example, the "hunt object" action can be scripted as a sequence of sub-actions: "hideFrom object", "face object" and "moveTo object" (when "object" is facing the other way). Any such sub-actions utilize the moveForwards, turn, playSound and playAnimation action primitives. In this manner the LLA offers an objective way of carrying out higher level actions by making combinations of more primitive ones. The HLA still has access to all levels in this action command hierarchy, if for example it is an illustrative feature of a character's personality to carry out an action in a certain manner. So an HLA can carry out a "hunt object" in another manner than the one pre-scripted into the LLA, should it so desire. This is a clear example of the fact that the borderline between the objective and subjective agent levels has to be fluid/dynamic. Sometimes the way something is done is at least as important as the fact that it is done (see Chapter 10 for more detail on this).

9.7.2 What Does It Mean to Be an Avatar?

Normally the avatar concept relates to the representation of a user in a virtual world. As such, an avatar does not have any capabilities in terms of sensing and acting on its own. All avatar actions are completely and directly controlled by the user via some interface, for example the mouse.

In our work an avatar is an agent where some functionality has been taken over by a human. One way of using an agent as an avatar is for the user to control the *movements* of the avatar, again using some interface. Another possibility is to control the agent's movements using the same level of abstraction as the HLA communicates to the LLA, i.e. using action commands such as "moveTo object". These two possibilities are currently supported in our implementation, but we are actively investigating alternative methods for avatar control.

Regardless of the abstraction level for avatar control, the agent is still "alive" when it is being used as an avatar. That is, it still receives percepts as it would if it were moving around on its own accord. Consequently it is continuously maintaining its spatial memory. Thus at any point in time the user can release the agent from the avatar function, and the agent can continue "as if nothing happened". When the agent is released from the avatar mode it will have a spatial memory which is consistent with what the agent sensed during its stint as avatar. This is a feature we are using in ongoing research projects, where the user is allowed to choose any character in the virtual world and use it as an avatar at any point in time. When an agent is chosen as an avatar, the "virtual camera" being used to visualize the virtual world to the user is attached to the head position of the chosen agent, such that the user sees the world from the point of view of the avatar.

9.7.3 Ongoing and Future Work

We are continually building upon the work described in this paper. Two of the more important active directions of work are investigating architectures for High Level Agents and expanding the interactive capabilities of agents to include a linguistic modality.

We are currently designing a High Level Agent based on many of the ideas behind the agent architecture proposed by Blumberg (1997) (see also Section 9.3.1). Drawing upon our experience as presented in the present paper, we are specifically focusing on designing an agent architecture which actively uses the spatial memory and associated functionalities. This is an aspect we have found to be missing in the original work by Blumberg, and others for that matter.

While working on High Level Agent architectures we are also making provision for incorporating spoken language understanding into agents. Together with a research group at the Centre for Language Technology in Copenhagen we have designed a way for a number of autonomous agents to share a module providing a speech recognizer, a parser and a dialogue manager. Ideally, each agent would have such a separate module, but this is not realistic from a computational point of view. So we have designed a system such that each agent uses the same speech module as a resource which translates whatever is said by the user into something meaningful for the agents. This translation is agent-specific, and only the agents within hearing range of the user's avatar will hear what is said. Conversely, each agent will be able "speak" by sending text to a text-to-speech generator.

In conclusion, we are working towards designing autonomous agents using a bottom-up approach, where we maintain a strong focus on ensuring that the agents do not cheat – What You Have Sensed Is What You Know. There is no such thing as a user; there may be another agent around who is in fact controlled by a human, but this is just a coincidence.

Acknowledgements

The work described in this chapter is all done in fruitful collaboration with numerous people. To mention but a few of the more important, the authors wish to thank Bo Cordes Petersen, Rasmus Agerholm and Paolo Pirjanian for their invaluable contributions.

Finally, the support of the European research project PUPPET, ESPRIT Long Term Research EP 29335 under the i3 Early School Environments programme, and the Danish Research Council research project STAGING is gratefully acknowledged.

References

Andersen, C. S., Madsen, C. B., Sørensen, J. J., Kirkeby, N. O. S., Jones, J. P. and Christensen, H. I. (1992) Navigation using range images on a mobile robot. *Robotics and Autonomous Systems* 10: 147–160.

Blumberg, B. (1997) *Old Trickes, New Dogs: Ethology and Interactive Creatures*, PhD thesis, Massachusetts Institute of Technology, Program in Media Arts and Sciences.

Brøndsted, T., Nielsen, T. D. and Ortega, S. (1999) Affective multimodal interaction with a 3D agent. In *Proceedings: Eighth International Workshop on the Cognitive Science of Natural Language Processing*, Galway, Ireland, pp. 102–109.

Brooks, R. (1986) A robust layered control system for a mobile robot. *IEEE Journal of Robotics and Automation* 1: 14–23.

Brooks, R. (1991) Intelligence without reason, computers and thought lecture. In *Proceedings: International Joint Conference on Artificial Intelligence*, Sidney, Australia.

Franklin, S. and Graesser, A. (1996) Is it an agent, or just a program?: A taxonomy for autonomous agents. In *Proceedings: Third International Workshop on Agent Theories, Architectures, and Languages*. Berlin: Springer-Verlag.

Huber, M. J. (1999) Jam: A bdi-theoretic mobile agent architecture. In *Proceedings: Third International Conference on Autonomous Agents*, Seattle, Washington, pp. 236–243.

Latombe, J.-C. (1991) *Robot Motion Planning*. Boston: Kluwer.

Madsen, C. B., Pirjanian, P. and Granum, E. (1999) Can finite state automata, numeric mood parameters and reactive behaviours become alive? In *Proceedings: Workshop on Behaviour Planning for Life-Like Characters and Avatars*, held in conjunction with the I3 Spring Days, Sitges, Spain, p. 4.

McCrae, R. R. and Costa, P. T. (1989) The structure of the interpersonal traits: Wiggin's circumplex and the five-factor model. *Journal of Personality and Social Phsychology* **6**(4): 586–595.

Monsieurs, P., Coninx, K. and Flerackers, E. (1999) Collision avoidance and map construction using synthetic vision. In *Proceedings: Workshop on Intelligent Virtual Agents*, Salford, UK.

Pirjanian, P. (1998) *Multiple Objective Action Selection and Behaviour Fusion Using Voting*, PhD thesis, Department of Medical Informatics and Image Analysis, Aalborg University, Denmark.

Pirjanian, P., Madsen, C. B. and Granum, E. (1998) *Behaviour-Based Control of an Interactive Life-like Pet*. Technical report, Laboratory of Image Analysis (unpublished).

Rich, E. (1983) *Artificial Intelligence*. New York: McGraw-Hill International Editions.

Silva, D., Siebra, C., Valadares, J., Almeida, A., Frery, A. and Ramalho, G. (1999) Personality-centered agents for virtual computer games. In *Proceedings: Workshop on Intelligent Virtual Agents*, Salford, UK.

10
Discussion

P. Bøgh Andersen, Claus B. Madsen and Erik Granum

The chapters in this section are written by people with rather different backgrounds: some come from the humanities, some from engineering. This is not unique to this book, but is rather the normal state of affairs in research and development of multimedia. But although these different qualifications are necessary, interdisciplinary cooperation and communication are not without difficulties (and joy!).

The present mini-chapter is an edited version of a discussion the authors had one cold day in January as the deadline for manuscripts relentlessly approached. We wanted to see whether we could tie some loose ends and discover unnoticed correspondences (or disagreements) in the chapters we had written. The half-fictive form we have chosen in order to present the gist of this discussion is an edited dialogue between Mr Engineer and Mr Humanist, the purpose being to illustrate the types of frustration and joy that interdisciplinary collaboration offers.

The dialogue starts when Mr Engineer describes the current way of implementing perception. For each visible object in the 3D world the perceptual mechanism will keep broadcasting the following items to all agents:

- Object identifier, position, speed and size
- Object type (e.g. hay, fox-food)
- Qualifiers (cold, sour etc.)
- Current activity (waving, running, jumping etc.)
- Sense modality (vision, audio)
- Speech act type (greeting, refusing, denying etc.)

"Aha!", Mr Humanist said to himself, this is a typical engineering point of view. They assume that there are objective perceptions of the world that are common to all its inhabitants. Positivists! Never heard of the idea that observations are relative to the observer. Well, this is to be expected, of course, but I seem to remember that they had some rather advanced ideas of letting actions influence perceptions half a year ago, so I shall not say anything yet, in order not to make a fool of myself. These guys *may* be really deep.

Instead Mr Humanist asked:

Mr H: But you need to allow the different agents to make different interpretations of the same sensory percept. I mean, a goose may be of type "fox-food" to the fox, but of type "scary animal" to a small child.

Mr E: Yeah, but we still need to broadcast basic properties – possibly the example "fox-food" was not the best one. We have another component that makes higher-level interpretations of the sensory input.

Mr H: *(Sees an opportunity for airing his relativistic tendencies.)* But you have just said that the user-representative – the *avatar* – is merely an ordinary agent with no behaviour inside. Consequently, if the screen representation of the 3D world is that of the avatar, then it too should be biased according to the *user's* emotions and intentions. If the user is to be afraid of the goose then it should be presented as frightening, for example in an ant's perspective and illuminated from below. They use these tricks in film you know.

Mr E: *(Has heard this stuff before – humanists do not seem believe in the real world at all, no wonder they are so ineffective.)* No, we want to maintain the idea that there is a real world that can be perceived in an objective way. We do not want to use the avatar's view as defining the screen image.

Mr H: *(Has heard this stuff before – engineers do not seem to notice anything when they go to the movies; no wonder they are so stiff-necked.)* But we are not creating reality, we are in the business of illusions. In all aesthetic products you need to distinguish between plot and story. The story is the sequence of events as they unfold in the fictive world, whereas the plot is the sequence in which the consumer of the product gets the information. These two time-scales are different in all *professional* products *(hope he got the subtle sarcasm)*. Can you imagine a whodunit where the time of disclosure is not later than the time of the crime? In movies there are standard plot sequences designed to distort plot and story time.

Mr E: *(These humanists are so traditional. If he wants to make a movie, he can use his video camera – but I must be obliging so as not to offend him.)* Well, if you want to make a movie you *can* do that in our system. You can record the events while you interact with the virtual world, and then ask the system to produce a movie to be viewed afterwards. But it does not make sense to twist the time during the interactive phase. This would destroy the illusion.

Mr H: *(He believes I am a conservative humanist locked to traditional media. But I really do have many modern views although I am past fifty. Think hard now, don't give in.)* But the idea of plot time *does* make sense in the interactive phase too. Suppose a rooster and a fox are on the scene. These agents are schizophrenic, half animals and half actors. They must know how to behave as animals but also how and when to present their behaviours to the user. In some stories it would be okay to let the user see the fox killing the rooster at the time it happens. But in other stories, the actor part of the agents might decide that this is a story involving deception of the user.

Therefore the user must not know whether the rooster has been eaten or not. On the screen there are some bushes, and the actor rooster therefore decides to flee behind them to prevent the user from seeing the actual killing. In this way, we can produce the information lacunae so important to suspense.

Mr E: *(Think hard now, don't give in.)* But how do you intend to eventually present the information to the user? You cannot just swap chronology as you please in interactive worlds, and you cannot compress and enlarge story time, as you do in movies.

Mr H: *(Sees the point.)* Well, an event can be presented in different modalities. In movies your often use verbal descriptions of events instead of showing them on the screen. You could do this here too. For example, the punchline of the story could consist in a goose – an eyewitness to the deed – narrating the real course of events to the deceived user *(how did I eventually get into this stupid story about pacifist foxes and talking geese?)*. But you are right, we can only delay the user's recognition of the event.

Mr E: *(Sees a vague possibility of generalizing the platform which may enable him to publish his work in a respectable journal in spite of the talking geese nonsense.)* I still do not like the idea of agents performing for an audience. But inside the virtual world, agents may perform for *other* agents, and agents may also try to *deceive* other agents...

Mr H: ...and the avatar is an agent, so you can just see the plot structure as a special case of agents trying to deceive other agents (*not a bad idea at all, not at all...)*

Mr E: In order to do this we will add a third kind of memory to the two other kinds we have, namely memory of what other agents have seen and know, and you can have your plot for free.

Mr H: Yes, that is not a bad idea.

At this point, both gentlemen had began to entertain warmer feelings towards one another, each being convinced that he had got the good idea. After a meal and a smoke, they began to look for other instances of agreement.

Mr E: We have made provisions for shifting geometrical perspective, you know. For example, you can shift from viewing the world through the eyes of the avatar to using the eyes of any agent – yes, you can even fly around in the scene like a bird.

Mr H: *(Remembers scraps of literary history and wants to show off at bit.)* That is very useful, and facilities for constraining the possible perspectives would be very useful, since such constraints have traditionally been used to define literary genres. For example, the flying camera possibility corresponds to the omniscient author so popular in the 19th century, whereas constraining the point of view to avatars heralds the dawn of naturalism in last decades of the century *(hope I remember correctly and that he does not look it up).*

Mr E: *(Leafs through Mr. Humanist's paper.)* I see you have some classifications of actions, for example there is one here by a Zeno Vendler that distinguishes between activities and achievements. I can recognize them in our behaviours. For example, MoveTo is clearly an accomplishment and Follow and MaintainSpace are activites. But why is that interesting? Our job is construction, and we judge concepts according to their usefulness.

Mr H: I can't prove that this process typology is useful, but I have this argument: Vendler's process types are formalized in language – elements such as adverbials and verb forms are sensitive to them. Therefore they must be basic to human perception of processes and consequently they ought to be useful for designing processes that users can immediately make sense of. But I recognize we use two different methods: you develop concepts through experimental work and I through analysis of empirical evidence from language, literature, film and games.

Mr E: It would be nice to know whether these two approaches lead in the same direction or not. What about our hierarchy of perception for example? Do you have anything corresponding to the low-level perceptions and the higher-level processing?

Mr H: Yes, in fact I suggest three levels: a basic continuous "Newtonian" level concerned with objects and their positions and velocities. Then an intermediate level of process chunks, and finally a superstructure of discrete representations of processes. It seems to me that your low-level agent contains the first two layers. The "Newtonian" level corresponds to your information of object position, speed and size, and my intermediate one to the rest of your low level. Your high-level processes correspond to my third level.

Mr E: I can see the similarities, but there is a difference: we too are interested in the distinction between the continuous and the discrete, but in our platform it is more a matter of degree: in our system there is only a huge collection of loops, and when you descend through our system, what happens is that the frequency of loops increases. But there is another difference that is more important: our distinction between high- and low-level processes is a functional one, and hinges on what is merely used as material and what is important from a dramaturgic point of view. This means that there is no fixed distinction between high- and low-level processes. For example, the detailed movement of the legs of an avatar is usually a low-level process, but in some cases, it is the very point. There is a good example in the "silly walks" sketch of *Monty Python's Flying Circus*. The funny thing in this sketch is the detailed way in which John Cleese moves his legs, and not his higher level intentions and plans.

Mr H: *(Quickly revising his ideas, feeling that he should have made this point.)* Yes, of course.

The discussion continued along these lines for a while, until both gentlemen became tired and began to repeat themselves.

However, two interesting ideas remained when the pacifist foxes and talking geese were mercifully forgotten. Firstly: plot structures are possible in interactive 3D worlds, but they must be implemented as agents hiding and disclosing information for one another within the virtual world. Secondly: the level structure of the agents must be variable, allowing low-level processes to become a part of the high-level dramaturgic schemes.

SECTION 3

Verbal and Non-Verbal Interaction with Virtual Worlds and Agents

Introduction

Patrizia Paggio

This section groups together three chapters all dealing with how users can interact with virtual worlds. In other words, the focus is narrowed down to one of the types of interaction discussed earlier in this volume in Chapter 2: human–machine interaction. Reflecting the fact that more and more attention is being given in the research community to multimodal interfaces, the chapters discuss verbal and non-verbal communication, as well as ways in which the two modes of interaction can profitably be combined.

Chapter 11, on Motion Capture (MoCap), addresses the issue of how the user's body movements can be captured and made use of in a computer interface. The idea is very simple: the user's movements could either be replicated in the virtual world to make avatars move in as nuanced and believable a way as possible; or they could be "understood" by the interface so that a specific movement had a specific effect in the virtual world – an example of this could be interpreting the user's nodding as an assent.

The chapter makes it very clear, however, that implementing this idea so that the user can interact naturally with the computer is not straightforward. Currently, MoCap devices producing the best results are based on the technique of active sensing, where the user has to wear devices that either transmit or receive signals. The use of devices makes the reconstruction of the subject's movements reasonably precise. The paper provides a brief overview of the various types of existing devices.

Moeslund points out that MoCap based on active sensing has enjoyed a considerable degree of success, especially due to the use made of it in the film and advertising industries, where MoCap data are recorded and stored to be used later in the creation of computer animation.

In spite of its widespread use, however, the author concludes that active-sensing MoCap suffers from a fundamental fault. Because of the mechanic sensors of various kinds the user has to carry, moving around will quickly become cumbersome. This may also explain the fact that this kind of MoCap is used especially in an asynchronous manner, where movements are recorded and then reproduced in the virtual world, but where the user does not interact directly with it. An important research goal, and a challenge, is therefore to try to get rid of the devices. This is done in a different MoCap technology called passive sensing.

Passive sensing is based on the idea of having one or more cameras film the user's movements. Since the cameras produce two-dimensional images, the problem consists in reconstructing the original three-dimensional motion. After a short historical survey of various approaches to the problem, some of which rely on the use of markers such as thin light tubes attached to the user's body, Moeslund discusses the various components making up a MoCap system, and the degree of complexity they need to have in the various system types. The discussion is not technical, and the quality of the achievable results is very clearly shown in a series of pictures. Finally, various possible MoCap applications in areas as different as surveillance, analysis and control, are described.

The main emphasis of the chapter is on the use and potential of MoCap technology for the reproduction of the user's movements in a virtual world. However, Moeslund points out that the mapping of MoCap data into the virtual world may also be indirect; in other words it may require an interpretation. This concept is addressed in Chapter 12, which deals with the issue of multimodal interfaces. The authors' background is that of language engineering, so their main concern in this chapter is how techniques used in Natural Language Processing (NLP) can be adapted to a combined processing of verbal and non-verbal input.

The authors argue that since the experimental data on users' reactions to different multimodal settings is not very conclusive, the design of a multimodal interface can draw on analyses of how gestures combine with language in human conversation. The first part of the chapter therefore presents a typology in which gestures are grouped according to the kind of interpretation they are given in human conversation. For instance, deictic gestures locate objects or events in the physical space, metaphoric gestures represent an abstract concept by a concrete image, and so on. It is also pointed out that gestures can interact with speech at the level of syntax, semantics, information structure and pragmatics.

Contrary to what is done in other approaches, where modality interaction is dealt with in very hard-coded specific procedures that are difficult to extend and reuse, the authors propose a general model in which gestures are represented as part of a more complex "sign", also comprising a representation of the speech input. They argue that in such a complex sign, information coming from as many different devices as possible can be combined (unified), provided of course that different modality data are expressed in a similar fashion. The way in which the proper merging of the various parts of the sign is achieved is by rules similar to the grammar rules used in NLP to analyse linguistic input.

Examples of such complex signs are given in the paper showing how the formalism chosen can be used to merge the interpretation of simple utterances with that of a few simple gestures. The point is also made that in case of an ambiguous gesture interpretation, the generalizations expressed in the rules on how certain gestures, preferably combined with certain linguistic expressions, can help the system understand the ambiguous gesture in the right way.

The correct interpretation of a gesture according to a system of signs, in fact depends on the accurate recognition of the gesture in question, which as made clear by Moeslund in Chapter 11 is certainly not always guaranteed. Paggio and Music then argue that, by combining gesture and speech recognition, the system has the possibility of constraining the interpretation of ambiguous gesture analyses. Although the point is not specifically discussed in the paper, it can be added that speech recognition is also still an imperfect technology. Therefore, at least in principle, gesture recognition could also be used to constrain the results of the speech recognizer.

The rest of the chapter explains how the model envisaged can be implemented in a concrete system. An architecture is presented, and the various components participating in the analysis of the multimodal input are briefly described. The component responsible for parsing the input, in other words for applying the rules for multimodal combination and producing the combined sign representation mentioned earlier, is discussed in slightly more (technical) detail. The reader not familiar with parsing and parse trees may wish to skip over this part without bothering about how exactly the general principles discussed earlier are actually formalized and implemented.

The kind of verbal input discussed in Chapter 12 is limited to isolated utterances, the interpretation of which is extended to include an interpretation of the accompanying gestures. In Chapter 13, which concludes this section on verbal and nonverbal interaction, the issue is addressed of how to design systems capable of engaging in a dialogue with the user. Modelling the human ability of carrying out conversations in such a way as to be able to implement at least part of it in a computer system, is a very complex task.

Navarretta starts out by identifying the main components of a dialogue system: a dialogue manager responsible for driving the dialogue, so that the system knows how to behave depending on how the dialogue is proceeding; a discourse interpretation component with the job of interpreting an utterance not in isolation but with respect to the preceding utterances; and a response generation component responsible for generating appropriate verbal responses.

She then discusses a number of theories and implemented systems that have contributed in different ways to theoretical advancement, especially in the areas of dialogue management and discourse analysis. The various theories and systems differ with respect to a number of parameters. One is how to define the smallest unit of analysis, where various possibilities taken into consideration are sentences, speech acts, intentions etc. Others are the nature and number of relations that are necessary to capture the interaction between the units, and the structures in which to combine them (trees, task descriptions, stacks etc.).

An important issue which bears on all these parameters of variation, is whether and how cognitive aspects playing a part in human dialogues, such as the intentions of the dialogue participants, or their inferential mechanisms, should be included in dialogue systems.

Navarretta argues that in planning systems, where the dialogue serves the purpose of helping the user and the system to carry out together a very specific and limited task, it is easier to interpret for instance the user's intentions. In systems where the dialogue is intended to be more flexible, as is the case in Staging, a more viable approach may be that of analysing the user's utterances as dialogue acts, or speech acts, such as "information_request", "answer" and so on. Dialogue segments are then defined in terms of acceptable sequences of different speech acts. It is clear that a model of this kind provides a more superficial, and therefore more easily implementable, analysis of the various dialogue units than a planning system trying to recognize the intention behind each utterance.

On the other hand, Navarretta also points out that restricting dialogue analysis to the recognition of speech act sequences may be too superficial. For instance, to show that it may be useful to distinguish different task levels she gives an example where the concrete task of ordering a drink is pursued in a dialogue in parallel with the more socially oriented task of flirting with the bartender.

In the last part of the paper, Navarretta works out the analysis of a few dialogue examples in an extended version of the influential Discourse Representation Theory (DRT) where the typical DRT boxes containing specifications of events and referents in the discourse (here the dialogue), are extended with information on the speech act.

Hopefully, after having read this section, the reader will be left with the impression that some progress is being made in making human–computer interfaces more natural than they are today by equipping the computer with at least some of the communication abilities characteristic of human interaction. It will also be clear, however, that even the most advanced technologies still only allow the computer to understand (and respond to) a limited portion of the possible communicative acts – both verbal and non-verbal – that humans can easily process, and that multimodal dialogues are only possible for restricted applications and limited domains.

I would like to conclude by pointing at two issues which are closely related to the themes explored in this section. One is the complex issue of response generation, which has not been devoted attention in this volume, but will no doubt be of concern to the project at a later stage. All dialogue systems have a response generation component which can either be based on a simple canned response strategy, or involve more or less sophisticated Natural Language Generation (NLG) techniques. In a system where the user can interact verbally with agents playing a role in a virtual world with its own activities and rules, response generation is not only a linguistic task, but involves deciding on the right kind of action, which may well be (and probably most often should be) a combination of a verbal reply and a physical action. This clearly complicates matters.

The second issue concerns a possible new application of the NLP techniques described in this section. If we allow not only multimodal communication between the user's avatar and the agents, but also among the agents, it is an obvious question to ask whether the same model used to manage multimodal communication with the user can be used to handle inter-agent communication. But this may be an issue for another book.

11

Interacting with a Virtual World Through Motion Capture

Thomas B. Moeslund

11.1 Introduction

Previously in this book the concepts of interactions, agents, avatars and virtual worlds have been discussed. In this chapter we will look closer at how the non-verbal interaction with a virtual world takes place.

The non-verbal interaction (hereafter interaction) to virtual worlds can be through a command/text window and keystrokes which are seen in many systems. But as the virtual worlds and the interaction with them becomes more complex so does the need for more advanced interfaces. One way of improving the interfaces is to use motion capture (MoCap). That is, the motion of the subject interfacing to the virtual world is used to make the interface more general and intuitive. As an example, say you want to make a creature in the virtual world wave its hand. Instead of using playback, with its inherent limitations, or using a complex combination of keystrokes and mouse movements, you could simply wave your own hand in the desired way and have a MoCap device register the movements and send them to the creature, making it able to duplicate your movements in real-time. The advantages of using MoCap are evident, but how exactly can the motion of a human or another object be captured? And how may it be used to interact with the virtual world? These are the questions we will try to answer in this chapter.

We will do this by first describing the different devices used for MoCap and their complexity, and then discuss how MoCap is used to control something, especially in a virtual world. But first we will give a more precise definition of MoCap, including a brief glimpse into its development.

11.2 Motion Capture

A fair question to ask in this context is what exactly is MoCap? Formally it is the process of capturing motion, usually human body motion, via a MoCap device.

However, a closer investigation reveals that this is not entirely true. Many devices, e.g. a computer mouse or a steering wheel in a car, are usually *not* considered MoCap devices, and their tasks are not considered to be MoCap, even though their sole purpose is to capture human motion. A precise definition covering all aspects of MoCap cannot be given, since it differs between applications and depends on the applied technology. Generally it can, however, be said that measurement devices which are associated with registering and/or storing of general human motion, and which do not have a predefined purpose (as, for example, a steering wheel does) are considered MoCap devices. Another characteristic is that most of these devices can be fitted to different humans and applications.

When we use the term MoCap in this chapter it refers to *the process of capturing the motion of a human body (part), at some resolution*. The phrase *at some resolution* is added to indicate that both the estimation of the overall human motion, e.g. his or her centre of mass, as well as the estimation of motion of each articulated joint in an object, is considered a MoCap problem.

The development in MoCap technologies and devices comes from two sources: research and industry. At first, for many years, MoCap applications were designed to measure, and thereby help understand, the motion patterns of humans (and animals). This was solely driven by research. Later medical aspects were investigated, resulting in an actual MoCap market.

Some 10–20 years ago, as computers were becoming widely available, a number of new application areas opened up and interest in MoCap exploded. Since then some of the interested parties have been big industries: military, entertainment, medical and advertising. They all have plenty of money to invest, resulting in a fast developing market with a continual flow of new and improved products. Beside these industries the research community has also contributed to the rapid development. Lately the research community has invested much effort in the area of Human–Computer Interaction (HCI). For complex HCI applications, such as sign language recognition and avatar control in a virtual world, MoCap is a very welcome (and in some cases necessary) tool.

Together the research community and various industries are constantly developing and improving MoCap devices. The most important devices and their underlying technologies are described in the following section.

11.3 Devices Used for Capturing Motion

This section gives an overview of the different types of devices used for MoCap and a glimpse into the history of visual capturing methods in particular. The different MoCap devices are based on either active or passive sensing.

The concept of active sensing is to place devices on the subject which transmit or receive real or artificially generated signals. When the device works as a transmitter it generates a signal which can be measured by another device located somewhere in the surroundings. When it works as a receiver it receives signals usually generated by some artificial source in the surroundings.

In passive sensing the devices do not affect the surroundings. They merely observe what is already in the world, e.g. visual light or other electromagnetic wavelengths, and generally do not need the generation of new signals or wearable hardware.

11.3.1 Active Sensing

Different devices for active sensing have over the years been invented to capture human motion in particular. Marey was the first to tackle the MoCap problem, as early as 1873. He used pneumatic sensors and pressure chambers, e.g. under the foot, to measure the pressure conducted by the foot (Marey, 1873). This kind of work, where the forces and movements of different body parts are measured, is known as kinetic-based MoCap.

In the last two decades different devices, such as mechanical sensors, accelerometers, electromagnetic sensors, acoustic sensors and optical fibres, have been invented; see Andersen (1998), Dyer *et al.* (1995), Frey *et al.* (1996), Ladin (1995) and Youngblut *et al.* (1996) for general descriptions of these sensors and Allard *et al.* (1995), Aminian *et al.* (1998), Badler *et al.* (1994), Molet *et al.* (1996, 1997) and Semwal *et al.* (1996) for examples of systems where they are used in practice. In the following a short description of the different devices is given.

Mechanical devices are attached to some movable parts which when moved, e.g. during bending, will output a signal directly reflecting the configuration of the movable parts to which it has been attached. In Figure 11.1 a glove (the CyberGlove) based on this technology is shown.

An **accelerometer** is a small device which measures the acceleration of the object it is attached to. This is done by measuring the deflection caused by the movements of the device and converting this into an electrical signal. Devices can be more or less sensitive to the Earth's gravitational field.

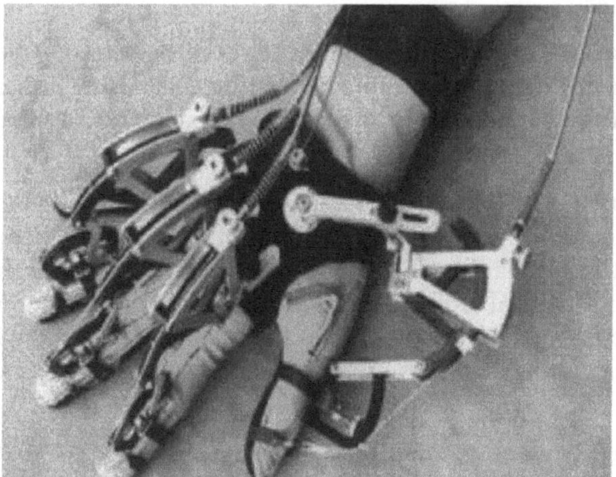

Figure 11.1 A mechanical glove for MoCap (Andersen, 1998).

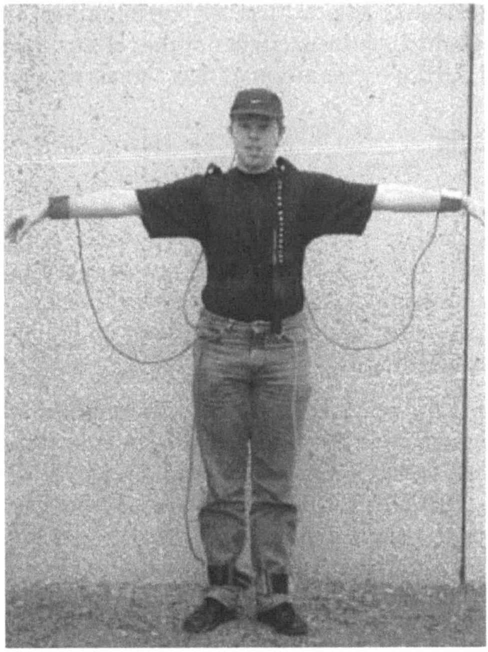

Figure 11.2 Electromagnetic devices mounted on a subject to capture his movements.

Electromagnetic devices are attached to different joints/segments on a subject and measures the orientation and position of each device with respect to the Earth's magnetic field, or a field generated by a transmitter. In Figure 11.2 a subject wearing seven electromagnetic devices is shown. All devices feed their signals to a box on the back of the subject from where they are send (via radio or through a wire) to a MoCap computer.

Acoustic devices use a set of microphones to receive a sound wave emitted from an acoustic sensor attached to a subject, or vice versa. Using either triangulation or the phase of the sound wave it is possible to calculate the 3D position of the device.

An **optical fibre device** is a special case of the mechanical sensor mentioned above. It it described separately because, first of all it is a very popular solution, and secondly the mechanics do not hamper the user in the same way as the other types of mechanical sensor do. Optical fibres are placed along the limbs of a subject, e.g. the finger, and a signal is produced which reflects the bending of the fibre/limb. An example of a glove where this technology is used can be seen in Figure 11.3.

Most of the above devices are mainly used in kinematic systems where the goal is to track spatial coordinates of segments or joints over time. The problems with them are that the subject whose motion is to be captured must be wired up, making it cumbersome to move around. This motivates the use of passive sensing.

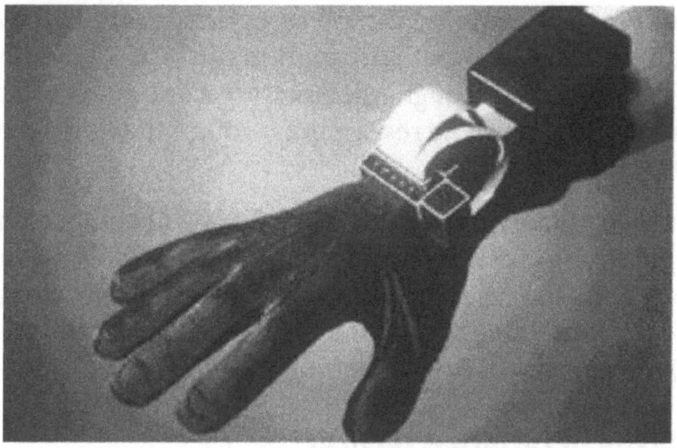

Figure 11.3 A fibre-optic glove (the 5th Glove) for MoCap (Andersen, 1998).

11.3.2 Passive Sensing

In passive sensing the idea is to use an image obtained from a camera[1] and capture the motion based on that image. The image is a 2D projection of the 3D world, so the trick is to find the 3D (human) motion that gave rise to the 2D projection. This problem is known as photogrammetric reconstruction (Allard *et al.*, 1995). The idea was first used by Muybridge back in 1887 where he set out to prove that a horse has a flight phase where all its limbs are in the air at the same time (Muybridge, 1957). Later Muybridge turned his research to human motion capture. Recently, Bregler and Malik have successfully tried to use state of the art computer vision algorithms to track the original data used in Muybridge's early experiments on capturing human motion (Bregler and Malik, 1998).

The idea of using passive sensing, e.g. a camera, to capture the motion of the subject is very noble but also very difficult. The difficulties arise because of the 3D to 2D projection and the amount of information in an image sequence. To reduce these problems many systems use markers attached to the subject, reducing the amount of information and making the photogrammetric reconstruction easier. Marey (Ladin, 1995) used this idea by attaching white stripes between the main joints of the user – the first passive marker.

In 1895 Braune and Fischer were the first to explore the idea of using active markers[2] (Braune and Fischer, 1987). They attached thin light-tubes to different body segments and generated short bursts of light synchronously photographed by four cameras. This type of active marker has become known as a Moving Light Display (MLD), where an image sequence is reduced to a sequence of moving lights (see Cedras and Shah (1994) for a review). A classical MLD example is the one done by Johansson back in the early 1970s (Johansson, 1975). He showed that human

1 More than one camera can be used.

2 Even though the markers might be active, the overall sensing technology is still considered to be passive.

activities like walking and running can be recognized from lights attached to the joints of an actor. This suggests that pure motion can be used for direct recognition instead of doing it indirectly through a geometric reconstruction. Today the idea of direct recognition is used by many researchers around the world (see e.g. Campbell and Bobick (1995)).

Even though the use of markers is a good idea, it is still cumbersome for the user. Therefore computer vision researchers have recently tried to move away from the marker approach and aim at more "pure" MoCap systems, where the "raw" input image is used to perform the photogrammetric reconstruction (see Moeslund and Granum (1999) for a review).

11.3.3 Complexity of Different Devices

When MoCap is used in practice the output from the MoCap sensor system (one or more devices) needs to be analysed before the motion data are available. This is illustrated in Figure 11.4. The complexity of the analyser module depends on the sensor module. The higher the level of the data that the sensor module produces, the less complexity is required by the analyser module, and vice versa. For the devices based on active sensing the output from the sensor module is usually very high, yielding only a little complexity in the analyser module. For devices based on passive sensing usually high complexity is required by the analyser module.[3]

In MoCap systems based on active sensing the overall performance depends on the number of devices and their quality. The latest versions of these devices are fast (up to 140 Hz) and rather accurate (down to 0.5 mm in a well-controlled setup) (Ladin, 1995). If more devices are placed on the subject a better performance is obtained. In the analyser module not much performance can be gained when using active sensing, but the use of inverse kinematics may improve the overall result to some extent.

For passive devices, especially without markers, the performance is totally dependent on the analyser module. The output from the sensor module does not contain any explicit information on the motion of the subject. The data needs to be analysed to extract the relevant motion data. A simple analyser module may only extract the motion of the silhouette of the subject, while a more complex analyser module may extract the actual pose of different limbs over time. In Figure 11.5 the captured data, at one time instance, from two different systems using two different

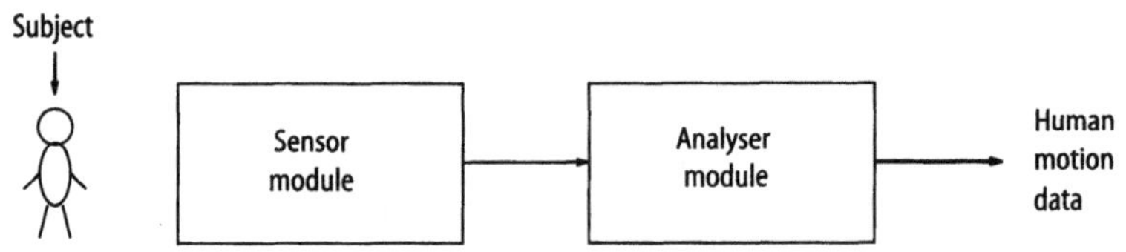

Figure 11.4 An illustration of the components in a MoCap system.

3 The analyser module becomes somewhat simpler when markers are used.

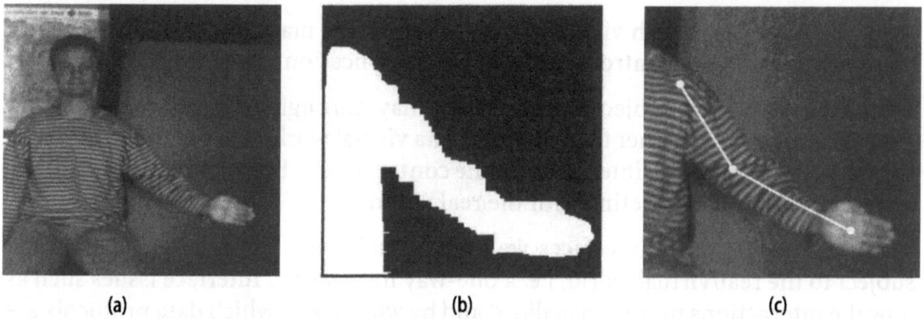

Figure 11.5 (a) An input image. (b) The estimated silhouette of the subject's left arm. (c) The estimated 3D pose of a subject's left arm superimposed on the input image (Moeslund and Granum, 2000).

complexities, are shown. Figure 11.5(b) shows the extracted silhouette of the left arm of the subject in Figure 11.5(a). This is obviously the result of a somewhat simple analyser module, but can still be used in, for example, motion detection and texture mapping. In Figure 11.5(c) the 3D estimated pose of the left arm is superimposed on the input image, and it can be seen that the estimation is rather good. This is the result of a complex analyser module and is comparable to the devices based on active sensing, but without being as cumbersome.

After having described the different MoCap technologies and devices, we will now see how these may be used, particularly in control applications.

11.4 Motion Capture Used in Control Applications

MoCap has over the years been applied in many different applications. These may be divided into three overall areas concerning *surveillance*, *analysis* and *control*, respectively.

The surveillance area covers applications where a subject or a number of subjects are being tracked over time and possibly monitored for special actions. A classic example is the surveillance of a parking lot, where a system tracks subjects to evaluate whether they are about to commit a crime, e.g. steal a car. Due to the nature of this area only passive sensing is applied in these applications.

The analysis area is concerned with the analysis of the raw motion data. This could be used in clinical studies of, for example, diagnostics of orthopaedic patients, or to help athletes understand and improve their performance. Magnetic sensors and marker-based vision systems are the most common solutions in these applications. This is mainly due to the fact that the applications are situated in a highly controlled environment and due to the requirement of very precise motion data.

The control area relates to applications where the captured motion is used to control something. It could be used as an interface to games, virtual worlds or animation, or to control remote located implements. Both active and passive sensing are used depending on the concrete application.

Since the interaction with virtual worlds is one of the main topics of this book we will look closer at the control area where this application is included.

After the motion of a subject is captured, it may, through an interface, be used to control something in either the real world or a virtual world. Clearly the interface to the virtual world is more interesting in the context of this book, but we shall still say a few words about interacting with the real world.

When discussing these interfaces we only consider the control signals from the subject to the real/virtual world, i.e. a one-way interaction. Interface issues such as how the interactions may be visualized and by whom, and which data protocols are used, are not considered.

11.4.1 Interacting with the Real World Through a MoCap System

In Figure 11.6 the interaction between a subject, through a MoCap device, and the real world is illustrated. The arrow indicates the interaction. One way of interpreting it, or the interaction, is to classify different interactions by the degrees of freedom (DoF) in the interface. Defining it like this, a device such as a button with one DoF will be located at one end of the axis, while a body suit or a full-blown computer vision system estimating all body parameters will be located at the other extreme.

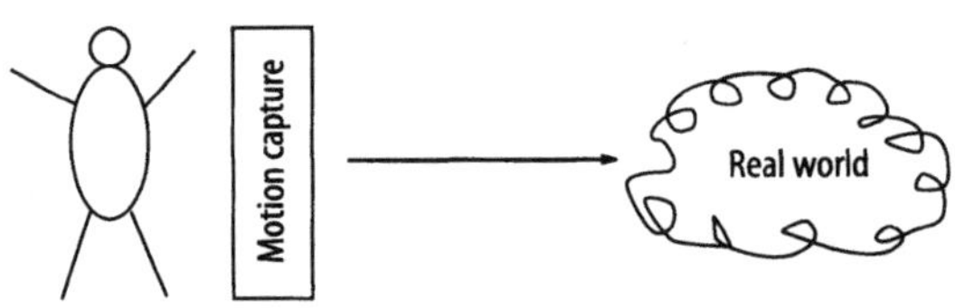

Figure 11.6 An interface from a subject to the real world through a MoCap system.

Another way of looking at the interaction is to divide interfaces into synchronous and asynchronous. This, we feel, will provide the best insight into different interaction methods.

Synchronous interaction is interaction carried out online. That is, the motion captured is immediately used to control something in the real/virtual world.

Asynchronous interaction is interaction concerned with recording. That is, when a subject's motion is captured it is not used immediately but rather stored for later use.

11.4.1.1 Synchronous Interaction with the Real World

Synchronous interaction can be seen a lot using devices which are normally not considered MoCap devices, such as steering wheels, brakes, gears and buttons. The use of devices which *are* considered to be MoCap devices (see Section 11.3), is still being researched. In several movies a view into what might be tomorrow's synchronous interfaces to the real world can be seen. In the science fiction movie *Aliens* (1986) Ellen Ripley (played by Sigourney Weaver) successfully fights off one of the meanest aliens ever encountered on film using a so-called powerloader – a mechanical device structured like the human skeleton which Ripley steps into. Her movements control the arms and legs of the powerloader and thereby multiply her strength by a factor of several thousand. In the movie *Dave* (1993) the President of the USA (played by Bill Pullman) during a visit to a factory controls a giant robot using the same technique as in *Aliens*. Besides the size of the controlled robot, the difference is that the President is not inside the actual robot but instead controlling it from a distance. In *Lost in Space* (1998) a boy (played by Jack Johnson) controls a fighting robot from a distance, as in *Dave*, using a so-called "Holographic Interface". It is not evident how the motion is captured, but it is definitely based on passive sensing.

Even though these devices are still science fiction they might actually be implementable in a not too distant future.

11.4.1.2 Asynchronous Interaction with the Real World

In many industries, especially where conveyer belts are used, a high number of repeated operations are seen. These are mainly carried out by machines/robots to ensure similarity in production and speed, and to avoid wearing humans down. As the operations become more complex it becomes more complicated to program them to carry out the operations. This problem has been tackled using asynchronous interaction. A human performs the operation, while a computer captures his or her motion. Afterwards the computer may use the captured motion data to control the same machine performing the operation. The best-known example is perhaps spray painting, where a human paints an object. The movements of the painting device are captured and can afterwards be replicated by a painting robot.

11.4.2 Interacting with a Virtual World through a MoCap System

Figure 11.7 shows a subject interfacing to a virtual world through a MoCap system. The arrow indicates the interaction between the subject and the virtual world. It may, as mentioned in Section 11.4.1, be representing the DoF in the interface. But, as before, we choose to use the synchronous/asynchronous division.

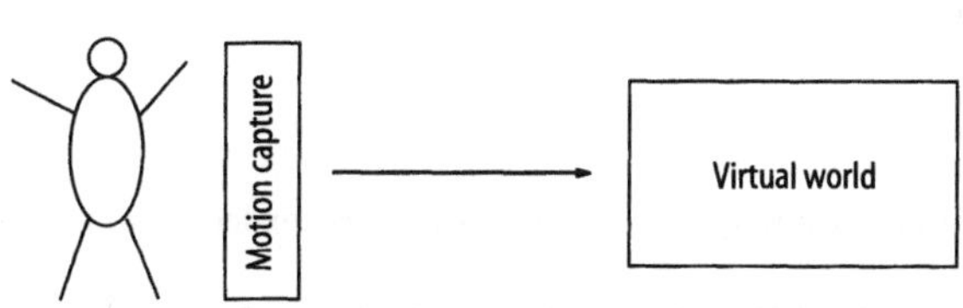

Figure 11.7 An interface from a subject to the virtual world through a MoCap system.

11.4.2.1 Synchronous Interaction with a Virtual World

Synchronous interaction with a virtual world may be carried out in two different ways: either as a one-to-one mapping or as an interpretation. That is, a **direct** or **indirect mapping.** The direct mapping covers the methods where the subject's movements are duplicated directly in the virtual world. In the ultimate system this means that one could not tell the difference between movements in the real world and movements in the virtual world. Indirect mapping is when the subject's movements are captured, interpreted, and *then* used to control something. That is, the signals send through the interface are discrete symbols rather than "raw" continuous motion data. The subject could wave his or her hand in the real world and it would be sent to the virtual world as a command, for example to close the connection between the two worlds.

In some systems both methods may be seen. For instance, in systems where the subject's movements are mapped directly into the virtual world there is the problem of moving around. The virtual world is usually bigger (in theory infinite) than the real world where the MoCap equipment applies. Therefore some methods must be designed to allow subjects to move around in the virtual world without having to move (as far) in the real world. This can be done using a special mapping, e.g. walking on the spot maps to walking in the virtual world. Clearly this requires some sort of interpretation, but still the rest of the motions conducted by the subject may be one-to-one mapped, i.e. a mix of both methods. The two different types of interaction will be described further below.

When a **direct mapping** takes place it is known as **performance animation**[4] and the object animated in the virtual world is known as the **avatar** of the subject. A good example of performance animation is the work by Wilson, where he defines performance animation as *animating a graphical character via a like human performance* (Wilson, 1999), i.e. the animation is based on performed motion as oppose to, for example, using key-frames. In his Luxomatic system a computer vision system captures the motion of the subject's hand and uses it to control a lamp in the virtual world. Figure 11.8 shows a snapshot from the system. The MoCap process can be seen in the bottom-right corner, while the rest of the figure shows the subject's avatar[5], the lamp, in the virtual world.

The term *performance animation* is mainly used when the animation is used as part of a performance, e.g. dance performance. That is, instead of viewing the performer the audience views the avatar. An example of this is shown in Figure 11.9, where six images taken from a performance animated sequence, *Ghost*, made at The Department of Dramaturgy, Aarhus University, Denmark, is shown. The motion of a dancer is captured and mapped to the virtual character, which is animated as a fuzzy stick-figure.

---

4 Performance animation may also be based on prerecorded data, i.e. an asynchronous interaction.

5 Other good examples of avatars may be seen in movies such as *The Lawnmower Man* (1992) and *Disclosure* (1994).

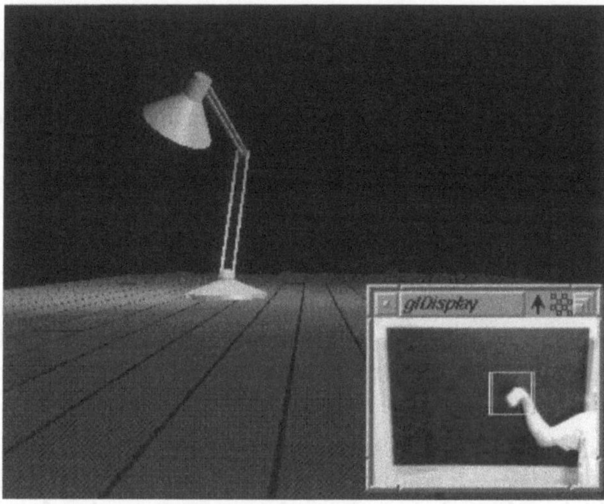

Figure 11.8 A snapshot from the *Luxomatic* system (Wilson, 1999).

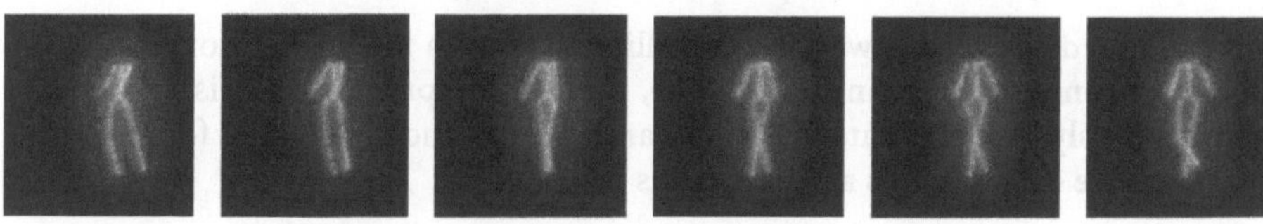

Figure 11.9 A performance-animated sequence of a dancer.

This idea can be taken a step further where the performance is the *interaction* between the subject and his or her avatar! The term *performance animation* is rarely used in other applications even though it is a rather good definition.

In the case of **indirect mapping** the captured motion is not reproduced in the virtual world but rather interpreted and represented as a few symbols which are sent to the virtual world. Chapter 9 describes how the motion of a subject's hand is captured by a dataglove and converted into one discrete symbol having one of three values (none/pointing/open hand). The symbol is send to a virtual world where an autonomous agent uses it, together with an auditory input and a number of internal parameters, to decide how to react.

In the work by Freeman *et al.* (1995) passive sensing without markers is used to capture the motion of a subject. The images are analysed and converted into a few symbols which explain the 2D orientation of the subject's hand. The symbols are used to control (steer) a car in a computer game.

11.4.2.2 Asynchronous Interaction with a Virtual World

Good examples of where asynchronous interaction with a virtual world is used are the movie and advertising industries. Here MoCap data are recorded and stored, and later used to create animations. Animations have been used in cartoons in particular for a number of years. But animating complex objects moving realistically over time is somewhat difficult using hand animations, and therefore MoCap is used extensively, since it allows exactly this through performance animation. Imagine movies such as *Jurassic Park* (1993) and *Titanic* (1997) without computer animations based on MoCap. In the former, MoCap devices were places on elephants and their movements were recorded. Later these motion patterns were applied to make the computer models of the dinosaurs come to life and move realistically. In the latter movie a number of people had their walking patterns captured and applied to human models to make them move realistically. Daily we actually also witness a number of computer animations based on MoCap. Look more closely next time you watch a computer graphic commercial on TV and wonder how they have made, for example, the small Colgate figure move so realistic – MoCap!

An entire industry specializing in MoCap for performance animation has emerged during the past five years. It consists of MoCap houses which all include a MoCap studio where high-tech equipment is used to capture motion for the movie and advertising industries in partuclar. A recent study found that about 30 to 40[6] MoCap houses provide a MoCap service for hire worldwide (Delaney, 1998).

As mentioned above, this way of controlling objects in the virtual worlds is based on asynchronous processing. Of course, the MoCap process itself is carried out synchronously, but the data are afterwards stored and fine-tuned for later use. Therefore we consider this asynchronous interaction.

11.5 Discussion

MoCap is a powerful technology for designing advanced interfaces, especially when the interface is too complex for keyboard and mouse. The MoCap technology may be based on either active or passive sensing. Active sensing is generally based on wiring the subject up, while passive sensing is not. Obviously this makes passive sensing most attractive in the context of this book.

Generally, active sensing gives rather precise data, but for many applications this solution is too cumbersome. Passive sensing may be based on either wearing or not wearing markers. When markers are used good results may be expected, but, as for active sensing, this is too cumbersome for some applications. When no markers are used a more general interface might be realized. The drawback is, however, that the complexity needed to extract and analyse the motion data is very high. Actually, no system has so far been able to capture the exact motion of an entire subject using only passive sensing without markers. This is therefore a large research topic and better and better solutions are being developed. In the future we might see workable systems using this technology.

MoCap may be used in either synchronous or asynchronous interaction with virtual worlds. Synchronous interaction is interaction carried out on-line, i.e. the

6 Today the figure is more likely 100.

motion captured is immediately used to control something in the virtual world. When the motion data is not used immediately, but rather stored, fine-tuned and *then* used, the interaction is considered to be asynchronous. This is seen a lot, especially in big Hollywood movies and the advertising industry, and an entire industry has grown up to support it.

In the context of this book synchronous MoCap is most relevant. It is, as described earlier, divided into direct mapping and indirect mapping. When the interaction is used in direct mapping it is known as performance animation and the object to be controlled in the virtual world is known as the avatar of the subject. Indirect mapping requires some sort of interpretation prior to use in a virtual world.

Whenever a human wants an avatar to mimic him or her the obvious choice is to use direct mapping. In all other situations, however, the motion data needs to be interpreted before an action is carried out in the virtual world, i.e. indirect mapping. Inspired by Andersen and Callesen's work (Chapter 7) the interpretation can be viewed as a matter of converting the continuous motion data (trajectories) to discrete symbols according to some known sign system.

Ad hoc sign systems are being designed to suit different virtual worlds and the interpretation of these is an integral part of the MoCap process. Actually this simplifies the required analysis of the MoCap data, since it is easier to extract specific motion patterns than to capture general motion parameters.

However, if we wish to build good interfaces for people other than the designers we need to use the (both formal and informal) sign systems used in everyday life. This means a lot of subtle signs which are extremely difficult to extract from the continuous flow of motion data. For example, consider a situation where a human moves his or her hand or head while saying: "They went that way". Clearly the movement indicates a direction, but unless the sign system is very limited or the context is known, it would be extremely difficult to convert the motion into a discrete symbol containing information about the indicated direction.

To reduce this problem, the continuous motion data can be combined with the speech data and a multimodal interpretation carried out. This idea is discussed further in Chapter 12.

Acknowledgement

The author would like to thank Lone Koefoed Hansen (The Department of Multimedia, Aarhus University, Denmark) and Andrew D. Wilson (The Media Lab, MIT, USA) for providing images for Figures 11.2, 11.8 and 11.9.

References

Allard, P., Stokes, I. and Blanchi, J. (eds.) (1995) *Three-Dimensional Analysis of Human Movement.* Champaign, IL: Human Kinetics.

Aminian, K., De Andres, E., Rezakhanlou, K., Fritsch, C., Schutz, Y., Depairon, M., Leyvraz, P.-F. and Robert, P. (1998) Motion analysis in clinical practice using ambulatory accelerometry. In *Modeling and Motion Capture Techniques for Virtual Environments.* Berlin: Springer-Verlag.

Andersen, C. (1998) *A Survey of Gloves for Interaction with Virtual Worlds*, Technical report, Laboratory of Image Analysis, Aalborg University, Denmark.

Badler, N., Hollick, M. and Granieri, J. (1994) Real-time control of a virtual human using minimal sensors. *Presence* 2(1): 82–86.

Braune, C. and Fischer, O. (1987) *The Human Gait*. Berlin: Springer-Verlag. (Originallly published in 1895.)

Bregler, C. and Malik, J. (1998) Tracking people with twists and exponential maps. In *Proceedings of IEEE Conference on Computer Vision and Pattern Recognition*, Santa Barbara, CA, June, pp. 8–15.

Campbell, L. and Bobick, A. (1995) Recognition of human body motion using phase space constraints. In *Proceedings of the Fifth International Conference on Computer Vision*, Cambridge, MA, pp. 624–630.

Cedras, C. and Shah, M. (1994) A survey of motion analysis from moving light displays. In *Proceedings of the Conference on Computer Vision and Pattern Recognition*, Seattle, WA, pp. 214–221.

Delaney, B. (1998) On the trail of the shadow women: the mystery of motion capture. *Computer Graphics and Applications* 18(5): 14–19.

Dyer, S., Martin, J. and Zulauf, J. (1995) *Motion Capture White Paper*, Technical report, Windlight Studios & Wavefront.

Freeman, W., Tanaka, K., Ohta, J. and Kyuma, K. (1995) Computer vision for computer games. In *Proceedings of the 2nd International Conference on Automatic Face and Gesture Recognition*, Killington, VT, pp. 100–105.

Frey, W., Zyda, M., Mcghee, R. and Cockayne, B. (1996) *Off-The-Shelf, Real-Time, Human Body Motion Capture for Synthetic Environments*, Technical Report NPSCS-96-003, Computer Science Department, Naval Postgraduate School, Monterey, CA, USA.

Johansson, G. (1975) Visual motion perception. *Scientific American*, pp. 76–88.

Ladin, Z. (1995) In *Three-Dimensional Analysis of Human Movement* (eds. P. Allard, I. Stokes and J. Blanchi). Champaign, IL: Human Kinetics, Chapter 1.

Marey, E. (1873) *Animal Mechanism: A Treatise on Terrestrial and Aerial Locomotion*. New York: Appleton. Republished as Vol. XI of the International Scientific Series.

Moeslund, T. and Granum, E. (1999) A survey of computer vision-based human motion capture. Submitted to *International Journal on Computer Vision and Image Understanding*.

Moeslund, T. and Granum, E. (2000) Multiple cues used in model-based human motion capture. In *Proceedings of the Fourth International Conference on Automatic Face and Gesture Recognition*, Grenoble, France. Los Alamitos, CA: IEEE Press.

Molet, T., Boulic, R. and Thalmann, D. (1996) A real time anatomical converter for human motion capture. In *EUROGRAPHICS Int. Workshop on Computer Animation and Simulation*, Poitiers, France.

Molet, T., Huang, Z., Boulic, R. and Thalmann, D. (1997) An animation interface designed for motion capture. In *Proceedings of Computer Animation '97*. Los Alamitos, CA: IEEE Press.

Muybridge, E. (1957) *Animal Locomotion*. Reprinted in Brown, L. S. (ed.) (1957) *Animal in Motion*. New York: Dover.

Semwal, S., Hightower, R. and Stansfield, S. (1996) Closed form geometric algorithms for real-time control of an avatar. In *Proceedings of the Virtual Reality Annual International Symposium 1996*. Los Alalmitos, CA: IEEE Press.

Wilson, A. (1999) *Luxomatic: Computer Vision for Puppeteering*, Technical Report 512, MIT Media Lab.

Youngblut, C., Johnson, R., Nash, S., Wienclaw, R. and Will, C. (1996) *Review of Virtual Environment Interface Technology*, Technical Report H 96-001239, Institute of Defense Analyses.

12

Linguistic Interaction in Staging – a Language Engineering View

Patrizia Paggio and Bradley Music

12.1 Introduction

B: Anything else I can tempt you with?

C: I don't know really.

B: How about a cognac?

C: That's not a bad idea.

B: I've got various brands. Any preference?

C. Just give me a good one.

B: This one is good.

In the dialogue excerpt above, a bartender and a customer are negotiating the best drink for the customer to order. Besides this practical goal, however, the bartender is also attending to a different concern: he is trying to make the customer feel at ease – he is probably even flirting with her. This is reflected in the way his questions are phrased. The customer on the other hand is not very decisive, but shows in her replies that she trusts the bartender's judgement. This dialogue, which has been constructed on the basis of a series of dialogues written for the Staging project by Niels Lehmann and his colleagues from the Institute of Dramaturgy at the University of Aarhus (Denmark), is a good example of the kind of linguistic interaction envisaged in Staging: the user and the agent engage in a conversation where the level of interpretation directly related to the task that has to be solved (making a decision about the drink to be ordered) is subordinate to the social character of the dialogue.

However, linguistic interaction between a user and an agent is usually characterized among researchers working with dialogue systems as typically task-oriented. Bunt *et al.* (1998a, p. 45), for example, state that:

> In the case of human–computer communication, social motivations do not arise, so we may assume that the user communicates with a computer in order to accomplish a certain task – what is called an *application.*

It seems more accurate to say that this restriction of the communication to task-oriented dialogue types, rather than being an intrinsic characteristic of human–machine communication, is a choice made in most current dialogue systems, whether multi- or monomodal. Thus systems have been built to deal for example with train enquiries as in Sundial (McGlashan *et al.*, 1992); hotel reservations as in Waxholm (Carlson, 1996); and managing various forms of equipment, from microwave ovens to electronic microscopes or railway systems as in Olga (Beskow *et al.*, 1997), DenK (Bunt *et al.*, 1998a) and TRAINS (Allen *et al.*, 1995).

Clearly, a reason for this limitation is the fact that building a dialogue system is a very complex enterprise, and that many technical and theoretical problems remain to be solved before more natural and flexible linguistic interaction with a computer will become possible.

During the past four or five years, however, a great deal of work has been invested in enriching dialogue systems with the ability to interact with the user in a multimodal fashion. Multimodal communication can be defined as communication involving two or more different modalities, such as speech, gestures, gaze, head movements and body posture. Depending on whether multimodal behaviour is implemented in the analysis or generation component, the system will be able to understand or produce multimodal messages, or both.

Opening up the possibility of a multimodal dialogue between the user and the system, we argue below, is a step in the right direction towards the goal of making more natural and flexible linguistic interaction in human–machine interaction possible (as argued also in Bernsen *et al.* (1998)). First of all, it is a well-known fact that non-verbal behaviour plays a crucial role in human communication, where it interacts with speech in a complex way (Allwood, 1998). One of the most interesting functions of non-verbal behaviour is that of giving communicative feedback (the hearer understands, confirms, shows an emotional response etc.) and of negotiating turn-taking. Clearly, if computer interfaces could provide at least some of the means available to humans to communicate in a cooperative way, human–machine interaction would be much more natural, appealing and efficient. Providing interfaces with the ability to interpret and react to complex messages where utterances are accompanied by non-verbal behaviour is a way of making them more reactive to the social implications of the interaction, rather than just cooperative in some task the system can be used for. Furthermore, as we shall discuss in more detail, modality integration may provide an interesting means to overcome some of the technical limitations still hampering natural language interfaces, and thus also in this way give systems more flexibility.

The goal for human–machine communication of the future can then be defined as giving the user the possibility of interacting with linguistically sophisticated agents, where semantically and pragmatically complex information can be expressed via verbal and non-verbal behaviour, choosing the combination of modalities which is most suitable at a given moment. This is a very ambitious goal, which it may well take years of work to achieve.

The initial focus of our work in Staging – and of this chapter – is on a single aspect of this scenario, i.e. a method for integrating information from multiple modalities into a unified semantic representation, which can be used by the action selection component of the system to decide how the agent addressed in the dialogue must react to the user's communicative act.

Before presenting our approach to multimodal communication, in Section 12.2 we discuss multimodality in more detail, and summarize some of the most interesting work on the integration of gestures in computer interfaces. To this overview follows a discussion of our proposal for modality integration in Section 12.3. Section 12.4 contains an overview of the components of a multimodal dialogue system, with specific reference to the first Staging prototype. Finally, in Section 12.5 we draw the conclusions.

12.2 Human–Machine Interaction as Multimodal Interaction

> We argue [...], that humanoid interface agents do indeed raise users' expectations... up to what they expect from humans, and therefore lower their difficulty in interacting with the computer, which is otherwise for them an unfamilar interlocutor. (Cassell, in press, p. 47)

Many sources argue that users generally prefer multimodal to monomodal systems, thereby providing a flexible design where users can express themselves via various preferred modalities. (See, however, Petrelli *et al.* (1997) and Carbonell and Mignot (1994), who call this general assumption into question). Many sources also indicate an overall preference for one modality over another. Which modality or combination of modalities is chosen by the user is affected not only by the availability of the modalities in question, but also by other factors, such as the layout of the experiment conducted to determine what the user's preferences are, the task to be accomplished, response time, previous computer experience, and so on (see Music (1998) for a discussion). Since the conclusions drawn from these sources are rather contradictory, Music argues that it seems advisable when designing a multimodal system to give priority to approaches for combining multimodal inputs, regardless of the particular types of modalities generating that information.

Users' familiarity with multimodal communication, however, can be studied not only in relation to the way they react to yet rather primitive multimodal computers, but also by looking at the use of multimodality in human communication. As we shall see, some interesting attempts have been made to transfer knowledge from the domain of human communication to the implementation of multimodal systems.

The first attempts at combining speech with another modality – deictic gesture – date back about twenty years to the Put-That-There system (Bolt, 1980). This work has provided inspiration for many later approaches. The system was speech-driven, and gesture was only taken into account if speech analysis alone was not enough to interpret a command.

But deictic gestures are only one type among a rich typology of non-verbal behaviours playing a role in human communication. A very interesting body of work on the use of non-verbal behaviour in the implementation of embodied conversational characters is that by Cassell and her colleagues at the MIT Media Lab. Most automatic spoken systems trying to integrate speech with other modalities have focused on emblematic or emotional gestures, and are usually speech-driven. In the design of their embodied conversational agents (Cassell, in press), Cassell and her colleagues take into account a wider range of non-verbal behaviours, and integrate them with speech on the basis of the function they typically have in human communication. The attention given in this work to the conversational functions of non-verbal cues such as head nods, body posture, beat gestures and gaze we find particularly interesting and relevant to Staging.

The way in which different non-verbal behaviours can be made part of the communicative competence of animated agents has been explored at the MIT Media Lab in a number of prototype systems. The first is Animated Conversation, where two agents converse with each other about bank transactions. They can generate and react to iconic, metaphoric and beat gestures (see typology below). Especially noteworthy in this work is the attempt at synchronizing beat gestures with the rhematic part of the sentence (Halliday, 1967). In the second experiment, users can react with an agent – Gandalf – via datagloves and a thin jacket allowing the system to sense the position of the user's body. Gandalf understands gestures pointing towards the screen as referents to planets, and turns towards the screen as initiations of task activity. The fact that Gandalf is sensitive to the interactional level of the dialogue makes it a relatively "believable" partner in the conversation. Cassell notes that after a while, users begin to show a more natural style of conversation: they move their hands, they turn towards Gandalf while he speaks and to the screen while things are shown on it. Rea, the most recent of these creations (described in Cassell *et al.* (1999a,b)), is a real estate agent that can show the user house models. She reacts to the user's unconscious cues related to turn changes, she reacts naturally to the user interrupting her, and is able to initiate repair sub-dialogues if she does not understand what the user says.

These experiments show in our opinion that insights coming from human communication can indeed be used in the domain of multimodal human–machine communication. In the following section, we look more closely at the various types of gestures that Cassell and her colleagues have analysed.

12.2.1 A Typology of Gestures for Multimodal Interaction

Although body posture, head movements and gaze are also important modalities in human communication, here we shall limit ourselves to a description of hand gestures. Cassell groups gestures into conscious gestures on the one hand and spontaneous ones on the other. Conscious gestures may be of two kinds:

- Emblems, which are culture-specific, e.g. the gesture associated with the concept *okay* in American English.
- Propositional gestures, e.g. the gesture of measuring the space at the same time as saying *this big*, or pointing gestures. At the speech level, propositional gestures are typically associated with *place holders* such as the demonstrative pronoun.

This type of gesture is very important in task-oriented applications, where the physical location of objects on the screen is a topic in the conversation. Cassell argues, however, that propositional gestures are not the most common ones in spontaneous human conversation.

Among spontaneous gestures the following can be distinguished:

- Iconic gestures, depicting some semantic feature of the event being described. This can be the manner of movement, or the path or the speed in an utterance containing a movement verb (Cassell and Prevost, 1996). Iconic gestures are also, like emblems, culture-specific. One language may lexicalize certain features so that others are best expressed by gestures. Another language may display different preferences for which features can be expressed verbally, while leaving others to non-verbal rendering.
- Metaphoric gestures, representing an abstract concept by a physical shape.
- Deictic gestures, locating aspects of the discourse in the physical space. These do not need to be pointing gestures (which according to Cassell's typology belong instead to the category of propositional gestures). A deictic can, for instance, also function as an interactional cue, for example by picking up a person in the audience who the speaker is addressing.
- Beat gestures, small baton-like movements accompanying the spoken utterance. These gestures may serve several pragmatic functions, e.g. signalling speech repairs or turn change. In particular, speakers bring their hands into gesture space when they intend to take their turn, and at the end of a turn the speaker's hands come to rest. Cassell seems to imply that this use of beat gestures is universal, without, however, referring to cross-cultural empirical data.

From the point of view of the way they are articulated, gestures are composed of either three phases (preparation, stroke and retraction), or two (movement into and out of gesture space). Iconic and metaphoric gestures are triphasic, while deictic and beat gestures are biphasic. In either case, the stroke, which is the most energetic part of the gesture, falls together with or immediately before the most prominent syllable of the corresponding utterance.

From the point of view of their contribution to the communicative act, gestures can be either redundant or non-redundant. Finally, they can interact with speech not only at the phonological level, where, as we saw, stroke corresponds to pitch accent, but also at several other levels, as listed below:

- Interaction at the syntactic level: a sentence constituent is expressed through a pointing gesture, while a place holder reserves space for it in the speech segment. An example is *Move that there*, while pointing at the object to be moved and the new location intended for the object.
- Interaction at the semantic level: a semantic feature is expressed through a gesture. An example from Cassell and Prevost (1996) is *Road Runner comes down* while showing with his hands that he is driving.
- Interaction at the level of information structure: beat gestures are synchronized with the rhematic part of the utterance, roughly corresponding to the part containing new information.

• Interaction at the pragmatic level: gestures are used to regulate turn-taking.

Keeping in mind this brief characterization of gestures and of the way they can interact with speech, we can now discuss the way in which we intend to treat non-verbal behaviour in Staging.

12.3 Combining Modalities in a Unified Representation

Given the complexity of the interaction between gestures and speech, and the fact that many technical difficulties still have to be overcome before a similar degree of complexity can be transferred to multimodal systems, it is reasonable to assume that concrete implementations will initially focus on the integration of the speech signal with a limited set of unambiguous non-verbal behaviours. Which gestures are chosen for the particular application will vary. The assumption made here is that for the user to be able to experience the interface as natural, the gestures chosen should have a similar function in the system to what they would have in human communication. (Other important factors contributing to the naturalness of the interface which we are not considering here, are, for example, response times and robustness). Therefore, rather than focusing on the interplay of two or more particular modalities, in this section we propose a general method for integrating input coming from different modalities.

The literature generally depicts multimodal systems implemented with hard-coded procedures checking individual feature values, treating information from different modalities differently, executing decision-making based on hard-coded information which may or may not be formulatable as rules. This makes it difficult to generalize either about a given implementation's multimodal behavioural description or its process of combining the various pieces of multimodal information. It also makes it impossible to rely on being able to extend or reuse the work from one system for another application and/or modality configuration.

In the current context, we take a cue from Natural Language Processing (NLP); we will separate descriptive information about multimodal behaviour from processes which apply the information, analogous to the grammar vs. parser distinction in NLP. We envision a multimodal grammar plus an algorithm for applying the grammar to input from multiple modalities.

This separation of process and data has advantages, such as allowing for generalities about either processing or data, which has been fruitful for NLP. The process of merging inputs from different modalities becomes more general, as the entire representation becomes media-independent and any processes/procedures defined for modality integration within the processing stages are then generally applicable regardless of which input modalities originate the information in question. Finally, it also increases the chances that components of the system can be extended and/or reused.

Given that we want to express all modality behaviour in terms of process-independent declarative rules, it is clearly most advantageous to use a compatible formalism for the individual modality grammar descriptions (e.g. linguistic, gestural), the multimodal grammar description, and for the domain-specific semantics. We agree with Gourdol *et al.* (1992) that "[f]usion is facilitated if it takes place among uniform objects", i.e. a common representation.

In addition, assuming we want to be able to parse complex linguistic utterances as part of the multimodal system, we need a formalism with open-ended expressive power. A formalism supporting typed features is interesting here, as they allow representation of hierarchical information, and thereby permit expression of non-linguistic information as part of the same structure as linguistic information while still maintaining the distinction in information types. The usual advantages of typed features, well known from formal linguistic theories (e.g. HPSG, (Pollard and Sag (1994)) are also available, such as the convenience and perspicuity of grouping particular mutually relevant features into a single feature type.

Unification is desirable as it provides a convenient means of integrating underspecified information from various modality sources, simultaneously disambiguating possibly highly ambiguous information from modalities. Johnston *et al.* (1997) give excellent examples of the usefulness of this approach, where gesture and speech recognition are mutually compensatory.

Turning now to the Staging bar scenario, which is one of a series of scenarios that are being studied by the project, let us assume for example that the user is playing the part of the customer, and that she points at a cake on the counter while uttering "I'd like that one". The input from the speech recognizer and the data glove would be combined in a feature structure like the following one, where the "lingsign" feature contains the output of the speech recognizer, and the "gesture" feature the output of the dataglove, which has been resolved as a gesture pointing at an entity in the virtual world:

```
sign = {lingsign = {I'd like that one},
         gesture = {pointing = {$1cake}
                   }
        }.
```

This structure can be analysed by a parser to build an interpretation where the meaning of the deictic gesture is merged with the meaning of the linguistic segment. In this particular case the two information types complement each other, in that the referent of the pointing gesture must fill the slot corresponding to the demostrative pronoun, as shown below:

```
sem = {speechact = request,
       reln = want,
       args = {arg1 = {reln = user},
               arg2 = {reln = cake,
                       index = $1cake}
              }
      }.
```

Note that in the semantic representation above, the distinction between information coming from speech and information originating from gesture is no longer made.

Iconic gestures can be analysed in a similar fashion. In the next example, the user utters "A small beer" when the bartender asks her what she wants. At the same time, she makes a gesture which can be interpreted as meaning *small*, for instance by bringing thumb and forefinger close to one another.

In this case, let us assume that the speech recognizer has missed a word in the user's message, so that the gesture, which was used by the user in a redundant way, must in fact be analysed as complementary to the linguistic sign. The input to the parser may then be something like:

```
sign = {lingsign = {a beer},
        gesture = {iconic = {small}
                  }
       }.
```

The parser should be able to interpret the property expressed by the iconic gesture as modifying the nominal phrase *a beer*, and create a representation like the following one:

```
sem = {arg2 = {reln = beer,
               defs = indef,
               mod = {reln = small}
              }
      }.
```

Imagining now a case where gesture recognition has delivered an ambiguous result, the same multimodal input may be presented to the parser as follows:

```
sign = {lingsign = {a beer},
        gesture = {iconic = {small};
                   pointing = {$2glass}
                  }
       }.
```

The interpretation of the gesture is ambiguous between an iconic and a pointing gesture. However, since the nominal phrase associated with the gesture is indefinite, the grammar should be able to discard the pointing interpretation as meaningless. In other words, merging of the two information types here has a disambiguating function. More generally, a representation combining inputs from different modalities into a unified whole would adhere to well-defined principles. For instance, information coming from the dataglove must contribute to (i.e. unify with) the linguistic analysis, otherwise the system will recognize this as an error situation.

A unification-based solution to modality integration, then, seems a viable solution that can integrate redundant, complementary or ambiguous information seamlessly. At least, integration of gestures and speech at the syntactic and the semantic levels lends itself to a representation in terms of feature structures, as illustrated by the simple examples just discussed. Integration at the level of information structure is probably also amenable to this kind of approach, in as much as proposals have been made in the literature for expressing the information structure in typed feature structures (Engdahl and Vallduví, 1996). On the other hand, it is unclear how feature unification could be used to capture the pragmatic information conveyed by gestures with respect to, for example, turn-taking. Since this kind of information does not pertain to the single communicative act, it should probably be sent directly to the multimodal interaction manager in charge of controlling the interaction (see Section 12.4) circumventing parsing.

12.4 The Ingredients of Automatic Linguistic Analysis

In the preceding section a formalism for integrating input from different modalities was proposed, but it was not discussed how exactly this formalism was to be implemented in a running system. In this section, we look at the various components making up the architecture of a multimodal dialogue system, with particular regard to the analysis process, and with reference to the first Staging prototype, which is under development at CST.

From the point of view of what happens in the system, linguistic interaction can be broken down into two steps: analysis of the multimodal input and generation of a response. The job of the analysis process is to take input from the various modality devices available in the system, combine these inputs into a meaningful whole and map it onto an abstract representation which, sent to the virtual world, causes the agent(s) to perform some action, possibly accompanied by a verbal reply. The generation of a verbal reply is carried out by the generation component.

In what follows we shall discuss in more detail what we see as the tasks of the analysis process. A reasonable list is the following:

- processing the speech signal to output a list of word hypotheses (speech analysis)
- processing input from other modalities (currently a dataglove) to output a list of gesture hypotheses
- synchronizing input from the different modalities
- transforming the word and gesture list corresponding to each user communicative act into a more abstract representation of the syntactic and semantic content of this utterance (parsing)
- interpreting the meaning of each utterance in relation to the rest of the dialogue and the current state of the virtual world so that the virtual world can react to the user's input in the correct way (discourse and dialogue analysis)

To these "basic" tasks must be added the ability to initiate repair sub-dialogues in situations where the system does not understand the speaker, either because too much information is lacking, or because the information present is contradictory. Although the issue of repairs is a very important one, we shall not treat it any further here. See, however, Music (1998), where various types of system repairs that could be added to the architecture shown here are discussed. Methods for the treatment of users' self-repairs, on the other hand, are discussed for example in Tischer (1997).

Different system components take care of the various tasks listed above. The architecture envisaged in Staging for the whole system is shown in Figure 12.1.

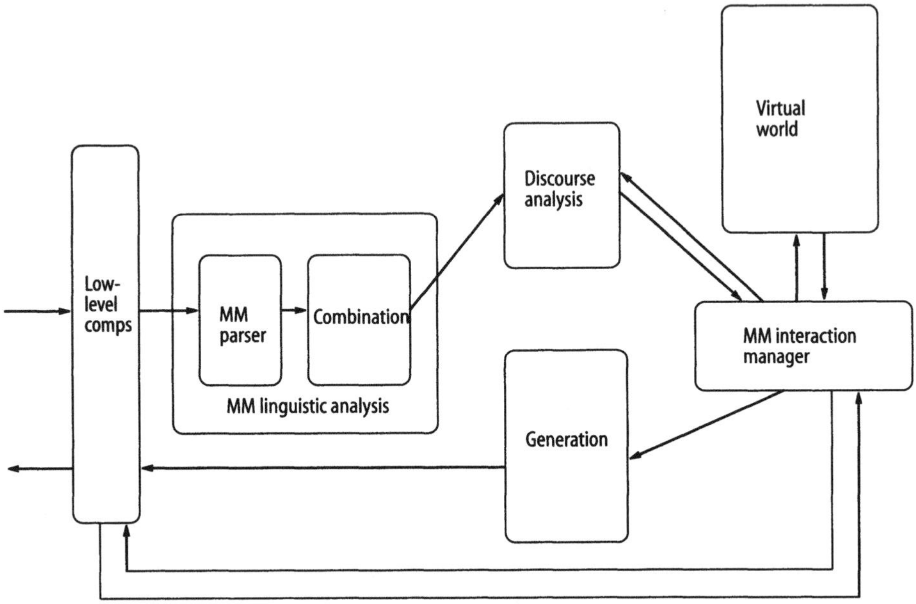

Figure 12.1 The system's architecture.

Information from various modalities is collected by the low-level components of the system and sent to further processing in a convenient format. Low-level components at this stage of system development are a speech processor and dataglove. An important requirement is that inputs from the two modalities are time-stamped, so that the system is able to synchronize them. Since the actual recognition of the speech signal or the signals sent through the dataglove are not the focus of our work, we assume here that existing software is simply plugged into the architecture, and possibly replaced with better products as they become available.

The speech processor currently in use is the commercial product Dragon NaturallySpeaking Professional, which provides word-based, continuous speech analysis trainable to different speakers' voices and accents. Dragon supports the Microsoft Speech Application Programming Interface (SAPI), which can be exploited to integrate the program with other components.

The low-level components send input containing information from one or both modalities either to the parser or the multimodal (MM) interaction manager, which will send it to the virtual world. The latter will happen if an entity pointed at must be identified, or if the user has signalled that he or she either wants the floor or is expecting the system to respond. In other words, the MM interaction manager is in charge of keeping track of turn-taking. In future, the MM interaction manager will also be responsible for initiating repair situations originating from failures to parse the user's input. Note that in such cases it must be an agent in the virtual world, and not an "omniscient" system that reacts to the failure, possibly initiating a repair metadialogue with the user.

MM parsing, as explained below, consists of two phases, one where grammar rules are applied to find an interpretation of the multimodal input, and another where an incomplete or fragmentary interpretation can be fleshed out. Parsing only looks at single communicative acts, a communicative act being an utterance (either a grammatical sentence or a phrase) possibly combined with a gesture. In many cases, however, a precise interpretation of the content of such a communicative act can only be determined on the basis of the preceding messages. The discourse analysis component of the system is responsible for this additional level of analysis. A detailed description of the requirements to be met by such a component, and of the approach to discourse analysis taken in the project is given in Chapter 13. Discourse analysis sends discourse interpretations to the MM interaction manager, which transfers them to the virtual world. Through the MM interaction manager, it can still access domain knowledge and knowledge about the preceding dialogue.

The last linguistic component of the architecture is linguistic generation, which is activated by the MM interaction manager if the Virtual World decides that the agent must reply to the user's input verbally. The actual shaping of this component will be the object of study at a later stage, and is therefore not discussed here.

In the next section, we explain in more detail how parsing of multimodal input is carried out, parsing being the central process in our approach to multimodal analysis.

12.4.1 Multimodal Parsing

Multimodal parsing comprises two stages, parsing proper and combination.

These correspond largely to "Partial Parsing" and "Combination" as used by Rosé and Lavie (1997), who argue that a "two stage repair approach" is demonstrated to provide the possibility of doing error recovery without the high performance overhead of single-stage approaches integrated within the parsing process. Although error resolution and repairs are not in focus in this paper, it is clear that the possibility of recovering from error situations is a very important requirement in any dialogue system, and therefore an architecture providing the possibility of adequate error resolution is to be preferred for our purpose.

In a multimodal context, separate parsing and combination stages provide both practical and conceptual advantages. Conceptually, the initial parsing phase can implement rule-based syntactic and semantic parsing where multimodal information is combined in an integrated feature structure via unification as outlined above, while the combination stage can implement modality-specific attempts at combining information in cases where the initial parsing phase is insufficient. From this derives the practical advantage that modality specific integration strategies need not complicate the already complex parsing process.

In the final part of this section, we focus on parsing proper.

The actual parser chosen for the implementation is an adaptation of Njal (Music and Povlsen, 1993), a bottom-up left-corner parser, which is being adapted to receive input from several modalities. Njal is a good candidate for the Staging prototype, since it is fast and is able to produce partial parses if the input is ill-formed or outside the coverage of the grammar. Njal has in fact also been used with success in another multimodal application (Brøndsted *et al.*, 1988).

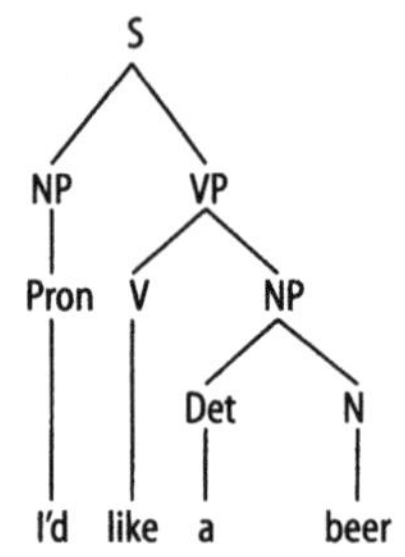

Figure 12.2 A phrase structure tree.

To build a representation of the input, Njal applies grammar rules like the following one (the rule is slightly simplified here for simplicity's sake):

```
s_1a = {cat=s}
              [
                {cat=np},
                {cat=vp, fin=yes}
              ].
```

The rule describes a phrase structure tree where the mother node is a declarative sentence (`cat=s`), and the two daughters are a nominal phrase (`cat=np`), and a finite verbal phrase (`cat=vp, fin=yes`). Assuming that other rules have analysed the nominal and verbal phrases, the application of this rule to the input *I'd like a beer* will result in the parse tree shown in Figure 12.2.

Associated with the parse tree is a feature structure containing the semantics of the sentence or phrase analysed. For instance, the semantics of the sentence under discussion will be expressed by a feature structure containing at least the following information:

```
sem= {speechact=request,
      reln=want,
      semtype=event
      args={arg1={reln=user,
                  defs=def,
                  semtype=human
                 },
            arg2={reln=beer,
                  defs=indef,
                  semtype=drink
                 }
           }
     }.
```

Semantic features are assigned as interpretations to the various nodes of the parse tree by the application of so-called semantic mapping rules. They are then collected in a unified representation associated with the top node of the tree. An example of a semantic mapping rule is the following:

```
vp_map = { sem={reln=REL} / {cat=vp}}
                            [
                            {cat=v, reln=REL},
                            {cat=np}
                            ].
```

The rule applies to the structure defined to the right of "/", i.e. a verbal phrase (cat=vp) consisting of a verb and a nominal phrase, and copies the relation name corresponding to the verb onto the semantic representation via the shared variable REL.

Assuming now that the structure built by the parser is a parse tree with gestural information attached, similar rules could also be used to make values coming from other modalities fill in slots in the semantic representation by unification. An example is shown in the following rule, where the information coming from an iconic gesture in a sign combining phrase structure (cat=np) and gestural information, is copied onto the semantics of the sign as the value for the feature mod via the shared variable MOD:

```
np_map = {sem={mod={reln=MOD}} /
                [sign = {cat=np},
                        {gesture = {iconic=MOD}}
                ].
```

In combination with the application of other semantic mapping rules, this will have the effect of generating the right semantics for one of the examples discussed in Section 12.3, where the user says "A small beer" or just "A beer" at the same time as showing with a gesture that the beer must indeed be small.

The task of defining the exact syntax and semantics of such rules, as well as the actual use of them to handle concrete examples, is currently being addressed in the project.

12.5 Conclusion

> One important limitation of human–computer interfaces is that they do not obey the Multimax Principle: not all modalities that the human partner naturally uses in a face-to-face situation can be used when facing a computer; one cannot speak in a normal way, one cannot use ordinary gestures, and one cannot use facial expression (smiles, frowns, ...); in fact, *none* of the natural modalities can be used! (Bunt *et al.*, 1998b, p. 3)

In the preceding sections we have argued that allowing the user to combine different modalities while communicating with the computer is a step forward towards more flexible and natural interfaces. However, we have also pointed out that studies on users' response in experiments involving real or simulated multimodal interfaces show little agreement as to what is the best choice and combination of modalities. Research trying to transfer insights from the use of multiple modalities in human communication, on the other hand, seems more promising. Users seem to respond well to systems capable of human-like, although of course limited, communication behaviours.

We have seen that in human communication, verbal and non-verbal signs may interact at the syntactic, semantic or pragmatic level. We have argued therefore that for a system to be able to understand multimodal behaviour of a kind similar to that which occurs in human communication, it must be able to merge inputs coming from different modalities at different representational levels.

To achieve this goal we have presented a formalism – based on typed feature structures – which allows for such an integration, irrespective of the particular choice of modalities implemented in a concrete system. Such an integration is implemented through unification, a well known and widely used operation in modern formal linguistics. We have argued that the adoption of such an approach, besides constituting a straightforward way of merging multimodal information, also provides the system with a way to handle ambiguous and contradictory analyses. Furthermore, in order to increase the system's ability to repair ill-formed input, we have proposed a two-stage analysis architecture where the multimodal input is parsed first and ameliorated if necessary in a combination phase.

An immense amount of work is still needed to be able to design and implement a multimodal dialogue system where users can engage in unrestricted conversation with a knowledgeable and cooperative human-like agent on any subject they like. Indeed, such a system may be impossible to build. But an intelligent use of multimodal devices in limited domains will make for better interfaces than we are accustomed to today.

Acknowledgements

The work described was carried out by the authors at Center for Sprogteknologi (CST) in Copenhagen. However, Bradley Music is currently employed at Microsoft Corp. in Redmond, WA.

In addition to the authors, Bart Jongejan, Bo Fleig Mortensen and Costanza Navarretta have also contributed to the work carried out for the Staging project at CST.

References

Allen. J. F., Schubert, L. K., Ferguson, G., Heeman, P., Hwang, C., Kato, T., Light, M., Martin, N., Miller, B., Poesio, M. and Traum, D. R. (1995) The TRAINS project: a case study in building a conversational planning agent. *Journal of Experimental and Theoretical Artificial Intelligence* 7: 7–48.

Allwood, J. (1998) Cooperation and flexibility in multimodal communication. In *Proceedings of the 2nd International Conference on Cooperative Multimodal Communication*, Tilburg, pp. 11–19.

Bernsen, N. C., Dyhkjær, H. and Dybkjær, L. (1998) *Designing Interactive Speech Systems*. London: Springer-Verlag.

Beskow, J., Ellenius, K. and McGlashan, S. (1997) Olga – a dialogue system with an animated talking agent. In *Proceedings of EUROSPEECH*, Rhodes, Greece.

Bolt, P. A. (1980) Put-that-there: voice and gesture at the graphics interface. *Computer Graphics* 14(3): 262–270.

Brøndsted, T., Larsen, L. B., Manthey, M., Kevitt, P. M., Moeslund, T. and Olsen, K. (1988) The Intellimedia WorkBench – an environment for building multimodal systems. In *Proceedings of the 2nd International Conference on Cooperative Multimodal Communication*, Tilburg, pp. 166–170.

Bunt, H., Ahn, R., Kievit, L., Piwek, P., Verlinden, M., Beun, R.-J., Borghuis, T. and van Overveld, K. (1998a) Cooperative dialogue with the multimodal DenK system. In *Proceedings of the 2nd International Conference on Cooperative Multimodal Communication*, Tilburg, pp. 44–61.

Bunt, H., Beun, R.-J. and Borghuis, T. (eds.) (1998b) *Multimodal Human-Computer Communication.* Berlin: Springer-Verlag.

Carbonell, N. and Mignot, C. (1994) "Natural" multimodal HCI: experimental results on the use of spontaneous speech and hand gestures. In *Proceedings of ERCIM Workshop Reports, Multimodal Human-Computer Interaction*, pp. 97–112. CRIN 94-R-188.

Carlson, R. (1996) The dialog component in the Waxholm system, in *Proceedings of Twente Workshop on Language Technology (TWLT 11) – Dialogue Management in Natural Language Systems*, University of Twente, The Netherlands.

Cassell, J. (in press) Embodied conversation: integrating face and gesture into automatic spoken dialogue systems. In *Spoken Dialogue Systems* (ed. S. Luperfoy). Cambridge, MA: MIT Press.

Cassell, J., Bickmore, T., Billinghurst, M., Campbell, L., Chang, K., Vilhjálmsson, H. and Yan, H. (1999a) Embodiment in conversational interfaces: Rea. In *CHI '99 Conference Proceedings*, pp. 520–527.

Cassell, J., Bickmore, T., Campbell, L., Chang, K., Vilhjálmnsson, H. and Yan, H. (1999b) Requirements for an architecture for embodied conversational characters. In *Computer Animation and Simulation.* Vienna: Springer-Verlag.

Cassell, J. and Prevost, S. (1996) Distribution of semantic features across speech and gesture by humans and machines. In *Proceedings of Workshop on the Integration of Gesture in Language and Speech.*

Engdahl, E. and Vallduví, E. (1996) Information packaging in HPSG. In *Studies in HPSG* (eds. C. Grover and E. Vallduví). Centre for Cognitive Science, University of Edinburgh, pp. 1–32.

Gourdol, A. P., Nigay, L. M., Salber, D. and Coutaz, J. (1992) Multimodal systems: aspects of events fusion and a taxonomy. In *Proceedings of IFIP*, pp. 156–162.

Halliday, M. A. K. (1967) Notes on transitivity and theme in English (part 2). *Journal of Linguistics* 3: 199–243.

Johnston, M., Cohen, P. R., McGee, D., Oviatt, S. L., Pittman, J. A. and Smith, I. (1997) Unification-based multimodal interaction. In *Proceedings of the 35th Annual Meeting of the Association for Computational Linguistics*, Madrid, pp. 281–288.

McGlashan, S., Bilange, E., Fraser, N., Gilbert, N., Heisterkamp, P. and Youd, N. (1992) Dialogue management for telephone information systems. In *Conference on Applied Language Processing.* Trento, Italy.

Music, B. (1998) *Robust Modality Parsing*, Technical Report Staging Deliverable 9B.1, Center for Sprogteknologi, Copenhagen, Denmark.

Music, B. and Povlsen, C. (1993) The NLP module of a spoken language dialogue system for Danish flight reservations. In *Proceedings of the 3rd European Conference on Speech Communication and Technology*, pp. 1859–1862.

Petrelli, D., DeAngeli, A., Gerbino, W. and Cassano, G. (1997) Referring in multimodal systems: the importance of user expertise and system features. In *Proceedings of Referring Phenomena in a Multimedia Context and Their Computational Treatment, a Meeting of the ACL SIGMM*, Madrid, Spain.

Pollard, C. and Sag, I. A. (1994) *Head-Driven Phrase Structure Grammar.* Chicago: University of Chicago Press.

Rosé, C. P. and Lavie, A. (1997) An efficient distribution of labor in a two stage robust interpretation process. In *Proceedings of EMNLP* (http://xxx.lanl.gov/abs/cmp-lg/9706021/; accessed 23 June 1998).

Tischer, B. (1997) Syntactic procedures for the detection of self-repairs in German dialogues. In *Dialogue Processing in Spoken Language Systems. ECAI '96 Workshop*, Budapest. Berlin: Springer, pp. 113–124.

13 Exploiting Recent Research on Dialogue to Model Verbal Communication in Staging

Costanza Navarretta

13.1 Introduction

Multimodal systems where the user interacts with one or more autonomous agents in a tridimensional environment must be able to interpret multimodal input from a user and react to it in a coherent way. The treatment of natural language dialogues in computer systems can be divided into three components: dialogue management, discourse interpretation and response generation. Dialogue management consists in implementing strategies that drive the dialogue, such as who can take the initiative and who controls the dialogue (the user, the system or both of them) and how the system must react to error situations. The choice of strategy depends, *inter alia*, on the application of the system and on the degree of robustness of the available speech recognition software.

The treatment of verbal interaction in unimodal and multimodal dialogue systems is similar. In unimodal systems a dialogue management component decides how to interact verbally with a user's utterance, after having interpreted it. In a multimodal system the non-linguistic input from the user is combined and interpreted together with the linguistic input. A multimodal manager module is responsible for choosing the most adequate modalities for presenting the system's response.

Discourse interpretation and response generation are built upon models of discourse structure. Such models have been proposed in different fields, among them sociology, psychology, linguistics and philosophy, and each of these focuses on specific aspects of discourse relevant to the actual field. Natural language engineers and scientists from artificial intelligence have been inspired by all these models. The dialogues determining the sub-language to be handled by dialogue systems are human-to-human task-specific conversations, or dialogues collected with Wizard of Oz experiments.[1] The conversations allowed in implemented systems are very limited and follow pre-specified schemata. The question which we will address is how to define strategies to implement dialogue systems which allow less bound and more "natural" dialogues between a user and agents than in existing implementations.

Although we focus primarily on discourse analysis, i.e. on the interpretation of linguistic and non-linguistic data from the user after this input has been processed by the parser and the multimodal combination components (see Chapter 12), we also address issues of dialogue management and of response generation.

In what follows we shortly present some of the components needed by a system to interpret dialogues and generate responses. We then review a few theories for modelling these components and look at the solutions implemented in existing uni- and multimodal dialogue systems. Then we discuss how the theoretical and implemented models fit in with less schemata bound dialogues than those allowed by existing systems. Finally we propose a preliminary model to be used in an implementation of dialogue management in Staging.

In what follows we use dialogues provided by the project's dramatist group. These dialogues, from now on called the *bar dialogues*, are conversations between a bartender, B, and a customer, C. The conversations are flirtatious, in that B flirts with C while he is asking what she would like to drink, whether she is feeling well and so on. These dialogues have more social implications and are less task-bound than dialogues supported by implemented systems.

13.2 Common Ground and Context

Most models of discourse[2] structure are based on the assumption that dialogue participants share a certain common ground and that, during conversation, they dynamically add information to this common ground. Defining and encoding the common ground, or background knowledge, of dialogue participants is quite a complex task. Background knowledge comprises linguistic and non-linguistic information, and general and domain-specific (sub-language-specific) information. In a computer system the knowledge encoded is necessarily a strong simplification of the knowledge that humans have and it is restricted to the sub-language and task which the system has to perform. The knowledge used by a system is both static and dynamic, the latter being the information which is changed or added to the system as a result of the interaction with the user.

---

1 In these experiments the users think that they are interacting with a real computer system, but, in reality, the system, or some of its components, is/are simulated by humans (Newell *et al.*, 1990).

2 In the literature "discourse" refers to both written and spoken texts/dialogues, including multimodal input, such as gestures and facial movements. We use the term with this broad reading. Also text must be understood with its wide meaning of "written or spoken passage" (Sinclair *et al.*, 1987, p. 1510).

One of the most important dynamic knowledge sources in a dialogue system is the so-called **dialogue history**, where the context of the interaction between the user and the system (or the system's agents) is registered. The dialogue history is useful to both the analysis and the generation process. The following example (1) from the *bar dialogues* illustrates a simple case of utterance interpretation against the previous conversational context.

(1) a. B: *Generer lyset dig?*
(Does the light annoy you?)

b. C: *Det er lidt skarpt*
(It is a little bit sharp)

If we assume that B is a system agent and that C is the user, the dialogue interpreter component has to "remember" utterance 1-a to find out that the pronoun *det* (it) in utterance 1-b refers to the light. In the isolated example above simple restrictions on the gender of the nominals in the two utterances are sufficient to resolve the pronominal reference. But, of course, there are many cases where the situation is more complex, as in the following example (2):

(2) a. *Anne gave presents to Carol.*

b. *She liked it*

If stress information is not available, sentence 2-b is ambiguous. The preferred interpretation is that Carol liked receiving the presents. However, in a broader context where the speaker is explaining why Anne has no money, the sentence could actually mean that Anne likes giving (and buying) presents. In many cases, the interpretation of utterances requires both knowledge of the structure of the ongoing dialogue (Hobbs, 1983; Asher, 1993), and knowledge of the intentions behind a speaker's utterance (Grosz and Sidner, 1986; Moore and Pollack, 1992). The structure of discourse is also necessary to generate appropriate responses. In example (1), a coherent response of the bartender to the customer who utters that the light is too sharp could be replacing it with a softer light or suggesting that the customer could sit at another table. If the bartender reacted by turning sharper lights on, his response would be perceived as peculiar.

13.3 Discourse Structure

In this section we look at some models of discourse structure presented in the fields of natural language engineering and artificial intelligence that have influenced the implementation of dialogue systems: the so-called Rhetorical Structure Theory, RST (Mann and Thompson, 1987), the coherence relation theory (Hobbs, 1983) and what we will call the GS86 model (Grosz and Sidner, 1986). The first two theories are inspired by linguistic studies investigating the relations that link clauses, sentences or other pieces of discourse to each other, for example Halliday and Hasan (1976), while the third approach is inspired by work on dialogues in task-oriented applications and on studies of the resolution of referring expressions in these task-specific sub-languages.

13.3.1 Hobbs

Hobbs (1983) assumes that conversations are planned and that people interact and produce text in order to achieve certain goals. He recognizes three interleaved levels of planning in conversation: the message level, the coherence level and the description level. The message level involves the main goals that motivate people to engage in a conversation and the coherence level is about how the speaker plans to present his message. The description level is concerned with the choice of lexical items, grammatical constructions and appropriate descriptions of entities and events. In modelling comprehension all the three levels must be taken into account. Hobbs' coherence theory only investigates the second level of planning, but it is part of a more general theory, according to which text interpretation means finding the most plausible explanation to a text using an abductive inference model (Hobbs *et al.*, 1993).

Texts are coherent and coherence can be characterized by means of inferable coherence relations between segments of the discourse. A coherence relation holds between sentences to a degree which depends on the salience of the axioms used to establish the relation. In Hobbs' coherence theory the basic elements of discourse are sentential units (clauses). The union of two sentential units linked by some coherence relation is also a sentential unit. The structure of discourse is built up as a binary tree whose terminal nodes are clauses and whose non-terminal nodes are coherence relations among them.

Elaboration is one of the recognized coherence relations and is characterized as follows:

> A segment of discourse S1 is an Elaboration of segment S0 if the same proposition P can be inferred from both S0 and S1, and one of the arguments of P is more fully specified in S1 than S0 (Hobbs, 1983, p. 31)

According to Hobbs a question–answer sequence is a kind of Elaboration, as is the case in the following example (3):

(3) a. B: *Hvad skal du have at drikke?*
(What do you want to drink?)
b. C: *En fadøl*
(A draught beer)

The information that C wants a draught beer elaborates the question of B in the required way, i.e. it fills in the object argument for the formula

A: $drink(c,X) \wedge customer(c)$

so that we get

B: $drink(c,b) \wedge customer(c) \wedge draught\_beer(b)$

The restricted set of coherence relations described by Hobbs have been used in many dialogue systems. His abductive theory of inference has also inspired theories which try to combine belief and dialogue models. The main problem with the abductive inference model is that it is not very efficient and requires the collection of quite a large amount of world knowledge which the participants in a conversation are supposed to share.

13.3.2 Mann and Thompson

Mann and Thompson's Rhetorical Structure Theory (RST) (Mann and Thompson, 1987) was originally a theory for generating explanatory texts. Later it was applied to deal with discourse interpretation. As in Hobbs' coherence theory (Section 13.3.1) RST texts are divided into units, called spans, which typically consist of a clause and form the terminal nodes in an RST tree structure. Spans are related by binary rhetorical relations. The union of two spans having an RST structure is also a span. The most prominent span in each relation is called the nucleus, while the less prominent one is called the satellite. The set of nucleus–satellite relations is open. Some of the relations recognized are: Antithesis, Background, Conditional, Elaboration, Enablement and Purpose. RST only permits one relation between two spans. If a text has multiple analyses, the most plausible one in terms of the writer's perceived overall goals must be chosen.

An RST analysis of sentence (4)

(4) *Jeg har også små peanuts, hvis det passer dig bedre*

(I also have small peanuts, if it is better for you)

would result in two RST spans:

1. *Jeg har også små peanuts*
2. *hvis det passer dig bedre*

Span 2 is in a **Conditional** relation to span 1, the nucleus. The graph for the obtained RST relation can be seen in Figure 13.1. RST theory has been used in many generation systems and in a few dialogue systems. The fact that it does not support multiple analyses of the same text has been criticized, because most texts are ambiguous (Moore and Pollack, 1992; Asher and Lascarides, 1994). The strong side of the theory is, in our opinion, that many of the rhetorical relations described in the model have been identified on the basis of the analyses of texts done by different people. We see it as a problem that cognitive aspects are not explicitly incorporated in the theory.

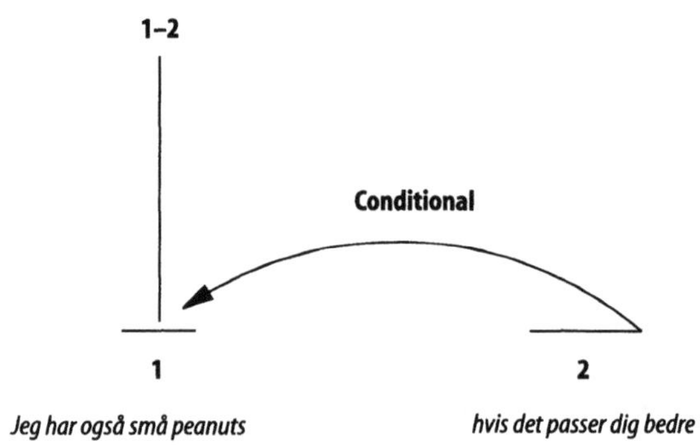

Figure 13.1 RST diagram for example (4).

13.3.3 Grosz and Sidner

Grosz and Sidner (1986) present a model of discourse structure which combines three interacting components: the linguistic structure, the intentional structure and the attentional state. The **linguistic structure** consists of the sequence of utterances in a discourse, aggregated into so-called discourse segments, and of the relations which hold between these segments. These relations are the surface reflection of the two relations holding among elements of the intentional structure: **satisfaction-precedence** (DSP1 contributes to DSP2) and **dominance** (DSP2 dominates DSP1).

The **intentional structure** deals with the purpose of the discourse. The intention that motivates engaging in a particular discourse is the so-called discourse purpose (DP). Each discourse segment has a corresponding discourse segment purpose (DSP) which specifies how the actual segment contributes to the achievement of the DP. DP and DSPs are intentions which the speaker wants to be recognized. To determine DSPs, information from different knowledge sources must be collected, such as linguistic markers (especially cue phrases), utterance-level intentions, general knowledge about actions and objects in the domain of discourse, and intonation.

The attentional state coordinates the linguistic and the intentional structures and is modelled by a set of focus spaces. The attentional state dynamically records the objects, properties, relations and DSPs that are salient at each point of the discourse. The relationships among DSPs determine pushes and pops from the focus stack. The focus space constrains the range of DSPs to be considered as candidates to be related to the current DSP and the search for possible referents of nominal phrases.[3]

In the GS86 model the utterances in (4) would be part of a Discourse Segment whose corresponding purpose is that of selling nuts to the customer. The main task (DP) for a bartender is, in fact, that of selling things and of serving the customer. Parallel to this overt task there is the flirtatious intention which is more difficult to formalize and to break down into subgoals.

Grosz and Sidner's theory is interesting because it relates linguistic, intentional and attentional aspects in the same framework. Grosz and Sidner's analysis of the relation between linguistic expressions and intentions, their implementation of the attentional state as a stack and the treatment of different kinds of phenomena such as anaphora resolution and interruptions, has also influenced later research on discourse and dialogue. For us the main problem with the theory is the identification of DSPs, which is not spelled out in the model. Segmenting discourse in fragments which reflect subgoals is nearly impossible when automatically treating dialogues which are not strictly task-oriented. The second problem with the theory is that the informational aspect of utterances is neglected.

---

3 A focus stack is used to resolve referents between discourse segments, which exhibit *global coherence*. The so-called centering theory has been proposed to resolve references to nominals among utterances in a discourse segment which are assumed to have *local coherence*, e.g. Grosz et al. (1986) and Kameyama (1998).

13.3.4 Combining Intentionality and Textual Relations

There have been several attempts to combine theories of discourse structure based on rhetorical relations and theories where intentionality plays a central role in the analysis of communication. Common to these "mixed" approaches is the fact that they state that both rhetorical and coherence relations and the recognition of the intentionality behind utterances are necessary to the task of interpreting dialogues (Moore and Pollack, 1992; Asher and Lascarides, 1994).

Asher and Lascarides (1994), in particular, present a complex formal model based on two parallel theories. The first theory specifies how rhetorical relations influence the structure of discourse. The second theory accounts for how different pragmatic knowledge resources must be used to infer the rhetorical and coherence relations holding between discourse units. Asher and Lascarides (1998, 1999) extend this framework so that it integrates discourse content and cognitive states. They use non-monotonic cognitive axioms to infer rhetorical relations at the discourse level, and these rhetorical relations have a semantics which constrains the resolution of anaphora.

Asher and Lascarides' work is interesting from a theoretical point of view because they actually present a framework for combining the different approaches to discourse structure. However, their model is much more complex than those used in practical applications and has to be tested in a real-time implementation.

13.3. Concluding Remarks

What in general characterizes the different theories and models which we have presented in this section is the attempt to identify the most important aspect(s) of discourse structure and the elementary units of discourse. RST concentrates on a single aspect of discourse, i.e. its rhetorical structure. This structure is useful in text generation and can influence the resolution of anaphora in text interpretation. However, RST alone does not provide enough information to model dialogue in interactions where both the informational and intentional aspect are relevant.

More complex are Hobbs' and the GS86 models, in which the importance of the linguistic structure together with the intentional and cognitive structure are recognized, although only some aspects of each level have been given priority in the authors' initial proposals. Recently researchers have argued for the necessity of combining the basic aspects of these three theories.

13.4 Dialogue Modelling in Planning and Information Retrieval Applications

Different approaches to dialogue modelling have been followed in the field of expert systems, especially planning systems, and in information retrieval or booking systems.

13.4.1 Dialogue Modelling in Planning Systems

Common to all the dialogue models adopted in planning applications is that they are inspired by Searle's speech acts theory (Searle, 1975). The speech acts relevant to a given application are treated and formalized as physical actions. An important aspect in the treatment of actions in expert systems is the recognition of the intentions (goals) which move an agent to perform these actions, similarly to the GS86 model. Following a tradition started with Fikes and Nilsson (1971) actions are considered to be *operators* described by the following elements:

- a *header* containing the name of the action
- a *precondition list* storing the conditions which must apply to perform the action
- an *effect list* representing what will be true after the action
- *bodies* storing the means or subgoals/sub-actions whose achievement constitutes the performance of the action

In the last decade the interest of researchers in the field of expert systems has moved towards the cognitive aspects involved in the processing of dialogues, i.e. the formalization of the effects of the illocutionary acts on the mental state of the conversants (Litman and Allen, 1990; Cohen and Levesque, 1990).

A dialogue system combining traditional linguistic modules with a plan-based dialogue model is the TRAINS system, developed at the Department of Computer Science of the University of Rochester (Allen *et al.*, 1995). The TRAINS system is a natural language conversation and plan reasoning system where the user and an agent must cooperation to manage a railway transportation system.

The architecture of the TRAINS system contains natural language interpretation modules and domain task interaction modules which both interact with the dialogue manager. The dialogue model is based on the so-called conversational act theory (Traum and Hinkelman, 1992) which states that speech acts must be grounded (Clark and Schaefer, 1989), i.e. acknowledged, by the listener before they are added to the common ground. The dialogue manager of the TRAINS system maintains a model of its mental state and the discourse context which includes the turn, the current domain plan, grounding and plan-based focusing information. The discourse context is implemented as a stack.

The TRAINS project is interesting because it combines planning techniques with a computational linguistic approach to the treatment of dialogues. In the analysis of dialogues the central idea is that of grounding, which has been followed by many researchers since then.

13.4.2 Dialogue Modelling in Information Retrieval Systems

Many real-time systems have followed a so-called dialogue grammar approach, for example, the Sundial (Speech Understanding and DIALog) systems (McGlashan *et al.*, 1992) and the LINLIN system (Ahrenberg *et al.*, 1990). In this approach it is assumed that the structure of the chosen textual units can be used to model dialogue and that a grammar can describe the dialogue's structure. Although the intentional perspective is still considered to be important, it is not central to the processing of dialogues. The idea of using a grammar to describe the most important elements of the surface structure and the semantics of dialogue and the description of suitable parsing strategies for such a grammar has been introduced by Polanyi's (1988) Linguistic Discourse Model (LDM). She was inspired by the theories of discourse structure which we presented in Section 13.3 and by studies of conversations made by American sociologists, also known as the ethnomethodologists. In LDM the basic units are sentences, here understood as clauses or false starts, hesitations and other linguistic noise. Sentences combine by rhetorical subordination and coordination relations and, on a higher level, into discourse genre units, such as stories and arguments, and Discourse Adjacency units, such as question/answer pairs and compliment/response sequences.

The models behind systems based on the dialogue grammar approach differ in the way and in the granularity in which the dialogues are divided into constituent units. In Sundial and in LINLIN the units are dialogue acts/moves, i.e. speech acts, enriched with dialogue relevant information. In the Sundial model more dialogue acts compose an intervention marked as initiative, reaction or evaluation. More interventions form an exchange or negotiation. More negotiations form a transaction, which corresponds to a DSP in the GS86 model. In LINLIN dialogue moves combined in initiative-response units form a dialogue segment. Initiative-response units are, for example, the pairs information_request/answer, information_request/assertion.

Another dimension along which these dialogue systems vary is to what extent they integrate non-linguistic aspects, such as task descriptions and cognitive aspects. The dialogue manager of the Sundial system, for example, operates on different structures corresponding to the three levels in the GS86 model. The LINLIN system, instead, has a simpler structure.

Apart from the above-mentioned differences, the systems are quite homogeneous and treat conversations in similar types of applications and domains such as information retrieval and booking of travel and hotels. The interaction allowed in these systems is topic-specific and follows a pattern which is defined on the basis of the chosen sub-language, in most cases obtained by Wizard of Oz experiments. The higher constituent units in the dialogue structure are also chosen on the basis of the current sub-language and task definition. These units can therefore, in most cases, be used to predict the next dialogue move. The dialogue analysis is effective and the error rate is low. Some of the linguistic generalizations in LDM are lost in the implemented systems.

13.4.3 Concluding Remarks

Dialogue models behind planning systems and information retrieval systems are task- and sub-language-specific. The former focus on the intentions behind the utterance of speech acts, the latter use the combination structure of speech acts in specific sub-languages. Interesting in these models are the study of speech acts and the inclusion into the models of phenomena studied by the ethnomethodologists, such as turn-taking mechanisms and grounding phenomena.

The analysis and formalization of the intentions and attitudes of the conversants in the plan-based theories of speech acts opens important perspectives on the analysis of dialogues. Problematic are the identification of the intentions of an agent and the efficient implementation of a plan recognizer which considers intentions. In such a recognizer the search space is extremely large, and it is necessary to adopt special strategies to make it efficient in real-time systems (Jönsson, 1997). This is a serious problem, especially considering the fact that the described plan-based systems are quite simple and very task-oriented.

Besides the clear necessity of simplifying the discourse interpretation process in order to implement real-time systems, dialogue systems based on the dialogue grammar approach try to combine different aspects of existing discourse models. They are efficient, but the interaction they allow is limited to pre-specified conversation schemata.

13.5 Dialogue Modelling in Multimodal Systems

Most multimodal systems have the same dialogue structure as unimodal dialogue systems. Non-verbal input from the user is combined with the verbal input and a multimodal manager decides which modality/ies is/are most appropriate to express the system output (McGlashan, 1996; Johnston, 1998). In multimodal systems the user can communicate by verbal (spoken or written) utterances and by pointing to objects in the virtual world with a mouse or a pen. The systems can respond with written or spoken utterances and with 2D or 3D graphics. Many multimodal systems are built reusing existing dialogue systems or some of their components. Thus the dialogue models behind these systems are not new with respect to those we discussed in Section 13.4.2. Also, the applications of multimodal systems are similar to those of unimodal dialogue systems, i.e. information retrieval and ticket booking, for example VOYAGER (Glass *et al.*, 1995), WEBGALAXY (Lau *et al.*, 1997), the Waxholm system (Carlson *et al.*, 1995) and Olga (Beskow *et al.*, 1997).

The new aspect in multimodal systems is the possibility of combining different modalities, and therefore researchers have focused on these aspects. Agents' behaviour and the way in which they use multimodality have been formalized on the basis of studies of inter-human communication. Examples are the Waxholm system, where labial and eye movements are synchronized with the spoken output, the Olga system which extends this setup to body movements, Gandalf and Rea (Cassell and Vilhjálmsson, 1999) where facial movements and hand gestures are integrated with verbal interaction.

Some experimental studies have been done to record the user's choice of modalities (Oviatt *et al.*, 1997) and possible ways of combining modalities have been described by Martin (1997). A first framework for choosing output modality from the media and the data characteristics has been proposed in Arens *et al.* (1993). Because we focus on discourse interpretation, the main issue, for our future research is how multimodal communication affects discourse structure and analysis.

Table 13.1 Variation of discourse units and structure.

Model	Unit	Relation	Structure
RST	Sentence	Rhetorical relations	Tree
Coherence theory	Sentence	Coherence relations	Tree
LDM	Sentence Questions/answers etc.	Conjunction, subordination Adjacency pairs	Parse-tree
LINLIN	Dialogue acts	Initiative–response pairs	Parse-tree
GS86	DS (intention) Satisfaction-precedence	Dominance	Tree
Planning systems	Intention (speech act)	is-a-precondition-of/is-a-way-to	Task description
TRAINS	Turn-taking, grounding Speech acts	Argumentation	Stack

13.6 The Staging Approach

As we have seen in the previous sections, there are many theoretical and applied models of discourse. The most important dimensions of variation in the models are the choice of the dialogue units and the relations which combine them, and the weight linguistic and non-linguistic aspects are given.

The first dimension is summarized in Table 13.1. Most models represent dialogue structure as a tree. In a few systems the dialogue structure is implemented as a stack or an array. In expert systems the interest is in the intentions behind the utterance of speech acts and the inference processes necessary to calculate goals from intentions and intentions from goals. The chosen component units are sentences, speech acts or the intentions behind a speech act. These units can be combined by textual or plan-related relations, or they can be analysed as components in adjacency pairs.

Although it is generally recognized that a variety of aspects interplay in conversations, the different theories and models focus on only a few of these aspects. This second dimension of variation is not as fixed as the former, because most of the theories of discourse structure have been presented as partial theories and are continually extended to cover more aspects.

In the following sections we look at how the different theories and practices can contribute to the treatment of fewer schemata-bound dialogues than those allowed in existing systems. Then we present the dialogue modules which will be used in Staging.

13.6.1 The Dialogue Structure

All dialogue models in computational linguistics and in artificial intelligence presuppose that communication is a cooperative task and we follow this assumption. Following the GS86 model we assume that linguistic, intentional and attentional levels interact in dialogue structure, but we do not base our analysis exclusively on the recognition of the intentions behind utterances, because these intentions cannot always be determined automatically, especially in not strictly task-oriented domains. Instead we choose dialogue acts as the basic elements of the dialogue structure, but recognize the importance of intentionality and, to a certain extent, follow a task-oriented approach.

Seen from such a task-oriented point of view, dialogues imply at least two task levels. The first level, common to all dialogue types, is that of controlling and planning the dialogue.[4] The second level is the overt domain-dependent task. In the bartender domain this level includes the tasks of selling drinks/food and serving the customer, which can be split up into sub-goals and plans, as is the case for tasks implemented in expert systems.

In dialogues other more covert "tasks" can be present, related to specific social relations. In the bar dialogues, for example, one such task is that of flirting with the customer. The flirt is a kind of social game whose main goal is keeping the flirt going. At this level the way and the style in which sentences are uttered and extra-linguistic factors are more important than what is said.

To treat the dialogue-task level we follow the dialogue grammar approach defining initiative–response pairs and sub-language specific pairs. Few coherence and rhetorical relations can also be used. The domain-specific task can be treated in a task module, where a task is divided into subtasks which are connected to specific linguistic expressions (here dialogue acts). The components at this level correspond to the discourse segments in the GS86 model. They are used in the interpretation phase to keep track of entities relevant at the current point of the interaction for resolving, for example, the referring expression and treating interruptions. The task structure is also used when the system has to plan the next move of the agent.

More socially related tasks can require the generation of specific types of sentences (in a flirting situation an agent's utterances could be ambiguous). Use of textual relations as in RST and in the coherence theory and commonsense knowledge could be useful at this level.

13.6.2 Dialogue Modules

A **dialogue manager** module is in charge of interpreting the user's multimodal response in the context of the ongoing interaction and of planning verbal reactions. The interpretation is made in a **dialogue analysis component** which receives a semantic representation of the user's input from the multimodal combination component (see Chapter 12). The dialogue analysis component is in charge of resolving referring expressions and of interpreting the output in the current interaction. The interpreted message is then passed to the multimodal manager, which is responsible for choosing an appropriate response from the agent. If the chosen

4 This dialogue task level is called the domain-independent plan in Litman and Allen (1990) and the dialogue control act level in Bunt (1995).

response includes verbal output, the dialogue manager passes an appropriate semantic representation of the utterance to be output to a **generation component** and then adds this representation to the dialogue history. A component describing the task structure is consulted by the dialogue manager during both interpretation and generation. In what follows, we focus on the interpretation process. In unimodal dialogue systems the universe of discourse, i.e. the entities that the user and the system can verbally refer to, consist exclusively of the entities that the user and the system/agents are expected to know at the beginning of the interaction (common background defined by the application sub-language and task) and the entities that are explicitly introduced during the interaction.

In multimodal communication, where the user interacts with agents in a 3D virtual world, the objects and agent(s) in this world are also part of the common ground. The ongoing changes in the virtual world must also be recorded, and the user and the agent(s) can refer to the entities of the 3D world verbally and with pointing acts.

The dialogue manager keeps track of the dialogue in the **dialogue history**, a representation of the user's and the agent's conversational contributions. The dialogue manager must also have access to another dynamic data structure recording the entities (objects, agents) currently present in the 3D world. The dialogue analysis component receives a simple semantic representation of the combined user's verbal and non-verbal input, together with information about the sentence-type, such as whether the sentence is a question, an assertion or an interjection.[5]

The dialogue history is composed of dialogue units. A dialogue unit is a dialogue act, i.e. a speech act to which is added information about the dialogue "situation", using Barwise and Perry's terminology (Barwise and Perry, 1983). In most cases a sentence corresponds to a speech act, but in some cases (e.g. complex sentences) it must be split up into more units. The dialogue analysis component adds to the original semantic formula the information about the utterance situation. If the representation corresponds to a single speech act it will be added to the dialogue history, represented as a tree, in conformity with LDM. If the sentence representation corresponds to more speech acts, it is split up before the resulting acts are added to the dialogue history. A dialogue act is part of an initiative–response pair and more pairs will combine into a transaction (a discourse segment in the GS86 model). Transactions in the bartender domain are, for example, selling a drink, selling food, asking how the customer is feeling.

The insertion and deletion of dialogue acts into and from the dialogue tree is made according to these structuring elements. For example, a transaction will start a new subtree, the daughters of which are initiative–response pairs. When a transaction is terminated, the corresponding subtree can be deleted.

We formalize dialogue using a variation of Discourse Representation Theory, DRT (Kamp, 1981; Kamp and Reyle, 1993). DRT is the first of a number of semantic theories based on a dynamic notion of meaning, i.e. where the meaning of a sentence is considered a function from a context to a context. DRT describes how to construct

5 *Sentence* must be understood here as words and/or gestures that can be interpreted as complete propositions.

semantic representations, called *Discourse Representation Structures*, DRSs, from natural language (English) sentences.

As an example we give the graphical DRS for utterance (1-a) (*Does the light annoy you?*).

(K0)

e1,x,y
light(x) *customer(y)* *annoy(e1,x,y)*

To the DRS is added the information that the sentence has been uttered by the agent and that it is a yes–no question.

(K1)

e1,x,y
light(x) *customer(y)* *annoy(e1,x,y)*

utterer: agent1; sentence_type:Yes-No-question

A "yes–no question" in the present example is an "information-request" act that in most cases is followed by an "answer" act (Section 13.4.2). Here we assume that K1 starts a new serving transition about the "light". A transition node is added to the existing dialogue tree and a daughter-node, marked as info-request/answer, is then attached to it. DRS K1 is added to this node.

The customer's response in (1-b) (*It is a little bit sharp*) can be represented by the enriched DRS K2.

(K2)

s1,x,z
sharp(s1,z) *little(s1)* *z=x*

utterer: customer; sentence_type:assertion

The dialogue analysis component resolves the reference of pronoun *it* to the *light*, for example on the basis of gender information from the parser. The problem at this point is to "understand" how K2 is answering K1, i.e. what is the "occasional" meaning of the utterance, using a Gricean expression. The dialogue model is based on the assumption that communication is a cooperative enterprise and that the user's intention in uttering (1-b) is to provide a coherent response to the agent's question. To interpret K2 as a coherent answer to K1, the dialogue manager needs more knowledge. This knowledge, called lexical semantic knowledge, could, in this particular case, be the fact that the adjective *sharp* modifying the nominal *light* means "strong" and that *sharp light* can be annoying. At this point the system can infer that the customer, by answering that the light is a little bit sharp, really means that she is annoyed by the light. This is in line with Hobbs' coherence theory and his abductive interpretation theory, but it involves also the notion of intentionality as presented in the GS86 model and in models behind planning systems. It most be noted that encoding all the knowledge necessary to make this kind of inferences is by no means a trivial task.

In the two extended DRSs K1 and K2 we have not included information about time and space. This information, comprising reference to the time and place in which an utterance has been performed, together with the time and place to which the current dialogue act refers, must be added to the representation of each utterance. Time and space information in the actual dialogue unit come from the parser (tense information and temporal and spatial adverbials). Spatial information must be related to the current 3D world. This information is used to interpret deictic expressions. If we add this information to DRS K1 we get K3. In K3, **t** stands for time, **p** for place, **n** stands for "now" and **b** stands for "in-the-bar".[6]

(K3)

e1,x,y,t,p,n,b
t=n *p=b* *light(x)* *customer(y)* *annoy(e1,x,y,t,p)*

utterer: agent1; sentence_type:Yes-No-question, place=p, time=n

The time and place to which the dialogue act refers are, of course, not always the same as the time and place in which the act is uttered.

If no deictic gestures combine with the utterance *Does the light annoy you?*, and if no reference to a *light* could be found in the preceding context, the definite nominal phrase *the light* must be interpreted using background knowledge of the 3D world, i.e. descriptions related to the light entity(ies) in the virtual world. If the agent points to a specific light in the bar while producing the utterance, the information of the gesture's type and direction, combined with the information of the entities in the 3D world, is used to interpret the nominal phrase as referring to the light which the agent is pointing to. Algorithms for resolving referring expression are usually restricted to anaphora and, in some cases, to temporal deictic expressions. They must be extended to treat other deictics.

6 A discussion of which theory should be chosen for representing temporal and spatial aspects is not in the scope of the present chapter, but see for example Barwise and Perry (1983), Kamp and Reyle (1993) and Asher (1993).

13.7 Conclusion

To analyse and coherently respond to user multimodal input, where language is one of the modalities involved, is a very complex task. In this chapter we have discussed how discourse structure can be modelled in a multimodal scenario. In particular, we have looked at how existing discourse structure theories and models can contribute to the formalization of complex dialogues between a user and an agent in 3D virtual worlds and we have proposed an approach to be used in the Staging project. We have also presented modules to process dialogues in a multimodal setup. In this setup the representation of the context of discourse must be extended to comprise the entities (agents and objects) in the virtual world and the changes in their status during the interaction. Although we have mainly focused on the analysis process, we have also discussed issues relevant to dialogue management and answer generation.

The theories and models of discourse structure which we have discussed are partial, focusing on few aspects of discourse. We argue that some of the aspects and strategies from the theories must be combined for tackling more natural (human-like) dialogues than those allowed in many implemented systems. In particular we propose a preliminary mixed approach where we combine the three level analysis presented by Grosz and Sidner with the analysis of speech acts and the use of a dialogue grammar typical of implemented models. We also argue for the importance of using commonsense background knowledge and of adopting a subset of textual relations (RST and coherence theory) in the interpretation and generation process.

Although we do not choose the intentions behind utterances as basic discourse units, because it is not clear how to extract them automatically, we follow a task-oriented approach and recognize different task levels in dialogues: dialogue-specific, domain-specific and social-related task levels. The presented model foresees actions at each level.

References

Ahrenberg, L., Dahlbäck, N. and Jönsson, A. (1990) Discourse representation and discourse management for a natural language dialogue system. In *Proceedings of the Second Nordic Conference on Text Comprehension in Man and Machine*, Täby, Stockholm.

Allen, J. F., Schubert, L. K., Ferguson, G., Heeman, P., Hwang, C., Kato, T., Light, M., Martin, N., Miller, B., Poesio, M. and Traum, D. R. (1995) The TRAINS project: a case study in building a conversational planning agent. *Journal of Experimental and Theoretical Artificial Intelligence* 7: 7–48.

Arens, Y., Hovy, E. and Vossers, M. (1993) On the knowledge underlying multimedia presentations. In *Intelligent Multimedia Interfaces* (ed. Maybury, M. T.). Cambridge: AAAI Press, pp. 280–306.

Asher, N. (1993) *Reference to Abstract Objects in Discourse*. Dordrecht: Kluwer Academic.

Asher, N. and Lascarides, A. (1994) Intentions and information in discourse. In *Proceedings of the 32nd Annual Meeting of the Association for Computational Linguistics*, Las Cruces, USA, pp. 34–41.

Asher, N. and Lascarides, A. (1998) Questions in dialogues *Linguistics and Philosophy* 3(3): 237–309.

Asher, N. and Lascarides, A. (1999) Cognitive states, discourse structure and the content of dialogue. In *Preproceedings of Amstelogue '99. Workshop on the Semantics and Pragmatics of Dialogue*, Amsterdam University.

Barwise, J. and Perry, J. (1983) *Situations and Attitudes*. Cambridge, MA: MIT Press.

Beskow, J., Ellenius, K. and McGlashan, S. (1997) Olga – A dialogue system with an animated talking agent. In *Proceedings of EUROSPEECH*, Rhodes, Greece.

Bunt, H. (1995) Dialogue control functions and interaction design. In *Dialogue in Instruction* (eds. R. J. Benn, M. Baker and M. Reiner). Heidelberg: Springer-Verlag, pp. 197–214.

Carlson, R., Hunnicutt, S. and Gustafsson, J. (1995) Dialog management in the Waxholm system. In *Proceedings of Spoken Dialogue Systems*, Vigsø.

Cassell, J. and Vilhjálmsson, H. (1999) Fully embodied conversational avatars: making communicative behaviours autonomous. *Autonomous Agents and Multi-Agent Systems* 2(1): 45–64.

Clark, H. H. and Schaefer, E. F. (1989) Contributing to discourse. Cognitive Science 3: 259–294.

Cohen, P. R. and Levesque, H. J. (1990) Rational Interaction as the Basis for Communication. In *Intentions in Communication* (eds. P. R. Cohen, J. Morgan and M. E. Pollack). Cambridge, MA: MIT Press, pp. 221–255.

Fikes, R. and Nilsson, N. (1971) STRIPS: a new approach to the application of theorem proving to problem solving. *Artificial Intelligence* 2: 189–208.

Glass, J., Polifroni, J. and Seneff, S. (1995) Multilingual spoken-language understanding in the MIT Voyager system. *Speech Communication* 17: 1–18.

Grosz, B. J. and Sidner, C. L. (1986) Attention, intentions, and the structure of discourse. *Computational Linguistics* 12(3): 175–284.

Grosz, B., Joshi, A. K. and Weinstein, S. (1986) Towards a computational theory of discourse interpretation, Unpublished MS.

Halliday, M. and Hasan, R. (1976) *Cohesion in English*. London: Longman.

Hobbs, J. R. (1983) Why is discourse coherent?. In *Coherence In Natural-Language Texts* (ed. F. Neubauer). Hamburg: Helmut Buske Verlag, pp. 29–70.

Hobbs, J., Stickel, M., Appelt, D. and Martin, P. (1993) Interpretation as Abduction. *Artificial Intelligence* 3(1–2): 69–142.

Johnston, M. (1998) Multimodal unification-based grammars. In *AAAI Workshop on Representations for Multimodal Human–Computer Interaction*, Madison, WI. Menlo Park, CA: AAAI Press, p. 31.

Jönsson, A. (1997) A model for habitable and efficient dialogue management. *Natural Language Engineering* 2,3: 103–122.

Kameyama, M. (1998) Intrasentential centering: a case study. In *Centering Theory in Discourse* (eds. M. Walker, A. Joshi and E. Prince). Oxford: Oxford University Press, pp. 89–112.

Kamp, H. (1981) A theory of truth and semantic representation. In *Formal Methods in the Study of Language* (eds. J. A. G. Groenendijk, T. M. V. Janssen and M. B. J. Stokhof), Vol. 1. Foris, pp. 277–322.

Kamp, H. and Reyle, U. (1993) *From Discourse to Logic: Introduction to Modeltheoretic Semantics of Natural Language, Formal Logic and Discourse Representation Theory*. Boston: Kluwer Academic.

Lau, R., Flammia, G., Pao, C. and Zue, V. (1997) WebGALAXY: beyond point and click – a conversational interface to a browser. In *Proceedings of the Sixth International World Wide Web Conference* (eds. M. Gemeresereth and A. Patterson), Santa Clara, CA, pp. 119–128.

Litman, D. J. and Allen, J. F. (1990) Discourse processing and commonsense plans. In *Intentions in Communication* (eds. P. R. Cohen, J. Morgan and M. E. Pollack). Cambridge, MA: MIT Press, pp. 365–388.

Mann, W. and Thompson, S. A. (1987) Rhetorical structure theory: description and construction of text structures. In *Natural Language Generation* (ed. G. Kempen). Boston, MA: Martinus Nijhoff, pp. 85–95.

Martin, J.-C. (1997) Towards "intelligent" cooperation between modalities. The example of a system enabling multimodal interaction with a map. In *Proceedings of the IJCAI'97 Workshop on "Intelligent Multimodal Systems"*. Nagoya, Japan.

McGlashan, S. (1996) Towards multimodal dialogue management. In *Proceedings of 11th Twente Workshop on Language in Texhnology*, Enschede, The Netherlands.

McGlashan, S., Bilange, E., Fraser, N., Gilbert, N., Heisterkamp, P. and Youd, N. (1992) Dialogue management for telephone information systems. In *Proceedings of the 3rd Conference on Applied Natural Language Processing*, Trento, Italy, pp. 245–246.

Moore, J. D. and Pollack, M. E. (1992) A problem for RST: the need for multi-level discourse analysis. *Computational Linguistics* 18(4): 537–544.

Newell, A. F., Arnott, J. L., Carter, K. and Cruickshank, G. (1990) Listening typewriter simulation studies. *International Journal of Man–Machine Studies* 3: 1–19.

Oviatt, S., DeAngeli, A. and Kuhn, K. (1997) Integration and synchronization of input modes during multimodal human–computer interaction. In *Proceedings of Conference on Human Factors in Computing Systems*. New York: ACM Press.

Polanyi, L. (1988) A formal model of the structure of discourse. *Journal of Pragmatics* 2(5/6): 601–638.

Searle, J. R. (1975) A taxonomy of illocutionary acts. In *Language, Mind, and Knowledge* (ed. K. Gundersond). Minneapolis, MN: University of Minnesota Press, pp. 344–369.

Sinclair, J., Hanks, P., Fox, G., Moon, R. and Stock, P. (eds.) (1987) *Collins Cobuild English Language Dictionary*, London: HarperCollins.

Traum, D. R. and Hinkelman, E. A. (1992) Conversation acts in task-oriented spoken dialogue. *Computational Intelligence* 3: 575–599.

SECTION 4

Interactive Narratives

Introduction

Søren Kolstrup

This section contains six chapters. In Chapter 14, Søren Kolstrup discusses the possible ways that narratives can be configured in different media and what the criteria for computer narratives could be. Jørgen Stigel (Chapter 15) emphasizes the communicative spaces created for narrative representations in television and the computer media. Jens F. Jensen (Chapter 16) presents film theory and how it can serve the analysis of computer-generated narratives. Edvin Kau (Chapter 17) offers a provocative discussion of the ways in which meaning is created in film and in computer narratives. Hanne Dankert and Niels Erik Wille (Chapter 18) discuss the implications of the absence of indexical foundation in computer-generated 3D representations, especially the 3D documentary. Finally, Peter Øhrstrøm (Chapter 19) presents the fundamentals of time structure in different narrative representations.

The six chapters use different strategies. Two use a bottom-up approach (from practical examples to theoretical demonstrations), three expose different theoretical viewpoints before they come to practical examples and one uses a continuous movement between the theoretical and practical poles. In particular, the chapters using bottom-up strategies contain controversial points of view.

There is (cf. the general introduction) some common ground for all the articles: the narrative tradition from Aristotle to Seymour Chatman! But the key dimensions within this tradition are often used in rather different, if not incompatible, ways. The differences or divergences can be ascribed to some few but important themes or problems: the notions of indexicality/truth, identification, space, time and narrative.

Beyond Indexicality

The first of these fields of diversity concerns the notions of truth, plausibility, realism, the level of narrative authority, the problem of indexicality etc. Edvin Kau proposes distinguishing between "transmission" (indexicality) and "transformation" (symbolic representation) and he contests the normal linking of film/documentary pictures with the photo's indexical origin and even more the utility of this

Peircian key concept and of the cognitivist trend in current film and television theory. Certainly within the fiction film/3D multimedia, but also in documentaries, the realistic effect is not the result of our daily life experiences, but is the product of the construction. Here Kau differs from Jens F. Jensen, for whom film is an indexical medium as opposed to 3D multimedia that are iconic or symbolic.

Niels Erik Wille and Hanne Dankert are equally sceptical about the (mechanical) indexical truth; they do not dismiss it, but 3D documentary has to rely on internal coherence and cannot rely on any direct link to the referent.

Identification or Involvement

Edvin Kau is sceptical about the traditional way of explaining the viewer's identification with the protagonists, especially through the POV or subjective camera. His analyses show that the camera movements are more complicated than that. In a horror film you occasionally may take over the villain's point of view, but nevertheless you experience involvement on the side of the victims. Kau proposes the dichotomy involvement and distance instead of the well-known dichotomy identification/detachment – a dichotomy that is taken for granted by Kolstrup and also by Niels Erik Wille and Hanne Dankert, even if they differentiate between types of identification or involvement.

Space

Space is equally a notion that varies from author to author. In fact, the word is used concretely and in different metaphorical registers.

Jørgen Stigel analyses communicative space, if not metaphorically then at least as "an elementary dimension of interpersonal communication". Thus this space is not cut off from the space represented on the screen and the space between viewer and screen, a space that can be seen concretely as well as metaphorically.

Edvin Kau (following Eugeni) uses the notion of space as a double-sided phenomenon: media space and real-life user space, where different interactions may exist (logical space, use space, screen space), thus assimilating the sense of space to the sense of time. Kolstrup uses space as represented space but with specific relationship to actions: locations making this or that action possible. Thus in fact making space take over the role of time as the general plot setter in 3D multimedia. As for Niels Erik Wille and Hanne Dankert, they use space more as space represented. The notion of space is broad, even polysemic; what is really divergent and even contradictory in these chapters are the space as frame (film) and space taking over the role of time (3D worlds).

Time

Time is less controversial. Ongoing chronological time seems to be common ground, but the importance given to the different temporal lines in the narrative process differs from author to author. The distinction between story (fabula) and discourse (sujet) is common ground to the authors; but the implications of the time of the telling (discourse) not only for the reconstruction of the storyline but also for the interaction time (game time) are different from author to author. This problem is made even more crucial if we look at the way the authors present the convergence between interaction and discourse. In any case, the reader should be especially careful reading Øhrstrøm's distinction between time seen from the outside and time seen from within, a distinction that is not represented directly in the other chapters, but which has some importance for Stigel's notion of communicative space. So at a closer look the first impression of a resemblance between the authors may be fallacious.

Narrative

Finally there are differences in the comprehension of the key word "narrative".

Jørgen Stigel draws an outline of the main features of the classical narratives as presented in literary and film theory. His definitions are broad and can in fact include non-narrative genres (the definitions are made up of necessary but not sufficient features); thus the notion of closure seems to play a very limited role. Stigel's conception of narrative is thus opposed to Kolstrup's, for whom closure is an important feature of narrative that is seen as a very formal structure. When Stigel makes a classification of representational spaces with important implications for the narration (forum, experimentarium, laboratory exploratorium, consultarium) he more or less excludes the exploratorium as basis for narratives. To Kolstrup exploratorium as space is the basis for interactive narratives. The aim of Niels Erik Wille and Hanne Dankert is a description of the documentary as narration. They too use a broad definition of "narrative" as an open-ended story.

Perspectives

All the chapters talk about user activity; the differences appear when the user activity is related to the dimensions of time, space, identification etc. The user activity is also seen differently according to the "medium of departure" of the authors: film, television, print media etc.

The six chapters, with all their similarities and differences, show that interactive narratives constitute a very fruitful field of research. Film gave rise to important theoretical work on narratives and documentaries some 50 years after its invention. Television began to be theorized some 30 years after its introduction as a mass phenomenon – this time a whole range of genres were taken into account: narratives, talk shows, games, news etc. There is a rich ongoing discussion of genres within the field of television studies.

Now we are confronted with an increasing number of new genres and formats for the computer medium and we are confronted with the necessity of describing the new genres. But we still rely very much on the theoretical framework of the preceding media. They are our point of departure.

In a recent book the French television and film researcher François Jost has mapped the existing television genres in a triangular model (Jost, 1999, pp. 28–34). The corners are named "Fictive", "Authentic" and "Plays/games". The model is necessarily incomplete when used for the computer medium, but it shows clearly the tasks of research in the coming years.

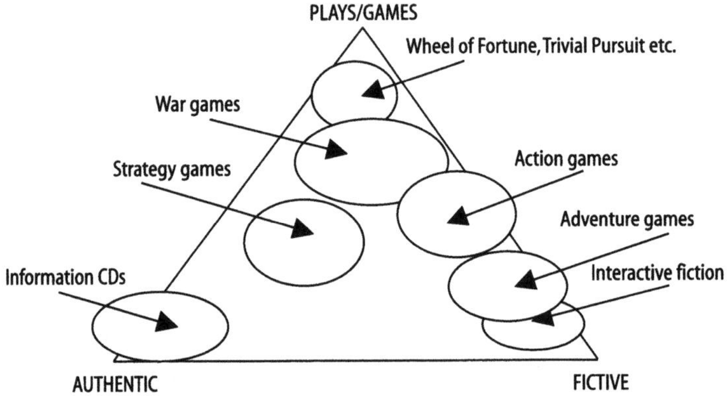

References

Jost, F. (1999) *Introduction à l'analyse de la television.* Paris, Ellipses.

14

Narratives: Different Narratives, Different Theories for Different Media?

Søren Kolstrup

Paintings *present* themselves as if they were holistic, verbal narratives, as if they were linear. They do so regardless of how any given spectator or reader goes about perceiving any given work. The structure is one thing; the perception another. Temporality informs narrative texts in a way that it does not inform paintings (or non-narrative texts for that matter). temporality is involved only in the spectator's *work* in perceiving a painting. But temporality is immanent to a component of narrative texts (Chatman, 1990, pp. 7–8).

14.1 Introduction: Could Any Text Be a Narrative?

Journalists don't write articles. They write stories. A story has structure, direction, point, viewpoint. An article may lack these.... Journalists are professional storytellers of our age. (Bell, 1991, p. 146).

This rather programmatic passage contains a good deal of the criteria normally used for the definition of "narrative". But Allan Bell, a journalist and media researcher from New Zealand, uses the notion without any true definition. He is eager to make a difference between the simple article and the news story. But why?

In a recent book based on interviews with the French architect and philosopher Paul Virilio, the interviewer asks: "And this means that (film) art has got free of the linear narrative?" And Virilio answers: "Yes and at the structural level it rediscovers the heritage of Eisenstein, the art of the montage" (Virilio, 1999, p. 38 – quoted after the Danish version).

Why has the notion of narrativity (story, tale etc.) become that popular? Why should news articles be stories or even narratives? Why does everyone wish to tell a story, to make a narrative? And the second point: why this dream of a non-linear story or narrative? What does word "non-linear" mean? Why do some researchers talk about the necessity of creating a non-linear interactive narrative? What is good about the interactive story? Is it more democratic – leaving the initiative to the user? How does it happen that in these discussions temporality is so often forgotten?

This article will discuss the notion of narrativity in relation to different media. To do this fruitfully it is necessary to discuss the notion of mediacy (Brügger, in press) and to consider narratives as what has been called "transmediatic" genres (Marion, 1997).

These last years have seen an increasing use of the notion of narrativity to characterize the texts (programs) in two fields: journalism and the interactive media. But what is a narrative in these media? Is the journalistic news story a narrative? Is the interactive story a narrative? Is "interactive story" a *contradictio in adjectio*? It might seem utterly trivial to discuss if this or that text is a narrative or not. If the author has decided to call her text "narrative" why not? If to Allan Bell the journalistic news report is a narrative, why not? But:

> If Description is treated as synonymous with Narration (or Exposition), then obviously no more can be said. But we are not doomed to such a terminological impasse. It is precisely the functions of theory building to coin new terms and to regulate old ones not in a prescriptive or proscriptive spirit but simply in an effort to facilitate communication. We are not the slaves of language (as some contemporary theorists doe fully contend) but its masters, and we can decide what we are talking about and how best to talk about it. (Chatman, 1990, p. 9–10)

Chatman talks about the confusion concerning the sense of *narrative* and *description*. His remarks are equally valuable in this article that discusses the (too?) broad sense of *narrative*. In fact, what is a narrative and what is not a narrative? We all feel when a story is a true narrative and when not. According to the Swiss text linguist Jean-Michel Adam, who refers to Bakhtin, the learning of the elementary discourse genres is a part of the learning of the mother tongue – or conversely: we cannot learn language without learning the discourse genres (Adam, 1992, p. 11). This means that whatever an author may wish to baptise "narrative", he or she is up against the practical, tacit everyday knowledge of everyone! And at this level we all know what a narrative is.

The discussion should take into account the manifold of the genre divisions. But to which extent should we use a set of well-defined hierarchically ordered features as criteria, and to which extent should we use prototypical criteria? Or could we simply use a unique criterion as a kind of catalyst? This article is based on a prototypical understanding and uses a specific device as touchstone or catalyst in order to extract the essence not only from different theoretical approaches, but also from our daily understanding of "narrative". A simple operative criterion, valuable for all media, should function as tool (=catalyst) to decide whether or not a given genre presented in a given medium can be classified as narrative. This criterion is the given medium's ability to create a cliffhanger or some similar kind of tension! There are not very many definitions of the notion of cliffhanger in film theoretical literature. The *Complete Film Dictionary* defines the notion this way:

> **Cliffhanger.** A film of great suspense with an especially tense ending, named after early serials in which the heroine hanging from a cliff was rescued at the last minute. Ridley Scott's Alien (1979) can be considered a modern type of cliffhanger. (Königsberg, 1987, p. 53)

Obviously Königsberg uses the word to indicate a subgenre. She defines suspense with the following words

> **Suspense.** A state of uncertainty and delay that builds up anxiety as one awaits the outcome of a situation. Suspense seems to elongate time and delay the inevitable, but without decreasing our interest or tension. (Königsberg, 1987, p. 364)

In fact we normally use the word *cliffhanger* to indicate a specific scene build on suspense. The cliffhanger combines the most important prerequisites for narration: the (linear) time skeleton (also time as omen and time as limit), the *mise en intrigue* (the putting into plot) of the French narratologist and philosopher Ricoeur. This *mise en intrigue* implies causality, the will of the subject, and the distribution and withholding of information. The cliffhanger is the frozen moment of the story where past actions are confronted with the possible coming actions. It is the moment where the identification mechanisms or the involvement mechanisms of the reader/spectator reach their peak. And in our everyday understanding of "narrative", the cliffhanger is often the point that leads us to the climax of the narrative. For a more succinct introduction to narrative principles see Chapter 15).

The discussion can follow different paths: one can make an investigation about what people think is a narrative. Or you can make an investigation of the notion of narrativity as described in central narrative theories within the different media: theory of literature, film theory, journalistic theory etc. You can dress a table of the different media and their mediacy in relation to narrativity. Finally, you can discuss specific products and their status as narratives/non-narratives.

14.2 The Notion of Narrative

14.2.1 What Do We Understand by "Narrative"?

Thus, even if people are not normally preoccupied by the definition of *narrative*, they should have a practical knowledge of *narrative* if Bakhtin is right. A small exploratory investigation at the Department of Information and Media Science, University of Aarhus showed that for most people the classical Aristotelian narrative is still *the* narrative. This narrative is characterized by the subjects with the following key words marked by *italics*:

> *Succession in time, causality, succession of events* (existence of plot, chain of actions) the existence of *changing, human involvement*, the presence of a *narrator, spatial succession*, the making of *decisions, actions, conflict, fiction, suspense* and the *movement towards a climax*. The existence of a *morale* or the *importance of content and values.*

Any popular television fiction can stand up to this "definition" – but hardly any item of a news bulletin. Which types of computer game can?

14.2.2 "Narrative" in Mass Media Research and in Cultural Studies

14.2.2.1 Story, Entertainment and News (USA, UK)

In *Narratives in popular Culture, Media, and Everyday Life*, Arthur Asa Berger presents a very broad definition of "narrative". His subject is all kinds of popular stories, his definitions or better characterizations of "narrative" can with his slightly ironic words be reduced to "Story about things that have happened or are happening to people, animals, aliens from outer space, insects – whatever" (Berger, 1997, p. 4). He talks about sequences of events related to or bound to "some kind of time", mostly a linear time. The closure of the story is the important feature. But Berger excludes one genre from the list of stories: the news report in newspapers. Even his broad definitions do not seem able to embrace this genre in the newspaper medium. This exclusion means that the closure can remain important, with the result that "narrative" is mostly seen as a fiction story.

When we turn to non-fiction, the theories change. In 1994, the *Journal of Narrative and Life History* produced a special issue edited by Tamara Liebes: *Narrativization of News*, an issue that covers a broad field of mass media stories.

Tamara Liebes is very circumspect in her definitions of narrative, because you have to leave out some of the normal characteristics or distinctive features of "narrative" if you want to embrace the news story "all seven articles regard narrative structure in terms of (a) conflict between characters" (Liebes, 1994a, p. 4). So she reduces the features to one outstanding one: the presence of *conflict between characters*.

Gurevitch and Kavoori follow Seymour Chatman and his well-known distinction between "story order" (the order of events) and "discourse order" (succession in the text) (Gurevitch and Kavoori, 1994, p. 11) (compare Chatman, 1978, p. 19). Even if Gurevitch and Kavoori pay much attention to time and temporal order, it appears clearly that the temporal order of events is not the decisive feature. Time is not considered as a constituting element of the narrative structure as such. They describe two methods of organizing the text: a succession with simple linear time and what they call *valens*: "the relative dominance of strength of specific elements in a story" (Gurevitch and Kavoori, 1994, p. 12). It is clear that the story/narrative in their perspective is a broad concept. A closer look at the article shows that their news story is in fact a descriptive and argumentative text. In the van Dijk model of news (van Dijk, 1988, p. 52–57) it would be a news story written with an emphasis on "comment". The notion of narrative has thus been enlarged spectacularly also by loans from dramaturgy (Gurevitch and Kavoori, 1994, p. 21). But one fundamental question remains open: is a story constructed not in a linear temporal order but according to van Dijk's relevance structure, the inverted pyramid, a narrative?

The understanding of news as narrative is strong in this tradition of mass communication research. On British and American (Israeli and Danish!) soil there is an emphasis on the referent, on the story (narrative) as a succession of events going on "out there". The narrative is hardly seen as a (re)construction told according to given structural models.

This also appears just as well if you turn to the notion of bardic television exposed in Fiske and Hartley's now classic book *Reading Television.* Television news is considered as an ongoing collective production of (mythic or mythological) information where the structure of the single item disappears. The important thing is that television makes social coherence and consensus possible (Fiske and Hartley, 1976, pp. 84–108, specifically p. 88). Bird and Dardenne follow the same lines as Fiske and Hartley (Bird and Dardenne, 1988, p. 71, in Carey, 1988).

14.2.2.2 When the Media Tell Society (Belgium)

The researchers of Comu, the Department of Communication at the University of Louvain-la-Neuve in Belgium, investigate the news story within the framework described by Paul Ricoeur. In their work on the "media narrative" the Comu researchers are indebted to Ricoeur, especially for his notion of the triple mimesis the *prefiguration* (our daily life understanding of actions and events), the *configuration* (the work of the narrative competence to make a story out of these actions and events) and the *refiguration* (the reader's restructuring of the text). The central point in the configuration is the *mise en intrigue*: the putting into plot. But the Comu researchers make rather free use of the three volumes of *Time and Narrative.* (Lits, 1996, p. 34 ff; Lits, 1997b, p. 5 ff; Lits, 1997c, p. 42).

In fact, Comu uses a broad or even a loose definition of "narrative" in order to make it compatible with the notion of *parcours mediatique* (Lits, 1997b, p. 6). By *parcours médiatique* is meant the way the stories are put into the media and recycled by the media, a conception very close to the ideas exposed in Bird and Dardenne (1988) and in Fiske and Hartley (1978).

"We prefer to extend the narrative as category": Marc Lits, Director of the "Media Observatory" of Comu, underlines the telling of stories as function or as activity instead of focusing on a narrow structural definition of "narrative" or "narration" with its closure (Lits, 1997c, p. 42). Storytelling is seen as fundamental for mankind and some lines further on Lits quotes Eco: "The novel as genre may disappear, but not narrativity. It is a biological function" (Eco in *Nouvel Obs*, p. 1318). Lits goes on to quote Michel de Certeau: "our society has become a told [récitée] society – and in three ways: It is defined by narratives [récits] (the fables/legends in the ads and in the news bulletins), by the quotations [citations] of the narratives and by their eternal "requotation" [récitation]". (Michel de Certeaus plays with the words récit, citation, réciter, citer) (Lits, 1997c, p. 43).

An event only becomes news when it has been mediated, i.e. when it has been "put to narrative" (*mise en récit*). The use of this term (*mise en récit*) might seem without much importance, but Marc Lits deliberately avoids the proper term in this context, *mise en intrigue* – a word that emphasizes that a narrative has specific structures and that this internal structure is decisive. Not so with *mise en recit.*

Lit's colleague Benoît Grevisse makes it even more clear. He opposes the small narrative (the closed text of the restrictive definition of "narrative", the text that cannot tell society) to the great narrative (all the stories about the event). In this way the narrative as isolated text explodes, the closure as defined by Berger, is transgressed. The narrative becomes a mythology. Theoretically the positions are clear, but not without problems (Grévisse, 1997, pp. 135 ff).

To sum up, mass media research shows that there is a clear tendency to see the notions of narrative beyond the frame of the single text and that the narrow definitions (and understandings) of "narrative" are discarded in favour of "narrative-as-all-the-stories-about-a-given-affair" or narrative as all the stories about a given aspect of society. This is probably the reason why Allan Bell does not see the discrepancy between his use of the Labov model for stories of personal experiences (a narrow definition with a linear time structure) (Labov, 1972, p. 363) and the actual structure of news reports in print media.

14.2.3 Formalized and Algorithmic Understandings

14.2.3.1 The Grammar of Narrative or the Living Story?

In some semiotic theories and in some theories about interactive stories and computer-generated stories we find the opposite tendency, everything is seen in small details from within the single text. The evolution of the plot and the evolution of the actions are seen as a long chain of choices and decisions, an algorithmic thinking. This is clear when we look at the semiotics of the 1960s. The perspective changes from the overall structure with its possible retrograde or retroactive determination (the theories of Gérard Genette) to the narrow focus on the single decision.

This is obvious in Brémond's algorithmic model for the progression of the narrative (Brémond, 1966, pp. 60–76). But the different formalizations of Greimas and Courtès show the same interest in details. This is valuable from Greimas' early reductions of the formulas of the fairy tale as analysed by Propp (Greimas, 1966, pp. 192–203) to the elaborate models of Courtès (cf. Courtès, 1993, pp. 72–86).

We can hardly ascribe the semiotic theories to a narrow field of investigation as we could in the case of mass media theory and the news stories. But the empirical material or basis of much semiotic narrative theory has been the short story, the detective story and the fairy tale (Greimas and the fairy tale, Todorov and Decameron etc.)

14.2.3.2 The Construction of the Planning

Marie-Laure Ryan is a genuine exponent of the construction tendency for at least two features.

The first feature is her research in the world of fiction: how is the fictional universe constructed as space, as world? A problem that literary theories about narratives pay rather little attention to. How do we distinguish between fictional worlds and factual worlds? What are the implications of the fictive/factual universe for the plot structure? Where is the borderline that distinguishes factual worlds and fictional worlds? (Ryan, 1991, pp. 109–123)

The second feature in her theory is the description of the choices – moves – the passing from one state to another. The development of the narrative is seen as calculation. The focus is on the single state or phase in the syntagmatic evolution. As she is dealing with the smallest units of narratives, her theory should in fact be equally valid for several media (Ryan, 1991, pp. 124–147).

The importance of the construction of world is stressed by Grodal (1998, p. 242) who interprets the action in some computer games as a passing from one space to another (in fact, the word "location" would be more appropriate). Thus he combines in his interpretation of games the two most important features in Ryan's description. See equally Eugenio (1997).

We should keep in mind that these theories are not in conflict with other narrative theories (except the ones we find in much mass media theory?). What they do is to focus on small narrative elements and they focus more on space and less on time than other theoretical approaches. They also focus just as much on production theories as on pure interpretative theories.

14.2.4 The Telling of the Story in Film Theory

Film theory is a vast field with different traditions and trends. Here I shall focus on the notions in mainstream discussions today. The emphasis is on the time of the narrative, the point of view, the narrator, the narrative structure and above all on the distribution of knowledge and the withholding of knowledge (Bordwell and Thompson, 1997; Branigan, 1992).

> **Narration.** The process through which the plot conveys or withholds story information. The narration can be more or less restricted to character knowledge, and more or less deep in presenting characters' mental perceptions and thoughts. (Bordwell and Thompson, 1997, p. 480)
>
> **Narrative form.** A type of filmic organization in which the parts relate to each other through a series of causally related events taking place in a specific time and space. (Bordwell and Thompson, 1997, p. 480).

Bordwell and Thompson focus on the notion of withholding of information – the holding back of information by the narrative process. Branigan focuses more on the uneven distribution of knowledge between the protagonists, and between some protagonists and the viewer. Here is what Branigan writes *in Narrative Comprehension and Film*:

> **Disparities of knowledge.** The second fundamental concept (after Knowing how) that is needed to analyse narration is the notion of a disparity of knowledge. Narration comes into being when knowledge is unevenly distributed- when there is a disturbance or disruption in the field of knowledge. Informally one can grasp the importance of disparity by imaging a universe in which all observers are perfect and all knowing. In such a universe, there can be no possibility of narration since all information is equally available and already possessed in the same ways. Therefore I will posit that the most basic situation which gives rise to narration will be comprised of three elements: a *subject* in an *asymmetrical* relationship with an *object*. (Branigan, 1992, p. 66)

The last lines are more or less a description of the main axis in the actant model, a subject trying to be reunited with its object along the project axis.

Mainstream (American) film theory is in accordance with our daily understanding and with most classical understanding of *Narrative*. But film theory necessarily has to investigate the ways in which the different semiotic systems are combined in film, how for instance music, pictures and the protagonists' talk may underline each other or contradict each other. The act of telling in film is a subtle interplay of channels: which channel tells what (or remains silent). Thus film theory has had to describe three types of distribution of knowledge: distribution between channels (sources of information), distribution between the narrative elements (protagonists, narrator and viewer) and distribution over time. The conflicts between channels/collaboration between channels have had as a result that the distribution of information/knowledge has gained a central position in film theory – more important than in the more classical theory of the novel.

14.2.5 Text Linguistics and the Narrow Definition of "Narrative"

The extreme case of a narrow definition of "narrative" is the theoretical construction of Jean-Michel Adam.

According to Adam the actual discourse is build up by small nuclear units called sequences, which can be ascribed to a relatively little number of prototypical genres; each "text" is normally a heterogeneous mix of discursive genres. Probably the most important is the narrative sequence, followed by the descriptive and the argumentative.

A "true" narrative text must fulfil the following five or six conditions: it should have a succession of events, tending towards a closure (linear time structure). There should be a humanized subject. The subject should undergo a change. The actions should form a unit or at least be integrated. The temporal progression should have the form of causal relations of a *mise en intrigue* (Paul Ricoeur). There may be a moral (cf. Chapter 15).

The narrative sequence has five (or six) phases: Initial stage (orientation), Rupture or introduction of a dynamic element, Actions and eventually evaluations, Resolution, Final stage and eventually a Moral (Adam, 1992, pp. 45–63; Adam, 1994, pp. 31–45).

It is obvious that at least some texts called narratives cannot stand up to these conditions. In particular, news reports are very far from this model. Can computer games stand up to the model? Adam focuses narrowly on the internal structural aspects of texts and not on the experience of texts. In doing so he underestimates some of the important narrative criteria that we find in other narrative theories:

- The notion of distribution of knowledge
- The hierarchy of enunciation, the levels and the positions of telling
- The criteria for the distinction of factual and fictional universes

Adam can be seen as a radicalization and a clarification of points of view that can be found in the works of Labov (his model for oral narratives) or in film theory.

14.3 Mediacy as Problem and Solution?

14.3.1 The Notion of Mediacy

The notion of narrativity seems thus to be divergent according to the field investigated. In some cases this is due to inherent theoretical traditions: semiotics never paid much attention to space. But the different theories of narrativity normally depend to some extent on the object of research. The divergences are due to the fact that the different media have different ways of telling "the same story". It is no wonder that Marie-Laure Ryan pays so much attention to space: in games and interactive stories actions and narration are linked to space, to locations.

General investigations into the specificity of each medium or of the different media as opposed to the others are not very common. What we normally have is comparisons between written narratives and film narratives (Seymour Chatman) or film vs. television (John Ellis). But there are some attempts to rethink the specificity of each media and the relations between media. This is the case of Joshua Meyrowitz, Philippe Marion (Louvain-le-Neuve) and Niels Brügger. You may also find some brief pages on this subject in different textbooks like Fiske's *Introduction to Communication Studies.*

In Brügger and Kolstrup (in press), Niels Brügger distinguishes seven *variables* for the definition of a media, four of which are important for the construction of narratives: matter (the physicality of the media), space, time and symbolic format. To the *variables* should be added the *areas*, here defined as production, distribution and consumption. For our discussion it is above all time, the symbolic form, and consumption in a large sense that are important. It is not quite clear if Brügger sees a notion like interactivity as a variable (it would be preferable in our case) or if it is simply seen from the outside as an area roughly similar to consumption.

Philippe Marion describes the potentiality of a medium as defined by the materiality of the media, its internal semiotic configuration, and its communicational and relational organization (Marion, 1997, p. 79).

According to Marion the media are "opaque": they are characterized by a fundamental opacity. Some stories are more easily told in one medium than in another, and "the same story" (the fabula) is never the same when told in a new medium, which has a bias in rendering the story. This is what Philippe Marion calls opacity or "*force d'inertie*" (Marion, 1997, p. 85).

But this opacity of the given medium is at the same time (paradoxically) described as that which gives the media its specific aesthetic expressivity.

To catch the differential specificity of a medium is to grasp its mediacy". Mediacy is the totality of parameters that define the expressive and communicative potentialities developed by a medium. Mediacy is a given medium's capacity to represent and to place the representations in a communicative dynamics (Marion, 1997, p. 79).

Fundamentally this is due to the fact that each media has a specific semiotic configuration of semiotic channels at its disposal. Each medium has a specific support, i.e.

materiality or technique (machine, newspaper – broadsheet or tabloid, book, screen). Each medium has a specific relation to time (and space).

The distribution and circulation systems are different from medium to medium. The same is true for consumption: interaction or reading, individual, collective, time of consumption, linear or non-linear consumption, identification mechanisms etc.

14.3.2 The Configurations of the Media

Let us begin with a brief reminder of matter and semiotic configurations of some media.

Book:	Paper of a specific format with written text.
Newspaper:	Paper of a specific format with written text (varying letters) + (still pictures).
Radio:	Specific technical device with text as (speech) + (music) + (sound).
Still picture:	Flat support of any kind: the rock walls of a cave, a sheet of paper etc.
Comics:	Paper of varying format with series of still pictures (varying formats) + (written text with varying letters)
Film:	Specific technical device with moving pictures + (speech) + (sound) + ((music)) + (((written text)))
Television:	Specific technical device with speak + moving pictures + (sound) + (written text) + (still pictures) + ((music))
Computers:	Specific technical device with all the semiotic channels

The decrease in importance is indicated by the increase of the number of parenthesises. The presentation indicates the normal combinations, but there are exceptions. The differences of use in film and on TV are due to the different sizes of screens, different technical devices, different relations between the viewer and the screen etc. The importance of speech on TV is the outstanding difference, not in principle, but in actual use (Ellis, 1982, pp. 38–61, 129–144).

But one cannot deduce the mediacy from the configuration of semiotic channels and the materiality of the media alone. You have to include other factors of mediacy. In the case of narrative as transmediatic genre you have to see how each medium treats time and space. In the case of narrative as transmediatic genre it is essential to see how the narrative constitutes the storyline and the discourse line (Chatman, 1979, pp. 19 ff).

Finally, how does the user interact with the medium? *Interact* here has a very broad definition: interaction is reading, flicking through the text, consumption.

If you want to find out the specificity of television and film you should not take into account the use of television for showing cinema films We should keep out all examples of a given medium used as "*medium vicarium*". And we should even keep out examples of one medium using another as a complement, such the use of illustrations in novels using the book as medium. In this case the illustrations could be left out without damaging the plot of the text – not so in true comics.

The aim is to extract the essence not only from different theoretical approaches but also from our daily understanding of "narrative" and to use this essence as a criterion.

14.3.2.1 The Book

The narrative in the book is a linear representation; the text (novel, short story) has a fixed beginning and end. Space has a modest role if any for the narrative progression. The book invites to a linear interaction with a text expressing a linear progressive time (even if exceptions are common). The story is time-bound, the withholding of information is used rather often. The cliffhanger is not only possible, in some sub-genres of written narratives it is fundamental. The narratives in books are a high-involvement genre.

14.3.2.2 The Newspaper

The newspaper medium is radically different. The matter is different from that of the book: 10 to 24 large pages that invite the reader to a non-linear interaction. The newspaper's system of headlines is a spatial or topographic display, a guiding tool for the individual interaction or travel through the pages. This specificity is linked with the particular shape of each article or story (the relevance order): you get the central information first and you are free to choose your own direction through the article or to leave out the rest. There is normally no trace of linear time structure, only some moments or dates (van Dijk, (1988, pp. 56–57); for more details on temporality and sequential succession see Jamet and Jannet (1999, pp. 23 ff). Storyline, discourse line and interaction diverge fundamentally. Space as locations for the different actions is fundamental for the news story. No cliffhanger is possible. We should not confuse our waiting for next day's news with a cliffhanger. Waiting for news is an ongoing process at the consumption level. The newspaper is a low-involvement medium.

The newspaper has been a powerful *medium vicarium* for novels, but the serial novel was (is!) totally different in temporal structure from the news story and is consumed in a radically different way. The serial novel from its very beginning was designed as a "stranger" in the newspapers. The newspaper is a *medium vicarium* in this case.

14.3.2.3 Comics

At a first level of presentation the comics are as linear as the book (narrative-in-the-book), but within the single frame it follows the still picture – except for what is said in the balloons. Thus the comics are marked by the doubleness of the linear progression between the frames and the different ways of progressing or stopping time within the frames, especially in large frames that invite a personal investigation. The mediacy of the comic is a specific configuration of still picture and linear telling principles. The story order and the discourse order are linear in the overall structure, but not in details, not within the same frame.

Comics are marvellous creators of cliffhangers, even if the identification force is rather weak in comics and the medium is thus a low-involvement medium.

14.3.2.4 Audio-Visual Media

The mediacy of the audio-visual media is different from that of the book. But in one respect they are rather close: if narratives in books are linear then the audio-visual narratives are even more strictly linear. The more the film is based exclusively on pictures the more it becomes linear (linear story, linear discourse and linear consumption). The interaction/collaboration of different semiotic channels that characterize the audio-visual media makes the use of disparities (and withholding) of knowledge a fundamental of the audio-visual narratives. The spatial setting is important. The cliffhanger is a term from film and TV production, and we consume cliffhangers every day.

14.4 The Computer as Medium for Narratives

14.4.1 Interactivity and Narrative

The computer is normally presented as an interactive medium! (Jensen, 1998b, pp. 208–214). What is interaction and what is interactivity? The word and the notion of interactivity have a wide range of uses and correspondingly a wide range of definitions. What kind of interactivity can serve narratives, stories that meet the cliffhanger criterion? If the computer is used in texts that are shaped like the old interactive books, it functions as *medium vicarium*. For the time being we may keep Jensen's definition of interactivity:

> Interactivity can be defined as a measure of the medium's potential ability to let the user influence the form and/or content of the mediated information. Or in more detail: the notions of interactivity and interactive media are related to media that, beyond the output from the media system, open possibilities to transfer different grades and types of input from the user to the system. (Jensen, 1998b, p. 232)

In this definition the user has, to a variable degree, the possibility of influencing the form and content of the output. The computer implies the active intervention of the user – if it is not used only as a *medium vicarium* for other media. When the computer is more than a *vicarium*, the intervention of the user becomes a part of the text. The combinations of the different media ont the computer screen are more than the sum of the basic media; it is a qualitative shift.

In the interactive narrative, discourse line and reading/interaction line are not only convergent, the interaction line is the discourse line (cf. Jensen's definition) and this is a fundamental difference from the other media. But according to the definition even the content and the storyline depend on the interaction. Users should in a way create their own story and discourse (syntagm) out of the paradigm stored in the computer. But which narratives are possible under these conditions?

From a narrative point of view this creates a problem! According to the narrative (film) theories that have been mentioned, the withholding of information is crucial for the creation of suspense and drive. If the user knows too much, suspense and drive may leave the story. We must add one feature to the definition.

The main point is that to communicate an interactive narrative, the computer as medium should also be able to resist the user. If not, the computer is not able to produce a cliffhanger, to create tension. The user cannot decide to have a cliffhanger. As soon as the user decides that there will be a cliffhanger – it vanishes! This was the problem for interactive books where the reader could choose among different directions. This way of organizing the text, where readers know that they can just go back and choose another direction, made boring books.

Not all computer games can be considered as narratives, but some can, e.g. adventure games.

Grodal classifiies computer games (Grodal, 1998, p. 249) into four groups:

1. visuo–motor games, such as flight simulators or ice hockey games
2. adventure games
3. war and shoot'em up games
4. construction games

To this classification we should add all the "true games" like "Wheel of Fortune" or the different variations of "Trivial Pursuit".

Of Grodal's four types only type 2 and some shoot'em up games can fulfil the conditions for being considered as narratives.

Grodal points out that action film and computer games in particular have common narrative structures, but he is not very explicit: "Often a computer game will have a kind of narrative structure" (Grodal, 1998, p. 239); "the relationship between computer games and film is articulated in several dimensions. It is not only the narrative structures that are common for film and computer games, very often they share theme and atmosphere and actors..." (Grodal, 1998, p. 241). Grodal seems to be in more doubt about the possibilities of erotic computer games structured in a narrative way, but does not exclude the possibility. The only comment on his doubts is that we are far from having seen the whole range of possible narrative computer games for the simple reason that until recently the computer game industry has focused rather narrowly on young males' interest in action. (Grodal, 1998, pp. 239–43).

Based on Grodal you can dress a scheme, an outline of actors, action, time and space for the interactive medium like the one made for narratives in books, comics and in the audio-visual media (see Section 14.3.2).

14.4.1.1 *Computer Narratives*

The consuming time (interaction) tends to be identical to the discourse line and the subject/story is attracted into the sphere of interaction. The cliffhanger has a tendency to be of a different type than the ones we find in paper fiction and in the audio-visual media. The strong identification with the hero in trouble that we know from film and novel is more difficult to create.

What we get instead is "the experience of control and the fight for control" (Grodal); the interactivity makes any passive fear and identification impossible. We can act, may be in vain, but we try to.

The narrator is now a combat field between the resistance of the system (author) and the player!

14.4.2 Crosstown, Tomb Raider and Riven

Crosstown is a Danish produced "interactive fiction" from 1998. In fact it is an adventure game constructed as a detective story (or a detective story in the shape of an adventure game). It is drawn with a very particular graphic design derived from comics and it has a restricted use of free camera movements.

Riven and Tomb Raider should need no presentation.

The adventure game looks pretty much like a fairy tale, a sub-genre where the cliff-hanger does not really exist in the normal sense of the word. The fairy tale has, as everyone knows a strong actant structure: there is a destinator/giver, a receiver, a hero (the player + avatar), opponents/villain, helpers and finally the object (and of course the magic tools/objects). In Crosstown the shopkeeper Ali is the giver. The player and his or her avatar, the journalist Minna, is the subject, the opponent or the villain is the engineer Hermansen (and also the personnel of the local newspaper the *Globe*). Some actors are between helpers and opponents: e.g. Bibi Bartholin.

The fairy tale did create some kind of space, a space for the different actants/actors: the king in his castle, the villain in his or her specific evil location, the helpers mostly in nature or in isolated houses in open country etc. They correspond to the access points (Grodal, 1998, p. 242). Computer games are like fairy tales in this respect: the actions are bound to the locations, only this or that action is possible in this or that location. To get information about Bibi's past you have to go to Mother Angelique in the monastery. Written information is found at the *Globe* except for the first letter, delivered by the shopkeeper Ali. The actions are stored in space and the narrative progress is linked to space, this is especially the case of all the setups.

But what about the cliffhanger? In the fairy tale they exist in some way: the hero tries first in vain to get into the location where the treasure/the princess is caught, but finally he succeeds. The hero flees from the villain; each time he is about to be caught some magic device makes him escape. But as the fairy tale does not change location in order to deploy another action, and as it cannot suspend time, it cannot create cliffhangers as we know them from any James Bond film, or as we know them in the serial novel in newspapers or in television crime stories.

Computer games have problems that can be considered similar to those of fairy tales. But some kind of tension at least exists in computer game, where it will often take on the aspect of a fight for control: we can't get into the location whatever we try – the doors of Chemoflex (Crosstown) remain closed after my first visit. I think I know that there is still something to get or to do there but I can't – and time goes on and I still can't find the solution to the problems (story, discourse or my time?). The game goes on but without progress (Crosstown). We can't escape the danger (we did not get the object). I die – at least for a moment (action games). I (or my avatar) thrive to save the world, but the poisonous gas becomes more and more dense. Every time the game allows me to get through the tunnels of the sewer and to ring at the door of the chief engineer of the sewers there is more and more poisonous gas. And I feel I have only a limited amount of time to save this poor world (Crosstown). The games resist our will; that is the way the interaction line and time can begin to replace the discourse line and the story line.

Tomb Raider is characterized most like an action game by the focus on each single action/reaction. Will Lara Croft be able to shoot the tigers before they kill her/me? Will she be able to escape the rolling rocks? Will she be able to jump to the top of the cliff etc.? There are plenty of small action sequences that create some kind of suspense, some kind of a cliffhanger, but not quite. The time preceding the action is too short; the suspense is not built up in the same way. What Tomb Raider lacks (in terms of narrativity) is the long construction of setups with uncertain payoffs. Tomb Raider has a short time and narrow space perspective.

This is not so in Riven, where you have to pick up objects or make small actions (powering the switches, the valves or the levers placed near the doors or the domes) whose utility is not always clear to you at the beginning. But you know that you have to fight the villain Gehn and to liberate Catherine and that you should activate these objects. The time perspective is long, and you even have a causality that sees things from a point in the future: you concentrate on actions that have a specific intention and that later on (at the story level!) may function as causes. *The Official Riven*, an instruction book to the game, has a chapter named "Walking through the Fifth Age" where a possible walk through the game is written as a novel with a personal hero, the first-person singular pronoun "I". This attempt to change the narrative game to a narrative text makes the distinctive characters of narrative games as opposed to narrative literature very clear. We get a totally linear story with no ramifications. The possible but unrealized paths through the game do not count, they cannot function as parallel actions to the main actions like the ones we have in most epic literature (except fairy tales!). This is equally the case if for some reason you return to zero to find a better path and therefore reject your first path. The story time becomes a thin linear line derived from the interaction. What counts is space as the locations, access points and setups. The only temporal dimension that counts is the future: what will happen or not happen in future if I execute or don't execute this action? (Riven, 1997, p. 75–105). Narrative games work like that. But up till now there has been a price: compared with film or literature computer games invite other identificational and involvement patterns, with a different (and lower) intensity of identification. Computer games (video or others) have in this respect a resemblance with comics. You are absorbed, but you never fear for the life of the hero in the intense way that you do in film or in novels. You cannot project your feelings into the protagonist, you are the protagonist or he or she is your avatar.

The important point is that computer games by their very origin on the one hand have narrative aspects, but on the other hand have similarities with games like chess or other board games. This similarity is particularly clear when we look at the time structure, the possibility of returning to the game or a new similar game. The closure of the "text" is temporary in computer games. It is a paradox that the fairy tale with its emphasis on closure (the hero marries the princess) has in fact a repetitive structure, the same one from story to story. This paradox can be explained if we look at Burkert's hypothesis about the genesis of the fairy tale. Action adventure games have got back to the very roots of the narrative. Burkert's hypothesis was that narratives have their origin in hunting and that any fairy tale at its most profound levels has this structure: go out and look for the prey, catch or kill the prey and run back to safety. In more common narratological terms: peace and no hunger → hunger → the killing of the prey → the eating of the prey → peace and no hunger. This structure is clearly what we find in computer games. We rush out to save the world according to the giver's wishes. We are happy as long as the system resists, because we are absorbed. When finally it gives in, the world is as boring as the world of the fairy tale after the hero's marriage with the princess.

The news producers' dream of being the storytellers of our time is an illusion. We do not enter the world of the narratives when entering the newspaper (or the television news bulletin). There are no cliffhangers (Lewis, 1994, pp. 25 ff). We only look forward to the next news bulletin, whose items will be forgotten as soon as seen (Mouillaud and Tétu, 1989, pp. 26 ff). Games are much closer to narratives: we concentrate at a particular point, we try to identify the narrative problem, we try our best to get to another point, to solve the problems, and we fight against the implicit author to get a status as implicit and explicit narrator. The world and the actions of narratives claim a certain closure: no closure, no cliffhanger. But games do not offer all the possibilities of closure, they are open because not only can you repeat your actions, but the system foresees that this is the case. The cliffhanger does not vanish, but it gets the low involvement that we know from comics. A new Danish media report "Det er bare noget de laver" [It's only something constructed] (Sørensen and Jessen, 2000) about children and adolescents playing computer games concludes that their personal involvement and their fears are much weaker when they play games than when they look at films. We fight to get to a specific point, to be saved at this access point. It is a not the strongest cliffhanger, but it is one.

References

Adam, J.-M. (1992) *Les textes: Types et prototypes*. Paris: Nathan.
Adam, J.-M. (1994) *Le texte narratif*. Paris: Nathan.
Bell, A. (1991) *The Language of News Media*. Oxford: Blackwell.
Berger, A. A. (1997) *Narratives in Popular Culture, Media, and Everyday Life*. London: Sage.
Bird, S. and Dardenne, R. W. (1988) Myth, Chronicle, and Story. In: *Media, Myth, and Narratives: Television and the Press*, (ed. J. W. Carey). London: Sage.
Bordwell, D. and Thompson, C. (1997) *Film Art*, 5th edn. New York: McGraw-Hill.
Branigan, E. (1992) *Narrative Comprehension and Film*. London: Routledge.

Brémond, C. (1966) La logique des possibles narratifs. In *Communications 8*. Paris: Seuil,.
Brügger, N. (in press) Theoretical reflections on media and media history. In *Media History, Theories, Methods, Analyses* (ed. N. Brügger and S. Kolstrup) (forthcoming)
Brügger, N. and Kolstrup, S. (eds.) (in press) *Media History, Theories, Methods, Analyses.*
Burkert, W. (1979) *Structure and History in Greek Mythology*. Berkeley, CA: University of California Press.
Carey, J. W. (ed.) (1988) *Media, Myth, and Narratives: Television and the Press.* London: Sage.
Chatman, S. (1979) *Story and Discourse.* Ithaca, NY: Cornell University Press.
Chatman, S. (1990) Coming to Terms. Ithaca, NY: Cornell University Press.
Courtès, J. (1993) *Analyse Sémoiotique Narrative et Discursive.* Paris: Hachette.
Ellis, J. (1982) *Visible Fictions.* London: Routledge.
Eugenio, R. (1997) Myst: multimedia, hypertexts and film semiotics. In *Iris* no 25: Film Theory and the Digital Image. Carlville, IA: University of Iowa Printing Department.
Fiske, J. (1982) *Introduction to Communication Studies.* London: Routledge.
Fiske, J. and Hartley, J. (1978). *Reading Television.* London: Routledge.
Greimas, A. (1966) *Sémantique structurale.* Paris: Larousse.
Grévisse, B. (1997) Récit et analyse des pratiques journalistiques. In *Recherches en communication* 7.
Gurevitch, M. and Kavoori, A. (1994) Global texts, narrativity, and the construction of local and global meanings in television news. In *Journal of Narrative and Life History* (Special Issue) 4(1,2).
Jamet, C. and Jannet, A.-M. (1999) *Les stratégies de l'information.* Paris: L'Harmattan.
Jensen, J. F. (ed.) (1998a) *Multimedier, Hypermedier, Interaktive Medier.* Aalborg: Aalborg Universitetsforlag.
Jensen, J. F. (ed.) (1998b) Interaktivitet og interaktive medier. In *Multimedier, Hypermedier, Interaktive Medier* (ed. J. F. Jensen). Aalborg: Aalborg Universitetsforlag.
Johansen, J. D. and Larsen, S. E. (1994) *Tegn i brug.* Copenhagen: Amanda.
Königsberg, I. (1987) *The Complete Film Dictionary.* New York, Meridian.
Grodal, T. (1998) Filmfortælling og Computerspil. In *Multimedier, Hypermedier, Interaktive Medier* (ed. J. F. Jensen). Aalborg: Aalborg Universitetsforlag.
Labov, W. (1972) *Language in the Inner City.* Philadelphia, PA: University of Pennsylvania Press.
Lewis, J. (1994) The absence of narrative: boredom and the residual power of television news. *Journal of Narrative and Life History* (Special Issue) 4(1,2).
Liebes, T. (ed.) (1994a) Narrativization of the news. *Journal of Narrative and Life History* (Special Issue) 4(1,2).
Liebes Tamar (1994b) Narrativization of the news: an introduction. In *Journal of Narrative and Life History* (Special Issue) 4(1,2).
Lits, M. (ed.) (1996) *Le récit médias et société.* Academia Bruylant, Louvain-la-Neuve.
Lits, M. (ed.) (1997a) Le récit médiatique. *Recherches en Communication 7*, Louvain-la-Neuve.
Lits, M. (1997b) Le récit médiatique: Approches narratologiques et ethnologiques. In *Recherches en Communication 7*, Louvain-la-Neuve.
Lits, M. (1997c) Le récit médiatique: Un oxymore programmatiqueet. In *Recherches en communication 7.*, Louvain-la-Neuve
Marion, P. (1993) *Traces en Cases.* Academia: Louvain-la-Neuve.
Marion, P. (1997) Narratologie médiatique et médiagénie des récits. In *Communication Recherches en Communication* 7: 70.
Mouillaud, M. and Tétu, J.-F. (1989) *Le journal quotidien.* Lyon: Presses Universitaires de Lyon
The Official Riven (1997) Indianapolis, IN: Brady Publishing.
Ryan, M.-L. (1991) *Possible Worlds, Artificial Intelligence, and Narrative Theory.* Bloomington & Indianapolis, IN: Indiana University Press.
Sørensen, B. H. and Jessen, C. (2000) *Det er bare noget der er lavet.* Copenhagen: Medierådet for børn og unge [Media Council for Children and Young People]
Van Dijk, T. (1988) *News as Discourse.* Hillsdale, NJ: Lawrence Erlbaum.
Virilio, P. (1999) *Cyberworld – det værstes politik.* Copenhagen: Introite. Originally published 1996 as *Cybermonde, la politique du pire.* Paris, Les éditions Textuel.

Games

Crosstown (1998) Vision Park, Bonniers Multimedia, Copenhagen.
Riven (1997) Cyan Productions, Crawley, West Sussex.
Tomb Raider II (1997–1998) Eidos Interactive, Aspyr Media.

15

The Limits of Narration

Jørgen Stigel

3D interactive multimedia (3DIMM) makes it possible to interact with virtually created, lifelike worlds, consisting of nothing but the stuff that dreams are made of. Thus a crucial limit in aesthetic constructs between on the one hand the audience and on the other actors has been abolished.

The audience are no longer just some people who attend, listen and watch, and who form their own ideas in relation to something that is or has been represented, and so can only act and relate to this by contemplating, reacting emotively, and identifying with it. They are not just "passive" participants,[1] but actors who can or must act, carry on and "move" according to patterns very much like those of real life.

In this way, 3DIMM is so far the last link in a long development chain of media and forms of representation within the aesthetic field. In this connection we must bear in mind that this is seen in a mimetic[2] tradition, i.e. the tradition within the aesthetic field aimed at developing various frameworks and forms of representation, within which reality can be reproduced, imitated and represented to the life in well-defined sequences and versions, including merely imaginary ones. Significantly enough this development begins with the so-called central perspective[3] and which – from this point on and in different ways – through an ever-increasing refinement of the symbolic tools and the reproductive abilities of the media techniques works ahead along those lines that attempt to suggest that the user of the artefact is at the centre of things and has reason to identify with the artefact and

1 The term "participation" is used in accordance with what will later become more explicit through the examples. So it is used in accordance with the fact that audio-visual narratives, for example, draw heavily on the audience's inferring abilities. Participation in this context is not to be understood as physical engagement, but as the more abstract mental phenomenon that you in a simular or parallel way "understand" what is going on in (fictitious) persons and what is at play in a given situation or act. You are able to reproduce what another person experiences on the basis of a few pieces of information and you become able to identify but without being able to interfere. In Danish the word *deltagelse* (participation) is used also in this more passive sense, while in English you would use "sympathy": "Må jeg udtrykke min deltagelse?" = "May I offer my sympathy?".

2 See e.g. Walton (1990).

momentarily feel an involved part of it. The word *momentarily* is decisive, for the user is also at a distance, outside, and not responsible.

Thus, so far 3DIMM is also a last element in that particular dimension of media and media development which has to do with media seen partly as an element of the illusion-making and partly as a surrogate for actual human interaction and communication. Also, as regards the different ways in which the media and their forms of representation attempt to create mental *space* and a communicative context with their receivers or users, the 3DIMM can be argued to have reached a new high. Finally, they will probably also represent a zenith when it comes to *how* the media are an extension of our daily scope and *how* perceptionally and experientially they give access to information that we would not otherwise get.

Until the computer medium began to manifest itself as an audio-visual, network-based medium, TV was the medium most able to represent reality in segments and within a well-defined framework. Among other things this was because TV is able to pass on picture and sound from/of reality in real time, i.e. simultaneously with the viewer's time. This very simultaneity, "live" as it is termed, is an essential dimension in connection with TV's special aesthetic strong points and power to fascinate in the area of reality.

But no matter which medium one is dealing with, there are some basic conditions for the forms of production and communication which have not changed decisively. It is no mere coincidence that Aristotle is still one of the most quoted authorities when it comes to basic problems within the aesthetic forms of communication and production. Nor is it a coincidence that problems about how to understand the basic mechanisms and constituents of the forms of representation keep cropping up and must be regarded separately from the ever-changing aspects when new media appear.

One of the forms of reproduction and mediation, which in the cognitive sense must also be understood as a fundamental and almost universally valid form of reproduction, is the narrative, because the narrative makes up a framework of understanding and a pattern for perceiving, processing and preserving reality and experiences of reality.

The intention in the following is to identify or encircle the narrative dimension *vis-à-vis* 3D interactive media and especially those particular problems posed to narrativity by interactivity. This will be done by first establishing a general understanding of narratives, seen partly as process structure/logic and partly as a kick-start to the receiver's inferring abilities and comprehension, and thus as a certain mode of information which in an aesthetic form calls forth features containing parallels to (sense perception of) reality. Next, narrativity will be perceived in the light of forms of address and narration of the TV medium and of the special potential of TV for interacting with the audience. On the one hand it is a question of clearly defining those modifications to narrativity that are due to the medium's dimensions of real time,

---

3 Although aspects of creating illusionary perspective are recognizable in ancient Greek and Roman painting and in medieval painting too (Giotto), the invention of the so-called central perspective or frontal perspective is normally dated at the Renaissance (15th century). Massacio's fresco "The Trinity" in Firenze (Florence) of 1427 is recognized as the first genuine work of art to represent a (mathematically) "correct" illusion of space. Likewise the theory of perspective begins with L. B. Albertis' *De pictura/Della pictura* from 1435–36.

simultaneity and simulated interaction. Despite all their limitations, these factors of closeness in relation to the user may be regarded as experientally parallel to certain features of 3D interactive multimedia. Thus they tell us something about the relativization of the importance of the narrative. On the other hand, it is a question of a more direct, cash-on-the-nail, exemplified definition of those features about audio-visually transmitted narratives by one-way media which make their priorities strikingly different from those of 3D interactive media, i.e. a definition of those exact features which play a great part in traditional audio-visually designed narratives, but which precisely are *not* decisive in interactive ones. This difference is first and foremost rooted in the changed mode of information caused by the radical change of the receiver's or user's role: from introvert ("passive", contemplative) participation into an extrovert ("active", controlling) role or perceived scope for action. The chapter concludes in an attempt to take a more functional view of (dimensions of) narrativity and the usability of narrative processes seen in relation to different types or genres within 3D interactive multimedia universes.

15.1 Narratives

The fundamental things about a narrative[4] are partly its narratedness and the intention built into this *act* of narration, and partly what is being told, i.e. the story or the process on which the narrative *reports*. The narration is *speech* and a statement from someone to or for somebody else about something that is taking place or has taken place *over time*. The temporal aspect is thus a double one. It relates partly to the time of the narrative (narrator's time) and partly to the time of what is being narrated. And as the temporal aspect is a double one, so may the intentional aspect be. The aggregate intention is not necessarily in accordance with the intention(s) being *expressed* in the story.

So the narrative is an *address* and a *lead card*. It is a *presentation* and thus a structured arrangement which is intentionally directed with a report on a progression or a process, the story which altogether gives *a promise* of some sort of meaning or point and which must be able to keep this promise. It is also a representation, however: the story is an artefact in the shape of a (re)construction referring to, standing for and reproducing a process in a factual or fictional manner.

On the one hand, the story itself is built on (a chain of) *events*, and on the other on "living" *human* (anthropomorphic) entities.

---

4 The section on narratives is inspired partly by a structuralist and semiotic tradition and partly by a pragmatist and cognitivist one, which takes a critical attitude to the former and concentrates more on the question of the role of the audience and their given forms of understanding in connection with narratives on the basis of, for example, gestalt and scheme theory, theories on prototypes and a series of other theories on deduction-based perception, categorization, expectation and knowledge. Central in this connection is Branigan (1992). But needless to say there is a long chain of forerunners as e.g. Propp (1968), Bakhtin (1981), Barthes (1988), Greimas (1981), Todorov (1970, 1977a,b), Bremond (1980), Genette (1976, 1980), Benveniste (1966), Metz (1974), Chatman (1978, 1990), Iser (1978), Eco (1979), Bordwell (1985), Adam (1985, 1992). In this connection no position is to be taken as the more principal points of disagreement and divergences between the various theoretical orientations.

The events may be designed partly as a number of *actions* following or consequential upon each other and/or *episodes* or coincidences. The living components may be shaped partly in roles or *characters* and partly in *environments* or configurations (settings).

As mentioned, the narrative is an invitation or appeal to a user. Taken abstractly, the gist of the appeal will as a rule aim at creating the framework round a (reading) process, which may create sense and coherence and point from a progression into which enter actors, barriers to the aims, plans, acting scope, and "struggle" to overcome the opposition and barriers. Seen *thematically* the progression will head in certain directions, and to ensure this direction the whole thing will usually be governed by a *cause–effect mechanism* and tied together by a *plot*. Often the actors may be seen as "pure" causal, processed *functions* of this plot or setup.

As a rule, the aggregate process will contain or produce a change, a *transformation* of conditions and predicates in the relationship between starting situation and end situation via the action of the actor. For example, the actor changes elementarily from the passive to the active voice. But not necessarily, since the actor may choose not to act. Thus a narrative consists of a succession of processes, which come into being from the following *successive basic pattern*: (1) (acting) opportunity to change condition A in the starting situation (which may be taken or not) (2) action (or non-action), and (3) achievement or non-achievement of the change to condition non-A or conditions B, C etc. in the end situation. At each of these stages, conflicts may arise. But the phrase "as a (chief) rule" is used advisedly, since narratives – or rather the story – are not always highly rated at this point-oriented and final structure. To make sense of this madness, however, the audience will typically induce or infer dimensions of narrative logic, as for that matter they infer and are expected to infer their expectations and foreknowledge – or maybe even prejudices.

The narrative is an appeal to the listener's/reader's imaginary powers and inclination to guesswork and speculation. It is the substratum of this capacity for imagination. On the one hand the injunction "Imagine!", and on the other the requirement of the narrative for "make-believe", i.e. to create an illusion of a symbolically designed kind of reality, which in a credible and plausible manner appeals to the receiver's conception of reality or his or her conception of causal and other procedural connections, patterns and values in reality, are two sides of the same matter.

Like any other form of symbolical design and aesthetic artefact, a narrative refers to itself and closes on itself. But in this connection it draws heavily on (reference to) the experiential patterns of reality, on imitation of reality (mimesis and verisimilitude), and the reader's own interests, anticipations and inferring abilities from, for example, cues, hints, fragments and the sequence in which the individual parts of the progression appear, are organized and juxtaposed. Thus a narrative progression is not only forward-oriented. It requires conclusions about something already shown/narrated on the basis of something successively narrated. In this sense narratives draw upon forms and patterns of understanding in the shape of experiential and cognitive *schemes or schemata*. Cognitive schemes may be defined as those patterns of understanding and that foreknowledge used to predict and categorize new sensory data within a certain domain. This is coherent knowledge, which for instance ascribes probability to events by, for example, basing itself on causality, expectations, assumptions based on categorization, and the linking of sense impressions from a stock of experiences regarding "how something typically takes place or is played out, including which intentions may be at play".

The receiver must be willing to enter into something purely imagined or pretended and into the framework and space erected for this pretence. The receiver must be prepared to adjust himself in a certain manner and be willing to make an effort at imagining and concluding things, a certain imaginative energy within the erected limited framework which is that of the narrative. The story must become *fabula* to the receiver.

In other words, the receiver has been endowed with a certain role as co-author, filler-in and fable creator within the framework, but the receiver cannot make any decisive changes to the framework and influence or manipulate the variables entering into it. The receiver's lack of opportunity to interfere and change the progression is taken as a tacit agreement between the narrator (who "owns" the narrative) and the audience. They must sit quietly and pay attention and leave things more or less to chance, for the narrative is structured and pre-structured. It is the expression of an overall or all-embracing survey oriented towards where everything, not least the actors, is heading, where the narrative is going pointwise, where the reader is going, and not least *how* the reader gets there.

If the receiver becomes a user and has to act and inter(act) with the narrative, the receiver is changed into a player, an intercepting actor who, for example, is allowed a number of options, which in the further progression may be minted out in a number of strings of progression, for instance. This may take place on one or more of the narrative's levels (cf. the following chapter).

In other words, a narrative is not just a definite structure or logic with a beginning, a middle and an end during which conditions and predicates are transformed. A narrative interacts to a very high degree with given typifications and patterns of understanding and not least of expectations and considerations of probability as to progress. As regards progress, this applies to the unwinding of progress within narratives (the genre in various media) as well as within the domains and situations of lived life, and to the conclusions which may be taken for granted in both fields.

In sum, what narratives, as well as other forms of interpersonal and media-borne communication, attempt to create, is a mutual *space* of speech and imagery.[5] This mutual space may give high priority to the narrating or relating situation itself, and in this way to the fact that there is a narrator who addresses us with the story. In this way,

5 "Space" in this context is neither meant to be taken literally nor metaphorically. In this context it is meant to indicate a rather elementary dimension of interpersonal communication, for instance: the parties build themselves a physical space of contact, conversation and interaction, which is constructed by different kinds of verbal as well as non-verbal behaviour. It makes up their immediate situative context and sensous and perceptive orientation, but it also delimits them from the surroundings (cf. parties, where it might be rather difficult to break into a group). In a parallel manner the addressing or presenter format on TV might be seen as a way of simulating traits of the same kind of conversational space (simulated interaction), while an audio-visual drama format, for example, will seek in quite another way to get a hook into the audience's imaginary capabilities by making it possible to identify with persons and actions and thereby identify with or mentally move into a certain universe. See also Stigel (2000).

the relater and mediator role is given weight, as also is the emphasis on the explicit address. However, it may also give low priority to the fact that we have a narrator with a story, and thus high priority to the universe that the story is about and its direct transmission to the audience, so that – "without intermediary" – the audience is brought face to face with this universe and the actions taking place in it, but needless to say in a selective manner.

15.2 The Construction of a Mutual Space of Imagination on TV

So far, the TV medium has been the one which has most extensively been able to create mutual spaces of imagination of a very varied nature together with an audience. At the same time, seen in relation to the audience, the TV medium is a medium without an arena. The TV set stands in the sitting room, and even if the individual programme may not be, the transmission itself is always direct and here-and-now. As in all other connections, the amount of priority given to representation and presentation varies. And, as in all other connections, the narrator is an (institutionally) staged figure, a role.

The narrators on TV may be physically visible as presenters of the story. The narrator role and the pronouncing location are important here, just as it is decisive that the narrator addresses him- or herself directly as a person with visual and other contact "to" the viewer. The form simulates contact and interaction as in the "I-you-here-and-now" relation of interpersonal communication. In this way, it is also a case of simulation and an allegation of a mutual speaking and contact space between persons, where for example the presenter or moderator plays the part of a mediating figure by addressing partly his own stage, partly the audience at the screen, where head movements and other pointing movements (deixis) play an important role.

However, the relaters may also be invisible and only speaking presenters. That is to say that they speak during a picture sequence (1) which either illustrates the statement and/or (2) which the statement comments upon, anchors and indicates. Moreover, picture and speech sequences may to a higher extent be combined, so that one plays up to and takes over from the other, so that each dimension gives its special contribution to the meaning of the aggregate plot, so that the gaps between spoken and shown play up to the audience's "own" conclusions. In this kind of voiceover-governed format, the speech location is, so to speak, not clear, and this gives the voiceover format a very wide scope for the filling of the narrator's role and its interplay with what is shown.

Finally, the narrators may be invisible as well as silent, and thus absent, it being only the story itself, i.e. the represented dimension which unfolds physically by being reproduced in action, dialogue, and events on their own dramatic level. That the narrator is invisible and silent does not mean, however, that the narrator is not there. It just means that the emphasis is not on the address dimension of the story itself (that someone is telling/wants to tell us something), but on the story as a story and how – in a physical and spatially processual manner – it may be captured, performed and created via actors, scenography, camera, sound and lights. This is done precisely in a spatiality which simultaneously manifests itself and, so to speak, joins the performance with a wealth of contextual information.[6]

But this also means that the "I-you-here-and-now" relation of the communication situation is not necessarily decisive. The viewer is not just a "you" who is being addressed, but an experiencing I, who is placed face to face with a reproduced world and its actors, and the intention is that this very world with its actors and events should captivate the viewer.

Thus, TV attempts in various ways to create a mutual space[7] with the viewer. Generally speaking, this may take place through the simultaneity of TV. More specifically, it may happen through the direct physical address of the presenter form, which establishes an alleged space of contact and conversation. The address may be subject to a picture sequence, and in this connection establishes a greater gap or clearance between spoken and shown. And finally the address dimension itself may be absent and replaced by a space formed by an identificatory movement into a made-up world which comes into being via deputizing characters and their viewpoints within this world.

While the imagination space is right on the surface of the screen and between screen and viewer in the two first formats, where the story to a higher extent is something spoken (about) and pointed out, in the third and last, metaphorically speaking it lies "inside" the screen and in its "depth" and in the shape of a world. The reason is that the viewer should be able to "enter into the spirit" of this world and accept it. The possibility of identification is established among other things by the viewer having to do a job of work, namely a job of deduction as to how even tiny components of the plot are to be understood and how it all hangs together. Arousal of the viewer's curiosity is necessary. An elliptic, a synecdochic, and otherwise suggestive and in this sense suspense-creating form of presentation will, for example, be able to initiate this work of deduction. And as a rule and to a very high degree, this work of inference functions automatically. As mentioned before, it rests on prototypical situations, types of situations, but it also rests on quite fundamental, trivial and self-evident understandings of (*open* and *closed*) spaces as the context of situations, including entries and exits from spaces and connections between spaces and localities. It equally rests on basic understandings of how persons build up a communicative space or field of tension between them. We might try to illustrate this by the following trite example (1),[8] which plays itself out in a prototypical situation.

> In close-up we see a section of a table with a mess of handwritten papers, notes, periodicals, and a coffee cup plus a hand with a pencil. A classical violin concerto sounds discreetly in the background. At the same time the sound of an ordinary, somewhat

---

6 Apart from the fundamental difference that narrating time equals narrated time in audio-visual media, one of the characteristic differences between literary/linguistic media and theatrical/audio-visual ones is how one may/is to understand the descriptive element. In the literary/linguistic field the descriptive elements are part of the progression of the text and are really pauses in this progression seen from the viewpoint of plot. In the audio-visual field the corresponding descriptive dimensions will be evidently connected with the plot and its spatiality and will rarely appear as properly descriptive passages. See for example Seymour Chatman (1980).

7 cf. Note 5.

shrill doorbell is heard, and with a slightly annoyed movement the hand puts the pencil away. In the next cut we see another hand in ultra-close-up, in fact only a woman's finger with a varnished index fingernail pressing a bellpush. The door is opened from the inside during the ringing, and a youngish woman only just manages to slip on her most ingratiating smile as the door opens. She is classy with gold jewellery on ears and throat and says, "Hello, I'm sorry to bother you". Reaction shot from the woman's viewpoint of youngish, slightly surprised man in the doorway. She is then seen again from the man's viewpoint, "I'm having a dinner party and I have run out of coffee". The man in close-up again, answers with a very open and obliging expression, "Come in", and his eyes follow her with a smile while she passes with a "Thank you". During the passage there is a cut so that the camera still focuses on the man's face, which with a slightly wrinkled forehead and a sideways glance indicates that either he does not know what to make of the situation or maybe he feels that she is somewhat importunate. Close-up of Nescafé Gold on kitchen shelf and hand taking the jar and cut to close-up of man with Gold, "Will Gold be too good for your guests?". With a slightly ambiguous look, which may be interpreted as slightly derisive, the woman answers, "Oh, I think they could get used to it". The man makes a roguish point, "It's a very sophisticated coffee", while regarding her very determinedly and intensely and advancing a fraction. The woman replies with a crisply sparkling smile, "They have very sophisticated taste" while with an equally aggressively flirtatious glance she also advances towards him. And during the man's, "Do they?", they are therefore face to face. "Yes. Well, I must be getting back", she ends, while her eyes slide slightly out of focus and she makes a little coquettish toss of the head. After this, pack-shot with Nescafé Gold, two cups and voiceover. Via close-up of the very same type of cup, which is drunk with enjoyment by the woman, the scene has now changed to a restaurant. "Have you met your new neighbour yet?", another woman asks in familiar girl-friendly way. "Well, I've popped in for coffee", she says through an ambiguous smile, which might indicate hopes for more.

This example shows something about elementary inferences as to action, space and location in the classic (also scenic) situation: "there is a ring (at the door)", as e.g. Eugene Ionesco in the play *La cantatrice chauve* (1950) exploited *ad absurdum* and which, to be sure, sounds quite absurd if made explicit. When "there" is a ring at the door, there is (1) *somebody outside* who rings, (2) *somebody inside* who must understand the ringing as a call signal and interrupt what this somebody is doing in order to see who this somebody outside is and answer the bell in the belief that the person outside has a relevant errand, because (3) the two "somebodies" banally and basically are not in the same space. In other words, in this example the sound of the bell justifies an almost direct jump from a fragmentary reproduction of an ongoing activity being interrupted (in one space) to the opening of the door on (another) space, and all intermediate stages are left out.

---

8 The Nescafé (Love for Gold) commercial spot was shown on Danish TV2 in March 1994. Apart from the inserted pack-shot it is in English, as there is no synchronization of speech, but translation in subtitles. In the English connection it has a considerably more comprehensive history, since – as indicated at the end of this particular spot – it developed into an episode serial with the two neighbours. In England it even began being published in book form and became a potboiler (cf. McAllister, 1996). In the USA a competition was launched between consumers as to how the story might continue. In the USA the history started in 1990. Here – along with other serials – the new episodes were pre-advertised (On ABC's soap magazine *Episode*, 1992 and in *TV-Guide*). The series ran for several years as an ad-as-serial.

But the above example does not only show something about automatic inferences regarding actions and actors in a space. It also demonstrates how withheld and implied information may be exploited to create elementary curiosity, suspense and a basis for identification. Obviously, the withheld information first and foremost concerns the male actor, from whose viewpoint and world or space we watch, but notably do so *before* he himself has been established as an identifiable, acting and seeing person *to us*. And that is the point. And analogously in a sense also as regards the female actor, whose hand we also first see in exactly the same way. So it is only at the door that the characters are to be revealed and the (only elliptically hinted at) unknown be visible, so that the audience experiences its first actionwise release.

In the subsequent chain of shots and reaction shots and the underlying, hinted flirtation with the coffee as cause or conversation piece, the whole ambiguity of the significance of the meeting at the door is established exclusively by intonation and face expressions. Now the emphasis is on the construction of the communicative space *between* the parties, which is built up by exclusively focusing on their open faces and (what is construed as) their mutual direct eye contact. But the hinting, suspense-creating play continues and is made more intensive – now only in the form of over- and undertones in the interaction of the actors and less of the sequence of information items.

The opportunity for identification (and experiencing space, too) is created by the curiosity and suspense arising (1) through the sequence of information given, including the withholding of information; (2) in the manner in which a character is established through whom – vicariously and momentaneously – one is allowed to experience "through", i.e. whose "eyesight" one momentaneously utilizes in the form of point-of-view editing (POV) and the establishment of a so-called focalizer (joint vision); (3) by the actors' eyes, looks and body language stating something other and more than what they state in the trivial verbal and semantic sense, i.e. that we get an uncertain added meaning in the interplay between said and shown; and (4) finally, it is characteristic that we receive information and views of something, where the reasons behind are not closely connected to the level of the focalizing persons, but is connected to the exterior vision of a higher narrative level. What is seen and heard is seen and heard because the narrative as an audio-visual progress and story simply makes a good point of seeing and hearing it, i.e. – via what is shown – to inform us as viewers from the superior level of a more general viewpoint, which might then e.g. be justified by the requirement for the continuity of the process (through characters as well as objects like coffee cups) and the requirement for *drive*. But they may also be rooted in the requirement to create tension between the level of knowledge at the disposal of the principal characters and the one at the viewers' disposal, and in this way create other types of chinks or cracks through which the audience's identification can be furthered. In other words, these direct tensions and shifts of viewpoint between *insight* and *overview* have the effect that now the viewer knows less, now more than the characters of the story, and it is characteristic that these can be communicated fairly seamlessly and only rarely lead to one asking, "Who is watching this?" or, "Why is this being dwelt on?". This only just happens when one senses that the camera begins to be an independent and demonstrative actor, who so to speak says, "This is to be seen!" without there really being an immediate justification for it in the plot. As the reader reads in good faith from left to right, so the viewers watch in the same good faith, i.e. do not necessarily question shifts of angle, let alone leaps between different worlds, but accept them and take them for granted, because they are usually incorporated in and justified by an entity of progression which (gradually) creates coherence. This and much more is what we are dealing with in the following example (2),[9] which also plays itself out in a prototypical situation, but expands into something totally different.

> The location is that of a museum with figures of an ethnographic character. A youngish male visitor walks around like a typical onlooker, regarding and scrutinizing one thing and another with a stare while masticating his chewing gum. This munching comes to a halt when something takes him aback. The stare is also emphasized by the actor's close-set eyes, oblong face, and by his looking at the things from all possible angles and by his opening his eyes wide at certain bodily extremities. But it is emphasized not least by the extremely rapid montage with several jump-cuts concentrating on recording nothing but this wandering stare. After having inspected a number of fairly large figures, he stops at some smaller ones on a small podium and focuses his stare on something that might resemble a tiny, frail voodoo or witch doctor figure. His look at the over-accentuated round eyes of the figure is turned into ours. Then the direction of the voodoo figure's look is turned into ours via our focalizing principal character and his turning his head in the opposite direction. The look turns out to be directed at a photograph on the opposite wall – a picture of US President Bill Clinton among African chieftains/presidents and with an African mark of honour on his chest. Suddenly the scenario changes. We are at a press conference at The White House with Bill Clinton greeting people from the rostrum to applause, and then just as suddenly back at the photo, where the voodoo figure's face is now superimposed on Clinton's. The principal character's look and the connection between the Clinton photo and the figure is stabilized by being repeated a number of times via the principal character's staring head movements 180° from right to left, i.e. from the voodoo figure towards the photo and back again cutting in tighter and tighter. The principal character ends by poking his nose right up to the little figure and looking into its eyes, which are finally seen in ultra-close-up and now shine red. Our onlooker looks more and more amazed and wants now to take another close look at the Clinton photo, bends down a bit, but also walks backwards a bit so that his behind collides with the figure's arm which falls down. Cut to Clinton, who makes a falling arm movement on the rostrum. Back at the museum our perplexed principal character struggles to put the arm back in place. Cut back to The White House where Clinton makes the same totally unmotivated and spastic arm movement, at first something like a "Heil Hitler" salute, and the second time round with both arms raised extremely high and twisted above his head and consequent worried reactions among his audience. Meanwhile back at the museum, the principal character is turning the figure between his hands. Likewise Clinton turns round on his rostrum and is now standing with his back to the audience. The principal character struggles on. Clinton is on the point of falling under the rostrum. Finally the principal character thinks he has put the figure back in its place and removes his hands very carefully. Nevertheless the figure falls off its stand. Likewise at The White House: Clinton topples sideways off the rostrum. Full view of empty rostrum and shocked audience. Slightly worried and burdened by guilt our principal character again holds the voodoo figure in his hands and regards the awl-like metal prong on the stand to which the figure has been fastened. Close-up on the point. Resolutely he slams the figure down on the prong, so that it is impaled through the rump. Exit our principal character from the

9 The commercial from Centraal Beheer won a Gold Lion in Cannes 1997 at the annual international advertising prize festival. The spot has a duration of 70 seconds and consists of almost as many cuts, i.e. an average of one cut per second (Cannes Lions 44th International Advertising Festival, 23–28 June 1997).

picture, but the text *Just call us*, followed by Centraal Beheer, the Insurance Company of Apeldoorn, appears upon the screen.

In this example, a fair amount of energy is expended on establishing an extremely heavy focalizer indeed, who very pointedly walks about and stares, and whose eyesight and – not least – whose mediating visual connnections are definitely quite crucial. He could be argued to be a peripatetic incarnation of the fact that vision or glances create connections and open up mutual spaces between entities in (different) worlds.

But in addition this example is full of obvious and quite unrealistic "absurdities" which just barely derive their logic from a staring person – in surrealistic and fantastic manner – creating a living connection between two arbitrary and inanimate objects: a picture of Bill Clinton and a voodoo doll, which (we gather) must be placed across from each other. In this sense the character is nothing but an exterior visually demonstrative mediator of "virtual reality". The photo is thus the only justification for cutting to the White House press conference, which is then without further ado alleged to take place simultaneously and so parallel at the same time. Likewise, the superimposing of the voodoo doll's face on Bill Clinton's is the only thing which at the outset indicates a connection between Clinton and the doll. This more or less arbitrarily created parallel-running space and the connection between the two entities thus initially comes into being on a superior authoritarian level of narration and cannot be seen as illusions or visions belonging to the principal character. The parallels and the interdependence are then amplified by the repeated stares and head movements of the principal character, but nonetheless he is happily ignorant of what he is causing – among other things possibly because he is happily ignorant of what object he is sticking his nose and eventually also his clumsy butterfingers into. In this way the principal actor's knowledge is clearly separated from that of the viewers, just as the context of his actions and their range is far narrower than the one placed at the viewers' disposal. What is accident and clumsiness in his tiny cramped world becomes a spastic, embarrassing performance within the public arena of the president and high politics. Among other things, it is this gap (of acted ignorance and "innocence") between a micro and a macro world, which makes the story exciting as well as amusing. But needless to say it is not just the gap, but also the joining of or bridging between otherwise disparate worlds and phenomena which contribute to the fun and games.[10]

Analogously with what the voodoo figure incarnates, and what our principal character incarnates on a slightly less magic level, connections can be created between

---

10 In this sense the narrative conforms to the familiar basic pattern of any kind of humour and – more generally – also of the formation of human ideas and consciousness: the unsuspected leap (of thought), which suddenly joins together two entities between which it is not normally possible to build a bridge. What also makes the story amusing is the created magical and elementary connection between the doll as "victim", but notably a victim with powerful abilities of transmission, and the (we must assume) thereby remote-controlled and powerless Bill Clinton as a parallel accident-stricken victim in a political world of power running parallel to the other. This magical connection rests exclusively on similarity and repetition, but its suppleness is due first and foremost to the contrast between the roles of power figure and victim, and its reversal by virtue of the voodoo figure having fallen into the clutches of an unskilled bungler. The voodoo figure is the simple symbolic incarnation of it being at all plausible for a plotwise parallel transfer or mimetic projection to take place from one universe to the other.

otherwise totally separate universes including their actors, it is possible via the techniques of narration and montage of the film media with very few repeated effects to create lightning-quick plausible connections between two widely different spaces and two widely different entities. Also, the ending of the story may safely be left to our own imagination, since the pattern has been laid.

Just the fact that an audio-visual narrative establishes two spaces with different actors really sets the scene for the parties in the two spaces to meet or to create a different kind of more or less intense connection between them (at some time or other). The fact that certain selected directions of glances and connections between glances indicate emphasis makes it possible to establish more or less arbitrary connection or coherence between otherwise totally separate entities, so that a semantic connection between them suddenly arises (cf. Eisenstein's and Kulechov's theories of montage). The fact that repetition of the same basic mechanism (such as "cause–effect" or "like x, so also y") create a certain structure or pattern enables one to deduce the point for oneself. In this case, this is attained through a combined and heavy-handed exploitation of the basic rules applying to an alternating syntagm as well as to a parallel syntagm (if one were to speak in Metz's categories[11]).

In this way narratives are governed by a certain economy where those principal ingredients which have been introduced and established and between which a gradual connection has been created are, so to speak, to be used up during the progression, as they are driven towards and are condensed in the point. And in this way narratives constitute a figure-borne processuality creating (a space of) time round a progression which in sensorily concrete symbolic forms displays or illustrates a point by making use of various forms of imitations, but also highly structured selections and representations of real, "lived" life and its culture-given, familiar entities.

But audio-visual narratives are also governed by a definite form of distribution of knowledge. They strike a balance between giving out information and withholding information. In deliberate and calculated manner this balance creates now suspense, now acceptance between the levels of knowledge of the actors and, respectively, the audience. The tension between the agent or actor, brought into this world by the narrative, and the rest of the information about this world, i.e. familiarity with the context of the actions of this agent, enables the audience to know more and to make guesses. It helps to make the audience find it interesting to stay tuned. The opposite might also be the case: that the audience knows less than the principal character, and are mystified as to where the whole thing is leading, precisely because knowledge of decisive parts of the context is more or less constantly withheld from the audience. In this way the audience is being put to the test and must accept at certain stages being without a clue, as with a jigsaw puzzle, in which the whole that the pieces are to form has been in no way revealed.

---

11 According to Metz (1968, 1974) an alternating syntagm as well as a parallel syntagm run in the form of A–B–A–B–A–B etc. But while the former is a chronological syntagm, the latter is non-chronological. So the difference is due to their relationship with time and space. In an alternating syntagm A and B will be part of the same time (and space in the widest sense), whereas in a parallel syntagm A and B are not. In a parallel syntagm the As and the Bs are meant to signify parallel meaning between, for example, separated objects and phenomenons.

The question now is how and to what extent this form of symbolic and highly structured artificiality is usable if you try to apply it to the kind of artificiality which may be played out in 3DIMM worlds where quite another kind of unknown and ungovernable variables of action come into the picture, not to say through the door and into the room in the form of the user's scope for action. And where presumably a great number of the features concerned with furnishing chinks, cracks, counters and lead cards for the user's approval and involvement assume a completely different character, since – in a totally different direct sense – the user "is present" at the scene of the action. So the user does not – via a number of perceptory and mental tricks and suspenses – have to be enticed into entering into it, but is rather to be incited to act on the scene of action and thereby also accept the particular scope and the special game rules placed at his or her disposal.

15.3 Narrativity and 3D Multimedia Worlds

In 3DIMM worlds one can create for oneself and act via deputizing characters, i.e. so-called avatars who are brought into the world and made to act within constructed virtual worlds and spaces among other avatars. This might of course result in various forms of actors' sociality, exchanges, situative communication and interaction, but it does not have much to do with narrativity. That is, not unless someone establishes definite setups with hustlers and con artists and other forms of consciously staged machinations or skulduggery, which may entrap naïve newcomers and other nitwits, give them a spanking and altogether teach them a lesson, because they have not yet decoded the world they are moving in – quite obviously in the first place its social norms.

In continuation of this, 3DIMM worlds encourage the user's forward-directed I-vision and direction of viewpoint to be predominant. This is surely not always the case, but the following will allow itself to rest on that premise.

In accordance with the user being the active party, this requires a continuous (i.e. compared with TV and motion pictures – "uncut") POV determined by one POV-bearer (first person or at least a point of view as close to an actor as "over the shoulder"). The user is the focalizer and in this sense is at the centre by being the POV-controller. This results in some decisive shifts and abolition of ambiguities. For example, a face directed towards the user is quite unambiguously a face to be understood as an I-you relationship, i.e. first to second person, and not as a her-him relationship, i.e. third person. What is seen is determined from a stable point of view, but it is precisely this that prevents the creation of narrative suspense via shifts of viewpoint and via the above-mentioned play between levels of information and (im)balance between overview and insight. In that sense we are close to the formerly mentioned presenter form which is manifest on TV.

In the world of motion pictures and TV a film or programme is very seldom consistently shown from a first-person POV. One of the few films which has made a largely consistent attempt at this is *The Lady in the Lake* (1946, directed by Montgomery).[12] It is unique in several respects, but mostly in not having had many successors. That it has not is presumably due to (1) the curtailed 90° vision of the camera and (2) some basic problems precisely regarding the suspense and drive of the story when there is only one point of view and one level to inform the viewer from or from which the viewer may draw conclusions and thus feel involved and feel suspense (cf. above).

The lesson that *can* be learned from the TV medium, however, is that its capacity for reporting here-and-now, i.e. the very simultaneity in connection with the media and its synchronization of time and place in relation to the viewer, may eclipse a number of the requirements incorporated in a narrative. TV is quite capable of transmitting extensive progressions which are largely point- and plotless, because the point is simply that of watching events and actions from the location in the world of "reality", while, or rather at the moment, they happen, and in this sense feeling in contact with them and close to them. The simultaneity and the effect of the moment (nearness in time) in themselves contribute to the formation of the mutual space, and the medium as such is also a generator of simultaneity. This not only manifests itself in the newscasts and their topicalization, but also in the intervals between programmes.[13] Mutual time to some extent becomes mutual space, and the hotness and topicality of the problems or people's very direct topicalization as speakers from the screen have the effect that more aesthetically sophisticated and condensed forms of presentation are not necessarily required. In this way one might talk about a cost–benefit relation, which is more generally in evidence in the case of TV, i.e. the factor that what is experienced as satisfactory TV aesthetics is made highly relative by a factor of closeness in time (topicality) and place. And – needless really to say – cultural closeness also plays a part, e.g. the topic's nature as to touching on a more or less obvious "common destiny" or at least a common field of experience. Because of the very nature of the medium one cannot talk about a similar cost–benefit relation with regard to the film medium (the cinema). In other words, the special thing about the medium is that certain features of interpersonal communication can be simulated, such as direct address and simultaneity, just as the simultaneity may be quite real in the form of live TV on location and not just in the form of "as live". Seen in this perspective, narratives are first and

---

12 Apart from a very short starting and closing situation, which altogether frame the main story as having taken place, the film is subsequently represented by the first person view. In Branigan (1992, pp. 142–160) The various (mis)understandings of *The Lady in the Lake* are comprehensively treated. Branigan also points out how the subjective POV reduces information to the viewers and makes contextualization difficult.

13 Simultaneity is a fundamental characteristic of the electronic mass media, TV and radio. Ellis (1982) defines TV counter-distinctively in relation to film and summarizes the special features of TV as, among other things, being more pervasive and having more general immediacy-effect, which is connected to its (original) dependence on live production and on direct address and general verbosity. Seen from more systematic genre-wise and aesthetic considerations of the aggregate programme landscape and address forms of TV I have emphasized (Stigel, 1997) that one (out of several) decisive qualities about the TV medium is its instant aesthetics, i.e. its opportunity to fuse the viewer's now with a now (or something that appears as a now or the now in which things happen) somewhere else. This closeness in time to reality and despite distance endows TV with a form of direct suspense and suppleness which in a wide range of TV programme types is able to outstrip more narratively elaborate constructions and programme types. In this way TV can allow itself to be far more extensive and pointless, because what happens here and now and what the viewer may personally watch with a feeling of being part of this here and now is enormously crucial. This could be summarized as cost–benefit, i.e. the viewer is ready to renounce the idea of a more final and suspense-oriented point and meaning (such as a narrative promises) for the price of being more directly and immediately involved in what is happening.

foremost a way of organizing material to compensate for the receiver having been silenced. Therefore the receivers must be accorded space and the opportunity to imagine so that they can enter the ring and invest their "imagination", i.e. suppositions, inferences, guesses etc., via the sequence of information items. The right to one-way communication is conditional on either the speech making an effort to enable receivers to participate with their own inferring abilities and powers of deduction and that these are played up to *or* on the receiver being simply immediately, motivationally and situationally able to relate to what is being shown and talked about.

Transferred to 3D multimedia it may be argued that the very fact of being able to do something, move "oneself" virtually, and influence something in a space which at the same time feels close among other things by being perceptually close to the perception and behaviour of real, "lived" life, and being able to do this in real time, means that narrative in a stricter, "economical", intensive and structural sense does not need to have a high profile. The extensive structure of time and progression which applies to parts of the TV medium and which is connected to its simultaneity and simulations of contact will therefore also be able to manifest itself in this context. On the other hand, a number of the more general basic elements on which audio-visual narrative constructs rest perceptionwise and cognitively may be important. Above all, it is a question of (1) space conditions (including moods and attractors, i.e. cues to create connections and take action), and also the role that sound and light play in the construction and indications of space and relations between spaces as well as how one may plausibly jump or move from space to space; (2) types of situations and actions (including time and means–end notions); (3) types of actors (including (attributed) intentions); and (4) themes.

In addition, as with any other type of medium/programme, it is decisive what prospects are held out by the "programme and its virtual space", i.e. which anticipatory contract or framing exists between user and programme or type of programme or perhaps one had rather say domain/universe or type of universe.

One part of the framework is thus the universe constructed and its delimitations, including also how and in which form the user as actor "is" or figures in the universe. Another part is what the aim or intention is or could be with being able to move and act within this universe. A third part of the framework is what actions can be taken or for which the groundwork is laid within the universe, and how these actions can be taken. A fourth part of the framework is what types of situation are (may be) established within the universe. A fifth part is which incentives to or requirements on inference and action may be inserted or installed in the universe *vis-à-vis* the user in the form of cues, hints, ambiguities, clues, barriers, routes of access and "tests".

What manifests itself in any circumstances is the spatiality and its character – just as in "lived" life. Presumably it will make a very great difference whether the framework is constructed to fill a need in the form of a meeting or gathering place, i.e. a *forum*, or to comply with a need to test oneself and experiment in the form of an *experimentarium* or *laboratory*, or whether it is simply to meet the need to go exploring for the unexpected in the form of an *exploratorium*, or finally that the framework has been established to give information, solve problems, give good advice and information in the form of a *consultarium*. This is not to say that these functions may not be mixed, but just that something will predominate.

A forum may be seen as a parallel to the town square, where you may run into one person or another, chat, discuss and in other ways interact, sit in on somebody's wedding, attend a cocktail party, and altogether walk to and fro and watch any happenings and coincidences that might occur, and from time to time be a "personal" party to these, but really without any guarantee that this will lead to something.

An experimentarium or laboratory may be seen as a parallel to the situation of a job interview, an examination, a crisis, a negotiation or ambiguous interplay, where you test yourself and your patterns of action and reaction far more determinedly in relation to a number of delimited, but all the same not quite clear and calculable situations and forms of interaction, and maybe also in relation to the consequences that one's choices or lack of them may have in relation to the subsequent situations that may arise. The testing consists among other things in how well one is able to *live up to and fill or master a role* in a given context. In short: how to cope.

An exploratorium has its progression parallel within the picaresque novel[14] or novel of chivalry, but for that matter one might as well use a forest or an area in the countryside or a town neighbourhood as the parallel. You sally "forth to" or "into" a universe to discover and explore it, run into temptation, peculiarities, and opposition, surmount it etc. Maybe you get lost in mazes, are misled by false clues, begin to walk round in circles, are exposed to one surprising, enigmatic, mysterious or horrifying thing or other, and may even stumble into situations, where (in Kafkaesque manner) you are made responsible for things you have not done. The decisive thing about an exploratorium is therefore "the road along which" you move and what gradually comes into being and may arise on this road.

A consultarium has its parallel in a location far easier to survey: a library, a museum, an information bureau or a salesroom. Consequently you seek it out on a far more limited errand: to be informed, taught, guided and to have a need (for knowledge) met. But as is characteristic of such places, you may (also) return home with something completely different from what you came determined to get, and in this way discover a need you did not believe or realize you had or could be sold on.

If it can be accepted that these are some of the typical basic functions, there will be a number of forms of address and aesthetic requirements that – relative to the basic function – will be more or less predominant.

In a consultarium and a forum it is not necessarily an absolute requirement that the actor(s) you meet should be 100% human as to figure or texture. It is enough for them (e.g. by animation) to mime (certain features) of human behaviour. Likewise, the universe need not be particularly realistic as to texture. On the other hand, it will probably be fairly important for the universe actor to be able to actively stand out as a (type of) character, and lead off with a direct address of the type seen in the presenter format – but in this particular case as a sort of (in some cases – serving) character with whom you can primarily make functional exchanges.

---

14 The novel of chivalry, or picaresque novel, is characterized by its additive structure. The progress is loosely tied together from episode to episode. The only thing that connects these episodes is a common principal character. The story may largely move in any directions and into any fancies or digressions.

In an experimentarium/laboratory – obviously depending on what is to be achieved – a higher degree of realism and credibility of the simulation as to universe, matter and figure will be important in order to ensure that, for example, a spontaneous pattern of action and reaction is maintained on the part of the user. But apart from this the underlying pre-organization or – calculation of the progression or strings of progression including various forms of plot structure, and thus a possible pre-organization on narrative patterns and logics – will not be a great problem, since the use is aimed at, for example (the handling of, training in, or acquisition of experience with) certain prototypical situations, within which a more or (especially) less delimited scope is granted and where the variables and unknowns the user may lead off with will be relatively limited precisely because of the nature of the setup. If one thinks beyond the individual, delimited situation and in connected chains of situations, making discontinuous jumps between situations will not be a problem either. While the micro-dimension should thus be or be felt as intense and lifelike, the macro-dimension need not live up to this requirement. In this way much may be legitimated by the fact that one is testing oneself, and by the creation of suspense depending on whether one can live up to the action demands of the situation.

It is quite another story in an exploratorium, which is a totally different open universe where both micro- and macro-dimensions should hang together via forms of continuity. If one should choose to enter such a universe rather than take a walk in the woods, there must necessarily be something exciting to experience and do – other than just moving straight forward in the universe. The question therefore is how to create coherent continua of suspense and incitement to action and in a plausible manner move or jump from one universe to another with the same POV. In this field one may make use of something elementary of the mechanisms in example (1) (signal calls, ambiguous figures) as well as example (2) (that a virtual world makes it possible for dead things to come to life and open up new universes and new contexts), but right here I shall not venture into further speculation.

15.4 The Narrative Feeds on Life. Life Is No Narrative. How About 3DIMM Life?

Within the film medium it was relatively soon realized that interminable reproductions of lived life, such as are still found represented even today in private home videos or movies, are rather boring, pointless and irrelevant – unless something surprising or unexpected sneaks in, which may then be cut out and sold to the TV stations' sample programmes of this kind. Sporadic reproductions of lived life are largely only interesting from a (later) historio-ethnographic point of view or because of the special relationship between actors, camera-holder and viewers and their intimate mutual references. The same experience was made in literature about 100–150 years before the film medium,[15] and is very amusingly exposed and travestied in, for example, the Danish poet Johannes Ewald's *The Life of Master Sewing Needle*, which is completely negated as progress by standing out as a vagrant structure – and pointless nonsense rattling along post-haste.

Life is no narrative, but people have a tendency to turn it into one said Samuel Johnson in the same century, when – seen from academe – narratives were above all something to learn from and which should make sense. It is against this background in particular that Ewald's anarchistic raid with *Master Sewing Needle* makes sense by pointing out that there is a lot of lived life and representations of it that do not make sense and then out-trumps his point by shortly after having the same Master Sewing Needle report on a *dream* he has had. In retaliation, this (of course) has the neat coherence of a Robinsonade.

3DIMM universes aim to a very high degree at lifelike behaviour and progressions based on an acting "I", as they supply spaces for development, the ambition of which, at least, is to be homologous with and simulate those of real life in the form of spatiality and acting into this spatiality. If 3DIMM universes are used for very definite delimited and predetermined purposes of an interactive, didactic or testwise character, then of course 3D may help to raise the experiential reality status of the simulation as well as the interactivity, first and foremost in the form of instantaneous actions/choices and instantaneous consequences of actions. In this connection, the framework will be given by the delimited purpose mentioned, just as the aesthetic design and the limitations herein may be legitimated to a very high degree by the governing appropriateness and functionality. This will apply to those abovementioned types of universe which have been termed the consultarium and experimentarium/laboratory, and to a considerable extent also to the forum.

To the extent that we are also dealing with a more open and unbound aesthetic use of 3DIMM universes it appears clearly that if there are no settings or various forms of setup which may have a natural structuring and framing effect on the scope for action and the actual development, then such universes will become as uninteresting as the home video. As in all other aesthetic connections it is the limitations, but in this case of the more imperceptible kind, which establish the suppleness. In other words, 3DIMM universes of the kind termed exploratorium in the above must have built-in *suspense* and uncertainty and create *suspense* and uncertainty in a way that will constantly see to it along the way that the user is kept up to the mark and on track. The manner of creating curiosity and suspense cannot be identical with that of the film medium, for example, and the (mediation) forms of the more traditional audiovisual media, because the point of departure of the 3DIMM universes is that one "is" in the universe and should not first be brought into it and then constantly held in it, and because the opportunity to intervene, absent in other media, is crucial here. A great number of the suspense-creating devices that we find in films and which are first and foremost aimed at creating suspense and drive via the distribution of

---

15 In the Age of Enlightenment and the 17th century the narrative is put on the agenda (novel and moral tale), but in the same breath so also is the question of the relationship between on the one hand the narrative's requirement for structure, point and logic, and on the other hand the reproduction of narrative – if not exactly the lack of it in actual life, then at least its difficulties with living up to the requirement. Laurence Sterne exposed the problem in his novels (*Tristram Shandy* and *A Sentimental Journey*), and on Danish ground Johannes Ewald was the first to describe the problem in the same way. This happened among other places in the fictive periodical *The Strangers*, which claimed to describe what happened in one of the predominant patriotic clubs (of the same name) during that period. This is the perspective in which Master Sewing Needle's two (intendedly didactive) – pointedly juxtaposed – stories should be seen. The obvious point is that while life is characterized by its workaday absurdity, routine and incoherence, the dream is characterized by suspense, coherence and logic.

information and points of view in interplay between the level of the actors and that of the audience are thus irrelevant. On the other hand, the type of suspense that has to do with the handling of situations and with what may "hide or reveal itself round the next corner", ambiguities, and not immediately precisely decodable signals and constellations, may be fairly decisive. Those dimensions of the audio-visual narrative which will be decisive are at most its progressional architectonics.

References

Adam, J.-M. (1985) *Le texte narratif.* Paris: Nathan.

Adam, J.-M. (1992) *Les Textes: types et prototypes. Récit, description, argumentation, explication et dialogue.* Paris: Nathan.

Bakhtin, M. M. (1981) *The Dialogical Imagination.* Austin, TX: University of Texas Press.

Barthes, R. (1988) Introduction to the structural analysis of narratives. In *The Semiotic Challenge.* New York: Hill & Wang.

Benveniste, É. (1966) *Problémes de linguistique générale.* Paris ("L'homme dans la langue", pp. 225–287).

Bordwell, D. (1985) *Narration and the Fiction Film.* London: Routledge.

Branigan, E. (1992) *Narrative Comprehension and Film.* New York: Routledge.

Bremond, C. (1980) The logic of narrative possibilities. *New Literary History* 11(Spring): 387–411.

Chatman, S. (1978) *Story and Discourse. Narrative Structure in Fiction and Film.* Ithaca, NY: Cornell University Press.

Chatman, S. (1980) What novels can do, that films can't (and vice versa). *Critical Inquiry,* 8.

Chatman, S. (1990) *Coming to Terms: The Rhetoric of Narrative in Fiction and Film.* Ithaca, NY: Cornell University Press.

Eco, U. (1979) *Lector in fabula.* Milano: Bompiani.

Ellis, J. (1982) *Visible Fictions.* London: Routledge

Genette, G. (1976) Boundaries of narrative. New *Literary History* 8(Autumn): 1–13.

Genette, G. (1980) *Narrative Discourse: An Essay in Method.* Ithaca, NY: Cornell University Press.

Greimas, A. J. (1981) *On Meaning: Selected Writings in Semiotic Theory.* Minneapolis, MN: University of Minnesota Press.

Iser, W. (1978) *The Act of Reading: A Theory of Aesthetic Response.* Baltimore, MD: Johns Hopkins University Press.

McAllister, M.P. (1996) *The Commercialization of American Culture. New Advertising Control and Democracy.* Thousand Oaks, CA: Sage.

Metz, C. (1968) *Essais sur la signification au cinéma.* Paris: Klincksieck.

Metz, C. (1974) *Film Language. A Semiotics of the Cinema.* New York: Oxford University Press.

Propp, V. (1968) *Morphology of the Folktale.* Austin, TX: University of Texas Press ((1928) *Morphologie du comte.* Paris: Seuil).

Stigel, J. (1997) The aesthetics of television, the quality of television: on distinctions and relations of programme form and quality of address. In *Quality Television* (eds. M. Eide, B. Gentikow and K. Helland). Bergen: University of Bergen.

Stigel, J. (2000) TV advertising virtually speaking. The invisible voice elaborating on the space between screen and viewer. In *The Aesthetics of Television* (eds. G. Agger and J. F. Jensen). Aalborg: Aalborg University Press.

Todorov, T. (1970) The two principles of narrative. *Diacritics* 1(1).

Todorov, T. (1975) *The Fantastic: A Structural Approach to a Literary Genre.* Ithaca, NY: Cornell University Press.

Todorov, T. (1977a) Categories of the literary narrative. *Film Reader* 2.

Todorov, T. (1977b) *The Poetics of Prose.* Ithaca, NY: Cornell University Press.

Walton, K. (1990) *Mimesis and Make-Believe. On the Foundation of the Representational Arts.* Boston, MA: Harvard University Press.

16

Film Theory Meets 3D: A Film Theoretic Approach to the Design and Analysis of 3D Spaces

Jens F. Jensen

16.1 Introduction

This chapter explores possible approaches through which 3D spaces or virtual 3D worlds can be conceptualized, designed and analysed from a film theoretic point of view. First, 3D space seen as a new form of interactive multimedia is defined. Second, similarities and differences between 3D space and the film medium are discussed. Third, key concepts from film theory are introduced, such as: *mise-en-scène*, cinematography, montage and the relation of sound to image. Finally, features of 3D space and virtual 3D worlds are described and discussed against the backdrop of these key concepts from film theory.[1]

16.2 What Is 3D, Anyway?

Considered as new media, 3D spaces or virtual 3D worlds can be characterized by the following traits:

---

1 Earlier and shorter versions of this chapter have been presented as full papers at WebNet 99, World Conference of the World Wide Web and Internet, Honolulu, Hawaii, 24-30 October 1999 (Jensen, 1999d), and at ICCE '99 – 7th International Conference on Computers in Education. New Human Abilities for the Networked Society, Chiba, Japan, 4-7 November 1999 (Jensen, 1999f).

- 3D spaces are generated from software and drawn as interactive computer graphics in three space dimensions (plus a fourth in time), i.e. they exist only in cyberspace: in the digital domain of the computer and computer networks.
- 3D space is build on coordinate geometry, i.e. a system of three imaginary lines or axes, X, Y and Z. Any point in 3D space can then be described with a set of three coordinates referring to a position on each of the three axes.
- 3D spaces are represented
  (i) either via 3D display systems based on stereoscopic technologies (3D films, 3D caves, hologram projections etc.), or
  (ii) on a two-dimensional screen, i.e. in the last case, 3D graphics are understood as a way of representing 3D data in 2D (as in film, television, painting, still photography etc.), so that it can be viewed on a computer monitor or a TV screen.

  Re point (i) – in the case of 3D display systems based on stereo vision – we perceive the *z*-axis as bidirectional. It points from the screen surface back toward the horizon, but also forward toward the viewer. As a result, the objects are perceived as relative to us, not to the surface of the screen, i.e. they appear to extend beyond the screen toward the observer.

  Re point (ii) – in the case of representation of 3D on 2D screens – we perceive the *z*-axis as unidirectional. The closest object seems to lie on the screen surface and the *z*-axis points from the screen backwards toward the horizon, away from the observer.
- In 3D spaces the user is
  (i) either represented by a point-of-view or a "virtual camera", i.e. by a position in 3D space in the form of a set of three coordinates (x, y, z) plus the point that the camera is aimed at, defining the line of sight, or
  (ii) by a so-called "avatar", a computer-generated representation of the user – in other words, these spaces are inhabited by their users, designers and developers. In this case the user has a viewpoint that is attached to his or her avatar, either in the form of a so-called first-person point-of-view, where you see the world from the position of your avatar, or in the form of a third-person point-of-view, where a virtual camera follows your avatar from positions and visual angles defined relative to the avatar.
- In both cases – (i) and (ii) – the point-of-view or the avatar (plus the attached point-of-view) can be moved around on the 3D scene, and the movement is controlled interactively by the user. Because the background and the objects in the scene are animated, the user can see the whole scene move relative to the point-of-view or the avatar. In short, the user can interactively control the point-of-view and/or the avatar relative to the 3D space.

It is these 3D spaces and Virtual 3D Worlds that are the primary objects of this study.

16.2.1 Similarities and Differences

Considered as media, films and 3D spaces resemble each other in several aspects:

1. Both films and 3D spaces are representational media, i.e. they use cultural and aesthetic conventions to create "texts" that can exist independently of their sender (similar to books, paintings, sculpture etc.) (Fiske, 1982), in contrast to presentational media that use the body as a transmitter and produce acts of communication and are consequently tied to the sender and to the here and now (similar to theatre, voice, body language, facial expression etc.).
2. Both films and 3D spaces are time-based media, i.e. they include development in time (in contrast to sculpture, architecture, painting etc. that are articulated primarily in space).
3. At the same time they also include spatial composition and movement or development in space (in contrast to, for instance, written or spoken languages that deal only with the linear aspect of construction).
4. Both films and 3D spaces are "multi"-media in the sense that they make use of several (sub-)media or sign systems. The French film semiologist Christian Metz points out five channels of information in film: (1) the visual image, (2) print and other graphics, (3) speech, (4) music and (5) sound effects (Monaco, 1981). The same is surely true, *mutatis mutandis*, of computer-based multimedia in general and of 3D spaces in particular.
5. Both films and computer-based multimedia, among these 3D spaces, can draw on the majority of the other arts (spoken and written language, graphics, music, painting, dance etc.) for much of their meaning, aesthetic power and various effects – for one thing because they can record them. That is one of the reasons why computer-based multimedia are among the most complex of all media in regard to sign systems, aesthetics, composition etc.
6. Multimedia aside, both films and 3D spaces are based on moving images as the dominant sign system.
7. Both films and 3D spaces are informed by representational conventions such as the relationship between stage and actor (known primarily from theatre and film) and the representation of the point-of-view (known primarily from painting, still photography, TV and film).
8. And last but not least: both films and 3D spaces are composed in three space dimensions, and just like all films are screen media, where the three-dimensional world is projected on a two-dimensional surface. The vast majority of current 3D spaces – i.e. with the exception of 3D display systems based on stereo-vision – are also screen media that represent the illusion of three-dimensional space on a two-dimensional screen.

However, there are important differences as well:

1. Monaco (1981) writes: "Cinema is not strictly a medium of intercommunication. One seldom holds dialogues in film. Whereas spoken and written languages are used for intercommunication, film ... (as well as language when it is used for artistic purposes), is a one-way communication. As a result, even the most utilitarian of films is artistic in some respect". Computer media and 3D spaces, on the contrary, are media of intercommunication. In other words, networked media resemble spoken and written languages in that they are used for intercommunication. In fact, one often holds dialogues in 3D spaces (e.g. 3D chat). Or, more

precisely stated: film is a one-way medium whereas 3D space is (often) two-way communication; film is an inherently passive medium, whereas 3D is strongly marked by interactivity and human–computer interaction (Jensen, 1997).[2]

2. Although both films and 3D spaces are representational media, which use cultural and aesthetic conventions to create "texts" that can exist independently of the here and now of the sender's act of communication, 3D space, in contradistinction to film, has a peculiar feature with regard to the here and now of the receiver. 3D space can be said to produce text on two levels. On the one hand the program, software or code is a "text", invisible to the ordinary user but visible to the programmer, and on the other the actually generated 3D space or picture on the screen is a "text". Whereas the program text, like film, exists independently of the presence of the sender and the receiver, the screen text is in a way dependent upon the receiver. The reason is that a given section of a virtual 3D world is only generated and drawn as computer graphics on the screen when a user passes by. In this way, the screen text can be said to be tied not to the sender's presence and here and now (like theatre, voice, body language etc.), but to the receiver's (virtual) presence and (virtual) here and now in the 3D space. Consequently, there may be parts of 3D spaces or virtual 3D worlds which are never drawn as 3D graphics and in this way never realized as actual screen text. That is surely one of the most unique features of 3D spaces compared with other media such as film.
3. Both films and the majority of 3D graphics project the three-dimensional space on a two-dimensional surface. However, while the film camera and its optical system perform this projection more or less automatically (although it certainly can be modified, cf. below), in 3D space we need a mathematical model or a 3D engine to construct or reconstruct the space from scratch.[3]
4. Both films and 3D spaces utilize the illusion of 3D and the movement of the point-of-view in the three-dimensional scene, but in film the fixed movements of the camera are controlled by the film director, whereas in 3D space the user is able to control movements and point-of-view interactively.
5. Finally, film is primarily an indexical medium (there is a physical connection between the images and the scene they represent) and an iconic medium (the images have a direct similarity to the object). In contrast, 3D space is first and foremost a symbolic medium, because there is no necessary existential bond between sign and object (and in some cases no direct resemblance), but only a contract or an arbitrary convention (Jensen, 1993), and possibly an iconic medium (on the assumption that the images resemble the object).[4] Thus, while

---

2 At the same time, however, multimedia and 3D spaces resemble film in that they are often artistic in some respects. This is another reason why multimedia and 3D spaces are some of the most complex of all media as regards semiotics and aesthetics.

3 Although elements of the automatic photographic process can be found in techniques based on digital photography, such as QuickTime Virtual Reality.

4 The concepts of icon, index and symbol as they are used here do not refer to the level of genre, as expressed in terms like *fiction* and *facta*. Following C. S. Peirce, they refer only to the relation between the representation and the represented (in Peirce's terms: the representamen and the object), in this case the relation between the picture and the depicted.

film is a medium with a strong bias towards the indexical and iconic, 3D space is a medium with a strong bias towards the symbolic and iconic.[5]

16.3 *Mise-en-scène*, Cinematography, Montage, and Sound and Image

Returning to film, Monaco remarks: "In film criticism, generally, the modification of space is referred to as *mise en scène*.... The modification of time is called montage" (Monaco, 1981). Both *mise-en-scène* and montage are principles of organization. But where *mise-en-scène* concerns the techniques of the shot (setting up the scene, organizing the space, staging the subject in front of the camera), montage concerns the techniques that relate shot-to-shot: editing or cutting. In Monaco's words: "montage simply did in time what *mise-en-scène* does in space" (Monaco, 1981).

These two dimensions are – according to Monaco – of paramount importance for the construction of meaning in film. To produce a film, the film director has to make specific choices. When the significance of a specific shot depends on having "been chosen from a range of other possible shots" then we can speak of meanings produced on the paradigmatic axis. That is, the "sense we comprehend stems from the shot being compared, not necessarily consciously, with its unrealized companions in the paradigm, or general model, of this type of shot" (Monaco, 1981). The paradigmatic aspect of film is thus associated with *mise-en-scène*. Conversely, when the significance of a specific shot does not depend "on the shot compared with other potential shots, but rather on the shot compared with actual shots that precede or follow it", that is, the other shots we do see, then we can speak of meanings produced on the syntagmatic axis. The syntagmatic aspect of film is thus associated with editing and montage.

"These two axes of meaning – the paradigmatic and the syntagmatic –", Monaco (1981) sums up, "have real value as tools for understanding what film means. In fact, as an art, film depends almost entirely upon these two sets of choices. After a filmmaker has decided what to shoot, the two obsessive questions are how to shoot it (what choices to make, the paradigmatic) and how to present the shot (how to edit it: the syntagmatic)". And likewise when we "read" a film, the sense of meaning, "depends on understood comparisons of the image with images that were not chosen (paradigmatic) and images that came before and after (syntagmatic)...". Thus, according to Monaco (1981), "the tension between these twin concepts of *mise-en-scène* and montage has been the engine of film aesthetics ever since... the turn of the century".

---

5 This is not to say that we never find indexical signs in 3D worlds or symbolic signs in films. Actually, photographic pictures, live feed videos, texture-based on photography etc. frequently occur in 3D worlds in the same way that animations, effects, computer graphics etc. often occur in films. It is only to say that indexical signs are not a fundamental, constitutional, and necessary part of 3D graphics as they are in film and symbolic signs are not a fundamental, constitutional and necessary part of films as they are in 3D space. Thus, the distinction points to a relative rather than an absolute contrast, i.e. a difference in emphasis.

In the following, we will structure the discussion around these two key concepts diverted from film: *mise-en-scène* and montage. However, we will have to supplement the twin concepts with a third, which also relates to the techniques of the shot. Usually, film theory distinguishes between two techniques of the shot: *mise-en-scène* and cinematography. While *mise-en-scène* concerns *what is being filmed* or what is put in front of the camera, cinematography concerns *how it is being filmed*, i.e. how it is inscribed on the strip of film.

In short, the domain of *mise-en-scène* is *what to shoot*, the domain of cinematography is *how to shoot it*, and the domain of montage is *how to present the shot*. Finally, we will supplement this with a short discussion of some of the techniques that relate sound to image.

First, however, we have to outline the basic concepts of "shot", "scene" and "sequence" (Bordwell and Thompson, 1997; Raskin, 1986b; Andersen, 1997).

In film theory, a "shot" refers to one uninterrupted run of the camera to expose a series of frames, that is, if defined in relation to "shooting". In the finished film, correspondingly – that is, if defined in relation to editing – a "shot" is one uninterrupted flow of image frames with a single static or mobile framing (Bordwell and Thompson, 1997) or, in other words, a segment of film between two splices. The shot is thus a sort of "minimal unit" in the film medium, although the concept of "minimal unit" has been heavily contested in film theory (Monaco, 1981). In 3D space, it would correspond to one continuous 3D walk-through or one tour in a 3D space without a change of point of view.

A "scene", on the other hand, is a larger segment of a film relating to the same logical unit of meaning, i.e. it is unified as to time and space and/or involves one complete stretch of action (Bordwell and Thompson, 1997). In 3D space, it would correspond to a series of consecutive actions or interactions in the same time and (3D) space that can be understood as a logical and meaningful unit – without regard to a change in point of view. In film theory the concept of "plan-sequence" refers to a long and usually complex segment involving much camera movement during which a whole scene is filmed in a single shot without cuts. While, in films, "plan-sequence" is an exception to the rule, in 3D it has, in fact, already established itself as the conventional way of representing a scene.

Finally, a "sequence" is a number of scenes linked together by time, location or narrative continuity to form a unified episode in a film, often equated to a chapter in a book. In 3D space, it would, for example, correspond to an accomplishment of a "level" in a 3D computer game, a sub-plot or episode in an interactive narrative, or the like.

As it appears from the above, while the concept of "short" pertains to *mise-en-scène*, the concepts of "segment" and "sequence" relate to montage or editing.

16.4 The Techniques of the Shot I: *Mise-en-Scène*

Mise-en-scène involves the techniques of the shot.

Mise-en-scène was originally a theatre term which reaches back into 19th century theatre. Here, the concept was applied to the practice of directing plays. The French phrase literally means "putting in the scene" or "staging an action". The term crossed over to film production, where it came to signify practices involved in the framing of *shots*. Now the concept is used to signify "the director's control over what appears on the film frame", i.e. the codes that operate within the frame; or rephrased: "In controlling the *mise-en-scène*, the director *stages the event* for the camera" (Bordwell and Thompson, 1997).

Following from the term's theatrical origins, *mise-en-scène* includes those aspects of film that overlap with the art of the theatre – notably setting, lighting, figures, movement, appearance and costumes – within the frame. Each of these general areas offers the filmmaker a range of possibilities for selection, choice and control. Thus, as a set of techniques or codes, *mise-en-scène* assists in the composition of the shot in space and time – and thereby modifies our reading of the shot.

In recent years, the filmmaker's control of *mise-en-scène* has been extended to a degree impossible with live actors shot in real time, first by means of animated film as seen in drawn or puppet animation, and later by means of computer-generated images and animations. Consequently, settings, figures, and movements created by digital computers are also considered part of the *mise-en-scène*. In the context of computers and 3D spaces, we can define *mise-en-scène* as every element that appears in the scene – and on the screen – and that the designer can control.

Obviously, aspects concerning *mise-en-scène* have a special relevance for the new virtual 3D worlds emerging on the Internet and as standalone applications (Jensen, 1998b, 1999a,c). Here, the designer literally has to create or stage a new scene, a new environment, or a whole new world. So Peter Bøgh Andersen (1997) is right in saying that the emergence of 3D worlds and 3D interfaces is the fulfilment and culmination of *mise-en-scène* in the computer medium.

In the cinema, *mise-en-scène* is often used to guide our attention across the screen, shape our sense of the space that is represented, and emphasize certain parts of it. That is, to guide our perceptions and hence to shape our understanding of and inferences about what we see and hear. The same can be said about 3D spaces. And as demonstrated, the techniques of *mise-en-scène* contain a host of ingredients to provide cues and direct the user's attention. Since, as a rule, we scan a frame for information, not only space but also time is brought into play. As a result, *mise-en-scène* can control not only *what* we look at but also *when* we look at it. For example, in cinema, lighting is much more than just illumination of the scene. Lighting shapes objects by creating highlights and shadows, articulates textures, and forms the overall composition of a shot. As perhaps the most important tool to modify the meanings of form, line and colour, lighting provides cues and guides our attention to certain objects. Correspondingly, in 3D spaces you often have to add (virtual) spotlights and lighting to illuminate the scene.

Each of the general areas under the techniques of *mise-en-scène* offers the designer a range of possibilities for selection and control. Due to a lack of space, we will only comment upon a few of these codes with special relevance to 3D, namely depth cues or the illusion of three-dimensional space: our ability to create and perceive 3D depth in 2D representation.

Needless to say, there is no real space extending behind the screen, but arrangement of the *mise-en-scène* and the way it is being transformed for the screen must prompt the viewer to imagine or construct that screen space. In other words, the techniques and codes of *mise-en-scène* must provide cues that enable the viewer to infer the three-dimensionality of the screen from the flat two-dimensional images projected on the screen.

Naturally, some of these codes concerning depth perception are shared with still pictures, notably photography and painting. The most important of these codes to simulate the effect of 3D depth or distance in 2D representation that can be observed in still pictures, film and 3D spaces are overlapping planes, linear perspective, relative size (proximity and proportion), height in plane, density gradient, aerial perspective, and light and shadows.

Overlapping planes. One of the most common ways of creating the illusion of depth in 2D representations is overlapping planes or partial overlap. If one object partially covers another object (although they obviously lie on the same plane) we perceive the first as being in front of the second and, accordingly, the one that is partially blocked from our view as being behind the object doing the covering. Thus, we readily interpret partially overlapping objects as a representation of the third dimension in the form of "behind" and "in front" positions. Arnheim writes: "Overlapping is of particular value in creating a sequence of objects in the depth dimension when the space conception of the picture relies on contour rather than on volume or light. For some painters, space is realized best through a continuous series of overlapping objects, which lead the eye like stepping stones from the front to the back".[6] This classic depth cue used in painting and still pictures is also used in 3D. For instance, the position of an avatar in relation to other objects or avatars in a scene is always indicated by a "behind" or an "in front" position.

Linear perspective. The best known of all means for creating the illusion of depth on a two-dimensional surface is of course linear perspective. Leonardo da Vinci defines it as "the diminishing perspective of objects as they recede from the eye",[7] or in the words of Donald Graham: "through convergence of line and plane, and with diminution of sizes and volumes, it is possible to simulate deep space".[8] The core principle of linear perspective is that horizontal lines converge and vanish at one point in the distance, the so-called vanishing point. The vanishing point always lies on the horizon line at eye level or camera level. As a result of the converging parallel lines, the horizontal as well as the vertical lines lie closer together the farther away they are from the observer.

Density gradients. Closely connected to linear perspective are density gradients. A density gradient is described by Arnheim as a "perceptual gradient of size", referring to the phenomenon of "objects becoming increasingly smaller as they recede, possibly with the intervals between them also becoming increasingly smaller".[9] Due to the fact that horizontal and vertical lines come closer together the farther away they are, the illusion of depth can be produced simply by

6 Arnheim (1969, p. 241), here quoted from Raskin (1986a, p. 45).
7 Da Vinci (1954), here quoted from Raskin (1986a, p. 42).
8 Graham (1970, p. 40), here quoted from Raskin (1986a, p. 42).
9 Arnheim (1969, pp. 268–269), here quoted from Raskin (1986a, p. 42).

crowding parallel lines, objects or dots toward the horizon. This depth cue – also referred to as the "crowding effect", "depth through crowding", or "depth through texture" – is a very common way of producing depth in computer-generated graphics.

Relative size (proximity and proportion). Another important depth cue with a strong affinity to linear perspective and density gradients is the technique of relative size. In real life, the father away an object is the smaller it appears. Consequently, the smaller a given object appears within a picture frame, i.e. relative to the borders (be it a painting or a screen), the father away it is perceived to be. The larger it appears within the picture frame, the closer it seems to the viewer. Furthermore, if we know how big an object is supposed to be or we can estimate its size from the context of other known objects, then we can infer the distance to the object – i.e. establish a third dimension – on the basis of how big the object appears relative to the frame of the picture. Correspondingly, if two or more objects are supposed to be identical in size, we automatically infer that the largest representation of the object is closer to us than the smallest representation. This depth cue is also referred to as proximity and proportion. In 3D graphics this technique is often used to create the illusion of depth. For instance, the relative size of avatars in a scene is automatically perceived in terms of the relative distance, and identical objects which reduce in size are always perceived as increasing distance on the *z*-axis.

Height in plane. Given that the camera is shooting parallel to the ground, the higher objects are positioned in the picture field up toward the horizon line the farther away they are perceived to be. This distance clue can also be found in 3D graphics, where the horizon line is often an important graphical feature.

Aerial perspective. In real life, because of moisture, dust etc. in the atmosphere, we usually see objects that are farther away less sharply than objects that are close to us. Thus, while the foreground is sharp and dense, the background is often less clear and textured. Correspondingly, with regard to pictures, if objects appear less sharp and if colours become less saturated and lose their density they are interpreted as being farther away from the observer or the camera, thereby creating the illusion of depth. In like manner, less saturated colours seem farther away than highly saturated colours, cold colours recede and warm colours advance the eye of the observer etc. This technique is often called aerial perspective or perspective of colours and it also goes back to Leonardo da Vinci. Arnheim writes: "So-called aerial perspective, first described by Leonardo da Vinci, produces a gradient of color by making objects paler with increasing distance from the observer".[10] This technique can also be found in 3D graphics.

Vanishing perspective. Closely connected to aerial perspective is vanishing perspective or gradient of sharpness. Objects "ought to be less carefully finished as they are farther away", writes Leonardo da Vinci. Or in the words of Arnheim: "In physical space, we see near objects more neatly defined than distant ones. In painting, the same effect serves to enhance depth.... In painting, the zone of greatest definition is generally in the foreground".[11]

---

10 Arnheim (1969, p. 269), here quoted from Raskin (1986a, p. 42).

Light and gradients of brightness. Arnheim again: "One way in which light produces depth is by means of brightness gradients. Maximum brightness appears at the level nearest to, or coincident with, the location of the light source. Thus brightness also establishes a key level of spatial distance, which does not have to be in the foreground.... From this base a gradient of decreasing brightness pervades space, not only toward the back and the front, but also sideways. Light creates a spherical gradient expanding in all directions from a chosen base in space".[12] Likewise, in many 3D spaces there are virtual light sources to enhance the illusion of 3D space.

Shadows. Light and light sources suggest another related depth cue: shadows. Because cast and attached shadows emphasize the volume of a given object and thereby indicate a third dimension, they are often used to produce the illusion of depth. However, in some 3D programs only attached shadows exist, not cast shadows.

In addition to these conventional techniques of creating the illusion of depth adopted from still photography and painting, 3D graphics has some unique methods not known from other media. One of them is the so-called "level of detail" or LOD. To avoid calculating and drawing all the polygons in a detailed model when the distance from the object to the viewer makes it impossible for him or her to see all the details anyway, an object often has a series of models of different degrees of complexity and detail. Then as the viewer moves closer to the object the level of detail increases, substituting richer detail, and as the viewer moves further away from the object the LOD is reduced. This technique is also applied to textures, showing more detailed textures as the viewer moves closer to the object (Wilcox, 1998). Although the primary purpose of LOD is to save calculating time and computer power, the effect for the viewer is a new depth cue with perceptual affinity to that of "vanishing perspective".

16.5 The Techniques of the Shot II: Cinematography

As mentioned above, film theory usually distinguishes between *mise-en-scène* and cinematography as two techniques of the shot. *Mise-en-scène* concerns *what is being filmed* or what is put in front of the camera. Cinematography *concerns how it is being filmed*, or how is it inscribed on a strip of film. Literally speaking, cinematography means "writing in movement", corresponding to photography, which means "writing in light". Traditionally, cinematography includes factors such as the photographic aspects of the shot, the framing of the shot and the duration of the shot (Bordwell and Thompson, 1997).

In the digital world and in the context of 3D spaces, the distinction between *mise-en-scène* and cinematography is no longer well founded, among other reasons because there is actually nothing in front of the "camera" and nothing is being inscribed on a light-sensitive film. Both the scene and the way it is being represented are, in a way, generated from the same machine. Thus, the "what" and the

11 Arnheim (1969, pp. 269–270), here quoted from Raskin (1986a, p. 42).
12 Arnheim (1969, p. 270), here quoted from Raskin (1986a, p. 44).

"how" are often indistinguishable. This collapse of a clear distinction between the aspects of *mise-en-scène* and cinematography is in fact one of the significant characteristics of 3D space as a medium. Nevertheless, some of the factors treated under the rubric of cinematography are still pertinent to our subject.

In this context, we will deal only with the codes most relevant to 3D, which are camera angles, mobile framing and camera movements.

Camera angles. Camera angles consist of sub-types such as eye-level shot, high-angle shot, low-angle shot, oblique framing and sideview angle. The most common types used in 3D are eye-level shots, for example in the case of first-person point-of-view, and high-angle shots, in the case of third-person point-of-view or God's-eye perspective (either relative to the scene or attached to the avatar). Furthermore, in 3D space the aspect of camera angles is often consigned to the domain of interactivity. In flight simulators, for instance, the user frequently can choose between different "views", defined relative to the aircraft.

In addition to camera angle, the direction in which a given actor faces in relation to the camera is perhaps worth noticing. Sub-categories are here front view, back to camera, in profile, three-quarter view etc. In this aspect, one of the more peculiar differences between films and 3D is the use of "back to camera". While extended use of this direction of face is very rare in films, it is not uncommon in 3D. For example, in games based on a virtual camera following the avatar – such as "Tomb Raider" or certain levels in "Crash Bandicoot" for the PlayStation, to mention just a couple of examples – the user actually sees the avatar-protagonist "back to camera" more often than not.

Besides the possibility of changing camera angle, another unique feature in 3D is the powerful capability of interactively changing the view or perspective. In certain CAD systems, for example, you can choose between the usual orthographic views (top, front, side), different non-perspectival 3D views (isometric, axomometric, oblique) and true perspective.

Depth characteristics of lenses. In films, the optical characteristics of lenses can influence other depth factors and thus strengthen or weaken the illusion of the third dimension. Obviously, this is most relevant to a camera *vis-à-vis* a motif in the real world. But, increasingly, 3D applications have techniques to simulate the functionality of the camera lens. For example, in 3D CAD software you can choose the angle of the cone of vision (measured in degrees) that determines the zoom setting of the virtual lens, from wide-angle to narrow-angle or telephoto views.

Another set of depth codes with high relevance for 3D space, which is not shared with still pictures, like photography and painting, but which is relatively specific to film, is the so-called mobile framing or camera-movement: the ability to change the camera's position within the shot, so that the frame moves with respect to the framed material. In some forms of mobile framing, the camera is fixed at a certain point, but is rotated around its own axis. Because the camera and the subject are located in three-dimensional space, there are three types of movement, corresponding to the three axes that intersect the camera (Monaco, 1981; Bordwell and Thompson, 1997).

In the *pan shot* (short for "panorama"), the camera is rotated on the vertical y-axis but the camera itself does not move, that is, it pivots horizontally in a sweeping motion. In the world of 3D graphics, where this rotation is often called *yaw*, a parallel can be found in QuickTime Virtual Reality (QTVR), which is essentially based on this panoramic view of a scene (up to 360°) fixed at a node in space.

In the *tilt shot*, the camera is rotated in the horizontal x-axis but the camera itself does not move, that is, it pivots upward or downward. The tilt thus decides the elevation of the shot: overhead, high-angle, eye-level, and low-angle. This type of rotation, which in 3D graphics is often called *pitch*, has its parallel in QTVRs (and video reality) too.

In the *roll shot*, the camera is rotated on the depth (z-)axis that corresponds to the axis of the lens (the horizontal axis that runs into the picture), but the camera itself does not move (also called *roll* in 3D graphics). This axis represents the relationship between the camera and the framed material. While the pan and the tilt shot change the framed material, the roll shot maintains the same focus of attention but turns it around. The roll shot thus destabilizes the subject as well as the horizon and the depicted space. Because of this (and perhaps because it does not correspond to any natural bodily experience in physical 3D space) it is very rarely used in film. In the province of computers and 3D, it can be observed, however, in simulation games based on car races, boat races etc., where it is used to represent accidents, collisions, overturning and so on. And in this case – if we observe the scene from a first-person point-of-view – the rotation actually corresponds to a natural bodily experience.

The zoom shot. In the interval between the still frame and the moving camera, or in the interval between a camera being fixed at a certain point and a camera that moves, we have the zoom shot. The zoom shot mimics the tracking shot (cf. below) in that it apparently moves forward or backward, but does so within the frame through the use of a variable focus lens while the camera is in fact fixed at a certain point. However, since the camera does not move, the observer does not have the feeling of physically entering the space, the spatial relationship between the objects in different planes does not change and, consequently, the perspective remains the same, even if part of the scene is magnified. As a result, the observer has the feeling of getting closer without getting nearer, an experience for which there seems to be no obvious standard of reference in real life. The effect of a zoom shot is thus very dissimilar to a tracking shot. Speaking of computers and 3D, the zoom shot can be seen in QTVR and the zoom function is, for example, standard in most CAD programs, making it possible to zoom in on an object. Depending on the technology, in 3D in contradistinction to films, the viewer may get a perceptibly lower resolution into the bargain.

In addition to being fixed at a certain point, but rotated around these three axes as in the pan, tilt and roll shots, the camera can be moved from one point to another within a shot in the form of the *tracking shot*, the *crane shot* and the *point-of-view shot* (Monaco, 1981).

In the *tracking shot*, *dolly shot*, or *travelling shot*, the camera itself is moved forward, backward, sideways or in any other horizontal direction along the ground. The tracking shot thus generates a feeling of physically entering the scene; the spatial relations between the objects in the scene continually change, and – consequently – so does the perspective. As a result, the tracking shot markedly strengthens the perception of depth.

In the *crane shot*, the camera is moved in the vertical direction above the ground. In the area of virtual 3D worlds, this technique is often used in the form of a so-called "out-of-body" viewpoint, "bird's eye", or "God's view" (Jensen, 1998b, 1999a) and in the domain of computer games it can be observed in, for instance, "Tomb Raider", where a virtual camera in a "bird's-eye" perspective is constantly tracking the movements of the protagonist, Lara Croft.

The concept of a *point-of-view shot* is perhaps best explained with reference to the literature. A story is always narrated by someone. This "someone" can either be a person who participates as a character in the story – in which case we speak of a *first-person narrator* – or it may be a person who is positioned outside the story – in which case we speak of an *omniscient narrator*. Film can, to a certain degree, mimic these literary codes (in this context, for the sake of simplicity, we will deal only with the images, not with a story told on the sound track, cf. below). The vast majority of narrative films are narrated from an omniscient point of view. We see the story not from a person participating in the narration but from an autonomous position separate from any given character in the story. We might call this a *third-person point-of-view*. In some cases, nevertheless, we see the events from the perspective of a character participating in the story. This is the *first-person point-of-view*.

In the context of the film medium, this point-of-view is, however, much more infrequent and, when used, only used on a limited scale. Monaco suggests that if the first-person rule is applied to cinema on a larger scale, it inevitably causes problems. In computer media in general and in 3D applications in particular, the first-person point-of-view has, on the contrary, already been established as a firm convention.

A particular version of the first-person-view is the *subjective camera*. In this case, the point-of-view is more or less permanently attached to a character participating in the setting or in the story. In other words, you see the world and the scene through the given character's eyes. This version is extremely uncommon in films, but very common in computer media, especially in 3D applications; presumably because of the medium's inherent interactivity, which presupposes that the user controls the action and participates in the events. Examples of first-person views of this kind – where you constantly see the (3D) world through your avatar's first-person point of view – can be found in most of the virtual 3D worlds on the Web as well as in the bulk of contemporary computer games.

In 3D graphics, correspondingly, the range of motions available to an avatar or a viewpoint is called the *degrees of freedom* (DOF). There are six possible DOFs in 3D. Movements along the *x*, *y* or *z*-axes (parallel to tracking, crane shot etc.), which determine the coordinates in the given 3D space, and rotation around any of these three axes: you can move your avatar's or virtual camera's viewpoint up and down (tilt/yaw), turn it right and left (pan/pitch), or roll it from side to side (roll) (Wilcox, 1998).

16.6 The Techniques that Relate Shot-to-Shot: Montage

While the concepts of *mise-en-scène* and cinematography refer to the "shot", montage refers to the techniques that relate shot-to-shot. The original French phrase literally means, "putting together". Montage may thus be described as the way shots are put together to make up a film. In like manner, editing may be defined as the process of selecting, assembling and arranging shots in coherent sequence and continuity. Consequently, montage or editing relates primarily to the temporal dimension.

The precondition for editing is that the human receiver has a tendency to perceive two joined shots as being in some way related, and thus to infer a whole on the basis of the parts. This phenomenon was examined by the Soviet filmmaker and theoretician Lev Kuleshov, who, during the 1920s, conducted experiments concerning relations between shots: "In order to demonstrate that editing is the truly decisive factor in film, Kuleshov... performed an experiment which has become a landmark in the history of film theory. He had identical copies printed of a shot of the Actor Mosjoukine's face – an expressionless close up – and alternated them with shots of a bowl of soup, a woman in a coffin, a smiling baby. And the public on which Kuleshov tried out this experiment, raved about Mosjoukine's ability to express appetite, sorrow and tenderness with such extraordinary subtlety" (Raskin, 1986b). Thus, not only did the audience immediately infer a whole on the basis of the parts, i.e. that the actor was reacting to events in the accompanying shots, but they also produced very different interpretations of the, in fact, identical shots of the actor's neutral facial expression, solely based on the editing of shots (Bordwell and Thompson, 1997). This phenomenon is now often referred to as the "Kuleshov effect".

In films, these joints can be of various kinds. The most common way of getting from one shot to the next is the unmarked or straight *cut*, the instantaneous junction of two shots, but there are a number of conventional ways of joining shot-to-shot: double exposure, dissolve, fade-in or fade-out, iris-in or iris-out, circle-in or circle-out, wipe, swish pan, zip pan, whip shot etc.

In the computer medium, these means of getting from one node to the next have practically exploded, owing to the flexibility of digital technology. A conventional program such as Microsoft's PowerPoint offers more than 40 transitions, i.e. ways of getting from one slide to another. While browsing the WWW, we currently have a peculiar way of getting from one node to another: the blanking out of the screen for an indefinite amount of time and a more or less slow build up of the new Web page, i.e. a combination of cut-to-white and a fade-in. Thus the dimension of "editing" is one of the most annoying aspects of the Web. In virtual 3D worlds, similar joints occur when the user changes views or "jumps" or is teleported from one place to another or from one world to another.

Whereas cuts and joints are frequent occurrences in film, they are more rare in 3D space. In the force field between *mise-en-scène* and montage, 3D space definitely has a bias towards the *mise-en-scène*.

Editing two shots together permits the interaction of qualities (graphic, rhythmic, spatial, temporal etc.) of those two shots. This interaction can be based on differences or similarities, producing abrupt contrast or smooth continuity, respectively. In film, it is the last style of editing that has been established as predominant, in the form of so-called *continuity editing*.

The basic principle of continuity editing is to produce seamless transitions from shot to shot – so-called "invisible cutting" – so that one event follows "naturally" from another and time and space are logically represented. The prime purpose is to maintain immediacy, to concentrate attention on the ongoing action, that is, to tell a story coherently. This is done by a multitude of different techniques: match cut (which links two disparate scenes via a graphic match or continuity), rhythmic relations of shot lengths, spatial continuity (establishing shot, the 180° rule), temporal continuity, and – most generally – by creating a smooth flow and avoiding clashes from shot to shot (Monaco, 1981). All of these techniques are also pertinent to 3D spaces.

16.7 The Fourth Dimension: Sound – or the Relation of Sound to Image

Sound as a supplement to images is often considered a secondary factor by the viewer. Nevertheless, sound is a powerful technique that influences and codifies the experience in many ways. Sound can guide our attention within the image and focus our perception by pointing to things of particular interest. And sound can thus actively shape the viewer's perception, interpretation, and understanding of images. In 3D spaces, in like manner, sound is an important factor, since it can bring about an overall sense of a realistic or convincing environment.

The term *sound* usually covers four types of aural phenomena: *speech*, *music*, *sound effects* and *silence*. In the following we briefly introduce a typology based on the relationship of sound to image, having its source in film theory, but of pertinence to 3D spaces as well. Sound has spatial as well as temporal dimensions. It has a spatial dimension because it comes from a source, and it has a temporal dimension because it is perceived as linked to visual events that take place at a specific time. In the spatial dimension, at the most general level, sound is divided into diegetic and non-diegetic sound, based on the identification of the source of the sound.

Non-diegetic sound is sound that is represented as coming from a source that can not be located in the scene, space or world. It is often called "sound over" because it comes from outside the represented visual space of the events. Non-diegetic sound can be subdivided into:

1. *Music* – so-called "background music", "movie music" or "wallpaper music" – that does not issue from, but is added to, the scene.
2. *The voice of the narrator*, in this case a heterodiegetic, omniscient third-person narrator, who introduces time, place and characters, but whose voice cannot be recognized as belonging to any of the characters in the space.
3. Non-diegetic *sound effects*, i.e. natural or artificially created sounds, other than speech or music, that are added to the sound track.

Diegetic sound is sound that is represented as coming from a physical source in the visually represented space or world. Diegetic sound can be subdivided into:

1. *Actual sound,* i.e. sound that the characters in the given space can or would be able to hear. In other words, we perceive the source of the sound as actually present in the here-and-now of the scene. Actual sound can be subdivided into on-screen and off-screen sound, cf. below.
2. *Subjective sound,* i.e. sound that can be heard only by a single character in the scene (inner voices etc.).
3. *The voice of the narrator,* in this case a homodiegetic, first-person narrator, that introduces time, place and events, *and* whose voice can be identified as belonging to a character in the represented events.

Diegetic actual sound can be either on-screen or off-screen.

On-screen sound refers to diegetic sound perceived as coming from a source that is visible within the frame at the time the sound is heard, e.g. we hear a voice and at the same time we see the lips of an avatar move.

Off-screen sound refers to diegetic sound coming from a source that is not immediately visible within the frame at the time the sound is heard; nevertheless the source is perceived as being present in the scene at the given moment, only outside the actual frame. In 3D applications, environmental sound would be a case in point. Consequently, off-screen sound can indicate space reaching beyond the immediately perceivable frame and may be used to cue the user's attention on and expectations about off-screen space. This technique is very useful and effective in 3D applications. For instance, in certain networked 3D shoot-'em-up games (such as "Quake") you are able to hear your opponents although they are actually out of sight. Thus, off-screen sound becomes an important cue to the opponents' movements and activities and, as a result, an important guide for your own navigation and strategy.

Another feature of diegetic sound with strong pertinence and applicability to 3D space is the possibility of *sound perspective* (Bordwell and Thompson, 1997). Corresponding to the depth cues that constitute visual perspective, it is possible to create a sense of spatial depth, distance or location that in turn can model a kind of three-dimensional sound environment. It goes without saying that sound perspective can be produced by stereophonic sound or, better still, surround sound channels. Utilizing these techniques, it is possible to represent a sound's placement in the three-dimensional space – on-screen as well as off-screen. Sound perspective can also be produced simply by volume, because volume by a conventional code is related to the perceived distance. A loud sound is thus perceived as coming from the acoustic foreground close to the listener; a quieter or softer sound is sensed as located in the acoustic background far from the listener.

In the same way that sound has a spatial dimension because it is perceived as linked to a source, sound has a temporal dimension because it is perceived as linked to visual events that take place at a specific time. The most common relation between sound and picture in the temporal dimension involves synchronization (Monaco, 1981).

Synchronous sound refers to sound that is matched with the projected image, i.e. we perceive the sound at the same time that we see the source produce it. Because of this definitory precondition, synchronous sound relates primarily to diegetic on-screen sound. However, it is also possible, in a more unrestricted manner, to speak of synchronous sound applied to off-screen sound, subjective sound, the voiceover, or even background music, sound effects etc.

Asynchronous sound refers to sound that is not matched with the projected image, in short: sound that is *out-of-sync*. This, of course, refers first and foremost to technical inaccuracies and time lags, which are not uncommon in this early stage of the technology. But asynchronous sound can also be utilized for expressive and aesthetic purposes. Again, this type of sound primarily has a bearing on on-screen diegetic sound. In this case, correspondingly, it is possible in a more vague manner to speak of asynchronous off-screen sound and asynchronous voiceovers, as well as asynchronous, or non-contemporary, background music, sound effects etc.

On a more abstract level or in the above-mentioned more unrestricted or vague manner we can also speak of *counterpoint* versus *parallelism*. *Parallelism* refers to a coincidence or redundancy in what is heard and what is seen; the sounds simply repeat the images. *Counterpoint*, on the other hand, refers to a non-coincidence of what is heard and what is seen. The sounds do not simply repeat or reinforce the images, but they can even be played off against one another.

16.8 Conclusions and Perspectives

The above-mentioned considerations have analytical, theoretical and methodological as well as practical implications. They are of interest in relation to the analytical and theoretical understanding of this new and rapidly growing medium and in relation to methods of examining these phenomena. The study shows that concepts and categories from the field of film theory are highly relevant to the area of 3D applications and it indicates that the concepts presented here can form the building blocks for a more comprehensive and coherent theory of 3D spaces and virtual 3D worlds. However, the study also has implications for construction and design aspects, since the design of 3D spaces must be based on actual knowledge of the conditions and possibilities for the construction of signs, codes and meaning in the new medium.

References

Andersen, P. B. (1997) Film og multimedier [Film and multimedia]. In *Design af Multimedier* [*Multimedia Design*] (ed. B. Fibiger). Aalborg: Aalborg University Press.

Andersen, P. B., Holmqvist, B. and Jensen, J. F. (eds.) (1993) *The Computer as Medium*. Cambridge: Cambridge University Press.

Arnheim, R. (1969) *Art and Visual Perception*. Berkeley: University of California Press.

Bordwell, D. and Thompson, K. (1997) *Film Art*. New York: McGraw-Hill.

Da Vinci, L. (1954) *Notebooks* (ed. E. MacCurdy). New York: Braziller.

Fiske, J. (1982) *Introduction to Communication Studies*. London: Routledge.

Graham, D. (1979) *Composing Pictures*. New York: Van Nostrand Reinhold.

Jensen, J. F. (1993) Computer culture. The meaning of technology and the technology of meaning. A triadic essay on the semiotics of technology. In *The Computer as Medium* (eds. P. B. Andersen, B. Holmqvist and J. F. Jensen). Cambridge: Cambridge University Press.

Jensen, J. F. (1996a) Mapping interactive television. A new media typology for information traffic patterns on the superhighway to the home. Invited paper at *Interactive Television 1996, The Superhighway through the Home? A World Conference Dedicated to Interactive Television*, 3-5 September. University of Edinburgh, Scotland (unpublished).

Jensen, J. F. (1996b) Mapping the Web. In *Proceedings of WebNet 96 – World Conference of the Internet, Intranet and World Wide Web* (ed. H. Mauer). Charlottesville, VA: AACE.

Jensen, J. F. (1997) "Interactivity" – tracking a new concept. In *Proceedings of WebNet 97 – World Conference of the WWW, Internet, & Intranet* (S. Lobodzinski and I. Tomek). Charlottesville, VA: AACE.

Jensen, J. F. (1998a) Road map of the information highway: Internet based education systems. In *Computers and Advanced Technology in Education (CATE '98)* (eds. J. Gil-Mendieta and M. H. Hamza). Anaheim, CA: IASTED/ACTA Press.

Jensen, J. F. (1998b) Interaction and representation in 3D-virtual worlds – from Flatland to Spaceland. In *Proceedings of WebNet 98 – World Conference of the WWW, Internet and Intranet* (eds. H. Mauer and R. B. Olson). Charlottesville, VA: AACE.

Jensen, J. F. (1998c) Communication research after the mediasaurus? Digital convergence, digital divergence? *Nordicom Review* 12(1).

Jensen, J. F. (1998d) Interactivity. Tracking a new concept in media and communication studies. *Nordicom Review* 12(1).

Jensen, J. F. (1999a) From "Flatland" to "Spaceland". Spatial representation, enunciation and interaction in 3D-virtual worlds. *WebNet Journal. Internet Technologies, Applications & Issues* 1(1).

Jensen, J. F. (1999b) The concept of "Interactivity" in "interactive television" and "interactive media". In *Interactive Television. TV of the Future or the Future of TV?* (eds. J. F. Jensen and C. Toscan). Aalborg: Aalborg University Press.

Jensen, F. J. (1999c) 3D-inhabited virtual worlds. Interactivity and interaction between avatars, autonomous agents and users. In *Proceedings of WebNet 99 – World Conference on the WWW and Internet* (eds. P. de Bra and J. Leggett). Charlottesville, VA: AACE.

Jensen, J. F. (1999d) Film theory meets 3D Internet. A film semiotic approach to the design and analysis of 3D virtual worlds on the Web. In *Proceedings of WebNet 99 – World Conference on the WWW and Internet* (eds. P. de Bra and J. Leggett). Charlottesville, VA: ACCE.

Jensen, F. J. (1999e) Trends in interactive content & services over multimedia networks. In *Proceedings of the IASTED International Conference on Internet, Multimedia Systems and Applications (IMSA 99)* (ed. B. Furht). Nassau, The Bahamas.

Jensen, F. J. (1999f) Film theory meets the Web. A semiotic approach to the design and analysis of Web pages and Web sites. In *Advanced Research in Computers and Communication in Education. New Human Abilities for the Networked Society, ICCE 99-conference* (eds. G. Cumming *et al.*). ISO, Tokyo.

Jensen, J. F. (1999g) The concept of "interactivity". Interactivity and interactive learning environments. In *Advanced Research in Computers and Communication in Education. New Human Abilities for the Networked Society, ICCE 99-conference* (eds. G. Cumming *et al.*). ISO, Tokyo.

Jensen, F. J. (1999h) Information traffic patterns in the networked society. Computer networks and educational applications and services on the Internet. In *Advanced Research in Computers and Communication in Education. New Human Abilities for the Networked Society, ICCE 99-conference* (eds. G. Cumming *et al.*). ISO, Tokyo.

Jensen, J. F. (1999i) Interactivity – tracking a new concept. In *Communication, Computer Media and the Internet. A Reader* (ed. P. A. Mayer). Oxford: Oxford University Press.

Jensen, J. F. and Toscan, C. (eds.) (1999) *Interactive Television. TV of the Future or the Future of TV?* Aalborg: Aalborg University Press.

Monaco, J. (1981) *How to Read a Film.* Oxford: Oxford University Press.

O'Neill, R. and Muir, E. G. (1998) *Guide to Creating 3D Worlds.* New York: Wiley Computer Publishing.

Raskin, R. (1986a) *Elements of Picture Composition.* Aarhus: Aarhus University Press.

Raskin, R. (1986b) *Film Terminology. Terminologie du Cinéma.* Aarhus: Aarhus University Press.

Wilcox, S. K. (1998) *Guide to 3D Avatars.* New York: Wiley Computer Publishing.

Zettl, H. (1990, orig. 1973) *Sight Sound Motion. Applied Media Aesthetics.* Belmont, CA: Wadsworth Publishing Company.

17

Shaping Meaning: On Action and Content in Unreal Worlds

Edvin Vestergaard Kau

17.1 A "Freak Show" and a Murder

17.1.1 Through the Maze of the Freaks

To form some ideas of what is characteristic of narration in computer-generated multimedia compared with that of film, the article opens with two short, exemplifying and comparative analyses of a game (*The Residents Freak Show*, which the introductory text calls a "theme park of imagination" – "envisioning the future of interactive stories, music video, and digital art") and a film scene (from Kurosawa's *Rashomon*).

The analysis of a sequence of *The Residents Freak Show* focuses on the player's (the user's) relation to a variety of available attractions in the fairground, because *Freak Show* is presented as a circus that has come to the local fairground, where people can enter and go to see a series of separate acts or shows – in this case so-called freaks or monstrosities. In this way it is more like a small, travelling amusement park, where the acts in fact are like booths, in which visitors can get their entertainment by performing or witness exciting and extraordinary actions. The show people arrive, offering experiences out of the ordinary and beyond the rules and framework of everyday life.

The following is a sketch of how *Freak Show* works: (1) The user can click to see each attraction in the circus tent. (2) Those acts can also be understood as stories about each freak's fate, e.g. a kind of concentrated narrative, which in this way are created through the users' exploration of the environments and things he finds. (3) One of the paths can be described as a "trap": you end up in a room where you are apparently forced to buy other examples of the designers' products! "Buy or Die!", as a sign says. (4) Last but not least, there is a route, where the user, having entered one of the caravans that it is possible to explore, is finally twisting himself through and past something that he gradually finds out looks like the inside of a brain – nerve fibres and the like.

Apart from rows of curiosity-arousing exhibits along the route (potential detours or dead ends – teasers!) you end up in front of something looking like peepholes and, if you open and take a look outside, you see – straight into the face of another visitor. Not only are you standing inside an eye, you are also positioned as a gaze yourself, meeting other gazes. The exploration of the freaky attractions leads to the encounter with the curious audience – that you are part of yourself.

17.1.2 The Player Sees His or Her Own Activity

The gaze meets itself; curiosity looks itself straight between the eyes. The narrative meets itself in the shape of the activity that is necessary to get anything told at all. In other words, you can say that *Freak Show* makes a theme out of the very relation between the seeing and the seen, or the distance between what is narrated and the narrator. In the context of interactive media we may put it in a perspective: user activity explored as a research into virtual 3D fiction.

While this is a meta-level that is built into *Freak Show* itself and which in this way positions the player or the viewer within the universe of the narrative, this practice also defines these positions of the user and the used – not just, as it may seem at first glance, as involvement, but as distance. Any media and communication practice will define a user, player or viewer position, and so it does in this case: the curious fairground visitor who is watching the strange characters, freaks of nature, and runs the risk of becoming aware of – him- or herself. The eye is turned to – the audience itself. This means that attention is drawn to an element of narration, which is of importance to our project in general, too: the *user and viewer activity.*

17.1.3 A Choreography of Eye-Lines

Akira Kurosawa's film *Rashomon* (1950) could very well be said to resemble a game. In the framing story three men discuss a murder case. A samurai has been found dead in a remote forest. He may have been killed in a duel with a notorious bandit, been stabbed by his own wife, or committed suicide. Before his eyes, the bandit assaulted the samurai's wife, or she eventually submitted willingly, perhaps provoked by her husband's cowardly behaviour. Two of the men (a poor woodcutter and a priest), whose discussion is the film's point of departure, have given testimony at the subsequent trial. In addition to their versions – and the third man's sarcastic doubt about everybody's statements and motives – we are presented with the versions of the three involved persons: the bandit, the wife and the dead man (speaking to the court through a medium). Thus we are presented with no fewer than five versions of the incident.

Naturally, the different testimonies given about the events in the forest hold different opinions about the question of guilt. Also, the scenes showing each account demonstrate the witnesses' possible motives to tell it the way they do. Through its narrative structure and its visual style the film arranges both the level of narrative authority (the narrator) and each of the witnesses in front of the viewer who, in his turn, will take different positions on the testimonies and the film in general. From an audience perspective, the important question really isn't to find *the* solution to the murder mystery, as much as it is the discussion of dilemmas, possible motives, credibility and the possibility of moral judgement etc. In other words: a game of possibilities.

A brief analysis of the camerawork in a scene can demonstrate the position of the viewer's gaze and the construction of the interplay between viewer and narration. In his version, of course, the bandit describes the incident in a way so as to show that from very early on we have a triangle, the samurai's wife willingly submitting to and choosing him at the expense of her husband. Therefore it wasn't really rape. Subsequently, according to the bandit, the woman provokes a fight until death between the two men. She will follow the winner.

The prelude to all this is: after having lured the samurai away from his wife, the bandit attacks him and ties him up. Then he leads the woman to the scene of the crime in order to show her the husband's powerlessness. From that moment on the following series of shots are composed and edited in a very special way which precisely establishes the literally triangular field of psychological tension between the characters.

One after the other, the three characters turn their heads slightly and move their eyes back and forth between each other. Traditionally this kind of cutting on eye-line matches is done by switching between the looking eyes and shots which from the exact watching position show what the characters are looking at. But, in this case Kurosawa has chosen another solution that becomes a remarkable "circular movement" between the parties of the triangle. When we see one of the characters turn his or her eyes towards one of the others, Kurosawa will cut not just to a shot showing this other character from the seeing character's point of view (POV), but to a camera position *behind* the looked-at character. As a result, the latter's back is in the foreground of the shot, while the character whose eye-line was changed in the previous shot is seen in the background, looking out towards the next person and the camera. Then, this character in the foreground turns his or her head/eyes, and a cut is made in precisely the same way to a shot from a position behind the character towards whom the gaze is directed, etc. This style figure is repeated five times, until the camera is finally moved from behind the head of the wife to an *en face* position, a moment before she tries (in vain) to attack the bandit, is overpowered, submits, and things happen the way they do.

17.1.4 The Film Viewer's Activity

As a result, this style practice (and other ways in which Kurosawa stylizes the cinematic narrative activity during the course of the film) has an influence on the viewer's way of seeing, and as a consequence on his very relation to the characters, their gazes and positions, as well as the position of the narrator. In this way, the film right from the start accentuates *the audience as privileged observers and participants in the discussion* – and on the other hand it also establishes a narrative authority with which it is possible to discuss. ("Narrative authority" is a crucial concept in Browne (1975), his pivotal article on "the spectator-in-the-text"). Thus, in this scene we have a whole system of gazes. As mentioned, the gazes of the characters are emphasized by the style of editing, and the same goes for "the point of camera view". *The audience can see this system of gazes see.* This necessary participation in the project of narration on the part of the audience, in the same way as in *Freak Show*, again draws the attention to *the viewer activity.*

On the one hand this dialectical approach of comparing cinema and computer games confronts (traditional and new) film theory, and on the other hand hopefully leads to new concepts of both multimedia and cinema. It involves reflections on multimedia as sign systems; montage-based meaning production, and narrative practice. This also means ideas for rethinking traditional concepts of sign, meaning and montage in the new media surroundings of multimedia, taking as a point of departure the inspiration from film theory. It is essential to start a renewed thinking through of the aesthetics and the theory of the moving image. Time and space as dynamic and basic features must be seen as integrated in the sign of the moving image, not least in the context of new computer-based developments within mass media entertainment and communication.

17.2 Involvement and Distance: Whose Point of View?

17.2.1 The Cop and the Machine

The analysed examples and the interplay between (1) style, (2) narrator and (3) user/viewer which I have emphasized point to a discussion of involvement and distance. Are they contradictory elements, or can they work simultaneously? One of the points of the following discussion is that the concepts of involvement and distance are preferable to those of identification and detachment. A telling articulation of the interplay between the three: the inherent statement of visual style, the narrator, and the user/viewer can be seen in *Robocop* (Paul Verhoeven, 1987).

Traditionally the film viewer is said to be put in a character's place (or even experiencing some kind of identification) through the use of a particular fictional character's point of view. That is, the camera is placed in the exact position of that character's eyes, the idea being that we as an audience see and experience the world not only through that person's eyes, but even through the character's mind, so to speak. Also, this stylistic figure is said to cause identification with or sympathy towards the character. Without denying that this may be the case in some instances, I shall nevertheless contend that there are numerous occasions where the subjective point of view does not lead to simple identification with or empathy for the person whose POV we "borrow".

In near-future Detroit a cop, Murphy, is killed in the line of duty. But the corporation which now runs the police department transforms him into a perfect cyborg cop. Murphy, the brain and the body parts that are left of him, has lost his identity. Neither his human nor his machine parts are able to remember anything by themselves. But the machine/computer part of Robocop the Cyborg is able to plug into the police department's computer system and retrieve information about a criminal that his built-in memory has recognized and about the gang he is working with. These are the gangsters who killed Murphy, and through the files he also learns about their victim, himself. All of this we are able to follow on-screen, because the

POV of Robocop is not only the representation of his gaze, but also the interface which gives access to the information he is able to get out of the department's server.

After that, Robo-Murphy and the audience are able to go a step further. His brain and his visual centre being linked to the cyborg's hard disk, he is able to "see", which means that he can go out and search for his former home, enter it and recall scenes with his wife and family. All this the film (e.g. the narrator) is able to show us on Robocop's inner screen, so to speak, since we have been "installed" in the cyborg's POV by way of a subjective camera – in a very literal sense! This is shown in much the same way as we saw the criminal who gave him the clue to his own identity, namely through Robocop's POV. That is, through his camera–monitor–display–computer–screen–cabled gaze: the film screen is transformed into a multi-layered interface representation – which becomes the viewer and user interface, too, during the cinema experience, and which also resembles the interface of a computer desktop or game. On the one hand we have the human side of the cyborg, his view of an earlier life, family, and the gaze that can show all this to us. But the gaze has literally become a screen, monitor lines and all. The view that is supposed to drag us into his mind and life is establishing a distance, too.

But the fact is that films with a more ordinary use of POV also work the same way, as does *Robocop*. In this film it is just made more obvious and built into his, the cyborg's, camera- and monitor-like "gaze". In principle, this gaze is the same (only here half-human, half-machine) as the audience can watch in movies where a subjective POV is "only" supposed to relate the viewing position of a human character. It is much too simplifying to argue that the viewer "is" or "becomes" the character with whose gaze he sees this or that in a scene. Whether or not people sit in the movie theatre and think that way, this is how it works. The viewer watches a camera watch (or mime) a gaze watching things or other characters in a scene.

So, the point is not that you identify with a character just because of the use of subjective POV. But this style figure may very well contribute to an involvement in the event that is being shown and the characters in it, because, in a way, you have access to the fictional world through the spatially free camera. The narrator has the power to find his vantage point anywhere; consequently in subjective points of view, too. But at the same time, the involvement has as its basis that the viewer, with the distance which is established partly through the camera position, often has a broader understanding of things than the characters in a scene (e.g. knowledge about other characters, their thoughts and the preceding events of the film).

For instance, it is not unusual in thrillers or horror movies that the subjective camera point of view is positioned with threatening villains or murderers. But in the context of the situation as a whole it is perfectly possible to experience involvement and engagement on the side of the potential victims.

17.2.2 Babysitters and the Killer's Eyes

Within the very first shot of a film like *Halloween* (John Carpenter, 1978) the camera is identified with the point of view of the psychotic murderer. Through this gaze he, and we, observe his victim and follow his deed. A six-year-old boy apparently for no reason slaughters his teenage sister. He is hospitalized, but after 15 years he escapes, returns to the small town – same street, same house – and starts looking for teenage babysitters! So, though we hardly see the murderer's face, the result of the opening scene is that many camera movements of a certain floating or gliding kind, and certainly every shot of that kind, which is also defined as a subjective point of view, is charged with the horrifying quality: *he is coming*. The viewers do not just look at the town and the girls, but do so through his eyes. But more than that: the audience sees his gaze see the victims. Involvement and distance are active at one and the same time – the former on the part of the victims, the latter by way of the knowledge of the circumstances and the threat – and both are equally necessary in creating the thrilling experience. As mentioned above in relation to *Rashomon* and *Freak Show*, users and audiences see a whole system of gazes see, and this includes the gaze of the camera and its demonstration of different characters' points of view.

17.2.3 Looking at the Looking. Playing with Distances and Involvements

The interplay between different positions and between media and users is a way of describing users' and viewers' involvement. But as the analyses show, an important element in the relation between the three levels is the distance inherent in the embedded indication of the difference from the narrative as plot or mere string of events (camera and editing style in *Rashomon*, the game's "own will" and the explicit display of the user position in *Freak Show*). The difference between user position and diegetic position lies in the question of how users/viewers become involved as such. This does not happen in terms of becoming part of something or identifying with somebody within the fiction. It may be brought about through the curiosity that people, from a certain distance, feel towards something which is told or presented in well-shaped (stylized) and well-defined forms (beginnings and endings as crucial breaks between reality and the worlds of fiction; see Kau (1996b) on beginnings and endings).

Thus, rather than talking about identification and/or detachment, it is practical and more suitable to use the concepts of involvement and distance. It is possible at a certain distance to get involved in the universe of the characters, watching them and their fictional world from a series of different positions in and around it/them. It is perfectly possible to get involved (feelings, sympathy and all), and at the same time be aware of one's distance from the fictional worlds of make-believe.

17.3 Transmission and Transformation

In his article "True lies. Perceptual realism, digital images, and film theory" (Prince, 1996), Stephen Prince has an interesting discussion of analogue versus digital imagery. And it has inspired some of my following reflections on computer games and cinema. Digital imaging technologies, both in the production of film (storyboarding, shooting and editing) and in the experience of it ("un-human" and "un-natural" transformations), create problems for parts of classical film theory, says Prince. New and creative possibilities are so many that they challenge traditional understanding of cinematic representation and viewers' response. Some of his examples are *Forrest Gump* (1994, President Kennedy talking to Gump), *Terminator 2* (1993, computer-generated supernatural effects) and *Jurassic Park* (1993, recreation of extinct species). Although I can agree with his idea and examples, I would like to add that while Prince contends that, in a digital and computer-crazed era, these possibilities are unprecedented, this is not entirely true. In principle, at least, they are not different from cartoons and the cinematic tricks of for instance Meliès: the fact that you are able to create credible pictures which are not naturalistically mimetic is a well-known part of film history. On the other hand, if you bring this pictorial reflection back to the cinematic picture, so to speak, we may as well conclude that the exercise only reinforces the conception of cinematic fiction as radical illusion, pure make-believe. This way of thinking may end the superstitious belief in the cinematic image as indexically connected to our real world (cf. my suggestion below: to distinguish between *transmission* (the domain of indexicality) and *transformation* or creation (the domain of symbolic meaning production).

The curious point about the many strange digital creatures in new films is that "no pro-filmic referent existed to ground the indexicality of its image" (Prince, 1996, p. 29). Hence the theoretical problems as well as the creative possibilities. But theoretically and from the point of view of the creation of fictions (games or VR as well as films), as models of fantasy worlds – and the meaning they may have other than documentary-like indexical anchoring in apparently photographic reality – indexicality is precisely not the interesting aspect. What is interesting in these worlds of fiction is what meaning they are able to create apart from indexical references.

17.3.1 Plausible Artificiality/Artificial Intelligibility

Instead of using indexical references as explanation, Prince argues that our understanding of digital imagery is also based on a correspondence theory: "film spectatorship builds on correspondences between selected features of the cinematic display and the viewer's real-world visual and social experience". (Prince, 1996, p. 31). But my point is that this has only to do with recognition, the simple understanding of what things and what dimensions and so on we see in the picture. The effort to bring the index theory, and the pseudo-natural-scientific so-called cognitivism, down from its pedestal, is an exercise trying to show that it is not so-called real-world experience that decides whether pictures are realistic in terms of credibility.

The aspect of recognition in this correspondence theory is but a starting point (a necessary precondition for production) for establishing an *artificial* world with the necessary amount of credibility. *The aim is plausibility, which is defined in an internal set of relations within the fictional and constructed world itself, rather that in an external reference or correspondence relation to the real-world experience of the viewer.* Just try to think of Donald Duck, Goofy, Bugs Bunny, *The Mask*, *The Matrix*, Pat and Billy in the film about Garrett and The Kid, *Edward Scissorhands*, or *The Godfather*. Or take a western, a film noir – all genre movies for that matter. Are they plausible because of any relation to our own everyday experiences?

Things that are the basis of the pure and simple understanding and recognition of characters and things are not the interesting parts of visual fiction. What we are able to respond to and see in (more or less) meaningful relation to the world and life of the audience, is not explained by the simple correspondence idea inspired by cognitivism. For instance, very often the interesting parts of visual narrative fiction are the *improbable ones*, things that add perspectives to ideas and thoughts and do not resemble anything. But they may offer new ideas or meaning to be taken into the viewer's world. Or we may call it an experience that is precisely *out of* one's own world (aesthetical, enjoyable, fantastic, entertaining, extravagant, surprising, thrilling, scaring etc.).

Two examples can demonstrate differences rather than correspondences: (1) watching a melodrama, you may sob because of the lovers' lack of understanding and the complications of which they are the victims; and (2) viewing crime films and thrillers, you may get angry or thrilled, maybe even outraged because of the villains' deeds. You sit in your seat and feel all this. But you would precisely not behave like that in real-life. Instead of just watching, you would explain how things really are and help the lovers, and in the other case call the police instead of just passively witnessing a fight or a robbery.

17.3.2 Acting and Understanding in What World?

We are able to understand the character-models, and we "know" from the way the world works (morality etc.), how to have an opinion about them, but even - or better: precisely the patterns of emotional reactions in the media experience are different from those of the real-world experience. In the former you have feelings when faced with examples that are put into a (narrative/aesthetic) system - and have your own views on the matter. In the latter you *participate* in and *act* with your surroundings. Recognition and perception of elements, models and prototypes that may recur from film/media to real world (or the other way around) do not result in the same or corresponding emotional reactions in those two worlds. Understanding and interpretation of the elements within the fiction trigger other things than does the involvement of oneself in events in the real world.

Neither agents nor their surrounding worlds in multimedia or films are real. Thus neither audience nor users will react to the media in the same ways as they would in real life. The consequences of this can be shown in analyses of examples from cinema, computer games and multimedia presentations, one of the questions being: how do members of the movie audience, game players and other users in fact interact with or respond to the media products or "surroundings" they are confronted with? In what way do aesthetic patterns and rhetoric of the media guide attention and action (interactivity)?

Virtual worlds and fiction are separated from the real world. Pictures and events are composed and structured in the former; the latter is neither composed, nor has it any narrative or dramaturgical structure. To keep things clear and to distinguish the use of media in fiction and in reality, I have introduced the concepts of *transmission* and *transformation*. In this understanding, transmission is a term dedicated to media practices and genres that depend on reference: much television production, documentaries, news, sports and live productions in general, whereas transformation (or creation) is dedicated to the production of different kinds of fiction: fiction films (and their computer-generated elements, of course), cartoons, soap operas, virtual 3D worlds (not VR used as a means to carry out for instance "distance surgery", though; people working with these tools have to use very precise references, hopefully), and computer games. (Further use of this idea obviously calls for a lot of work, defining possible combinations and crossovers between transformation and transmission (for instance the use of one type in the other?), and perhaps even genres, some of the possibilities being: (1) live on tape: transmission material used to construct/edit an end product that is a transformation; (2) does the editing of an overwhelming number of camera positions during a transmission of a sports event turn it into a transformation (creating an experience of a kind of fiction)?; (3) the use of documentary type footage as raw material for otherwise computer-generated fictions/games; and (4) or the other way around, using computer-generated material to be mixed with footage containing real actors, landscapes etc.). In the present context my point is that all of the examples of this article and their described mechanisms represent elements of transformational use of the computer and film media.

17.4 From *Riven* and *Myst* to San Francisco and Ferrara. The Power of the Spaces

17.4.1 The Role of the Player

The game *Riven* is the sequel to one of the most successful games worldwide to date, *Myst* (Eugeni, 1998, p. 9). Apart from the account of the success of *Myst*, Eugeni's article is one of the best texts I have read on the subject and some of my discussions of *Riven* and games in general take it as their point of departure). Like *Myst*, the world of *Riven* is constructed as a combination of several types of elements. Video clips show the main characters inhabiting the world of the game. Actors play the parts, meeting the player at different crucial point of the game, sometimes giving information, sometimes asking questions, or handing over diaries or other books. The world of *Riven* is based on thousands and thousands of computer graphic pictures, combined with a series of impressive 3D-animations. The iconography is characterized by fantastic landscapes, uncanny jungles, idyllic beaches, ancient-looking dwellings, a medieval temple, steam-driven machinery from the industrial age and fantasy creatures. Most of it is in a style resembling the work of cartoon artist Enki Bilal. Also, the impression on the player is enhanced by the use of music and sound effects. Stone and metal doors and elevators and machines move with echoes, rumpling and clanking and creaking that literally make you hear their weight and material.

Like films and other computer games *Riven* tries to involve the user by "offering him a camera position". Right from the start the user meets the game and the first character in it from a so-called first-person point of view. The camera is defined as a subjective POV, and as a player you are positioned in it! The man, Atrus, in front of the user asks his help, and so we are on our way into the plot. Briefly, it goes something like this. Years ago, in another world, Atrus's father, Gehn, was able to create worlds – by literally writing them. Writing a book about a world would make this world exist, and through the so-called link-books it was possible to travel between the worlds. But Gehn's worlds were not perfect, at least not in his own view, and instead of trying to make them better and perhaps save them and their inhabitants, he would abandon them and go on to new projects. He saw himself as the god of these worlds, but Atrus, who became at least as good at writing and creating as his father, couldn't bear to see whole ages collapse and their inhabitants just disappear. This fate would also be that of Riven, named the Fifth Age by Gehn, but in this case Atrus also had a personal interest, since his wife, Catherine, came from the Fifth Age. Atrus and Catherine have managed to trap Gehn in Riven. While Gehn is trying to create a new world to flee to, the user's task is to help Atrus save Catherine and her people before the inevitable collapse of Riven, trap Gehn, and let him disappear with the Fifth Age.

Apart from the paradox of this metaphorical status of the book (the power of the letter, and the literary sources for the worlds of *Riven*) in the genesis of the digitally generated life and space of the game, it is also part of the characteristics of many games, CD-ROM productions and multimedia presentations that, to a very large extent, they depend upon introductions, explanation of pre-histories, narrators or other written "sources" to get a plot going.

To reach his goal, finding the necessary tools and information, as he goes along, the user has to find his way through maze-like structures, solving a wealth of puzzles, finding all kinds of clues, and restoring power to machines and vehicles in order to make his travels between different parts of the Fifth Age possible. To do all this, the user must navigate through the space of this virtual hypertext-structured world. Basically, this of course is done by using the cursor/pointer. In Both *Riven* and *Myst* it has the shape of a hand on the screen. On moving it to different positions it changes according to what actions are possible. When looking into a landscape or a building, the user can move the hand pointing upwards/into the picture to the desired spot or path that he wants to go to and click. This will change his position moving forward. It is also possible to click on left or right pointing hands. This of course turns the view in the respective directions. In some quarters the pointing finger may be bent as though pointing over one's shoulder. Clicking in this instance turns the user 180°. Likewise the user may move up/look up or move down/look down/move back, according to hands pointing up or down with the palm turned against the player.

17.4.2 Working at a Distance

Movements and different positions are reached by transitions from picture to picture, resembling fairly fast dissolves in film. Left or right turns, on the other hand, appear like medium slow wipes or swish pans; this is not always very elegant, especially since the position of the user may change in jump cut-like fashion from one frame to the next. Each frame or computer graphics picture of *Riven* is very delicate work, many of them even beautiful. But the fact remains that the user moves through a world composed of separate graphic plates. This, combined with the manipulation of the pointer, makes the built-in distance mentioned above in relation to camera position and point of view in the film *Rashomon* and the game *Freak Show* present, in spite of what Eugeni calls the first-person point of view of the user.

Besides moving things and opening doors and so on, the user travels and manipulates vehicles (trams, a small submarine, and the like). When set in motion, these means of transportation run as animations, and they are impressive with sometimes rollercoaster-like effects. Nevertheless, as mentioned, both involvement and distance are at play in games as well as in films, and involvement is not accomplished through subjective POV alone. You have to have something, characters or events, to get involved in, in the narrative. Were it not for the introduction to the plot by Atrus or a booklet or something else, the staging of the user's POV in relation to the graphics and the systems of movement together with the lack of events and characters during long sequences would have let the feeling of distance dominate the interaction. This is made even more evident by other characteristics of the camera of *Riven* = the user's supposedly subjective point of view. In a variety of ways it is limited. First visually/kinetically: in some positions it is impossible to look or move in certain directions – parts of the universe simply haven't been drawn. The only paths and areas available are those belonging to the routes of solutions. Secondly, the camera-eye is limited through the workings of the puzzles: range of sight and freedom to move depend on the amount of solutions the user has been able to reach. Again, we are reminded of the interplay between distance and involvement, and often in games users/players are very much aware of their role both in the game and outside the game, e.g. the player with the pointer, the mouse, the hand.

17.4.3 Four Spaces

From this description and the analytical points we may summarize elements at different levels. (1) The user is introduced into a narrative context with certain plot structures, too. (2) On the screen it is possible to move different versions of the pointer "over" the world of *Riven*. We know it as the interface, and it corresponds to the surfaces or screens that make it possible to experience other media. It is the kind of physical layer or "scene" where we can meet television productions or films. (3) From his own position, the user can observe the screen and what is happening on and in it, and get more or less involved, and by using the mouse act according to the development of the game. You might say that from his chair the user is able to touch the diegetic world of fiction. (4) All of this is governed and structured by the system of the game: its programmed script.

In his analysis of *Myst*, Eugeni calls these levels spaces, and they are useful as descriptions of the mechanics of *Riven*, too. This is the way he describes the relations between the spaces:

> First, we have seen how the logic space [my No. 4 in the above, EK] is one of the conditions for the existence of the diegetic space continuum [my No. 1, EK]. Such an underlying space, although invisible, integrates the diegetic space through metaphors: think of the many communication trenches, corridors, bends, doors, and switches that render the routes in the diegetic space navigable. So the diegetic space turns out to be

> completely structured by the underlying (and invisible) logic space, constantly depending on it and permeable to it. Second, the screen space [my No. 2, EK] is never completely transparent: the pointer is always present on the surface of the screen indicating the directions of the navigable routes in the diegetic world. Third, the diegetic space is open, through the screen space, to the use space [my No. 3, EK]: the pointer can often "penetrate" the represented world and change things (e.g., open doors, alter meter figures, turn pages of a book, press levers and buttons), displaying the user's personal participation in the fictional space. (Eugeni, 1998, p. 15)

17.4.4 Open Games, Closed Films?

Eugeni's view on film: the diegetic space is characterized by its conclusiveness; it is an "enclosed space that cannot be crossed by either screen or use spaces" (Eugeni, 1998, *ibid*), and the exhibition of that space is the goal of the organization of the other involved spaces. The screen space is said to be transparent, and "the use space is wiped out in the concealing darkness of the cinema" (Eugeni, 1998, *ibid*). But, as I have demonstrated in my comparative analyses of examples, this is not so. The organization of the cinematic screen space and the composition of shots (and editing, and camera movement, and...) is pivotal to the resulting diegetic space. The only way you find out about the diegesis and its space is by concentrating on the screen, and it is not to be forgotten or just seen through. The example I have used is the camera position and the concept of (subjective) point of view. This is something which you see on the screen and which is working in the screen space. Similarly, use space is what brings screen and diegetic space together as meaning production. True, the viewer cannot manipulate elements on the screen or in the diegetic space as in a computer game, but for the film to work as a semiotic meaning-producing machine the viewer has to be (inter) active in relation to the film, as foreseen by its originator, the director.

Much as I find Eugeni's work on game analysis innovative and inspiring, his views on film analysis and theory draw on traditional opinions about film that through repetition have apparently become a preconceived "truth", and it is time to think about the interplay between these spaces or levels in new ways. It is not true that screen space and use space do not "cross" or in other ways are active in the diegetic space. This is a blind spot in some traditional film theorists' misconception, embedded in an almost mythologizing view of the audience's self-forgetting experience, imagining that the viewers plunge themselves into the story space of the diegesis, almost disappearing there, leaving their bodies behind and forgetting the theatre and fellow-viewers around them. Furthermore, the logic space of the game corresponds to the narrator or narrative authority of the film, and in this respect, too, I find that the two media resemble each other more than Eugeni thinks. Film fiction is more open, and computer games more closed in structure, than he argues.

In its determination of what action can be taken in the use space (how, as a user, to act in the screen space in order to navigate in the diegetic space), the logic space in this type of game makes its world as conclusive as the narrative chain of events is in a film. As long as you, as a player, are within the game's fiction world (without banging against the limits of any given level), you can move about in a relatively free manner. But as soon as you want to go beyond the limits (perhaps having missed a clue, forgotten to solve a puzzle, or the like) that are set by the logic space (e.g. what the narrator or designer as narrative authority has decided upon as the governing structure of the diegetic space and development of this particular game), you are thrown or held back within this part of the narrative space, this level of the game. Users experiences this as a limitation of their ability to move; it is a spatial limitation. The result is that not only is the space frozen, in a way, and you cannot get any further in your manipulation of things and navigation in space, but also, as a consequence, time has come to a standstill. The *spatial* trap *blocks the development over time* in the experience of narrative progress.

As a comment on this *relationship between game time and user time* you might think of examples from CD-ROM multimedia productions in the presentational genre. These do not have goals or ends that are supposed to take place in another time and space than that of the user. Games or other narratives in computer-generated simulated worlds have levels, stages or solutions to be reached within the spaces and times of those worlds themselves. Whereas multimedia presentations, too, on the one hand may construct elaborated spaces and more or less firmly organized time-relations, on the other hand the answers and solutions are to be reached at and delivered, so to speak, in the eyes and ears of the beholder in the time and space of the user's world. The user has the power to choose where to go and what information to seek. The user decides upon the pattern of movement and the moment to do this or that. To take an example, parts of the multimedia presentation *Michelangelo* (Oliver Nolin, 1995) are staged like pieces of theatre, or animated chapters with music and the voice over of a narrator. You can choose a presentation of Michelangelo's biography ("Narrative"), and in the main menu of this chapter it is possible to go to no fewer than 33 entrances about parts of his life (1475–1551). Three other chapters are (1) The Work, (2) Characters (with relation to his life) and (3) Places (where he lived and worked). Within these, you can choose between a large number of subjects, such as drawing, fresco or sculpture (in 1), politics, philosophy or religion (in 2) or Chapel, Sistine or Duomo (in 3). At any given point in this Michelangelo world you may choose to jump to any other or leave. It is even possible to go to a special menu to get information about what and how much "ground" you have covered in this material. (Similarly one could refer to many other CD-ROM productions of the presentational multimedia kind, of course. Fine examples are *Blood Cinema* (Marsha Kinder, 1994) and *Film, Form, and Culture* (Robert Kolker, 1999). Although they are of the reference book type, like *Michelangelo*, they also have the advantage of live video examples to illustrate their introductions to film history and theory).

17.4.5 The Game's Space as User's Time Trap

As we have seen, the important result of the interplay between different points of view, possible actions, and the involvement/distance dialectic is the crucial role of user activity in the dynamics and meaning production in the game. This means that the perhaps frozen time in the game fiction spreads into the time of the user space. Suddenly the otherwise involved player finds himself not in game time but in his or her own user time, and the time spent in game space is transformed into time wasted in real time. The otherwise effective and meaningful dialectic between involvement and distance which defines the experience of being "in there" (in the game) and at the same time out here having fun, may lose the element of involvement and turn into too much distance for the game to be successful entertainment.

This is the potential problem with games: their narration is a way of organizing and structuring space and time. If successful, the user can move about in the game's space from his or her own place, and the user's time is integrated as an understandable and reasonable interactivity with the game's fiction. But if the user's activity in time is not integrated successfully in/or met in a reasonable way by the narrative and logic space of the game, the balance between the world of the narrator and that of the user is lost, and the user is, so to speak, thrown back into his or her own, real, time. As a consequence, the attention is focused on the time that is spent *in vain* in *the use space* trying to find solutions in the *diegetic space.*

17.4.6 Stylized Shapes of Unreal Worlds

To compare with film once more, the user gets involved in the game travel in the same way that the viewer does in, for instance, Hitchcock's *Vertigo* or *Rear Window.* We experience the events in San Francisco and Greenwich Village "with" the main characters, Scottie and Jeff, in a special way: we do so, not just because viewers see "with" or through the characters' gaze, but also because we can see them see. Viewers have (1) the camera and (2) their own gaze on the camera and on what it is telling/showing, including the character. This is just one of the mechanisms that contribute to the difference between real-world experience and the experience of fiction film (and several other media). Also, it adds to an understanding of the fact that the experience of the computer game and its world (things, landscapes, architecture, characters, narrative, time and space as part of its structure) is radically different from the way we experience and understand our own world, reality. At the same time as we are presented with Scottie's experience of the events in *Vertigo,* and sometimes even his visions or nightmares, we are clearly defined as audience: we see him having these visions and dreams and see him seeing what he sees. Again, we have involvement and distance in one.

In Michelangelo Antonioni's last film, *Beyond the Clouds* (1995), there is a scene with two young people who are in love but haven't seen each other for some time. They meet, and while they are walking across a square in Ferrara, Antonioni lets his camera follow them. But in doing so, he moves the camera in such a way that their position within the frame in relation to the Duomo (cathedral) in the background does not change. While we can see them walk, and therefore are aware that they are moving in space, this is strangely contradicted by the way this shot is constructed. If they actually move (and if screen practice is like everyday practice), their bodies should move across the background. But, having the camera move in a certain direction and at precisely the right pace, Antonioni creates the impression that they are *moving on the spot.* The camerawork articulates the screen space (cf. above about screen space in games) so as to produce meaning or give shape to it. This strange experience of static movement (some might call it poetry in motion) is open to any viewer's interpretation, but it is fair to say that the moment is isolated and taken out of the flow of the ordinary continuity of time. Curiously and telling enough, this *time* magic is a result of *spatial* articulation, of the relation between foreground and background when articulated in time and space. That is, as movement.

In *Riven*, as well as in *Vertigo*, *Beyond the Clouds* and other games, VRs and films, the users and viewers are presented with constructions, stylized shapes of visual and unreal worlds that are referentially fictional, as Prince calls them. In a combination of involvement and distance we understand, interpret and react to them as fictional constructs. If we connect to or even like these games and film worlds and the way their meaning is shaped through stylistic construction, we do so from a position outside the fictions; and if we have difficulty in understanding and accepting them or following the rules or demands of the games, we are thrown back into our position in real time and space.

Different kinds of actions in and in front of different, yet connected, spaces of games and films shape the content which users and viewers experience in their encounters with the media. Different kinds of dialogue or interaction between audiences and media have to be analysed and theorized. Hopefully, this chapter has articulated a journey through virtual and film worlds which has contributed to the understanding of the practical and theoretical potentials of games and other computer-generated, fictional spaces, and in doing so demonstrated that it pays to practise a style of analysis which takes as its point of departure a comparison with moving pictures of film and an inspiration from film theory.

References

Bordwell, D. (1985) *Narration in the Fiction Film*. London: Routledge.

Bordwell, D. (1996) Contemporary Film Studies and the Vicissitudies of Grand Theory. In *Post Theory* (eds. D. Bordwell and N. Carroll). Madison, WI: University of Wisconsin Press.

Bordwell, D. (1997) *On the History of Film Style*. Cambridge, MA: Harvard University Press.

Browne, N. (1992) The Spectator-in-the-Text: The Rhetoric of Stagecoach. In *Film Theory and Criticism*, 4th edn (eds. G. Mast, M. Cohen and L. Braudy). Oxford: Oxford University Press.

Carroll, N. (1996) Prospects of Film Theory: A Personal Assessment. In *Post Theory* (eds. D. Bordwell and N. Carroll). Madison, WI: University of Wisconsin Press.

Eugeni, R. (1998) Myst: Multimedia Hypertexts and Film Semiotics, Special Issue of *iris* (revue de théorie de l'image et du son, 25, spring 1998/French–English: Film Theory and the Digital Image).

Kau, E. V. (1986) Nothing is what it seems. *MacGuffin* 57: December.

Kau, E. V. (1995) "You are the camera. The camera is your eye". The Staging of the Gaze in Orson Welles' Work. In *Nordisk Filmforskning 1975–95* (ed. P. Grøngaard). Nordicom-Danmark.

Kau, E. V. (1996a) Filmtilskueren som levende død. Eller hvordan film er konkret leg, der bliver til symbolske billeder; Den ex-centriske billedfortælling. Eller hvordan film er fortællen, uden centrum; and Hvem ser Pauls hemmelighed? Eller hvordan film er sindbilleder, uden identifikation. All three articles in *POV* 1: March.

Kau, E. V. (1996b) Great beginnings – and endings. Made by Orson Well. In *POV* 2: December.

Kau, E. V. (1997a) Sense of emotion – in space. Sense of place – in time. *POV* 3: March.

Kau, E. V. (1997b) Tid og rum i Filmen og Multimediet. At tænke med øjne og hænder. In *Multimedieteori – om de nye mediers teoriudfordringer* (ed. H. Juel). Odense Universitetsforlag.

Kau, E. V. (1998) Separation or combination of fragments? Reflections on editing. *POV* 6: December.

Kau, E. V. (1999) Collapsing time. In *POV* 7: March.

Prince, S. (1996) True lies. Perceptual Realism, Digital Images, and Film Theory. *Film Quarterly* 3: Spring.

Games

Riven, Cyan Inc. (1993).

Myst, Cyan Inc. (1997).

The Residents Freak Show. Ludtke, J. and The Residents (1994). Voyager, New York/The Cryptic Corporation, San Francisco.

Films

Antonioni, M. (1995) *Beyond the Clouds.*
Carpenter, J. (1978) *Halloween.*
Hitchcock, A. (1954) *Rear Window.*
Hitchcock, A. (1958) *Vertigo.*
Kurosawa, A. (1950) *Rashomon.*
Verhoeven, P. (1987) *Robocop.*

CD-ROMs

Nolin, O. (1995) *Michelangelo*, Montparnasse Multimedia, Paris.
Kinder, M. (1994) *Blood Cinema*, Cine Discs, Los Angeles (and book, California University Press, 1993).
Kolker, R. (1999) *Film, Form, and Culture* (and book, McGraw-Hill College, 1999).

18

Constructing the Concept of the "Interactive 3D Documentary" – Film, Drama, Narrative or Simulation?

Hanne Dankert and Niels Erik Wille

18.1 Introduction

This chapter aims to establish a new genre concept, the "interactive three-dimensional documentary" – as opposed to analysing and implementing a pre-existing genre concept.

The work reported is part of a project on (script) writing for interactive works that communicate factual information to the user of the work. The objective of this project is to systematize existing guidelines and established practices of script writing in order to optimize the production process, seeing the script as a tool for planning and coordinating the work of a production team consisting of persons with a wide variety of skills and talents and a variety of educational and experiential backgrounds.

The term "interactive 3D documentary" was adopted from the very beginning of the project, but all along the need for a more precise definition (or construction) of the implied concept was recognized. This is a concern that at the present time one will meet in connection with most other emerging genres in the "new media".

A typical approach is to regard an interactive work as a variety of some well-established genre. And the corollary for script writing is to adopt the formats and conventions of scripts for that model genre. One such approach is to regard interactive works as varieties of "film narratives" and so to see the script writing in terms of "screen writing" – writing for the film screen or television screen. This approach is adopted in several influential handbooks on writing for interactive media, such as Jon Samsel and Darryl Wimberley's *The Interactive Writer's Handbook* (1996) and its sequel *Writing for Interactive Media. The Complete Guide* (1998), Timothy Garrand's *Writing for Multimedia. Entertainment. Education. Training. Advertising. World Wide Web* (1997), and Michael D. Korolenko's *Writing for Multimedia. A Guide and Sourcebook for the Digital Writer* (1997). These books draw heavily on examples from the multimedia industry, demonstrating that this is not only a textbook approach, but reflects actual practices in the industry.

In this framework an interactive work concerned with factual information has then to be conceptualized as a variety of "documentary", following the dichotomy of "fiction film" and "documentary film". The prime examples of "interactive fictions" or "interactive narratives" (the equivalents of "fiction films") are normally taken to be computer games, typically of the adventure type, but other possibilities are discussed in the literature, for example in Espen Aarseth's *Cybertext. Perspectives on Ergodic Literature* (1997).

The film, televison or videogram documentary is by now a well-established genre, although dynamic and still developing. Discussions of script writing for this rely on many years of practice and teaching. But interactive documentaries (whether 2D or 3D) cannot to the same extent take genre conventions and practices for granted. Actual examples of the genre are relatively few, but we have found at least one company that has marketed factual interactive works as "interactive documentaries". In the manual of FlagTower's *The Unexplained* (1996) it says: "FlagTower has named this concept the Interactive Documentary, a title which reflects the televisual appeal of our style of production". But other works of course exemplify the same basic idea without actually adopting the term.

Attempts at theoretical characterization and systematization are almost non-existent, since interactive fictions have drawn the most attention.

A constructive clarification of the term "interactive 3D documentary" will have to address several problems, typified by the three terms: "interactive", "three-dimensional" and "documentary".

This chapter then takes its point of departure in a discussion of salient features of the documentary film, in order to investigate to what extent it is feasible and valuable to transform concepts, devices, tools and modes of expression and representation from (documentary) film production to interactive works, and to what extent these new types of work call for new concepts. We then proceed to discuss interactivity and the complexities introduced by three-dimensional representations as opposed to the two-dimensional representations of space normally used in film.

18.2 Film and Theatre as Interface Metaphors

Brenda Laurel in *Computers as Theatre* (1993) proposed drama, understood as theatrical productions, as a general model or "metaphor" for computer interface design. This puts the user in the double role of spectator and director of the "play" unfolding on the screen and other output devices. The screen etc. is conceptualized as a stage with actors, props and scenery, and the idea is to focus on the action unfolding rather than on "static" displays of information.

It should be stressed that Brenda Laurel is not proposing to use the theatre as an "interface metaphor" in the normal sense of this term. This would mean actually dressing the screen up as a stage with actions represented by actors and props, and perhaps even representing the director and his or her tools directly in the interface. She mentions Ellis Horowitz's ScriptWriter system from 1987–88 as an actual example of the use of a theatrical interface metaphor. Multimedia designers of today will be familiar with MacroMedia Director, where the interface is built on a film director metaphor. Laurel underlines the "distinction between using the theatre as an interface metaphor and using it in the deeper way that this book advocates – as a fundamental understanding of what is going on in human–computer interaction" (Laurel, 1993, p. 19).

This statement by Brenda Laurel seems a natural stepping stone for a short explanation of the use of film as a model for understanding interactive 3D documentaries in the present chapter. The aim is neither another interface metaphor (like the one used in Director) nor a conceptual model for human–computer interaction as proposed by Brenda Laurel. Both the writers on interactive media referred to above and those of the present article see the film as a model in a fairly literal sense: events and actions represented by moving images and sound, and projected on the computer screen as a medium of display. Since a computer is used, some sort of interface will have to be provided for human–computer interaction. This may employ a film metaphor, thus underlining the film-like nature of the work. But all sorts of other metaphors and interaction devices are feasible, as demonstrated by scores of computer games and multimedia presentations.

18.3 The Interactive 3D Documentary as Film

The core of an interactive 3D documentary is, like the film, an interrelated sequence of moving images projected on a screen and giving the user/spectator a view of a world including agents, "props" and scenery, organized in one or more locations. In the present article we concentrate on works that use a single computer screen for projection, not taking was has become known as "Virtual Reality" into account. The reason for this is that while there are many similarities, some of the differences are crucial and entail a different approach both in production and in analysis and evaluation of the final results.

With a computer screen the viewport to the represented world is an image cropped at the edges of the screen, not a direct view of the scene as in normal space. The viewport cuts off large parts of the world as well as giving access to selected parts of it. As with film this creates the possibility of an illusion of a partial view of space extending in all directions, to both sides, above, below and behind the position of the spectator, who is both "in the world" and outside it. The part of the world that the spectator has access to through the viewport of the image has to be worked out in such detail as is needed according to the purpose, style and technique of the work, but everything outside the view is filled in by the imagination of the spectator, and can be left without details or even not worked out at all.

In typical documentary films, of course the assumption is that the world in front of the camera is real and actually extends in all directions, but it is still acknowledged that a specific selection of the viewpoint, the images created and the way that sequences of images are edited together may create illusions or distortions from "authentic" footage. This may result in works that are experienced as "false" as well as works that are experienced as "true" representations of the depicted world. The photographic registration of what is in front of the camera does not automatically guarantee "true" representations. In the literature one will find many demonstrations of the fact that something just outside the viewport of the camera might have changed the impression created by the film considerably if it had been included rather than – consciously or unconsciously – left out.

The images produced with the film camera may vary: close-ups, medium shots and long shots; panoramic views and interiors; panning, tilting and moving with the actors; employing various types of perspective (frog's-eye view, bird's-eye view, personal point-of-view); partially blurred and clearly focused images; images with natural light or carefully contrived artificial light; colours enhanced or distorted by "filters"; etc.

In film this is created with the use of a photographic film camera that intervenes between the spectator and the depicted world. In interactive 3D presentations no physical camera is needed, but it is fruitful to conceptualize the device generating and projecting the images of the three-dimensional world as a kind of "virtual" camera. This device could render whatever is supposed to be in front of it in a very unsophisticated way, typically using a mathematically constructed "central perspective" as "seen" from a specified point in the virtual space of the depicted world.

But the idea of a "virtual camera" effortlessly leads to reflections on the "creative" role of the physical camera in film, as suggested above. And this again generates ideas about possible alternative designs of the "virtual camera" and the restrictions and possibilities that any specific design will impose on the "director" of an interactive 3D documentary. The virtual camera should typically be capable of doing what a physical camera can do, as well as something more; a camera that is enhanced as well as virtual. But in some cases one might want to impose restrictions rather than enhancements, depending on the overall design of the planned interactive work.

The film camera, virtual or otherwise, creates the possibility of a whole range of pictorial representations that are specific to film, and makes theatrical space and film space two fundamentally different phenomena, in spite of all their obvious similarities. These pictorial representations are found as well in the animated film, even though the "world" in front of the camera is drawn, painted or modelled rather than "real". Factual films (documentaries in a broad sense) created with animation techniques are of course not relying on "photographic documentation", but on the statements created with words, moving images and sound being in accordance with reality as the creators conceive it.

For obvious reasons the world in front of the virtual camera of an interactive 3D documentary is not the real world or a carefully selected part of it. The 3D world is represented in or generated by the computer and displayed on the computer screen using the virtual camera. The closest relative in the film world is actually the animated film, where painted pictures or models are used to represent the world, but historical re-creations and drama documentaries in the same sense aim at displaying images that make true statements about the real world, but without any of the normal "authenticity" of a photographic documentation.

Since our concept of the documentary film is closely associated with this type of photographic documentation, some "deconstruction" of the concept of the "documentary" is in order. But first we will try to exemplify what we mean by an "interactive 3D documentary".

18.4 An Illustrative Case: Life and Death in the Danish Bronze Age

In order to do this we will introduce a specific example which is only in the planning stage, but will be worked out in more detail at a later stage of our script writing project. This was partly inspired by a documentary film produced by the Danish National Museum in the 1950s and involves among other thing the re-creation of some famous Danish Bronze Age burials.

Another inspiration was the exhibition *Gods and Heroes of the Bronze Age. Europe at the Time of Ulysses*, a European collaboration shown first at the Danish National Museum in 1998.

In 1921 a burial mound in Egtved was excavated; the burial site held among other things a big coffin made from a hollowed-out oak trunk, 2 metres long. In the coffin were the remains of a young woman ("the Egtved girl") complete with skin, hair and teeth, as well as well-preserved clothes and jewellery. The modern excavation methods used made a very detailed analysis of the burial possible. The burial was dated to about 1400 BC.

An excavation in 1935 at Skrydstrup disclosed another burial of a young woman in an oak coffin. This, together with earlier excavations of burial mounds, mainly of men, has given us a substantial amount of knowledge about Bronze Age burials. The burials are some of our most important sources about this period of Danish prehistory, but other archeological findings have disclosed weapons, artefacts used for ceremonial purposes, symbols carved in stone, remnants of buildings etc. Earth samples with, among other things, seeds and other botanical, zoological and geological indicators, give a very good picture of the climate, landscape, domestic animals and wildlife of the time. The Bronze Age is the period between 1800 and 500 BC in Denmark and the other Scandinavian countries.

The excavations inspired the National Museum to commission in 1958 a documentary film to illustrate how the researchers had reconstructed life in the Bronze Age using the Egtved and Skrydstrup burials as the main focus. Other well-known objects from the same period, such as the ceremonial bronze horns known as "lur" in Danish, were included in the reconstruction. For the location of the film a landscape similar to that thought to exist in Denmark in 1400 BC was used. The actors were dressed in the type of clothes found in the coffins and used the jewellery, weapons and other utensils known from the burials and other archeological finds. Everything was done to implement the knowledge about the period available to the researchers, but of course the movements and gestures of the actors, as well as the actual ceremonies depicted in the film, were based on conjecture.

The basic idea was to help the spectator visualize life in the Bronze Age in Denmark, and to create a possible context to the artefacts and other objects that had survived. This was done through discursive presentations, combining spoken commentaries with photographic descriptions, as well as dramatized sequences; for instance one covering the time span from the death of a young man to his burial in an oak coffin and the erection of the mound.

Three other devices used by museums and heritage sites to illustrate life in former time should be mentioned in this context. The first is the use of scale models to illustrate how a bit of landscape or a specific village or town might have appeared at the time. This normally allows the visitor a bird's-eye perspective of the area, but mirrors may be used to give a more horizontal perspective from different angles. The second is the use of full-scale dioramas to show a group of people in some sort of (social) action, with dummies dressed in reconstructions of clothes etc. The third device is full-scale reconstructions of buildings and their environments. This may even be peopled by "actors" dressed in reconstructed clothes and enacting daily life and ceremonies etc. Depending on the setup, the visitor may be allowed to interact with the players to get more information about the time and our present knowledge of the time.

An interactive multimedia documentary would use the one or more of these devices, cinematographic reconstructions, virtual models of buildings and landscapes, virtual dioramas and images of actual artefacts, allowing the user to explore a segment of the Bronze Age world, investigating the artefacts of the time and observing the people of the age go about their business, in this case focused on the burial of an important member (or the offspring of an important member) of the society.

The user might be placed in the role of an unobserved observer, moving around at will, or as a participant observer, an outsider, interacting with the people in the rendered world to elicit information. The user might even play the role of a specific person in that world, directly influencing the flow of the "story" by his or her actions.

The equivalents of discursive presentations could of course be included in the work as a whole, in the form of written or spoken text, supported by illustrations in all relevant media: graphics, photographs and film strips, 3D representations of artefacts, sound and music.

The designer of this multimedia work would have a choice of still pictures (graphics and photographs), animated 2D graphics, video sequences with live action actors, or animated 3D graphics. Of course only the use of 3D graphics would make the work an "interactive 3D documentary", in part or as a whole.

Other possible modes of expression for such a simulation have been demonstrated in the Viking age multimedia installation in Ribe, Denmark (Laursen, 1997a,b, Laursen and Andersen, 1993).

We will now return to our discussion of the concept of "documentary".

18.5 The Concept of "Documentary"

The term "documentary" is in general associated with film and television documentaries, but actually has a wider use as illustrated by this extract from *Webster's Third New International Dictionary* (1961 edition):

> 1. **documentary** [...] 1: being or consisting of documents : contained or certified in writing <~evidence> 2: of, relating to, or employing documentation in literature or art <~annotations> <a careful~writer> *broadly*: having or claiming the objective quality, authority or force of documentation in the representation of a scene, place or condition of life or of a social or political problem or cause: FACTUAL, OBJECTIVE, REPRESENTATIONAL – used of literature, the theatre, art, photography, radio and TV programs.
>
> 2. **documentary** [...] a documentary presentation (as a film or novel).

This dictionary entry underlines the relation between some aspects of reality and the documentary work: the intention of a faithful or "true" representation of those aspects of reality, using actual "documents" or other means. With documentary films or television programs that relationship has both conceptually and practically been integrated with the use of photographic images and sound recording for the registration of selected parts of the reality to be represented.

This of course has everything to do with the very nature of the photographic image and sound recording, but it has just as much to do with what is put in front of the camera and the tape recorder (or whatever). Fiction film uses exactly the same equipment to register scenery and playacting carefully organized in order to create the illusion of events and actions unfolding in front of the camera (and so in front of the spectator).

Erik Barnouw in his *Documentary. A History of the Non-fiction Film* (1974) tells how film from the very beginning developed into two types of popular entertainment: one openly fictional – photo plays – and one claiming to be factual: war reports, travelogues, shots of famous people and royalty, etc. Also, various forms of "fakes" very soon entered the factual films, sometimes under the name of "reconstitutions":

> Reconstitutions and fakes have an impressive record of "success." Memorable genuine footage came back from the 1906 San Francisco earthquake, but other footage of the event, contrived in table-top miniature, was equally applauded. Several volcanic eruptions were triumphantly faked, as in Biograph's 1905 *Eruption of Mount Vesuvius.* Film companies did not want to ignore catastrophes or other headline events merely because their cameramen could not get there; enterprise filled the gap. In this spirit the British producer James Williamson shot his 1898 *Attack on a Chinese Mission Station* in his back yard, and some of his Boer War scenes on a golf course. The snows of Long Island and New Jersey provided settings for such action as Biograph's 1904 *Battle of the Yalu* and a competing Edison film, *Skirmish Between Russian and Japanese Advance Guards.* In the latter we see soldiers surge back and forth before the unmoving camera, while many fall in their tracks. To help audiences

> identify the players, Russians were dressed in white, the Japanese in dark colors. The acceptance of such items probably discouraged more genuine enterprise – at least among some competitors.
>
> A different kind of fakery was exemplified by a project of Doublier [...]. The court-martial of Dreyfus had taken place in 1894, before the debut of the cinémathographe, but agitation by Emile Zola, along with the confessions of forgery by a colonel in the French War Office and the colonel's subsequent suicide, brought interest in the scandal to a new pitch in 1898. Doublier proceeded to satisfy it with footage that originally had no connection with Dreyfus. A few words to the audience, and their own imagination supplied connections. Footage of a young French officer at the head of an army parade was promptly accepted as "Dreyfus." A large Parisian building became the "scene of the court-martial." A tug going out to meet a barge became "Dreyfus taken to a battleship." A long shot of the Nile delta became "Devil's Island," scene of the imprisonment.
>
> Audience imagination was often relied on for such services. A curious instance involved a much-publicized 1907 African hunting trip by Theodore Roosevelt. William Selig, working in Chicago, found a Roosevelt look-alike and photographed him stalking through a studio jungle, followed by black "native" porters, also from the Chicago area. He encountered an aged lion, who was then shot on camera. The film was a great financial success. The name "Roosevelt" was never mentioned. The item was merely titled *Hunting Big Game in Africa*. (Barnouw, 1974, pp. 25–26)

So the important issue was not the "realism" of the photograph but the ethics of the photographer, or the relation of authenticity between film representation and the reality represented. The emerging documentary film genre became preoccupied with how best to transform reality, actuality and facts, observed from a certain position through a camera lens and a microphone, via the editing process, into a coherent statement about the historically given world. This implies very much an awareness of the element of construction and artistic approach, putting documentary films on par with fiction films as "works of art". Documentary film makers were preoccupied with the "Creative Treatment of Actuality", but drawing a line with the sort of "reconstitutions" illustrated by Barnouw. The distinction between fact and fiction has to be upheld as an underlying rationale for the documentary film, no matter how blurred in practice.

This basic relationship between the reality depicted and the pictures and sounds recorded is at the core of our concept of documentary. However, in interactive 3D documentaries the world depicted does not exist as such, but is generated from data represented digitally in the computer. No matter the degree of photorealism attained, the image is not a photograph of something existing outside the "camera" and independently. While the traditional documentary film sought to establish its credentials through the authenticity of the events and actions in front of the camera, the interactive 3D documentary has to rely on the verisimilitude of the data and the images generated from them, and the veracity of the statements about the real world that it conveys. This in many ways puts it on a par with historical reconstructions and animated films, rather than the prototypical documentary.

This may remind us that "documentary" since the beginning – as outlined by Barnouw – has developed into a specific film genre which is a sub-genre of what could be called the "fact film": Other related genres are instructional films, news reporting, promotional films, scientific documentation etc. The "documentary film" in this narrow sense is very much like the literary genre called the "essay". It has the status of an art form and is a vehicle for personal expression, as well as a representation of reality. These features we see as important features of the new genre too, challenging naturalistic modelling and photorealism as the main criteria for success in interactive documentaries.

The predominant conception of the documentary film was formulated in the 1920s by John Grierson, the Grand Old Man of British documentary. He was the author of the "definition" of the documentary film as the "Creative Treatment of Actuality". His point was that a good documentary should not be a mechanical or unreflecting registration of what happened to be in front of the camera, but a partisan statement by a director with a strong sense of social responsibility. In "First Principles of Documentary" (1932) he makes a distinction between what he sees as the documentary film proper, and the "newsreel" ("a speedy snip-snap of some utterly unimportant ceremony"), the "lecture film" ("their... form is cut to the commentary, and shots are arranged arbitrarily to point to the gags or conclusions") and the "film symphony" ("the orchestration of movement"). It is important to understand that Grierson was not aiming at a formal definition, but was trying to construct a genre that to him seemed worthy of special attention and further development. In this respect he was very successful.

After Grierson it is taken for granted that "documentary would photograph the living scene and the living story", not "acted stories against artificial backgrounds". Secondly that "the original (or native) actor and the original (or native) scene, are better guides to a screen interpretation of the modern world". And thirdly "that the materials and the stories taken from the raw can be finer (and more real in the philosophic sense) than the acted article".

Perhaps these statements should be taken as prescriptions about means rather than ends, and mainly directed against established practices of the commercial studios at the time, rather than against filmic reconstructions as such. Read this way, Grierson preferred real coal workers to play the parts of coal workers, and stories taken from real life rather than the inventions of novelists and screenwriters. Grierson also stresses the need for a strong storyline and dramatization rather than discursive (argumentative) presentations in his preferred form of the documentary. This view is, we think, supported by the two documentaries normally associated with Grierson: *The Drifters* (1929), directed by Grierson, about the life of fishermen and the sea they depend on for living, and *The Night Mail* (1936), produced by him, about the night express between London and Scotland and the men working on it, which focused on the role they play in the delivery of letters and other mail services.

The conceptual core that may be distilled from this, is that the documentary film is a fact film (a representation of the real world) which is dramatic in form, organized around a story (an interrelated sequence of events) and making a statement about some aspect of the reality depicted. This characterization makes it possible to include both animated documentaries and dramatic reconstructions of historical events and situation with live-action actors ("faction" films) (for a discussion of the term "faction" see Harms Larsen (1990)). John Halas and Roger Manwell in *The*

Technique of Film Animation (1971) draw a direct line from Grierson's *Night Mail* to animated films used in Public Relations and propaganda, as well as instructional and educational animated films (Halas and Manwell, 1971, pp. 116–138). For a discussion of the use of film to "restage" the past, see Sorlin (1980).

This paves the way for a smooth transition to a characterization of the interactive 3D documentary as a dramatized representation of (selected aspects of) reality, created by one or more "directors" (or authors in the wide sense of the word) in order to communicate statements ("views") about that reality.

What this implies in terms of storyline and narrative structure will be discussed later. But first we would like to discuss some further lessons to be learned from documentary films.

18.6 The Modes of Production in Documentary Film

The discussion of the relationship between reality and film representation by documentary film makers has given rise to several ways of approaching the reality to be represented during the production process.

Bill Nichols, in *Representing Reality. Issues and Concepts in Documentary* (1991), calls them Modes of Representation, and he makes a distinction between four basic types: "expository", "observational", "interactive" and "reflexive". While they obviously have to do with how thing are finally represented in the finished and published film, these modes are just as much ways of approaching the reality to be depicted during the production of the film. That is why we prefer to refer to them as Modes of Production.

The *expository* mode of production aims at producing a discursive exposition of the facts as seen by the director or producer of the film. The organizing principle of the film is the statement and its supporting evidence, and any footage recorded in the field is seen as photographic evidence or illustration for this statement. It will often take the form of interviews and testimonials by key persons. Reconstructions (carefully declared as such) are acceptable. The film may include pre-existing documents, including footage made for other purposes, as long as they fulfil their rhetorical as well as documentary function within the film.

Some of the characteristics of the expository mode are the construction of a coherent world, presented from a god-like perspective, neatly arranged and structured to fit a certain purpose of an ideological or idealistic nature. The backbone of the exposition is often a "Voice of God" spoken commentary that explains or sums up the intended message. The expository mode intentionally leaves little room for self-reflection and interpretation on the side of the spectator. This mode is in many respects what was in John Grierson's mind when speaking (derisively) of "lecture films".

In the framework of the interactive 3D documentary the expository mode would be something like a guided tour of the depicted world. The ongoing activities could be broken into independent pre-recorded sequences, with the user interaction focusing on the selection of which sequence to initiate and in what order. Like a real-life guided tour this might involve some exploration of selected areas where it is judged safe to let the user roam, for instance to get more information about artefacts and scenery. The feel would be very much like Hypertext, with the pre-recorded actions and the commentary taking the place of written text with illustrations.

The *observational* mode of production aims at exploring a piece of reality or a "slice of life" and to leave it to the user to get something out of it, or rather what to get out of it. The camera (and microphone) registers whatever happens in front of it and this is conveyed to the spectator of the film with a minimum of editing. The viewer becomes the "fly on the wall" which the director tries to imitate. In film terms this has been labelled "*cinema verité*" or "direct cinema" and is associated with series of stylistic devices that signal the non-intrusive nature of the recording. A handheld camera could be one such device, but of course the most important one is that none of the participants in front of the camera demonstrate any awareness of the cameraman and other members of the film crew.

Typical examples of *cinema verité* aim at getting public access to otherwise (to the public) closed institutions, environments etc. in order to explore the interaction going on between e.g. user/inmate/client and those in power/skilled staff of different kinds. It is left to the audience to make sense of what is going on and eventually take sides in the confrontations and power plays depicted. The camera – so it seems – "just" registers daily life inside the institution. It is in the editing process, first and foremost, that the separate takes are organized into a coherent testimony about a particular institution.

In an interactive 3D documentary the awareness of the use of a virtual camera rather than a physical one may actually make it easier to establish the illusion of unobserved observation. A roving camera could be used to explore a situation full of ongoing activities, allowing the user to select camera position, zoom factor, angle, panning etc. at will. The "story" could be a pre-recorded sequence, like the burial ceremony of the Bronze Age, or it could be a sequence generated in real time, like a market scene, where several typical actions and characters could be selected and activated more or less at random. One would probably invent ways of avoiding collisions with people or ghost-like passing through them, while perhaps accepting that the roving camera can pass through walls (or look out from walls), fly through the air, and jump from location to location.

In terms of avatars and agents, the camera in this case becomes the user's avatar, invisible in the world of observation, but with tools of operation visible or otherwise perceptible in the interface to the interactive work.

The *interactive* mode of production, on the other hand, makes a virtue out of the fact that any film recording necessarily interferes with the activities that are being recorded. (Here of course "interactive" is used in an entirely different meaning from that in "interactive 3D documentaries" or "interactive multimedia work".) The director and/or the crew interact with the characters/people "being or playing themselves" and with expert witnesses, events, daily life situations, historical moments etc. depicted in the film, and so lay bare or expose "the scene behind the scene" or the attitude and intended meaning behind the surface of the construction.

The actual presence in front of the camera of the creator/director and the interaction between her or him and the "protagonists" occasionally creates an intense feeling of commitment and equality. The revealing of the attitudes and intentions of the director/crew may create a kind of transparency, which allows the spectator to form his or her own opinion about the subject matter.

The equivalent form of interactive 3D documentary is one in which the user has some presence in the depicted world, and is allowed to interact with agents present in the picture space (and perhaps the avatars of other users).

Several varieties of this interaction may be envisioned, making for different types of documentaries. Three of them are outlined below:

1. The camera functions as the avatar of the user (as in the observational mode), but this time his or her presence in the virtual space is recognized, allowing conversation and other sorts of social interaction. This means that the position and the movement of the camera will have to mimic realistic eye positions and body movements for a person of specific height and physical abilities. The camera would be what in film terms is known as a "subjective camera" with a "first person view". The only parts of the body visible in the picture could be the hands (as well as any tool held in the hands).
2. The avatar of the user is present in the space visible through the viewport created by the camera. All parts of the body are in principle visible. The user is only able to see what happens in the immediate environment of the avatar, so the interaction is limited to props and agents within that environment. Movement to other parts of the virtual world depicted will follow natural rules (no passing through walls and closed doors, no flying etc.). The camera would be the "subjective camera" with a "third person view" in film terms.

   In some cases the camera is fixed in a specified position in relation to the avatar, e.g. behind the back of the avatar looking forward over the shoulder. The user moves the avatar and the camera automatically adjusts its position.

   In other cases the program allows a more flexible positioning of the camera, for instance according to the needs of the action or the position of the avatar in the depicted space. The use of the camera may also include "first person view" with close-ups of other agents in certain forms of interaction.
3. The user could have visual access to the whole of the virtual world, using a roving camera as outlined in (1), but only be able to interact with props and other agents when an avatar is present as in type 2. More than one agent in the depicted world could be controlled by the user, for instance in a complex simulation.

   Movement of the camera could be restricted in specified ways, for instance restricted to areas of the virtual world that have been visited by one or more avatars controlled by the user. Movements of the avatars will normally be restricted by "natural" rules like those in type 2.

The fourth mode of production, the *reflexive*, is the most self-aware. It plays on a meta-level with conventions regarding film language, genre and audience expectations. The very presentation of the story poses a variety of questions concerning the relationship between form and content; reality and fiction; and true and false. "It uses many of the same devices as other documentaries but sets them on edge so that the viewer's attention is drawn to the device as well as the effect" (Nichols, 1991, p. 33). This actually demands very careful planning at the production stage in order to get the necessary material for the final result.

This mode is also interesting from the point of view of interactive 3D documentaries, even if the implied relationship between reality and photographic reproduction does not exist. It is of course possible to design an interactive work that draws attention for instance to the artificiality of the interaction of a present day user with a strange, past world, rather than trying to make the user forget it as a precondition for the "suspension of disbelief" aimed at.

One such device could be the use of certain agents ("guides") that recognize the user-avatar as a stranger in need of explanation of what is going on and who is able to communicate with the user on the user's terms. To all other agents the user-avatar would be invisible and they would go about their business without having to take account of a stranger in their midst.

The alternative to this would be a user-avatar that had to act in a strange world as if he or she belonged there, but without the necessary knowledge and experience. The interface would then have to provide the user with tools to overcome this, such as an encyclopaedia, explanatory discourse, tutorial guides etc., breaking the illusion of total immersion.

Another alternative could be to cast the user-avatar in the role of a "time traveller", recognized by everybody as a stranger to be treated accordingly. This would "solve" the problem of differences of knowledge and experience, but at a cost: the events are no longer running their "natural" course but have to take into account this strange agent.

Anyway, in a 3D interactive context the user could be the co-creator/co-editor of the material available and enabled to play with genre conventions and to turn these upside down. Besides, the user could be able to exploit different narrative strategies in the construction of a story or plot or an argument. The user might choose to see the world or study the subject matter from unusual and surprising angles (provided these are worked out by designer and programmer), or employ a multilayered perspective in order to gain alternative kinds of knowledge and insights within the field of interest.

18.7 Story and Discourse. Dramatic, Narrative and Discursive Presentations

Seymour Chatman, in his two books on narrative structures in fiction and film, has underlined an important analytical distinction between the story (series of events with actors, props and scenery) communicated in a narrative, and the narrative forms used to communicate that story to the reader, listener, spectator or whatever. He prefers to call the two aspects "story" and "discourse"; other terms may be found in other authors (what he calls "discourse" is called "plot" in the tradition of Russian structuralism). And both his terms are slippery, especially "discourse", probably one of the most overused terms in modern humanistic and social research.

To Seymour Chatman and many other modern writers any rendering of an interconnected series of events (a story) is a "narrative", but the means used for narration may differ. So both a novel and a film may in this sense be a narrative, one based on a verbal (textual) presentation of the story, the other on moving images of actors, props and scenery (together of course with dialogue, sound effects and music).

In his first book Chatman (1978) takes the stand that films are normally "non-narrated", that is without a Narrator in the sense implied in all verbal narratives. A Narrator is then a special case found in some films, either a first-person Narrator – one of the characters represented in the film – stepping forward at times to speak to the audience, or an off-screen Narrator's voice presenting certain information about the Story and its characters. (The use of written text for the exposition at the beginning of the film is a special case of this type of Narrator.) It is interesting to note that documentary films are often "narrated" in this sense, having a verbal commentary binding the image sequences together and explaining their meaning.

In his second book Chatman (1990) then changes his analysis and insists that all film narratives imply a Narrator, using the language of film rather than verbal language for the narration.

This may be seen as a mere terminological problem, but underlying this is a real conceptual one. If we turn to the father of all narrative theories, Aristotle, we find that he insists that there are two distinct forms of presentation of a "story': the Dramatic and the Narrative. In the dramatic form the story is enacted in front of the spectator, the drama is a spectacle arranged to convey the story by the actions unfolding in the "present" of the play and by whatever is made known about the past through these actions (primarily the dialogue). The narrative, on the other hand, is "told" by a narrator, using only verbal means, and describing agents, props and scenery, rendering their dialogue and exposing relationships and motivations through the comments included with the narration proper. This distinction is underlying the whole of the discussion in *De Poetica*, but the following four quotations bring out the point:

> A third difference in these arts is in the manner in which each kind of object [= action] is represented. Given both the same means and the same object for imitation, one may either (1) speak at one moment in narrative and at another in an assumed character, as Homer does; or (2) one may remain the same throughout, without any such change; or (3) the imitators may represent the whole story dramatically, as though they were actually doing the thing described. (*De poetica*, Ch. 3, p. 1448)

> [Epic poetry] differs from [tragedy], however, (1) in that it is in one kind of verse and in narrative form; [...] (*De Poetica*, Ch. 5, p. 1449)

> A tragedy, then is the imitation of an action that is serious and also, as having magnitude, complete in itself; [...] in a dramatic, not in a narrative form [...] (*De Poetica*, Ch. 8, p. 1452)

> In a play one cannot represent an action with a number of parts going on simultaneously; one is limited to the part on the stage and connected with the actors. Whereas in epic poetry the narrative form makes it possible for one to describe a number of simultaneous incidents [...] (*De Poetica*, Ch. 24, p. 1459)

An equally useful distinction between narrative and discursive presentations on the other hand comes out of rhetorical theory. In the presentation of a law case the actual events to be discussed are normally presented in a so-called "narration" (Latin *narratio*), while the arguments *pro et contra* are presented in a discursive text (discursive in the sense of arguing step by step, exemplifying another well-established meaning of the term "discourse").

Taking works of historical research as an example, we can make a distinction between narrative and discursive presentations of what in Chatman's terms is a "story", for instance a sequence of historical events. The narrative will focus on the action, the actual doings of the agents, and the way that actions lead to other actions. While the discursive presentation will focus on causes and consequences, and the arguments *pro et contra* a specific interpretation of what is going on.

We may then talk about three fundamentally different ways of presenting a sequence of events that form a "story": (1) a dramatic re-enactment in the form of a spectacle taking place in front of the viewers (this is the Drama of traditional Poetics); (2) a verbal re-telling of the events, focusing on actions, motives and feelings of the agents, and describing the setting and the "props" involved (this is the Epic of traditional Poetics, but also the modern Narrative in a narrow sense of the term); and (3) an analytical, argumentative presentation of the events (this should be called "discourse", but as mentioned above this term is dreadfully overused by modern theoreticians; we shall use "discursive presentation" for lack of a better term).

In all the three forms, somebody – the Author of the work – is responsible for organizing the presentation, but this is not the same as the Narrator. In the case of the Drama, a Narrator may be part of the enactment, but if we follow Aristotle, the Drama is not narrated. In the discursive presentation it would again be best not to talk about a Narrator, since the text is not a narration, though the presentation will of course have an Implied Author.

This takes us back to Seymour Chatman and his problem with the narrative status of film, or rather the problem of "narrated" versus "non-narrated" films. We think that this problem reflects an important issue that also has bearings on our understanding of interactive 3D documentaries.

Basically the types of film we are talking about are dramatizations. The actors in front of the camera are "imitators" in Aristotle's terms. And "They [...] represent the whole story dramatically, as though they were actually doing the thing described". A Narrator may be part of the spectacle, either on-screen as part of the "play" or off-screen as an external commentator (or both). But in the absence of such a Narrator we would have to say that the film was "non-narrated".

On the other hand, in film we find the same type of intervention between story and spectator that is found in the typical narrative, such as a novel, short story or fairy tale. In verbal presentations there always is a distinct narrative "voice" describing the actions, telling us about the motives of the agents, clarifying relations of time and space, colouring the story with feelings and interpretations, establishing a "narrator's point of view" that has to be kept separate from the points of view of other agents etc.

As has been amply demonstrated by Seymour Chatman and many other students of film, the use of camera movement, camera angles, montage, shots and cuts, sound effects, music etc. implies a strong narrative presence that does not (or only to a limited extent) use verbal language as a means of expression but a special film language. Seen in this light we would say that yes, all films that present a story are narratives, they are "narrated" even if they don't have an explicit Narrator.

So with film it seems that we have to make a distinction between two different types of Narrator: The Implied Narrator, who is always there and who organizes the way the Story is represented in the "Discourse" of moving images and sound, and the Explicit Narrator that may be used sometimes for special effects.

In documentary film an Explicit Narrator is often used, typically combining narration and commentary. The Narrator is normally talking from the position of a knowledgeable observer who is not part of the situation described in the film action, but a mediator between the depicted world and the spectator. But it is important – in documentaries as well as in fiction – not to identify the explicit and the implicit Narrators. The explicit Narrator is one of many tools that the implicit Narrator has at hand to tell the Story.

New problems arise when we try to apply these principles to an interactive documentary.

18.8 Are Interactive 3D Documentaries Narrated or Non-Narrated? Narrative Versus Explorative Modes

This analysis then leads to the conclusion that a film "telling" a story is also a narrative with an Implied Narrator. This covers the typical documentary film as well – though the "lecture film" is discursive rather than narrative. The role of the Implied Narrator is to organize the flow of the story, to select which parts of it to disclose when, to direct the viewer's attention using camera movements, close-ups, selective focus etc., to create meaningful contrapositions using a montage of shots and to organize the temporal "rhythm" of the moving images for timing, suspense, relaxation etc.

But what happens when the flow of events is controlled by the user, not an Implied Narrator? Conceptually we will still have an interrelated sequence of events, with agents, "props" and scenery, in one or more locations, that is a Story. But is it a Narrative?

One way of answering this question – and the one typically chosen – is to say that the user has taken over the role of Author, Director or whatever. So why not the role of Narrator? He or she is so to speak telling the story to himself. This is about as meaningful as talking of somebody seriously playing chess with him- or herself. A vital part of the game of chess is that the two players have to figure out the intentions of the other player, while it is not possible if the two players are the same person – in the normal case – to prevent one player from knowing what the other is thinking.

When the user is in control of the flow of events and of the camera displaying the flow of events, he or she is not – as a director – using the camera to direct his or her attention – as a spectator – to something that might otherwise be missed, or making sure that this is done with the right timing to create a pleasing aesthetic experience. The user is – as a spectator or participant – turning his or her attention to something in the virtual world and directing the camera accordingly.

When reading the books on writing for interactive media mentioned in the introduction (Samsel and Wimberley, 1996, 1998; Garrand, 1997; Korolenko, 1997) one is struck by the fact that exactly the lack of control over the normal narrative tools is a main concern for writers nurtured on film and turning to interactive multimedia. They want to have a strong Story with interesting characters and a setting that provides fascinating images. And they want narrative control for fear of boring the user. Hollywood script writing conventions that focus on dialogue, rather than the development of characters and settings, support this tendency when imported into multimedia productions.

For practical reasons it is not possible, nor economically feasible, to work out all possible outcomes of user interaction so that the resulting "narrative" is always optimal. The result is often a reduction of user intervention in the virtual world and a reliance on longer pre-recorded action sequences using traditional film techniques of presentation. In such cases it of course seems very meaningful to talk about an interactive narrative with a typical implied Narrator.

But in the many cases where user intervention is frequent and the user is allowed to explore the virtual world and its potential for events and actions more or less at will, the term "narrative" seems unnecessarily contrived. And no presence of a Narrator is felt. In this case "explorative" would be a much better word than Narrative. The user is an "explorer" of the world created by the Author or Director of the work. And their role is that of creating characters, props and settings, the rules governing their behaviour, and the tools that allow the user to interact with the world – and to interact with the characters (agents) encountered as part of the exploration. Levinsen (1997) also makes the point that "exploration" seems a much better conceptual model for multimedia presentations than "narration". The same point is made by Stigel in Chapter 15. In the gaming world this kind of work is known as a "simulation". They include working models of aeroplanes ("flight simulators"), racing cars, tanks, submarines etc. Most war games that aim at historical accuracy are simulations. Less warlike are the "sim"-series: *Sim City*, *Sim Life*, *Sim Earth*, *Sim Ant*, and no end of managerial and economic simulations like *Railroad Tycoon*, *Pizza Tycoon*, *The A-train*, *Capitalism* etc.

From the tentative examples of interactive 3D documentaries given here and earlier, it should be obvious that these works will lie on a continuum from predominantly narrative presentations to predominantly explorative presentations, with some discursive presentations thrown in. So the answer to our question is not a simple yes or no. It depends on the sort of control that the designer has built into the user intervention and the purposes served by different types of intervention.

18.9 Interactivity and Three-Dimensionality

A more detailed discussion of the term "interactivity" is outside the scope of this chapter. Other contributions to this volume as well as other sources have dealt with the intricacies of the term and the related concepts. But we think that one aspect has to be discussed and that is the relationship between interactivity and the perception of three-dimensionality in an interactive work.

In one sense any traditional film is a rendering of a three-dimensional world on a two-dimensional screen. This is simply the result of using photographic images. And many animated films use graphical techniques that underline the three-dimensionality of the space depicted.

A good question then is: what is the difference between the 3D to 2D projection of any documentary film and the sort of 3D we are talking about? What makes the question really intriguing is the fact that nowadays 3D digital modelling is used extensively for special effects in fact and fiction films.

With film the user has to accept the rendering of the three-dimensional world that was selected by the director, including the specific sequence of 2D images. A film shot or sequence of shots may give the user the illusion of moving around in the depicted space, and camera movements and other devices may actually enhance this perceptual experience. Looking at the scenery the user may feel that some exciting or existential experience is waiting around a certain corner, but is bound by the director's decision whether or not to disclose it. This is an important part of the toolbox of the film narrator.

Interactive 3D on the other hand allows the user to turn that corner and to explore parts of the townscape not immediately visible at first. Objects may be turned around and monuments looked at from all sides. This is – we think – the crucial difference between the two types of 3D to 2D projection, and this is only possible in interactive works.

But it is a special type of interactivity. Interactive documentaries may involve interactive selection of film-like sequences in a form of interaction which, as already mentioned above, should perhaps be categorized as a type of hypertext. And other forms of user–system interaction could be included, but only if the user has the possibility of actively "entering" the depicted spaces and exploring at least part of it in depth and at will, does the work seem to deserve the term "interactive 3D documentary".

This implies the use of a digital model of the space depicted and not simply a series of a "flat" bitmaps of the projected images. But the use of such a model does not in itself imply this type of interactive 3D, since it could just as well be used to generate a film-like "pre-recorded" sequence.

Again the space depicted does not have to be photorealistic or realistic in any other sense – apart from the fact that it has length, width and depth. Moving around a highly stylized or abstract three-dimensional space would fulfil the criteria as well.

18.10 The Film Camera and the Virtual Camera of the 3D Documentary.

The physical camera is built to capture what's in front of it and is able to pan, track, tilt and zoom, and also to speed up (resulting in "slow motion" pictures) or down ("fast motion"). Its ability to function as an extension of the camera person, to be his or her eyes and body, is one of the camera's distinctive features. The built-in ability to represent or simulate reality masks the built-in distortions of the camera lens.

Creators and audiences have learned to see the world through the camera representations and distortions and have accepted this artificial view of reality as reality. And with the highly artificial principles of "continuity" "masked" as "seamlessness" (see Chapter 16) the feeling of "being there" was established as a convention hardly ever questioned when it comes to the notion of naturalism. The set of rules that apply to representing or simulating reality are constructions that we, creators and audiences alike, have come to accept as natural. The shifting viewpoints between first and third person are constructed and conceived effortlessly. And as a film audience we do not fall in and out of our engulfment due to the limitations or shortcomings of the camera's ability to cover the whole scene and fluidly shift from one position to the other following what is going on. So when we talk about filmic representations or simulations of reality, we as an audience are well conditioned to expect a very high level of credibility and plausibility. These expectations are in certain ways transferred to all media representations of reality and the actual world, which in some cases prove to be a drag to the new media.

The "virtual camera" is in a way non-existent. It is not a fixed artefact with specific properties. It has to be constructed from one production to the next and may be programmed with specific limitations as far as camera movements and shifting perspectives go. The virtual camera's range of possibilities is put to the test when it comes to notions of representation of reality, simulation, continuity, narration and *interactivity*, all of which except the latter are simultaneously closely related to film editing principles.

In many computer games that rely on a film like presentation of the game world (such as certain adventure games or role-playing games) the first person point of view is preferred in order to make room for, or for the use of, different degrees of interactivity. This is in contrast to most film representations. In film a first person view is seen as an artificial form of narration, which is normally used for very specific purposes only, since it attracts attention to the camera technique itself and is thus perceived as an expressive tool suitable for creating special effects or moods. The usual third person narrative device allows for spectator immersion and character involvement and at the same time ensures acceptability and credibility as far as representation of reality goes. And the film camera then has no problems showing the movements of the protagonist or conveying the action.

The algorithm-based virtual camera on the other hand has – historically seen – had to take into consideration and overcome some limitations of movement, continuity and range of view (as had the physical camera of the early days of film). The designer and programmer will often be placed in the dilemma of constructing camera movements and camera angles which emanate from film and which "look good" and thus hold a visual fascination, or accept the "limitations" (seen from a specific filmic point of view) and instead explore the advantages of the interactive components.

Suspending disbelief is considered to be one of the key aspects of narrative engagement; and now we are talking first and foremost about fiction. When it comes to documentary, suspension of disbelief is usually replaced by questions of authenticity, reliability, credibility and honesty. And this indeed has to do with the camera as a tool for representing the actual world as well as imposing meaning on that world. But in an interactive 3D documentary the screen images have little or no credibility in the traditional sense, seen in the context of the documentary tradition. The notion of reliability and credibility is substituted by notions of immediacy, transparency and interactivity, all of which further the expansion of mediated reality.

18.11 Time and Space

Film language has established a number of conventions regarding, among other things, time and space. In film you have a vocabulary of "how to" when it comes to dealing with time and space in regards to genre, theme, story and style. The conventions are based on the fact that the individual film has a specific running time: the actual time it takes for the viewer to watch it, or rather the time it takes for the film to run through the projector. And within this hour and a half or whatever the narrative unfolds with its own sense of time: the time frame of the story or plot. In 3D interactive spaces these two different "time frames" are substituted in certain key genres with game time, which in some way controls the user, timewise. But within this calculated time limit the "author–director" and designer has little control over narrative time, i.e. compression and expansion of time, unless they make use of *cut scenes.*

Cut scenes enhance the narrative use of time and space. They constitute a linear continuity, but at the same time take control out of the hands of the user. The user will find him- or herself "lifted out" of the game or the interactive 3D world and "put into" a movie/film, which for some may be quite enjoyable and for others rather frustrating. At the same instance the user will be "removed" from the present scene of action or from the present time (time in the present tense) and find her- or himself in other surroundings, settings or circumstances and in another time (of the day, the year, the century); maybe without the possibility of returning to the former situation/location.

In the construction of time and space some creators may be obsessed with reality and the accurate, detailed accounts of the real world and the specificity of time. So far it is difficult to create autonomous agents/avatars that live up to the demands of photorealistic representation, moving "freely" and naturalistically in space and time, satisfying the user's need for simulation. But this might not be so bad after all. The craving for realistic images of the world together with simulation and interactivity could actually hamper the development of new or alternative visual representations of reality, based on a different kind of perception and knowledge about the senses and other layers of the mind. Within this latter way of thinking the creators are free to exploit all sorts of possibilities for constructing images of reality that combine elements from an infinite variety of sources, such as painting, animation, photography, poetry, film, theatre, writing, sound art and music, and float freely between different time spheres and spaces. The advantages of 3D virtual reality are obvious: you experience the world we live in as adventurous, absurd, surreal, fantastic and consisting of many layers of reality.

The advantages of exploring alternatives to photorealism have been stressed by our colleague Bjørn Laursen in various publications (Laursen, 1997a,b; Laursen and Andersen, 1993).

18.12 Script Writing and the Creative Matrix

Is it possible to adjust the typical film script to a sort of work manual for constructing 3D interactive virtual spaces (seen in a documentary context)?

When you look at the discipline of script writing from a filmic point of view it obviously has proved its extreme importance and is a well established handicraft and art form. In *The Art and Science of Screen writing*, Parker (1998, p. 12) operationalizes the script-writing process by way of a creative matrix. The concept of a creative matrix:

> ...provides a means of seeing the various elements which make up a screenplay in conjunction with each other, without allowing any one element a determining role over all others.
>
> [...] Within the matrix, story, theme, form, plot, genre and style are seen to be the key reference points when writing a screenplay. Each of these elements will be shown to have a different weight in relation to each other, depending on which type of screenplay is being written.

Seen in connection with the New Media it seems evident that some of this might prove very useful in production design. However, one must differentiate between various screen narratives and narratives designed for inhabited 3D worlds constructed to take place in actual spaces like caves, theatrical surroundings or amusement parks. In this particular connection we are only concerned with what we might call the screen writing, and not the script writing for virtual performances in "real" theatrical spaces.

In script writing for feature films among other things you need to make sure to strike a balance "between original elements, genre parameters and the style of the narrative" (Parker, 1998, p. 165). In script writing for documentaries at times you may not even know what to expect, especially when you are working within the observational mode of production.

But when designing for 3D documentaries you have to plan carefully (for) every single detail, whatever the mode of representation. Which means that you need something similar to the elaborated script and storyboard of the fiction film, even when you are dealing with factual, observational elements.

Looking more closely at the art and science of screen writing for works of fiction, we will notice that:

> As story provides the motivational framework and is illustrated by a development of events, so theme provides the emotional framework and value system of the narrative and is illustrated by the use of repetition. (Parker, 1998, p. 19)

> In this context form is the dramatic shape of the narrative while plot is the way the story and thematic elements are dramatically revealed within this dramatic shape. (Parker, 1998, p. 21)

In this elaboration of "story", "theme", "form" and "plot" in accordance with feature film traditions we are made aware of the important differences in design and the structuring of material in the old and the new media. As far as the differences between fiction and documentary go, the picture is rather blurred when we think of the contemporary scene with its multiple choices of genres, sub-genres, hybrids and mixed formats. But we won't enter further into that particular discussion!

Clearly, one of the most important features of the New Media, the ability to hand over control of the presentation to the user (the interactivity), has no place in Parker's concept of screen writing. In order to activate the following question which the "plot" is supposed to answer, you need to reconsider the structuring of the film narrative and deconstruct it from a user interactivity point of view: "What is the most interesting way to tell the story/ies or explore this theme, within this narrative ?" (Parker, 1998, p. 24).

According to the traditional film script:

> The key purpose of the plot as a whole though is to work at the emotional level in terms of engaging the audience in the narrative's development.

It is the plot that reveals theme but it is the theme which makes a plot worth following. (Parker, 1998, p. 25)

This kind of emotional involvement paramount to film (documentary as well as fiction film) in the New Media has to be transferred to or substituted with the playfulness of interactivity, which creates another kind of engagement with the theme. The notion of plot is expanded to comprise the skills, fascinations, interests and personality of the user. Thus the designer has to construct multiple possibilities when it comes to plot structure and "accept" and arrange for open-ended storylines and narratives without conclusions or final solutions. So the prerequisite of the plot to reveal the story and thematic elements in the most interesting or engaging way is radically changed. Some users may (still) be interested in revealing a story with a beginning and an end and try to create a plot in order to do so. Other users may be engaged in the learning process, in fact-finding, in the exploration of a subject or theme. And some may interact with the virtual world for the sheer fun of playing without a specific purpose and without finding an answer or a coherence.

The emotional involvement thus has to do with the kind of interactivity invested and not so much with story, plot and the narrative, and this of course significantly influences the screen-work.

So when Parker (1998, p. 29) states that: "These three different aspects of the narrative – active questions, engagement and act structures – are the essence of screen language", we need to problematize at least the latter aspect from the point of view of the user.

Consider the notion of the *Three-Act Structure*, which takes the form *Establish* (Act 1), *Develop* (Act 2) and *Conclude* (Act 3). Within this structure the writer/creator/director of the "classic" media has a firm grip on the unfolding of the narrative. But it does not leave much room for interactive components, and thus there is no variety of choices for the user to play with.

Parker (1998, p. 25) advises that: "Themes may come and go in the development of a screenwork, but recognizing and holding on to them at the end is vital".

Again we are dealing with a complex statement of the world created from the directional point of view, which is furthermore underlined in the next passage:

> If you are working with a theme, then using the emotional power of a story's means of engaging an audience will significantly enhance the impact of the theme. (Parker, 1998, p. 96)

But when it comes to the emotional power seen from an interactive user's point of view, this has first and foremost to do with the level of immersion made possible by the system of interaction.

Within the art of script writing for fiction films, character development and emotionality, feeling/mood and atmosphere are foregrounded as a necessity for spectator involvement. The three-act structures "provide a means of understanding the development of characters, stories and ideas within the narrative, and that emotional engagement is essential for a plot to work" (Parker, 1998, p. 100).

Much of a plot's emotional power arises from the genre and style of the narrative. Audience expectations concerning a particular genre play an important role regarding emotional engagement, and various stylistic devices enhance this engagement. When it comes to "classic" Hollywood movies, character development and emotional engagement are closely connected with "continuity", timing and pace, all of which help the spectator to "effortlessly" absorb or immerse oneself in the gradually unfolding (unfolded) story. "Continuity", rhythm and tempo are essential elements of dramatic structure: rhythm as the "overall pacing of a narrative" and tempo as the "level of activity within scenes" (Parker, 1998, p. 132).

Thus the feeling of "being there" constructed by means of an unobtrusive style, a certain rhythm and tempo according to genre conventions and the type of story, naturalistic acting and photorealistic approach are characteristics of most popular audio-visual narratives. In opposition to this mode of conception, production and representation we are interested in various deviations as far as genre and style go. Among the early experiments we find surrealism and expressionism. The expressionistic approach is concerned with form in a non-naturalistic sense. And the expressionistic style is obtrusive and draws attention to itself as a style and aesthetic form. In that sense you may as an audience on one level experience the unfolding of a plot and a storyline, and on another level an expressive "commentary" pointing to the fact that this whole thing is clearly an artificial construction, and not a make-believe story for you to step right into and be absorbed by.

These characteristics relate the expressionistic approach to the more self-aware and self-reflective *reflexive* documentary mode of production and representation that creates a kind of "transparency" (in the sense that you as a spectator/user are invited, so to speak, to see through the technical or artificial devices, which are laid bare to you in a demonstrative way). Also this approach or mode creates interruptions in a flow (continuity) or deconstructs a linear storyline, conceived to seduce the spectator into believing in the complex statement about the world made by the (writer–)director of the documentary.

In an interactive 3D documentary you are not bound by these genre conventions and the demand for linearity, continuity and pacing, i.e. pacing across the narrative or within a single scene. Due to the possibilities created by interactivity the writer–director should be able to avoid problems like these facing his or her counterpart in the world of film-making:

> The importance of the tempo arises from the problem of either overloading a scene or moment – and thus making it difficult for the audience to take in all of what is being given to it – or achieving too little, in which case the attention of the audience wanders. (Parker, 1998, p. 133)
>
> [...] However, the moment this sequence of shots ends, the audience needs to be given time to relax and take in all that has happened because is has been overwhelmed. The problem is, you cannot stop the narrative. There is still something on the screen and it is a judgement call as to how long you take before the next significant piece of narrative information is provided. (Parker, 1998, p. 134)

The major limitation on the pacing of scenes and sequences is the capacity of the human brain to absorb certain levels of narrative information. The two extremes of this produce either a sensation of confusion or of boredom. (Parker, 1998, p. 134)

The challenges and advantages for the designer of multimedia works are to a certain degree linked to this particular set of problems, which in many ways can be overcome by providing sufficient interesting material for the user to interact with. In as much as the designer/creator in the new medium is met with considerations concerning narrativity, due to tradition or traditional thinking within the established media institutions, he or she is at the same time expected to free us all from the limitations of spectatorship and provide us with multiple choices with a wide range of possibilities in the form of interactivity. The quotations given above point to the idea of one evident use of the New Media: as a source of information on many levels, provided for the user in a multilayered fashion free to be explored from a personal point of view, at any time and anywhere, in an individual rhythm and tempo. The pleasure of the "narrative" is replaced by the pleasure of playful interaction (with elements representing facts, fiction or faction).

18.13 Concluding Remarks

The answer to the question posed in the title of this chapter is – as shown by the discussion in between – that the interactive 3D documentaries, as outlined, are something of all the categories mentioned: film, drama, narrative and simulation.

In singular instances these features may be mixed in varying proportions from film-like expositions to explorative simulations.

Some problems that were encountered in answering the question were actually the results of terminological ambiguities and inconsistences in terms and concepts between various disciplines and schools of thought. Sorting out the relationship between film, drama and narrative is a difficult matter for this reason, but reveals also that film and film-like presentations combine both drama and narrative in an interesting way worth exploring further. For this purpose it might be fruitful to draw on the idea of the stratified structure of works of art developed by the philosopher Roman Ingarden in the 1930s (Ingarden, 1989). This has already been applied by the author himself to novels, theatrical performances, film and music, all based on temporal organization, and some on rendering worlds and actions organized as stories.

In general the idea of drawing on filmic representations and script-writing techniques seems to be worth further elaboration, but has also been shown to have serious limitations, especially in relation to interactive 3D. Film narrative and interactive 3D are not compatible in any obvious sense. Still, using documentary and fiction film as a board to play against has revealed interesting features of the new genre "interactive 3D documentary", and this deserves further development.

References

Aarseth, E.J. (1997) *Cybertext. Perspectives on Ergodic Literature.* Baltimore, MD: Johns Hopkins University Press.

Aristotle (1946) *De Poetica.* In: *The Works of Aristotle*, translated into English under the editorship of W. D. Ross, M.A. Oxford: Oxford University Press.

Baddeley, W. H. (1975) *The Technique of Documentary Film Production.* London: Focal Press.

Barnouw, E. (1974) *Documentary. A History of the Non-fiction Film.* New York: Oxford University Press.

Chatman, S. (1978) *Story and Discourse. Narrative Structure in Fiction and Film.* Ithaca, NY: Cornell University Press.

Chatman, S. (1990) *Coming to Terms: The Rhetoric of Narrative in Fiction and Film.* Ithaca, NY: Cornell University Press.

Crawford, C. (1984) *The Art of Computer Game Design. Reflections of a Master Game Designer.* Berkeley, CA: Osborne/McGraw-Hill.

Crawford, C. (1990) Lessons from computer game design. In *The Art of Human–Computer Interface Design* (ed. B. Laurel). Reading, MA: Addison-Wesley.

Culhane, S. (1988) *Animation. From Script to Screen.* New York: St Martin's Press.

Dunnigan, J. F. (1992) *The Complete Wargames Handbook. How to Play, Design and Find Them.* New York: Morrow.

Garrand, T. P. (1997) *Writing for Multimedia: Entertainment, Education, Training, Advertising, and the World Wide Web.* Boston: Focal Press.

Grierson, J. (1971) *Grierson on Documentary.* (ed. F. Hardy). New York: Praeger.

Halas, J. (1976) *Film animation: a Simplified Approach.* Paris: UNESCO.

Halas, J. *et al.* (ed.) (1976) *Visual Scripting.* New York: Hastings House.

Halas, J. and Manwell R. (1971) *The Technique of Film Animation.* New York: Hastings House.

Harms Larsen, P. (1990) *Faktion – som udtryksmiddel* [*Faction – as a means of expression*]. Copenhagen: Forlaget Amanda.

Hayward, S. (1977) *Scriptwriting for Animation.* London: Focal Press.

Ingarden, R. (1989) *Ontology of the Work of Art: the Musical Work, the Picture, the Architectural Work, the Film.* (transl. R. Meyer with J. T. Goldthwait. Athens, OH: Ohio University Press. (Orig. German edn. 1961.)

Kau, E. (1997) Tid and rum in film and multimedier – At tænke med øjne and hænder [Time and Space in Film and Multimedia – thinking with eyes and hands]. In *Multimedieteori – de nye mediers teoriudfordringer* (ed. H. Juel). Odense: Odense Universitetsforlag, pp. 29–63.
Korolenko, M. D. (1997) *Writing for Multimedia. A Guide and Sourcebook for the Digital Writer.* Belmont, CA: Integrated Media Group/Wadsworth Publishing Company.
Laurel, B. (1993) *Computers as Theatre*, 2nd edn. Reading, MA: Addison-Wesley.
Laursen, B. (1997a) Den klassiske fortælling and den postmoderne [Classic and post-modern narration]. In *Design af multimedier* (ed. B. Fibiger). Aalborg: Aalborg Universitetsforlag, pp. 259–264.
Laursen, B. (1997b) Trække eller pege-system in multimedieinstallationen Odins Øje [Pull or point system in the multimedia installation Wothan's Eye]. In *Design af Multimedier* (ed. B. Fibiger). Aalborg: Aalborg Universitetsforlag, pp. 318–339.
Laursen, B. and Andersen, P. B. (1993) Drawing and programming. In *The Computer as Medium* (eds. P. B. Andersen, B. Holmquist and J. F. Jensen). New York: Cambridge University Press, pp. 236–262.
Levinsen, K. T. (1997) Pædagogiske erfaringer ved undervisning in multimedieproduktion [Reflections on teaching multimedia production]. In *Multimedieteori – de nye mediers teoriudfordringer* (ed. H. Juel). Odense: Odense Universitetsforlag, pp. 107–123.
Murray, J. H. (1997) *Hamlet on the Holodeck. The Future of Narrative in Cyberspace.* Cambridge, MA: MIT Press.
Nichols, B. (1991) *Representing Reality. Issues and Concepts in Documentary.* Bloomington & Indianapolis, IN: Indiana University Press.
Parker, P. (1998) *The Art and Science of Screenwriting.* Exeter: Intellect.
Rosenthal, A. (1996) *Writing, Directing, and Producing Documentary Films and Videos.* Carbondale & Edwardsville, IL: Southern Illinois University Press.
Samsel, J. and Wimberley, D. (1996) *The Interactive Writer's Handbook.* Los Angeles & San Francisco, CA: Carronade Press.
Samsel, J. and Wimberley, D. (1998) *Writing for Interactive Media. The Complete Guide.* New York: Allworth Press.
Sorlin, P. (1980) *The Film in History. Restaging the Past.* New York: Basil Blackwell.
Strothotte, C. and Strothotte, T. (1997) *Seeing Between the Pixels. Pictures in Interactive Systems.* Berlin: Springer-Verlag.
Swain, D. V. and Swain, J. R. (1988) *Film Script Writing. A Practical Manual.* London: Focal Press.
Vince, J. (1992) *3-D Computer Animation.* Wokingham: Addison-Wesley.
Wille, N. E. (1968) Fortællingens multidimensionelle verden. En studie in formalistisk litteraturteori [The multidimensional world of the narrative. A study in formal theory of literature]. In *Romanproblemer. Teorier and analyser* (eds. M. Gerlach-Nielsen, H. Hertel and M. Nøjgaard). Festskrift til Hans Sørensen den 28 September 1968. Odense: Odense Universitets-forlag, pp. 65–78.

Other Sources

Bronzealderen. Director: Carl Otto Petersen. Production: Dansk Kulturfilm in collaboration with a.o. Nationalmuseet. Copenhagen (1958) (7 min).
Gods and Heroes of the Bronze Age. Europe at the Time of Ulysses. National Museum of Denmark. 25th Council of Europe Art Exhibition [and others]. Copenhagen, Bonn, Paris, Athens (1998).
The Unexplained. FlagTower (1996) (CD-ROM).

19 Temporal Logic as a Tool for the Description of the Narrativity of Interactive Multimedia Systems

Peter Øhrstrøm

In the study of interactive multimedia systems we are obviously dealing with temporal series or structures of events. It seems natural to make a distinction between two kinds of series of events which are relevant for the study of interactive multimedia systems. Firstly, the user's interaction with the system itself constitutes a series of events, some of which are counted as past, others as present and still others as future, possible or even counterfactual. This *discourse structure* is relevant for any use of interactive multimedia systems. Secondly, the system may itself, prior to any use of it, presuppose a narrative, i.e. a structure of events, which the user comes to learn during his or her interaction with the system. Many multimedia systems presuppose such *event structures*, although they may be absent or not very interesting in other cases, for example in some strictly dictionary systems. The relations between the discourse structures and the event structures have been studied in some detail in Andersen and Øhrstrøm (1994).

In this chapter I intend to investigate the temporality of interactive multimedia systems. In particular, I shall focus on the temporal features of simulation systems. In order to build a simulation system it will be very important to have a description of the virtual scenario formulated in some appropriate formal or semi-formal language. Moreover, a notion of causality is needed. The implementation of this notion of causality must include information about which events necessarily follow from and after any possible situation in the virtual scenario of the system. Furthermore, the system must for each possible situation include information regarding the alternative possibilities that are left open for the user's choice.

Obviously, any interactive system can be described from the perspective of the system developer as well as from the user's perspective. Seen from the system developer's point of view the emphasis is probably mainly put on the study of the event structure of the virtual scenario. Seen from the user's point of view it appears more important to focus on the discourse structure, which for any given (present) situation includes a representation of the past as well as a representation of the range of future possibilities left open for the user.

In my opinion, neither discourse structures nor event structures can be studied entirely without involving some kind of formal or semi-formal representation of time and tense. In the following, I shall discuss how these series of events may be represented and studied in terms of concepts and ideas from temporal logic. The study of the relation between the temporalities in the two kinds of structures gives rise to a number of interesting problems.

In Section 19.1 I shall deal with some basic components from temporal logic which can be used for the description of interactive multimedia systems. In Sections 19.2 and 19.3, I shall discuss the temporal analysis of linear and non-linear systems, respectively. In Section 19.4 I shall intend to discuss a particular interactive simulative system in which ethical notions play an important role.

19.1 A- and B-Logic: Two Kinds of Temporal Logic

With respect to a proper description of the event structures and the discourse structures, it will be important to use the so-called A-logical notions (past, present and future) along with the so-called B-logical notions (earlier, later and "simultaneous with"). The distinction between A- and B-notions goes back to McTaggart (1927), who studied the relation between what he called A-series and B-series, respectively.

A. N. Prior was the founder of modern temporal logic. Among other things he suggested a further elaboration of McTaggart's distinction between A- and B-series. Since Prior's development of the tense-logical field in the 1950s and 1960s, logicians have been discussing the relations between A- and B-logic. Prior and his followers have argued that A-logic (often called tense-logic) is fundamental and that the notions of B-logic should be derived from the notions of A-logic. Other logicians (e.g. D. H. Mellor (1981)) have argued that the notions of B-logic should be regarded as fundamental. According to these B-theorists, tenses should be considered as mere meta-linguistic abbreviations. They simply reduce A-logic (tense logic) to a by-product of the introduction of some practical definitions into a fundamental B-logic. In other words, they see tense operators as nothing but a handy way of summarizing the properties of the before–after relations. In their opinion, the B-concepts determine the proper understanding of time and reality, and they deem tenses to have no independent epistemological or experiential status. According to the B-theorist, truth should be understood as relative to temporal instants. In their opinion, a statement is true "at an instant", and consequently the idea of "nowness" is irrelevant within logic. A. N. Prior rejected the idea of temporal instants as something primitive and objective. In fact, he claimed the reality of tenses:

> So far, then, as I have anything that you could call a philosophical creed, its first article is this: I believe in the reality of the distinction between past, present, and future. I

> believe that what we see as a progress of events is a progress of events, a coming to pass of one thing after another, and not just a timeless tapestry with everything stuck there for good and all. (Copeland, 1995, p.47)

For philosophical reasons these two kinds of temporal logic have been intensively discussed since the rise of modern temporal logic in the 1950s and 1960s. Furthermore, it can be argued that these basic ideas and their mutual relations are very important for the study of interactive systems. The structure of discourse can naturally be represented in terms of the basic A-logical notions, whereas the structure of events is more appropriately represented in terms of the basic B-logical notions. If the focus is on the user's choice, it seems straightforward to describe the use of the system in terms of A-logical notions. On the other hand, if the attention is on the totality of the system as it is in itself (independent of anything else) then the B-logical notation appears at first glance to be the more applicable. I shall, however, argue that the latter point of view is likely to by fruitless in the context of the development of interactive systems.

It was Prior's conviction that tense logic was not merely a formal language together with rules for purely syntactic manipulations. It also embodied a crucial ontological and epistemological point of view according to which "the tenses (it will be, it was the case) are primitive; only present objects exist". (Prior and Fine, 1977, p. 116) To Prior, the present and the real were one and the same concept. Shortly before he died he formulated his view in the following way:

> ...the present simply is the real considered in relation to two particular species of unreality, namely past and future. (Prior, 1972)

It is obvious that Prior was strongly attracted by questions concerning the relation between time and existence. In *Time and Modality* he proposed a system called "Q" which was specifically meant to be a "logic for contingent beings" (Prior, 1957, pp. 41 ff.). System Q can deal with a certain kind of propositions, which are not always "statable". Such propositions are particularly interesting from a tense logical point of view. The system Q also appears to be relevant for the logical description of the user's potential for communication with an interactive system. The point is that as the system is used, the communication potential grows more and more in the sense that the user gradually obtains the ability to formulate more kinds of statements. Some statements or ways of interactive use of the system, which were unstatable in the past, are now possible simply because the vocabulary has grown with new names and new concepts during the use of the system.

The event structures correspond to the B-logical notions according to which the propositions take the form "p is true at time t", where t is an element belonging to a set of times organized with a "before–after relation". This B-logical framework is often employed in the process of system development where the developers try to see the system as a whole from the outside.

However, if the system is seen from "the inside", i.e. from the user's point of view, we cannot do without the A-logical notions. In this case, we need a logical description corresponding to the inter-subjective notion of time, i.e. an A-logic (tense logic). An A-logic involves primitive tense operators for the past and the future, i.e. $P(n)q$ (read: "it has been the case n time units ago that q") and $F(n)p$ (read: "in n

time units it is going to be the case that q"), whereas q alone can be read "it is now the case that q". In terms of these basic operators we may define other operators for corresponding to "it will always be the case that ..." and "it has always been the case that...".

Within Prior's A-logic the times (instants), which are fundamental in the B-logic, are understood as rather special propositions which are only true once. In fact, all B-notions can be presented in terms of A-notions, but not vice versa, since there is no B-logical equivalent to the A-logical "now".

19.2 Temporal Analysis of a Linear System

Let us assume that we are dealing with an interactive multimedia system, but more than just a dictionary system, in the sense that it includes some kind of event structure. The representation of the narrative may be understood as a text which the user can study by means of interactive access to it. This means that the system presupposes some kind of story, which in some way has already been implemented as the crucial component of the system. Let us assume that the story can be represented as a linear sequence of events.

Even if the event structure of the system is linear, the discourse structure can be rather complicated, since the user can in principle be given access to the events in any order. In their excellent paper Keisuke Ohtsura and William F. Brewer (1992) have studied some interesting aspects regarding the relation between the event structure and the discourse structure of a narrative text. They have introduced five kinds of passages, which differ with respect to their relations between the two structures, and which can be defined as follows:

- In a canonical passage the order of the discourse structure is the same as the event structure.
- In a backward passage the order of the discourse structure is the reverse of the event structure.
- A flashback passage is canonical, but an event is omitted and given later in the narrative.
- A flashforward passage is canonical with the exception of an event, which is late in the event structure but given earlier in the narrative.
- In an embedded passage some of the events are postponed whereas the others are given in the canonical order.

Ohtsura and Brewer have tested the comprehension of different passages empirically. The subjects in these tests were 100 undergraduate university students. The results of the tests showed that flashforward passages are the most difficult to understand.

Obviously, Ohtsura and Brewer present the discourse structure as closely related to the temporal process of communication. During the discourse more and more information regarding the events (and their mutual relations) is communicated. It seems natural to relate the discourse structure to an inter-subjective notion of human time of experience, whereas the event structure seems to be on the whole independent of human cognition. The discourse structure clearly depends on the choices of the story-teller in a very straightforward way, whereas the structure of events is supposed to be reflecting a mind-independent reality. This seems even clearer when it comes to interactive systems. In this case the user is directly involved in the structure of discourse by his or her successive choices, whereas the structure of possible events is given as a crucial part of the implementation of the system prior to any use of it.

It has to be admitted that A-logical descriptions can be very complex compared with B-logical descriptions. In the case that Ohtsura and Brewer are dealing with, the event structure is just a linear order of a finite set of events. This means that the B-logical description is very simple. But even in this simple case, the A-logical description of the discourse structure becomes rather complicated. A description of the interactive use of the system is nevertheless unacceptable without A-logical concepts. Only by involving the A-logical notions may one provide a satisfactory description of the excitement, the choices, the awareness etc. which are crucial for a proper understanding of the interactive use of the system.

Prior's tense logic seems very relevant for a proper description of the use of interactive systems – even in the simple case which Ohtsura and Brewer are dealing with. A description of an interactive system alone from a B-logical point of view cannot be satisfactory, since such a description would imply the ignoring of the user's "nowness" and therefore also the proper description of the user's choice, without which the system should not be counted as interactive at all. If we, on the other hand, make a conceptual start from the Prior's tense logic (i.e. the A-logical point of view), all notions normally counted as B-logical can be defined in terms of the A-language. In this way it can be argued that A-logic is much richer than B-logic, and that the difference between the corresponding two languages is essential for the description of interactive systems.

The need for an A-logical description becomes even clearer when we turn to a temporal analysis of systems which are non-linear even from a B-logical perspective.

19.3 Temporal Analysis of Non-Linear Systems

Many interactive systems presuppose non-linear event structures. In fact, the event structures of the virtual worlds which become accessible through the interactive multimedia systems are normally non-linear. Among such systems games and simulation systems appear to be particularly interesting. As pointed out by Marie-Laure Ryan, a simulation system is not a static representations of a specific state of affairs, but

> ...a "garden of forking paths" (to paraphrase the title of a short story by Borges), containing in potentia may different narrative lines threading together many state of a affairs. Through the choices of the user, every session in the simulative system will send the history of the virtual world on a different trajectory. (Ryan, 1998, p. 4)

Here Ryan is obviously employing the notion of branching time. A. N. Prior formally developed this notion, but it had been used much earlier in literature (Øhrstrøm and Hasle, 1995, pp. 180 ff.). In the 20th century the idea of branching time has become more acceptable than it was in the 19th century. In this connection the authorship of Borges, to which Ryan refers, stands out prominently. Apparently, Borges was the first intellectual to give a detailed description of the new model of time, namely in his short story from 1941 *The Garden of Forking Paths* (in Borges, 1962). In the following I shall account for the new understanding of time anticipated and compellingly unfolded by this story.

Throughout Borges' short story the description of time as a gigantic branching system gets still more precise. Towards the end of the story we get the an explanation, according to which "The Garden of Forking Paths" is a picture, incomplete yet not false, of the universe that can be described as

> ...an infinite series of times, in a dizzily growing, ever spreading network of diverging, converging and parallel times. This web of time – the strands of which approach one another, bifurcate, intersect or ignore each other through the centuries – embraces every possibility. (Borges, 1962, p. 100)

Borges' conception of time bears many similarities to Leibniz's idea of possible worlds. The different futures represent different possibilities, and this aspect assumes a particular importance with respect to the existence of persons. Even though a person exists in one series of time, it cannot at all be taken for granted that he or she exists in another series of time. Moreover, the question about the existence of persons in the different series of time gives rise to some considerations on the extremely difficult philosophical problems concerning temporal and counterfactual identity. This problem is also relevant in the context of interactive systems like simulation systems and games, in which the user is allowed to "undo" decisions. In which sense can virtual persons, for instance in a game, be said to keep a cross-world identity? That is, how can such "persons" keep their identity in spite of the fact that they have different histories and are in mutually exclusive situations at the same date?

Borges' idea about time is represented in a literary figure, and therefore it is no wonder that a number of philosophical and logical problems remain unanswered. In particular, the question about the branching towards the past is conspicuous. How can Borges accept an idea about a branching past? What does it mean when "the web of time – the strands of which approach one another ..., intersect" (Borges, 1962, p. 100) and "Sometimes the pathways converge" (Borges, 1962, p. 98)? Does Borges actually mean that it makes sense to talk about alternative possibilities of the past in the same way as one may operate with alternative possibilities of the future? Clearly it is meaningful to talk about an alternative past in an epistemological sense, since we do not have a full or definite knowledge about the vast majority of questions about the past. This epistemological limitation is different from an ontological assumption that there be several different courses of events in the past which are equally real. However, there is hardly any evidence of such a distinction being made in Borges' story. On the other hand, it is difficult to believe that Borges would really make room for a liberty of choice regarding the past. The story repeatedly stresses the observation that the past is irrevocable. The ethical tension arises exactly out of the wilful and forced projection of this property of the past onto the future. Nobody else can repeat or alter the past.

Apparently, Borges is relying on a certain concept of "state of affairs" in his depiction of a temporal branching system. Borges' idea of state of affairs may be understood as "a snapshot". From the viewpoint of the present state of things (i.e. the present "snapshot") it is possible to imagine different past courses of events which have in various ways led to the present situation. These different pasts would be possible in so far as they among themselves make no (recognizable) contrast to the present state of affairs, for if they did we could rule some of them out.

In his development of the formal idea of branching time A. N. Prior used an idea of "a state" which differs from that of Borges. According to Prior a full description of the present includes much more than just the present "snapshot" of things as they are right now. In his opinion a complete description of the present instant should also contain information about all past states of things. Using this idea of the present instant (and of instants as such) it becomes clear that there can be no branching into the past. This was very important to Prior. He had a strong commitment to what he called "a belief in real freedom", and in his opinion one of the most important differences between the past and the future is that

> ...once something has become past, it is, as it were, out of our reach – once a thing has happened, nothing we can do can make it not to have happened. But the future is to some extent, even though it is only a very small extent, something we can make for ourselves... (Copeland, 1995, p. 48).

Prior wanted to develop an indeterministic tense-logic. Prior related his belief in real freedom to the concept of branching time. He would agree that the determinist sees time as a line, and the indeterminist sees it as a system of "forking paths". Inspired by some ideas from Saul Kripke, Prior worked out the formal details of several different systems, which constitute different and even competing interpretations of the idea of branching time. Eventually, he incorporated the idea of branching into the concept of time itself.

We may refine the intuitive picture of branching time using Figure 19.1. In this picture, it makes sense to say that for every event there is one unambiguous past. For instance, in relation to event E5, the past contains the linear arrangement of events represented by E0, E1 and E2. In relation to E5 considered as the present time, events E9 and E10 are alternative future possibilities. Relative to E5, events E4, E6 and E7 will be counterfactual; that is, if E5 is ever "realized", E4, E6 and E7 are indeed "by now" (E5) beyond possible realization. Each E-node really represents a set of events and facts; if two facts both "belong to" one and the same node, say E5, they are of course genuinely simultaneous at E5. E4, E6 and E7, on the other hand, represent a pseudo-simultaneity with E5 for what would have been real under different and counterfactual conditions.

It is, however, still possible to interpret this general idea in various ways. Prior himself worked out two different interpretations, inspired respectively by Ockham and Peirce (Prior, 1967, pp. 122 ff.). This fundamental work has led to a large number of articles in various journals. A significant number of these papers are concerned with the problem of determinism versus indeterminism. Øhrstrøm and

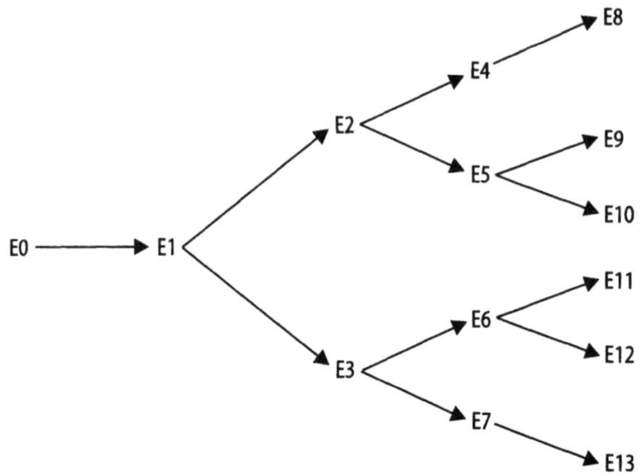

Figure 19.1

Hasle (1995) discuss in detail how indeterministic tense-logics based on the idea of branching time can be worked out.

In order to shed light on the concept of time, Prior's procedure was basically to work out different temporal systems and then to examine their logical consequences. Other researchers have taken a more "ontological approach", focusing on the concept of time itself; from an analysis of that concept, one can then construct the corresponding logic. (Needless to say, the two procedures cannot be kept strictly apart, but they do differ somewhat in their methodological consequences.) Nicholas Rescher (1968), for one, has reacted against Prior's rendition of branching time, arguing that time itself is not really branching, in spite of the fact that a wealth of possibilities for the future course of events can be found (as seen from the present). To Rescher and Urquhart (1971, p. 173), we have a "branching in time", but not "branching of time". Storrs McCall (1976), on the other hand, has argued that the passing of time is genuinely related to the understanding of time as a branching system: the passing of time is equivalent to a loss of possibilities! This observation emphasizes how the branching of time is directed towards the future only, that is, for any point in the system there exists only one possible past. Of course, the problem of the ontological status of the possible futures is a very difficult one.

It has to be admitted, however, that the representation of the idea of branching time in terms of Figure 19.1 appears to be rather B-like. This means that the branching time system is viewed from the outside. In this figure there is no representation of the present. In Øhrstrøm (1996) a different representation in terms of Charles Sanders Peirce's existential graphs has been suggested. Using this alternative representation and assuming that E5 is present we find that the relations in Figure 19.1 can be illustrated as in Figure 19.2, where a dotted enclosure stands for something in a possible future, whereas a dashed enclosure stands for the past.

I will suggest that the representation of branching time in terms of existential graphs is much more appropriate from a tense-logical point of view that the traditional representation (as in Figure 19.1). Clearly, the representation in terms of

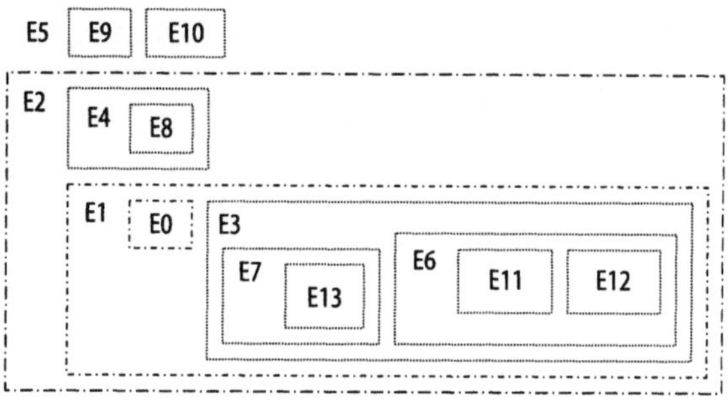

Figure 19.2

existential graphs presupposes that the present state of affairs is taken into account as such, as well as that of the past and the possible futures. In this way the representation becomes clearly A-logical. But what about the B-logical representation of the branching time system? It seems to us that strictly speaking the B-description of the system is only relevant from "God's perspective", i.e. when the system is seen from the "outside". But this kind of description is inappropriate from an ordinary human perspective, i.e. when seen from a human being who is a part of the system or who interacts with it in a causal way. Within computer science circles, the B-logical representation becomes relevant only if we want a system description corresponding to a traditional system developer who does not pay very much attention to the user's point of view. I suggest that in many cases the B-logical description is insufficient even from the system developer's point of view. In my opinion, a proper B-description would be relevant if we were creating a virtual universe completely independent of the real world and the "nowness" we experience. In many cases, however, we would like to maintain a clear relation between the real world and the virtual scenario. This is at least to some extent the case when it comes to interactive systems. This means that for such systems the virtual scenario should be seen as an extension of the real world rather than as an independent or new world. This is due to the simple fact that the unfolding of the interactive system depends strongly on the user's free choice. For this reason the virtual scenario has to share its "nowness" with the real world.

In the following section I will discuss a simulation system which is designed to simulate not only some medical reactions and processes but also the ethical perspectives related to this medical reality. It is assumed that the use of the system to a large extent can generate the same responsibility and ethical judgement as the reality that is being simulated. In this case the virtual scenario is supposed to share with the real world not only its "nowness" as such but also its present ethical values. Consequently it becomes even more evident that the virtual scenario should be seen as an extension of the real world rather than as an independent or new world.

19.4 An Example: a Simulation of a Cardiac Care Unit (CCU)

In Holm *et al.* (1999) and Holm *et al.* (2000) a computer simulation of a six-bed cardiac care unit has been described. The system has been named CARDIO. This

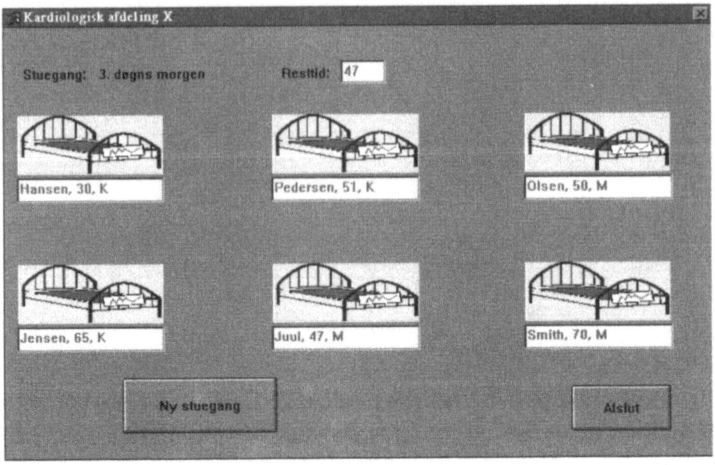

Figure 19.3 The virtual CCU in CARDIO.

simulation is based on models of a limited number of possible cardiac diseases. In this way a virtual universe has been established. It is "inhabited" with virtual patients, and it is equipped with a number of "laws of nature" as well as with a certain degree of randomness. This means that users can play the role of a doctor, in the sense that they can treat the "patients" according to their decisions. In CARDIO the reactions of a patient over time are on the whole predictable given the disease and the treatment. In this system users are actually supposed to be real-life physicians, and it is assumed that they will make decisions in the virtual scenario which are similar to the decisions they would make if they had to treat real patients in a real cardiac care unit.

The CARDIO interface (see Figure 19.3) is made as graphical as possible, although there is at present no real-time video or speech involved. Under each virtual bed there is a field displaying the name and age. Other basic information such as the pulse, blood pressure and pain level of the patient in the bed can also be found here. The interface also contains a clock displaying the remaining time for the present ward round and buttons for ending a ward round or ending the program.

The simulation can display a number of data about the individual (virtual) patient (see Figure 19.4). A picture of the patient is presented together with a field showing the patient's name, occupation and age. There is also a scrollable patient record and a continuous one-lead monitoring ECG. The patient record window is designed to give a quick overview of the state of the patient, and enable the physician to make initial decisions about further information gathering or initial treatment decisions.

The system has been developed as a possible tool for the study of ethical and other aspects of medical decision-making. It attempts to make the system quite realistic in order to make it likely that the reaction pattern of a physician who is running the system will be similar to the pattern in real life. If such a similarity can be assumed, then the simulation system provides a nice tool for the study of decisions concerning individual patients, as well as decisions concerning prioritization.

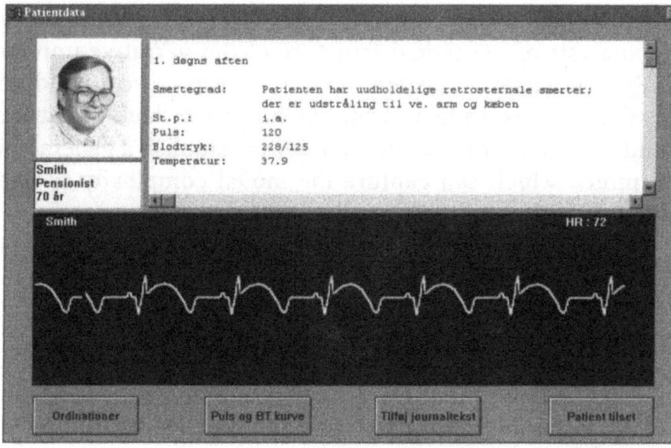

Figure 19.4 The patient record in CARDIO.

In order to obtain data relevant to the analysis of ethical values, certain decisions have been made obligatory in the simulation. The construction of CARDIO is partly based on information gathered from real life. This work has, for instance, shown that it is routine in many CCUs in Denmark to decide whether or not a given patient should be resuscitated, and whether or not the patient can be moved to an "ordinary" medical bed following each ward round. Therefore these two decisions have been made obligatory, since they provide a pointer to the priorities of the physician running the simulation.

It is very clear that this simulation system is based on a rather complicated structure of events involving a mathematical model of the development of the various diseases over time and the reaction to various possible treatments. This model corresponds to a branching time system, which is in fact a B-logical system. On the other hand, the system also gives rise to an A-logical description of the many decisions and choices the user has to carry out when running the system.

As mentioned above the need for an A-logical description makes it necessary to see the virtual scenario of a simulation system like CARDIO as an extension of the real world rather than a separate world. The understanding of the virtual scenario as an extension of the real world rather than as a new world becomes even more evident when we are discussing systems (like CARDIO) with which the ethical choice is simulated. In this case the virtual scenario not only shares its "nowness" with the real world. Some or perhaps even most of the values of ethical importance are also supposed to be shared with the real world.

It may be considered to allow CARDIO users to "undo" their decisions when they realize that a certain treatment leads to unwanted results. Such a feature would, of course, make the system a bit unrealistic. It is, however, an open question to what extent such a facility would reduce the possibilities of transferring the results regarding ethical behaviour from the virtual scenario presented by CARDIO to the scenario in a real CCU at a real hospital.

Clearly, various ideas of modality are needed in order to give a formal or semi-formal description of simulation systems like CARDIO. This topic has been thoroughly investigated by Marie-Laure Ryan (1991, pp. 111 ff.) who has published an interesting analysis of the modal structure of the narrative universe as such. According to Ryan a narrative system outlines an actual world and a number of alternative possible worlds. In fact, Ryan has suggested that at least four kinds of modality should be taken into account in order to establish a general and satisfactory semantic model which can capture the modal complexity of narrative and interactive systems:

- *K* (representing belief and knowledge)
- *O* (representing moral obligation and permission)
- *W* (representing wishes and desires)
- *I* (representing goals and plans)

All of these kinds of possible worlds seem to be relevant within the context of a system such as CARDIO. For our purpose, however, it even seems useful to make a distinction between knowledge and belief including an independent modal notion corresponding to "belief" in the description language. In the present chapter I shall limit the discussion to the use of the following modal operators:

K (read: "the agent knows that ...")
B (read: "the agent believes that ...")
W (read: "the agent wants that ...")
O (read: "it ought to be that ...")

We also need a predicate "act" which take as its arguments the set of instants and the set of possible acts, which can be carried out in the present situation. The proposition $act(i,i',a)$ is read "at the instant i the instant i' can be necessarily be obtained by performing the act a". It should be noted that the instant i' is supposed to be one time unit later than i.

Things become more complicated if several agents are involved. In this case we have to introduce references to the identities of the various agents who are active in the virtual scenario. For instance, we may use the expression $perform(x,a)$ as meaning "the agent x performs the act a".

In the case of many agents acting in the virtual scenario, we also have to relate knowledge, beliefs and wishes to the identities of the agents. This means that we'll have to use an approach slightly different from that suggested by Ryan:

$K(x,q)$ (read: "the agent x knows that q")
$B(x,q)$ (read: "the agent x believes that q")
$W(x,q)$ (read: "the agent x wants that q")

It is assumed that the description language allows quantification over the set of possible acts. Let us assume that e is a possible user with a number of ethical qualities in the sense that he actually ought to act according to any wish he may have. If this user believes that i is the present instant, and if he wants to obtain the situation i', and if there is an act for which $act(i,i',a)$, then because of this user's extraordinary ethical qualities he also ought to perform such an act now which can lead to a new instant according to his wish. In symbols:

$$(B(e,i) \wedge K(x, \exists a{:}act(i,i',a)) \wedge W(e, F(1)i')) \supset O(\exists a{:}(act(i,i',a) \wedge perform(e,a)))$$

There is obviously a lot to do in order to establish a full-fledged theory in terms of which the features of the virtual scenario can be described. A further elaboration of such a formal language is outside the scope of this chapter, but it is worth mentioning an idea that is being considered for the further development of CARDIO. According to this idea, we may want to implement virtual doctors in the CARDIO environment corresponding to various ethical positions. For instance, it seems obvious to include a strongly utilitarian doctor (u) and a strongly deontological doctor (d). In order to implement these virtual doctors, we have to define functions *util* and *deont* from the set of Priorean instants into the set of possible actions. This means, that for an arbitrary Priorean instant i, $util(i)$ and $deont(i)$ will be the well-defined actions which the two virtual doctors may choose to carry out at the present instant, i. It seems that the relation between such functions and the tense-logical setup can be formulated in the following way:

$$(i \wedge a = util(i)) \supset perform(x,a)$$

It is obvious, however, that for an agent to behave in a utilitarian manner the fulfilling of this condition is not necessary. The reason is that the user normally does not know exactly which instant is the present one since the complete state of affairs is normally unknown for the agent. Instead we have to deal with some kind of ethical reasoning based on incomplete knowledge and beliefs.

If the utilitarian agent u believes that i is the present instant, and if she knows that $a = util(i)$, then she will, if she is a genuine utilitarian, at any time carry out the calculated action, i.e.

$$(B(u,i) \wedge K(u, a = util(i))) \supset perform(u,a)$$

Similar descriptions can be formulated for the deontological agent d in terms of the *deont* function:

$$(B(d,i) \wedge K(d, a = deont(i))) \supset perform(d,a)$$

One may even be able to define other functions representing positions in between the utilitarian and the deontologist. An obvious ambition for the further development of CARDIO would be to implement a number of virtual agents with which the actual user can be compared. If such an virtual inhabited world can be successfully implemented as an extension of the real world, it will be possible to evaluate the ethical behaviour of the physician who is using the system in relation to the various ethical positions which have been implemented. However, a number of problems have to be solved before such a goal can be reached. In particular, the implementation of a satisfactory model for the user's belief and knowledge may turn out to be extremely difficult.

19.5 Conclusion

I have argued that interactive systems should be described within an A-logical manner. If we want to take the choice of the user into serious consideration a B-logical language will be insufficient. I have also argued that interactive systems share their "nowness" with the real world, for which reason the virtual scenarios of interactive systems ought to be seen as extensions of the real world and not as independent worlds. Moreover, I have argued that this conclusion becomes even more evident if we are dealing with simulation systems such as CARDIO in which the focus is on ethical behaviour and ethical values. Finally, we have also seen that in order to describe the kind of features which could be imagined for the further development of systems like CARDIO a number of modal operators will be needed in addition to the basic Priorean tense logic. Obviously there is still a lot to do in order to establish such a tense-logical description language which can be used for the description of the narrativity of interactive multimedia systems. It seems rather clear, however, that such a tool can be introduced in detail within the Priorean tradition of modal and tense logic.

Acknowledgements

The ideas presented in this chapter are related to research in progress together with Per Hasle and Søren Holm, to whom I am indebted for important comments.

References

Andersen, P. and Øhrstrøm, P. (1994) *Hyperzeit, Zeitschrift für Semiotik* 16(1–2): 51–68.

Borges, J. L. (1962) *Ficciones*. New York: Grove Press.

Copeland, J. (ed.) (1995) *Logic and Reality: Essays in Pure and Applied Logic in Memory of Arthur Prior*. Oxford: Oxford University Press.

Holm, S., Øhrstrøm, P., Rossel, P. and Pedersen, S.A. (2000) Cognitive studies of ethical reasoning based on the KARDIO-simulator. In *Mathematical Modelling in Medicine*, IOS Press, pp. 217–227.

Holm, S., Øhrstrøm, P. and Donner, C. (1999) KARDIO – A simulation of a cardiac care unit intended for the study of the ethical components of medical decision-making. In *Proceedings of the 12th International Florida AI Research Society Conference*, Orlando, FL. Menlo Park, CA: AAAI Press.

McCall, S. (1976) Objective time flow. *Philosophy of Science* 43: 337–362.

McTaggart, J. M. E. (1927) *The Nature of Existence*, ii. Cambridge: Cambridge University Press.

Mellor, D. H. (1981) *Real Time*. Cambridge: Cambridge University Press.

Øhrstrøm, P. (1996) Existential graphs and tense logic. In *Conceptual Structures: Knowledge Representation as Interlingua* (eds. P. Eklund, G. Ellis and G. Mann). Berlin: Springer-Verlag, pp. 203–217

Øhrstrøm, P. and Hasle, P. (1995) *Temporal Logic. From Ancient Ideas to Artificial Intelligence*. Boston: Kluwer Academic.

Ohtsura, K. and Brewer, W. F. (1992) Discourse Organization in the Comprehension of Temporal Order in Narrative Texts. *Discourse Processes* 15: 317–336.

Prior, A. N. (1957) *Time and Modality*. Oxford: Oxford University Press.

Prior, A. N. (1967) *Past, Present and Future*. Oxford: Clarendon Press.

Prior, A. N. (1972) The notion of the present. In *The Study of Time*, Vol. I (eds. J. T. Fraser, F. C. Haber and G. H. Müller). Berlin: Springer-Verlag, pp. 320–323.

Prior, A. N. (1995) Some free thinking about time, Box 7, Bodleian Library, Oxford. In *Logic and Reality: Essays in Pure and Applied Logic in Memory of Arthur Prior* (ed. J. Copeland). Oxford: Oxford University Press, pp. 47-51.

Prior, A. N. and Fine, K. (1977) *Worlds, Times and Selves*. London: Duckworth.

Rescher, N. (1968) Truth and necessity in temporal perspective. In *The Philosophy of Time* (ed. R. Gale), London: Macmillan, pp. 183–220.

Rescher, N. and Urquhart, A. (1971) *Temporal Logic*. Berlin: Springer-Verlag.

Ryan, M.-L. (1991) *Possible Worlds, Artificial Intelligence, and Narrative Theory*. Bloomington & Indianapolis, IN: Indiana University Press.

Ryan, M.-L. (1998) *Cyberage Narratology. Computers, Metaphor and Narrative* (unpublished)

SECTION 5

Methods for Designing Interactive Inhabited Virtual Worlds

Introduction

Kim Halskov Madsen

Whereas the previous sections have addressed a set of issues concerning how to come to grips with the nature of virtual inhabited 3D worlds, this concluding section is concerned with some of the methodological challenges that multimedia production people face.

Chapter 20 considers the interface and the experience of the user and addresses the methodological issues when designing an entire application, the mcpie. The mcpie is an interactive installation questioning control in human–computer interaction. Chapter 21 addresses the very specific question of how software engineers work with the task of designing the interactive aspect of software as illustrated by how three designers solve a classical software specification problem – the lift control problem. Finally Chapter 22 takes us into the business domain of multimedia production and discusses process management issues when handling both the software and the content aspect of multimedia production.

All three chapters share the common characteristic that they take an empirical study as point of departure – but of quite different nature. Skov and Stage (Chapter 21) have set up an experiment in a lab-like setting where three individual software engineers, within a time frame of hours, are given the task of solving the lift control problem using three different software engineering paradigms. Although Skov and Stage primarily take a qualitative approach they also to some extent do quantitative analysis, for instance by counting the number of concepts used in various categories during the design of the process-architecture. In Chapter 20, Horn, Svendsen and Madsen provide an analysis of a four-month multimedia production process in a university setting which took as its starting point a fairly loose idea of an interactive multimedia installation. The analysis offered in this chapter is primarily concerned with how the product is shaped throughout a series of experiments. Rosenstand, in Chapter 22, takes us out into industry, where he starts out from an analysis of the insight he has gained through interviews of a large number of multimedia practitioners. In this way the three chapters takes the reader from the world of software engineering in the direction of where the software industry meets the media industry.

The methodological approaches of the first two chapters each represent the two main traditions within information systems design, i.e. the system-oriented approach and the experimental approach. According to the system-oriented approach, design is a matter of transforming a set of specifications into the software implementing the application, whereas the experimental tradition has taken the position that product quality is established in processes of experiments in use like settings. In the former tradition quality is a matter of whether the software fulfils the specifications, whereas in the latter tradition quality evolves during the process through a series of encounters between the user and sketches and prototypes. Chapter 22 offers the additional tradition of business and management, where quality is seen as a parameter strongly dependent on time and resources. In particular, Rosenstand makes the claim that quality must be defined as part of the business contract, but he also points out the fact that the narrative quality, i.e. the quality as experienced by the user, is of a rather subjective nature.

One of the main conclusions made by Skov and Stage is that when it comes to the design of the dynamic aspect of interactive systems the object-oriented paradigm may benefit from a combination with the declarative paradigm and the principles of operating systems design. The message of Horn, Svendsen and Madsen is that using a diverse set of materials in a series of experiments is a key factor in creative multimedia design. Rosenstand argues that when the software industry merges with the media industry the management strategy must be reconsidered. In addition he suggests how the production of different types of narrative multimedia systems must be managed in different ways.

Clearly much can be learned from both the traditional software industry and the media industry when producing 3D multimedia products. The challenge of the future is to transform the practices of the past in a way where the new circumstances are taking into account without dismissing the wisdom of the two industries and domains of research.

20

Experimental Design of an Interactive Installation

Bjarne Horn, Ernest Holm Svendsen and Kim Halskov Madsen

In this chapter we start out from the notion of an experimental design approach which emphasizes the importance of experimenting, throughout the design process, with different kinds of design representations in a use-like context. Such approaches to design have been particular successful in the domain of design for work settings, as reflected in book titles such as *Design at Work* (Greenbaum and Kyng, 1991), and particularly successful when it comes to setting up design processes where end-users actively take part; see also Schuler and Namioka (1993). As the conceptual platform for introducing the idea of experimental systems development we apply Schön's (1983, 1988, 1992) theoretical but strongly empirically grounded conceptual framework.

In the main part of the chapter we report on the compelling use of an experimental approach to the design of an interactive installation questioning control in computer-based human–nonhuman interaction. Through motion capture equipment a person's movements are used to interact in real time with a virtual 3D figure (the mcpie) projected on a 3 × 2 metre screen. A related piece has been produced by Krueger (1983). The design of the mcpie has been part of the *Digital Theatre*, a collaborative research effort between the Department of Dramaturgy and the Department of Information and Media Science, Aarhus University. The Digital Theatre (`http://www.daimi.au.dk/sdela/dte/`) is an exploration in the domain of multimedia performance of the use of motion capture technology, 3D animated worlds, projection technology and other kinds of new information technologies. The mcpie installation was set up in the foyer at the Kasernescenen in Aarhus, Denmark, during the presentation of "Bodybuilding – a 3D poem", a stage performance that took place from 4–6 June 1999.

Motion capture equipment is a technology which enables the identification of the position of an object or a person in 3D space. In the specific case we have used the MotionStar wireless capture system from Ascension Technology Corporation (`http://www.ascension.com/`), which is a system based on active sensing by applying electromagnetic sensors whose positions and orientations are detectable in a magnetic field. MotionStar wireless components include sensors, a unit for data processing, and an external range transmitter for emitting detectable magnetic fields. The MotionStar star system is an active sensing system as opposed to a passive sensing system; see Chapter 11. The core element of a passive sensing system is the use of visually reflecting markers on the body and one or more cameras recording 2D pictures. Dedicated software calculates the 3D position of markers based on the position of the cameras and the corresponding images recorded by the cameras. Computer vision research has tried to move in the direction of passive sensing systems that work without the use of markers. Motion capture equipment has been widely used as a cost-effective way of creating computer animations in games and films (Thalmann and Thalmann, 1996), but is also being used for a large range of other kinds of applications, e.g. biomechanical studies.

The mcpie installation is unique compared with the conventional kinds of product previously developed applying an experimental approach:

1. Rather than using a standard interface consisting of monitor, mouse and keyboard, the interaction is based on motion capture gear.
2. The system is not designed as a tool for a work setting but as an artistic piece.
3. The system is not designed for any particular profession, but for people in general.

20.1 Experimental Design

According to Schön (1983, 1988, 1992) the design process is a "kind of experimentation that consists in reflective 'conversation' with materials of the design situation" (Schön 1992, p. 135). The interaction with materials is a conversation between the designer and the materials in a metaphorical sense. For instance when "working in some visual medium... the designer sees what is 'there' in some representation..., draws in relation to it, sees what has been drawn, thereby informing further designing" (Schön, 1992, p. 135). Keeping with the metaphor, the materials talk back to the designer, which guides further moves and the process becomes one where the designer sees, moves while taking account of the previously unanticipated result of his moves, and sees. The move causes the designer to appreciate things in the situation that goes beyond his initial perception of the problem. The designer shapes the situations and "...plays his game to a moving target, changing the phenomena as he experiments" (Schön, 1983, p. 153).

The designer works selectively in different materials experimenting with different aspects of his design at different stages in the design process. The design representations may facilitate experimentation at low risk and cost by eliminating or inhibiting the constraints of the built world. In this way, several alternatives can be easily created and explored. The designer is able to move in the virtual world and experience what it would be like in the real world. Events that take a long time in the built world can be made to happen immediately in the virtual world, and variables that are interlocking in the built world can be separated from one another in the virtual world. "But the virtual world of drawing can function reliably as a context for experiments only insofar as the results can be transferred to the built world" (Schön, 1983, p. 159).

When it comes to software design one of the advantages is that software itself is a very flexible material for creating design representations in terms of prototypes; see for instance Budde *et al.* (1984). Another kind of design representation that has proved particularly productive in the domain of software design is "mock-ups" which are design models built from non-digital materials, e.g. cardboard and paper. Ehn and Kyng (1991) report how they early on in the UTOPIA project used cheap materials like paper, slide projectors and cardboard boxes to mock-up the computer technology for newspaper page make-up. As in industrial design the benefits of using mock-ups in software design include:

1. They encourage practical experiments.
2. They are cheap; hence many alternatives can easily be created and explored.
3. They are easy to modify on the spot (Ehn and Kyng, 1991, pp. 172 ff.).

Another important issue in design is that of context. Since successful design requires a match between the future system and its context we need to have representations of the future context of use as well – we need to mock-up the context as well, so to speak. A way to address the issue of context is working with scenarios. Scenarios are different from conventional representations like data structures and data flow by focusing on the context of use of the computer system and the interaction between the two. Or in John Caroll's (1995, p. v) words: "When we design systems and applications, we are, most essentially, designing scenarios of interaction". The definition of what constitutes a scenario has been a much debated issue, but as observed by Kuutti (1995, pp. 20 ff.) there seems to be a general agreement that:

1. A scenario describes a process or a sequence of acts.
2. A scenario refers to a situation or an episode.
3. A scenario is a sequence of actions.
4. A scenario represents the system as seen from the users' point of view.

A much more debated issue concerns whether a scenario is an external description of what a system does or whether a scenario sees the system in a much broader context of use.

20.2 Designing the mcpie

Having introduced these general issues regarding experimental design, we provide, as seen through the lens of Schön's conceptual framework, an account of how the mcpie has been designed using such an approach. As already mentioned, the mcpie is an interactive installation questioning control in computer based human-nonhuman interaction. Through motion capture a user's physical movement is used to interact in real time with a figure (mcpie), which responds to the interaction according to its own will and interest in the user and so appears to be a self-reliant

Table 20.1 Overview of the design process.

1.	The original idea
2.	The first video brainstorm
3.	Technological and aesthetic experiments
4.	Another video brainstorm
5.	The user's perspective
6.	Structuring the interaction
7.	Video user study
8.	2D prototype in Director
9.	Version 1
10.	Version 2

figure with which a user can engage in a communicative process. Table 20.1 offers a brief overview of the design process.

20.2.1 The Original Idea

The idea for the mcpie project actually came out of an entirely different project altogether. We were working with motion capture equipment, considering using it as a foundation for an animated user interface to an interactive fiction engine that we had created, when we were introduced to the Bouncy project at the University of Aalborg (see Chapter 9). Bouncy is a virtual dog, capable of responding to simple hand gestures and sound through a data glove and a microphone. The interaction, however, is based on a simple causal system, and we wanted to experiment with a more complex style of interaction, involving a user's entire body and installing a will of its own into the virtual figure. Over the cause of a few meetings, this idea came into shape as the concept of a virtual self-reliant being, projected on a large screen. A user would interact with this figure through physical movement, exploring the emotions of the figure – its different moods, levels of interest and general activity.

20.2.2 The First Video Brainstorm

Having established this idea as our foundation, we began considering the design and behaviour of the figure through a series of brainstorming sessions. In the first one, we used an overhead projector and a video recorder to quickly sketch and capture ideas we could work with later (see Figure 20.1). By drawing on transparencies and moving them about on the projector we could simulate a very rough approximation of how the system could be set up and experimented with freely, trying out new ideas as they occurred and immediately getting a feel for them. In this way we produced a number of ideas that were later implemented in the final system. We experimented with having the figure's eyes follow the user's movements, making it wave back, projecting it on the ceiling and suddenly zooming in to make it fill up the entire screen. We did this using multiple sheets of transparent plastic, each with a part of the figure drawn on them. For instance we used two

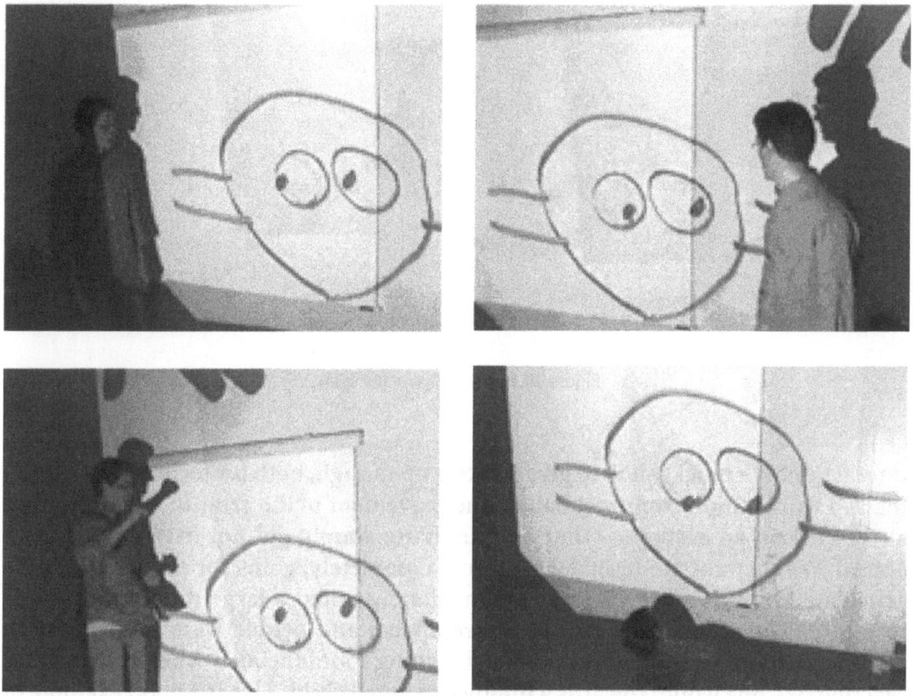

Figure 20.1 Early mock-up.

sheets to make the figure's eyes follow the user, one with the pupils of the eyes and one with the rest of the figure, and then one of us would move the sheets around (see Figure 20.1). For waving we used another sheet with an arm, which we were then able to move independently of the body of the figure.

This first very simple technique was in fact the easiest-to-work-with mock-up we created in the series of tests and setups we did towards the final installation. Its ease of use combined with its strong power of visualization generated a number of ideas that we would probably never have thought of had we just been sitting by a table, talking things over.

20.2.3 Technological and Aesthetic Experiments

On the basis of the ideas generated in this session we had a rough estimate of what the figure should be able to do. We therefore went on modelling our first prototype in the 3D-programming environment we were working with, Alias Wavefront: Maya™ (`http://www.aw.sgi.com/`) to begin technological and design experiments right away.

During the course of design, we worked with two very different versions of the virtual figure. The first one was made primarily of spheres and cylinders (Figure 20.2). It also had arms, which we wanted to use as an extra support in the user

Figure 20.2 Early version of the figure.

interaction. We quickly had to give this one up though, both for technical reasons – the SGI workstation could not handle the movement of the arms in real time – but also based on an aesthetic criterion: the figure simply did not have enough user appeal. We therefore redesigned the figure completely, going for a cuter and more articulated look (Figure 20.3), and immediately noted a large difference in user response. The second one had far more appeal and people were more eager to attract its attention and interact with it, laughing spontaneously when seeing it and reacting like one would towards a puppy or a small child. This is a good example of the immeasurable factors of a design that play an important part but which are very much of a qualitative nature. Our experiences here are very much in line with observations made by Mogensen (see Chapter 5) about the significance of considering the aesthetic aspects when creating an experience of autonomy. Since the mcpie is not a tool to be used in a particular work setting, decisions as to when it "works" cannot be tested against the particular work practice that the system is

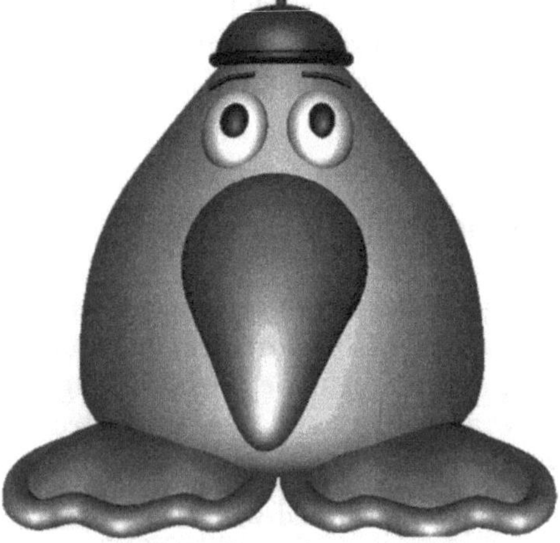

Figure 20.3 A cuter and more articulated look.

intended to support or improve. Instead, such decisions are primarily based on the designer's feel for the product and a general sense of users' responses. In our case, the users' reactions played a vital role in the success of the entire project, and we were consequently eager to find a design that as many users as possible found appealing. We believe we found one, but even now it is hard to say precisely why it works – it simply does.

20.2.4 Another Video Brainstorm

With a prototype of the virtual figure well on the way, and still experimenting with the technology, we were now able to do another video brainstorm. This time we involved a "test user", that is, a person experiencing the mocked up system for the first time and giving us feedback through her actions and explaining her thoughts and experiences (Figure 20.4). Since no system was implemented and we only had a rough sketch of its interface, we simulated the computer's responses through a technique named after the Wizard of Oz (Kelley, 1983). The Wizard of Oz technique is a prototyping technique where a human being is simulating the computer behind the screen.

During this session we realized that the actions of the figure had a tremendous impact on the user interacting with it. The process of interaction went both ways – it was not just the figure responding to the users' actions – the user responded equally to the figure's behaviour.

Out of this the issue of control came up: who controls who in the process of interaction, and how does the response of the computer system affect the user's next actions? This quickly became the main topic of our continued examination and we decided to do some enquiries into the field of basic behaviourist psychology to find a theoretical framework for the issues. We came out with a few central topics that could be used as an overall framework for the interaction design – the primary concept being the behaviourist notion of shaping. The idea is that you can affect the behaviour of animals as well as humans by positive reinforcement. This in turn brought up a number of new questions, primarily: what is positive feedback for the user? And is it technologically possible to support gesture recognition at a level that

Figure 20.4 User test.

is precise enough for the shaping to work; that is, to make focused feedback possible at all times?

20.2.5 The User's Perspective

To answer these questions and to get a bit closer to a final design solution, we needed a better idea of what kind of users we were designing for and how they would experience the setting. Since we were not designing a system to improve an already existing tool or in some other way had a work situation that we could study, we had to use our imagination to try to put ourselves in the user's place once the installation was set up. This led to two documents, a "user's perspective" and a "design scenario"; see Figs. 20.5 and 20.6. The two documents represent the vision of mcpie as the installation was imagined at that particular point in the process.

Working with the project from the user's perspective in this way drew our attention to a number of issues that we realized we had not yet considered properly. Most of them were minor things; however, one issue needed clarification: for the shaping to work, the user had to be given the impression that by trying just a little bit harder she would get her reward. We therefore had to find a way to convey to the user that she was "close" to some sort of payoff, without the payoff actually being evoked. Our solution became the foreshadowing of actions with others, for instance a gentle bobbing before a complete somersault. We felt confident that the user trying to attract the figure's interest and the tricks that the figure would perform if the user performed well would be sufficient to serve as positive feedback for the shaping.

20.2.6 Structuring the Interaction

Our first shot at a set of system specifications revolved around the notion of phases. We divided the system into four distinct phases, each with its own purpose in the process of shaping the user:

1. First you have to catch his interest, make him move from below the edge of the screen to the middle.
2. Secondly you have to move about a lot if the figure is not to lose interest and leave below the edge of the screen again.
3. After a while even this gets boring, and now all the figure really cares about is you getting closer to patting your head – which he really likes.
4. When you succeed in patting your head, his mission is completed, and the figure will vanish in the virtual distance of the screen.

The motivation behind these phases was all along to be able to shape users into jumping about like a madman and eventually patting themselves on the head, which would, if successful, allow us to make our claims about the computer literally controlling the user. The first phase was intended to be very easy, to establish a feeling of control in the user: if you moved your arms upward, the figure would move towards you. After this was completed we figured we could use the notion of "extinction" to make the user frantic for a few seconds, just so that we would get some movement. In this phase any movement at all would make the figure happy.

User Perspective
g1: "Using motion capture as interface"
Ernest Holm Svendsen, Bjarne Horn

Due to the special nature of our project, this will not be a user study in the classic sense. It will rather be a description of the project seen from the user's perspective.

The setting
The setting is an installation in a large room, with other artistic activities going on. An audience is drifting about in the room, speaking softly and experiencing the different installations.

Our installation is positioned in a corner, and consists from the user's point of view primarily of a large screen (min. 5 by 3 meters), a computer with an operator and a backpack with sensors attached to it. The installation is dimly lit, to add an intimacy to the experience, as well as to make the projection stand out clearly.

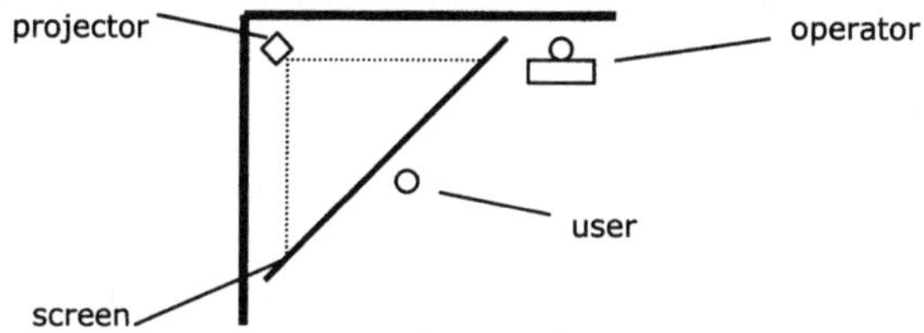

The user

The user is a younger person without much experience with computers (?) apart from the basic word processing and perhaps an occasional computer game or two. The user is open to experiencing and experimenting with the installation.

To try out the installation, the user has to wear a motion-capture pack. This is a psychological boundary that the user has to cross, and will be likely to ensure that the users are indeed willing to experiment openly. The process of getting the equipment strapped on is a process that will automatically filter away uninterested users.

To attract users it will probably be necessary to have a pre-made animation of our creature running on the screen. When potential users stop to figure out what the installation is about, the operator can approach them and invite them to try it out.

Putting on the motion-capture pack involves wearing a backpack and having three sensors attached to your body: one on the head (wearing a cap) and two others on your wrists (Velcro). Before the interaction begins the user has to stand over a mark on the floor for a few seconds so that the computer can locate her precisely.

The interaction
During this initiation, the creature has disappeared from the screen. But now that the user is ready, he reappears at the very bottom of the screen, only his top visible. The user now approaches him and tries through movement to attract his attention and get him to come out in the open. She quickly learns that what is needed is large movement to attract him. He comes out and interacts with her for a while – when she jumps, he jumps etc. At this point a small crowd of spectators has gathered, and are enjoying the event, possibly suggesting things for the user to do. If she has friends with her, they certainly do. At one point, she turns around to face the spectators, and as she does so, she is confused by laughter among them. Her friends explains, that when she turns her back, the creature comes very close to the screen, looking at her, but she can only catch a glimpse of this when she turns back.

The creature, however, begins to lose interest after a short while. The user continues her effort to attract his attention, and realizes that he appears especially interested in the movement of her right arm. She waves it a little, and gets a reaction, and after a while she finds, that what he really likes is when she pats herself on the top of her head - he does somersaults and flips around. Suddenly, however, he loses interest altogether and leaves.

Figure 20.5 User's perspective.

Design Scenario
g1: "Using motion capture as interface"
Ernest Holm Svendsen, Bjarne Horn

Louise is a 2nd year student of dramaturgy at the University of Aarhus. She has read a notice on a bulletin board at the institute which says that an event involving the institute is taking place today, investigating "inhabited 3D spaces", and has heard from one of her lecturers that it involves a combination of computer projections and actual set design in a number of installations. She has invited her friend, Lisbeth, to join her visit at the event.

They enter the big hall with a lot of other visitors wandering about looking at and trying out different installations. As they too walk about, Louise's eye is caught by a cute figure moving on a large 5 by 3 metres screen in one corner of the hall. They walk over to the screen and look at the figure for a while, trying to find out what it is about. An operator is sitting by a computer next to the large screen, and Louise asks him what the installation is about. He briefly explains that one can interact with the figure using motion, and asks if Louise is interested in trying it. With a little laugh she says "Okay".

The operator now brings a small backpack with three wires attached to it. He helps her put it on and attaches the wires to her wrists and a cap that she places on her head. He then points to a cross on the floor and asks her to stand there for a second. Then he goes to the computer, presses a few keys and tells her "Okay, you can start now."

"What am I supposed to do?" Louise asks. "I don't know... Whatever you feel like – try to get him to come out" the operator says, pointing to the bottom of the screen, where Louise now notices the rotating propeller on the figure's head.

"Well...", she says, laughing again, "okay...". She steps a bit closer and waves her arms, obviously feeling a little strange about it. But then she sees that her movement has made the figure come up a little to look at her. She moves some more, and he comes out completely, his eyes following her.

"Hey, it works", her friend Lisbeth says. "He's watching you!" As the figure comes out and starts to respond to her actions, Louise forgets her initial uncomfortable feeling. She moves about, waving her hands, and the figure moves with her. She jumps and he jumps, looking very happy. At one point, as she moves very quickly from one side of the screen to the other, he moves up and down a few times, and then makes a complete somersault, which both the girls and the people that have gathered around find very amusing. Louise tries to make him do it again by repeating her action, but he doesn't seem very interested any more. She tries to jump, but he doesn't respond to that any more either, and his eyes begin to look in other directions. "Oh, now he's bored", Louise says, lifting her hands. That seems to catch his interest though, and makes him move a bit closer. She lifts her hands again, and he moves up and down, just like before he did the somersault earlier. She lifts her hands up high, and he moves up and down again, a little quicker. When she does something else, he loses interest, but as soon as she lifts her hands he responds.

After a while, he stops responding to just lifting the hands though, and only jumps up and down when she waves one hand over her head. The more she moves the hand, the more he jumps, until finally, as she moves her hand up and down in a straight line above her head, he does the somersault.

"He did it!", Lisbeth says. "Yes", Louise says, as the figure loses interest in her completely and after a short while disappears into the distance.

...cut...

Figure 20.6 Design scenario.

After generating a predefined amount of movement, phase and focus would shift once again, this time towards the goal of actually making users pat their head. We used an approach where initially any movement of a hand close to the head would make the figure happier, and then gradually increasing the demands toward the user, until only a distinct pat on the head would get a reaction from the figure.

20.2.7 Video User Study

We were now ready to do another prototype session, once again using the Wizard of Oz technique and a new set of users. Until now we had suspected that users would respond very differently when placed in front of a large screen with an orange figure on it, some would bounce around like the user in our earlier video brainstorm and some would be more timid. This suspicion was confirmed when we conducted the prototype session. The second set of users were far more reluctant to use their whole body in the interaction; mostly they resorted to attempting direct manipulation of the figure with their index finger – something which neither we nor the figure were particularly happy about. The users' reluctance to really move around was cause for concern in our project, and something we wanted to address before the final installation.

20.2.8 2D Prototype

After having reconsidered our specifications based on the input we got from the prototype session, we decided to implement a prototype in Macromedia Director instead of starting with a full-fledged Maya™ version (Figure 20.7). We wanted to work on the balance of the different phases to make them appear as coherent as possible to the user, to define its different states and the progression of the system. We chose to work in Director mainly because we are more familiar with that environment. A lot of tweaking and elaboration of the initial specification was done during the work on this 2D version of the project. For instance, while working with the mock-up we implemented a "shyness" in the creature, a new concept that subsequently generated ideas about arrogance for the creature and the possibility of implementing a gesture that would tell the creature to go away – the figure would respect this for a short while, but then forget about it – all through manipulation of the basic "shyness" property.

Figure 20.7 Prototype in Macromedia Director.

20.2.9 Version 1

With the results from the mock-up we could finally go on to an actual implementation of the system in our 3D environment. After converting what we made in the 2D prototype to a 3D version, we learned an important lesson about the importance of interface and presentation. When we worked with the 2D version there were some things we could not do easily, such as detailed experiments with the figure's facial expressions and the motion pattern, but we decided that "when we do this in 3D, it will work". Also we assumed when using the mouse and keyboard as the interface in the 2D mock-up instead of the actual motion capture equipment that some tweaking would be enough for the same actions to work in 3D. As the 3D version neared completion, unfortunate signs were showing. The differences between 2D and 3D, and between motion captured gestures and mouse and keyboard, are much larger than we had anticipated, and what had seemed reasonable simply did not work. In particular we found, by using the system ourselves, but primarily by having a user try out a beta version, that the rigid structure of phases and progression was not conveying the impression that you could actually influence the figure. Because of the rigid structure, it was hard to use it without knowing this particular structure – so a user who did not know anything about the underlying structure simply did not get any response from the system, quickly dismissing it as boring. We could have tried lower thresholds for when a "wave" is a wave, and thus make it easier for a user to get a response from the system. This, however, would create new problems for the shaping part of the experiment, and we decided that we had to make more fundamental changes.

We realized that for an interaction that is more of a communicative event than a rigid and rule-based point-and-click structure, it has to be very free and fluid indeed. The key thing was to make the computer act as little like a computer as possible, which translated into hiding all signs of the rules controlling the "life" of the figure.

20.2.10 Version 2 – the Final One

So in a sense we ended up returning to the idea that had originally spawned the entire project: the engine for creating interactive fiction. Inspired by the work of Peter Bøgh Andersen (Andersen, 1997, 1998), this original system had been based on the notion of a "primordial soup". The idea was that instead of viewing an interactive fiction as a puzzle, where four good stories has been cut up and mixed, and in which it is the user's job to recreate one or more of the stories, one should rather create a soup of story elements – potential stories. It would be a universe living a life of its own, whether the user is active in it or not, which can only be influenced indirectly by the user's actions – a user is just another element in the universe; a "primordial soup" holding the possibility of a theoretically infinite number of stories emerging through a sequence of interaction outside the total control of user as well as of teh author. There are a number of problems with this metaphor of course, but for accomplishing the task of bringing fluency into the project at hand, using the "primordial soup" metaphor seemed an appealing possibility.

Instead of basing our system on phases, we built a new version that consists of a number of dynamic force fields (Andersen, 1997), which are able to both attract and reject each other. These fields indirectly and dynamically control the attention of the figure (which is represented in the system as just another field), his mood, where he is positioned, where he is going and how fast he is going there. If no user is using the system, the figure seems to have a life of its own, playing with its bat or hiding behind a tree, two artefacts that we introduced into his world to serve exactly this purpose of giving him something to do on his own. When a user is interacting he or she is treated by the system as another field, the most significant difference of which from the others is that it cannot be physically manipulated by the system. This user-field then influences the other fields based on some simple rules; if the user jumps, for instance, the figure might jump if it is happy, but if it is sad, or if the user keeps jumping a number of times, it will quickly lose interest and respond less. As long as it is interested, however, it will also follow the user, watching as the user moves and moving with the user, sometimes eagerly, sometimes a little timidly. If the user does nothing of interest for a while, it will begin playing with its toys and as time goes by and it gets to "know" the user, it will demand more activity to be interested. In this way its responses vary over time in this new version of the system as well, but now in a far more dynamic and fluent way than the rigid phases used earlier. Our concern about the users' reluctance to move was alleviated by the added fluency, as it turned out that small reactions from the figure encouraged users to move about more to get even bigger reactions. In order to shape the user, the new version also has the figure doing tricks (pirouettes, somersaults, cartwheels etc.) trying to gently push the user in the direction of eventually patting him- or herself on top of his or her head.

During the period in which the system was set up it was used by a number of different users, and we adjusted it many times, improving minor parts in response to our observations. We quickly realized that the motion capture equipment was not precise enough for the gesture recognition to work optimally. We therefore had to give up the shaping, which was totally dependent on exact recognition of gestures, and chose instead to focus our attention on the aesthetic/entertainment issues, improving this part of the system and gathering very interesting empirical data. It is not the focus of this chapter to discuss these data in any detail, but the general issues that surfaced revolved around the use of the body as an interface; the different ways in which users respond to a completely new interaction setting and from which fields of experience they draw their material; the relation between the user and the audience; the balance between confusing and rewarding users to keep them interested; and finally the users' enormous desire to generate rules about the system and interpret causality between actions that are, from the system's point of view, totally unrelated. Very interesting fictions were brought about in this way: users talked to the figure, danced with it, flirted with it, tried to scare it, felt sorry for it, made friends with it and annoyed it – they extracted a world of personality out of it that was never there, but which made the system a great success from an aesthetic point of view.

20.3 Concluding Overview of the Process

The design of mcpie may be seen as a series of experimental activities through which ideas have emerged and shaped mcpie. Table 20.2 shows an overview of the main activities and illustrates how the use of various materials and techniques were instrumental in the development of mcpie.

Table 20.2 Activities and use of materials and techniques.

Experiments	Key ideas
The original idea	The idea of the project was sparked by two other systems.
The first video brainstorm: Drawings on transparencies and use of overhead projector.	The figure's eyes follow the user's movements, making it wave back, projecting it on the ceiling and suddenly zooming in to make it take up the entire screen.
Technological and aesthetic experiments: 3D model in Maya running on an SGI workstation.	Reducing the complexity of the geometry of the figure and at the same time making it appealing to people.
Another video brainstorm: No motion capture equipment but simulating the system's responses via the Wizard of Oz technique using the mouse and keyboard as interface.	The actions and appearance of the figure have tremendous impact on the user. The idea of shaping the user emerges.
The users' perspective: Scenarios.	The user must be stimulated to interact with the figure by offering the user some kind of reward or positive feedback.
Structuring interaction: Text documents.	The idea of phases.
Video user study: Wizard of Oz technique.	The users are quite different; there is a need to accommodate both bold and timid users.
2D Prototype: Prototype in Macromedia Director.	Balancing of the phases and evolving the shy mood of the figure.
Version 1: Prototype in Maya and motion capture interface.	The need for a more fluid user interaction.
Version 2: Prototype in Maya and motion capture interface.	The system must be as enjoyable as possible for both the users using it and the audience watching.

A diverse set of materials and design representations have been used, ranging form transparencies, projections, video, scenarios and prototypes to conventional design specifications. Setting up experiments with the purpose of creating a process where it was possible to try out what it would be like to use the final system has been a key characteristic throughout of the process. Each experiment has had its own focus, for instance the mood of the figure and the behaviour of the user.

The process did not started out from a clear-cut idea of how the installation was going to be. On the contrary, a significant portion of the ideas behind mcpie emerged during the experimental activities.

Clearly the various prototypes and materials are not passive entities but play as active a role as the human subjects: both kinds of elements are mutually stimulating a creative conversation or interactions. The materials have been modifying the designer, which in turn has modified the materials.

References

Andersen, P. B. (1997) The force dynamics of interactive system. Towards a computer semiotics. *Semiotica* 103(1/2): 5–45.

Andersen, P. B. (1998) Multimedia phase-spaces. *Multimedia Tools and Applications* 6: 207–237.

Budde, R. *et al.* (eds.) (1984) *Approaches to Prototyping*. Berlin: Springer-Verlag.

Caroll, J. M. (ed.) (1995) *Scenario-Based Design: Envisioning Work and Technology in System Development*. New York: John Wiley & Sons.

Ehn, P. and Kyng, M. (1991) Card Board Computers: Mocking-it-up and Hands-on the Future. In *Design at Work: Cooperative Design of Computer Systems* (eds. J. Greenbaum and M. Kyng). Hillsdale, NJ: Lawrence Erlbaum Associates, pp. 169–195.

Greenbaum, J. and Kyng, M. (eds.) (1991) *Design at Work: Cooperative Design of Computer Systems*. Hillsdale, NJ: Lawrence Erlbaum Associates.

Kelley, J. F. (1983) An empirical methodology for writing user-friendly natural language computer applications. In *Proceedings of CHI'83 Conference on Human Factors in Computing Systems*, Boston, MA. New York: ACM.

Krueger, M. (1983) *Artificial Reality*. New York: Addison-Wesley.

Kuutti, K. (1995) Work processes: scenarios as a preliminary vocabulary. In: *Scenario-Based Design: Envisioning Work and Technology in System Development* (ed. J. M. Caroll). New York: John Wiley & Sons.

Schuler, D. and Namioka, A. (eds.) (1993) *Participatory Design: Principles and Practices*. Hillsdale, NJ: Lawrence Erlbaum Associates.

Schön, D. (1983) *The Reflective Practitioner*. New York: Basic Books.

Schön, D. (1988) Designing: rules, types and worlds. *Design Studies*, 9(3).

Schön, D (1992) Kinds of seeing and their role in design. *Design Studies* 13(2).

Thalmann, N. D. and Thalmann, D. (eds.) (1996) *Interactive Computer Animation*. London: Prentice Hall.

21 Using Software Engineering Approaches to Model Dynamics in Interactive Software Systems

Mikael Skov and Jan Stage

21.1 Introduction

Software engineering comprises all aspects of designing and implementing computer-based systems. Pressman (1992) defines software engineering as "the establishment and use of sound engineering principles in order to obtain economically software that is reliable and works efficiently on real machines". Tradition has formed a classical life cycle for software engineering to consist of systems engineering, analysis, design, code, testing and maintenance, (cf. Pressman, 1992; Sommerville 1992). Modelling and constructing future computer-based systems primarily take place in the analysis, design and coding phases where the objective is to describe the systems in terms of software components. Various methodologies have proposed specific solutions to these three phases, such as the recent object-oriented methodologies (cf. Booch 1994; Coad and Yourdon 1991a,b; Jacobson *et al.* 1992; Martin and Odell 1993; Rumbaugh *et al.* 1991; Shlaer and Mellor 1988, 1992; Wirfs-Brock *et al.* 1990). These methodologies have primarily been designed and created based on experience from the development of traditional computer-based systems, e.g. administrative systems such as a bank account system.

With the evolution of hardware technologies, new types of computer-based systems have emerged during recent years, one of them being multimedia systems. Multimedia systems share many similarities with other kinds of computer-based systems, yet there are also fundamental differences. Compared with typical software systems, multimedia systems are often more interactive and involve a considerable number of elements that are produced in other ways. These elements provide content in the multimedia system; examples are graphics, sound and video clips. They are often denoted as the assets of a multimedia system. A high level of interaction between the user and the system is characteristic of most multimedia systems. The system processes and presents a large amount of information to the user by means of several media, and the user is expected to continually respond to that information. It has been suggested that multimedia system development should start by defining the fundamental requirements of the system in question. After this initial phase, development should then proceed along two parallel tracks, where the first track deals with development of the software, and the second track with the production of assets. Finally, the last phase should involve the integration of assets into the software system.

The development of multimedia systems can be viewed from different design perspectives, e.g. movie-making, storytelling or as a software engineering design process (Eriksen *et al.*, 2000). In this chapter we adopt the latter view. Research within multimedia systems development shows that contemporary multimedia systems are designed and created primarily by intuition, and therefore lack methodological support and systematic work practices (Sutcliffe and Faraday 1994, 1997). A fundamental lesson learned through many studies and experiments in software engineering is that improvements in design and quality assurance processes require systematic work practices that involve well-founded methods (Sommerville, 1992).

In this chapter, we focus specifically on the software aspect of multimedia system development. Skov and Stage (1996) state that software designers who employ software engineering techniques and notations during the modelling process are able to gain and express a fundamental understanding by means of static structural diagrams, but at the same time they face a key challenge: it is difficult to understand and design the dynamic collection of objects that are collaborating during the execution of a software system and the properties that the system as a whole will possess. In the development of software systems with a strong element of interaction, like multimedia systems, this challenge becomes a key characteristic of the design activity. A high level of interaction increases the dynamic nature of the collection of objects and their collaboration. The design and implementation of multimedia systems is a fundamental challenging process with a particular focus on the dynamics of the interaction. For these reasons we have set up two questions to be answered in this chapter:

- What are the key characteristics and challenges of designing multimedia systems?
- How do experienced software designers work with the task of designing the dynamic element of an interactive software system?

In the first question, we will address the characteristics and complexities imposed by the development of multimedia systems in order to set up an experiment which addresses the second question. The chapter provides qualitative interpretations from an empirical study of three software designers. Section 21.2 addresses the first question by discussing key characteristics of typical multimedia systems. The next section provides an overview of the empirical study; complete documentation is available on the WWW (Skov and Stage, 1995). The results are presented in the following four sections where each section presents a key observation that partially answers the second question raised above. Finally, the last section summarizes the lessons learned from this limited study and points out avenues for further research.

21.2 Designing Multimedia Systems

Multimedia systems can be compared with traditional software systems in order to emphasize similarities and differences. Two key differences that emerge from such a comparison are that multimedia systems generally engage the user's senses more intensively and involve a higher degree of interaction. Below, these two aspects are illustrated by three examples.

The first example is of a multimedia system that is used by people who are learning to drive a car in order to train them in certain kinds of traffic behaviour (Bergman and Møller, 1998). Thus the purpose of this system is education and training. The system presents the user with video clips or animated sketches of realistic traffic situations, and the user must act to handle the situations that arise. The output from the system is video and sound that presents a traffic situation to the user. The input may take different forms; in a simple version, the user may select an action from among a set of options that are presented by a kind of menu, whereas in a more elaborate version the user may be able to operate devices similar to the wheel and pedals of a real car. Other examples of this category are systems for training and evaluating decision-makers in an organization or umpires in a sailing match (Eriksen *et al.*, 2000). This example illustrates how multimedia systems engage the user's senses much more strongly than traditional software systems. The use of graphics, animations and video transcends the potentials of traditional screen-based output, and the combined use of sound adds a completely new dimension.

The second example is a game where the user moves around in a virtual world that is created by exposing the user to different images and sound (see Chapter 7). Thus the purpose of this system is entertainment. The user controls a certain character or group of characters by means of an input device and thereby acts in the virtual world. The action of the controlled character often requires considerable input from the user. This example illustrates how a multimedia system requires a high degree of interaction with the user. If the user wants to stay in the game, it is necessary to respond continually to the changes that are displayed on the screen, and this response clearly influences the further development of the game.

The third example is a system for teaching children about wildlife (Hansen *et al.*, 1999). The purpose of this system is edutainment, i.e. simultaneous education and entertainment. Thus the system was developed as a prototype for a zoo in order to illustrate how multimedia technology could be used to teach children of between five and ten years of age about the animals in the zoo. The system enables the user to view photos, drawings and video clips of animals and obtain various information about them. Moreover, users can exercise their knowledge by answering quiz-like questions on the animals.

The basic characteristics of these and other multimedia systems are summarized in this definition (inspired by Eriksen and Skov (1998)): *A multimedia system is a computer-based system that integrates a multitude of assets to facilitate user immersion and activity in a virtual situation. The assets represent fragments of the virtual situation and are based on modalities such as text, graphics, pictures, video, animations, sound, tactile information and motion. The activity involves interaction with objects in the virtual situation and is limited by certain temporal and spatial structures. The development of the virtual situation is defined by a plot.* This definition emphasizes the main challenges of designing multimedia systems. First, the plot, the virtual world and the limitations imposed by temporal and spatial structures must be created and described. The result is a design of the story that provides the foundation of the system. Second, a large number of assets must be specified, typically in detail. Third, the software system that integrates the assets, handles their interplay, and enables interaction with the user must be designed.

This design task requires both static and dynamic conceptions. The static conception is necessary in order to identify objects and their properties. In software design, this process of identifying basic elements is referred to as abstraction (Booch, 1994). The behaviour of the system as a whole can be designed by describing how objects are created and disposed, and how they interact with each other. This process requires a dynamic conception where the focus is on the collection of objects and their interplay. Many of the existing software development methods provide considerable support for the design and understanding of the static aspects; for example, this applies to the object-oriented methods that were referred to in the introduction. Even though different traditions emphasize and employ different concepts, they share a strong focus on static aspects. The existing methods provide much less support for the dynamic aspect of software design. Because of the dynamic nature of multimedia systems, the limitations of the existing concepts and notations reduce the advantage of using a software development method. This fundamental problem leaves us with two different research approaches.

One approach is to employ a more experimental approach. In the design of mcpie, the developers engaged in a number of cycles where different prototypes of the system were developed and evaluated (see Chapter 20). A second approach is to employ other concepts or notations. In the design of a training and evaluation multimedia system, the developers produced descriptions that were inspired by storytelling and movie production (Eriksen *et al.*, 2000).

Our aim in this chapter is to contribute to the second approach. In the following sections, we focus on an empirical study of three software designers. The aim of this study was to identify the basic concepts that the designers used to design and understand the dynamic aspects of a software system and their usefulness in that design process. The details of this study are described in the following section.

21.3 Empirical Study

The empirical study reported in this chapter was designed to explore the second question raised in the introduction. The question is of a qualitative nature, since no variables are defined *a priori*. The study can be characterized as being a descriptive *in vitro* qualitative case study based on observation of an individual designer (Basili, 1996). The detailed design of the study was inspired by an earlier more general experiment by Guindon *et al.* (1987). A complete description of our study is publicly available on the WWW (Skov and Stage, 1995). Three different software engineering design approaches were chosen for the study, representing different design perspectives and abstractions. The three approaches were an object-oriented approach, an operating systems approach, and a mathematical–logical approach. The first is primarily founded as a practical approach widely used in the systems development industry, while the other two are more formal approaches building on strict semantic definitions and notations. The study involved three designers with the following personal characteristics:

- *OO Designer (object-oriented)*: He has a Ph.D. in Computer Science and more than 10 years of experience with research, teaching and software development, with an emphasis on programming, programming languages and programming environments.

  He applied no specific method and used only an informal notation inspired by Smalltalk (Goldberg and Robson, 1989) and Beta (Madsen and Møller-Pedersen, 1993). Smalltalk and Beta are based on traditional object-oriented concepts such as modularity and information hiding, and objects constitute a natural medium for analysing and describing concurrent processes.
- *OS Designer (operating system)*: He has a Ph.D. in Computer Science and more than 20 years of experience with research, teaching and software development, with an emphasis on operating systems and distributed systems.

  He applied the Phase Web notation (Manthey, 1988; Manthey *et al.*, 1994), which is inspired by the Actor model (Satoh and Tokoro, 1992). The Phase Web notation is a method for analysing and describing concurrent and communicating processes. The Phase Web notation uses entities called sensors in the description of different states of the entire system. The Phase Web notation is mainly based on aspects of synchronization and co-exclusion.
- *ML Designer (mathematical-logical)*: He is a Ph.D. student in Computer Science with about three years of experience with research and application of formal methods related to protocol design and verification.

  He applied the Calculus for Communicating Systems (CCS). CCS is a general calculus or theory for analysing and describing concurrent and communicating processes. However, CCS is not only applicable for describing concurrency and communication, but can also be applied for studying machines, architectures, programming methods and languages in general (Milner, 1989).

Each designer was given the task of designing the process architecture for an interactive software system controlling a set of elevators in a building (see below). In solving this standard classical problem from software specification and software requirements research (Guindon *et al.*, 1987), they were required only to use their "own" paradigm as a development methodology.

The Lift Control Problem

An *N*-elevator system is to be installed in a building with *M* floors. Your assignment is to design the process architecture for a software system which controls the movement of the elevators. The processors can described as follows:

- There is one processor at each of the *N* elevators. This processor controls the engine and the doors, and reads the push buttons and sensors associated with every elevator.
- There is one processor at each of the *M* floors which reads the push buttons associated with that floor.
- There is one processor which is able to control all requests from all push buttons.

It is your choice whether you want to design a centralized or a decentralized solution to the problem. The design has to be elaborated according to the following rules:

1. Each lift has a set of buttons with one button for each floor. These illuminate when pressed and cause the lift to visit the corresponding floor. The illumination is cancelled when the corresponding floor is visited (i.e. stopped at) by the lift.
2. Each floor has two buttons (except ground and top), one to request an up-lift and one to request a down-lift. These buttons illuminate when pressed. The buttons are cancelled when a lift visits the floor either while travelling in the desired direction or while having no requests outstanding. In the latter case, if both floor request buttons are illuminated, only one should be cancelled. The algorithm used to decide which of these requests to service first should minimize the waiting time for both of them.
3. When a lift has no requests to service, it should remain at its last destination with its doors closed and await further requests (or model a "holding" floor).
4. All requests for lifts from floors must be serviced eventually, with all floors given equal priority (can this be proved or demonstrated?).
5. All requests for floors within lifts must be serviced eventually, with floors being serviced sequentially in the direction of travel (can this be proved or demonstrated?).
6. Each lift has an emergency button. When pressed, it causes a warning signal to be sent to the site manager. The lift is then deemed "out of service". Each lift has a mechanism to cancel its "out of service" status.

It is a requirement that the task is solved using object orientation, Phase Web or CCS. A final solution shall be delivered. It shall be possible for another person to evaluate this solution.

None of the three designers knew the problem in advance. They were given two hours to solve it and they were required to produce a solution that could be handed over to another person for later evaluation.

The designers were instructed to think aloud during their design process. During the whole session, they used only pencil and paper. All three design sessions were videotaped and the paper-sheets produced were enumerated to enable later identification and relation to the video recordings.

In the data analysis, the videotapes were examined with the purpose of describing each designer's process as a sequence of activities where a change from one activity to another was identified as a situation in which the designer broke the ongoing line of reasoning (Guindon *et al.*, 1987). Furthermore, the activities were characterized in terms of the problem considered, the concepts used to analyse and solve this problem, and the approach taken by the designer. This procedure was developed because of the highly dense and complex nature of video material as a documentation medium. For each of the three sessions, this transcript was elicited by viewing the videotape five to six times, amounting to approximately six pages of text. These transcripts are available on the Web; see Skov and Stage (1995).

The second part of the data analysis focused only on the solutions produced by the three designers. Their solutions were evaluated by two independent reviewers who were both associate professors in computer science and had many years of experience in areas related to the focus of the experiment. The documentation produced by the three designers was examined and evaluated in about an hour by each of these reviewers. To summarize their evaluation, they were also asked to mark the three solutions with a grade representing how well the assignment had been solved. These reviews are also available on the Web; see Skov and Stage (1995).

21.3 Conceptual Basis

The first observation focuses on the concepts that were used by the three designers throughout the process architecture design.

> The OO designer uses a broad variety of different concepts with unclear mutual relations. In several situations, the same aspect of the problem is characterized in terms of two or three concepts with almost the same meaning.
>
> The OS designer and the ML designer both use a limited set of well-defined concepts with clear mutual relations.

The OO designer used a broad variety of different concepts during his design of the process architecture. To analyse this in detail, we distinguish between the three levels of concepts used, specified in Table 21.1.

Table 21.1 shows that the OO designer used a total of 25 different concepts during the design process. Level 3 includes concepts that were used to analyse the problem or express a solution in an explicit manner and were consistent with the notation he used. We have attributed 11 of the concepts to this level. Level 2 include concepts that were stated explicitly and used to characterize the problem or evaluate

Table 21.1 The number of concepts used during process architecture design.

Level	Description	Legend	OO designer	OS designer	ML designer
3	The concept was used as an integrated element of the paradigm	•••	11	9	6
2	The concept was stated explicitly during the process	••	10	7	7
1	The concept was not stated, but was used implicitly in the process	•	4	2	1
	Total		25	18	14

alternatives but were not used to express a solution. We have attributed 10 concepts to this level. Finally, Level 1 includes concepts that were used in thinking about the problem but not used explicitly in analysing the problem or expressing a solution. We have attributed 4 concepts to this level. It is characteristic that the OO designer has less than half of the concepts on Level 3. A total of 14 concepts are on Levels 1 or 2, which indicates a shallower use of these concepts, and one sixth of the total number of concepts used are only on Level 1.

Table 21.2 shows the distribution of the concepts that were used by the OO designer on a selection of essential issues in process architecture design. These issues have been used by either of the three designers or serve as a key concept in major object-oriented analysis and design methods. These issues have then been organized under the three overall concepts that are indicated in the table. The

Table 21.2 The specific concepts used during process architecture design.

	OO designer	OS designer	ML designer
Concurrency	•••	•••	•••
– Parallelism	(•)		•••
– Active objects	(•••)		
– Process	•••	•••	•••
– Processor	(••)	••	••
– Multitasking		••	
Communication	•••	•••	•••
– Message	•		•
– Broadcast	••	•	••
– Interrupt	••	••	
– Polling	•••	••	
Synchronization	•••	(•••)	•••
– Mutual exclusion		•••	
– Starvation	(••)	(••)	(••)
– Deadlock	(••)		
– Rendezvous	••		
– Race condition	•		

table shows only 15 out of the total of 25 concepts that were applied. Ten concepts, including robustness, time aspects, and independence, have been left out for brevity. The bullets in the table refer to the three levels of use that are shown in Table 21.1. Parentheses indicate that the concept was only used upon request of the observer.

Table 21.2 emphasizes three important characteristics. First, it shows that the OO designer focused primarily on communication issues. Communication between objects was analysed and specified explicitly. There are fewer concepts on concurrency and synchronization and about half of these have only been introduced on behalf of the observer. Second, it shows that three of the essential concepts are used only on Level 1. Some of these concepts embody aspects that are critical to the success of the solution. Third, it shows that synchronization received least attention. Only the overall concept was used on Level 3, whereas the concepts reflecting more specific aspects of this issue were at most treated on Level 2. These include concepts like deadlock, starvation etc. These concepts played only a minor role in the design process, since the OO designer did not employ them for systematic reflection.

The multitude of concepts used by the OO designer were characterized by unclear mutual relations. In several cases, he did not define the concepts he used, nor did he express their semantics clearly. For example, he did not make clear what active objects versus processes meant to him:

> *OO designer*: I view all elevator objects as active objects... there may be introduced some processes later on, but I will not treat such aspects on this design level.

The OO Designer also used different concepts with almost the same meaning to describe the same aspect of the problem. For example, he did not distinguish between process, processor and active object in his solution:

> *OO designer*: I do not make a distinction between processes and processors at this design level.

In fact, the three concepts were used interchangeably. In the beginning, he used the concept of processor for the entities in his solution. Later on, he began to use the concept of process for the same entities, and finally he mentioned that all these processes could be compared to active objects. In all three cases, he did not provide an explicit definition, nor did he consider how it might affect his solution.

The OS designer and the ML designer both used considerably fewer concepts than the OO designer. Table 21.1 shows that the OS designer used a total of 18 concepts, of which 9 were on Level 3. The ML designer used a total of 14 concepts, of which 6 were on Level 3. Compared with the OO designer, they also have significantly fewer concepts attributed to Level 1.

The use of specific concepts is shown in Table 21.2. The overall concepts, concurrency, communication and synchronization are used actively by both designers. These concepts served as natural and well-defined components of their design processes. However, both designers seemed to emphasize concurrency and communication more than synchronization.

Another characteristic of the two paradigms is that the key concepts have generally accepted definitions and their mutual relations are usually clear. For instance, the concept of process has a well-defined meaning in both paradigms. This was very apparent in the study, since none of these two designers switched randomly between different concepts in their description of a certain aspect.

21.4 Abstraction and Complexity

The second observation focuses on the role of abstraction in the whole design process and the extent to which the descriptions made reflected their intuitive understanding of the problem.

> The OO designer changes rapidly and unsystematically between different aspects of the problem and between different levels of abstraction. In this sense, his approach is controlled by the nature of the problem. The description made is closely related to his intuitive understanding of the problem.
>
> The OS designer and the ML designer both approach the problem systematically, often working continuously with the same problem and on the same level of abstraction. In this sense, their approaches are controlled by the nature of their paradigms. They are forced to introduce inexpedient reductions because the complexity of their descriptions is growing dramatically with the size of the task.

The entire approach employed by the OO designer reflects frequent and unsystematic changes between different aspects of the problem. Typically, he immediately began to perform a test once he had specified a certain aspect of the problem. During the execution of these tests, he often discovered a related problem in his solution. This initiated an attempt to design a modified solution that also handled the new problem. The following scenario illustrates approximately 15 minutes of the design process: (1) he specifies the static aspects of an elevator object; (2) he begins to test whether an elevator moving in one direction is able to satisfy a request in the opposite direction; (3) he tries to describe the various states of an elevator; (4) he realizes that there may be a potential problem with the push buttons in the elevator; and (5) he starts to specify actions for the push buttons. While coding the solution, he still returned to further specification and experimentation with the solutions that were expressed in the code.

In the early analysis, it was characteristic that the OO designer relied only to a very limited extent on specific object-oriented concepts. For example, he had worked for 15 minutes before he introduced even the first object-oriented concept; this happened when he turned his focus to the definition of processes and objects. Similarly, his overall design choices were governed more by his general knowledge and intuitive understanding than by specific object-oriented concepts or perspectives.

Two additional characteristics contribute to the impression that his approach was controlled by the nature of the problem rather than the nature of his paradigm. First, turning from specifying to simulation seemed to be random. Sometimes this change was triggered by a recognition of a potential problem or an aspect he could not describe clearly. In several cases, the latter was caused by the inherent concurrency of the problem. Second, after testing a partial solution he often returned to a different problem.

While working with the task, the OO designer was able to specify on a level of detail that was appropriate for his momentary intentions. During his first analysis, the OO designer tried to obtain a general overview of the elevator problem by drawing a sketch of a building with a number of floors and a number of elevators. He defined elevator and floor objects without describing them in greater detail. Thereby, he obtained a first intuitive understanding of the problem at hand. Later on, elevators and floors constituted the objects upon which he specified more detailed aspects and evaluated potential solutions. This was possible because the object-oriented concepts do not require description at a specific level of detail. The adding of details can be done continuously during the design phase. Moreover, his intuitive model resembled the real-world complexity when considering objects and static relations.

The OS designer and the ML designer both began their design process by drawing a sketch of a building with a number of floors and elevators. Once this frame for an intuitive understanding was established, they changed to a mode of operation that was far more rational than the experimental process conducted by the OO designer. In some situations, they *did* test partial solutions, implying that they changed from the rational mode in which they were specifying in terms of their paradigm to a more experimental mode where they were testing partial solutions. But it was on a much smaller scale, and they never switched randomly between different issues or levels of abstraction. Both designers spent significantly more time specifying the actions for the solution, and the majority of their effort was spent on systematic work that was carried out in a mostly sequential order. The paradigms seemed to force the focus of the designers in certain directions and to maintain this focus for longer periods of time.

The OS designer and the ML designer both faced severe problems with complexity as their descriptions grew radically with the size of the task. This led them to reduce the task considerably by imposing restrictions on the number of elevators and floors. The ML designer chose to restrict the task to three floors and only one elevator. The OS designer initially reduced the problem to three floors and three elevators, and later on he considered reducing the task further by dealing only with two floors and two elevators:

> *OS designer*: Normally I would not solve such a task with three floors. I would only involve two floors in order to reduce complexity.

This problem was emphasized by Reviewer R2 who stated that the solutions made by both the OS designer and the ML designer were characterized by enormous complexity. The problem was that the design of a solution is described by a set of rules that are expressed in the notations defined by the paradigms. These rules are not intended for manual execution by people, but have been made to support automated processing. The OS designer stated it this way:

> *OS designer*: Solutions made with the Phase Web paradigm quickly become complex and enormous because of the many actions.

The OS designer was very familiar with his paradigm. Thus he was able to foresee problems that would emerge in a solution as a consequence of certain design choices. For example, he had no problem envisioning the actions needed to move an elevator from one floor to another. Due to more limited experience with the paradigm, the ML designer had a less clear relation between his thinking and the notation used for expressing it. Nevertheless, he never seemed to have problems that were comparable to those of the OO designer.

Despite the fact that both the OS designer and the ML designer had to restrict the task in order to reduce complexity, it seemed that they used the relevant concepts and their notations coherently. Both designers were able to think of the problem in terms of their respective paradigms. In this sense, there was no leap or semantic gap between their thinking and notation. They were able to use the notation in accordance with their thinking, once the problem had been reduced to a size that was practical compared with the capability of the notation.

A more severe leap occurred in the relation between the descriptions and solutions on the one hand and an intuitive understanding of the real-world problem on the other hand. The task was reduced considerably at an early point in time. The restrictions that followed from this reduction gradually narrowed the scope of the designers' work, and in the end both designers turned out to have solved a very limited problem. This was expressed very clearly by Reviewer R2 who claimed that the intuitive understanding of the actions in the paradigms was not clear to him:

> *Reviewer R2*: It easily becomes signs and strange actions, where you cannot associate anything with these widgets. A semantic gap is introduced between your intuitive understanding of the problem and the actions in the paradigm.

This statement illustrates the problems that arise when a paradigm forces designers to reduce the task inexpediently. The reduction is necessary due to the complexity of the descriptions made, but it seems to imply that the semantic content of these descriptions contradicts an intuitive understanding of the problem. The reduction introduces a leap between the intuitive understanding and the descriptions made.

21.5 Identifying the Problem

The third observation focuses on the part of the design process in which the designers identified whether concurrency was an issue and the nature of this potential issue.

> The OO designer identifies the inherent concurrency of the problem through experiments and simulations. In this way, he uses a considerable amount of time obtaining a clear understanding of the nature of the concurrency involved.

> The OS designer and the ML designer both identify the inherent concurrency of the problem in terms of mechanisms from their paradigms. In this way, they quickly achieve a sufficient understanding of the nature of the concurrency involved.

One of the major difficulties during process architecture design is the identification of potential sources of concurrency (Jacobson *et al.*, 1992). Early in the design process, the OO designer was able to identify that the elevator problem involved inherent concurrency. However, this identification was not based on a systematic and methodical analysis but rather on an intuitive understanding of the problem. Moreover, he was unable to indicate where concurrency could turn out to be a problem and what consequences it would imply for his solution.

The process conducted by the OO designer was characterized by frequent and random changes between specifying and simulation. Now and then he was specifying actual code of his solution; now and then he was testing a partial solution by performing simulations. Typically, he was working approximately ten minutes on specifying and then about five minutes on testing. During the entire design process, he made this kind of change between specifying and testing six or seven times.

This approach to identification of concurrency can be characterized as being highly experimental. Potential problems caused by the inherent concurrency were discovered through execution of simulations on partial solutions. Another example of this occurred when he performed minor simulations on his solution in order to determine whether an elevator was able to satisfy an up-request when it was going down. He also simulated what would happen when an elevator was waiting for requests. A consequence of this approach was that he used a considerable amount of time on the identification of concurrency in order to gain the necessary overview. In fact, aspects of concurrency were identified and handled every now and then during the entire design process. For example, after having made his first overall design choice, he spent six to seven minutes trying to apprehend a very minor and simple concurrency problem. Thus the overall impression is of a very ineffective and irrational mode of operation.

The OO designer also faced problems when he attempted to evaluate the consequences of his design choices. At first, he chose a centralized unit for coordination of requests. Through simulations, he later realized that this centralized unit was a problem because the elevator had to delete a request when it arrived at a floor. Instead, he began to design a decentralized solution:

> *OO designer*: A decentralized solution attracts me because it is more robust. Such a system (the lift control system) is of course subject to breakdowns.

This redesign caused other problems, as he could no longer guarantee that only one elevator would service a request from a floor:

> *OO designer*: I have some problems with the concurrency involved here, but I would rather have two elevators trying to service a request from a floor than none.

This approach to identification of concurrency indicates that the OO designer never became totally certain whether the problem was fully understood or whether important concurrency issues still had to be addressed in order to design a satisfactory solution.

Both the OS designer and the ML designer quickly identified the key problem of the task. They benefited from their paradigms, which respectively enabled them to identify and describe the inherent concurrency in terms of the mechanisms that were provided by the paradigms that they applied.

Both paradigms represent a long tradition of dealing with the concept of concurrency and related issues, and they have been designed specifically to handle such aspects. As a result, the OS designer and the ML designer could avoid dealing explicitly with many detailed aspects of the concurrency involved. All they had to do was to specify the conditions that have to hold during the execution of the system. In fact, it was often hard to see that they addressed the problem at all, since their paradigms handled the concurrency:

> *ML designer*: It is a formalism where you can put things in parallel for free. Communication and concurrency have been built into the language.

The two designers with backgrounds in classical concurrency paradigms employed a conception of concurrency that is very different from the view held by the OO designer. Their identification of sources of concurrency was more systematic because their paradigms imposed a sequential order on the issues they had to deal with. Both paradigms can be seen as media for capturing and describing concurrency aspects and this enables users of the paradigms to invest a very modest effort but still achieve sufficient understanding of the concurrency involved.

21.6 Expressing the Solution

The fourth observation focuses on the part of the design process in which the designers developed and expressed their solution to the problem.

> The OO designer has difficulties describing how communication and synchronization are handled because he lacks a notation to describe the dynamic behaviour of objects on an overall level.

> The OS designer and the ML designer both describe communication and synchronization without any severe problems as they simply express themselves in terms of the mechanisms that are available in their paradigms.

When the OO Designer started drawing a sketch of the real-world situation, his focus was primarily on objects and their dynamic behaviour. For instance, he thought of and described the dynamic behaviour of an elevator: what happens when it reaches a specific floor, what happens when it awaits requests etc. This led him to determine the heart of the lift control problem as being the design of a good algorithm to control the behaviour of the lifts:

> *OO designer*: ...all rules in the problem statement imply that the algorithm for the elevators has to be rational... the design of the algorithm is the core of this task.

His attempts to map this behaviour into an object-oriented description caused fundamental problems. He tried to express the dynamic behaviour of the whole system as procedural code in the abstract classes of the objects involved. After having spent only 31 minutes on the task, he started coding both essential and unessential aspects on a very detailed level. His third and fourth sheets of paper already contain program statements; for example, he specifies a constructor function that initializes an elevator object to be generated on floor 1. He worried about such details even though he still lacked a coherent overall understanding of the problem. He gave the following reason for specifying with code:

> *OO designer*: It is easier for me to see how the objects interact when I specify them with actual code.

This statement can, however, be questioned, since later on he had difficulties describing certain aspects of the dynamic interaction between objects. For example, he had to incorporate additional attributes to represent the motion of an elevator going up or down and this in turn introduced difficulties in realizing whether his solution would be able to service the various request from push buttons in the elevators and on the floors.

The heart of the difficulty he faced was caused simply by the lack of an overall notation for analyzing and designing solutions in terms of specific objects and on a relevant level of detailing. Instead, he became burdened with isolated and unessential issues that occurred only because he had to express himself in detailed code belonging to the individual classes. As he gained new insight and wanted to modify his design on the overall level, he had to express these changes in several different fragments of code. This also implied that he modified the same part of the code several times.

To circumvent the lack of a suitable means of expression, he tried to employ concrete knowledge about the hardware and software that would be available on the underlying implementation platform. In designing the experiment, we had anticipated this problem. The problem statement of this study was originally taken from Guindon *et al.* (1987). Yet this description lacks specific information about the facilities of the technical platform. In order to support the designers in developing an appropriate solution, we had extended the original problem statement with a detailed specification of the available hardware. However, two contradicting characteristics illustrate that this description was of very limited value to the OO designer. On the one hand, he did not distinguish between processors and processes (cf. the first observation on conceptual basis). This indicates that he relied on the assumption that it would be a simple task to map the processes he designed onto the processors that constituted the technical platform. By making this assumption, he was able to refrain from solving a key problem of the process architecture design and this in turn allowed him to ignore the information about the available hardware that was provided in the problem statement. On the other hand, he faced several situations in which he requested even more specific and detailed information about the features of the platform:

> *OO designer*: I assume that this is handled by interrupts, but I cannot specify it in more detail without additional knowledge of the underlying hardware.

The lack of a specific platform with a distinct semantics was obviously a problem for the OO designer. He chose to virtually ignore the problems of describing how communication and synchronization should be handled. In Table 21.2 this is illustrated by his limited focus on concepts like broadcast, interrupts, starvation, deadlock and race conditions. These issues were treated only marginally during the design process, even though some of them may significantly influence the success of the final solution. Later on, he realized that a problem could arise with his solution when an elevator was trying to service a request. The problem was that an elevator could move to a floor in vain because another elevator had already serviced the same request:

> *OO designer*: Some of the elevators may move in vain... this is a synchronization problem... some communication is, of course, taking place between the processors, but I need more information about the hardware to specify such aspects.

These characteristics clearly emphasize that the object-oriented paradigm lacks a means to express the overall aspects of communication and synchronization. Instead, users of the paradigm are forced to deal with the actual features of the underlying hardware and software.

The paradigms employed by the OS designer and the ML designer have been built deliberately to handle key aspects of communication and synchronization. Of course, this influenced the experiment. Both designers were able to describe and express aspects of communication and synchronization in terms of the notations provided by their paradigms. This was clearly in contrast to the work of the OO designer, because he had to deal explicitly with these topics.

None of the two designers made any use of the information that was given in the problem statement about the available technical platform. Instead, they made assumptions about features that had to be available:

> *OS designer:* I assume that features of the underlying hardware make it possible for me to turn off the lights in the pushbuttons when a request has been serviced.

Both designers expressed that problems concerning communication and synchronization played a very minor role in their designs because their paradigms would take care of such aspects:

> *OS designer:* I know you might think that I am getting over the problem easily, but I am sitting on a synchronization machine which solves a lot of my problems. All I have to do is to write down the synchronization conditions that have to hold.

The ML designer described the key aspects of synchronization by means of labels on his entities. In order to synchronize an elevator and a floor, he could specify a specific action on each of the entities involved. The actual synchronization of the two would then be handled by the paradigm.

21.7 Conclusion

This chapter has explored how three experienced designers worked with a realistic and complex problem related to designing the dynamic element of a software system. The preceding sections have expressed the results of this exploratory approach in terms of four observations that are summarized in Table 21.3.

The OO designer faced several situations in which he needed stronger conceptual or methodical support. His design process conveyed four essential deficiencies. First, he wasted much effort because he lacked a coherent conceptual framework and a related set of methodological guidelines to support the design process. Second, a notation for relating the dynamic behaviour of objects to the static definitions of classes would have improved his design process and solution significantly. Third, his design suffered from the lack of an abstract machine that served as the underlying technical platform of a design solution. Fourth, his solution describes the structuring of processes but the overall design is largely missing.

Table 21.3 Summary of observations.

		OO designer		OS and ML designers
Conceptual basis	–	Many similar concepts with unclear mutual relations	+	Few well-defined concepts with clear mutual relations
Abstraction and complexity	–	Rapid changes between different aspects of the problem and different levels of abstraction	+/–	Continuous but un-reflected work on the same aspect of the problem and on the same level of abstraction
	+	Close relation between description and intuitive understanding	–	Reduced description due to dramatic growth in complexity
Identifying the problem	–	Unstructured and experimental approach, slowly accomplished	+	Structured and systematic approach, quickly accomplished
Expressing the solution	–	No abstract notation for specifying communication and synchronization	+	Simple, abstract mechanisms for specifying communication and synchronization

These observations are based on a small experiment with only one object-oriented designer and a comparison with two other designers; and all three designers represent fundamentally different and very heterogeneous paradigms. Thus our experiment cannot form the basis of quantitative and statistically valid conclusions concerning all object-oriented designers. The advantage of this limited experiment is that it has facilitated a rich, qualitative insight into the problems and breakdowns faced by each individual designer and the reasons why they occurred (Basili, 1996). Video observation and exhaustive qualitative data analysis of a large number of designers is practically impossible. The qualitative exploration is a first step towards a better understanding of object-oriented process architecture design. Later on, the four observations can be examined quantitatively in a more ambitious study that involves more designers and a varied selection of process architecture problems.

This exploratory approach also opens other avenues for further research. A related effort would be to study the extent to which specific object-oriented methods support the process architecture design activity. Finally, it could be investigated how the process architecture has been designed in a number of complex software systems. All of these efforts would contribute to improving the work practices of software designers dealing with realistic concurrency problems.

Acknowledgements

The research behind this article has received financial support from the Danish Natural Science Research Council under grant No. 9400911. We owe a special thank to the five participants in the experiment: Kasper Østerbye, Michael J. Manthey, Kaare J. Kristoffersen, Arne Skou and Bent Bruun Kristensen. Without their participation, the experiment would not have been possible. We are also grateful to Lars Mathiassen. Peter Axel Nielsen, Dan Sletten and Heinz Züllighoven for their comments and suggestions to different versions of this article.

References

Basili, V. (1996) The Role of experimentation in software engineering: past, current, and future. In *Proceedings of the 18th International Conference on Software Engineering*. Los Alamitos, CA: IEEE Computer Society, pp. 442–449.

Bergman, H. and Møller, H. R. (1998) *Method for Development of Multimedia Systems for Training and Education* (in Danish). University of Copenhagen.

Booch, G. (1994) *Object-Oriented Analysis and Design with Applications*. Redwood City, CA: Benjamin/Cummings.

Booch, G., Jacobson, I. and Rumbaugh, I. (1997) The *Unified Modeling Language Version 1.0*. Santa Clara, CA: Rational Software Corporation.

Coad, P. and Yourdon, E. (1991a) *Object-Oriented Analysis*, 2nd edn. Englewood Cliffs, NJ: Prentice Hall.

Coad, P. and Yourdon, E. (1991b) *Object-Oriented Design*. Englewood Cliffs, NJ: Prentice Hall.

Eriksen, L. B. and Skov, M. (1998) A critical look at OOA&D in multimedia systems development. In: *Proceedings of the 21th Information Systems Research Seminar In Scandinavia*, 8–11 August, Sæby, Denmark.

Eriksen, L. B., Skov, M. and Stage, J. (1998) *A Multimedia System Development Project: Documentation*. Available at the following URL: `http://www.cs.auc.dk/~dubois/manager/`.

Eriksen, L. B., Skov, M. and Stage, J. (2000) Multimedia systems development methodologies: experiences and requirements. Submitted for publication.

Goldberg, A. and Robson, D. (1989) *Smalltalk-80. The Language*. Reading, MA: Addison-Wesley.

Guindon, R., Krasner, H. and Curtis, B. (1987) Breakdowns and processes during the early activities of software design by professionals. In *Software State-of-the-art: Selected Papers* (ed. T. DeMarco and T. Lister). New York: Dorset House Publishing, pp. 455–475.

Hansen, K. K., Harbøll, B., Høegh, R. T., Lorentzen, K. H., Madsen, R. Ø. and Pedersen, M. S. (1999). *Zoomedia. A Multimedia System Developed for Aalborg Zoo* (in Danish). Aalborg University.

Jacobson, I., Christerson, M., Jonsson, P. and Övergaard, G. (1992). *Object-Oriented Software Engineering*. Wokingham: Addison-Wesley.

Jackson, M. (1983) *Systems Development Software*. Englewood Cliffs, NJ: Prentice Hall.

Madsen, O. L. and Møller-Pedersen, B. (1993) *Object-Oriented Programming in the Beta Programming Language*. Reading, MA: Addison-Wesley.

Manthey, M. (1988) *Maskinel II*. Technical report. Aalborg University, Denmark.

Manthey, M., Andersen, L. U., Arent, J., Christiansen, H., Nielsen, T. K., Simonsen, J. and Sørensen, T. B. (1994) *A Topsy Example*. Aalborg University, Denmark.

Martin, J. and Odell, J. (1993) *Object-Oriented Analysis and Design*. Englewood Cliffs, NJ: Prentice Hall.

Milner, R. (1989) *Communication and Concurrency*. Englewood Cliffs, NJ: Prentice Hall.

Pressman, R. S. (1992) *Software Engineering: A Practitioner's Approach*. New York: McGraw-Hill.

Rumbaugh, J., Blaha, M., Premerlani, W., Eddy, S. and Lorensen, W. (1991) *Object-Oriented Modelling and Design*. Englewood Cliffs, NJ: Prentice Hall.

Satoh, I. and Tokoro, M. (1992) A formalism for real-time concurrent object-oriented computing. *ACM Sigplan Notices: OOPSLA*. 27(10): 315–326.

Shlaer, S. and Mellor, S. J. (1988) *Object-Oriented Systems Analysis: Modeling the World in Data*. Englewood Cliffs, NJ: Yourdon Press.

Shlaer, S. and Mellor, S. J. (1992) *Object Lifecycles: Modeling the World in States*. Englewood Cliffs, NJ: Prentice Hall.

Skov, M. and Stage, J. (1995) *Object-Oriented Design of Process Architecture: An Exploratory Study – Documentation*. Available through the WWW at the following URL: `http://www.cs.auc.dk/~jans/procarch/`.

Skov, M. and Stage, J. (1996) Object-oriented design of process architecture: an exploratory study. In *Proceedings of the 19th Information Systems Research Seminar In Scandinavia*, 10–13 August, Lökeberg, Sweden, pp. 975–1000.

Sommerville, I. (1992) *Software Engineering*, 4th edn. Workingham: Addison-Wesley.

Sutcliffe, A. G. and Faraday, P. (1994) Designing presentation in multimedia interfaces. In *Proceedings of Computer-Human Interaction Conference '94* (eds. B. Adelson, S. Dumais and J. Olson). New York: ACM Press, pp. 92–98.

Sutcliffe, A. G. and Faraday, P. (1997) Designing effective multimedia presentations. In *Proceedings of Computer–Human Interaction Conference '97* (eds. C. Ware and D. Wixon). Available at `http://www.acm.org/sigs/sigchi/chi97/proceedings/paper/pf.htm`.

Wirfs-Brock, R., Wilkerson, B. and Wiener, L. (1990) *Designing Object-Oriented Software*. Englewood Cliffs, NJ: Prentice Hall.

22 Managing Narrative Multimedia Production

Claus A. Foss Rosenstand

This chapter on methodology introduces two very different approaches to multimedia production. In chapter Chapter 20 the focus was on how to use prototyping to learn about users' perception of the content, while Chapter 21 concentrated on the functionality of the software. Actually, the latter proposes that development of a multimedia system should proceed along parallel lines: the first dealing with software development, and the second with the production of assets. This approach is a problem in a multimedia production with a high level of content complexity.

Methods in multimedia production draw on traditions from both software and the media. Traditional software production uses methods dealing with problems of functionality: system requirements, object orientation, functional prototyping etc. Traditional media production uses another methodology to deal with content problems: storyboard, script, relations between roles etc.

Methods from the software tradition converging with methods from the media tradition means that problems from both traditions also converge. Often this results in the emergence of significant new multimedia challenges, and it sometimes leads to interference, where substantial new multimedia production problems emerge. My empirical studies show that interference occurs when functionality and content need to be handled at the same time. The interference problem then becomes extremely relevant, since functionality and content very often converge during the production of a multimedia system with high content complexity, demanding that the two aspects be combined and handled at the same time.

In order to analyse this problem, I have chosen an empirical approach, with its point of departure in my practical background as head of the board of InterAct, a multimedia company. InterAct produces narrative multimedia systems with a high level of content complexity, based mainly on interactive video. Because of this background, I have chosen to focus on the production of narrative multimedia systems in an industrial context.

In this context, resources and quality become essential interrelated parameters. *Resources* are designated as *time* and *cost*, *time* being how long it takes to make a production (all processes included), and *cost* being the money used during the production process. During the production process, resources are converted into people's work, where the use of material and tools results in a product. This is why the knowledge, attitude, skills and personality of the people in the production process are integrated elements of the resources.

Since the software and media industries converge, management of functionality and content becomes an important methodological problem: how can functionality and content be managed in an integrated way? In order to study this problem I have visited companies, institutions and people with different traditions and interests in the multimedia market.[1] For example, RWD Technologies in Baltimore (who implement new technology in the automotive industry, among others), PriceWaterhouseCoopers in London, DR-Multimedia in Copenhagen (the multimedia department of the National Danish Broadcasting Corporation), London Business School, and the University of Westminster. During these visits I discussed management methods in the narrative multimedia industry, with discussions mostly structured as open interviews.

From a management perspective, narrative multimedia systems are normally regarded as one item. However, there are varying demands on management with regard to the type of narrative multimedia system to be produced. In this chapter I differentiate between two types of quality: business quality and narrative quality. In short, business quality implies the satisfaction of the client, which means that the business quality of a product is or should be formalized by a "content and treatment agreement" with the client (England and Finney, 1999, p. 17). Narrative quality concerns the narrative experience of the user(s), which I will be returning to

---

1 WM-Data (large traditional IT consultant firm moving into the Danish Multimedia Industry), Deadline Multimedia (Multimedia game producer), DR-Multimedie (DR is the largest Danish public TV broadcaster), Shavana (Multimedia game producer) and SAS-Data (100% owned by Scandinavian Airlines), Nykris Digital Art (a company with a background in design and media production), SkillChange (a very professional business approach), PriceWaterhouseCoopers (multimedia department for internal training), Change Partnership (only top management training, and interested in the understanding of narrative multimedia tools for training), RWD Technologies (using multimedia to bring technology and people together, e.g. in the auto industry. They are interested in narrative multimedia tools), London Business School (interested in using multimedia in courses and for distance learning), University of Westminster (investigating the possibility of starting a new media cooperation with InterMedia, University of Aalborg), Andy Finney (multimedia consultant and author), Elaine England (multimedia consultant and author), Bob Hughes (multimedia consultant and author), Alexa Robinson (multimedia producer and interactive author), Peder Mervil (IT consultant and MBA student), Hellen Mousley (multimedia consultant and saleswoman). Thanks to everyone.

In March 1999, I arranged a seminar on the narrative multimedia industry for people representing different multimedia companies. The keynote speakers were Elaine England and Andy Finney. At the time, they had just published the successful book *Managing Multimedia – Project Management for Interactive Media*. It is their presence at the seminar that has made many of the points in this chapter possible.

in Section 22.3. When I use the term *quality*, I am referring to both business quality and narrative quality.

The chapter is structured in four sections:

In Section 22.1 my empirical observations of the narrative multimedia industry are represented as two opposing categories: the function- and content-orientated multimedia industries.

In Section 22.2 the opposing categories of the industry are used as second-order observations of the empirical narrative multimedia industry, giving a new point of view on the industry. The analysis leads to eight normative suggestions on how to manage a narrative multimedia production in an industrial context.

In Section 22.3 narrative multimedia systems are investigated from a managerial point of view. What narrative multimedia systems exist? What is quality in a narrative multimedia system?

Finally, in Section 22.4 I discuss the reasons why management of different types of narrative multimedia systems makes differing demands on the management of the production process.

22.1 A Function- and Content-Orientated Industry

To prevent any misunderstanding, I disregard two management problems which are not specific to the narrative multimedia industry. Nevertheless, they are often and wrongly designated as such.

The fact that lack of communication arises because of the interdisciplinary character of the production process is frequently emphasized as a particular problem in multimedia production. This can also be found in various other productions, e.g. in traditional media production, where technicians and creative people work closely together. The problem seems to appear more often in a multimedia production, but it is not particularly related to multimedia production. It is a symptom of a general lack of a specific multimedia language, resulting in misunderstandings which lead to frustration, incorrect work, re-work etc.

The fact that clients do not have sufficient understanding of the technology behind the products is also frequently pointed to as a particular problem in multimedia production. This problem is also found in software development, where, however, there are various methods to deal with it. Again, the problem seems to appear more often in multimedia production. It is a symptom of the clients' ignorance of the content made possible by the technology behind the products. The clients become uncertain of what they want, which often leads to lack of decision.

Section 22.3 defines the quality of narrative multimedia systems as a measure of the user's narrative experience. The narrative experience of the user is directly proportional to the level of narrative quality. In industry, it makes no sense to define quality only from an ideal or individual point of view. Instead, it is important to use the resources available in the specific context, i.e. to produce high business quality and to give the individual user the best possible narrative experience. A clear-cut definition of business quality must take its starting point in the specific industrial circumstances.[2] Thus, business quality and narrative quality are important subjects of discussion in every single production process.

Since the business quality of narrative multimedia systems is defined as agreement between content and treatment, a contract on the narrative content and structure should be formulated, beginning with the general level. Putting things in writing will not in itself improve the narrative quality, but it ensures communication about narrative quality, which could lead to improvement. This relationship between business quality and narrative quality implies that narrative quality is an added value[3] from the client's point of view.

The central aspect of the quality discussion is the link between resources and quality. As the use of resources is a serious issue for the client, the client should participate in the discussion of quality. In a multimedia company, this discussion must take place within the core team producing the narrative multimedia system, thereby involving key people and their qualifications. As the quality discussion takes place in a particular organization, it includes the employees, material and tools into which the company is able to convert the resources.

My empirical observations in different companies dealing with narrative multimedia productions identified a couple of interesting differences in the way the companies work. It paved the way for establishing two types of multimedia industry. The types accentuate some important aspects regarding management in the narrative multimedia industry, and they are characterized as two opposed categories, which can be perceived as two extremes in a continuous empirical reality: a *function-orientated industry* and a *content-orientated industry*.[4]

The specific characteristics of the function- and content-orientated industries are summarized in Table 22.1.[5]

In the function-orientated multimedia industry, the focus is on the functionality of the multimedia system in the production process. This is an appropriate focus in

2 Where quality is concerned, I distinguish between a purely academic discussion of ideal quality and a discussion of quality in an industrial context, where time and cost are always major parts of the quality issue. This discussion would be extremely fertile when dealing with basic research. I am certain that it will lead to perceptions which could be used to optimize product quality in some, but not all, industrial matters.

3 If the client receives what is agreed on in the contract, he or she should (in theory) be satisfied. But if the narrative quality (experience of the end-user) is higher than expected, the client will be happy – and the contrary if the narrative quality is lower. High narrative quality is a good way to get return business.

4 The method I use (with two opposite categories) is a sociological method, which Max Weber described at the beginning of the 20th century. In every social observation it is a prerequisite that ideal types of rational human action can be identified. Ideal types are idealized models, which can be perceived as extremes in a continuous empirical reality.

5 I presented the two business types for the first time at the seminar on "Organizing Multimedia Production in the Narrative Multimedia Industry", March 1999. Later, they were discussed and developed at a seminar at InterMedia Denmark, April 1999 and during an academic three-month stay in London, September–November 1999.

Table 22.1 Two extreme narrative multimedia industries.

	Function-orientated industry	Content-oriented industry
1.	People with competence in software production	People with competence in media production
2.	Use of shovelware	Development of new concepts
3.	Conventional	Creative
4.	Solutions based on clients' needs	Ideal solutions
5.	Tested methods	New methods
6.	Structured work	Seek and learn
7.	Reuse of code, methods and techniques	Use and throw away
8.	Calculated risk and fear	Danger and anxiety

many contexts of computer system productions. For instance, an air traffic surveillance system should be produced with a maximum reliable surveillance function. However, in narrative multimedia systems, functionality is mainly used for the distribution of narrative control; the functionality supports the user's narrative experience (cf. Section 22.3). That is why the content must also be in focus when producing a narrative multimedia system.

In the following, Table 22.1 is developed further, and in Section 22.2 I have used it to establish eight normative characteristics for how functionality and content can be managed at the same time.

22.1.1 People with Competence in Software Production <> People with Competence in Media Production

The key persons working in the function-orientated industry are experienced in producing functionality, typically with software backgrounds as programmers or system developers. Compared with the content-orientated industry, people in the software industry have a greater understanding of the technical aspects of the computer, meaning that attention is drawn to the risks of dealing with technological solutions, e.g. online vs. offline solutions. The key persons working in the content-orientated industry are trained in media production, typically with media backgrounds as authors, publishers or television producers, making them better qualified than people working in the function-orientated industry when it comes to the choice of content.

22.1.2 Use of Shovelware <> Development of New Concepts

"Shovelware" means to shovel the product onto the computer. Shovelware is a case of making, for example, a computer test for management recruitment based on a traditional paper text. Instead of exploring the potential of the computer media, e.g. animations of a situation, the computer is used just like a paper test. Such solutions are often found in the function-orientated industry, the reason being that the function of, for example, paper tests is directly copied into a computer test. In some cases, particularly when the intention is to carry out a well-known function (e.g. the automation of speed control), it is not necessarily a bad idea to shovel the product into the computer. However, as in the content-orientated industry, it is also important in a multimedia production to pose the question: will different content[6] mean better product quality? An answer to this question will often lead to the development of new concepts and another production process.

22.1.3 Conventional <> Creative

The development of new concepts in the content-orientated industry means that one must be creative. Smart but not necessarily rational solutions may be created, often resulting in an artistic performance. Since the client may not approve of the "smart" artistic solutions, this may cause problems in the relationship between the client and the multimedia company. If the producer is the creative type, he or she will probably see the client's disapproval as a personal attack, questioning his or her individual taste and professional pride. Similarly, products in the function-orientated industry are known to be conventional. Consequently, the result of a production process is predictable. This may turn out to be an advantage in a relationship with the client, because the client is acquainted with the product. On the other hand, the client cannot expect a smart solution, even if it has an unconventional problem requiring an unconventional and smart solution.

22.1.4 Solutions Based on Clients' Needs <> Ideal Solutions

When dealing with a production, the function-orientated industry takes its point of departure in the business needs of the client. As a consequence, solutions are normally based on careful identification and analyses of the clients' needs in terms of problems and wishes. In the content-orientated industry, creativity and "smartness" are the most important issues. Therefore the people in this industry tend to focus on ideal solutions. As a consequence, ideal solutions have their point of departure in the producers' personal creativity. This difference is found in the expression "you are only as good as your last product", in contrast to the expression "you are only as good as your last idea".[7]

22.1.5 Tested Methods <> New Methods

Contrary to the content-orientated industry, the function-orientated industry is known for using tested methods, including work methods, meaning that the risk of functional mistakes is greater in the content-orientated industry. The products of the function-orientated industry are more reliable than those of the content-orientated industry. As a matter of fact, in the function-orientated industry, reliability is often equated with product quality. In my understanding of the narrative multimedia industry, this is deemed only partly correct, to the extent that functional errors have a negative influence on the narrative experience of the user, which, of

---

6 By *different content* I mean different from content that could be shovelled.
7 Adrian Snook (interview, 1999), Manager, SkillChange, is quoted for this observation.

course, is often the case.[8] In that respect, the difference between the function- and content-orientated industries is the computer metaphor in use. In the functional multimedia industry, the computer metaphor is *machine*, like thinking of a car that can break down. In the content-orientated industry, the computer metaphor is *information system*.[9]

22.1.6 Structured Work <> Seek and Learn

The use of tested methods in the function-orientated industry makes the work process very structured. A structured work process is a very good aid in observing the deadlines and budget of a production. The work process in the content-orientated industry is characterized by a "seek and learn" process. Unpredicted needs in terms of problems and wishes are identified during the production process, and only during this process does the production team learn how to find solutions to particular needs. In the content-orientated industry, which is known to use new methods, work is very often unstructured. This is why planned budgets and deadlines in the content-orientated industry are often unrealistic. A doubling of the scheduled time and cost is not unheard of.

22.1.7 Reuse of Code, Methods and Techniques <> Use and Throw Away

In the function-orientated industry, reuse is common. In addition to the reuse of methods, program coding and techniques are also reused. A technique could, for example, be a certain way of integrating video and animation; this technique may very well be reused. Contrary to the function-orientated industry, the content-orientated industry has a use and throw away culture, because content is more important than the choice of method, technique and code.[10] The shape of the content depends on the choice of method, technique and code, which is why a new production in the content-orientated industry must always be started from scratch.

22.1.8 Calculated Risk and Fear <> Danger and Anxiety

Prior to the initiation of the actual production in the function-orientated industry, there is already a lot of knowledge concerning the production process.

---

8 An example of a functional error, which has no negative influence on the quality of the product, is in the multimedia computer game for children "Spøgelse med forkølelse" ["A Ghost with a Cold"]. In this game, a certain combination of interactive events results in a colour error. I was able to see the error because I have some computer knowledge, but the child (Teis Semey) showed it to me as a special and interesting feature of the narrative universe.

9 This difference between a machine and an information metaphor is comparable to the cultural metaphor of the modern and hypercomplex society (Qvortrup, 1998, pp. 71 ff.).

10 Simon Jon Andreasen, Multimedia Director at Deadline Multimedia, producing multimedia computer games, states that reusing program code, techniques, methods or content in an artistic production is an artistic choice independent of the resources.

This is why it is possible to work with a calculated risk. In a production process, risk is characterized by the predictability of possible damage during the process. This is not to be equated with danger, which characterizes the content-orientated industry. In this industry, only a little knowledge concerning the production process exists before the actual production. In contrast to risk, danger means being unaware of the consequences of the choices made. An example could be the choice of a new technique to obtain a better video quality – a technique not tested along with the chosen platform(s). Choosing a new technique exposes the production process and the product to danger, namely the possibility of a non- or poorly working multimedia system.[11] On a psychological level, the distinction between risk and danger deals with a distinction between fear and anxiety.[12] Risk and fear are aimed at something; danger and anxiety are about something which cannot be predicted.

22.2 Suggestions on Management

In the above, the function-orientated industry represented an industry with appropriate methods for handling problems of functionality, and the content-orientated industry represented an industry with appropriate methods for handling problems of content. This created a *form*, which accentuated important aspects of management in the narrative multimedia industry. In this section, I use this form as a *medium* for a second-order observation of the empirical narrative multimedia industry.

11 The example is taken from InterAct. We wanted to implement video with broadcast video quality in a new product (Virtuel VærdiLedelse [Virtual Value Management]). We were able to include the video format on the computer with Director (a programming language/general production tool). It was possible to compress the video satisfactorily. However, it turned out that the compressed video clips could not be united interactively in Director. This is an example of a danger to which we chose to expose the production process and InterAct.

12 A parallel is drawn between Niklas Luhmann's distinction between risk and danger (Luhmann, 1997, pp. 155 ff.) and Søren Kierkegaard's distinction between fear and anxiety (Kirkegaard, 1962, pp. 135 ff.). The text shows my understanding of Luhmann's distinction between risk and danger. Kierkegaard deals with fear as something that refers to an object, though, "Angest er Frihedens Virkelighed som Muligheden for Muligheden" ["Anxiety is the Reality of Freedom as a Possibility for a Possibility"]. Anxiety is connected to innocence and innocence is defined as being unaware – meaning the absence of the possibility of determining the future. However, at the same time, anxiety in this sense provides a feeling of seeking after something ("...i sin søde beængstelse" ["...in the sweet anxiety"]). For instance, one can seek the possibility of the use of a better quality of video in a narrative multimedia production. In the social dimension, fear and risk are closely connected to danger and anxiety. The risk that one person may fear may to another person be a danger that makes him or her anxious. As usual, one takes a risk and accepts the possible damage to obtain an advantage. To get an order, a multimedia company may take a risk while negotiating the deadline of a project with the client. If, for instance, the product must be ready on a certain date, then the producer's risk exposes the client to a danger.

Table 22.2 Eight suggestions on management.

1.	Competence in convergence of functionality and content
2.	Early consideration of the potentialities of the media
3.	Decide on the creative constraints
4.	Produce industrialized optimal solutions
5.	Make a distinction between development and production
6.	Reserve resources for contingencies in production process
7.	Use production tools for reuse
8.	Transform danger and anxiety into risk and fear

This re-entry of my observations into the empirical field has been an analytical process, primarily carried out through open interviews and conversations with people in the field. During this process, possibilities for combining high narrative quality with limited use of resources were discussed. The work has resulted in eight normative suggestions on how to manage a narrative multimedia production process in an industrial context, including suggestions on how to manage functionality and content at the same time.

Furthermore, I make suggestions on how to achieve higher narrative quality, because quality in narrative multimedia systems must be reached though a successful convergence of content and functionality. This refers to an industrial context, which means that the relationship between resources (time and cost) and quality is also taken into consideration.

In Table 22.2, specific normative characteristics of management in the narrative multimedia industry have been listed. The numbers (1 to 8) refer to the numbers in Table 22.1 in Section 22.1. The suggestions are the results of an empirical analysis, and the analysis is most likely incomplete.[13] In the following, I elaborate on exactly what is meant by each characteristic.

It is essential to keep in mind that functionality is what supports the content of a narrative multimedia product, and not the other way around (cf. Section 22.3). This aspect is important in the choice of the design of a particular production, and it is also important in communication with the client – including the user. It is important to remember the relationship between the elements of time, cost and quality. If one of these is changed, it will influence the two other elements. This implies, for example, that the impact on time and cost of a change in quality has to be estimated before a change is agreed with the client. What might seem to be a small change in the content could result in a complex change in functionality, and as a result, a major difference in resource requirements. This is why no change should be agreed upon with the client before the consequences have been checked in the core team.

---

13 This is not an attempt to avoid critique of the actual analysis. The point is that critique should be aimed at the validity of the results or at a lack of consistency. The critique should not be aimed at the empirical imperfection.

22.2.1 People with Competence in Software Production <> People with Competence in Media Production

→ Competence in convergence of functionality and content

To understand how to converge functionality and content, the production process of a narrative multimedia system must include people who have competence in both software production and media production. To have this competence in the convergence of functionality and content is a matter of both knowledge and skills. Knowledge can be taught, while skills are knowledge transferred into practice, which requires quite a lot of experience. In a traditional software production, it is a common problem that the client does not know how to express what he wants from the product so that it can fulfil his needs. Often, the project manager deals with the problem by producing different prototypes in order to improve communication with the client. In traditional media production, the problem is reversed: everyone, and particular every client, thinks they know what is a good or a bad media production. For instance, everybody has an opinion on whether a video is good or bad. This is why the client is very rarely invited to participate in the actual editing of a video. Even though the producer knows exactly how the production will end up, it is difficult for a client to imagine. This is one reason why interference exists between the working methods and the relationship with the client in software and media production.[14] Because the client understands the content and normally not the functionality linking the contents, it is important to communicate with the client about the content and not about the underlying functionality. The client should not worry about how functionality and content are converged. The only thing the client needs to know is how many resources it takes to produce the agreed content. When producing a narrative multimedia system, it is not possible to describe in writing everything about the narrative quality from the beginning – that would be the same as producing the actual system. Thus, the actual cooperation with the client must be split into sections. The first step is to make a deal on things in general: how is the control over the narrative premise and structure distributed between the computer and the user (cf. Section 22.3)? What is the product used for? Who is the user? And so on. When an agreement on these general issues has been reached, the narrative multimedia organization works for some time at a more specific level, without interference from the client. This could, for instance, result in an interactive script, to be used for further communication with the client on the content at a more specific level. In this case, it is important that the multimedia company does not accept changes at a general level – unless the client is prepared to change the resources and deadlines. To ensure this, it is necessary to include it in the contract with the client, who is able to authorize the content created in the production process by a signature. A minor change at a general level could very well lead to a big change at a more specific level, and consequently affect the entire multimedia company – for example, it might mean that an author has to rewrite a

14 Karen Vibeke Jacobsen, Danmarks Radio (Radio Denmark), made this point in March 1999.

manuscript. Indirectly, it will often have an impact on the whole production. For instance, the interactive script could be the point of reference for the implementation of the underlying functionality and the recording of a video. In this case, the programmers have been scheduled and video photographers, sound recordists, actors etc. have been employed. In addition to the problems in the actual production, the interactive author's time is usually scheduled for other parallel productions, which must now wait – and so on. The example illustrates that small changes in the content at a general level at the wrong time can very well lead to a doubling of the budget and a considerable postponing of the deadline. The question should always be whether the client will offer the necessary resources in terms of time and cost.

22.2.2 Use of Shovelware <> Developing New Concepts

→ Early consideration of the potentials of the media

Multimedia systems have a different and greater potential for presenting content than any other information medium.[15] Thus a particular story can very well be told differently than it would have been in a traditional media. The kind of relationship composed between the *story level* and the *telling level* is very important for the quality of the product. The story level is the imagined reality where the story is displayed – it is the fictional universe. The telling level is the way in which the story level is communicated (Ryum, 1982, p. 2). It is possible to improve the narrative quality considerably by using a smart way of composing the relationship, without an increase in expense. The way in which the relationship is created has a great effect on the resources that must be used for the production of text, video, animations etc. Thus it is important to reflect on or consider the potential of the narrative media in the early phases of the production process.

22.2.3 Conventional <> Creative

→ Decide on the creative constraints

To compose a smart connection between the story level and the telling level demands room for creativity. There are many ways in which a story can be told. Therefore there must be room for the playing with, and testing of, different compositions. This requires resources, which is why there has to be a decision on the creative constraints – on when, and how much, creativity there is room for. Because

15 In this case, a multimedia system is the ultimate medium. Theoretically, it can be exposed to the user like any information media. Allan Turing showed how a computer (as a Turing Machine) can configure itself. Thus, the point is semiotic, while the computer can be understood as a *media machine* – a machine which can be used to produce every media system imaginable. A computer can create the relationship between the signifier and the signified itself (it just has to be started).

the way the media potential is used seriously influences the need for resources and scheduling, it will not be possible to calculate how many resources a production will take if the narrative quality in general is undecided. Thus, the creative work must take place at the beginning of the project process . The creative constraint could, for instance, be determined by a demand for the use of a certain well-known narrative structure – this would restrict the use of functionality. Because a certain structure constrains the way in which the content is integrated, the experienced multimedia company will know how many resources it will take to implement the narrative multimedia system. It is important to ensure a high level of creativity, which can be done by moving the creative work into a clearly defined framework, within which the artistic person must be as creative as possible. This does not mean that it is not necessary to talk about creative ideas that lie beyond the creative constraints, or ideas created late in the production process. First of all, ideas are more likely to be forgotten if they are not shared with other people. Perhaps an idea could be used in another context – either in the current production or some other. Secondly, it is possible that the idea can be slightly altered by someone else in the multimedia company, placing it within the creative constraints. Thirdly, it is possible that a production will have unused resources that make it possible to implement an idea late in the production process.

22.2.4 Solutions Based on Clients' Needs <> Ideal Solutions

→ Produce industrialized optimal solutions

To allow the need for resources to be calculated, it is necessary to be familiar with the production circumstances in terms of time and costs. Usually, industrial circumstances do not allow the development of ideal solutions. Thus one has to optimize the quality of the product in the constraints already decided upon. This is why adjustments of the narrative quality should only be within the agreed constraints. An adjustment will often be an adjustment of how resources should be used. The necessary use of artistic people in a narrative multimedia production may very well lead to the desire for an ideal solution and make it difficult to make the necessary artistic compromises without using more resources than are available. To keep the work on track, it is important to communicate the connection between resources and the quality of the solutions inside the core team. It is vital that individual employees understand that their work is not about being as good an instructional designer, graphic designer or author, etc., as possible. The objective is to show how good they are within the arranged constraints. If they fail to understand this, the creative energy will be transferred into frustration over the ideas that it is impossible to put into effect. This not only results in a poor working environment, but also in a substantial reduction of the possibility of reaching a potentially high product quality. In the end, it will leave the clients dissatisfied. This is why it is so important to optimize solutions instead of making them ideal. Naturally, the needs of the client should still be a starting point for creativity, but there may very well be many different solutions that satisfy the same need.

22.2.5 Tested Methods <> New Methods

→ Make a distinction between development and production

New concepts, creativity and optimization often mean that things must be dealt with in new and different ways. This means that new implementations and working methods are used that may lead to unreliable products and thereby a possible weakness in the quality of a product. In this case, the management process must be very painstaking. However, first of all, it is to be considered whether it is possible to predict the consequences of a new method or not. In reality, that means that one can choose to use some of the resources to test a new method. An example could be the use of a new *extra* (additional tool) to play a certain kind of audio in the development tool known as Macromedia Director. In this case, the *extra* must be bought, and an audio segment must be produced as usual – including the use of compression techniques. Then a test must be carried out to make sure that it fits the environment (platform, computer, other programs etc.) in which it is to be integrated. It is not possible to make a safe choice before the test is effected. Will the new work method and technique be used? The choice is dependent on quality optimization criteria. If the test turns out successfully, it may be possible to save time in programming and to improve the quality of a product. If it demands too many resources to test the new method, or if the method does not optimize the production process, then it must be excluded from the production. Now the point has been reached when a new method chosen for testing would have been able to optimize the process of production, but it is still too demanding on resources for testing to be possible inside the constraints of the particular production. Not developing (and using) this method is something that can be done in the current production, but ignoring the method in a business organization is not acceptable. If the multimedia company does not develop new methods it will stagnate, which is the same as decline in an environment where technology changes and competitors optimize their production processes. Thus the company must take note of the particular method and then distinguish between production and development. Development is something which is *not* integrated in a current production. This is the reason why narrative multimedia companies have to establish development environments which are not tied to particular productions.

22.2.6 Structured Work <> Seek and Learn

→ Reserve resources for contingencies in the production process

Since it is not possible to calculate the entire risk connected with a certain method, some of the resources must be reserved for contingencies in the production process. *Contingency resources* are the resources covering the arbitrary aspects of a production process. Contingency resources can, for example, be used to investigate, test and learn about opportunities and problems which were not foreseen at the beginning of the project, and still keep the project on track. The amount of contingency resources that should be reserved differs from project to project. In any case, it is a good idea to save contingency resources for the last phase of the production process. A minor portion of resources used for a good finish may considerably increase the quality of a narrative multimedia system. Caution should be shown in the use of contingency resources – there is always a need for more than reserved. The more structured the production process, the fewer the contingency resources needed. This means that the project manager has to reserve a larger allocation of contingency resources for new and different projects, requiring the use of new and untested methods. In this case, a reservation of 25% of time and cost for contingencies in the process is common. The production manager and the production team are likely to want as many resources as possible to optimize the quality of a product in a particular production. In this case, it is important that everybody understands why it is important to distinguish between individual productions and development in general: the resources used as contingency resources within a particular project are resources withheld from potential development. If the production team does not have a proper understanding of this, it could lead to frustration, which of course has a negative impact on quality. A better way of ensuring this understanding among the people involved is to distinguish between roles and persons. The same person can be a designer (one role) in certain matters and in other matters be involved in a developmental environment (another role). This ensures an exchange of experience between a production and a development environment. Development costs which are not a part of individual productions must be included in the budgets of individual productions, meaning that clients pay for development that is of no importance to them. However, the clients benefit by the development costs that previous clients have paid. This is a significant reason why it is so resource-demanding to get a foothold in the market of narrative multimedia. It is important to be able to use substantial resources in the first steps of the development of a multimedia company.

22.2.7 Reuse of Code, Methods and Techniques <> Use and Throw Away

→ Use production tools for reuse

Reusing material may mean saving on resources. It is important to realize that reuse of material narrows the creative constraints. This could reduce the quality of a product, but not necessarily. A clear delimitation of the creative constraints may also increase the creative process, because less energy is required to define the delimitation. A good way of defining the creative constraints is to demand a production kept within the framework of a specific production tool. A large number of production tools are available on the market, but they are often designed for the production of a certain kind of content. Thus it is very often necessary for the business organization to develop its own production tools. An example could be a production tool designed for the making of video-based conflict narrative multimedia systems[16] (cf. Section 22.3). The tool could be continuously developed in the development environment and not developed in the individual productions, in order to optimize individual productions. A production tool consists of a

16 InterAct has developed such a production tool.

template that is filled in, and afterwards the production tool automatically uses the filled template to create code and/or material. The result can be either a large or a small part of a final product. A production tool may be simple; however, it can lead to a considerable reduction in the use of resources. An example could be the production of a Norwegian version of a Danish product, with a lot of speech for various small animations. It is possible to put the duration of the Danish speech fragments into a production tool (the template) with the corresponding Norwegian speech fragments. The smart little production tool then automatically makes sure that the durations of the Norwegian speech fragments are equal to the durations of the original Danish speech fragments. In this way, the Norwegian speech and the original Danish animation will fit together. The production tool makes it possible to reuse the entire animation material.[17] This example illustrates the importance of being aware of the possibilities and consequences of using production tools. When a production tool is produced and tested, it can be reused for the fast and relatively cheap serial production of narrative multimedia systems with relatively high reliability. Thus, production tools offer a technique of reuse based on reusable program code (template). With a production tool, the work will be formalized. It is easy to forget that the development of a production tool also forces one to reflect upon working methods. This is why attention should be paid to the possibility of optimizing the cooperation within a production team by developing a production tool; it forces the employees to focus on the way they work.

22.2.8 Calculated Risk and Fear <> Danger and Anxiety

→ Transform danger and anxiety into risk and fear

In the narrative multimedia industry, it is, of course, important to be proactive. To be proactive is basically about being able to successfully predict occurrences in the production process. Thus it is about being able to look forward in time, and where the future seems blurred, one estimates the need for contingency resources. A production should never be initiated if it is impossible to calculate the need for contingency resources. If the contingency resources are calculated correctly, the project will not be exposed to danger, only to a calculated risk. Now, there could be attractive possibilities with the potential to improve product quality. If one wishes to examine this dangerous possibility, the danger should be transformed into risk. In reality, that means encompassing the danger in calculated risk. In proactive management, a predetermined amount of contingency resources is used to test the dangerous possibility. As such, the project is "only" exposed to a calculated risk, namely losing the predetermined portion of contingency resources. As said before, there is a connection between risk and fear and between danger and anxiety. On a psychological level, proactive management is about encompassing anxiety in fear. By testing a dangerous possibility with a predetermined amount of contingency resources, the worst a proactive manager needs to fear is that the tested method does not work. In proactive management, there is no need for anxiety, because the

17 Simon Jon Andreasen (seminar, 1999), Multimedia Director, Deadline Multimedia, is quoted for this example.

consequences of failure are well known. The big question is, of course, whether the proper amount of contingency resources is available. This danger always exists. The use of contingency resources must be measured against the possible improvement of product quality. Perhaps an idea must be abandoned. Or perhaps the ideas should be put into a development environment, where dangers are precisely encompassed by calculated risks.

22.3 Narrative Multimedia Systems

So far, we have analysed management in the narrative multimedia industry in general. This section identifies four different types of narrative multimedia system. The production of each type requires a different type of management, which I will return to in the next section.

The dictionary defines the concept *narrative* as *the advancing of a story*. In relation to traditional media, interactivity is a new and central aspect of computer-based multimedia systems. Therefore I have focused on the unique new opportunity that interactivity creates when it is combined with the narrative: user control. It has made way for a division between, on the one hand, who controls the narrative structure and, on the other hand, who controls the narrative premise when the product is in use. Does the user or the computer control the narrative?

The narrative structure in a narrative multimedia system is to be defined as the way in which the narrative is built up in time and space. The narrative structure does not include the content, which the user interprets or selects by means of the interactive possibilities.

The narrative structure in multimedia systems thus includes the way in which a computer controls the integration of the assets, such as animation, speech and music. As regards the narrative structure, there are both narrative multimedia systems where the computer controls and those where it does not control the structure on which the advancing story is based.

When the computer controls the integration of the assets on behalf of the integration of an existing structure, the computer also controls the narrative structure. When the computer controls the integration of the assets on behalf of the interactivity of the user, the user indirectly controls the narrative structure.

A narrative premise is the claim which the advancing story supports. A premise is often morally orientated (Harms Larsen, 1990, p. 104). A premise could, for example, be: *it is good to be an analytic manager*. The premise does not include the structure, which is invisible to the user. Users are only indirectly exposed to the structure, because they can choose to interpret the montage of assets as an index of a part of the structure.

The premise in narrative multimedia systems deals with the way in which a computer controls the integration of the *content* (truth, diplomacy, correctness etc.). With regards to the premise, there are narrative multimedia systems where the computer controls the premise supported by the advancing story and those where it does not.

Table 22.3 Four types of narrative multimedia system.

Premise	Structure	
	Computer controls the narrative structure	User controls the narrative structure
Computer controls the narrative premise	Determined narrative	Explorative narrative
User controls the narrative premise	Conflict narrative	Creative narrative

When the computer controls the integration of the content on behalf of the integration of an existing premise, the computer also controls the narrative premise. When the computer controls the integration of the content though the interactivity of the user, the user indirectly controls the narrative premise.

Based on the above analysis, four different types of narrative can be defined. They characterize different narrative multimedia systems: determined narrative, explorative narrative, conflict narrative and creative narrative (Table 22.3).[18] The four types of narrative are labelled from the user's point of view.

In a *determined narrative*, the advancing story is decided with regard to the structural composition and the claim supported by the story. An example of this could be a PowerPoint-created slide show of *The Ugly Duckling* by Hans Christian Andersen, where the production team, though the computer, has already decided the order of the different screens. This means that the user has no control of the structure or premise. Therefore it is called a determined narrative. A lot of the so-called "edutainment" products belong to this category of narrative. In my opinion this is also the reason why they are often boring, particularly when you expect narrative control. Why interact with the narrative if you do not have any control over it?

In an *explorative narrative*, the advancing story is decided with regard to the claim supported. However, the user decides the structural composition of the story. An example of this is the standard offline version of "Quake" (a 3D shooting game). By using the keyboard, for example, the player can decide where to move in three-dimensional cyberspace. The morally orientated claim is simple and already decided: kill everything that moves – or cyber-die. The user is thus in a situation where the environment must be explored – hence the term "explorative narrative". Game producers for the Sony PlayStation, Nintendo and some PCs are the main competitors in the market for explorative narrative multimedia systems.

In a *conflict narrative*, the advancing story is decided with regard to structural composition. However, it is the user who creates the claim that the advancing story supports. Examples of this are some of InterAct's assessment multimedia tools, e.g. Virtual Management. By clicking on interactive symbols, the user has to choose parts of the content of the advancing story. The user chooses between different claims that should lead to the right or most suitable way of being a manager in different situations (producer, analyst, entrepreneur or integrator type), thereby

18 I presented a variant of the matrix for the first time at the seminar I arranged on Organizing Multimedia Production in the Narrative Multimedia Industry, March 1999.

exposing the user to different conflicts. Consequently, this is called a conflict narrative. Conflict narrative multimedia systems are classics. They have been known in the shape of text-based adventure games since the early 1980s.

In a *creative narrative,* the user creates both the structural composition and the claim that the advancing story supports. An example of this is "The Puppet Motel" by Laurie Anderson (1995). The user can freely navigate in 33 different rooms (love, ugly-one-with-the-jewels, palm reader etc.) and it is possible to interact with different objects of choice. The user creates everything regarding the narrative in the advancing story, so it is called a creative narrative. "The Puppet Motel" fascinates me, but I quickly get bored. Could it be because I have to do all the narrative work in a constrained cyber-world?

It could be discussed whether "The Puppet Motel", for instance, turns out to be a narrative experience or not. In this context, I find the discussion of terminology unprofitable. It is more relevant that a narrative multimedia system is normally a hybrid between the different narrative types. Actually, I only know a very few multimedia products which represent one of the narrative types in its pure form, not excluding the examples above. For instance, Virtual Management does contain a narrative structure which can be controlled by the user, although it is relatively simple.

The typification of different narrative multimedia systems implies that they must contain a premise and a structure. The premise and the structure must be controlled by a computer and/or a user. Thus I have defined a narrative multimedia system as follows:

- The integration of the *assets* is built on a narrative *structure*, which is controlled by a user through the use of interactivity and/or by a computer.
- The integration of the *content* is built on a narrative *premise*, which is controlled by a user through the use of interactivity and/or by a computer.

In a narrative multimedia system, the distribution of the computer's and the user's narrative control of content is controlled by the system. This is why a spreadsheet, a word processor or a drawing tool is not a narrative multimedia system – there is no control of the narrative premise and structure to distribute.

The definition could be used in a theory on interactivity in narrative multimedia systems. It could be relevant to find out more about different degrees of interactivity as a function of the user's, vs. the computer's, control of the narrative. Here, the different hybrids of the above-mentioned narrative categories could be examined.

To the user of narrative multimedia applications, it makes a difference whether the user or the computer controls the narrative structure and premise when the system is in use. A definition of narrative quality must be relative: what is low narrative quality to one person can very well be high narrative quality to another person. This means that the *narrative quality of narrative multimedia systems is a measure of the user's narrative experience.* This is why a narrative quality discussion will always be normative to some extent. This is also why Table 22.3, listing narrative types, contains no dimension of narrative quality.

The narrative experience contains different shapes, all depending on how the narrative control is distributed. This is what separates narrative multimedia systems from other multimedia systems in general, and leads to a very important aspect when dealing with management in the narrative multimedia industry: Functionality in a narrative multimedia system is not an aim, but rather the means of creating a narrative experience. Thus, functionality in narrative multimedia systems supports the experience of the narrative, and not the other way round. This is why content comes before functionality when dealing with narrative multimedia systems. Actually, it is possible to create the same narrative experience with different narrative structures.

22.4 Different Management Demands

Both structure and premise define a narrative multimedia system. This means that structure and premise must be integrated in the production process. From the software perspective, nodes are connected in a normally advanced data structure, where each node has a pointer to at least one other node (except the last node(s) of the story). Therefore the way the nodes are connected has to do with functionality – from a software perspective. From the media perspective, scenes are connected to support the claim supported by the advancing story (the premise). Consequently, connecting scenes has to do with content – from a media perceptive. To the computer there is no difference in nodes and scenes, and this is why functionality and content always converge in a narrative multimedia production, although they converge in different ways.

A functional and content dimension can be applied to Table 22.3, as shown in Figure 22.1. The more the user has control of the narrative structure, the more complex is the creation of the underlying structure. Conversely, the more the user has control of the narrative premise, the more complex is the creation of the premise of the story.

This means that functionality and content are converged differently in the four types of narrative multimedia system. This is exemplified below with the possible use of different kinds of production tool.

When producing a determined narrative multimedia system, the convergence between functionality and content is low. This means that there are few problems with handling the functionality and the content at the same time. A determined narrative multimedia system can very easily be produced with a production tool such as PowerPoint or Macromedia AuthorWare. Using these types of production tools means a certain convergence between functionality and content in the production process.

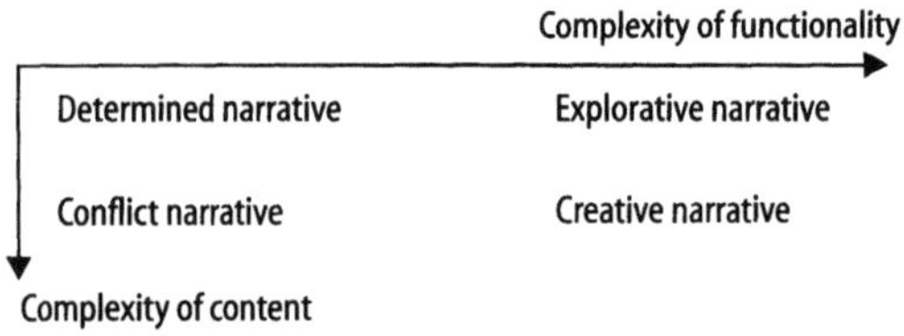

Figure 22.1 Complexity of creating a narrative multimedia system.

When producing an explorative narrative multimedia system, there is some convergence between functionality and content. The complexity of creating functionality is higher than the complexity of creating content. This requires a good understanding of the underlying functionality in the management process. An explorative narrative multimedia system is often produced with production tools labelled *gameboxes* and *engines*. The narrative multimedia company develops its own gameboxes and engines, which have distinct and specific purposes. Such a production tool can be very time- and cost-effective in the multimedia company in question, but cannot normally be used to optimize the relationship between time, cost and quality in other multimedia companies.

When producing a conflict narrative multimedia system there is also some convergence between functionality and content. The complexity of creating content is higher than the complexity of creating functionality. This requires a high understanding of the interactive content in the management process. Conflict narrative multimedia systems are often produced with production tools labelled *author tools*. Like the production tools for explorative narrative multimedia systems, the author tool is produced for a particular purpose inside the multimedia company, and can only be used for optimizing the relationship between time, cost and quality inside the multimedia company.

When producing a creative narrative multimedia system, there is high convergence between the functionality and content. This requires both a good understanding of the underlying functionality and of the interactive content. Production of a relatively large creative narrative multimedia system requires the use of *gameboxes*, *engines* and *author tools*, and it is an advantage if the different production tools are integrated, so that the convergence of functionality and content is integrated into the production tool.

As stated early in the chapter, management problems in the narrative multimedia industry arise when functionality and content converge. The more functionality and content converge, the more interference can be expected. Interference means that traditional methods from the traditional software and the traditional media industry, respectively, are insufficient, and new narrative multimedia production methods, in particular, are needed.

The greater the complexity of functionality and content that have to be handled at the same time, the more competently the production process must be managed. In terms of convergence of functionality and content, it is easier to manage the production of a determined narrative multimedia system than the production of an explorative or a conflict narrative multimedia system. And it is easier to manage the production of an explorative or a conflict narrative multimedia system than the production of a creative narrative multimedia system.

From the management perspective, the complexity of the convergence of functionality and content in the production process seems to increase with more narrative control distributed to the user. Higher complexity means that more effort must be put into organizing the complexity in order to gain a high narrative quality. And more attention should be paid to the eight normative suggestions (cf. Table 22.3).

It is beyond the scope of this chapter to go into detail on the production process of the four types of narrative multimedia systems. However, more research in this field is needed.

References

Aldrich, D. F. (1999) *Mastering the Digital Market Place.* New York: Wiley.

Decker, R. (1989) Data Structures. Englewood Cliffs, NJ: Prentice Hall.

England, E. and Finney, A. (1999) *Managing Multimedia – Project Management for Interactive Media,* 2nd edn. Harlow: Addison-Wesley.

Finneman, N. O. (1994) *Tanke, sprog & maskine* [*Mind, Language & Machine*]. Copenhagen: Akademisk Forlag.

Grøn, A., Husted, J., Lübcke, P., Rasmussen, S. A., Sandøe, P. and Stefansen, N. C. (1983) Politikens filosofi leksikon [*Politikens' Encyclopaedia of Philosophy*]. Copenhagen: Politikens Forlag.

Kierkegaard, S. (1962) Begrebet angst [The concept of anxiety], 5th edn. In *Søren Kierkegaard – Samlede værker* [*Collected Works*], Vols. 5 and 6 (ed. A. B. Drachmann, J. L. Heiberg and H. O. Lange HO). Copenhagen: Gyldendals Bogklub, pp. 101–240.

Harms Larsen, P. (1990) *Faktion – som udtryksmiddel* [*Faction – as a means to signify*]. Viborg: Amanda.

Luhmann, N. (1993) Zeichen als Form [Token as form]. In *Probleme der Form* [*The Problem of Form*] (ed. D. Baecker). Frankfurt am Main: Suhrkamp.

Luhmann, N. (1994) *Soziale Systeme – Grundrisz einer allgemeinen Theorie* [*Social Systems – The Framework of a General Theory*]. Frankfurt am Main: Suhrkamp.

Luhmann, N. (1997) Fare og risiko [Danger and Risk]. In Iagttagelse og paradoks [Observation and Paradox] (eds. F. Tygstrup, I. W. Holm, M. Hesseldahl and F. Sternfelt). Copenhagen: Gyldendal.

Qvortrup, L. (1998) Det hyperkomplekse samfund – 14 fortællinger om informationssamfundet [*The Hyper-Complex Society – 14 Stories about the Information Society*]. Copenhagen: Gyldendal.

Ryum, U. (1988) Om den ikke-aristoteliske fortaelleteknik [On the Non-Aristotelian Technique of Storytelling] (abstract). *Nordiska Teaterkommitten.*

Semay, I., Hansen, G. S. and Rosenstand, R. (1997) Projekt Virtuel Ledelse [*The Virtual Management Project*]. Aalborg: University of Aalborg.

CD-ROMs

ID Software (1996) Quake

ID Software (1999) Quake III

InterAct (1997) Virtuel Ledelse [Virtual Management]

InterAct (1998) Virtual Management

InterAct (1999) Vituel VærdiLedelse [Virtual Value Management]

InterAct (2000) Virtuel Skat [Virtual Tax]

PriceWaterhouseCoopers (1999, Beta version) In$ider

SkillChange (1999) Jarvis Hotel

Voyager (1995) The Puppet Motel

Author Index

MIX
Papier aus verantwortungsvollen Quellen
Paper from responsible sources
FSC® C105338
FSC
www.fsc.org

If you have any concerns about our products,
you can contact us on
ProductSafety@springernature.com

In case Publisher is established outside the EU,
the EU authorized representative is:
Springer Nature Customer Service Center GmbH
Europaplatz 3, 69115 Heidelberg, Germany

Printed by Libri Plureos GmbH
in Hamburg, Germany